TACTICS

and

TECHNIQUES

in Psychoanalytic Therapy

edited by

Peter L. Giovacchini, M.D.

Science House, Inc.

Designed by Gordon Lander

Library of Congress Catalogue Card Number: 72-144143. Standard Book Number: 87668-047-3.

Manufactured in the United States of America

Table of Contents

PART IV   Technical Factors and the
             Psychoanalytic Process

PART V   Specific Clinical Situations:
            Theoretical Viewpoints

Contributors

Bruno Bettelheim, Ph.D.

Stella M. Rowley Distinguished Service Professor of Education.
Professor of Psychology and Psychiatry, University of Chicago.

Gustav Bychowski, M.D.

Clinical Professor of Psychiatry, State University of New York, Downstate Medical Center. Lecturer, Institute of Psychiatry, Mount Sinai School of Medicine.

Elaine Caruth, Ph.D.

Clinical Assistant Professor, Division of Medical Psychology, University of California, Los Angeles. Senior Clinical Research Psychologist, Child Psychosis Program, Reiss-Davis Child Study Center.

Rudolf Ekstein, Ph.D.

Director, Reiss-Davis Child Study Center. Research, Child Psychosis Program. Consulting Editor, Annals of Adolescent Psychiatry.

Alfred Flarsheim, M.D.

Clinical Assistant Professor of Psychiatry, University of Illinois College of Medicine. Consultant, The Sonia Shankman Orthogenic School, University of Chicago. Editor, Bulletin of the Chicago Society for Adolescent Psychiatry.

Peter L. Giovacchini, M.D.

Clinical Professor of Psychiatry, University of Illinois College of Medicine. Co-editor, Annals of Adolescent Psychiatry. Chairman, Committee on Post-Graduate Education, Chicago Psychoanalytic Society.

Edward Glover, M.D., LL.D., F.B.P.S. (Hon.)

Chairman of the Institute for Study and Treatment of Delinquency. Consultant, Portman Clinic. Co-editor, British Journal of Criminology.

Martin James, M.R.C.P., D.P.M.

Member, The British Psychoanalytic Society. Consultant to National Association of Mental Health.

Otto F. Kernberg, M.D.

Director, C. F. Menninger Memorial Hospital, The Menninger Foundation.

M. Masud R. Khan, B.A., M.A.

Member, The British Psychoanalytic Society. Editor, International Psycho-Analytical Library. Co-rédacteur Étranger, Nouvelle Revue de Psychanalyse. Associate Editor, International Journal of Psycho-Analysis. Visiting Professor, Deutsche Akademie für Psychoanalyse.

John Klauber, M.A. (Mod. Hist.), B.M., B.Ch. (Oxford), M.R.C.Psych., F.B.Ps.S.

Honorary Scientific Secretary of the British Psycho-Analytic Society.

John A. Lindon, M.D.

President of the Psychiatric Research Foundation.
Associate Clinical Professor of Psychiatry, University of California, Los Angeles.
Editor, The Psychoanalytic Forum.

Margaret I. Little, M.R.C.S., L.R.C.P.

Member, The British Psychoanalytic Society.

Gilbert J. Rose, M.D.

Associate Clinical Professor, Department of Psychiatry, Yale University Medical School.

Donald W. Winnicott, F.R.C.P.

Was Consulting Physician, Paddington Green Children's Hospital and London Clinic of Psycho-Analysis.

Acknowledgments

Chapter 3: Copyright © 1971 by the Psychiatric Research Foundation. *Chapter 4:* Adapted from "A Contribution to the Ego-Psychological Critique of the Kleinian School," *Int. J. Psycho-Anal.* 50:317-333. Reprinted with permission of Otto F. Kernberg, The Institute of Psycho-Analysis, and Ballière. Tindall & Cassell, Ltd. *Chapter 9:* Adapted by Alfred Flarsheim with the permission of The Macmillan Company from The Empty Fortress, copyright © by Bruno Bettelheim. *Chapter 13:* This paper, from the work of the Psychotherapy Research Project of the American Psychoanalytic Association, Detroit, 6 May 1967. This investigation has been supported by Public Health Research Grant MH 8308 from the National Institute of Mental Health. The work of this project was previously supported by the Foundation's Fund for Research in Psychiatry and the Ford Foundation. Adapted from "The Treatment of Patients with Borderline Personality Organization," *Int. J. Psycho-Anal.* 49:600-619; and reprinted with permission of Otto F. Kernberg, The Institute of Psycho-Analysis, and Ballière, Tindall & Cassell, Ltd. *Chapter 20:* Copyright © 1972 by Donald W. Winnicott. *Chapter 23:* Copyright © 1972 by Donald W. Winnicott.

Preface

THE CONTRIBUTORS to this book were encouraged to accept the freedom to express themselves personally as well as scientifically. One can still communicate precisely and clearly without being stylistically mechanical and antiseptic. If the personal element at times sacrifices absolute clarity, it creates a more readable and human essay. The arousal of the reader's interest, in turn, will make the material more understandable.

There is variation, of course, in these chapters; some of the authors are more relevant and understandable than others, and what they reveal of their personal orientation helps enormously in shedding light upon the many obscurities of therapeutic interactions.

Treatment is a personal affair; many of us want to know about the intimate thoughts and even idiosyncrasies of highly skilled and experienced analysts. Students, especially, display their curiosity and eagerness to learn in their enthusiasm for tape-recorded interviews and videotapes. There seems to be a need to know how the contemporary analyst works and to penetrate the secrecy that is so often associated with what goes on in the consultation room. No matter what the orientation of the therapist might be, the tactics and techniques of psychoanalysis are of crucial importance, and there is an eager interest by most clinically oriented professionals to learn as much as possible about them. This book tries to serve that need and to dispel the mystique that has often obscured the frank discussion of technical issues.

Psychoanalysis has been frequently criticized for both its

esoteric attitude and its almost ecclesiastical self-reverence. The psychoanalyst has been described as a high priest engaged in mysterious and secret rituals which cannot be revealed except to a privileged, sacred minority. The authors of this volume, and some of them are among the pioneers of psychoanalysis, will soon dispel these lofty notions. They have a robust, earthy quality with an almost rough-readiness to share their experiences.

Initially I planned to include the topic of psychoanalytically oriented psychotherapy as well as more standard psychoanalytic treatment. When I asked each contributor to write a chapter, I told him about the scope of the book, but only Glover included the subject of psychoanalytically oriented psychotherapy in his essay. The other contributors simply chose not to do so. Later questioning revealed that they had feelings similar to mine. We felt that we had little experience in practicing modified analysis. This was especially curious since many of us had practiced all kinds of psychotherapy early in our careers, but with the passage of time paradoxically we thought that we knew less and less about forms of treatment other than psychoanalysis.

The principles underlying psychoanalytically oriented treatment are familiar enough. Our difficulties, not unlike those of students and beginning practitioners, are in the area of implementation. We do not seem to know how to reassure or support a patient effectively, how to help reestablish defenses and institute repression, or how to limit transference to positive transference (see Chapter 1). There was a time when I believed I understood how to accomplish the above maneuvers, but either I was deceiving myself or I have lost the ability.

With respect to ability, further involvement with analysis (including personal analysis) led to the loss of my ability to hypnotize patients. Some time ago I had had reasonable success in hypnotizing subjects — both patients and nonpatients. Today, however, I can no longer do so, partly because I have no desire to use this procedure, and partly because the melodramatic atmosphere and gestures required to hypnotize some subjects are at variance with my orientation and I can no longer incorporate them in an ego-syntonic fashion.

Consequently, I wonder if there might be a similar inhibition with respect to modified analysis. It is possible that the various maneuvers and manipulations required for such therapies can no longer be smoothly integrated into a professional self-representation ;

perhaps our identity is based upon another orientation. Naturally, I cannot assume that all of the contributors react in a similar fashion. Some have written about modification of analytic technique and they seem to be quite comfortable with it. These modifications are usually reactions to especially difficult clinical situations with patients suffering from severe psychopathology. Still, in spite of an occasional need to adopt another stance, all of the authors preferred to remain in an analytic context.

The contributors' selection of clinical material was also quite interesting. Rather than using so-called classical psychoneurotics for their clinical illustrations, most of them chose to write about patients who suffer from severe psychopathology. They described cases that are considered borderline, narcissistic character disorders, and even outright psychoses. The question of whether such cases could be treated psychoanalytically was seldom raised; it was simply assumed that they could.

Despite Freud's belief that patients suffering from character-ological defects could not be treated psychoanalytically, an increasing number of psychoanalysts are therapeutically optimistic. At two recent workshops, the topics of which were "The Psychoanalytic Treatment of Schizophrenia" (American Psychoanalytic Association, Boston, May, 1968) and "Clinical Aspects of Identity Disorders" (American Society for Adolescent Psychiatry, San Francisco, May, 1970), the question of whether psychoanalytic treatment was feasible was never asked. In fact, at the identity disorder workshop, there was almost unanimous agreement that psychoanalytic treatment was the treatment of choice. The audience and panelists' response was especially noteworthy because I can recall that only recently many analysts were bitterly attacking the idea that psychoanalytic treatment might be indicated for patients who cannot be nosologically subsumed under Freud's transference neuroses. To these analysts the psychoanalytic treatment of patients suffering from characterological disorders or schizophrenia was unthinkable.

The revelations of the contributors to this volume have an added dimension in view of what appear to be shifts in therapeutic orientation. Some of the chapters are open demonstrations of analytic technique. In fact, the last chapter is an account by Dr. D. W. Winnicott of a fragment of a five-year analysis of a patient suffering from severe psychopathology. Dr. Winnicott tells us in detail what the patient said and how he responded. The number of clinicians who practice psychoanalysis with other than psychoneurotic patients is difficult to ascertain. Certainly many of this book's contributors do, and they tell us exactly what they do. I doubt, however, whether they are a representative sample.

For, even though the *idea* that this group of patients is in general psychoanalytically treatable is rather widespread, therapists are still quite reluctant to put it into practice. I have repeatedly had the experience of referring cases to colleagues who believe that the indications for psychoanalysis are too constricted, and yet they refused to consider psychoanalysis when confronted with an actual patient. This has happened even when the patient asked for analysis and said that he would not remain in treatment if the therapist attempted to conduct any other form of treatment. The discrepancy between intellectual acceptance and clinical application is perhaps representative of a *therapeutic lag*.

Thus, some psychoanalysts cannot or will not conduct analysis except with a very select group of patients; even then one wonders how much such treatment depends upon having the patient's behavior conform to the therapist's moral standards and value systems. Although some of us find that treating patients non-analytically is difficult and tedious, others find it easier to interject their personal values and manage the patient's life than to be non-intrusive observers. There must be multiple determinants to account for these different orientations, including the analysts' training and identification with teachers and training analysts.

Apparently, there is a group of analysts who have freed themselves from those identificatory factors that prevent them from going beyond the status quo. I believe that the contributors to this volume are eminent representatives of such a group. Since I believe that psychoanalytic treatment is much more applicable than I was taught, I probably chose analysts to write for this book who, to a large extent, share and practice my viewpoint.

One often finds "schools" forming in a particular location, for example, in some areas the main orientation may be Kleinian and in other places there may be a uniform acceptance of Hartmann's ego-psychological orientation. Lately, however, there has been diffusion, and groups do not maintain a distinct identity, preferring to incorporate what is useful from many different frames of reference. Concerning treatment, however, there has been unusual homogeneity until relatively recently.

In Chicago, the group that practices on the basis of a more liberal attitude regarding the indication for analysis is very small, although, as stated, intellectual acceptance of such attitudes has now increased considerably. Still, these attitudes are far from provincial, for, as can be readily seen here, similarities of orientation do not correspond to geographical location. It is gratifying to know that there are analysts in other parts of the world who share an orientation similar to one's own, even though such attitudes may not be particularly popular locally. It is further gratifying to note that generations, as well as locations, are not fixed. Changing ideas about treatment have not always been initiated by "young rebels"; indeed, many were first formulated by the "older" generation. So we do not have either provincialism or a generation gap.

There are, of course, many others, especially from other countries, who could have made significant contributions to this volume. I could not ask everybody to write; I limited myself to people whom I have known personally or who were especially influential in shaping my orientation when I was a student. Since collecting material for this book, I have met and acquired considerable respect for many of our Mexican and South American colleagues. I believe that their ideas will have an increasing influence on our thinking in the near future and that the reciprocal benefits derived from collaboration will enrich all of us.

One final comment about the contributors should be emphasized. As far as I can ascertain, none are unorthodox. They all accept basic analytic tenets such as the importance of psychic determinism (the dynamic unconscious), developmental and genetic factors, and resolution of the transference as the basic therapeutic instrument. They may differ with other aspects of psychoanalytic theory, but in many instances their differences consist of extensions rather than sharp distinctions. Regarding treatment, the contributors differ, not so much in the matter of instituting innovations but in applying psychoanalytic technique in areas that previously were not considered feasible. Perhaps, once again, one can think of extensions and refinements as conceptual rather than procedural. Still, some of these ideas should be stressed because they are sufficiently unique.

The ideas presented in the following chapters fit easily into an organized sequential structure. After Part I, which deals with broad issues and was written by request, the remainder of the book is somewhat spontaneous. The essays I reviewed could be placed in a continuum, focusing on clinical material. They vary in the relative amount of theoretical discussion of the therapeutic process.

At the beginning the papers deal mainly with theoretical and even diagnostic issues with little or no attention to technical factors. The book ends with an account of an analysis that demonstrates therapeutic technique. There is, therefore, a flow from the theoretical to the practical. However, even in the presentations devoted primarily to clinical demonstration, there is a conceptual framework with which to organize and understand the data derived from therapeutic interaction.

I wish to thank the Department of Psychiatry at the University of Illinois, for their secretarial help in editing this book, and Miss Mabel Glisan, in particular, for her patient and diligent attention to all the details that make this manuscript intelligible. I thank all the contributors and other colleagues who have struggled with the same problems I have and who have both stimulated and encouraged me to persist in the task of bringing this book to light, a task that has had both painful and joyous aspects.

Peter Giovacchini, M.D.

Prologue

Tactical Approaches: An Overview

PETER GIOVACCHINI

THE TREATMENT of emotionally disturbed persons has undergone many changes since antiquity. One might consider that the modern era began with the unshackling of the insane and the adoption of humanistic attitudes, including a scientific frame of reference with a central deterministic focus rather than a religious-superstitious demonology.

Freud carried this focus to its ultimate with his firm adherence to the principle of psychic determinism. Even though both psychotics and neurotics were categorized as patients, the scientific viewpoint before Freud was restricted mainly to organic considerations, and the specific content of the patient's affects, thoughts, and behavior was thought to be epiphenomena. Irrational behavior was believed to be the product of organic dysfunction and, in some instances, the outcome of constitutional degeneracy.

This orientation was not felicitous to the development of psychotherapeutic approaches. With the exception of Charcot and his school, as well as Bernheim and his group at Nancy, most therapeutic endeavors were organically directed. Etiologies, especially after the discovery of Treponema pallidum as a causal agent in general paralysis of the insane, were thought of in terms of hidden but potentially discoverable anatomic or physiological disturbances. Charcot's and Bernheim's approaches were based upon hypnotic suggestion and in themselves were not incompatible with the principle that ultimate causes were mainly organic. In fact, Charcot and many of his followers believed very strongly that they were.

Freud, who had been a neurophysiologist for many years, also believed in a fundamental organic factor, defined as constitutional. His vision, however, encompassed much more; he had greater breadth in that he could also look at the patient's symptoms in etiological terms as being caused by the psychic sphere. If symptoms, behavior, and dreams could be viewed as having purpose or as being the outcome of *psychic factors,* then a rational, systematic therapeutic approach was possible. Thus, psychoanalysis was born. The remainder of Freud's life was devoted to constructing a theory that was relevant to the treatment of emotionally disturbed patients. Treatment and theory were inseparably interwoven, and each complemented the other in a manner that today we would call "positive feedback." In essence Freud established the basis for the psychotherapeutic approach, and since his book with Breuer, *Studies on Hysteria* (1895), there have been changes in both the theoretical fundamentals underlying psychopathology and the technical factors.

Throughout the years many other types of psychotherapy have been developed that differ radically from Freud's methods and goals. Along with changing psychotherapeutic approaches, general psychiatry has introduced many innovations, either alone or combined with an effort to engage the patient in a relationship type of therapy. I am, of course, referring to physiological, pharmacological, and shock therapies. Many such innovations were enthusiastically seized upon (a not uncommon situation in medical practice generally) and usually found a sizable group of adherents who initially reported good results. However, with the passage of time, enthusiasm waned and many of these approaches became obsolete.

I do not know whether one can postulate a sequential pattern of the areas to which various treatment approaches belong. For example, is there a cyclical pattern such as the introduction of drugs and enthusiasm for surgical approaches, followed by a preoccupation with psychotherapy, and finally a return to organic approaches? Undoubtedly this unilateral spectrum is over-simplified and naive, but from a gross outlook one can discern such a cycle since World War II. Shortly after the war there was an intense interest in psychoanalysis, and I recall that the prestige of a psychiatric residency to a large measure depended upon the percentage of residents who gained admission to a psychoanalytic institute. Then came a short period when psychosurgery was considered a breakthrough, but its scope was limited. Following this came an interest in tranquilizers which did, indeed, revolutionize many aspects of psychiatric management. In spite of their acknowledged worth, however, tranquilizers did not become the panacea that many had predicted.

Whether the impact of psychoanalysis or the purely psychotherapeutic approach was weakened during these developments cannot be precisely ascertained. Nevertheless, I had the impression while I was teaching psychiatric residents that there was less enthusiasm for the psychoanalytic approach and a greater emphasis on organic and pharmacological methods.

Recently interest has shifted back to interpersonal relationships. Still, there is a difference in that the one-to-one relationship has been transcended and the family, group, and community are in the forefront. The dynamic, theoretical frame of psychoanalysis has not been abandoned altogether, but the conceptual emphasis, when a rare attempt is made to put matters on a scientific basis, is usually restricted to phenomenonology. "Engagement" and "involvement" are the current shibboleths and seem to have an existence of their own apart from any internally consistent conceptual system. Indeed, many frown upon attempts at scientific systematization, believing that this introduces a barrier to a meaningful, affective relationship.

This book is not intended as a critical discussion of recent trends. Perhaps it is too early to make a really objective appraisal because the trends are still current; we are either involved in them so that it is difficult to be objective, or we are trying to preserve another orientation (such as the psychoanalytic) so that we tend to overreact negatively.

It is also difficult to predict how long the present trend will last and whether in the future there will be a swing back to therapeutic approaches that will primarily focus upon intrapsychic processes rather than upon group or environmental management. I do not wish to give the impression that these trends completely dominate and then just as completely disappear. Obviously, individual therapy is ubiquitous, and community and group approaches are neither entirely new nor will they some day vanish entirely. Similarly, physiological and pharmacological methods are being effectively utilized. I am simply referring to approaches that now seem to be in the forefront and others that may take their place in the future.

Changes in what is fashionable do not occur by chance. This is a complex problem, and to understand the relevant variables would require extensive research utilizing frames of reference that go beyond the scope of this volume. Still, if psychoanalysis has lost ground, it behooves us to take a retrospective glance and clarify its current position.

The need for such clarification seems essential when we consider the problems that psychiatric residents and students of psychoanalysis are facing. Many residents were taught that the "pure" psychoanalytic approach is sacrosanct and limited to a select group of patients; in some instances the patient also becomes sacrosanct. During my residency I recall my own and my colleagues' reactions to a patient in psychoanalytic treatment who had to be hospitalized because of some psychic decompensation. We stood in awe of him and were afraid to approach him except in the most gingerly manner, fearing we would either disturb a delicate balance or intrude into a mysterious and lofty sphere that confused and frightened us.

This reaction is not so common today, but residents continue to be confused. They are interested in the question of treatment in general and want help and guidance in to how to "do" therapy. Inherent in this need is a further question regarding the differences among various treatment approaches such as psychoanalysis and psychoanalytically oriented psychotherapy, which includes supportive treatment aimed at reestablishing defenses. Residents understand the supervisors' direction and advice, but they find themselves in the midst of an impossible dilemma when they attempt to translate what in principle is an abstraction into a concrete action with an actual patient.

For example, a well-known and highly respected analyst told a group of residents that, since they were not trained psychoanalysts, they should not "allow" their patients to develop transference; if transference occurred, it would be because they had committed a technical error. Several residents then asked how it is possible to prevent something that occurs spontaneously. The answer they received was vague and unsatisfactory; the most they could understand was that by focusing upon reality rather than upon intrapsychic processes, transference could be avoided. Experience, however, had taught some of these residents that even by trying to restrict their interchange with a patient to reality, irrational transference reactions still developed. All that they could avoid was an acknowledgment or recognition of the transference phenomenon.

The frustration of these residents was further increased when they asked what to do with a patient if the main focus is not upon intrapsychic processes and interpretation within the transference context. Technical concepts such as support, the institution of repression, or helping to reestablish defenses are simple enough to understand; but what are the specific methods, that is, what should one say or do to achieve those measures designed to secure a better equilibrated ego state? When asked for specific examples, this famous analyst recounted two anecdotes — one in which he established rapport with a rabbi patient by speaking Hebrew with him, and the other in which he belched back at a patient whose belching presumably had a psychogenic origin. If the residents could not speak Hebrew or belch spontaneously, how could they hope to be psychotherapists?

What has just been described may be a caricature of a problem that residents face, but it is nevertheless poignantly characteristic. True, many analysts have pointed out more specifically and helpfully how to deal with patients. Some of the chapters in this volume give precise examples of how skilled and experienced analysts effectively deal with fairly common problems and situations. The techniques they describe have universal applicability and can be incorporated into the residents' therapeutic armamentarium. Still, the problem continues in spite of occasional glimpses into the therapeutic process and the acquisition of skills. *A gap definitely exists between theoretical understanding and the technique of therapy.* More specialized training such as that received at psychoanalytic institutes does not completely solve the problem; in some instances it becomes compounded.

The psychoanalytic candidate benefits from innumerable case presentations where technique is discussed and demonstrated. He learns about the fundamental principles Freud expounded, such as free association, resistance, interpretation, the utilization of transference, and working through. He also learns about indications and contraindications for analysis. At some stage in his training a case is selected for him which is presumably analyzable, that is, a committee has decided that this patient, known as the first control case, meets the criteria of analyzability that the candidate has been taught in the classroom. This case is eventually discussed in a clinical conference by an experienced analyst and fellow students. In attending such conferences, I recall that my fellow students and I were quite surprised and confused as we listened and participated in discussions about the schizoid core of many of these first control cases and were told that they were probably not analyzable or, at most, only partially so.

During my early days of practice my colleagues and I were dismayed at the types of cases referred to us. Practically none of them met the criteria of analyzability we had been taught, and yet we were able to "keep" them in treatment. At a recent workshop attended by experienced analysts representing over seven different psychoanalytic societies, I asked if anyone in our group had ever seen a patient who might be considered "classical," that is, one who met the criteria of analyzability — a patient without a schizoid core whose problems were primarily at the oedipal level. *Not one analyst reported ever having seen such a case* (Lindon, 1968). Later, we reviewed some of Freud's cases and wondered if they fulfilled his requirements for analyzability (Reichard, 1956).

From such experiences, it now seems important — even vital — to review the question of indications for psychoanalysis and to reappraise the "classical" technique. There have been advances and modifications of theory — and with the development of ego psychology, exciting and novel ideas — but little has been done about technique within the psychoanalytic sphere. Modifications of technique or different approaches are not uncommon, but these are casually dismissed as nonanalytic. To a large extent, the dismay of both students and practitioners is due to this technical lag. I further believe that because the early definition of psychoanalysis was a narrow one, clinically speaking, it has lost ground in this period of pragmatism.

Psychoanalytically oriented psychotherapy seemed to be the answer to the pressing demands of a practically oriented community which could not afford the time or money to support long, drawn-out, arduous, expensive classical analysis. This treatment often had lesser goals than characterological change. Dr. Edward Glover, a pioneer who has participated in the development of psychoanalysis and has witnessed innumerable polemics on both theoretical and technical issues, discusses the subject of brief psychotherapy within a psychoanalytical frame of reference in Chapter 2.

Initially I had asked a senior resident and several candidates of psychoanalytic institutes to write on this topic because I believed that, as relative newcomers to psychoanalysis and yet having considerable experience with all types of patients, they could introduce a fresh perspective because they were not yet committed to any fixed position. Since I had heard them speak so much about their dilemma regarding psychotherapy in general, I also believed that much could be learned by making their confusion explicit. In this way it would be possible to examine various definitions of analytically oriented brief psychotherapy. Apparently there are rather strong feelings about these topics, which may touch upon deeper personality factors because everyone (candidates and residents) whom I asked to write enthusiastically agreed to do so (to some extent they even felt flattered), but no one actually came through. They were almost paralyzed when they tried to write. This paralysis did not stem from inexperience because several of the candidates had written a great deal and were able to express themselves coherently and lucidly. The topic I had placed before them was of foremost interest, but when the candidates and residents tried to give their thoughts some secondary process organization, some of them nearly panicked. Only veterans like Dr. Edward Glover seemed to be able to approach this subject candidly and with equanimity.

Whether brief psychotherapy is really "brief" and how one manipulates a transference to achieve specific goals are questions that have bothered both neophytes and senior therapists. I find that as the years go by I am less and less able to distinguish such treatment approaches from psychoanalysis, either in principle or in practice.

Returning to the psychoanalytic sphere without purposely introducing the technical modifications that are avowedly counter to analysis, for example, parameters (Eissler, 1953), one is impressed by the paucity of technical innovations introduced by practitioners of psychoanalysis. Ferenczi and Rank (1923) attempted to revolutionize analysis, but their ideas have not become established in the mainstream of psychoanalysis. With some modifications they were expanded by Alexander (1946); at that time Alexander's ideas caused a large degree of excitement in psychoanalytic circles, but today they are largely thought to be a nonanalytic form of treatment where the deviations are so gross that the treatment procedure bears little resemblance to analysis. Reich (1933) wrote extensively about technique but did not, in fact, propose any new principles. He explained how he handled specific types of resistance (character armor). Some of his techniques were based upon particular personality traits of his own that enabled him to deal effectively with certain types of patients. Because Reich actively demonstrated what he did, the reader could incorporate certain aspects of this technique when dealing with his own patients, but few, if any, of the suggestions have widespread general applicability. Other authors, that is, Fenichel (1953), Glover (1955), Greenson (1969), and Tarachow (1963) have written about technique; although they introduce some novel ideas, they largely restate and clarify Freudian dictums. Fairbairn (1954) focussed upon object relationships, making them (rather than libido theory) the cornerstone of his theoterical system. His concepts about object relationships have far-reaching implications for treatment.

Probably the most influential and controversial innovator (of both psychoanalytical theory and treatment — even at the present time) is Melanie Klein. She claimed that she remained within a psychoanalytic frame of reference but believed that her methods (exclusively interpretative) could extend the range of applicability of psychoanalysis, that is, to children and adults suffering from psychopathology to a degree that had previously been considered a contraindication to analysis. She encouraged many analysts (who do not necessarily agree with many of her theoretical formulations, especially those referring to developmental stages) to work with patients suffering form severe character pathology and psychoses, for example, Byschowski (1952), Boyer and Giovacchini (1967), Kernberg (1968), Khan (1960), Searles (1965), and Winnicott (1963), to mention a few.

One still speaks of the Kleinian school, and her ideas and principles are eagerly supported by many analysts, particularly by those in South America (see Litman, 1966). In any case, if one can speak of any major breakthrough in the theory and technique of psychoanalytic treatment, Melanie Klein's ideas constitute the only system that has had sufficient impact to be considered a school with significantly unique characteristics. It can be identified as distinct yet within a psychoanalytic context. Others, such as Sullivan (1940), have also been influential, but their influence has been parochial, never having achieved Klein's universality.

Klein caused considerable controversy in England when she first stated her main ideas. Even today, one still hears about the Kleinian school and its antagonist, the Anna Freud school. However, speaking with British analysts who are well represented in this book, I was not aware of any fanatic adherence to either "school". Klein was ignored for many years in the United States; I recall that when I was a student at the Chicago Institute for Psychoanalysis (1950), I was assigned to review Melanie Klein's principles because, since so few knew anything about them, it was thought desirable to learn about them. Some of the students and faculty knew absolutely nothing about her work.

Today, American analysts are better acquainted with Klein. Those who have studied her articles and books, in my opinion, seem to be more optimistic about psychoanalysis as a treatment method. This does not mean that they totally agree with her, but they are willing to extract ideas from her that they find useful when dealing with patients suffering from severe psychotherapy. The chapters that follow discuss Klein's work from both an expository and critical viewpoint. Any book that attempts to review current thinking and developments in psychoanalytic treatment must include her ideas, at least in capsule form, since so many of us have been influenced by her, either consciously or unconsciously.

In any discussion of psychoanalytic technique, one is inevitably faced with the question of what types of modifications (to use a mild term) are necessary when dealing with cases that Freud believed to be unanalyzable. Many believe that psychoanalysis is useful for patients who fit Freud's diagnostic category of narcissistic neuroses (which also includes psychoses). However, other analysts think that special ego-building measures are required. Klein's approach minimizes all activity, except analytic activity, and it focuses principally upon transference interpretations.

Some of this book's contributors, for example, Byschowski and Kernberg, specifically discuss the matter of "special" procedures for patients suffering from severe psychopathology. I have supported Klein's position, maintaining that deviations are not only unnecessary but, in many instances, actually detrimental. Still, after discussing this point with colleagues, especially Kernberg, I think it is likely that what one therapist calls a "modification" may be an intrinsic aspect of the psychoanalytic process.

Consequently, the analytic process itself has to be discussed further. Today there is a tendency to examine the therapeutic interaction utilizing the conceptual tools of ego psychology. Parts II, III, and IV consider various elements of psychoanalytic therapy, ranging from the selection of cases to the metapsychology of the transference relationship with patients suffering from severe characterological problems.

Finally, in Parts V and VI, these questions are examined further in a more extensive clinical context. Anyone practising psychotherapy has had to face many of the questions and dilemmas that the clinically experienced contributors to this book have confronted. By sharing their experiences with us, by candidly expressing their confusion which eventually leads to the definition of a problem, our work becomes challenging rather than frustrating. It is always reassuring to know that we are not alone and that our problems are not unique.

REFERENCES

Alexander, F., and French, T. (1946). *Psychoanalytic therapy*. New York : Ronald Press.

Boyer, L. B., and Giovacchini, P. L. (1967). *Psychoanalytic treatment of characterological and schizophrenic disorders*. New York : Science House.

Breuer, J., and Freud, S. (1895). *Studies on hysteria*. Standard Edition, vol. 2. London : Hogarth Press, 1955.

Bychowski, G. (1952). *Psychotherapy of psychosis*. New York : Grune & Stratton.

Eissler, K. (1953). The effect of the structure of the ego on psychoanalytic technique. *J. Amer. Psychoanal. Assoc.* 1 : 104–143.

Fairbairn, W. R. D. (1954). *An object relations theory of the personality*. New York : Basic Books.

Fenichel, O. (1953). *The collected papers of Otto Fenichel*. Edited by H. Fenichel and D. Rapaport. New York : Norton.

Ferenczi, S., and Rank, O. (1923). *The development of psychoanalysis*. New York and Washington : Nervous and Mental Disease Publishing Co.

Glover, E. (1955). *The technique of psychoanalysis*. New York : International Universities Press.

Greenson, R. (1969). *The technique and practice of psychoanalysis*. New York : International Universities Press.

Kernberg, O. (1968). The treatment of patients with borderline personality organization. *Int. J. Psycho-Anal.* 49 : 608–619.

Khan, M. M. R. (1960). Clinical aspects of the schizoid personality : affects and technique. *Int. J. Psycho-Anal.* 41 : 430–437.

Lindon, J. (1968). On regression : a workshop. *Psychoanal. Forum* 2 : 293–316.

Litman, J. (1966). *Psychoanalysis in the Americas*. New York : International Universities Press.

Reich, W. (1933). *Character analysis*. New York : Orgone Institute Press.

Reichard, S. (1956). A re-examination of "Studies in Hysteria." *Psycho-anal. Quart.* 25 : 155—177.

Searles, H. (1965). *Collected papers of Harold Searles.* New York : International Universities Press.

Sullivan, H. S. (1940). *Conceptions of modern psychiatry.* Washington, D.C. : W. A. White Psychiatry Foundation, 1947.

Tarachow, S. (1963). *An introduction to psychotherapy.* New York : International Universities Press.

Winnicott, D. W. (1963). *The maturational processes and the facilitating environment.* New York : International Universities Press.

PART 1

General Tactical Considerations

Psychoanalysis and Psychoanalytically Oriented Psychotherapy

EDWARD GLOVER

HAD THE topic "the relation of psychoanalysis to psychoanalytically oriented psychotherapy" been submitted to the late Ernest Jones at any time between 1919 and 1932, his contribution to the discussion would scarcely have filled one page of manuscript. For during those formative years, that doughty champion of what nowadays is frequently called "classical" psychoanalysis minced no words. Psychotherapy, he never tired of maintaining, could be divided into two parts, namely, psychoanalysis and suggestion; or perhaps, to preserve historical precedence, suggestion and psychoanalysis. This was regarded as a hard saying, by many therapists who then practiced exploratory techniques; however, at the time it served official British psychoanalysts as a testamentary declaration or credo. Indeed, it was also implicit in many of Freud's statements regarding the history and practice of psychoanalysis as, for example, when, dealing with the problem of terminating the process, he remarked that the best way to end an analysis was to carry it out "correctly," clearly implying the existence of an "orthodox" and obligatory technique.

"Classical," "correct," "orthodox": these are terms that in this context cry out for accurate definition, as do their antonyms,

17

"modern," "incorrect," "unorthodox." The latter set can of course be paraphrased as "neo-Freudian," "nonanalytical," and "analytically oriented" psychotherapies, respectively. But, alas, crisp definitions are hard to come by. Indeed, in the old 1919-1932 period, only one British writer attempted to define psychoanalysis in an aphoristic fashion. The credit for this goes to T. W. Mitchell (1927), an unusually brilliant philosopher, physician, and successful hypnotist who, encouraged by Ernest Jones, graduated in and contributed to the theory of psychoanalysis. Mitchell maintained that whoever believed in the existence of the unconscious, in infantile sexuality, in repression, in unconscious conflict, and in transference believed in psychoanalysis. At that time "belief" in psychoanalytic treatment went a long way toward securing a license to practice it.

But returning to Ernest Jones and his ex cathedra pronouncements on psychotherapy, it must be noted that from 1930 until his official retirement from the presidency of the British Psychoanalytical Society, Jones found himself compelled — or rather induced, for he was not a man to submit to compulsion — to father a split in the theoretical and practical (clinical) orientations of a society that owed its continued existence to his unremitting efforts. The result is that even today theories and practices that differ radically in principle are taught to unfortunate candidates for admission to the British Society. In this fashion both groups when "qualified" are officially entitled to call themselves "psychoanalysts," and do so.

Having closely studied the disastrous effects of this internal dissension, I published a paper (Glover, 1931), the essence of which can be summarized in an aphoristic form closely resembling some of Jones's earlier pronouncements. It runs as follows: When any two practitioners employ modes of "analysis" that differ radically in principle and practice, then one or the other of them is practicing a refined or occult form of suggestion. Of course, it is open to either of the antagonists to say, "My method is true analysis," adding *sotto voce*, "this other fellow isn't really an analyst." This happens. And I have no doubt that if pressed closely on the matter, the more timorous of the two would end by conceding, "Well, anyhow, mine is a form of "psychoanalytically oriented therapy.'" But I also doubt whether the average psychiatrist would accept either of these explanations, unless perchance he was himself pursuing similar lines of approach.

A lengthy and somewhat gossipy exordium this. Nevertheless it is essential to thrash these matters out before venturing even the most tentative conclusions on the issue that lies at the heart of the problem, namely, What *is* psychoanalytically oriented psychotherapy? For clearly, if there were no differences between "psychoanalytic" psychotherapy and "psychoanalytically oriented" psychotherapy, there would be nothing to discuss.

Now psychotherapy is an ancient craft or cult employed, unwittingly no doubt, in the earliest human communities and still practiced in modern institutions devoted to "human" or "interpersonal relations," if I may borrow these rather otiose paraphrases much favored nowadays by general practitioners of "clinical psychology." By comparison psychoanalysis, despite its three-quarter-century duration, is still the "new boy" in psychological scholastics, preaching doctrines that are still regarded by most therapists as subversive, if not crazy. So perhaps we had better begin with the definitions and particulars of psychoanalysis and work our way back to general psychotherapy before discussing the vital implications of the term "orientation."

C'est le premier pas qui coûte, or so we have been told. No sooner do we seek to apply logical processes of definition to the term "psychoanalysis" than we are confronted with an obstacle that is difficult to surmount. For the most cursory survey of psychoanalytical history establishes the fact that psychoanalysis is a fissile science. Indeed, the more pedantic of its hostile critics would maintain that it is a "fissiparous" science because it is propagated by spontaneous fission into *minute* parts (or parties) with the accent on "minute." But that, of course, is to exercise polemic license. Still, there can be no doubt that psychoanalysis is prone to fission and that the resulting fragments are often substantial enough. And this is not taking into consideration, for the moment, that many individual members who retreated from psychoanalysis had once been leaders and active contributors to the Psychoanalytical Association. However, these departures or defections (sometimes excommunications) do not matter too much. What does matter is the existence of schisms and cleavages *within* psychoanalytic groups, although these groups can and do preserve a superficial semblance of solidarity by flying, and sometimes waving, the official banner of "psychoanalysis."

Lest these affirmations appear unduly captious or partisan, or expressly designed *pour épater les bourgeois,* I would refer the reader to some research on psychoanalytic techniques and cognate conceptions Marjorie Brierly and I carried out as far back as 1930 — 1933 (Glover, 1940), that is to say, toward the end of the simon-pure period of psychoanalysis in Britain. Two extensive question-naires were sent to 29 practicing analysts, and their replies were collated and submitted for discussion to the society. No doubt our modern statisticians will look down their scriptural noses at the meagerness of the numbers, at the absence of control groups, or at our failure to check probability and significance by running such figures as were available through (or around) a chi-square. To these criticisms we can only plead guilty, for after all : a. there were only 29 practicing analysts available at the time ; b. control groups were impossible to secure ; and c. in the absence of statistical checks, there is no reason for not screening material for apparent "tendencies" or "trends."

Briefly, we found that already at that relatively early period, there were striking differences on matters of both practice and theory. Of the 63 items submitted for investigation, 21 showed a marked division of opinion; on only six points was there (almost) complete agreement, leaving 36 issues on which there was only a *consensus of opinion* among *two-thirds* of the contributors. Of the six items representing complete agreement (all of them concerning technique), only one was of any importance, namely, the necessity for transference-analysis. With respect to the relationship between theory and practice the results were equivocal, but on the whole not too disappointing. Later, however, it became clear that the society was composed of two groups that held sharply opposing views on theory, and consequently on practice.

Because these observations referred exclusively to the current ideas and practices in only one branch society of the International Association, it is obvious that they had to be complemented by similar investigations at an international level. In fact, in 1951, due to the foresight and good graces of Leo Bartemeier, I succeeded in obtaining sanction to form an International Research Committee, of which I was appointed chairman. I sent out a questionnaire to determine whether or not there were any *new developments in theory and practice*. But, alas, the project was sabotaged by the British Society, some of whose members refused to cooperate. And at the next Congress of the International Psycho-Analytic Associa-tion, a new committee appointed itself which, at the instance of the British group, quietly and unobtrusively committed hara-kiri.

So, despite the existence of "annual surveys" and the publication of sundry encyclopedias and psychoanalytical dictionaries, the definition of psychoanalysis has been left exactly where it was in 1930 — 1933 when it first became confused.

To revert to this first detailed examination of psychoanalytical standards and practices, it is interesting to note the reaction in the British Society to the "new" ideas presented in the form of papers and discussions and reflected in the answers to the questionnaire. Those who supported the ideas formed a distinct group; its members regarded their own ideas as advanced conceptions, constituting what would now be called a breakthrough or, at least, essential emendations of standard Freudian theory and practice. The conventional conservative group, on the other hand, treated the ideas with profound reserve and actively opposed them. The most interesting group was that which came to be called the "middle" (and later the "independent") group, the policy of which was essentially one of compromise, that is, trying to merge the two systems. Sensitive to the suggestion that they were hidebound to a closed system of psychoanalytic theory and tending to be carried away by the vigorous affirmations of the proselytizers, they maintained that these fissions should be welcomed as a sign of progress in a freely advancing science.

There can be no doubt, of course, that fission is the touchstone of a pure science without which little progress can be made. What if a *few* errors are perpetrated? This is better than to endure the tedium of reading platitudinous repetitions of stock formulas. Yes, but with one reservation: the new *principles* productive of fission must be valid; they cannot be a mere rattling of metaphysical bones, if I may be allowed a mixed metaphor. Otherwise it is like pouring an ersatz wine into old bottles without apologizing for retaining the old label. At some congress, now dimly remembered, I once suggested to Otto Fenichel — a brilliant and most reliable psychoanalytical entrepreneur — that he made an etiological fetish of the castration complex, adding that disparate disorders called for diverse etiologies. He replied, "That's all very well, but we must not neglect our priorities."

All this time we have left our proselytizers chanting that self-satisfied paean that runs, *"Nous avons changé tout cela."* This was a tendency that first manifested itself during the early 1930s in Britain and took the form of a covert suggestion that Freud was just a little bit old-fashioned. It continued until, following the prewar influx of Viennese expatriates to London, discretion prevailed over valor and criticism of Freud was muted for the time being. But not for long. In casual articles but more particularly in open discussions in Britain, in the United States, and in some of the rejuvenated countries of middle Europe, it is sometimes postulated that psychoanalysis has made great advances in recent years. This is, of course, the natural reaction of those who have been carried away by "new ideas," have merely subscribed to a fashionable trend, have propagated ideas of their own, or have become bored with what they conceive to be the sterility of older formulas. But in law it is recognized that a judge and jury should not prejudice an investigation by revealing their own prejudices. In psychological science it is equally essential to exclude any form of autosuggestion, to say nothing of self-adulation. Admittedly this is difficult to achieve, for, after all, on matters of unconscious psychology, who is going to judge the judges? Certainly not those general psychiatrists, neurologists, psychoneurologists, neuropsychiatrists, or behaviorists who have no knowledge of, but are nevertheless ready to oppose or modify beyond recognition, the "findings" of dynamic psychology.

To the utopist all this is no doubt a very sad and regrettable state of affairs, but it cannot be altogether helped. In the meantime we are obligated to arrive at provisional conclusions on the subject; otherwise, we shall never get anywhere. Allowing, therefore, for considerable subjective prejudice, and conceding the absence of accurate information on the international status of psychoanalysis, I would maintain that while there is a solid body of opinion in most (but by no means all) psychoanalytical groups that supports the "classical" approach, this is offset by the existence of systems that deviate strikingly from the standard pattern. So how are we to estimate the influence of "psychoanalytical orientation" on the body psychological? Faced with this dilemma we must obviously consider the definition and position of what we may for convenience designate as "general" psychiatry.

Here I must freely confess that I welcome the opportunity to proffer some sauce to the gander, for I have found that whenever I write a critical survey of psychoanalytical deviations, I can count on enthusiastic quotations from a number of psychiatrists and behaviorists, saying, "Well, what did we tell you — psychoanalysis is just mincemeat." These views percolate no doubt from professional circles to certain newspaper supplements in England and the United States that help to fashion "educated" opinion; this opinion is then reflected back to the original professional circles where it serves as confirmatory evidence for their point of view. Let us therefore see how the concept of general psychiatry fares under fresh inspection.

A psychiater! A good word soundly derived from the Greek — " a physician of 'disorders of the soul' " — which our dictionaries paraphrase as "mental disorders." A little bit cramped, say those psychoanalysts who are prepared to treat any form of characterological disorder, whether or not it conforms to customary captions, such as "neurosis," "psychosis" (or even "neuroticism," that question-begging caption). Of course, this definition excludes the neurologist, the psychoneurologist, and the behaviorist (no bad thing in my opinion) unless these specialists are prepared to confine their formulations to the constitutional factor in mental disorder. Let us, therefore, justly canonize the term "psychiatry."

Having done so, we must submit the fraternity to a form of catechism. What, for example, is their theory of mind (or soul)? Now, it is characteristic of many psychiatrists that, unless they have picked up a theory of mind from "normal" psychologists (who, by the way, seldom possess such an appurtenance) they leave the question of basic theory severely alone, thereby distinguishing themselves from the neurologists or their first cousins, the behaviorists, who, attracted by the term "central nervous system" or "brain" are prepared to explain quite crisply and in physiological terms why an infant may come to hate his nearest sibling. This, again, is natural enough, for their only alternative is to acquire from dynamic psychology a few slogans and convey these to their patients in a patois of their own invention.

This form of bowdlerization frequently creates the impression in the unoriented reader that he is dealing with new ideas and advances. Read the general psychiatric literature (or rather that part which does not deal with neo-Pavlovian theories): read particularly the literature devoted to child guidance and familial social science and you will almost certainly find many of the slogans of early psychoanalytical science, however attenuated or transmogrified.

At this point I feel sure that the discriminating reader will promptly inquire, "Well, isn't this just what we are talking about? Surely this constitutes an example of psychoanalytically oriented therapy; moreover, doesn't it produce satisfactory results?" Now, I should not like it to be bruited abroad that I subscribe to the seductive fallacy that the validity of any system of psychotherapy or neuropsychiatric therapy can be established by applying therapeutic standards. I can't remember now whether it was the late James Glover or me who, in a flippant mood, advanced the proposition that in certain cases it would be sufficient to leave a golliwog in the chair (which had been geared up mechanically) to say every five minutes, "What does that bring to your mind?" so that the analyst could retreat for morning coffee. Whichever of us said it, I regard it as a pronouncement of high significance, bearing on the problem of suggestion therapy.

Setting out to characterize "psychiatry," and no doubt influenced by the "tit-for-tat principle," I had resolved to describe general psychiatry as a "fissiparous" science. But since embarking on this review, I have come to realize that the term is inapt. Psychiatry is not originally a unitary system divided into subsections, but rather it is an aggregation of disparate approaches. A more apt simile might compare psychiatry to an aggregation of colonies living in uneasy symbiosis. Indeed, it is not clear whether such accredited approaches as the neurological are alien intruders in the body psychiatric. But leaving that matter aside, we may well ask, What are the essential differences between a psychoanalytical approach and a general psychiatric approach?

Had Mitchell been asked this question in the old days, he probably would have repeated his quinary list of psychoanalytical standards (Mitchell, 1927). Had he, however, been pressed to be more specific, it is pretty certain that he would have chosen the "analysis of the transference" as the touchstone of orthodox procedure. And Jones would certainly have agreed with him. For a number of reasons this analytical shibboleth is of supreme significance. In the first place, by maintaining the importance of transference phenomena, our predecessors in analysis were affirming their belief in the existence of the unconscious mind, in unconscious mechanisms, in an unconscious infantile sexuality, and in an unconscious ego. Some latter-day psychoanalytical pundits seem to be under the impression that their forebears neglected the "negative" transference and the importance of unconscious aggressive impulses. But this is surely a myth. Is the positive Oedipus complex a Sunday School fairy tale, or does it take cognizance of the profound conflict and consequent ambivalence of son to father or daughter to mother? What, after all, is ambivalence? Perhaps a more intriguing possibility is that in choosing transference analysis as a psychological tape measure, we are employing a two-edged weapon. For the analyst can and does maintain that the non-analytical psychotherapist (employing any system from the exhibition of aspirin to lobotomy) who does *not* seek to analyze the various forms of transference is rendering hostages to suggestion and should be rated accordingly. Naturally, the nonanalytical psychotherapist may retort that the vaunted claim of the analyst that he analyzes and dissolves the transference in all cases is in the nature of a myth. In many instances this may well be so, for therapeutic modesty is not one of the analyst's besetting sins; in any case, the pukka analyst can counterclaim that in all cases he *endeavors* to do so.

But this, emotionally speaking, is a perilous and parlous clinical field, and, after all, it is possible to describe the relation between analytic and nonanalytic psychotherapy in terms that will ruffle no one's beliefs. To be sure, the terms were originally coined by Freud when he set out his topographical theory of the mental apparatus; but they do not call anyone's therapeutic method, skill, or reputation into question. Stating the matter as briefly as possible, and operating with the concept of different psychic systems, each having special relations with or routes to the system perceptual consciousness (pcpt-cs), it would appear (or at any rate it can be suggested) that the general psychotherapist, however much he wants to analyze the perceptions and introspections he garners from his patient and supplements by self-observation, is inevitably confined to the interpretation of *preconscious content*. To be sure, the deepest layers of the preconscious are archaic enough in all conscience and can tax the skill of the most devoted psychotherapist. Nevertheless, his forte as a psychological analyst is and remains *analysis of the preconscious*. But it may comfort him to think that a substantial number of psychoanalysts appear to neglect the preconscious and the stimulating or depressing impact of everyday life.

An even simpler way to describe the difference, yet one that takes into account dynamic and functional factors, is to say that while the analyst's compelling interest lies in the "primary processes" of the mind, the nonanalytical, general psychotherapist is willy-nilly limited to the study of the "secondary processes." No hard feelings or imputations are called for on either side; therapeutic competition is keen enough and laudable enough as it is.

We are still left with the real problem: How does one make the transition from an analytical to a nonanalytical approach? What and where is "psychoanalytical oriented psychotherapy"? What, in fact, is "orientation"; and, by the same token, who effects the orientation — the tutor or the self-taught?

I think we would do well to consider the last question first. Having agreed, as we must, that the term "orientation," although originally a canonical concept, has, psychologically speaking, come to connote a "clear understanding" (of the significance of external and internal perceptions and ideations), we must also admit that in psychology this understanding can be acquired by the student either on his own or from his psychoanalytical preceptors. To be more precise, the psychotherapist can either read the literature of psychoanalysis or attend (if permitted) lectures on the subject[1] conducted preferably by qualified training analysts under the aegis and regulation of the training committee. Both approaches are perfectly legitimate because the official training of psychoanalysts includes both lectures and reading courses. Assuming, then, that these efforts have led to a "clear understanding" of the function of the mind and have consequently influenced or supplemented whatever other varieties of psychotherapy the psychotherapist may have pursued, *then, in principle, he is entitled to dub himself a "psychoanalytically oriented psychotherapist."*

If this were just a polemical affray between the psychoanalyst and his natural enemies, at this point he would call up his reserves and deploy his highest powered artillery. This could be described as the *cave canem,* or "heads I win, tails you lose" principle — one that naturally infuriates his opponents. He would say that when his patients begin to read psychoanalytical literature or listen to analytical lectures, this is only a resistance and therefore he discourages patients from adopting this protective device. Nevertheless,

---

[1] In Britain this would include lecture courses at university or mental hospital centers for students working toward a Diploma in Psychological Medicine (D.P.M.). Having taught for a number of years at the Maudslay Hospital (London's psychiatric college), I look back (nostalgically) to the days when I was scheduled to give *four* lectures to each group of students on "dynamic psychology." I may add that the accomplishment of this feat of *leger d'esprit* did nothing to raise my already inflated self-esteem. Things are different now; nevertheless, I maintain that if psychiatrists wish to be oriented in psychoanalysis, their teachers must plan a more extensive and thorough intellectual baptism of their unsophisticated charges.

he would be sure to add that psychoanalytical candidates must really *read up* on the subject. This is nonsense, for it can be demonstrated through experience that the analysis of a candidate in training is as difficult as that of a schizophrenic. I claim no particular merit for this insight. Many years ago, in the course of personal reminiscences, David Eder, who had spent a short time in analysis by Victor Tausk, said to me, "You know, Tausk had the diabolic insight of a schizoid mind." And when I replied, "You mean that he thought this was the state of mind of the average 'normal' person," he said rather sadly, "Well, yes."

If, however, there is any uncertainty about the efficiency of "intellectual orientation," one should ask : What other measures of orientation are available? The obvious answer is to consider what other programs are *obligatory* for the training of officially selected psychoanalytical "candidates." These consist of "training analysis," "controlled analysis" of selected patients, and attendance at clinical seminars.

It would take us too far afield to recapitulate the developmental history of these clinical training devices, for even the preliminary question of "selecting" psychoanalytical candidates (an essentially clinical problem) raises a number of issues that have not yet been settled. Leaving this aside, we still have to face the fact that *no* research has been carried out on what might be the most reliable evidence of the influence of these clinical (as distinct from "intellectual") measures of "orientation," namely, the after-history of psychoanalytical candidates who have either given up training on their own or been advised to do so by *training boards* and then began to practice general or eclectic psychotherapy.

Without comprehensive research of this order conducted on an international scale, all we have are "impressions" of individual training analysts, who, incidentally, are noted for their lack of published work. My own impression is that, with a few outstanding exceptions (as, for example, when a retired or rejected psychoanalytical candidate proceeds to practice unlicensed psychoanalytical psychotherapy on, shall we say, "a 75 per cent scale"), the majority of the rejected acquire a D.P.M. and practice whatever forms of psychotherapy they choose — whether it be fish, flesh, or good neuropharmaceutical *cum* neurosurgical *cum* behavioristic red herring. One can ask what is implied by the term "75 per cent scale,"? for to the psychoanalytical purist a miss is as good as a mile.

At this point I can well imagine our long-suffering editor throwing up his hands in despair, demanding to know why all this time has been spent on a discussion of "orientation" in the psychoanalysis of general psychiatrists. "We are not greatly concerned," he may say, "with the relation of psychoanalysis to general psychiatry; what we want to know is: *May fully trained psychoanalysts modify their techniques to meet the exigencies of private or public practice without detriment to their fundamental principles?*"

And so, at last, we are compelled (as so often happens in the psychological sciences) to return to our starting point. Unable so far to describe and define precisely the orienting influence of psychoanalytical theories on nonanalytical psychotherapists, must we alter our terms of reference? Must we shamefacedly confess that the issue is a narrower one — that "psychoanalytically oriented psychotherapy" is simply the prerogative of "trained" and officially labeled "psychoanalysts"?

Endeavoring to answer this question, we must agree that, as a citizen, a psychoanalyst is entitled to stand on his theoretical head if he wishes, so long as he does not infringe on the rights of other psychologists or of the public. We can also sympathize with the recalcitrant's plaintive defense that in his sphere of influence so many people have psychological problems that he must be excused if, in the interest of psychotherapeutic shortcuts, he tempers his more puristic standards. It was precisely this reason that led to the development of so-called "psychoanalytical" group psychotherapy and the inclusion of pharmacological, neurosurgical, and behavioristic (Pavlovian) agents in psychotherapy. Of course, the psychoanalyst is entitled to resort to these expedients but with two provisos: first, he should not claim that his modified technique constitutes a psychoanalysis *secundum artem*; and second, in all communications on the subject, he should clearly label what other constituents or techniques have been merged with or controlled by psychoanalytical "orientation." This is the only honest course. There is surely nothing to be ashamed of in confessing that "transference treatment" has continued to govern human relationships since the family was first established. Granted this formulation, I think we can arrive at a harmless and noncontroversial conclusion, namely, that the issue between "psychoanalysis" and analytically oriented psychotherapy as conducted by qualified psychoanalysts and general psychotherapists who have been "oriented" (either by reading or by clinical instruction by accredited psychoanalysts) is largely an academic issue because in principle there is no difference between the two groups. Of course, this conclusion can be modified by quantifying the various constituents of each therapeutic system, but such preconscious formulas would merely beg the question. A more radical distinction is necessary, similar to that made by Ernest Jones, namely, that psychotherapy can be divided into two parts — suggestion and psychoanalysis.

If, this conclusion appears too summary, too question-begging, or (remembering that psychoanalysis is sometimes alleged to have made great advances in recent years) too antediluvian, I would like to add a sort of conciliatory epilogue. I think that behind the present issue of terminology (which is restricted to therapeutic problems) there lies a matter of vital importance to the development of psychology, namely : What fate does the future hold for the present triad or triangle — psychoanalysis, psychoanalytic oriented psychiatry, and nonanalytical general psychiatry? We might, indeed, make the issue quadrangular, were it not for the fact that academic psychology lingers so persistently on the superficies of the mind that for the time being it can be regarded *hors concours*. Granted that there is such a thing as psychoanalytical orientation, however exiguous, what will be the future relations of the three angles of the psychological triangle? Will psychoanalysis gradually merge with general psychiatry, or will it continue alone? If it should merge, will it abandon or modify any of its fundamental principles for the always dubious advantage of a diplomatic bargain?

These problems are not of recent origin. I can recall a small discussion group (circa 1923 — 1924) in which the late Professor Flugel, a "classical" psychoanalyst, if ever there was one, raised the question of whether or not the concept of the "unconscious" could be "lost" or modified to meet the needs of an expanding psychology of the "(pre)conscious." The finding, incidentally, was in favor of the analytical *status quo,* but it was significant that the topic was even discussed.

The real impetus to *Gleichschaltung* of psychological concepts and method was not derived from the prewar regulations imposed in Nazi Germany. (I omit the regimentation of psychology in the Soviet Union, for we are not primarily concerned with Pavlovian theories or economic explanations of "physiological" behaviorism.)

The impetus in Britain resulted from the administrative status that psychiatry acquired during and after the war which almost obliterated its previous "alienist" limitations. In recent years the desirability of co-opting other sciences (most often ethology, but of course there is no limit) has been assessed by some accredited psychoanalysts. There seems to be a pacifistic urge or need to abandon "ancient feuds" in favor of a United Psychology (patterned after the United Nations, no doubt).

How would this millenial aim be achieved? To this, I think there can be only one answer: It could be brought about by a rapid expansion of dependable research, whatever its origin. In psychoanalysis the lines of investigation are clear enough; they must follow the lead of metapsychology, namely: investigators must closely examine the sources of mental energy in order to delineate accurately the early stages of ego formation, and they must study the influence of hereditary mental tendencies (later, mechanisms) that come to be exploited by an emergent ego.

The part can be played by psychiatrists is equally clear. Since they have closer access to the more extreme forms of mental regression than do psychoanalysts[2], psychiatrists can use their clinical descriptions to enrich the material that illuminates and illustrates the theories advanced and established by psychoanalysts. For this reason alone, it is extremely important that psychoanalytical theory not develop into a metaphysical exercise without clinical control. In return for these services, psychoanalysis could well extend its research (and experiments) in the etiological classification of mental disorders. For if it is true that the neuroses, and possibly the minor psychoses, are either statistically diminishing or assuming a less dramatic form in certain areas of the West, we may be sure that the existing imbroglio concerning "character disorder" or "perversion" will become more chaotic. To clarify this antiquated hotchpotch will present students with a task that, psychologically

---

[2] This applies only to those countries where lay analysis is officially recognized by the International Psychoanalytical Association or where medical analysts do not undergo thorough psychiatric training. Credit should be given to Laurence Kubie whose diatribes on the training of medical analysts or, indeed, of other kinds of psychiatrists, are well taken. I am not overlooking the fact that some psychoanalytical folklorists claim that no candidate should be licensed who has not studied the immortal legend of the *"three blind mice"* or that devoted psychoanalytical students of Shakespeare (like Ella Freeman Sharpe, writing on *Lear* and *Hamlet*) have unobtrusively advanced a similar claim.

speaking, is reminiscent of the fifth labor of Hercules. Here, surely, is the point at which there are possibilities of *mutual orientation* between psychoanalysis and other branches of psychological science.

I am not sure whether it is proper literary form to add a post-script to an epilogue. But I cannot refrain from saying that, on read-ing over the foregoing homily, I feel like Rip van Winkle awaken-ing from his sleep to find that he has been indulging in timeworn clichés. Yet, unless I am very much mistaken, the fundamental issue behind this discussion is not exclusively a therapeutic one : It concerns the future of psychoanalysis. Granted that Freud himself, using a metallurgical metaphor, visualized a time when, owing to the increasing demand for psychotherapy, the pure "gold" of psychoanalysis might be allowed to form a therapeutic amalgam with the "copper" of suggestion ; granted also that a *trained analyst* practising *preconscious* interpretations might have an advantage over the interpretive efforts of a *nonanalytical* therapist ; granted further that nonanalytical therapists gamble on the powers or virtues of "transference suggestion," there still remains an un-resolved problem : Is psychoanalysis merely an exhibition of psycho-logical mumchance? Or, is metapsychological mincemeat designed to both stimulate and assuage the appetite of the curious? If psycho-analysis should continue to maintain its (often disputed) reputation as the core and caretaker of a fullblown system of mind, will this be eroded by an increasing need or wish to explain irrationality by paying lip service to rationality?

One thing is certain : The psychotherapeutic neophyte, aspiring to consultant rank, cannot have it both ways. If he insists on it, how-ever, he can always quote the good libertarian Terence, whose Phor-mio immortalized the apothegm : *quot homines tot sententiae.* Anxious to emphasize his point, Terence added for good measure that tastes differ *(suus quique mos)*. If that is, indeed, the case (and Terence was no fool), there is no future for the fratricidal state of psychology. Although the application of Pragmatic Sanctions (the laws of succession) does not bode well for the progress of psycho-analytic principles, it is — in the case of eclectic psychotherapy — a perfectly legitimate device.

REFERENCES

Glover, E. (1931). The therapeutic effect of inexact interpretation : a contribution to the theory of suggestion. In *The technique of psychoanalysis*. London : Ballière, Tindall & Cox, 1955.

————. (1940). An investigation of the technique of psychoanalysis. In *The technique of psychoanalysis*. London : Ballière, Tindall & Cox, 1955.

Mitchell, T. W. (1927). *Problems in psychopathology*. London : Kegan Paul, Trench, Trubner.

3

Melanie Klein's Theory and Technique: Her Life and Work

JOHN A. LINDON

MELANIE KLEIN was born in Vienna on March 30, 1882, the youngest of four children. Her father was from an Orthodox Jewish family and had trained to be a student of the Talmud. At 37, he broke away from his Orthodox background, managed to acquire an academic education, and then became a doctor of medicine. At 44 he married a 25-year-old girl who had great strength and resourcefulness. Because of his meager income, his wife opened a shop in order to earn enough money to provide a good education for the children; she also managed the household and raised the children. Melanie Klein greatly admired the independent spirit and scientific attitude of her father, Dr. Reizes, but their relationship was never very close; this may have been due in part to the more than 50-year age difference. She felt closer to her mother, Libussa; she was deeply fond of her and admired her for her beauty, intellect, and desire for knowledge.

As a small child Melanie came into intimate contact with death. Her siblings Emilie, Emmanuel, and Sidonie were six, five, and four years older than she. Sidonie died at the age of nine, when Melanie was about five. Sidonie was bedridden for a year before her death and spent a great deal of her time teaching Melanie what she knew. Melanie felt that this knowledge was given to her in trust, and to please her sister she learned to read, write, and do some arithmetic before she was five. When she was older she had a similarly inspiring relationship with her brother Emmanuel, five years her senior. He was a gifted boy — interested in literature, art, and music. As an accomplished pianist and budding writer, he encouraged Melanie to share his interests. He believed in her potentialities, and under his influence she developed a passion for literature and music. But this relationship, as with Sidonie, was tinged with impending death. Her brother suffered from heart disease and died at 25, when Melanie was 20.

When Melanie was 14 she decided to study medicine, and, coached by Emmanuel, she passed the entrance examination to the Vienna Gymnasium, the only school preparing girls for the university at that time. Soon after her matriculation at the age of 17, she became engaged to Arthur Klein, an industrial chemist. Her early engagement and her marriage at 21 made her change her plans; she studied art and history at the University of Vienna, but never received a degree. Melanie Klein retained her interest in medicine and always regretted that she had not studied it.

Because of her husband's work, the family traveled a great deal. They had three children: Melitta was born when Mrs. Klein was 21, Hans three years later, and Eric seven years after Hans (Jaques, 1962). A few years before World War I, the family settled in Budapest, where Melanie Klein came across a book by Sigmund Freud. Immediately she became interested in the new science of psychoanalysis. The manner of her entry into the world of psychoanalysis, which would be almost impossible today, was remarkable even then. There she was, a Budapest housewife in her thirties with a husband and three young children, without any medical training or academic degrees, when she sought analysis with Sandor Ferenczi during World War I. She was in analysis for several years. During this time she began to observe and give analytic interpretations to the emotionally distressed child of a relative.

Ferenczi, who was greatly interested in the advancement of child therapy, recognized the talent of his analysand because of her skillful handling of the disturbed child. He discussed her aptitude with her and encouraged her to work in this new field of child therapy. He did all he could to help her with her first professional efforts in 1919. She felt Ferenczi's "strong and direct feeling for the unconscious and for symbolism and the remarkable rapport he had with the minds of children had a lasting influence on her and her understanding of children" (Klein, 1932).

She read her first paper on July 19, 1919, to the Budapest Psychoanalytic Society. Later it was expanded and appeared as her first published work, "The Development of a Child" (Klein, 1921). Late in 1919 she was elected a member of the Budapest Society. At the Psychoanalytic Congress in The Hague in 1920, she met Freud as well as Abraham, Deutsch, Groddeck, Hug-Helmuth, Jung, Reich, Roheim, and others. Karl Abraham was impressed with her and invited her to practice in Berlin.

In January, 1921, her husband went to Sweden and she and the children moved to Berlin. This separation was the first step leading to a divorce, which took place in 1923. She never remarried. In Berlin, Abraham invited her to work as the first child therapist at the Berlin Psychoanalytic Institute, which had opened the previous year. Her first case was a five-year-old boy, who was treated in his own home. From the start she recognized that he expressed his fantasies and anxieties mainly in play with his toys. She tried interpreting what he dramatized in a manner similar to Freud's interpretation of dreams. Thus began the development of her psychoanalytic play technique.

For the next five years she worked in Berlin, laying the foundations of her technique and describing the complex role of oral aggression in childhood development and the linked mechanisms of introjection and projection. This work flowed from the earlier insights of Ferenczi and others, but she was impressed with the universality and complexity of aggressive impulses and emphasized their dynamic nature and results. These years in Berlin were hard and turbulent. Her findings about the horrifying and unrealistic nature of her young patients' fantasies led to dissension among many of her colleagues, especially those who only worked with adults. Her insistence on the feasibility of child analysis without any educative or reassuring concomitants was rarely accepted. Anna Freud's technique and findings in Vienna sharply contrasted with Melanie Klein's. She needed all her courage and tenacity to persist in the face of passionate criticism and even harsh personal attacks. In 1946, she seemed to enjoy noting that Anna Freud had come to feel that child analysts could concentrate on purely analytic work without educative concomitants and that in other areas Anna Freud had moved closer to the views Klein had expressed 20 years earlier and still held (Klein, 1950b).

But in all her difficulties, another great analyst, Karl Abraham, president of the Berlin Psychoanalytic Society, supported and steadily encouraged her. He fully grasped the practical and theoretical possibilities of child analysis; at the First Conference of German Psychoanalysts at Würzburg in October, 1924, while he was summing up Klein's paper (the Erna case, in *The Psychoanalysis of Children*) on her treatment of an obsessional neurosis in a child, he declared, "The future of psychoanalysis lies in play analysis" (Money-Kyrle, 1955).

In spite of Abraham's repeated misgivings about the wisdom of engaging in analytic relationships within the small Berlin Psychoanalytic Society, Klein persuaded him to do further analysis of her at the beginning of 1924. This came to an end 14 months later when Abraham became ill and later died. This analysis made a strong impression on her, and she spoke with the deepest admiration and gratitude of Abraham as an analyst and teacher. After his death she carried on regular and daily self-analysis.

At the invitation of Ernest Jones, she gave a course of lectures in London during the summer of 1925. After Abraham's death she found the Berlin Society with its heavy criticism and personal attacks unpleasant; anti-Semitism was growing in Berlin; her children were growing up and no longer needed so much of her attention. Therefore, in 1926 when Ernest Jones asked her to move to England and work in the British Psychoanalytic Society, she gratefully accepted and moved to London with her youngest son. It was a decision she never regretted.

Ernest Jones was the third great analyst to recognize and personally sponsor her talents; with his support she continued her work with children. Many British analysts were eager to learn child analysis from her, and she undertook the supervision of their child cases. Edward Glover, Susan Isaacs, and Joan Riviere particularly welcomed her ideas. By the early 1930s she had begun to analyze adults as well as children and to develop her technique of adult analysis, which derived from her findings about the earliest internal anxieties.

While her analytic work flourished, her private life was marked by tragedy when her 27-year-old son, Hans, was killed in a mountaineering accident in the spring of 1934. Her daughter, Melitta Schmideberg, studied medicine, as her mother once had intended to do, and became an analyst. Earlier, when the mother and daughter both lived in Berlin, they had become intimately acquainted with the spirit and methods of the psychoanalytic pioneers. In later years, their scientific opinions differed, and Melitta Schmideberg became an outstanding therapist and analytic research worker in New York. Recently she returned to London.

Klein found much pleasure in her relationship with Eric, her younger son, who married and had three children in London, where he is a business executive. She was devoted to her grandchildren and found much happiness through them. She also found lasting pleasure with her friends and pupils, and derived deep enjoyment from art, particularly in her last years (Bion *et al.*, 1961 ; Clyne, 1961).

During the thirties her work grew in scope and depth ; she wrote prolifically, enlarging her earlier concepts. She was successively occupied with the appearance of the Oedipus complex and the superego in infancy, and then she developed her concept of the depressive position and began her work on psychotic processes. However, there was controversy.

The technique to which she was led by her findings about the fluctuations of mood caused by immediate introjection and projection processes required early and frequent interpretations and was out of line with the views of other analysts. The terms she used to describe her work involved concepts that were not universally accepted, and her need to teach her views and methods to others was considered by some as a danger to classical analytic teaching. By the late thirties Viennese analysts began arriving in London to escape Hitler. Their work with ego psychology had led them to different conclusions about the child's capacity for early experience. With their arrival opposition to Melanie Klein seemed to start in earnest (Jones, 1950 ; Segal, 1961b).

The ensuing decade of controversy cost Klein the full support of many British analysts who had previously welcomed her. She drew around her a group of pupils who later became known in the British Society as "the Kleinians." These pupils were able to work with her concepts and support one another without serious controversy, and yet could present their findings to their analytic colleagues. Some of the controversy was personal. Klein was at the center and vigorous in the defense of her work.

Shortly before World War II a group within the British Society was established to increase mutual understanding and communication, but the war intervened and dispersed a number of its key members. Meanwhile, increasingly bitter differences of opinion were expressed about Klein's work at meetings of the British Society; eventually a series of papers were presented on opposing points of view. Instead of increasing mutual understanding and communication, these papers reinforced the major points of difference beyond the possibility of reconciliation. Although the Society-Institute avoided a formal split, the schism was deep and persisted. Within the Institute there is a large Kleinian school that has trained many analysts who practice in England, South America, and on the Continent. Although Kleinian theories have considerably influenced analytic thinking in much of the world, they are not well known in the United States.

As a supervising analyst at the London Institute, Klein was considered to be a perceptive, illuminating teacher who did not insist on "Kleinian" interpretations but who continually emphasized transference interpretation at every stage of clinical psychoanalysis. She indicated to the student how her own formulation differed, particularly with respect to interpretations of internal objects, but she didn't insist on this interpretation. Non-Kleinian candidates found it possible to profit from her perception of deep transference material. At the same time the candidates were able to maintain an open-minded, skeptical attitude regarding the theoretical assumptions implicit in her reconstruction of the inner psychic world (Zetzel, 1961).

Klein treated her last child patient in the late 1940s, but until her death in 1960 she kept in close touch with child analysis by supervising many students who used her technique and conceptual systems. In her later years her main work was to teach and analyze psychoanalytic students, to treat adult patients, and to write. She remained creative to the end, as her writings show; she studied schizoid mechanisms and the psychoses, formulated the paranoid-schizoid position, and did work in infantile and oral envy. *Envy and Gratitude* (Klein, 1957) was written four years before her death, and during the succeeding two years she completed one of her most ambitious works, *Narrative of a Child Analysis* (Klein, 1961). Before she died at 78 years of age, she was writing "The Psychoanalytic Study of Oresteia of Aeschylus," which she was preparing for the Edinburgh International Psychoanalytic Congress (Klein, 1963).

During her last ten years, with the thinning of her own generation, she supported and was supported professionally by her friends and pupils. Her pupils worked with her ideas and pursued their implications in the fields of neuroses, character disorder, psychoses, sociology, and industry. Now that there were many others who would continue Klein's work, she arrived at a serenity that allowed her quiet pride in her work. Those who knew her only during her last ten years would see a woman whose frailty contrasted with a sharp mind and an enduring femininity and freshness. This picture gave only occasional hints of the militant strength and vigor of her earlier years. Some were surprised to find that this cartographer of the destructive instincts was herself not a fierce giantess (Bion *et al.*, 1961 ; Lester, 1959b).

Her pleasure in living showed itself in many ways, none more infectious than her chuckle that bubbled out of her even in scientific meetings and that could reduce her to laughing helplessness. She regularly conducted continuous case conferences for the senior analysts of the Kleinian group and was frequently amused when she had to point out that material which had been presented as evidence of oral envy or some other of her own findings was actually a regressive disguise of classical oedipal conflicts. She remained a true Freudian analyst (Evans, 1962).

She sought peace from the controversy that had surrounded her for so many years in the company of those who sympathized with her work — those whom she could count on to extend that work. An enthusiastic teacher even at 78, she was happy with young people who learned from her (Klein, 1959). She leaned a great deal on her younger friends and liked to accompany them. In 1959, she accepted an invitation to fly to Los Angeles, California, to conduct several weeks of case supervision and lecturing, and was most disappointed when her physician would not allow her to make the trip (Jones, 1952).

The following year a slowly growing malignancy was discovered and successfully removed by surgery. Her postoperative course seemed satisfactory. Two hours after an enjoyable visit with her son Eric, she suddenly and quietly died of a pulmonary embolus on September 22, 1960, in a London hospital (Clyne, 1961).

MELANIE KLEIN'S WORK

Melanie Klein considered herself a faithful adherent of Sigmund Freud; at no time did she regard her work as an independent set of theories of mental functioning, complete in itself and replacing Freudian theory. She believed that her work contributed to psychoanalysis, extending psychoanalytic understanding into the very early stages of infancy and the deeper layers of the unconscious.

Her Work With Children

In 1919, when, with Ferenczi's encouragement, she began to work with children, some psychoanalytic work had already been done, particularly by Dr. Hug-Helmuth. Klein treated her first child analytic patient, Fritz, a five-year-old boy, in his own home. She soon recognized that the child was using his toys in play mainly to express symbolically his experiences, fantasies, and anxieties. She recognized that this mode of expression was also the language of dreams; using Freud's method of dream interpretation as her guide, she interpreted these meanings to him. As a result additional material came into his play and verbalization. By interpreting both the child's verbalizations and his play, she applied the basic principle of free association. She was also guided throughout by two other tenets of psychoanalysis established by Sigmund Freud which from the beginning she regarded as fundamental: that psychoanalytic therapy is based on insight and that the analysis of transference is the usual means of achieving this aim.

At times Klein became perturbed by the intensity of the anxieties that were brought into the open through her interpretations to her five-year-old patient. She sought advice from Karl Abraham, who assured her that since her interpretations had often produced relief and since the analysis was obviously making progress, he saw no need for changing the approach. She was much encouraged by his support; as things turned out, in the next few days the child's anxiety, which had come to a head, greatly diminished. The conviction that she gained in this analysis strongly affected the course of her work (Klein, 1955a).

A definite step in the development of play technique was made in 1923 when she analyzed Rita, aged two years and nine months, her youngest patient. With Rita she decided that treatment should not take place in the child's home because she believed that transference could only be established and maintained if the patient felt that the consulting room or play room — indeed, the whole analysis — were something separate from his home life. Only under such conditions could the patient overcome his resistances against experiencing and expressing thoughts, feelings, and desires that were incompatible with convention and (in the case of a child) were felt to be at variance with much of what he had been taught (Klein, 1932, 1945).

She was convinced that one could achieve with a child a relationship free from educational, moral, or reassuring interferences so that a proper analysis could be carried out. (In *Narrative of a Child Analysis* [written in 1960], she noted that any time she deviated from her purely analytic role she subsequently regretted it [Klein, 1961].) Klein observed that every therapist who worked with children found to his surprise that, even in very young children, their capacity for insight often exceeded that of adults. She felt the explanation was that in part there are closer connections between the conscious and the unconscious in young children, that infantile repressions are less powerful, and that the infant's intellectual capacities are often underrated. Her conviction that it was necessary to reach the level at which unconscious anxiety was active led her deeper and deeper into the mind of the child. With Karl Abraham's encouragement she persisted in her approach, although it required a radical change in technique.

From her work with children, she became convinced that the superego, as conceived by Freud, was the end product of a development that began in early infancy. She observed that the superego was experienced as consisting of a variety of figures that the child unconsciously felt existed within him and functioned within his body. These internal figures or objects were once external objects in the child's experiences but had been introjected. She discovered the vital part that reparation plays in mental life; she believed that it includes a variety of processes by which the ego undoes the harm committed in fantasy and restores, preserves, and revives objects. The importance of reparation, bound up as it is with feelings of guilt, also lies in the major contributions it makes to all sublimations, and thus to mental health. As she continued to work with young children, she became increasingly convinced of the fundamental importance of oral sadistic impulses and their role in destructive fantasies, as discovered by Karl Abraham (1924).

From 1924 to 1926 her analysis of a paranoid girl, Erna, eventually helped her formulate a number of conclusions, especially the view that the early superego, built up when oral sadistic impulses and fantasies are at their height, underlies psychoses (Klein, 1928a, 1930a). By 1930 Klein had begun to work with adult neurotics, and she found it especially valuable from clinical and theoretical points of view to analyze adults and children simultaneously. Her work with neurotic adults and with neurotic and psychotic children led to her hypothesis that anxiety of a psychotic nature is, in some measure, part of normal infantile development and is expressed and worked through in the course of infantile neuroses. These psychotic-like paranoid and depressive anxieties are transient. She emphasized that she was not suggesting that children go through an infantile psychosis, but rather suffer with transient periods of psychotic-like anxieties.

She attributed considerable importance to symbolism and formulated certain theories about the processes of symbol formation. Play analysis had shown that symbolism enables the child to transfer not only objects but also fantasies, anxieties, and guilt to objects other than people. Her findings were in line with Ernest Jones's (1916) paper, "The Theory of Symbolism." Klein believed that in children a severe inhibition of the capacity to form and use symbols, and so develop fantasy life, indicated a serious disturbance. Such inhibitions and the resulting disturbance in relation to the external world and to reality are characteristic of schizophrenia.

At this time she published *The Psycho-Analysis of Children* (Klein, 1932). Although some of her major ideas appeared in this book, she modified her views considerably with later analytic experience; for example, it was late in her career when she discerned the fundamental importance of envy and its essentially aggressive nature (Evans, 1962). The major steps in the development of her ideas were :

1. Discovery of early forms of the ego, projective and introjective mechanisms for building up the child's internal world, and early forms of the oedipus complex.
2. Discovery of the crucial place in development of the depressive position, linked with the infant's awareness of his mother as a whole and separate person.
3. Discovery of the anxieties and the mechanisms that she termed the paranoid-schizoid position, a point of fixation in psychotic illness.
4. Discovery of early oral envy and its influence on the early stages of development.

Her study of the changes in ego structure and the types of anxiety in object relationships that occur between the paranoid-schizoid and the depressive positions was particularly important. Her followers believe that these discoveries are fundamental milestones in understanding early development.

Her Theories on the Very Early Stages of Infancy
and the Deeper Layers of the Unconscious

In describing her theories to her critics, Klein pointed out : "Allowance must be made for the great difficulty of expressing a young child's feelings and phantasies in adult language. All descriptions of early unconscious phantasies — and for that matter of unconscious phantasies in general — can therefore only be considered as pointers to the contents rather than to the form of such phantasies" (Klein, 1945).

The newborn baby experiences anxiety of a persecutory nature; the young infant feels évery discomfort as though it were inflicted on him by hostile forces. If he is comforted, he experiences happier emotions that appear to come from good forces; these forces enable the infant to have his first loving relationship with an object. The infant has an innate awareness of the existence of the mother, comparable to that of newborn animals who immediately turn to the mother to find their food. The human animal is exactly the same in that respect, and this knowledge underlies the infant's primal relation to his mother. One can observe that a baby of only a few weeks already looks up to his mother's face; recognizes her footsteps, the touch of her hands, and the smell and feel of her breast or the bottle.

In the earliest stages, love and understanding (or hate) are expressed by the mother's handling of her baby and lead to a kind of oneness — an unconscious feeling between the mother and the child of being in close relation to each other. The infant's feeling of being understood underlies the first and fundamental relationship in his life — his tie with his mother.

At the same time he experiences love, he also feels discomfort, pain, and frustration. Frustration, which to some extent is unavoidable, strengthens hate and aggressiveness. Frustration means more than going without food at certain times. There are unconscious desires — not always perceptible in the behavior of the infant — demanding the mother's continuous presence and her exclusive love. That the infant is greedy and wants more than even the best external situation can provide is part of his emotional life. He experiences these painful emotions as persecution and they form part of his feelings about his mother, who in his first few months represents his whole external world; he has both good and bad impressions of her, leading to a twofold attitude toward her, even under the best possible circumstances.

Both the capacity to love and the sense of persecution are traceable to the infant's earliest mental processes, and the mother is the first focus of these feelings. Destructive impulses and their concomitant emotions — resentment and the resultant feelings of hate, the incapacity to be reconciled, and envy of the all-powerful object — all arouse persecutory anxiety in the infant.

Innate aggressiveness in the young child is bound to be activated by unfavorable external circumstances, and, conversely, to be mitigated by love and understanding. Although the importance of external circumstances is now increasingly recognized, the importance of internal factors is still underrated. Destructive impulses, varying from individual to individual, are an integral part of mental life even under the best circumstances; the development of the child and the attitudes of adults both result from the interaction between internal and external influences. The struggle between love and hate can be recognized to some extent by carefully observing babies. Some babies experience strong resentment about any frustration and show this by their inability to accept gratification when it follows a deprivation. Such infants have stronger innate aggressiveness and greed than those whose occasional outbursts of rage are soon over. Babies in the latter group feel loved again when they receive gratification.

In her analyses of children Klein saw the strength and speed of introjection and projection and the importance of their constant fluctuations. From the beginning of postnatal life introjection and projection function as some of the earliest activities of the ego. *Introjection* implies that the situations and objects encountered by the infant are taken into his self and become part of his inner life.

Klein discovered that the external objects that are introjected are experienced as being concretely present within the body. She always made it plain that she followed Abraham's theory that the infant could only introject "part objects" until he was old enough to realize that his mother was a whole and separate person. In the child's perception, mother's breast, face, hands, and other parts only come together as part of a whole person in the latter half of his first year. The internalized breast, face, hands, and so forth are the precursors of the internalized mother herself. The core of the ego structure is the internalized breast. Klein's theories on "internal objects" constituted a milestone in her work and are used extensively (Evans, 1962).

Mental life cannot be evaluated even in adults without considering additions to the personality that come from continuous introjection. *Projection,* which goes on simultaneously, is a process in which the infant attributes his own feelings to others around him. Love and hate toward the mother are bound up with the infant's capacity to project all his emotions onto her, thereby making her into a good as well as a bad object.

Projection alters the infant's impression of his environment; by introjection this changed picture of his environment influences what goes on in his mind. Thus, an inner world is built up that partly reflects the external one. In this way, introjection and projection go on throughout life; although they are modified in the course of maturation, they will always affect the individual's relationship with the world about him. Therefore, even in the "normal" adult, the judgement of reality is to some extent influenced by his internal world.

The processes of projection and introjection must be thought of as unconscious fantasies. "Fantasy is in the first instance the mental corollary, the psychic representative of instinct. There is no impulse, no instinctual urge or response which is not experienced as unconscious fantasy. . . . A fantasy represents the particular content of the urges or feelings dominating the mind at the moment" (Isaacs, 1952).

Unconscious fantasies are activities of the mind that accompany every impulse experienced by the infant. For example, a hungry baby can temporarily deal with his hunger by hallucinating the satisfaction of receiving the breast with all its attendant pleasures: the taste of milk, the warm feeling of the breast, and being held and loved by the mother. But similarly unconscious fantasy can also lead the infant to feel deprived and persecuted by the breast that refuses to give satisfaction. As fantasies become more elaborate, their richness and their influence cannot be overrated.

The continuing interplay between introjection and projection, if it is not excessive or dominated by hostility, leads to enrichment of the inner world and improvement of relations with the external world. These are all mechanisms of maturation and may be significant in the dynamic understanding of the growth of the personality.

Another primal activity of the infantile mind is *splitting* — the tendency to separate impulses and objects into various aspects : good, bad, undamaged, damaged, etc. This occurs in part because the early ego lacks coherence ; the child's persecutory anxiety reinforces his need to separate the loved object from the dangerous one, thereby leading to a split between love and hate. The young infant's self-preservation depends on his trust in a good mother. By splitting the two aspects and clinging to the good one, he preserves his belief in a good object and in his capacity to love it. This is an essential condition for staying alive. Without at least some of this belief, he feels exposed to a hostile world and fears that he will be destroyed by it ; this hostile world will also be built up inside him by introjection.

Some babies without organic pathology perish because they have not been able to develop a trusting relation with a good mother. (René Spitz's studies of infants who suffer maternal rejection in the first year of life seem to corroborate this. He found that 29 per cent of the infants in a prison nursery who had lost their maternal objects died in the first year ; many more become schizophrenic, although they received the identical good care as other infants in the same nursery [Spitz, 1946].)

Splitting processes diminish during normal development as the ego becomes integrated. The infant's increasing capacity to understand external reality and bring together his contradictory impulses also leads to a greater synthesis of the good and the bad aspects of the object. People can be loved in spite of their faults ; the world need not be viewed only in terms of black and white.

Splitting processes change in form and content as development progresses but are never entirely eliminated. During the first three to four months of life, omnipotent destructive impulses, persecutory anxiety, and splitting predominate ; introjection is of "part objects." Klein called this combination of mechanisms and anxieties the *paranoid-schizoid position* ; in extreme cases it may lead to paranoia and schizophrenic illness when excessive persecutory anxiety interferes with the gradual integration of the ego.

Allied with splitting is another primal activity of the infantile mind that Klein called *projective identification*. It occurs when the weak, infantile mind splits off of those qualities it experiences as dangerous or endangered and projects them into some other person and then identifies with that person. This defense is employed before the ego is strong enough to use repression. Projective identification has many repercussions: the ego feels depleted; the infantile mind wishes and fears to regain its split-off fragment; one needs omnipotent control over the person who has the projected part of one's own mind so that the dangerous impulse will not be acted out and that one will not forever lose that portion of the mind.

Klein and her coworkers made many clinical contributions to the understanding of schizophrenia, paranoia, and manic-depressive psychoses. Projective identification, splitting, introjection, and projection were shown to be the major defenses employed in these psychoses because excessive persecutory anxiety had interfered with the gradual integration of the ego, leaving it fixated at the paranoid-schizoid position.

Klein believed that the infant's destructive feelings come from a death instinct that is projected onto the external world to protect the self. She believed that anxiety does not spring from the libidinal component of the fused Eros-Thanatos drives, but from the child's fear of his own agression which he can only partially control. The child is anxious about damage he does to himself by uncontrolled aggression (for example, in screaming fits) and about the harm he may do to others. Even the adolescent does not feel anxious about his increasing libidinal drives as such, but only about the sadistic component of these drives (Evans, 1962).

The concomitants of destructive feelings are significant; greed and envy are particularly disturbing factors, first in relation to the mother, then throughout life. *Greed* varies considerably from one infant to another because of constitutional factors. At one extreme are babies who can never be satisfied. With greed goes the urge to empty the mother's breast and to exploit every source of satisfaction without considering anyone else. A very greedy infant may enjoy whatever he receives for the time being, but he soon becomes dissatisfied and is driven to exploit, first, the mother and then anyone in the family who can give him attention, food, or other gratification — initially only in fantasy but later in both reality and fantasy. Greed is increased by anxiety — of being deprived, of being robbed, and of not being good enough to be loved. The infant who is so greedy for love and attention is also uncertain about his own capacity to love because of the hate that is aroused by his frustration. These dynamics, fundamentally unchanged, can be seen in the greed of the older child and the adult.

Whenever the infant is hungry or feels neglected, his frustration leads him to fantasy that the milk and love are deliberately being withheld from him or being kept by the mother for her own benefit. Such suspicions are the basis of *envy*. Inherent in this feeling is the urge to possess the object and also to spoil the object itself. If envy is strong, its spoiling quality leads to a disturbed relation with the mother and with other people later on; it also means that nothing can be fully enjoyed because the desired thing has already been spoiled by envy. Furthermore, if envy is strong, goodness cannot become assimilated as part of one's inner life, thereby giving rise to gratitude.

By contrast, the capacity to fully enjoy what has been received and to experience gratitude toward the person who gives it strongly affect the child's character and his relations with other people. *Gratitude*, a component of love, mitigates hateful feelings; therefore, through continuing projection and introjection, the child experiences both the real external world and his psychic inner world as friendlier environments.

Klein believed that the superego begins to operate much earlier than postulated by Freud. From babyhood on, the mother and eventually others are taken into the self as part objects; this leads to a variety of identifications, favorable and unfavorable. In the fifth, sixth, or seventh month of life, as the ego is increasingly integrated, the infant begins to realize, at first only intermittently, that the gratifying objects he needs and loves are aspects of the frustrating ones he hates and in fantasy destroys. Thus, he has matured to the point of perceiving whole objects.

With this discovery, he begins to feel concern about these loved objects, for he cannot yet distinguish between his fantasies and their lack of actual effects. He experiences feelings of guilt as well as the urge to preserve these objects and to make reparation to them for harm done. The anxiety he experiences now is of a predominantly depressive nature; its accompanying emotions and the defenses employed against them, which are part of normal development, are termed "the depressive position." Feelings of guilt that occasionally arise in every one have very deep roots in infancy, and the tendency to make reparation plays an important role in one's sublimations and object relations. This is a completely new approach to the understanding of Adam and Eve's original sin and guilt.

A *working-through process* occurs in all normal development. The infant increasingly adapts to external reality, thereby achieving a less fantastic picture of the world around him; for example, the return of the mother makes her absence less frightening and so the child becomes less suspicious of her. In this way the infant gradually works through his early fears and comes to terms with his conflicting impulses and emotions. At this stage depressive anxiety predominates and persecutory anxiety diminishes. Many apparently odd manifestations, such as inexplicable phobias of infancy, are indications of working through the depressive position. If guilt is not excessive, the urge to make reparation brings relief. Depressive and persecutory anxieties are never entirely overcome; they may recur temporarily under pressure, but a relatively normal person can cope with them and regain his balance.

In talking of the paranoid-schizoid position and the depressive position, Klein used the terms "positions" rather than "stages of development" to emphasize the fact that, owing to fixation and regression, earlier stages coexist with later ones (Money-Kyrle, 1955).

External experiences are of paramount importance throughout life. However, even in the infant, much depends on the ways in which the external influences are interpreted and assimilated by the child; this, in turn, largely depends on the strength of destructive impulses and persecutory and depressive anxieties.

The early wish to make reparation adds to the innate capacity for love. In the sublimations that arise from the earliest interests of the child, constructive activities predominate; the child unconsciously feels that such activities will help restore loved people whom he has damaged in his inner world. The fact that no one is entirely free from guilt is valuable in that it implies that he has never fully exhausted his wish to make reparation and to create in whatever way he can. Melanie Klein's views could lead to completely new insights into the dynamics of creativity as variations of reparation.

Even if the individual's development is satisfactory and leads to varied enjoyments, some feeling of mourning for the irretrievably lost pleasures of infancy, real and imagined, and unfulfilled possibilities can still be found in deeper layers of the mind. Emotional maturity means that these feelings of loss can be counteracted up to a point by the ability to accept substitutes, and that infantile fantasies do not disturb adult emotional life. The ability to enjoy available pleasures is bound up at any age with a relative freedom from envy and grievances. Contentment in later life can be found by enjoying vicariously the pleasures of young people, particularly of one's children and grandchildren. Another source of gratification, even before old age, is the richness of the memories that keep the past alive (Klein, 1960a, 1960c, 1963).

Klein believed that the infant's fear of losing the loved object as a result of his hatred and agression enters into his object relations and oedipus complex from the beginning and influences his passage through subsequent conflict-filled anal, phallic, and oedipal stages of development. "The infant's emotional life, the early defenses built up under the stress of the conflict between love, hatred, and guilt and the vicissitudes of the child's identifications — all these are topics which may well occupy analytic research for a long time to come . . . and lead us to a fuller understanding of the personality which implies a fuller understanding of the Oedipus complex and of sexual development" (Klein, 1945).

Some Comments About the Controversy

Aside from Sigmund Freud, probably no analyst has aroused as much controversy as Melanie Klein during her more than 40 years of psychoanalytic work. Originally I had intended to examine the controversy in a third section of this chapter; when that part of the manuscript alone grew to more than double the space allotted for the whole chapter, it became clear that a separate paper would be needed.

The criticisms of many analysts were presented in 1945 by Edward Glover who formulated his critique in a manuscript of book length (Glover, 1945). In 1962, additional criticisms appeared in reviews of Melanie Klein's last book, *Narrative of a Child Analysis,* published after her death. Some critics say that her work "constitutes deviation" from Freudian theory (Lorand, 1957); that she has "carried psychoanalysis *ad absurdum,*" that no distinction is made "between neurosis and schizophrenia, in any case, for 'psychotic' and 'persecutory' anxiety is supposed to be present in all cases," and that "the child's productions are severely distorted by interpretations" (Mosse, 1962).

Four of the most careful, scientific evaluations were made by Brierley, Fairbairn, Guntrip, and Winnicott, none of whom are Kleinians. Yet each showed that he understood the theories even if he disagreed; unfortunately, this was not true of many of the critics.

Marjorie Brierley (1951) devotes much of her book *Trends in Psychoanalysis* to a detailed examination of Kleinian theory.

Brierley, one of the senior training analysts at the London Institute, was trained by Edward Glover. She was one of the key members of the group that was formed within the British Psychoanalytic Society to evaluate Kleinian theory. Brierley states that Glover's critique "contains much sound criticism but is so polemical that it amounts to an exposé of the worst that could happen if the majority of psychoanalysts accepted quite uncritically every considered and unconsidered word uttered by Melanie Klein and regarded them as constituting a self-sufficient theory of mental life."

Brierley became convinced that "one of the major difficulties in coming to grips with Melanie Klein's views is that her generalizations tend to be expressed in perceptual rather than conceptual terms." She also criticized the Kleinians for "lack of clarity in definition and use of terminology . . . and a tendency to personification." She presents evidence to support the "view that Melanie Klein had not so far paid enough attention to the role of regression in the retrospective crystallization of depressive fantasies or in the etiology of manic-depressive states." She believes that there has been an overemphasis on object-relationships that can be corrected by correlating this work with that of those who have followed instinct vicissitudes.

Brierley, like Mendelson (1960), finds much in the writings of Freud (for example, 1915–1933), indicating that Klein was following his lead. For example, Brierley points out that in *The Ego and the Id* Freud (1923) described the ego as a precipitate of abandoned object-cathexes and the superego as a combination of parental identifications. Brierley (1951) states: "One is often tempted to wonder whether, if Freud had recognized the internal economy of melancholia before he formulated his theory of narcissism, he and Abraham would not themselves have carried further their exploration of intrapsychic animism."

Like Ernest Jones (1916, 1950, 1952), Brierley does not accept all of Klein's theories. She believes that certain corrections have already been made and that others will be made with further clinical work. She says that Melanie Klein's "work can justly be assessed only in the contribution [it makes] to psychoanalysis, a contribution in adding to legitimate growth and expansion which is still in the process of determination. Just and impartial assessment requires time; it cannot be effected by logic alone but must be put to the test of clinical experience and thus many years may be needed to stabilize judgment."

Brierley concludes: "the work of Melanie Klein cannot and should not attempt to stand alone but neither should it be dismissed as a deviation without value. . . . Melanie Klein has focused attention on the formative pre-history of the oedipus phase, and, apart from the vexed questions of precise chronology and etiology, she has in fact greatly enriched our appreciation of the complexity of the interplay of object-relationships, internal and external, identificatory and definitive, which result in a decisive pattern of post-oedipal ego organization, the ground plan of future personal development."

Ten years after Brierley's assessment, Guntrip (1965) published *Personality Structure and Human Interaction,* a massive work in which he evaluated psychoanalytic theories and sifted out inconsistencies; as Wisdom (1963) stated in a highly favorable review, "the overall aim of the book is to put Fairbairn squarely on the map and portray Fairbairn's work as a major system."

Guntrip credits Melanie Klein with major discoveries but criticizes her for adhering too closely to Freud's theories. He cites many examples in which Klein accepted Freud's theories of a death instinct and tried to incorporate them into her own theoretical formulations even though logically her own discoveries should have led her to new reformulations. He, like Brierley, feels that Klein's "loose and ill defined use of terms lends an element of confusion and lack of conceptual precision." Guntrip believes that Fairbairn "was able to follow up Klein's discoveries and lead to a new formulation of personality development which Melanie Klein logically should have come to expect for her loyal adherence to Freud's ideas."

Winnicott (1965), a brilliant, independent thinker, synthesizes in my view the best of Freud, Klein, and Fairbairn with his own original contributions. Winnicott criticizes Klein for what he feels are her "more doubtful contributions" — her utilization of the theory of the life and death instincts and her attempts to describe infantile destructiveness in terms of hereditary envy. However, he also feels that she made many valuable contributions:

1. Developed a strict orthodox technique for the psychoanalysis of children.
2. Used tiny toys in the initial stages to facilitate the technique.
3. Developed technique for analysis of two-and-a-half-year-old children and older.

4. Recognized fantasy as localized by the child (or adult) — inside or outside the self.
5. Understood internal benign and persecutory forces or "objects" and their origin in satisfactory or unsatisfactory instinctual experiences (originally oral and oral sadistic).
6. Recognized projection and introjection as mental mechanisms that arise in relation to the child's experience of the bodily functions of incorporation and excretion.
7. Emphasized the importance of destructive elements in object relationships, that is, apart from anger and frustration.
8. Developed a theory of the individual's attainment of a capacity for concern — the depressive position.
9. Related constructive play, work, potency, and child bearing to the depressive position.
10. Understood the denial of depression (manic defense).
11. Understood threatened chaos in the inner psychic reality and the defenses related to this chaos (obsessional neurosis or depressive mood).
12. Postulated infantile impulses, talion fears, and the splitting of the object prior to the attainment of ambivalence.
13. Attempted to state infant psychology without referring to the quality of the environmental provision.

Maxwell Gitelson may have answered one of the major criticisms of Klein : that she denigrates the role of the oedipus complex and is even anti-Freud in focussing on the pregenital stages of development. At the "Symposium on Re-evaluation of the Oedipus Complex" at the Seventeenth International Psychoanalytic Congress, Gitelson stressed that a satisfactory mother-child relationship was required in order for an individual to enter into and solve the problems of the oedipal period. He said that many borderline patients in current analytic practice, far from being able to deal with oedipal problems, had never successfully solved the primary problems of the mother-child relationship. Implying, then, that one who had begun to cope with oedipal situations has already gone far in his development, Gitelson (1952) concluded that "the Oedipus complex thus has special importance, not so much as the nucleus of the neurosis but as the nucleus of normal character structure and as basis of mature life."

It is interesting that many analysts are now arriving at conclusions that are similar to the most controversial ones of Klein, but almost none of them mentions her pioneering research. In "Toward the Biology of the Depressive Constellation," Therese Benedek (1956) describes the same theoretical and clinical formulations as Klein's "depressive position." In "On Identification," Roy Grinker (1957) uses different conceptual formulations to arrive at conclusions similar to Klein's. In "Anaclitic Depression," René Spitz (1946) arrives at many similar theoterical conclusions, as does Erik Erikson (1950). Edmund Bergler's prolific writings reveal marked similarities to Melanie Klein's theories (Bergler, 1949, 1950, 1952; Lester, 1959a). In "Negativism and Emotional Surrender," and in "Oral Invasion and Self-Defense," Anna Freud (1951) and Richard Sterba (1957), respectively, theorize about the earliest negative oral attitudes of the infant in a way that is strikingly similar to Klein's theory.

In his book, *Psychoanalytic Concepts of Depression,* Myer Mendelson (1960) found that there was "surprisingly widespread agreement on various points" of Klein's theories by such authors as Michael Balint, Fairbairn, Karen Horney, (the 1936 papers), Therese Benedek, Edith Jacobson, Maxwell Gitelson, and René Spitz.

In examining Sigmund Freud's writings (1915, 1917, 1921, 1923), Mendelson, like Brierley, found much that seems to support Klein's theories, thus showing that Klein was following Freud's lead. In examining what Freud (1936) had to say in *The Problem of Anxiety,* Mendelson concluded that Freud conceived of anxiety, "the central problem of neurosis," as only a signal of the real danger — the danger of loss of the object as experienced in its various forms in the various phases of development. Mendelson (1960) suggested that there are "more than superficial resemblances to Klein's theories in Sigmund Freud's progressively increasing conceptualizations of the central problem in neurosis as the danger of the loss of the actual and introjected love objects."

Perhaps Ernest Jones (1950) provided the best summary of the controversy :

> The division in the British Society will presently, I doubt not, be reproduced in all other psychoanalytic societies, and in the absence of colleagues with first-hand experience of Mrs. Klein's work she must expect adverse critics to be in the

majority. In England itself the storm was heightened by the advent of the Viennese colleagues whose life in their home-land had become literally impossible. They added to the other criticisms the opinion that Mrs. Klein's conclusions not only diverged from, but were incompatible with Freud's. This, I find myself, a grossly exaggerated statement. Not that it should be in any event a decisive consideration, if experience showed that her conclusions were nearer the truth; I yield to no one in my admiration of Freud's genius, but on several occasions I have not hesitated to put forward reasons for thinking that certain of his inferences were imperfect. We had, however, become so accustomed to regard on good grounds, the various analysts who had separated from Freud, such as Adler, Jung, Stekel, and Rank, as being influenced by subjective motives — a rationalization of inner resistances — rather than by a profounder insight, that it seemed to many less presumptuous, and certainly easier, to place Mrs. Klein in the same class. Yet, if psychoanalysis is to remain a branch of science it is evident that, now that Freud's ability to continue his mag-nificent impetus has been extinguished, advance beyond the limits he reached is inevitable.

Freud's investigation of the unconscious mind, which is essentially that of the young infant, had revealed unexpected aspects of childhood, but before Mrs. Klein there had been little attempt to confirm these discoveries by the direct study of childhood. To her, therefore, is due the credit of carrying psychoanalysis to where it principally belongs — the heart of the child. Mrs. Klein with the high psychological gifts and the amazing moral courage that so distinguish her was not to be deterred by any difficulties. She developed fearlessly the play technique of interpretation, using it in combination with various other devices, and was soon in the position to confirm first hand all that Freud had inferred from adult material concerning the hitherto unknown unconscious mind of the child. Encouraged by this she exploited to the full the favor-able opportunity she had created for herself and determined to pursue her investigations to their uttermost limit. . . .

But Mrs. Klein has taught us much more about these mechanisms (introjection as formulated by Ferenczi in 1909) than was previously known. Not only do they apparently operate from the beginning of life, as was indeed implicit in

Freud's own description of the "pleasure ego," but they alternate and are interwoven with each other to such an extraordinary extent that the greater part of early infantile development can be described in terms of them. It is indeed becoming increasingly difficult to distinguish clearly between the processes of introjection, incorporation and identification. The whole theory of "internal objects," "good" and "bad," has thus been enormously extended, with important results both for our understanding of early development and for our daily therapeutic practice.

Mrs. Klein . . . extended her study into the field of insanity itself. . . . There must be an interrelation between these psychotic-like reactions and phases in the infant and the efflorescence of them in actual insanity. I am confident that Mrs. Klein's work will prove as fruitful in this field as it has always shown itself to be in the more familiar one of neurotic and normal development.

It would, it is true, be tempting to explain all criticisms of her work as a flinching from the rigorous and uncompromising penetration of psychoanalysis into the utmost depths of the child's mind. Indeed some of them (the criticisms) often remind me of the same phrases that were applied to Freud's own work in its inception: words like "far fetched," "arbitrary," "one-sided," have a familiar ring to me but, however much truth there may actually be in this suggestion, it is not only a consideration from scientific discussion but would certainly be unfair to most of the critics in question. They have adduced a number of arguments that have to be dealt with very seriously and indeed already have been by Dr. Heimann, Mrs. Isaacs, Mrs. Riviere and others besides Mrs. Klein. Nevertheless some of Mrs. Klein's more abstract formulations will no doubt be modified in the future theoretic structure of psychoanalysis. What seems to be a probable example of this is her literal application to clinical findings of Freud's philosophical concept of a "death-impulse," about which I have serious misgivings. I quote it not for this reason however, but because I find it a little odd that I should be criticizing her for a too faithful adherence to Freud's views and odder still that certain Viennese analysts see in it a divergence from his views.

ACKNOWLEDGMENTS

References have been indicated in the text where feasible. Of course, Melanie Klein's own writings were the major resources and wherever possible I have quoted or near-quoted her. In addition, papers by Hanna Segal, W. R. Bion, Herbert Rosenfeld, Ernest Jones, R. E. Money-Kyrle, T. F. Main, Willie Hoffer, and Elizabeth Zetzel were of particular value (Segal, 1961a, 1961b, 1964; Bion et al., 1961; Jones, 1950, 1952, 1955; Money-Kyrle, 1955; Main, 1961; Hoffer, 1961; Zetzel, 1961).

Of great help were my personal communications with Melanie Klein, her daughter Melitta Schmideberg, her son Eric Clyne, and Elliott Jaques, Honorary Secretary of the Melanie Klein Trust. Especially helpful was Margaret Evans, a Senior Training Analyst of the Melanie Klein group of the London Institute and a long-time personal friend of Mrs. Klein, who considered Dr. Evans "my personal representative in the United States who speaks for me" (Malin, 1962).

REFERENCES

Abraham, K. (1924). A short history of the development of the libido. In *Selected papers*. London : Hogarth Press, 1927.

Benedek, T. (1956). Toward the biology of a depressive constellation. *J. Amer. Psychoanal. Assoc.* 4.

Bergler, E. (1949). *The basic neurosis*. New York : Grune & Stratton.

———. (1950). *Impotence, frigidity and homosexuality*. New York : Grune & Stratton.

———. (1952). *The super ego*. New York : Grune & Stratton.

Bion, W. R.; Rosenfeld, H.; and Segal, H. (1961). Melanie Klein. *Int. J. Psycho-Anal.* 42.

Brierley, M. (1951). *Trends in psychoanalysis*. London : Hogarth Press.

Clyne, E. (1961). Personal communication.

Erikson, E. (1950). *Childhood and society*. New York : Norton.

Evans, M. G. (1962). Personal communication.

Fairbairn, W. R. D. (1952). *Psychoanalytic studies of the personality*. New York : Basic Books.

———. (1956). A critical evaluation of certain psychoanalytical concepts. *Brit. J. Phil. Sci.* 7.

Freud, A. (1951). Negativism and emotional surrender. Paper read at the Seventeenth International Psychoanalytic Congress, Amsterdam. (For discussion of this paper, see Richard Sterba, "Oral Invasion and Self-Defense.")

Freud, S. (1915). *Instincts and their vicissitudes*. Standard Edition, vol. 14. London : Hogarth Press.

———. (1917). *Mourning and melancholia*. Standard Edition, vol. 14. London : Hogarth Press.

———. (1921). *Group psychology and the analysis of the ego*. Standard Edition, vol. 18. London : Hogarth Press.

———. (1923). *The ego and the id*. Standard Edition, vol. 19. London : Hogarth Press.

———. (1929). *Civilization and its discontents*. Standard Edition, vol. 21. London : Hogarth Press.

———. (1933). *New introductory lectures*. London : Hogarth Press.

———. (1936, orig. pub. 1926). *The problem of anxiety*. New York : Norton.

Gitelson, M. (1952). Re-evaluation of the role of the oedipus complex. *Int. J. Psycho-Anal.* 33.

Glover, E. (1945). Examination of the Klein system of psychology. *Psychoanal.* Study Child.

Grinker, R. (1957). On identification. *Int. J. Psycho-Anal.* 38.

Guntrip, H. (1965). *Personality structure and human interaction*. New York : International Universities Press.

Hoffer, W. (1961). Melanie Klein. *Int. J. Psycho-Anal.* 42.

Isaacs, S. (1952). The nature and function of fantasy. In *Developments in psychoanalysis,* by Melanie Klein, Paula Heimann, Susan Isaacs, and Joan Riviere. London : Hogarth Press.

Jaques, E. (1962). Personal communication.

Jones, E. (1916). The theory of symbolism. *Brit. J. Psychol.* 9.

———. (1950). Introduction to *Contributions to psychoanalysis,* by Melanie Klein. London : Hogarth Press.

———. (1952). Preface to *Developments in psychoanalysis,* edited by Melanie Klein, Paula Heimann, Susan Isaacs, and Joan Riviere. London : Hogarth Press.

———. (1955). Preface to *New directions in psychoanalysis,* edited by Melanie Klein, Paula Heimann, and R. E. Money-Kyrle. New York : Basic Books.

Klein, E. See Clyne, E.

Klein, M. (1921a). Der Familienroman in Statu Nascendi. *Int. Z. fur Psychoanalyse* 6.

———. (1921b). The development of a child. *Int. J. Psycho-Anal.* 4. (First published in German in *Imago* 9, 1921.)

———. (1922). Hemmungen und Schwierigheiten in Pubertatsalter. *Die Neue Erziehung* 4.

———. (1924). The role of the school in the libidinal development of the child. *Int. J. Psycho-Anal.* 5.

———. (1926a). Infant analysis. *Int. J. Psycho-Anal.* 7.

———. (1926b). A contribution to the psychogenesis of tics. *Int. Z. fur Psychoanalyse* 2.

———. (1926c). The psychological principles of infant analysis. *Int. J. Psycho-Anal.* 7.

———. (1927a). Contribution to "Symposium on child analysis." *Int. J. Psycho-Anal.* 8.

———. (1927b). Criminal tendencies in normal children. *Brit. J. Med. Psychol.* 7.

———. (1928a). Early stages of the oedipus conflict. *Int. J. Psycho-Anal.* 9.

———. (1928b). Notes on a dream of forensic interest by Douglas Bryan. *Int. J. Psycho-Anal.* 9.

———. (1929a). Personification in the play of children. *Int. J. Psycho-Anal.* 10.

———. (1929b). Infantile anxiety situations reflected in a work of art and in the creative impulse. *Int. J. Psycho-Anal.* 10.

———. (1930a). The importance of symbol-formation in the development of the ego. *Int. J. Psycho-Anal.* 11.

———. (1930b). The psychotherapy of the psychoses. *Brit. J. Med. Psychol.* 1.

———. (1931). A contribution to the theory of intellectual inhibition. *Int. J. Psycho-Anal.* 12.

———. (1932). *The psycho-analysis of children.* London : Hogarth Press.

———. (1933). The early development of conscience in the child. In *Psychoanalysis today,* edited by Lorand. New York : Covici-Friede.

———. (1934). On criminality. *Brit. J. Med. Psychol.* 14.

———. (1935). A contribution to the psychogenesis of manic-depressive states. *Int. J. Psycho-Anal.* 16.

———. (1936). Weaning. In *On the bringing up of children,* edited by John Rickman. London : Routledge.

———. (1937). Love, guilt and reparation. In *Love, hate and reparation,* edited by Melanie Klein and Joan Riviere. London : Hogarth Press.

———. (1940). Mourning and its relation to manic-depressive states. *Int. J. Psycho-Anal.* 21.

———. (1942). Some psychological considerations. In *Science and ethics,* edited by C. H. Waddington. London : Allen and Unwin.

———. (1945). The oedipus complex in the light of early anxieties. *Int. J. Psycho-Anal.* 26.

———. (1946). Notes on some schizoid mechanisms. *Int. J. Psycho-Anal.* 27.

———. (1948). A contribution to the theory of anxiety and guilt. *Int. J. Psycho-Anal.* 29.

————. (1950a). On the criteria for the termination of psychoanalysis. *Int. J. Psycho-Anal.* 31.

————. (1950b). *Contributions to psychoanalysis, 1921–1945.* London : Hogarth Press.

————. (1952a). Some theoretical conclusions regarding the emotional life of the infant. In *Developments in psychoanalysis,* edited by Joan Riviere. London : Hogarth Press.

————. (1952b). On observing the behavior of young infants. In *Developments in psychoanalysis,* edited by Joan Riviere. London : Hogarth Press.

————. (1952c). Limits and possibilities of child analysis. *Psychoanalytische Bewegung.*

————. (1952d). The mutual influences in the development of the ego and the id. *Psychoanal. Study Child.*

————. (1952e). The origin of transference. *Int. J. Psycho-Anal.* 33.

————. (1955a). The psychoanalytic play technique : its history and significance. In *New directions in psychoanalysis,* edited by Melanie Klein, Paula Heimann, and Roger Money-Kyrle. New York : Basic Books.

————. (1955b). On identification. In *New directions in psychoanalysis,* edited by Melanie Klein, Paula Heimann, and Roger Money-Kyrle. New York : Basic Books.

————. (1955c). Psychoanalytic play technique. *Amer. J. Orthopsychiat.* 25.

————. (1957). *Envy and gratitude.* New York : Basic Books.

————. (1958). The development of mental functioning. *Int. J. Psycho-Anal.* 39.

————. (1959). Personal communication.

————. (1960a). On mental health. *Brit. J. Med. Psychol.* 33.

————. (1960b). A note on depression in the schizophrenic. In Symposium on depressive illness. *Int. J. Psycho-Anal.* 41.

————. (1960c). Our adult world and its roots in infancy. Tavistock pamphlet no. 2. London : Tavistock Publications.

————. (1960d). The emotional life of the infant. *Psyche* 14.

————. (1961). *Narrative of a child analysis.* New York : Basic Books.

————. (1963). *Our adult world, and other essays.* New York : Basic Books.

Lester, M. (1959a). Lecture to seminar in current literature, Institute for Psychoanalytic Medicine of Southern California.

————. (1959b). Personal communication.

Lindon, J. A. (1958). Castrophilia as a character neurosis. *Int. J. Psycho-Anal.* 39.

————. (1966). Melanie Klein : her view of the unconscious. In *Psychoanalytic pioneers,* edited by F. Alexander, S. Eisenstein, and M. Grotjahn. New York : Basic Books.

Lorand, S. (1957). Review of *New directions in psychoanalysis. Int. J. Psycho-Anal.* 38.

Main, T. F. (1961). Obituaries : Melanie Klein. *Brit. J. Med. Psychol.* 34.

Malin, A. (1962). Personal communication.

Mendelson, M. (1960). *Psychoanalytic concepts of depression.* New York : C. C. Thomas.

Money-Kyrle, R. E. (1955). Introduction to *New directions in psychoanalysis,* edited by Melanie Klein, Paula Heimann, and R. E. Money-Kyrle. New York : Basic Books.

Mosse, H. L. (1962). Book review of *Narrative of a child analysis. Amer. J. Psychiat.* 119.

Schmideberg, M. (1962). Personal communication.

Segal, H. (1961a). Obituary : Melanie Klein. *Brit. J. Psychol.* 52.

———. (1961b). Personal communication.

———. (1964). *Introduction to the work of Melanie Klein.* New York : Basic Books.

Spitz, R. (1946). Anaclitic depression. *Psychoanal. Study Child.*

Sterba, R. F. (1957). Oral invasion and self-defense. *Int. J. Psycho-Anal.* 38.

Winnicott, D. W. (1965). *Maturational processes and the facilitating environment.* New York : International Universities Press.

Wisdom, J. O. (1963). Mid-century developments within psycho-analytic theory. *Brit. J. Phil. Sci.* 14.

Zetzel, E. R. (1961). Melanie Klein. *Psychoanal. Quart.* 30.

4

Critique of the Kleinian School

OTTO F. KERNBERG

In an effort to reexamine and update the egopsychological critique of the Kleinian orientation, stressing the areas of potential convergence, I will begin with a review of the principal criticisms that authors favoring the ego-psychological approach have formulated regarding Kleinian theories.

Waelder (1937) questioned the possibility of obtaining the kind of knowledge of fantasies during the first year of life that Kleinian authors felt justified in assuming on the basis of their experience. He stated that fantasies obtained from children past the second or third year of life do not justify assuming a similar complexity of fantasy during the first few months of life. He also questioned the universality of strong inborn aggression as assumed by Melanie Klein and her use of the term "superego" for what he would prefer to call the "antecedent basis of the superego" in the first few years of life. Waelder agreed that these early phases might also be called "superego" if it were acknowledged that only in the fifth year of life was a decisive step taken in the development of the superego, namely its integration. He also criticized the relative neglect of reality factors in the child's life as compared with the overemphasis on fantasy life in Melanie Klein's report of her case histories. Waelder warned against misuse of the term "psychotic" when referring to early anxieties and defensive operations of normal development, and stressed that psychotic phenomena represented regression both to earlier stages of the ego and to primitive modes of functioning that may never have had an independent place in ego development or even to new reaction formations by the damaged organism. Regarding technique, Waelder questioned the exclusive focus on deep unconscious material because human conflict involves conflict between the higher strata of the ego and repressed or dissociated instinctual needs. He said that early defensive processes such as introjection and projection are examined sufficiently in the Kleinian approach, but later levels of defensive operations seem to be seriously neglected.

Glover (1945) criticized what he felt to be liberties that Melanie Klein took with metapsychological terms leading to a condensation of psychic mechanisms, structures, and fantasies. Much of his paper is taken up with a discussion of "the new Kleinian metapsychology" from the viewpoint of classical psychoanalytic metapsychology, a discussion that is probably outdated in view of more recent developments within both the ego-psychological and the Kleinian approaches. The emotional tone of Glover's paper, reflecting the atmosphere at the British Psycho-Analytical Society where these issues were discussed, also illustrates the emotional complications and the consequent mutual distance between the two psychoanalytic orientations that developed over the years.

Bibring (1947) expanded the egopsychological critique of Melanie Klein's theories of infant development. He pointed out that a "mechanism of spreading of tension" represented a theoretical conception of the first order in Klein's reconstruction of development: the spreading of instinctual tension in cross section onto a variety of existing functions and in longitudinal section along what one might call "developmental lines."

Bibring agreed with the spreading of oral sadistic tensions in "cross section" along existing functions: oral frustrations may lead to an intensification of the need to suck, to an intensification of desire for the object (fluid, milk, nipple, breast), to rage expressed directly as well as projected, and to global physiological reactions experienced as internal destructive impulses. Sadistic needs to suck the mother's breast, to scoop it out, to bite it, to devour it, may now combine libidinal needs with defense against a dangerous object; thus, oral libidinal, oral aggressive, and self-preservative tendencies are blended into one functional whole. The spread of accumulated aggressive and libidinal tensions to other functions of the child's body makes crying, squeezing, pinching, gripping, and eliminating the "vehicles" of sadism.

Bibring considered the spread in "longitudinal section" along developmental lines more difficult to understand. Melanie Klein implies, he said, that expanding oral tensions help to arouse the genital function in the infant of a few months of age; a transition between oral and genital development is made by assuming that the infant is fully capable of unconscious understanding of symbols. A symbolic understanding of the nipple as a penis image supposedly establishes a link between the oral and the genital zones, causing oral tension to spread to the genital functions. Bibring criticized this aspect of Kleinian theory because it implies a concept of early ego and instinctual development that is largely independent of the total biological growth of the child. While the motors of development are represented by severe anxiety related to oral frustration, the tension thus generated activates a largely intra-psychic process that centers around unconscious knowledge of instinctual aims and objects. Bibring pointed out that experimental observation of the development of instincts in animals shows that phylogenetically determined instincts are directed predominantly to external stimuli — stimuli that if offered before a certain stage of development of the instinct have little or no effect. Conversely, lack of proper stimulation at a particular stage of development may result in the loss of certain instinctual functions. In humans, instincts are replaced by the interplay of drives and ego in the process of learning. In Klein's system, Bibring said, an infant's sexual drives develop according to an inherited plan, but these inherited tendencies are activated exclusively by anxiety, tensions, and symbolic equations that are far from being biological. Bibring stressed that in Klein's theory, there is a conception of the objects of instinctual need and of relationships with such objects and between such objects long before there is any corresponding per-ceptual knowledge. In Bibring's opinion, we have no evidence to justify accepting innate knowledge in the form of ideas that are not representations of sensations, impulses, and emotions. Biological functions may well be represented in the unconscious as urges, drives, or tendencies, but not as conceptions of the parts of reality toward which instinctual functions are directed.

Bibring concluded by suggesting that Mrs. Klein discards the theory of regression; he felt that she underestimated the extent to which genital conflicts may by regression reappear in oral terms or instances in which pregenital residuals may be carried over to later genital positions. In brief, he said, "Mrs. Klein has 'retrojected' into the earliest phases of physical development much that belongs to later stages." I have summarized Bibring's paper in some detail because he probably gives the most explicit analysis of one of the most controversial aspects of Melanie Klein's theories, namely, that oedipal conflicts develop in the first few months of life and that there is related innate knowledge of the genitalia of both sexes and of sexual intercourse.

Commenting on the terminological difficulties created by Melanie Klein in presenting her work, Brierley (1939) pointed out that the term "internal object" may refer to different entities according to whether "internal" means mental, imaginary, or imagined as being inside the body. In more general terms, she said, one has to distinguish between the clinical language used in giving interpretations to patients and the theoretical conceptualization underlying the interpretation. A patient's statement describing his perception of a bodily pain in terms of a fantasy has to be differentiated from the actual mechanism that has caused the perception of such pain. Brierley criticized Melanie Klein for mixing the language of fantasy with abstract terminology, thus laying herself open to misunderstood generalizations. For example, Brierley said that the expression "whole object" is used to distinguish a person-object from an organ or part-object, and also to distinguish it from a damaged object: a fantasy of a dismembered object cannot be equated to a mental process by which a mental object is "literally shattered." Brierley agreed that the contents of infantile fantasy described by Melanie Klein are important, but regretted her lack of conceptual clarity in relating such contents to mental functions, especially the development of psychic structures.

Brierley believed that Klein's contributions to psychoanalytic object relations theory were fundamental. Melanie Klein, Brierley said, has broadened our understanding of early instinctual development, connecting it with the development of object relationships and early mental mechanisms.

Zetzel (1951), in the first of several contributions to the ego-psychological critique of Kleinian theories, stressed the importance of Klein's conception of the growth of object relationships in an ambivalent setting. While criticizing the concept of the "depressive position," Zetzel said that there is much clinical material supporting the belief that the struggle between love and hate leads to depressive fears that the hating impulses will prove to be stronger; she concluded that the concept of the "depressive position" may well prove, under a more suitable name, to be important in our growing knowledge of the development of object relations. Zetzel suggested that this clinical contribution be separated from some of Klein's controversial theories, such as the existence of a primary death instinct directed from the outset against the self, the existence of innate sexual knowledge, and the hypothesized relationship of early introjections to definitive superego formation. She suggested that Melanie Klein's work does not need to be accepted or rejected *in toto* and that there is no need to base important clinical observations of aggression on the death instinct.

Zetzel also suggested that Klein's concept of full oedipal developments in the first year of life and the related establishment of the superego at that time may reflect a too faithful adherence to the classical analytic hypothesis that superego and Oedipus conflict are intimately related. She referred to the work of Edith Jacobson (1964) on the presence in the superego of formations related to infantile narcissistic desires as well as oedipal strivings and prohibitions. Early pregenital parental introjections may be regressively reactivated as a result of disappointment by the parents at the Oedipal level. In referring to Jacobson, Zetzel implied that Melanie Klein underestimates the part played by a real failure of the parents in the development of a predisposition to depression and neglects the possibility of different superego introjects stemming from successive developmental phases. In stressing the continuity between normal and pathological mourning, Zetzel pointed out that Klein neglects the very important qualitative differences between depression in non-psychotic patients and manic-depressive illness. Zetzel referred to the crucial difference of whether the weaning process is linked with a significant, real loss of the mother or not. The overt depressive state precipitated in infants forcibly separated from their mothers during the second six months of life may initiate a radical difference between normal and pathological development. Excessive feelings of helplessness of the infant in the face of frustration combined with rage may constitute a response to a specific traumatic experience, a viewpoint that is not incompatible with Melanie Klein's conception of the growth of object relationship in an ambivalent setting. Zetzel suggested that the combination of excessive helplessness and a capacity for awareness of the situation long before the development of effective modes of reaction may result in the early appearance of aggression as well as preverbal precursors of fantasies involving helplessness, omnipotence, and the conviction that the absence of the wished-for breast has been caused by an omnipotent destructive impulse.

In two other papers Zetzel (1956a, 1956b) pointed out some basic differences in theory and theory of technique between the Kleinian and the ego-psychological approaches. In the first of these papers (1956a), she criticizes the lack of sufficient differentiation between concept and content in Melanie Klein's contributions. Regarding content, Zetzel said, Melanie Klein's observations about the important role of aggression in early mental life, her recognition of the importance of object relations — the relationship between difficulties with the mother and early depressive tendencies — are all important contributions, compatible with egopsychological work in this area. However, Klein's concept that anxiety originated in the fear of the death instinct operating within the ego seems to be a highly questionable condensation of Freud's death instinct theory with the observable clinical contents. Zetzel stressed the confusion that such condensation between concept and content creates with respect to the clinical facts under scrutiny and how this lack of differentiation between concept and content led Melanie Klein to overemphasize the intrapsychic sources of conflict while neglecting the environmental contributions to it.

In her second paper, Zetzel (1956b) compared the ego-psychological and Kleinian concepts of transference and transference neurosis and the related differences in technique of these two psychoanalytic orientations. She pointed out how the emphasis on early object relations and related primitive defense mechanisms as the paramount determinants of the transference led Kleinian analysts to early, deep transference interpretations, with the hypothesis that interpretation of primitive object relations as activated in the transference situation is the main factor bringing about changes in ego functions and therapeutic progress. In contrast, egopsychologists emphasize later developments within the ego, structuring of ego and superego defenses derived from all developmental levels, and conflict-free ego functions reflected in the capacity for self-observation and cooperation with the analyst. This orientation led ego-psychologically oriented analysts to differentiate the therapeutic alliance from the transference neurosis; to differentiate early transference manifestations from later, full-blown transference neurosis; and to interpret, according to classical technique, from the surface down, and from the defensive aspect to the content aspect of the material. Although she does not develop her own position on the two approaches in this paper, Zetzel does provide the framework on which her more recent criticism of Kleinian theory and technique are based.

In discussing a paper by Rosenfeld (1964), Zetzel (1964a) pointed out that what she sees as Dr. Rosenfeld's current emphasis on the importance of the therapist as a real (even if only a part) object, with which the potentially healthiest part of the patient's ego forms a relationship, represents a significant new area of convergence. The real relationship is, for Zetzel, the primitive core around which a more mature therapeutic alliance may hopefully develop, even in the case of a psychotic patient such as the one described by Dr. Rosenfeld. She also agreed with Dr. Rosenfeld's distinction between normal infancy and normal development on the one hand, and psychotic regression and pathological development on the other: this distinction, she said, has often been lacking in the Kleinian school.

In her presentation to the First Pan-American Congress for Psychoanalysis in Mexico City, Zetzel (1964b) focused on the Kleinian technique, especially on their early interpretation of the transference in terms of primitive object relationships and primitive ego mechanisms. Zetzel pointed out that the analysis of the transference presupposes that the patient has the capacity to develop a therapeutic alliance with the analyst. This therapeutic alliance permits the patient to identify with the observing, analyzing function of the analyst, to split his ego into a part that observes and one in which transference regression occurs. The capacity for establishing a therapeutic alliance depends on certain basic ego functions, such as the capacity to maintain basic trust in the absence of immediate gratifications, the capacity to maintain self – object differentiation in the absence (relative or absolute) of the needed object, and the potential capacity to accept realistic limitations. Zetzel suggested that the early anxiety that develops at the beginning of the analytic relationship is, indeed, related to the reactivation of these functions (and conflicts or failure regarding these functions) as the patient enters into the relationship with the analyst. This relationship taxes the patient's capacity for basic trust, for self – object differentiation, and for accepting realistic limitations. In this respect Zetzel agrees with the Kleinian's belief that early anxiety in the analysis is related to early infantile conflicts, although Zetzel doubts that the appearance of unconscious fantasy in the transference repeats the actual unconscious fantasies of the first few months of life.

Zetzel warned, however, against the deep interpretation of early infantile material as related to the early anxiety in analysis because, in her opinion, there are realistic aspects of the analytic situation that foster regression. With this regression, there is a decrease in reality testing and the capacity for insight; these need to be overcome by an objectively helpful attitude of the analyst as an ordinary human being, in order for the specific process of transference regression and the ensuing analytic working-through of the transference to be accomplished. In short, Zetzel agrees with some of the theoretical considerations underlying Kleinian technique regarding the first few hours of analysis, but she does not agree with the technique itself because of its contradiction with the initial goal for establishing the therapeutic alliance by protecting the observing, reality testing, insightful functions of the ego.

In her contribution to the Second Pan-American Congress for Psychoanalysis in Buenos Aires (1966), she further elaborated her viewpoint. She stated that in the psychoanalysis of potentially mature, adult neurotics, in which early defensive operations of the ego, early object relationships, and early unconscious fantasy have been integrated into later levels of ego structure and function, premature transference interpretations of early anxieties in terms of early infantile conflicts will be ineffective and may be harmful because of preventing the gradual transference regression from occurring.

Zetzel said that in the case of severely regressed patients, such as borderline or psychotic conditions, primitive object relations may indeed come to the surface immediately, but in the context of a loss of those advanced ego functions such as self-observation and reality testing that are indispensable for the development of the therapeutic alliance and the eventual working through of the transference. In these cases, premature interpretation of deep transference determinants may trigger off in the patient even further regression and further incapacity to deal analytically with the transference. Here transference can no longer be contrasted with an ongoing reality, and the interpretation, however correct, may assume magical properties and/or be understood as a formal seduction, without genuine insight following.

In a review of Rosenfeld's book *Psychotic States: A Psychoanalytic Approach,* Zetzel (1967) pointed out that several changes in the Kleinian orientation are becoming manifest in Rosenfeld's writings. First, Kleinian theoreticians are making sharper differentiations between the development of the future healthy or neurotic adult, and the pathological development that characterizes the potential psychotic. Second, Rosenfeld's understanding of and response to the intense, variable, and ambivalent transference reactions of a psychotic patient appear to have much in common with the approach of many contemporary American psychotherapists. Zetzel stressed that Rosenfeld makes no dramatic claims for his therapeutic results but reminds us that any analysis of psychotic states will enrich our understanding and facilitate the treatment of other psychotic patients. Zetzel also acknowledged here that the Kleinian belief that psychotic patients are capable of transference reactions is now recognized not only by the Kleinians but by many other psychoanalysts as well. While repeating her rejection of the Kleinian hypothesis that the neonatal ego is capable of developing specific defenses and that these defenses are necessary responses to an innate, self-destructive death instinct, Zetzel also stated that in clinical pratice some of the mechanisms described by Rosenfeld may readily be recognized by the experienced therapist. In this regard, Zetzel pointed to a convergence of Kleinian psychoanalytic theory and technique relating to borderline and psychotic patients and the theory and technique of other psychoanalytic orientations with respect to these same kind of patients. I will return to this point when reviewing Searles's criticism of Bion and Rosenfeld.

Geleerd's detailed analysis (1963) of Melanie Klein's book *Narrative of a Child Analysis* further developed the ego-psychological critique of the clinical implications of Kleinian formulations. Geleerd stressed that many of Melanie Klein's clinical observations were astute and accurate, and that her observations in two-year-old children, of death wishes to siblings, castration fear, oedipal strivings, reactions to the primal scene, anxiety, and guilt were important contributions to psychoanalysis. Geleerd also acknowledged Melanie Klein's discovery of the ease with which unconscious fantasies are available to the young child and of the discharge in play and in sublimation of masturbation fantasies. Referring to Klein's criticism in 1927 of Anna Freud's work, Geleerd agreed with the validity of Klein's criticism of the manipulative preparation of the child for child analysis as then proposed by Anna Freud. She said that children develop many more transference reactions than Anna Freud had suggested in 1926, thereby agreeing with Melanie Klein.

Geleerd, however, criticized what she considers the loosely written, somehow not quite logical, statements that Melanie Klein first presented as an interpretation of her clinical work and later used as facts to support her hypothesis about early development: for example, the interchangeability of the terms "introjection" and "identification" for the same mechanism and the duality implied in assuming, on the one hand, a free communication between unconscious and conscious in the child and, on the other hand, the need to lift repression. Geleerd criticized Klein's overuse of symbolic interpretation and her rather symbolic, not sufficiently based, translations of clinical material. The child is able to develop transference reactions, Geleerd stated, but there are also important reality aspects in the relationship between the child and the analyst as a real, grown-up person; in evaluating Melanie Klein's relationship with the patient in her book, Richard, such reality considerations were at times overlooked.

Geleerd criticized what she thought was a process of contamination in Melanie Klein's work, such as the overextension of certain concepts. For example, the fact that delusional persecution is a symptom of paranoia does not mean that any manifestation of spying or torture is always paranoia. The fact that certain clinical manifestations represent ego, id, or superego functioning does not justify an ongoing personification of these structures in interpreting clinical work. Geleerd believed that Melanie Klein accurately traces certain mechanisms in psychotic patients whose object relationships are disturbed and that represent a regression to genetically earliest phases. Geleerd implied, however, that this does not justify the concept that all early development must be described in terms of psychotic states.

Geleerd's presentation of a careful, balanced analysis of Melanie Klein's interventions regarding Richard points to areas of agreement as well as disagreement. Geleerd stressed Klein's intuition and sensitivity, while criticizing her tendency to make early interpretations of a completely symbolic nature dealing with processes of destruction and reparation as postulated by her. Geleerd also criticized the fact that analysis of the defenses seems to be limited to the mechanisms of projection, introjection, manic defense, and denial, and that even these defenses were analyzed in a non-systematic way. The first and every other session, Geleerd said, give the impression of a similar level of interpretation, without any un-folding or deepening of the analytic process, and without clarifying the conflict between opposing forces — drive derivatives against defences, past against present, fantasy against reality.

Jacobson (1964, pp. 46–48, 94–95) added an additional dimension to the ego-psychological critique of the Kleinian school. Evaluating Melanie Klein's contributions from the viewpoint of ego-psychological object-relations theory, Jacobson criticized the Kleinian failure to distinguish the endopsychic representation of external objects from "introjects" and from the infantile superego. In Jacobson's opinion, Melanie Klein fails to distinguish the constitution of self and object representations and of object relations and ego identifications from superego formation. It should be stressed that this criticism has been formulated in the context of a very careful attempt, on Jacobson's part, to describe the vicissitudes of self and object representations as they enter both ego and super-ego formations and the various developing ego and superego structures that are related to the internalization of object relation-ships. In more general terms, one might say that Jacobson criticized the lack of structural analysis in Kleinian object-relations theory.

Fairbairn (1952), while starting from a different frame of reference from Jacobson, also criticized Melanie Klein for not explaining satisfactorily how fantasies of incorporating objects orally could give rise to the establishment of internal objects as endopsychic structures. Although his description of schizoid factors became closely linked with Klein's description of the mechanisms of the paranoid-schizoid position, he strongly rejected the instinctual basis of the establishment of object relationships and especially Klein's emphasis on the death instinct.

Guntrip (1961), in criticizing Melanie Klein's work from Fair-bairn's orientation, agreed with the latter that Klein underestimated the influence of the child's environment on his intrapsychic develop-ment and that she wrongly attributed the development of intra-psychic structure to the intrapsychic operation of the death instinct. Sutherland (1963) implied that the clarification of structural intra-psychic development provided by Fairbairn's modification of

Kleinian object-relations theory provided a helpful model for early development.

The last three authors (Guntrip, Fairbairn, Sutherland) represent a "middle group" orientation, bridging in a way the distance between the ego-psychological and the Kleinian approach. Two further criticisms of the Kleinian school from a "middle group" viewpoint, namely, Winnicott's and Balint's, focus on the clinical rather than the metapsychological question raised by the Kleinian orientation. Winnicott (1962) listed an impressive number of Kleinian contributions to phychoanalysis : the application of orthodox technique in the psychoanalysis of children through the use of toys; the understanding of internal benign and persecutory forces or "objects" as they are related to satisfactory or unsatisfactory instinctual experiences; the importance of projection and introjection as mental mechanisms; the emphasis on the importance of destructive elements in object relationships and on the development of the capacity for concern (depressive position); the understanding of manic defenses, and the splitting of the object prior to attainment of ambivalence. Winnicott criticized Klein's tendency to push the age farther and farther back at which mental mechanisms appear and her neglect of the environment in her writings. He expressed doubts regarding use of the theory of life and death instinct and attempts to state infantile destructiveness in terms of heredity and envy.

Balint (1968, pp. 104–109) sharply criticized the use of conventional language mixed with nouns (like breast, milk, inside of the body) whose meaning became both extended and comprehensive in the clinical work of Kleinian analysts. He suggested that their constant stretching of words was an effort to give names to things and experiences that did not previously have names and, therefore, could not be expressed in words; thus, the Kleinian analysts developed a "mad" language that was learned by their patients and was used in printed publications. Balint suggested that the patient, prompted by his need to be understood, would learn the analyst's habitual language so that he could express his associations in it, and that this was detrimental to the analytic relationship. Balint stated that the interpretations of Kleinian analysts, as reported at scientific meetings and in the literature, create the impression of a confident, knowledgeable, and perhaps even overwhelming analyst – an impression apparently shared by their patients. He wondered if this might be one reason why there is so much aggressiveness, envy, and hatred in their patients' material and so much concern about introjection and idealization. Balint suggested that introjection and idealization are common defense mechanisms in a partnership between an oppressed, weak person and an overwhelming powerful one. In addition, Balint criticized the relative reluctance of the Kleinian group to admit therapeutic failure.

Searles (1963) examined the recent contribution of two Kleinian authors, namely, Rosenfeld (1965) and Bion (1967), from the viewpoint of a clinician under the influence of the Sullivanian school who is mainly interested in the intensive, psychoanalytically oriented treatment of schizophrenic patients. Searles began by agreeing with Rosenfeld on the concept of transference psychosis rather than the old psychoanalytic viewpoints, which hold that the schizophrenic patient has regressed to an autoerotic level of development and is therefore incapable of forming a transference. In contrast to Rosenfeld and other Kleinian analysts who believe that psychotic transference is dominated by projective identification on the part of the patient, Searles proposed, in agreement with other ego-psychological authors, that the transference psychosis is a phase of symbiotic relatedness between the patient and the therapist. He suggested that verbal transference interpretations of projective identification, such as Rosenfeld and Bion provide in their case material, are a form of intervention that appeals to the nonpsychotic area of the patient's personality for collaboration. In many regressed, long-hospitalized, chronically schizophrenic patients, such verbal statements may not register; even in Rosenfeld's and Bion's cases, Searles continued, it is impossible to know to what extent the illuminating accurate verbal content of the therapist's words helped the patient or to what extent the feelings of confidence, firmness, and understanding that accompanied his words helped the patient. Searles added that he has worked with patients who were so deeply dedifferentiated that it took many years of therapy before they could distinguish between an "outside" and an "inside." With such patients the clinical formulations of Kleinian authors would not seem helpful. However, Searles concluded, Kleinian formulations, which imply that the patient has a higher psychic differentiation and a capacity to rely upon verbal interpretations, are frequently pertinent with schizophrenic patients.

Searles stressed the usefulness of Bion's clinical observations, for example: the schizophrenic patient's projection of his own "sanity" onto the therapist, the schizophrenic patient's "hatred of reality," and the advantage to the therapist of having a basically neutral attitude, even with severely regressed patients. He criticized, however, Rosenfeld's and Bion's neglect of the reality situation in the early life of the patient. He illustrated this point with examples of the "invasiveness" of parents of psychotic patients to such an extent as to prevent the child from meeting a genuine reality either outside himself or within himself as an individual. Some aspects of the schizophrenic patient's transference are reflections of an identification with a real, psychotic parent, and, in the process of "delusional identification," the patient's crazy behavior might include, along with a psychotic transference root, some aspect of an expressed identification with a therapist that possesses a kernel of reality in terms of the therapist's real personality functioning. Implicitly, Searles criticized the Kleinians' neglect of the reality of the future schizophrenic patient's childhood experience and their neglect of the schizophrenic patient's perception of the reality of the therapist in the treatment process.

The importance of Searles's critique is due to his extended experience in the application of psychoanalytic theory and technique to the treatment of chronically and severely regressed schizophrenic patients. Coming from an entirely different orientation, Searles has been able to confirm many clinical observations of Bion and Rosenfeld, and of the paranoid–schizoid mechanisms described by the Kleinian school. At the same time, Searles's implicit questioning of the "accuracy" of verbal interpretations of the kind presented by Kleinian authors, and his stress on the importance of the reality of the patient's life — both past and present — in contrast to the purely intrapsychic developments stressed by the Kleinian group, warrant serious consideration.

SUMMARY OF THE EGO-PSYCHOLOGICAL CRITIQUE

What follows is a brief summary of the main ego-psychological criticisms of Kleinian theory and technique, as presented above. Regarding Kleinian theory :

1. The concept of an inborn death instinct and the concept that such a death instinct is the crucial determinant of anxiety are rejected as an unwarranted extension of

Freud's speculative hypothesis of a death instinct and as a dogmatic statement without convincing evidence.

2. The concept that there is innate knowledge of the genitals of both sexes and of sexual intercourse is rejected because there is no evidence of such inborn knowledge and there is a contradiction between such elaborate knowledge and the very immature quality of psychic functioning in the first few months of life.

3. Klein's theory of early development is criticized because she does not take into consideration either anatomical or physiological development, on the one hand, or psychical development, on the other. Her stress on constitutional and instinctual factors in her theories, together with her neglect of epigenetic development, is seen as a pseudobiological orientation.

4. The "pushing back" of intrapsychic development, especially of complex relationships between oedipal and pre-oedipal conflicts, into the first few months of life appears to be unjustified from the clinical evidence presented. The cases of children analyzed at the age of two years and older, where early oedipal material and relationships between pregenital and genital conflicts can be found, may present a regressive pregenital expression of genital conflicts — a "retroactive" coloring of early experiences with later material; direct observation of children in the first year of life shows a capacity for anxiety, depression, and probable fantasy formation, but not of the complexity and kind that Kleinian authors accept as facts.

5. Ego-psychological authors criticize the Kleinians' neglect of environmental factors in their writing, although they pay lip service to the importance of these factors.

6. There is strong criticism of the Kleinians' failure to consider structural differentiation within both ego and superego formation, and of their relative neglect of development within all psychic instances. How "internal objects" are integrated into the ego and superego, how later developments differ from earlier ones, how progression, fixation, and regression determine an individualized history of psychological development, are neglected within Kleinian formulation.

7. The lack of differentiation between normal and patho-

logical development is criticized, as well as the implicit equalization of neurotic, borderline, and psychotic personality development. Clinically this is reflected in the neglect of differential psychopathology and of the relationship between diagnosis and treatment.

8. The vagueness and ambiguity of Kleinian terminology are criticized as major stumbling blocks preventing the clarification of Kleinian theory, of internal inconsistencies within that theory, and of possible relationships between that theory and the mainstream of psychoanalysis.

Regarding Kleinian technique :

1. The application of the same, non-modified psychoanalytic technique to patients with all levels of severity of illness — from neurotics to psychopaths and schizophrenics (Segal, 1967) — a consequence of the neglect of descriptive psychopathology by Kleinian authors, is criticized from the viewpoint of overwhelming clinical experience that psychotic patients and a good number of borderline conditions and antisocial personality structures do not respond well to the psychoanalytic approach.

2. The relative neglect of reality in understanding the psychoanalytic situation has been criticized as well as the related overextension of the concept of transference. This criticism and the three that follow are especially important in the opening phases of a Kleinian analysis.

3. Ego-psychological authors criticize the Kleinians' neglect of the defensive organization of the patient, especially the natural structuring of defenses in the early phases of analysis. The premature, "deep" interpretations of unconscious fantasy and transference manifestations, bypassing the defensive structure, create the danger of an intellectual indoctrination of patients in contrast to the natural upsurge of deep, unconscious material when the defenses against it are resolved through interpretation.

4. As a consequence of premature transference interpretations and the neglect of advanced ego defenses, especially of the patient's character structure, there is no deepening of the analytic relationship as the same constellation of primitive conflicts is interpreted again and again, from the beginning of the analysis on.

5. The combination of a peculiar use of terms related to infantile development, the consistently active behavior of the analyst, and the atmosphere of certainty within which interpretations are given may bring about a special situation as part of some Kleinian analyses in which the patient submits his productions and language to an indoctrination, thus, in appearances, confirming the analysts theories by associations centering on those theories and the language associated with them.

Let us now examine those aspects of Kleinian theory and technique that have been accepted and integrated into the mainstream of psychoanalysis. Some of these have already been mentioned or implicitly acknowledged as part of the ego-psychological critique of the Kleinian orientation. Regarding theory :

1. The importance of early object relations both in normal and in pathological development has been generally accepted. The importance of the development of a potential for depressive reaction in the first year of life, and of its fundamental importance for future development, is also generally accepted. The simultaneous development of narcissism and object relationships in contrast to the older model of an objectless stage of development is a definite feature of recent psychoanalytic thinking (van der Waals, 1965).
2. The importance of the defensive constellations described by Kleinians as paranoid–schizoid, depressive, and manic has been acknowledged by authors of the ego-psychological orientation working with borderline and psychotic patients. Although neglect of later defensive operations (such as repression, reaction formation, and other related defenses of the fully developed ego) within the Kleinian orientation and overemphasis on pregenital conflicts (those underlying the defensive operations described in the Kleinian "positions") are criticized by ego-psychological authors, selective use of the new understandings of early defensive operations provided by the Kleinian orientation has improved the over-all diagnostic and therapeutic armamentarium of psychoanalysis (Kernberg, 1966, 1967).
3. The importance of aggression in early development is now generally accepted, although not with the overriding emphasis that Melanie Klein gave to it.

4. There is a general tendency to accept early superego formation, probably starting with the second year of life, and to
recognize the importance of early superego structures on
early and later psychic development (Jacobson, 1964).

5. The relationships between early genital development and
pregenital conflicts, and the influence of pregenital factors
on the sexual development of both sexes and on the pathological sexual developments in severe character pathology
have been integrated by many non-Kleinian authors. The
presence of oedipal conflicts from the second or third year
on has been acknowledged by ego-psychological child
analysts (A. Freud, 1951).

Regarding Kleinian technique:

1. The application of classical psychoanalytic technique to
children is a generally acknowledged, major contribution
of Melanie Klein. Geleerd's acceptance of Klein's viewpoints regarding the Anna Freud–Melanie Klein controversy of the 1920s probably reflects the general attitude of
many non-Kleinian child analysts. There is a growing
consensus that children are able to develop full-blown transference neuroses (Harley, 1966).

2. There is an increasing technical utilization of the new
understandings of early defensive operations provided by
Melanie Klein and her followers. These include the interpretation of the splitting of ego states as a defense, the
understanding of negative therapeutic reaction as a possible consequence of unconscious envy, the focus on
projective identification and its relationship to countertransference, and the interpretation of omnipotence and
devaluation as narcissistic defenses (Kernberg, 1968;
Searles, 1963; Winnicott, 1962).

3. The understanding (if not necessarily management through
interpretation) of the above-mentioned mechanisms and
other early defensive operations as the predominant problems in the transference development of borderline and
psychotic patients has led to increased diagnostic refinement and therapeutic hopefulness for these previously
unapproachable forms of psychopathology. In this regard,

the interest of Searles and others from the Sullivan group in Kleinian concepts is an indirect indication of the relevance of these concepts for work with regressed patients. In general, the fact that psychotic patients do present transference reactions — a transference psychosis in contrast to a transference neurosis of less regressed patients is quite generally accepted now (Zetzel, 1967).

4. The focus on regressive features and the activation of early defensive operations in the opening phase of psychoanalysis have been acknowledged as important contributions from the Kleinian orientation. Zetzel's acknowledgment that such early determinants of ego development are activated in the opening phase is relevant here.

ANALYSIS OF THE KLEINIAN REACTION TO THE EGO-PSYCHOLOGICAL CRITIQUE

The theories of an inborn death instinct and of inborn sexual knowledge

First of all, Melanie Klein's theory of an inborn death instinct and of that death instinct as the first cause of anxiety (1946, 1948) continue to be accepted by the Kleinian school as far as I can tell. Their disregard of the criticism of these concepts, despite the total lack of clinical evidence to support them, appears to be an unfortunate dogmatic rigidity of the Kleinian group. Segal (1964) reaffirmed without discussion that "the immature ego of the infant is exposed from birth to the anxiety stirred up by the inborn polarity of instincts — the immediate conflict between the life instinct and the death instinct." There is the same unwavering adherence to Melanie Klein's concept (1945) of the inborn knowledge of the genitals and sexual intercourse. Segal (1964), while acknowledging that some analysts think that these fantasies arise later and are restrospectively projected into babyhood, affirmed that "this is surely an unnecessary additional hypothesis." Bion (1962, 1963) elaborated on Melanie Klein's hypothesis of inborn knowledge of the oedipal conflict by postulating an inborn preconception of the Oedipus myth as part of the apparatus of the ego for contact with reality: "the mating of this alpha-element oedipal preconception with the realization of the actual parents gives rise to the conception of parents" (1963). Bion's concept of inborn preconceptions, "thoughts" that require the development of an apparatus for "thinking," is based on a particular development of the meta-psychology of the development of cognitive processes, occasionally illustrated by clinical observations of psychotic patients but without direct evidence of either analytic or direct observational material from normal or psychologically disturbed children. Thus, it seems fair to state that Bion simply translates Melanie Klein's concepts into a new formulation, reaffirming the inborn knowledge of the genitals and sexual intercourse, and the oedipal conflict.

If one agrees with Zetzel's suggestion that neither the concept of an inborn death instinct and the concept that such a death instinct is the main source of anxiety, nor the concept of inborn knowledge of the kind postulated by Kleinian authors is indispensable to other aspects of the theory and technique (I, for one, agree with Zetzel on this point), it is really puzzling why these concepts continue to be held regardless of the lack of supporting evidence.

The problem of the formation and development of psychic structures

Bion (1962, 1963) and Segal (1964) have attempted to meet the criticism of Kleinian theory regarding the neglect of structural considerations. Bion has presented a complex system of cognitive development based on the Kleinian theories of splitting and projective identification, of transition from the paranoid–schizoid to the depressive position and vice versa, and of symbol formation. Insofar as he has presented the hypothesis of a hierarchy of intellectual processes ranging from the most primitive to the most abstract capacity for mathematical thinking, his system reflects a structural development — at least, with respect to cognitive structures — within Kleinian theory. Unfortunately, however, his theory of the development of thinking appears to be quite divorced from other available knowledge of the development of perception and cognitive functions in the child. Bion's rather personal style of presenting the material and his lack of sufficient supporting evidence, which might be utilized to contrast his constructions with other structural formulations, make it very difficult to evaluate his theory of cognitive development. His structural theory is developing within the Kleinian orientation, but I find it difficult to see how these structural formulations might relate to the usual structural concepts of the psychoanalytic mainstream.

Segal's structural analysis (1964), while closer to the more traditional concepts and language of psychoanalytic metapsychology than Bion's, still does not answer certain questions about psychic structure raised by Melanie Klein's theory of internal objects. Segal stated that

> these internal objects are not "objects" situated in the body of the psyche : like Freud, Melanie Klein is describing unconscious fantasies which people have about what they contain.

In her glossary, she defined internal objects as objects introjected into the ego. The ego identifies with some of these objects, which thus become assimilated into the ego, contributing to its growth and characteristics. Others remain as separate internal objects and the ego maintains a relationship with them. Segal stated that the superego is such an object, thus equalizing in my opinion what in egopsychological terms might be described as object representations with a complex structure such as the superego. (This viewpoint is puzzling, considering the abundant evidence regarding the development and changes within the superego and the complex intrasystematic components within the superego itself.) Segal also stated that

> the structure of the personality is largely determined by the more permanent of the fantasies which the ego has about itself and the objects that it contains.

Granting the probability that the term "ego" here means what ego psychologists would probably refer to as the "self" rather than the ego as a complex psychic instance with multiple autonomous and conflictual structures and functions, it is still difficult to see how fantasies are the main aspects of psychic structure. If internal objects are fantasies and the structure of the personality is largely determined by fantasies that the ego has about itself and its internal objects, structure in this sense seems to imply largely fantasies about fantasies, and, I propose, reaffirming my analysis of an earlier paper (1966), that this is an unsatisfactory basis for structural analysis, certainly insufficient to do justice to the complexity of integration of object relationships into the psychic apparatus.

Serious efforts, however, have recently been made by the Kleinian group to develop the structural implications of the constellations of defense mechanisms they have described, such as the difference between normal and pathological forms of splitting (Bion, 1967) and clarification of the structural implications of the depressive position (Segal, 1964). Segal (1964) stated that the depressive position, in which the infant recognizes a whole object and relates himself to this object, can be perceived when the infant recognizes his mother. Segal said that this means that the infant perceives the mother as a whole object in contrast to "both part-object relationships and split-object relationships." She further stated :

> These psychological changes help along, and are helped by, physiological maturation in the ego, the maturation of the central nervous system allowing a better organization of perceptions arising in different physiological areas and allowing for the development and organization of memory.

Her analysis explicity integrates maturational features into psychological development.

The problem of the ambiguity of terminology

It is possible to criticize the ambiguity of terminology in the psychoanalytic writing of all orientations : for example, the concept of identification is still not completely agreed upon and lends itself to ambiguous use.

I have mentioned the ego-psychological criticism of the problems posed by vagueness and ambiguity of terminology in Kleinian theory and technique. Recent efforts by Kleinian authors to be more precise in their terminology and to relate it to other psychoanalytic approaches are illustrated in Segal's "glossary" (1964) and in Rosenfeld's paper on depression (1959).

Rosenfeld carefully compared psychoanalytic studies of depression made by authors representing different psychoanalytic orientations, thus facilitating the relating of Kleinian concepts and terminology to corresponding ego-psychological developments. Indirectly he is making it easier to relate Kleinian mechanisms to structural concepts in general.

In my opinion, however, ambiguity of terminology — a general problem in psychoanalysis — is especially troublesome in certain Kleinian formulations. There are shifts in the way the terms "ego" and "self" are used throughout Kleinian literature that make it difficult to grasp the exact meaning of important concepts such as projective identification. Melanie Klein (1946) described projective identification as the projection of split-off parts of the self into another person. One aim of this process is the forceful entry into the object and control of the object by parts of the self. At this point Klein seems to use the concepts of ego and self rather interchangeably. Elsewhere (1963), however, she described the ego, referring to Freud, as the organized part of the self, while

> the self is used to cover the whole of the personality, which includes not only the ego but the instinctual life which Freud called the id.

Rosenfeld (1964) described projective identification as

> not only a term referring to the taking over or identification with an envied role or function but it also implies a projection of unwanted parts of the self into another object causing this object to be identified with the projected parts of the self.

Here the concept of projective identification is broadened to include the reaction of the object, that is, an interpersonal process is described as part of an intrapsychic mechanism. While I think many analysts working with borderline and psychotic patients would agree with the clinical phenomena described by Rosenfeld (see, for example, Searles, 1963), the shift in the definition of the underlying concept creates clinical as well as theoretical problems when one attempts to relate projective identification to other defensive operations of the ego. Segal (1964) also provided another, somewhat different definition of projective identification.

The definition of the mechanism of "splitting," as important in Kleinian terminology as projective identification, is another example of shifting meanings attached to the same term. Throughout much of her work Melanie Klein described splitting as an early mechanism related to the paranoid–schizoid position that is largely replaced at a later stage by other defenses such as repression, but at one point she practically equated splitting and repression (1952):

The mechanism of splitting underlies repression (as is implied in Freud's concept); but in contrast to the earliest form of splitting which leads to states of disintegration, repression does not normally result in a disintegration of the self. Since at this stage there is greater integration, both within the conscious and the unconscious parts of the mind, and since in repression the splitting predominantly effects a division between conscious and unconscious, neither part of the self is exposed to the degree of disintegration which may arise in previous stages.

The broad use of the term "splitting" by Kleinian authors in their published clinical material thus illustrates once more the general difficulty presented by Kleinian terminology when efforts are made to integrate it with the mainstream of psychoanalytic thinking.

The predominant focus on primitive conflicts and mechanisms

I have already mentioned that there is an increased utilization of the new understandings of early defensive operations as described by the Kleinian school. The Kleinian contributions are especially relevant in the diagnostic study and treatment of severe character pathology, borderline personality organization, and schizophrenia (Kernberg, 1967, 1968; Searles, 1963). The clinical contributions of Segal (1964), Rosenfeld (1965), Bion (1967), and Racker (1968), as well as the later ones of Klein herself (1957) are probably the most important recent contributions of the Kleinian group in the area of clinical psychoanalysis. There remain, however, some basic questions regarding the universality of the defensive operations described by the Kleinians, in their almost exclusive focus on these mechanisms in their clinical work.

There is a certain ambiguity in the Kleinian linkage of paranoid–schizoid, depressive, and manic defenses to the respective "positions," positions reflecting very primitive or early conflicts that were due to pregenital factors. Even without considering at this point the issue of normal versus pathological interrelationships between pregenital and genital conflicts, the question remains why these early mechanisms are so pervasively interpreted even in patients whose instinctual development and ego structure is of a much higher level than that of borderline or psychotic cases and in whom, presumably, shifts toward later defensive operations and conflicts have taken place. In other words, either the Kleinian mechanisms are linked to early conflicts and thus would predominate only in certain cases, or they are not linked to such early conflicts and may be interpreted in the context of later, predominantly genital or late oedipal developments.

Kleinian authors would reply that these early mechanisms may be used as defensive operations in later developmental stages, implicitly acknowledging that the content of such defenses may be entirely different in the typical neurotic case as compared with a borderline patient. In practice, however, the clinical material published by the Kleinian group invariably links these defenses to early conflicts so that a practical, if not a theoretical, contradiction remains. It is as if in this area Kleinian authors were paying lip service to their own theoretical flexibility as stated, for example, by Klein herself (1950):

> I shall now draw a conclusion from the definition already given, namely that persecutory anxiety relates to dangers felt to threaten the ego and depressive anxiety to dangers felt to threaten the loved object. I wish to suggest that these two forms of anxiety comprise all anxiety situations a child goes through. Thus, the fear of being devoured, of being poisoned, of being castrated, the fears of attacks on the "inside" of the body, come under the heading of persecutory anxiety, whereas all anxieties relating to loved objects are depressive in nature.

The importance of this issue lies in the need to relate the defensive operations of the patient with other defenses and contents according to the stage of development with which the conflict is connected. For example, manic defenses may have become integrated in the character structure, acquired the function of a reaction formation, and be utilized as such against impulse configurations that are completely different from those that originally brought the manic defenses into existence. Thus, a patient's use of manic mechanisms may reflect the activation of a character defense in the transference directed, for example, against fear of punishment or incestuous strivings. One frequently sees defenses against envy linked not only with oral conflicts, but with oedipal rivalry and as part of narcissistic character defenses.

Character analysis and the issue of early, deep interpretations

The Kleinian group's almost exclusive interpretation of

Kleinian defenses as related to early conflicts and primitive object relationships is associated with their relative neglect of later defenses of the ego that center around repression, especially character defenses. The neglect of character analysis in Kleinian technique is, in my opinion, an important shortcoming and results from an underemphasis of structural development of the ego. The issue of premature, "deep" interpretations in the early analytic hours is also related to the problem of neglecting the diagnosis of character defenses in the analytic situation.

In defending the early interpretation of transference in Kleinian technique, Segal (1967), gave an example of a candidate-analysand who started the first session by saying that he was determined to be qualified in the minimum time and then spoke about his digestive troubles and, in another context, about cows. The analyst interpreted "that I was the cow, like the mother who breast-fed him, and that he felt that he was going to empty me greedily, as fast as possible, of all my analysis-milk; this interpretation immediately brought out material about his guilt in relation to exhausting and exploiting his mother." Oral greediness probably was implied in the patient's associations. However, one might wonder to what extent this "eager" patient-candidate would accept such a "deep" interpretation as part of his wish to learn the new, magic language of the analyst; and to what extent such "learning" would feed into related defenses of intellectualization and rationalization, including the intellectual acceptance of transference interpretation. The patient's greediness might also reflect a narcissistic character structure, and the extent to which such character defenses might later interfere with a deepening of the transference should be clarified by exploring that defensive structure further, rather than by gratifying the patient's eagerness with a "direct interpretation" of the possible ultimate source of the trait. In other words, deeper levels of the defensive organization, especially the patient's character structure, may be seriously neglected by this approach; the defensive organization may go "underground" resulting in possible serious complications at later stages of the analysis. Working down from the surface does not mean going merely into the depth of the content, but into the depth of the defensive organization. The natural ordering of the material may be seriously interfered with by interpretation "in depth," by-passing important defenses that lie along the road of the conflict in its genetic development and its development in the transference.

An additional example may illustrate this point. In describing the analytic hour of a patient with antisocial behavior, Joseph (1960), another leading Kleinian analyst, summarized her interpretation of the deep, unconscious meaning that was implied in the patient's reaction to his losing his job. The patient said that he did not know why he had lost his job and expressed the view that his boss was a crook. Later in the hour the patient talked about tears coming into his eyes when he watched a film of a plane crash in which 14 people were killed. The analyst felt that these were "strikingly sincere" depressive feelings. It turned out, however, that the patient had lost his job because he stole something, as he told the analyst three days later. This stealing was seen by the analyst as "not just an acting out of greedy impulses, but a more complex method of avoiding the deeper guilt and anxiety about stealing by the spoiling of his good object — at depth the mother's breast." What is interesting is the analyst's lack of focus on the patient's lie; one might wonder what additional meaning the analyst's deep interpretations have for the patient when he knows that they are based on obviously incomplete information about the situation. Rather than speculating about deep conflicts around the avoidance of guilt, the first question one might ask is whether or not the patient had any conscious guilt about lying to the analyst, and what reaction he would have when confronted with this: guilt or anger, fear or indifference? In other words, guilt and the defenses against it operate throughout a complex layer of defense-impulse configurations, and to interpret such configurations only at their "ultimate" depth appears to be unreliable without considering the other aspects.

One may wonder to what extent a patient with severe character pathology who undergoes Kleinian analysis may surprise the analyst many months or years after beginning treatment with a completely unexpected misuse or distortion of all the analytic understandings that have been conveyed to him. Perhaps an awareness of this problem is what prompted Bion (1963) to discuss the "reversed perspective," by which he refers to a situation in which the patient and analyst apparently agree on an interpretation but actually the patient has taken an ambiguity in the analyst's phrasing or intonation in order to give his interpretation a slant that the analyst does not intend.

Rosenfeld (1965), in his important article on narcissism, acknowledged that the intelligent narcissist often uses his intellectual insight to agree verbally with the analyst and recapitulates in his own words what has been analysed in previous sessions. . . . The patient uses the analytic interpretations but deprives them quickly of life and meaning, so that only meaningless words are left. These words are then felt to be the patient's own possession, which he idealizes and which give him a sense of superiority.

Here Rosenfeld's thinking appears to differ from the view of other Kleinian authors regarding character defenses. It is interesting that in this same paper Rosenfeld concludes:

Often the attempt at integration fails because mechanisms related to the omnipotent narcissistic self suddenly take over control of the normal self in an attempt to divert or expel the painful recognition. However, there are patients who gradually succeed in their struggles against narcissistic omnipotence, and this should encourage us analysts to continue our research into the clinical and theoretical probems of narcissism.

This seems to be a far cry from the optimistic attitude regarding the analyzability of all kinds of patients expressed by other Kleinian authors.

The relationship between unconscious fantasy and defensive mechanisms

Segal (1967) attempted to deal with the criticism that Kleinian analysts interpret the content of unconscious fantasies and neglect the analysis of defenses. She states that

it is far safer to analyze pre-psychotics now, when we do not analyze predominantly resistance of defenses, leaving the ego defenseless but have some understanding of the psychotic fantasies and anxieties that necessitate these defenses and can modify these anxieties by interpretations, which are directed at the content as well as at the defenses against it. The concept of mental mechanisms as one facet of fantasy life implies also that there is less division between interpretation of defense and those of content, and interpretation can deal more readily with the patient's total experience.

She quoted Isaac's (1948) statement, "Thus fantasy is the link between the id impulse and the ego mechanism, the means by which the one is transmitted into the other," and added (1967), "This applies to all mental mechanisms, even when they are specifically used as defenses." The rationale for generalizing Isaacs's statement is Segal's earlier description (1964) of the mechanisms of introjection and projection as related to fantasies of incorporation and ejection:

> Clinically, if the analysis is to be an alive experience to the patient, we do not interpret to him mechanisms; we interpret and help him to relive the fantasies contained in the mechanisms.

Her description of mechanisms such as introjection and projection as closely related to fantasies of an incorporating or ejecting kind seems clinically justifiable, although one would still wonder to what extent such a relationship holds true for later forms of projective mechanisms. However, her generalization to the effect that all defensive operations are expressed by fantasies is questionable. Repression, intellectualization, and isolation are defenses in which it is much more difficult to accept concrete unconscious fantasies as representing these mechanisms. Segal (1964) stated that

> patients frequently describe their experience of the process of repression, for instance, by speaking of a dam inside them which may burst under the pressure of something like a torrent. What an observer can describe as a mechanism is experienced and described by the person himself as a detailed fantasy.

She illustrates this concept with the dream of a patient in his first week of analysis. The patient, a naval officer, dreamed about a pyramid. On the bottom layer was a crowd of rough sailors; they carried on their heads a heavy gold book on which stood a naval officer of the same rank as the patient; on his shoulders, there stood an admiral. Segal concluded:

His main defense mechanism, repression, is represented in fantasy by the combined pressure of the admiral — superego, and the naval officer — ego, trying to keep the instincts under. His personality structure is also clearly represented by the three layers, the instincts pushing upwards, the superego, pressing down from above, and his feeling of his ego being squashed and restricted between the two.

This seems to be a questionable translation of manifest dream content into structural theory, but the problem is even greater if we consider how to "translate" a defensive operation such as reaction formation or character defenses in general. These defenses usually have multiple functions and are structurally linked with different conflicts — and fantasies — as well as more or less autonomous ego functions. In character defenses, a direct relationship between defense and content in the sense of an unconscious fantasy expressing the mechanism is hard to imagine. Segal's effort to justify the Kleinian technique of "deep" interpretation of unconscious fantasy, by stating that these fantasies also represent the defensive operations, does not, in my opinion, answer the ego-psychological criticism of the Kleinian's neglect of defense analysis.

It seems to me that, while some of the ego-psychological criticism of the Kleinian theory and technique continues to be valid, there are hopeful changes in theory and technique such that Kleinian and ego-psychological thinking seem to be reaching an integration. The dialogue between the ego-psychological and the Kleinian orientation must continue. Mutual enrichment in theory and technique, as has already taken place, will, we hope, continue to develop.

REFERENCES

Balint, M. (1968). *The basic fault: therapeutic aspects of regression.* London : Tavistock Publications.

Bibring, E. (1947). The so-called English school of psychoanalysis. *Psychoanal. Quart.* 16 : 69–93.

Bion, W. R. (1962). *Learning from experience.* New York : Basic Books.

———. (1963). *Elements of psycho-analysis.* New York : Basic Books.

———. (1967). *Second thoughts: selected papers on psycho-analysis.* London : Heinemann.

Brierley, M. (1939). Problems connected with the work of Melanie Klein. In *Trends in psycho-analysis.* London : Hogarth Press, 1951.

Fairbairn, W. R. D. (1952). *Psychoanalytic studies of the personality.* London : Tavistock Publications.

Freud, A. (1951). Observations on child development. *Psychoanal. Study Child* 6.

Geleerd, E. R. (1963). Evaluation of Melanie Klein's "Narrative of a child analysis." *Int. J. Psycho-Anal.* 44 : 493–513.

Glover, E. (1945). Examination of the Klein system of child psychology. *Psychoanal. Study Child* 1.

Guntrip, H. (1961). *Personality structure and human interaction.* New York : International Universities Press.

Harley, M. (1966). Transference developments in a five-year-old child. In *The child analyst at work,* edited by E. Geleerd. New York : International Universities Press, 1967.

Isaacs, S. (1948). The nature and function of phantasy. *Int. J. Psycho-Anal.* 29 : 73–97.

Jacobson, E. (1964). *The self and the object world.* New York : International Universities Press.

Joseph, B. (1960). Some characteristics of the psychopathic personality. *Int. J. Psycho-Anal.* 41 : 526–531.

Kernberg, O. (1966). Structural derivatives of object relationships. *Int. J. Psycho-Anal.* 47 : 236–253.

———. (1967). Borderline personality organization. *J. Amer. Psychoanal. Assoc.* 15 : 641–685.

———. (1968). The treatment of patients with borderline personality organization. *Int. J. Psycho-Anal.* 49 : 600–619.

Klein, M. (1945). The oedipus complex in the light of early anxieties. In *Contributions to psychoanalysis.* London : Hogarth Press, 1950.

———. (1946). Notes on some schizoid mechanisms. In *Developments in psychoanalysis,* edited by J. Riviere. London : Hogarth Press, 1952.

———. (1948). On the theory of anxiety and guilt. In *Developments in psychoanalysis,* edited by J. Riviere. London : Hogarth Press, 1952.

———. (1950). On the criteria for the termination of a psychoanalysis. *Int. J. Psycho-Anal.* 31 : 78–80.

———. (1952). Some theoretical conclusions regarding the emotional life of the infant. In *Developments in psychoanalysis,* edited by J. Riviere. London : Hogarth Press.

———. (1957). *Envy and gratitude.* New York : Basic Books.

———. (1963). *Our adult world.* New York : Basic Books.

Racker, H. (1968). *Transference and countertransference.* New York : International Universities Press.

Rosenfeld, H. (1959). An investigation into the psycho-analytic theory of depression. *Int. J. Psycho-Anal.* 40 : 105–129.

———. (1964). Object relations of the acute schizophrenic patient in the transference situation. In *Recent research on schizophrenia,* edited by P. Solomon and B. C. Glueck. Washington, D.C. : American Psychiatric Association.

———. (1965). *Psychotic states: a psychoanalytical approach.* New York : International Universities Press.

Searles, H. F. (1963). Transference psychosis in the psychotherapy of chronic schizophrenia. In *Collected papers on schizophrenia and related subjects.* New York : International Universities Press, 1965.

Segal, H. (1964). *Introduction to the work of Melanie Klein.* New York : Basic Books.

———. (1967). Melanie Klein's technique. In *Psychoanalytic techniques: a handbook for the practising psychoanalyst.* New York : Basic Books.

Sutherland, J. D. (1963). Object-relations theory and the conceptual model of psychoanalysis. *Brit. J. Med. Psychol.* 36 : 109–124.

van der Waals, H. G. (1965). Problems of narcissism. *Bull. Menninger Clin.* 29 : 293–311.

Waelder, R. (1937). The problem of the genesis of psychical conflict in earliest infancy. *Int. J. Psycho-Anal.* 18 : 406–473.

Winnicott, D. W. (1962). A personal view of the Kleinian contribution. In *The maturational processes and the facilitating environment.* New York : International Universities Press, 1965.

Zetzel, E. R. (1951). The depressive position. In *Affective disorders,* edited by P. Greenacre. New York : International Universities Press, 1953.

———. (1956a). An approach to the relation between concept and content in psychoanalytic theory. *Psychoanal. Study Child* 11.

———. (1956b). Current concepts of transference. *Int. J. Psycho-Anal.* 37 :-369–376.

———. (1964a). Discussion of paper by H. Rosenfeld, "Object relations of the acute schizophrenic patient in the transference situation." In *Recent research on schizophrenia,* edited by P. Solomon and B. C. Glueck. Washington, D.C. : American Psychiatric Association.

———. (1964b). The analytic situation. In *Psychoanalysis in the Americas,* edited by R. E. Litman. New York : International Universities Press, 1966.

———. (1966). The analytic process. Unpublished paper read at the Second Pan-American Congress for Psychoanalysis, Buenos Aires, Argentina, August.

———. (1967). Psychosis and the very young infant. Book review of *Psychotic states: a psycho-analytical approach,* by H. Rosenfeld. *Contemp. Psychol.* 12 : 126–128.

PART II

Tactics of Evaluation

Editor's Introduction

Ordinarily, clinical treatises begin with discussions of diagnosis and therapeutic indications and contraindications. To be sure, much has been written about these topics in expositions on psychoanalysis.

In discussing treatability, Freud divided emotional disturbances into two fundamental categories — the transference neuroses and the narcissistic neuroses. In the first he included the psychoneuroses and in the second, what he called narcissistic neuroses and psychotic disorders; he concluded that psychoanalysis was not indicated for the latter category. Consequently, many discussions on the amenability of psychoanalysis emphasize finding the narcissistic or psychotic core before deciding on treatment. Most assessments of analyzability consist of evaluating the personality structure; from this one can predict whether a workable (therapeutically useful) transference will occur. At this point, distinctions among transference, transference neurosis, and transference psychosis are superfluous. The purpose of a diagnostic appraisal is to determine whether the transference projections can be resolved, that is, worked through.

Experience has taught many of us that the problem of assessment is not simple. One cannot make predictions about the potential resolution of transference exclusively on the basis of diagnostic labeling. In my opinion determining what is treatable is beyond diagnosis and depends upon many variables that are inherent in the patient-analyst dyad. (This issue will be discussed in Chapter II.)

The next two chapters will deal with the traditional viewpoint (Dr. Klauber, Chapter 5) and one where the patient rather than the analyst makes the decision regarding analysis (Dr. Flarsheim, Chapter 6); Dr. Flarsheim says that since the recommendation for treatment can be viewed as a manipulation, that is, an intrusion into and an attempt to manage the patient's life, it is preferable for the patient to decide this matter for himself.

The differences, on the surface, between Dr. Klauber and Dr. Flarsheim seem to be enormous. However, closer scrutiny reveals that they are not so far apart, and each of them has told me how much he esteems the other. Dr. Klauber seems to be writing about specific conditions, but a closer examination reveals that he is really talking about his convictions which are the outgrowth of his very extensive clinical experience. He does not present rigid rules but comfortable and effective ways of viewing and approaching clinical problems. His insight and skills can serve as a guide for many practitioners. Dr. Flarsheim develops a fascinating theme that seems to be antithetical to psychoanalytic principles, but actually he stresses an even stricter adherence to psychoanalysis than usual. This is where he contributes something novel, not by deviation or departure, but, in a sense, by being more Catholic than the Pope.

Chapter 5 is a contribution from Great Britain and Chapter 6 is a product of the United States. To me, it is particularly interesting that Dr. Flarsheim's ideas have been fairly well accepted in England. They have not appeared in print before in the United States; if they had, they probably would have met with considerable resistance in some quarters. Seeing these two chapters juxtaposed, I want to stress the positive values of each in expanding our clinical horizons.

5

Psychoanalytic Consultation

JOHN KLAUBER

To RECOMMEND psychoanalysis for a patient is a great responsibility. It implies an enormous investment of hope, and often of family involvement, money, and time. Analysis will dominate the patient's psychic life for several years, and he may become more depressed or disturbed (and certainly more dependent) in the course of treatment. A conflict of value systems between patient and analyst may cause the patient to develop a permanent underlying discontent that he is unable to articulate, but that may force him to make painful psychic adjustments which can only gradually be thrown off after the analysis is ended. Failure of the analysis may result in the impoverishment of the personality of the patient and, if too often repeated, of the analyst. Similarly, if the analyst, confronted with what appears to be a stalemate, forces termination before the patient is fully ready and willing, this can be destructive to both. The psychoanalyst is left with a sense of failure and guilt, and the patient feels like the rejected victim of a broken home. In some cases analysis lasts for 20 years or more, usually with the patient changing analysts several times. Successfully analyzed patients sometimes want to return, and no one knows in what proportion of cases the habit of analysis, once established, cannot be permanently broken. It is remarkable that so little attention has been paid in the psychoanalytic literature to the criteria upon which analysis is recommended.

When a patient seeks a psychoanalytic consultation, he presents the analyst with a core problem. He comes during a time of crisis in his relationship to life, whether he brings this overtly as the final instance of a repetitive failure, as a self-critical depression, or as symptoms that represent the acute expression of permanent unconscious conflicts. Since only a partial understanding of a life problem can be reached during the consultation, since the concept of "cure" for problems rooted in the character structure is only partially applicable, since psychoanalysis is not an entity in itself, but a complex relationship between two individuals whose understanding of one another will inevitably also be partial, it is clearly inappropriate to recommend psychoanalysis like a medicine. Recommendations of this kind are frequently made, however, especially by doctors who are not psychoanalysts or by inexperienced analysts.

If a man's difficulties are rooted in his life and character, he will need more than a recommendation in order to understand how psychoanalysis can help him. Here a problem arises. The patient will need to know more about his situation and about what may or may not be expected from analysis. But because analysis works by providing access to unconscious emotions, this understanding cannot be achieved by intellectual means alone. It can only be fully grasped by the actual experience of analysis, but at the outset the patient has only come for consultation. *Therefore, he has to get some experience of analysis within the framework of the consultation. This is the essence of consultation,* and achieving it is a delicate procedure. The consultant cannot and should not conduct a miniature analysis; if he did, it would either overwhelm the patient or cause him to become too attached to the consultant at the expense of a smooth transference to his eventual analyst. But successful consultation can offer enough tentative explanation and interpretation to give the patient a glimpse of the emotional and intellectual processes involved without unduly seducing him. It is primarily the quality of the rapport formed that will enable the consultant and patient to judge if the latter can make further use of this type of experience.

How should this experience be given? The technique of analysis and the technique of consultation are not the same. The aim of analysis is to free the patient to make his own decisions. Consultation inevitably is advisory, however much we may try to bring the patient to his own point of decision. After all, even the consultant's referral of the patient to another analyst is loaded with control on the basis of his assessment of factors of which the patient has little or no awareness (for example, his assessment of prognosis or of the capacities of other psychoanalysts). Its aim is a plan of action to be discussed in rational terms at the end of the sampling procedure of consultation; therefore, consultation must be directed primarily to the functioning ego. So, in a sense, must analysis. But there is more than one psychoanalytic technique, and there is considerable variation in the extent to which different psychoanalysts approach problems from the standpoint of the id or of the ego. If the patient is to commit himself to a procedure lasting an indeterminate number of years, after which, for better or worse and sometimes both, he may never be the same, it is only fair that he should do so exercising his powers of judgment as fully as possible. He will greatly appreciate the care that is taken to ensure that he makes his decision without being pressured. This is especially important because, once analysis is started, transference has the power to hold the patient in an unsatisfactory situation. *This attempt to give the patient as much freedom of choice as possible by rational means is actually his first glimpse of the ethos and method of psychoanalysis.* The difference between analysis and consultation is that consultation requires that the conscious functioning of the ego be sustained and paramount. Even more than in analysis, there should be no playing of the doctor game (Simmel, 1926) or any of its variants, such as the silent analyst.

This orientation toward the ego also enables another aspect of psychoanalysis to be demonstrated. The patient needs to know that psychoanalysis is sensible and that decent analysts are reasonable, not mad. Even more, he needs to understand that psychoanalysis can make good sense of what he feels as madness and that it will not initially compound the madness with the omnipotent symbolic or "deep" interpretations that he may expect or consciously hope for.

All this implies that if the consultant can grasp something about the function of the symptoms in preserving the patient's stability and communicate this to him, it will be the best possible demonstration of the rationality and depth of insight of psychoanalysis. To take a simple example, a woman architect in her late twenties would break down with crying attacks and psychic paralysis whenever she was insufficiently supported by her male superior. She has a pleasant personality and is successful in her work, but she has achieved her present position in order to personify her father's ideal of his own father. The question is: "Where is she now?" It is surely better to interpret this to the patient and to discuss her need for emotionality (which her parents suppressed in her), than to interpret the oedipal contributions to her breakdown. This I take as obvious. But in practice the hardest test of a consultant is to wrest the contribution of the ego regularly and clearly from the disguises produced by the patient's fear of his unconscious aspirations. It is emotionally difficult to try persistently to obtain the rational and human from people who may present themselves in a bad light. It is also difficult to combine the capacity to listen, to respond appropriately, and to observe with the intense intellectual activity required to construct a coherent picture of the patient's life pattern and to formulate it (or at least begin to formulate it in the time available) as a living response. However, I believe it is possible for a consultant to gain enough information in most cases to arrive at a fairly good understanding of the patient's presenting problem in the context of his life from childhood to the present day.

There is the administrative and technical matter of how much time should be allotted for a consultation. To some extent this will depend upon the taste and temperament of the consultant and, to a lesser extent, upon the capacity and needs of the patient. A few patients are too inhibited to make use of an extended first interview, but this will not happen very often with an experienced interviewer. Obviously there must be enough time for the patient to feel that some contact has been made, for otherwise how could the consultation continue? To set aside one session may be enough for a first interview in some instances, but it is dangerous to permit a period that may prove frustrating or, in some cases, may be too short to deal with unexpected developments. Rather, the aim should be to give the patient time to state his problem fully enough to be able to wait peacefully for the next interview, if another interview is necessary. The majority of patients come to consultation in a state of anxiety and tension. The functioning of their ego has been impaired by regression so that it tends to operate under increased pressure from the primary process, that is, on an all-or-none basis. Behind their politeness, their unsatisfied fantasies (libidinal or aggressive) contribute to the events of the interview. This means that for the patient to feel really satisfied with the consultation, he must have discharged his tension and reached the feeling that he has said all that he needed to say at that particular time and that what he has said has registered. This needs considerable time. For my own speed of working, 50 minutes is rarely adequate, though to allot more time may on occasion be a counsel of perfection for a busy psychoanalyst. I cannot agree with the view (Glover, 1949) that a period longer than an hour imposes an excessive strain on the patient, except in the rare cases already mentioned. The vast majority of patients come with a great load of accumulated tension and do not find that time spent talking about their problems passes slowly, as later analysis shows. On the other hand, the consultant has to consider himself, and he should not become the masochistic victim of compulsive delayers. I find that if I allow an hour and three-quarters, I can complete most consultations or at least reach a satisfactory stage for breaking them off; a total of two hours allows ample time for making a few brief notes at the end. When I review the information I have gleaned in this time, however, I frequently find important gaps and I may have to see the patient a second or third time to continue the assessment and think over my recommendation in the light of further developments. After the initial consultation it is usually possible to fit the patient into a 50-minute schedule.

A consultation, then, is an extended private talk between an analyst and a patient, in which the analyst tries to understand something of the patient's personality while giving the patient some understanding of the character of psychoanalysis. The psycho-analyst also learns how he may employ his individual personality to enrich his professional role.

How the patient judges this introduction may be revealed in his subsequent analysis. A good consultation should not make the patient feel that, in being referred to a second analyst, he is being fobbed off with second best, but it should allow the analysis to get under way without impediment. However, the personality of the consultant should make a sufficiently positive impression on the patient so that he will return for future reference if difficulties occur. It could be that the initial transference of the patient to the consultant makes a more lasting imprint than we usually allow for in our egocentricity when we analyze patients who are referred to us.

Advising patients who have already had one or more analyses is an important and difficult part of a consultant's work. The deficiencies of the earlier analysis are always consciously or uncon-sciously exposed, and the consultant's feelings of professional rivalry are easily aroused. It is important not to get drawn into criticisms of the previous analyst, even when there seems to have been a gross failure. For the purpose of the present consultation, it is more relevant to disentangle the repetitive elements in the patient's history (without using them to blame the patient for the analyst's failure) and to assess the significance of the patient's attitude toward his previous analyst. For example, a patient may present criticisms, perhaps valid, of an analyst who has helped him considerably and who has advised him to see the consultant. Interpreting these positive elements may clarify the patient's confused feelings in his immediate crisis and may indicate a possible underlying paranoid process.

I shall attempt to outline some of the main criteria that a consultant can try to use in making referrals and some of the pitfalls he may encounter, but I am aware that I can give no more than a sketchy and personal presentation. Much of it may turn out to be an unpleasant combination of the dogmatic and the banal, but it has taken me a long time to orient myself to the tasks of consultation and my most common mistakes have been of an elementary kind.

The first thing I set out to do is to make contact with the patient about his problem. I regard psychoanalytic consultation as a traumatic event in a patient's life, and I do not think he should be further traumatized by being left almost entirely on his own — naked, frightened, and ashamed. It is usually possible to build some sort of bridge of shared experience without guiding the patient's responses or engaging in insincere irrelevant communication. This bridge can be very slight, for example: "I have heard a bit about your problem from Doctor So-and-So, but I would like to hear about it directly from you." The quicker the patient is put at ease, the freer the communication and the fuller the consultation. Since this is obvious, I would not stress it unless I believed that the ethos of the detached analyst (in my opinion, a misunderstood concept) could sometimes be used as a cover for sadism.

The consultation inevitably begins with certain preformed ideas in the consultant's mind. He may have first spoken with the patient on the telephone. Probably he has already seen other patients sent by the referring doctor: he may start with some suspicion of the general practitioner who tends to send patients on his own rather than their initiative; he may lack confidence in the woman gynecologist whose own conflicts lead her to make her cases sound worse than they are; and he may have a reliable colleague who wants his considered opinion on a relative of one of the colleague's patients who has a difficult character problem. Above all, the consultant forms certain impressions as the patient enters the room and begins to talk. None of these impressions or preliminary ideas should be discounted, but, above all else, they should be carefully balanced in the consultant's mind in the light of the total interview. He must beware of judging by impression even though he may sometimes rightly allow his impression to overrule his judgment. It is possible to be convinced of the correctness of one's feelings when one's apparent reason suggests the opposite. Nonetheless, to rely too much on impressions is to ask for difficulties. Perhaps the consultant's most common pitfall is to blame the ignorance or ineptitude of other doctors for the failure of previous treatment and to believe the patient's assurances of serious intentions. So, too, patients who present themselves poorly may demonstrate by their history that they have a greater reliability than they permit themselves to show. Increasingly I find that I need time after the consultation has ended — at least several days and often a week or two — to weigh my impressions and form a considered judgment.

A consultation is an interaction between two personalities, previously unknown to each other, in which the patient is trying to express himself on highly emotional topics. Therefore, there is latitude for the unpredictable to occur and for errors of judgment to be made — that is, for the analyst to make an irrational response to the patient's transference. I believe that it is wise for any psychoanalyst to remember this before accepting a patient for analysis, no matter who the consultant has been. My suggestion contradicts the advice that is sometimes given: to make the preliminary interview as short as possible or even to convert it into an analytic session. It does, however, have the advantage of ensuring from the start that the analyst can act on his own judgment and that this can be seen by the patient.

What is to be evaluated at consultation, and how is this to be done? But first it should be asked: Is there any need to evaluate a great deal at consultation? If the patient has "a fairly reliable character," can respond with nondelusional transference, wants psychoanalysis, and has the money to pay for it (or has possibilities for obtaining it), can he decide for himself? In this view psychoanalysis is the treatment of choice for the moderately ill, and consultation consists largely of excluding psychosis and making referrals. This is the view of psychoanalysis as a medicine that I have already criticized. Psychoanalytic diagnosis must of necessity be more sophisticated than psychiatric diagnosis; it is a complex assessment of defenses and motives that yields a richer and more relevant picture of the personality stretching far back into the patient's history. But, most important, it recognizes the strength of the compulsion to repeat patterns of relationship inside and outside analysis and can therefore attempt to prognosticate how an analysis will run. This attempt may be inexact, but at least it alerts the potential analyst to some of the possible complications. Besides, since the patient knows so little about possible impediments, he needs and deserves the opportunity to avail himself of the consultant's experience. For example, the patient may benefit from discussing his difficulty in making full use of opportunities he may value. If he is to embark on analysis, to decide against it, or begin a course of analytic psychotherapy fully convinced of the wisdom of his choice, he needs to have defined as far as possible the nature of his crisis and its place in his life history.

It follows that the essential factor to define at consultation is the nature of the patient's motivation in its widest sense, for his sustained and realistic engagement with analysis is clearly the most important requirement for success. Actually, however, when a patient comes for consultation, his motivation, even at a conscious level, is the factor most frequently overlooked by those who refer the patient to the consultant. What commonly brings the patient is the pressure of his immediate suffering, usually on himself, but not infrequently on his doctor or his family. But in any case his conscious motivation, whether for analysis or against it, is only a partial indicator of his unconscious motivation. It is his unconscious motivation that has to be determined — the repressed wish, so to speak, behind the manifest content of his presentation and the relevance of this wish to the immediate crisis in his life. Ideally, therefore, the whole illness must be scrutinized to elicit and make clear to the patient the nature of his motive for seeing the consultant, but this requires a complex evaluation based on real contact with the patient.

The first requirement is to assess the patient's desire to communicate and his potentiality for communication at a deep level. The emotional level of his speech must be compared with the emotional level that the consultant infers for his illness. The "illness" is, of course, essentially the product of a character problem, and an accurate evaluation of the symptoms can only be made by evaluating the character defenses. A successful professional man came for consultation at his wife's suggestion, although he felt no need for it. His complaint was that her constant criticism was getting him down. He added that he had come to believe that he had "feet of clay" professionally; he recognized that he was being overtaken by younger men. It turned out that his wife was a substitute for his father. In considering this man's problem, it would be necessary to evaluate the total extent of his masochism, not merely the sexual masochism that led him to marry his wife. The consultant can only estimate the danger or imminence of a serious depression and understand what has kept this man's marriage going for 30 years by determining the relative balance between the turning of his aggression against himself and his masochism.

Some of the patient's character defenses — the turning of aggression against the self, denial, or isolation of affect — can be interpreted immediately, and the patient's response noted. In discussing the patient's life pattern, the consultant also has the opportunity to point out some of the patterns of repetition, or unconscious equations and identifications, and to observe the nature of the analytical engagement that usually follows. In this connection the significance of organic illness should not be neglected, either as an indicator of psychological crisis or for evaluating fixation points. Whatever comments or interpretations are made can still be general in nature and within the capacity of the conscious ego to appreciate. If they are not too "wonderful" or startling, they need not interfere with a subsequent analysis by another analyst. If the patient's power of communication is blocked, even transference interpretations can be given provided they are made in general terms so that the patient will not be ruined for analysis (and for the consultant) by overwhelming his ego with unconscious impulses. A woman, married to a perpetually tired man with a low spermcount, was depressed because she had not conceived a second child. To help the patient overcome her reluctance to speak, it would not necessarily be traumatic to tell her that it may be difficult for her to discuss her marital sexual problems with another man. On the other hand, she might be aroused in an uncontrollable way if she were told that she could not speak to the consultant because she was afraid of falling in love with him.

The overall concept of motivation represents that motivation available despite the inhibiting forces of the illness — the rigidity of the defenses and the degree of traumatization.

Indications for the future also depend on another balance of forces. If the patient's motivation is to be assessed primarily by his history of past struggles against regression, then the potential outcome has to be evaluated in terms of the feasibility of change within the patient's life situation. Failure to take into consideration the difficulties of his life situation is, in fact, an important reason why the final therapeutic results of analysis are sometimes disappointing when compared with all the information gained about psychopathology. Is a full analysis really indicated for the woman with the tired husband if she finally conceives a second child and still complains of some depression? Other balances may require more difficult decisions, for instance: Would analysis be indicated for an émigré who may continue to work in this country for some years, but who has a discontented wife who looks forward to returning to their own country?

I will list some of the types of patients and situations of which I am wary. I am deliberately suspicious of charming patients and of those described as "very good cases for analysis." When one is in a state of distress, the narcissism required to charm is liable to be excessive, and how can anybody be described as a "good case for analysis"? When we do achieve splendid results, what was the trick? While the quality of the analysis in these cases was usually good, the result may have been due to considerable rapport. I am hesitant to accept patients who try to make unrealistic arrangements, for I do not think that analysts should agree to arrangements that may turn psychoanalysis into a burden, or cause it to break down, or lead a patient to hate it. A young mother who lives in the suburbs should not be expected to park her baby five times a week in order to come into town. An analyst who encourages a patient to change his place of residence and work for analysis is either brave or foolhardy. An analyst who charges a patient more than he can afford for four or five "necessary" sessions a week instead of adjusting his therapy to what the patient can pay misses the forest for the trees. Psychoanalysis (it seems to me) is a way of understanding people, and whether the patient sits or lies or takes a walk round the town like Gustav Mahler is to some extent peripheral. Similarly, an analyst who consents to treat a patient whose only funds are fixed capital has a bad bet, especially with a masochistic patient; what a temptation for him to express his resentment by not getting better until all his capital is exhausted! I am wary of patients who have only one symptom : the lack of capacity for varied forms of displacement implies a near-delusional mechanism. Similarly, a psychosomatic complaint without other conflicts or anxieties makes me suspicious of the patient's power to sustain analysis. I do not believe all that has been written about ulcerative colitis either with respect to the patient's dependency or his paranoid tendencies, but I am inclined to believe with de Boor (1946) that it is characteristic of bronchial asthmatics to hold their love objects at an intermediate distance, neither allowing them to come close nor to go, and I do not welcome this form of transference. Like others, I regard hypochondriasis with suspicion. While hypochondriacal patients clearly have serious problems with projected and reintrojected aggression and may have great difficulty forming stable love relationships (including analytic relationships), I do not regard hypochondriasis as necessarily an indicator of near psychosis. I will end this list with the most dogmatic statement of all : While I believe that patient psychotherapeutic work can greatly help severely disturbed patients and sometimes transform their lives, I believe that the greatest pitfall of analysis is an excessive belief in our power to reconstitute the character. The best results can generally be obtained with those who, in Freud's words, "have a fairly reliable character" to start with.

There remains a class of patient who "needs" analysis because he is making someone else's life or analytic treatment impossible, although he is not aware of it. Occasionally there seems to be no alternative except to send this patient to analysis as one might send a child. An example of such a patient is a man who was in a double second marriage that was characterized by constant quarrels provoked by both partners. These quarrels often centered on the husband's sexual seduction of his children, all of whom required psychiatric help. In spite of her propensity to provoke arguments, the wife had a genuine concern for her stepchildren, but she could not communicate her point of view to her husband. Without some solution to this problem, the wife's analysis would probably have been futile, and the marriage could easily have broken down. Therefore, the husband was advised to seek treatment. Would the consultant have been justified in exploiting this man's most agonizing fears of harming his children in order to get him into analysis (in this case by connecting the man's fantasies of keeping his wife in chains while she begged to go to the lavatory with his 11-year-old daughter's symptoms of urinary and fecal retention)? Such a decision must depend on the consultant's estimate of the patient's ultimate good sense and power of forgiveness as well as the skill of the analyst to whom he will be referred to mitigate the trauma. For other patients the policy of "isolating the symptoms from the observing ego" (that is, telling the patient what a mess he is in) may result only in trauma and a revulsion toward analysis. To succeed it is usually necessary to wait until the patient is ready for the risky and cooperative venture of analysis. Only a naïve analyst doesn't know that other therapies also have their successes, and will never consider recommending them.

However, a more common problem than that of forcing patients into analysis is the matter of how to keep them out of it. Patients may feel ill and ask for treatment, but if one analyst will not accept them, they will go on to the next. Of course, it should be agreed that a person in distress, or suffering from a psychiatric illness, who asks for help has to be helped; also, that the type of patient who consults a psychoanalyst needs some deeper understanding of his illness. Actually he needs psychoanalysis as I have defined it: a particular way of understanding people. But in a technical sense this definition is not specific enough. Patients are treated differently if they just discuss their problems, or if they sit in a chair and engage in an analytic exchange twice a week for a year or two, or if they lie on couch three, four, or five times a week for many years while their unconscious fantasies about the analyst are consistently explored and related in detail to the totality of the problems in their life. It is difficult to define the difference, but perhaps one valid generalization is that patients in skilled psychotherapy seem to be spared a great deal and to fare remarkably well. In Freud's time there was no acceptable alternative to full psychoanalysis, but today, with a greater social and possibly psychological range of patients, psychoanalysts are experienced in applying analysis to groups and individuals.

The main object of consultation, therefore, is to make a tentative estimate of a feasible aim for treatment by answering a series of questions:

First: Should this patient have a full analysis from the start? Or, if he is not able to use a complete anlysis, is some completely different type of therapy indicated (such as relaxation therapy for a tense, elderly obsessional of limited intelligence who has a history of depressive breakdown) or some form of anlytic psychotherapy that wouldn't prejudice a possible later analysis?

Second : What type of analyst would be able to understand this patient's problem? This answer must be intuitive, but some similarities of character agree and some do not. I am not suggesting that an inhibited violinist should be recommended to an intensely musical analyst who may in part share the virtuoso's obsession. But the perverse husband who seduced his children would be suitably placed if he were referred to an experienced woman analyst who had special experience in child analysis.

Third : How should the patient's needs be matched with his financial resources? Suppose the patient is a young academic with a transvestite perversion who rightly feels he needs a full analysis in spite of his modest income. Should he be allowed to go to a clever but newly qualified analyst four or five times a week at a low fee, or should he be sent to a more experienced analyst at a higher fee twice a week? My answer would be very clear. It takes a long time to acquire the necessary experience to understand, and I do not think that I and my colleagues did our best work with our first patients. I hope that it is not cynical or harsh to take the view that a psychoanalytic consultant's first obligation is to his patient, and only secondly to support newly trained analysts. This, of course, again raises the question of what is psychoanalysis. Clearly a patient may receive more psychoanalysis (in the sense of analytic understanding) by sitting in a chair twice a week opposite someone who understands him easily than by lying on a couch five times a week talking to an analyst who has difficulty grasping the continuity.

I end a consultation when I feel satisfied that I have a reasonable understanding of the patient's problem and when I feel that he is satisfied with what I have to tell him. Since a whole analysis is not enough to understand a person's problems, this point must be determined by affective indicators. But affects are, after all, the arbiters of all our judgments. Having formed a judgment, I like to share it with whoever else may be involved — certainly the patient's doctor if possible. I often suggest to my patients that in times of stress they turn to their family doctor if, for any reason, I am unavailable. He can be of great help to the patient and analyst in a crisis, and especially when the analyst is away on holiday. If the analyst gives a patient the name of a colleague, the colleague may be reluctant to offer interpretations; if he should give interpretations, however, he may become the object of the patient's transference fantasies. If the analyst is lucky enough to find a friendly general practitioner, who is in no sense a rival, the latter may be able to handle the patient reasonably without undue transference complications. Moreover, the reputation of psychoanalysis will not be damaged by the analyst's subsequent discovery of crises handled without his knowledge. The general practitioner can also be of great help in illuminating the patient's family background or even in disclosing medical information that the psychoanalyst may consider important in his assessment.

The other people with whom I like to share my judgment may be the patient's relatives. If a relative pays for the treatment he deserves to know something about what he is paying for. I ask a wife to discuss it with her husband. With a young adult (I do not see children), I generally ask for permission to discuss at least the general nature of the problem and its implications with his parents.

Finally, I do not think that the patient should have to commit himself under pressure. If the potential analyst is oneself it is especially important to make certain (without driving him away) that the patient can gracefully get out of it.

REFERENCES

de Boor, C. (1966). *Zur Psychosomatik der Allergie ins besondere des Asthma Bronchiale.* Berne : Hubert; Stuttgart : Klett.

Glover, E. (1949). *Psycho-analysis.* London : Staples Press.   -

Simmel, Ernst. (1926). The doctor-game : illness and the profession of medicine. *Int. J. Psycho-Anal.* 7.

Treatability

ALFRED FLARSHEIM

In *Analysis Terminable and Interminable* (1937) Freud uses the term "forcible technical device" in discussing the setting of a time limit in the case of the Wolf-Man as a means of overcoming his resistance against analytic exploration of his infantile neurosis and against mature independent behavior, free from the need for analysis. Freud points out that the patient's subsequent symptoms included paranoid "residual" transference reactions. He does not go quite so far as to conclude that the patient's paranoid residual transference reaction was partly precipitated by the "forcible technical device," but his description of the patient's reaction leaves room to consider this possibility.

When the Wolf-Man returned for consultation five years after the end of the treatment, Freud learned that "immediately after the end of the treatment" there had been a reversal of the patient's helpless, clinging, dependent attitude toward him. The patient "had been seized with a longing to tear himself away from my influence" (Freud, 1918). The patient's paranoid feelings toward Freud were certainly overdetermined; he had also experienced similar feelings toward others (for example, tailors) during his analysis. In addition, the patient had reacted with guilt and anxiety to his knowledge of Freud's cancer, but Freud's footnote permits one to speculate that the "forcible technical device" may have contributed to the patient's difficulty in working through his paranoid transference within the therapy.

The patient was in reduced economic circumstances when he returned to Vienna five years after the end of his analysis, and for the next six years Freud gave him a small sum of money annually. During this time the patient began to manifest disabling hypochondriacal delusions, and so Freud eventually arranged for him to see Dr. Mack-Brunswick, without fee. In his work with Dr. Mack-Brunswick, the patient's "residual paranoid transference reaction" to Freud came to light, together with conflict about useless "alms thrown to a crippled beggar" (Mack-Brunswick, 1928).

In *Analysis Terminable and Interminable* Freud says that after his experience with the Wolf-Man he continued to use the "forcible technical device," but with many reservations about its utility.

My interest here is not in the specific device of setting a time limit for a patient's treatment, but in the broader question, What is the effect upon treatment of the *possibility* of the use of *any* "forcible technical devices" at all? Was Freud's pessimism regarding the treatment of psychotics related to his emphasis upon the technique of insisting that the patient overcome resistances to free association as a pathway to achieving synthesis and integration? Can we take other elements from Freud's discoveries that are more helpful in the treatment of psychotic patients?

Freud referred to the analyst as the active partner and the patient as the passive partner in the analytic situation (Freud, 1937). The therapeutic setting that he created is, however, one in which the patient can have the *greatest possible* freedom for the active expression of megalomanic and mutually contradictory urges. Freud did in fact report successful work with patients who would be judged psychotic by present-day standards. He reports having been very active and controlling with them, but this was certainly outweighed by another factor — his intense interest in understanding his patient's psychic processes. Freud attached great value to the way in which the patient affected him, and he was the eager recipient of the patient's "educational" activity (Szasz, 1957).

Lubin (1967) points out that the Wolf-Man considered himself to be an important contributor to psychoanalysis. I am distinguishing this from the fact that he believed he was "Freud's favorite patient." The latter includes a transference projection, in contrast to the genuine opportunity Freud provided for the patient to participate in creative activity. We would expect his feeling that he was "Freud's favorite patient" to have contributed to two kinds of restrictions while he was seeing Freud : 1.) A restriction of the patient's perception of Freud's feelings toward him to positive feelings only, and 2.) A corresponding restriction to positive transference reactions.

However, identification with Freud as an observer making creative use of his reception of the patient's productions would be consistent with awareness of the negative as well as the positive aspects of the total transference. As I read Lubin's report (1967) of his contact with the Wolf-Man, I received the impression that the enhancement of self-esteem that the Wolf-Man derived from feeling that he had taught Freud was the crucial therapeutic factor for him. It permitted an identification with a self-created deity which could not have been achieved simply by considering himself "Freud's favorite patient."

The patient who feels that he is at the mercy of omnipotent, ego-alien, intrapsychic forces seeks megalomaniac delusional promises of rescue. This expectation is frequent, and, if fostered, can lead to ego disintegration when the magical expectations fail to be realized. Insofar as we are learning from the patient, we are not offering to teach him magical solutions to his problems. As observers we are genuinely students and the patients are our teachers. We value what the patient can teach us. Interpretations can take the form of tentative statements for evaluation, revision, or confirmation by the patient as the final authority who possesses the answers in potentially understandable form (Bruno Bettelheim, personal communication, July, 1968). The patient who feels depreciated and worthless, perhaps having megalomanic defenses, gains a genuine feeling of worth from the opportunity to help us understand the workings of the mind. Insofar as we have this interest, we thus have a therapeutic instrument that can be utilized by the patient. Fortunately, we do not need to have Freud's creative genius. Freud subordinated all other interests to the investigative one, and we can certainly extend our ability to deal with the psychotic patient by deliberately defining the observational frame of reference. Experiences in another area of study are relevant here.

ANIMAL OBSERVATIONS

In his popularly written account of a scientific investigation, Schaller (1964) discusses the habits of free-living jungle animals. This is not the usual animal adventure story. There are unparalleled observations of behavior that may interest the general reader and the specialist in animal behavior as well as other behavioral scientists. But my main impression was that it is unusually unspectacular. This came as a surprise since it is the record of a man living in close contact and communication with free-living gorillas. There are no hair-raising episodes of escape from attacking gorillas. The *reason* the book is so unspectacular has special relevance for the psychotherapist.

Dr. Schaller points out that in order to conduct his close-range observation of the gorillas he had to go into the jungle among them completely unarmed. If he had carried a firearm, his psychology would have been affected in such a way that he would have provoked retreat or attack by the gorillas. But unarmed, he had to depend upon his ability to adapt to the powerful animals — to respect, for example, their indications that he should retreat from them — and to do so in a way that would not provoke them.

We can profit from the author's description of the requirements of the observer. Schaller says, "It is really not easy for man to shed all his arrogance and aggressiveness before an animal, to approach it in utter humility with the knowledge of being in many ways inferior . . . even the possession of a firearm is sufficient to imbue one's behavior with a certain unconscious aggressiveness, a feeling of being superior, which an animal can detect" (Schaller, 1964).

It was not a matter of being weaker than the animals, but of operating in a consistently observational frame of reference. To carry a firearm introduced the possibility of killing; therefore, it changed the frame of reference from that of pure observation to one that included potential killing or being killed. A gun, rather than being a protection, was thus a source of danger, which increased the possibility of being attacked, and reduced the ability to observe the animals closely.

This has direct relevance to our work. The possibility of introducing any forcible technique for the purpose of overcoming a patient's resistance or of controlling his life — for example, by directing his activities, hospitalization, drugs, or shock — affects the psychology of the psychotherapist in a way comparable to the effect of a firearm described by Dr. Schaller. Our ability to observe and to communicate with patients on their own terms does not depend upon our being weak and helpless, but upon our remaining in an exclusively observational frame of reference. Such an orientation requires the maximum ego integration of which the therapist is capable.

DIAGNOSIS

Phenomenologically a patient might be labeled psychotic on the basis of overt manifestations of primary-process functioning. A history of the development of his illness can be obtained in order to make a clinical diagnosis of established psychotic process. There is, however, another more relevant question, namely, can the patient use the treatment offered? We can try to infer the answer to this question from the patient's history, or we can answer the question more reliably by direct observation, which can lead to a "therapeutic diagnosis" (Winnicott, 1954).

The therapeutic diagnosis is a statement concerning the patient's capacity to utilize therapy; it depends principally upon two factors :

First, can the patient sustain himself between the therapy hours in the outside world and get to and from his appointments? This depends not only upon the ego state of the patient, but upon the attitudes of others — the patient's family and those in his wider environment — their interest in helping the patient, and their particular tolerances and sensitivities. It is here that casework management may be required. *In the extreme this can mean hospitalization, not as an inherent part of psychotherapy but to enable the patient to survive between his therapeutic sessions.* The second factor is whether or not the patient behaves in the office in ways that the therapist can tolerate. Since this depends upon both the ego state and psychopathology of the patient, as well as the idiosyncratic personal interests and sensitivities of the particular therapist, it will not be the same for any two therapists. A theoretical understanding widens our tolerance, as does a structured therapeutic setting, which defines and limits the responsibility of the therapist to the patient, thus expanding the freedom of the therapist to work with whatever the patient brings into the therapy. The therapist's own personal therapy can increase the range of conditions in which each individual therapist can function within an observational frame of reference. There are always limits to this ability, and each therapist has his own specific personal sensitivities and conditions that are required in order for him to achieve his maximum freedom of integrative and synthetic ego functioning. This corresponds to the fact that the facets of the therapeutic setting that are emphasized will not be the same for any two patients because the sensitivities of each patient differ.

In applying this concept to psychiatric clinics, Dr. Doris Wheeler (Seminar, Family Service Center of Wilmette, Illinois, November 13, 1967), pointed out another important factor. A meaningful therapeutic relationship develops spontaneously between the patient and the therapist. The exact form of therapy is a joint creation that evolves from the interaction between two unique personalities; it cannot be prescribed by a third person, such as a supervisor or the intake caseworker of a clinic or social agency. In a clinic much can be gained by having the patient seen initially in a therapeutic situation rather than in a traditional "intake interview." Thus, the patient's initial hopes and fears, as well as his transference expectations, can be utilized; otherwise, he is interviewed by several people and asked to maintain hope that a therapeutic relationship will be established in the dim future.

If we can define the conditions we need for our work, that is, conditions in which we can operate with maximum freedom within the framework of observation and understanding, we do not need to select patients for treatment on the basis of symptoms, absence of primitive mental mechanisms, and so forth. Each patient can select or reject us and the setting in which we work, on the basis of his ability to use the therapy we can offer. Since every therapist has a different personality, the conditions each one needs will be different (Lindon, 1967).

If one includes various manipulative procedures in his armamentarium, he is likely to find the use of them necessary. The very possibility of using forceful or manipulative techniques to control the patient helps to precipitate violent acting out, which must then be controlled. *For example, therapists who do not hospitalize patients rarely find that their patients need hospital care.*

Schaller mentions repeatedly that all sensory modalities are experienced more vividly in the quiet of the jungle. He points out several times that his understanding of the animals developed to the point of some slight intercommunication with them. Schaller stressed that this had not been experienced by earlier writers on the subject of free-living gorillas because they had gone into the forest with the preconception that they were going to encounter dangerous animals that would take the initiative and make unprovoked attacks on them, and were always prepared to counterattack by shooting the animals. The earlier explorers were not in a position to understand the gestures of the animals as signals or to notice how the animals reacted to the gestures of the observer because, as Schaller points out, the earlier observers were operating under the assumption that they would kill or be killed. As a result, they misinterpreted the animals' intent as aggressive and found it necessary to use their weapons. Schaller thus found that these writers distorted "the whole nature" of free-living animals.

I am comparing Schaller's observations with the reports in our literature about the dangers of working with the paranoid and the depressed patient, and the need for therapists to have "forcible technical devices" (such as hospitalization or drugs) for working with such patients. If we feel that we can forcibly control a patient, we tend to operate in a framework of controlling or not controlling him, rather than providing a setting in which he can develop control of himself.

In order to operate without trying to control a patient, we must have confidence in his potential for spontaneous maturation and development (Giovacchini, 1965). Rather than focusing on the patient's resistance to change, we can focus on the adaptive value of his behavior, including both his impulse to change and his impulse to maintain unchanging, predictable constancy in his life. The same behavior can be viewed as naughtiness, resistance, compromise, defense, adaptation, ego mechanism, or an achievement of the patient's ego, depending upon one's viewpoint (Bettelheim, 1967). Interpreting the adaptive value of behavior from the way in which the ego reconciles the demands of the id, the superego, and the external world implies acknowledgment of symptomatic behaviour as an achievement of the patient's ego. Primitive mental mechanisms, such as splitting, projection, or denial, imply extreme latent anxiety. The patient who uses these cannot conceive of a more integrated state without the need for such massive defenses, but can experience anxiety related to the loss of these mechanisms. When we can acknowledge the value of these mechanisms as defenses against anxiety, we enable the patient to share a successful experience with us rather than feel criticized and attacked.

Insofar as we attempt to intrude and to control the patient, as, for example, to coerce him to talk openly, we stimulate the same massive defenses that he uses against any threat to his equilibrium (Boyer and Giovacchini, 1967). Insofar as the patient can recognize that we respect and acknowledge the value of such defenses, he has less of a need to use them in his relationship with us. He can thus become aware of conflict within himself. This is well illustrated by a patient who needed to remain silent most of the time for many months.

CLINICAL ILLUSTRATION

Beginning of Treatment

A 22-year-old man telephoned for an appointment; after some confusion because he could not tell my office the correct number of the public telephone from which he was calling, he finally arrived at the time when I had offered to see him. He told me that he had run away from another city where he had been living at his parents' home, seeing a psychoanalyst, and treated for "perceptual defect," characterized by an inability to read, write or speak accurately in school; this condition was diagnosed to be the result of a neurological disorder without localizing neurological signs. He professed to be completely helpless with respect to finding a place to live in Chicago, supporting himself, or arranging to come to the office for appointments. He said he could not understand the function of street signs because when he looked at them they either "got broken up" or became a part of his eyes and changed their positions as he looked in different directions. This, he said, was an example of the perceptual "defect," or "handicap." He had considered both murder and suicide, particularly when he experienced any "bad luck" (meaning the failure of magical expectations). For example, he said that he was certain he could make a reliable income from winning things that were raffled off in advertising campaigns.

The patient remembered that he had acted aggressively toward his previous therapist by screaming, pounding, and kicking the couch; threatening to attack the analyst physically; proclaiming his helplessness and inability too care for himself; and "threatening suicide." He said that his analyst had "placated" him by pointing out the former's helpful intentions, advising him about practical affairs, having him sit in a chair rather than continue to use the couch, and "threatening" to hospitalize him or to give him drugs if he could not manage his life.

I was impressed that, despite his dazed and incoherent manner, he had found my office at the correct time for his appointment. He expected me to hospitalize him. I told him that there were psychiatric facilities at all major hospitals in Chicago and that a taxicab could take him to one if he decided to go into a hospital. I offered to see him in my office, regardless of whether he decided to live in a hospital or elsewhere, and for my regular fee. He said that he could not possibly pay the regular fee and asked to be referred to someone who would reduce the fee, as he said his previous therapist had done. I suggested that it would be all right if he could find someone whose regular fee was lower, but I advised him against seeing anyone who reduced the fee as a special adaptation. This was a fairly forcible recommendation, but at that time I did not expect to see the patient again and had no power to enforce the suggestion. He left saying that he would not be back because of my failure to recognize his need for guidance and to accept a lower fee since he "could not possibly work."

About a week later he telephoned again and sounded quite different. He wanted to start treatment in my office and at my regular fee. I was still influenced by our first meeting and was, therefore, hesitant over the telephone. He argued logically that I had offered to see him and that, since he had decided he would come to my office and pay my fee, I had no right to reject him now unless I did not want him as a patient or unless I no longer had time for him in my schedule. I found his logic impressive and gladly accepted him for treatment.

When he arrived I learned that he had an apartment and a job and had arranged for his parents to pay part of his fee. He said that my earlier failure to assist him had been a "vote of confidence" in him — an indication that I was "willing to take a chance" on him. He felt confident in the treatment, he said, because he believed that I had demonstrated to him that I had no guidance, drugs, or hospital with which to threaten him if he were anxious, helpless, or suicidal. He said that his previous analyst had reduced his fee because his parents had failed to pay the bill. This made him wonder why the analyst was seeing him. The analyst had sent the bill to his parents.

His parents wrote to me that they wanted to discuss their son with me, and they expected me to send them the bill. I preferred to give the bill directly to the patient, allowing him to deal with his parents. Although the father wrote to the patient that he considered treatment very important and promised to help pay for it, he was not consistent in doing this. I preferred to see the patient less frequently rather than reduce my fee; I explained to the patient that I would resent working for a reduced fee. I pointed out to him that I do not select patients; I explained to him my conditions for work and told him that the selection was up to him. The patient experienced this as a consistency between my statements and my actions. He said that this was reassuring to him because it made him feel that he might be able to "understand people," that is, correlate signs and signals with meanings.

He expected me to request records from his previous therapists and to take a formal history. I asked him why he expected this. He had not only experienced such procedures as a routine part of his initiation with previous therapists, but he expected me to use diagnostic assessment in order to choose my "therapeutic weapon" as well.

History-taking, leading to a diagnostic assessment, implies to many patients that we have an instrument, a technique, or some powerful medicine to prescribe once we have decided that the case is suitable for treatment. It is perfectly logical for a patient to wait passively for us to prescribe for him if we have taken the initiative from the start and after the patient has passively acquiesced to our request that he give us a history. If we do not select patients, but rather set the conditions that we need for our work, permitting patients to select or reject us, then we can offer them the opportunity to try treatment. *A "trial period" can permit a patient to find out whether he can use the therapeutic setting we offer.*

The 22-year-old patient found the treatment helpful and wanted to continue. In his helpless state, he needed to idealize me and sought security by trying to see his therapy with me as superior to his previous therapy and by depreciating his previous therapy.

Although he had found an apartment and a job, the patient began treatment by repeating that he could not manage his life because he "wandered around aimlessly" and could not "steer himself." I told him I assumed he was telling both of us that he needed to relax in my office because apparently he expected to relax further on the outside through his "aimless wandering" (Winnicott,

1954). His behavior became manifestly crazy in the office, with disjointed, polymorphous perverse, sadomasochistic fantasies, while his behavior on the outside became progressively more organized. (See Chapter 11.)

I am not certain why the patient so quickly experienced such marked clinical improvement. Although he did not refer to it explicitly, one factor may have been that I "forbade" him to see someone who would reduce his fee. I felt free to take this strong stand because he had asked to be referred and I did not think of him as my patient. The fact that I could not profit economically from my recommendation may have affected the patient because he seemed to suspect that I might want to exploit him economically. With his knowledge of the case, Dr. Bruno Bettelheim suggested that my recommendation was probably interpreted by the patient to mean that I wanted him to have complete and satisfying treatment rather than a repetition of infantile oral frustration.

The patient may have used my behavior as a focus for identification. He told me clearly what he wanted after I had specified what I wanted and had abstained from managing his affairs. He was unable to change the conditions of treatment that I considered essential. Testing the boundaries of the therapeutic setting may have assured him that it would be safe for him to manifest his primary process functioning within the treatment. Freud (1922) said that when an individual forms delusions and hallucinations there is an element of reality (illusion) because he does not project "into the blue"; he relies upon external reality in selecting actual characteristics of the outer world. In this passage Freud was particularly interested in the paranoid patient's selective awareness of the unconscious motivations of other persons. Khan (1953) points out that the concept of "illusion" (Winnicott, 1945) underlies the therapeutic function of transference and that it extends to the non-human as well as to the human environment (Searles, 1960). The patient reveals a certain creativeness when he revises external reality with his own mind. Khan calls creative "illusory" modification of the outer world while still respecting its actual qualities "an essential tool for the understanding of transference cure."

"Perceptual Handicap" ("Strephosymbolia")

As the patient recalled, his treatment for "perceptual handicap" had consisted of repetitive exercises to enable him to correct his perceptual "distortions." This had been partially effective with respect to his academic work, but it had left the underlying dynamics untouched and had not reduced his anxiety. Lacking any therapeutic techniques to try to force the patient to perceive the external world as others see it, all I could do was to observe his way of perceiving and consider it as a potentially meaningful communication. We could regard his idiosyncratic way of perceiving things (for example, street signs) as a special talent rather than as a "handicap"; that is, he omnipotently manipulated his perception of external reality as a defense against anxiety. If street signs, for example, came to mean the same thing to him that they meant to other people, they would be independent of his control; thus, he would have no better "luck" than anyone else and might find himself in some "unlucky" place. As it was, his location was always "unknown"; therefore, it was not surely "terrible" and had the potentiality of being "perfect." He told me that, although street signs were "meaningless," he could magically predict external events: he said he could be absolutely sure of winning contests. Actual failure to win specific contests did not shake this confidence.

Exploring the goals of his omnipotent manipulation of the mental representations of my actions and of things in my office so that they became signs and signals indicating his victory or defeat replaced his confusion about street signs. On the other hand, the limits of his power were important; the following episode illustrates the organizing function of the time framework of the treatment:

The patient was talking, without manifest anxiety, about a very frightening nightmare in which he sought "all the breasts in the world" and they turned into threatening flaming mouths. Suddenly the patient started to scream, "Forever, it goes on forever," with great apprehension. When I looked at my watch I discovered that I had neglected to stop him at the usual time but had allowed our time to run over about five minutes. I pointed this out to him, and his anxiety immediately subsided as we terminated the session. I think that he had come to depend upon my terminating the session after 50 minutes and that he could discuss frightening material without manifest anxiety so long as that was dependable. My failure to end the session when he sensed the time had come represented my failure to provide him with a reliable setting to support his defenses against anxiety; as a consequence of the importance of the time framework to him, he felt that my delay was "forever" (Klauber, 1967).

His orientation in space is illustrated by the following : We found that he had to control his body parts, particularly his arms and legs, as though they were parts of a complex machine, and that if he relaxed his control he could not be certain whether he had done things that he saw me doing, such as opening or closing a door. He was extremely sensitive to any changes in my routine behavior. He could acknowledge that certain actions were exclusively mine, rather than having to believe that they were his only when he could predict them on the basis of having seen me perform them frequently. This recognition led him to feel less of a need to observe me closely and to be able to exercise greater freedom in his own behavior ; there was also a marked improvement in his appearance and motor coordination. When his movements appeared smoother, I realized, in retrospect, the degree to which he had previously been uncoordinated. His earlier uncoordination had taken the form of propelling himself toward an object with too much force and then forcibly restraining himself in order to avoid a collision with the object.

In the waiting room, he could read articles in magazines that had been there for several months. When I would replace them with new magazines, however, he could not read the new ones because his eyes would be on a page looking at him rather than in his head looking at the page. Instead of reading new magazines, he "knew" their content by magic or else decided it was not worth knowing.

He recalled something interesting about his mother in connection with his reversal of numbers or letters in words he wrote or read. The patient said that his mother was dead : "She has always been dead." Gradually, I came to realize that he meant that his mother still said that she was dead and blamed the patient for her "deadness." He said, "Mother kisses me while accusing me of killing her." In connection with this, he remembered that, as a child, he became sick after eating a piece of chalk that his mother had told him was a piece of bread. He wondered whether he had changed bread into chalk or whether his mother had done so. He felt that by reversing symbols he might reverse fantasied actions — his own and his mother's — and thus avoid their consequences (Rosen, 1950; Witty and Kopel, 1936).

In retrospect, the "perceptual defect" consisted of : 1.) a correct and appropriate response to parental inconsistency ; 2.) an effort to communicate that signals and meanings, and symbol and object symbolized, were not predictably linked; 3.) a defense against omnipotent destructive fantasies (for example, by reversal); and 4.) an effort to make sense out of the relation between signals and meanings by keeping them tentative, pending an opportunity to link them in a meaningful and consistent object relation.

As we discovered these connections, the patient secured a more skilled and higher paying job that required precision. He began playing with risk investments on the side; although his belief in magic persisted, he only acted it out in controlled ways with small amounts of money, although with continued fantasies of enormous winnings.

At the same time that these events were taking place, there was another sequence that consisted of silence, whispering, and speaking.

Silence, Whispering, and Speaking

The patient was largely silent during his early sessions. He would lie quietly, but then he would suddenly kick his feet, pound the couch, or scream. Whenever I started to say something, he would jerk convulsively, and so I generally remained silent too.

The setting for the treatment was particularly important to me during the patient's prolonged silences, which sometimes lasted for several sessions, and on one occasion lasted for about three months. During the prolonged silences I had no idea what was going on. Whatever understanding I reached usually came later; it was retrospective. The setting was important because I relied on it to provide a framework to bridge the silences, enabling me to tolerate them without feeling pressed to interfere.

During these silences, when I had no idea what was going on, I read or did paper work. I told the patient that I was doing this in order to make myself comfortable so that I would not feel inclined to intrude into his silence, which seemed to be important to him, as evidenced by the fact that he was silent so much of the time. I would be startled, however, whenever he suddenly screamed; eventually I told him this, wondering whether his sudden screams were intended to show me how it felt to be startled. He agreed that this might be true and told me that he had been magically controlling me by being silent, that is, preventing me from speaking. Eventually the meaning of his silence progressed to a communication, a signal. Rather than being a magical device to control me, it became a way to show me how he wanted me to treat him, that is, not to intrude. This came about in the following way :

The patient complained that his parents had never been able to understand him and that he had never understood them. He said he felt hopeless about ever understanding anyone or being understood; in retrospect we linked this with his feeling that he had to have magical ability to predict and control events. We reached this understanding after he began talking very softly, so that I could understand only some of his words. At first I thought that he had made a compromise between talking and not talking to demonstrate how fragmented he felt, and to let me know what it felt like to receive a tantalizing fragment of a message. But when he said that he feared I might say "unexpected, nasty things" to him and that he was "trying to digest what came from other people," I realized that he was showing us his way of seeking increased trust in our relationship. When he spoke softly, whatever understanding I achieved was a joint creation, derived from those of his words that I heard, plus my own contribution to fill the gaps.

He wanted me to talk to him in the same soft way in order to "digest" what came from me rather than feel "dominated" by me. He wanted to use whatever I said for his own purposes and not feel that it was a "command from the outside." When he contributed to the formation of an idea, it became "digestible," or ego syntonic (Bettelheim, 1967; Little, 1966; Milner, 1952). Two changes in his outside life accompanied these events: 1.) he changed from expecting magical victories in contests to making potentially more realistic investments; and 2.) he began to live with a girl friend, whom he later married, saying that marriage is a situation in which two people create something together.

I want to stress again that it was only in retrospect — after several months of whispering, when he finally talked about "digesting what came from other people" — that I began to understand the meaning of the whispering. In linking the whispering with his statements about needing to be able to make events acceptable, or ego syntonic, there is a tendency to condense the data. There is a danger of giving the false impression that I understood the meaning of his silences and his outbursts while they were happening; as a matter of fact I had no idea why he was behaving as he did, and I could only assume that the patient must have a good reason for his behavior, and that my responsibility was to be prepared to understand it when he was ready to make its meaning clear. I want to stress that because I did not try to direct the patient's behavior but sought to provide a setting in which he could control it himself and find his own reasons for acting as he did, he was able to discover that the whispering was a creative accomplishment rather than a "resistance" against some other kind of behavior (Bettelheim, 1967). It would have been impossible not to be fascinated by this material, which revealed the basis of behavior that had been so disturbing both to him and to me.

Termination of Treatment

After three years of treatment, he felt more comfortable and wanted to terminate his treatment, and to use his earnings for other purposes. He was very "grateful" when he discovered that I did not have "conditions" that he would have to meet in order to be "allowed" to reduce the frequency of his appointments and then to terminate entirely. When he asked about coming in less often, he expected me to react by refusing to let him continue at all; he was surprised and grateful when I said that he could make his own decision about the frequency of his visits. His surprise and gratitude were so great that I was reminded of James's report (1964). James describes a patient who was able to relinquish delusions of omnipotent control after feeling fused with his therapist and actually controlling the therapist's actions in reality. It seemed particularly important for my patient to be able to tell me what he was going to do and have me agree with his wishes, rather than have me terminate his treatment when I thought he was "ready." In light of how he terminated his treatment, we were able to understand — retrospectively — the way he had started treatment three years before. At that time he had not complied immediately with my conditions for treatment, but had arranged things so that he could feel that I was meeting his demands. The patient compared the way in which he tapered off his appointments with his earlier drive to run away from home. He felt that he could never return to live in his parents' home; although he no longer needed to see me regularly, he felt it was important to know that he could return at any time in the future.

One could wonder if this patient's way of terminating treatment was an example of pathological acting out. However, it was my impression that he was not fleeing from me because of anxiety but because he had developed new object relations; I had therefore become less important to him. We expect the healthy young adult to replace the relationship with his parents with relationships to new objects; at the same time, in health, he will unconsciously retain a relationship with his parents. If the patient turns away from his parents because of anxiety in an attempt to destroy his relationship with them, new object relations must be used as defenses against the tie with his parents. We can compare this with the way in which patients mature in treatment. This particular patient's feeling that he could return at any time and the fact that he eventually married his girl friend (I later learned that the marriage was sustained and stable) seem to indicate that he had been able to introject me and the therapeutic situation as sustaining and ego supportive. Thus, he was able to replace me with new objects, while drawing upon the therapeutic introject in the new relationships; he did not need to use the new relationships as defenses against his relationship with me. Therefore, I believe that the way in which he left me was not a defensive flight or pathological acting out, but was an exercise of autonomy as he moved on to higher integration.

SUMMARY

The use of any forcible technical device to control a patient's affairs or to overcome his resistance to behavioral change introduces a disruptive power struggle between the patient and the therapist. Although Freud referred to the patient as the "passive partner" in a therapeutic relationship, he also showed us the therapeutic value of appreciatively receiving the patient's activity. Freud's observational frame of reference can be applied in the treatment of both the neurotic and the psychotic patient.

In describing the treatment of a confused young man, his "perceptual defects" were viewed not as residuals of unspecified organic neurological lesions but as meaningful ego processes. His idiosyncratic functioning was interpreted as an effort to communicate rather than as resistance to be overcome or as a distortion to be counteracted educationally (Freud, 1901).

The patient had run away from his parents' home just before seeking consultation. He showed an unusual potential for integration and a readiness to use therapy to organize his life. What he needed from me was that I not try to do anything about his "crazy" and threatening behavior except want to understand it. Much of the improvement in his outside life took place as soon as he decided to enter therapy, but before he actually began formal therapy. Carlson (1958) has described this phenomenon in the "confusional syndrome of late adolescents." The patient gained a feeling that he was managing his affairs voluntarily, while he lost the feeling that he was controlling things magically (Lipton, 1955). Magical control had served as a defense against his feeling of total helplessness, which had resulted from his failure to integrate signals and meanings; this failure had been the product of the simultaneous incompatible signals he received from his parents (Bateson *et al.*, 1956) and their unpredictable responses to him.

REFERENCES

Bateson, G.; Jackson, D. D.; Haley, J.; and Weakland, J. (1956). Toward a theory of schizophrenia. *Behavioral Science* 1 : 38–47.

Bettelheim, B. (1967). Regression as progress. In *The empty fortress.* New York : Free Press.

Boyer, L. B., and Giovacchini, P. (1967). *Psychoanalytic treatment of schizophrenic and characterological disorders.* New York : Science House.

Carlson, H. B. (1958). Characteristics of an acute confusional state in college students. *Amer. J. Psychiat.* 114 : 900–911.

Freud, S. (1901). *The psychopathology of everyday life.* Standard Edition, vol. 6. London : Hogarth Press.

———. (1918) (1914). *From the history of an infantile neurosis.* Standard Edition, vol. 17. London : Hogarth Press.

———. (1922). *Some neurotic mechanisms in jealousy, paranoia, and homosexuality.* Standard Edition, vol. 18. London : Hogarth Press.

———. (1937). *Analysis terminable and interminable.* Standard Edition, vol. 18. London : Hogarth Press.

Giovacchini, P. (1965). Transference, incorporation and synthesis. *Int. J. Psycho-Anal.* 46 : 287–296.

James, M. (1964). Interpretation and management in the treatment of preadolescents. *Int. J. Psycho-Anal.* 45 : 499–511.

Khan, M. M. R. (1953). Review of "On not being able to paint," by M. Milner. *Int. J. Psycho-Anal.* 34 : 333–336.

Klauber, J. (1867). On the significance of reporting dreams in psychoanalysis. *Int. J. Psycho-Anal.* 48 : 424–432.

Lindon, J. A. (1967). On regression : a workshop. *Psychoanal. Forum* 2 : 293–316.

Lipton, S. D. (1955). A note on the compatibility of psychic determinism and freedom of will. *Int. J. Psycho-Anal.* 36 : 355–356.

Little, M. (1966). Transference in borderline states. *Int. J. Psycho-Anal.* 47 : 476–485.

Lubin, A. J. (1967). The influence of the Russian Orthodox Church on Freud's Wolf-Man : an hypothesis. *Psychoanal. Forum* 2 : 145–174.

Mack-Brunswick, R. (1928). A supplement to Freud's "History of an infantile neurosis." *Int. J. Psycho-Anal.* 9 : 439–476.

Milner, M. (1952). Aspects of symbolism in the comprehension of the not-self. *Int. J. Psycho-Anal.* 33 : 181–195.

Rosen, V. H. (1955). Strephosymbolia : an intrasystemic disturbance of the synthetic function of the ego. *Psychoanal. Study Child* 10.

Schaller, G. (1964). *The year of the gorilla.* Chicago : University of Chicago Press.

Searles, H. (1960). *The nonhuman environment.* New York : International Universities Press.

Szasz, T. S. (1957). On the theory of psycho-analytic treatment. *Int. J. Psycho-Anal.* 38 : 166–182.

Winnicott, D. W. (1945). Primitive emotional development. *Int. J. Psycho-Anal.* 26 : 137–143.

———. (1954a). Withdrawal and regression. In *Collected papers.* New York : Basic Books, 1958.

———. (1954b). Metapsychological and clinical aspects of regression within the psycho-analytic setup. In *Collected papers.* New York : Basic Books, 1958.

Witty, P., and Kopel, D. (1936). Causation and diagnosis of reading disability. *J. Psychol.* 2 : 161–191.

PART III

Tactical Aspects of the Psychoanalytic Process

The goals of psychoanalysis are to reach "deep" into the personality and to effect character changes rather than simply symptomatic improvement. Freud reviewed such changes in terms of overcoming repression and the progressive development of the libido in attaining higher stages of psychosexual organization.

The developmental process and regressive and progressive shifts, as they appear both in and out of treatment, are of current interest since they are relevant to the understanding of the psychoanalytic process in general. The inevitable regression that is set in motion by analysis often reveals psychic states that cannot be adequately conceptualized in terms of the traditional psychosexual stages.

Nor do therapeutic interventions always require the patient to reveal himself fully. Higher states of ego integration can sometimes be achieved if the patient withholds from the therapist, that is, keeps his "secrets" to himself.

The study of characterological factors, a more detailed approach to the structural and functional aspects of the ego, gives us a conceptual framework in which to view developmental factors, the regressive ego state in a more extended fashion, and therapeutic management.

During the past decade, the importance of the symbiotic phase, both as a developmental stage and a point of fixation in regression, has been increasingly recognized. A derivative need of the symbiotic phase, which often has bizarre behavioral manifestations, is the need to fuse. The latter is frequently acted out in an attempt to maintain a precarious psychic equilibrium. The wish to fuse with the analyst is also a frequent transference manifestation.

I have written the next chapter in order to outline both the developmental aspects and the psychopathology that relate to the symbiotic stage. Disturbances during the symbiotic phase affect various ego systems specifically, and these are reflected in the patient's general character structure and the way he relates in the psychoanalytic situation. Dr. Rose discusses psychoanalytic theory from a similar frame of reference, emphasizing the need for fusion and the lack of a structuralized autonomous identity in patients who have never "emerged" from the symbiotic phase.

The generally adaptive, as well as specifically defensive, aspects of fusion have to be considered too. Dr. Bettelheim gives us a general survey of the regressive process as it reproduces fusion states and its potential for the establishment of future structure and autonomy. He not only refers to regression as a necessary therapeutic factor that has to be overcome by transference interpretation, but says that the regressed state has an inherent potential for structuralization, provided the therapist does not introduce a disapproving attitude. The latter is encountered more frequently than many of us care to believe; some therapists cannot stand prolonged periods of infantile behavior and demands.

Drs. Ekstein and Caruthers view the patient in terms of primitive developmental levels and the adaptive aspects and potential therapeutic benefits that can be derived from such infantile ego states. They see in positive terms certain aspects of the patient's behavior which many analysts would consider resistive and detrimental to analysis. The authors specifically discuss the withholding patient, for very few analysts believe that "keeping secrets" is a developmental focus around which ego boundaries can be consolidated and an autonomous identity constructed.

Concentrating upon developmental factors and primitive ego states also emphasizes the adaptive and disruptive aspects of early object relationships and their significance for later relationships, including the transference projection.

From insights about these general characterological factors, one can construct a therapeutic rationale. In many instances, the latter takes the form of a firmer adherence to psychoanalytic therapeutic principles rather than a desire to modify them. On the other hand, some of the patients' reactions that have been considered undesirable can be positively utilized. This point will be discussed and illustrated further in later parts.

7

The Symbiotic Phase

PETER L. GIOVACCHINI

THE CONTRIBUTORS to this volume make clear that the psychoanalytic viewpoint extends to the so-called deeper and more
primitive layers of the personality. Eventually most clinical formulations center on an early and important developmental phase —
the symbiotic phase. Here I wish to explore further both the clinical
and the theoretical aspects of this early ego state which seems to be
so relevant to understanding psychopathology, emotional development, and treatment.

Since Freud's revolutionary discoveries, early childhood experiences have been fundamental to our assessment of character
structure, defensive and adjustive modalities, and general psychic
equilibrium of both child and adult. Since such experiences always
include another person, they must be considered in terms of the
adaptive or disruptive qualities of object relationships.

Freud (1918) reconstructed the infantile neurosis retrospectively while analyzing adults. Study of the transference neurosis
enables one to evaluate how early object relationships have contributed to the current ego organization. Memories of the adult
patient about his childhood may be the product of considerable
distortion. Some analysts do not think that the exact reconstruction
of past realities is particularly important for therapeutic management. But in order to assess the etiological significance of early

object relationships on later psychic structure, one has to deal with more than the adult patient's fantasies or memories in which external objects are more or less revised. Still, there is always a reality basis for the archaic transference projections that occur during analysis.

Another research method that has recently achieved popularity is the longitudinal approach. Here one can observe early relationships that do not necessarily lead to psychopathology and are therefore more relevant to the study of normal development. However, as is true of experiments in general, introducing an observer changes the data, but this factor can be minimized and taken into account. Observing a continuum from the neonatal state to adulthood is valuable, and the data collected have a different kind of relevance than those obtained from studying the transference neurosis.

THEORETICAL CONSIDERATIONS

Data acquire significance only when they can be placed in a conceptual framework. Etiology can be established when process connections can be made among various phenomena and these intermediary links are placed in a consistent theoretical system. Theoretical elaborations frequently lead to predictions about heretofore unnoticed phenomena.

Freud (1900) constructed a comprehensive theoretical system based primarily upon a topographic framework and oriented chiefly around what he later referred to as the id. His metapsychology was biologically oriented, and he postulated a sequence of developmental stages that are determined by increasing maturation. The influence of external objects was recognized but not particularly emphasized except for their traumatic potential.

With the addition of the structural hypothesis to metapsychology (Freud, 1923), the ego was given a more central position in the psychic apparatus. Both reality and psychic systems (the superego and the id) were considered relative to the ego. Introducing the ego viewpoint enabled certain areas, such as object relations, to be more meaningfully integrated into the theoretical edifice.

Ego psychology is a particularly appropriate conceptual frame of reference for studying both efficient adaptation and disruptive psychopathology. This is especially true if the vantage point of observation is the transference neurosis. As the patient regresses to earlier modes of adaptation and projects archaic introjects onto the analyst, both the analyst and the patient have the opportunity to learn how these introjects ("precipitates of past object cathexes," [Freud, 1923]) are utilized in the service of adaptation and structuralization or how they impede development and cause characterological defects and fixations.

The study of the transference neurosis is essentially a study of different grades of psychopathology, including the psychoneuroses, since psychodynamic conflicts also involve significant persons in the patient's past. However, as implied above, ego psychology, by conceptualizing the influence of early object relations on the operations of ego systems (perceptual, executive, and integrative), focuses upon developmental factors in a microscopic fashion. The latter also has implications for the therapeutic process (see pages 164–166).

Ego psychology is also a useful framework for a phenomeno- logical approach, which is characteristic of longitudinal anterospective studies. More subtle (unconscious) motivations and "microscopic" ego operations are not discernible when surface behavior is studied. However, such reactions as aggression and techniques of mastery can be viewed in the context of object relations and maturation and development. Behavior, therefore, can be scrutinized in terms of its affective and motoric components; object relationships are the axis around which adaptive techniques become increasingly refined or psychopathologically fixated.

In a psychotherapeutic context Freud discussed adaptation in terms of psychoeconomics, which was based upon a hydrodynamic, drive-energy-discharge hypothesis. Energy resides in the libidinal reservoir (Freud, 1915) of the unconscious (later referred to as the "id"), as it pushes forward, it creates a tension state that seeks discharge. This is essentially a stimulus-response model where the stimulus originates within the organism, although Freud also acknowledged the influence of the external world upon inner impulses and needs. Nonetheless, the chief emphasis was on how organic tensions become psychologically elaborated and seek gratification.

The concept of psychic energy in the context of a dualistic instinct theory has been fundamental to our understanding of a developmental hierarchy. Both Freud (1923, 1926) and Hartmann et al. (1949) wrote about the fusion of drives — a process, when proceeding toward integration, called "neutralization." Others (Colby, 1955) have criticized the chemical analogy implicit in the term. Neutralization is the outcome of the fusion of libidinal and aggressive energies and leads to secondary-process-directed activities. If one restricts this process to energic considerations without including ego structure, it is difficult to understand how the fusion of two primary-process-oriented elements can lead to secondary-process operations. Rapaport (1966) and Gill (1963) have discussed the "taming" of affects insofar as primitive energies become bound to "higher" ego structures. But here again energy is considered in terms of a drive-discharge hypothesis with an implied independent status.

A psychology based upon a centrally placed regulatory ego is more internally consistent when energic sources are not restricted to instinctual impulses (Boyer and Giovacchini, 1967; Giovacchini, 1966a). The gratification of an impulse by setting the ego's executive apparatus into motion requires energy. The impulse is the psychic representation of a need that results from an upset of homeostatic equilibrium. The ego's sensory systems perceive changes in the homeostasis unless repressive forces are operating. Energy is required for repression as well as for perception and the cathexis of adaptive techniques that will gratify the impulse. Energy, however, is not part of the need but is mobilized from an organic-metabolic reservoir in response to homeostatic shifts; energy then makes possible the operation of various ego systems. When either external demands are made or internal needs are stimulated, appropriate psychic systems are cathected (energized) in order to master the problem created by such demands. In some instances this can lead to a feeling of tension, but the mastery of tension-producing needs does not require a discharge concept. Nothing is discharged; no quanta of energy are involved. Rather, various ego systems become functionally active as a response to these needs and reestablish homeostasis. The achieved homeostasis is not necessarily a quiescent state but merely a well-balanced one. After satisfying certain basic needs a person may seek other gratifications; he may create his own needs and pursue more integrated levels of adaptation.[1]

The course of emotional development can be viewed as a series of adaptations of varying degrees of complexity. The passage from childhood to adulthood, a developmental continuum, can

---

[1] Experiencing a need is not necessarily painful. The psyche may feel stimulated but instead of experiencing disruptive tension it reacts with pleasurable anticipation. Freud's (1905) remarks on forepleasure are particularly apt.

easily be conceptualized as a hierarchical structuralization of the psychic apparatus. All psychic elements, drives, and sensory and adaptational systems undergo progressive structuralization. The neonate's requirements are fundamentally biological and his techniques of mastery and adaptation are minimal. He is totally dependent upon external objects. With maturation and satisfactory nurture (somatic and emotional) and as his range of perceptual sensitivity widens, his needs become more structured. More avenues of satisfaction are open to him; as he learns to introject and assimilate gratifying experiences with external objects, his executive capacities also expand.

From a state of primitive biological helplessness, the psychic apparatus becomes progressively refined. However, the more advanced state of integration is a structural accretion to earlier states of organization. Just as the soma contains numerous types of cells and organs, ranging from primitive embryonic tissue and unstructured connective tissue cells to highly complex systems (such as the brain), the psyche also contains its developmental origins. Freud's (1900) concept that the ego evolves from the id is a prototype for a theory of psychic structure that contains a series of elements representing all stages of development.

All psychic structures, therefore, can be viewed as a hierarchical continuum that recapitulates the various stages of emotional development. Psychological systems are not rigidly fixed; earlier types of adaptation can become recathected under specific circumstances such as psychopathology, environmental stress, and others that are not necessarily pathological (for example, creativity). This hierarchical ego-psychological model does not require a hydro-dynamic-energic-discharge hypothesis; instead, it emphasizes structure-producing factors. These factors, in turn, focus upon the structure-promoting or psychopathology-producing qualities of object relationships.

DEVELOPMENTAL FACTORS

The newborn is not fully developed neurologically, and, as recent experiments suggest (Reisen, 1947), there is considerable autonomic instability and an incomplete perceptual sensory organization. From these findings and the neonate's global dependency, it seems plausible to postulate an early stage of development in which the child does not feel that he is a separate unit apart and distinct from the surrounding world.

A study of adults during regression in analysis indicates the existence of an early phase in which the boundaries of the ego are not yet formed and the self and the outer world are not separate and distinct. This phase is supposedly characterized by a megalomanic omnipotence where wishes are magically fulfilled. Insofar as the child feels that he is part of his mother, his needs and their gratification are not separated. From the study of infants and the retrospective reconstructions of adults, this early stage of development is conceptualized as a symbiotic phase.

Benedek (1938, 1949, 1956), who focuses upon the mothering process, and Mahler (1952, 1953) who is primarily interested in childhood psychosis, have discussed symbiosis extensively and presented convincing arguments for its usefulness as a postulate. For the sake of clarity it should be emphasized that the mother's need for the infant is not quite the same as his need for her (Giovacchini, 1967). If symbiosis refers to an "equality" of needs, this early relationship has some parasitic elements. Still, mothering is a need that has developmental potential for the mother (Benedek, 1959). From the initial symbiosis there is a progressive maturation and development which leads to separateness and object relations (Mahler's separation-individuation phase). Spitz (1965) outlines certain crucial points in time, for example, at two to three months and at eight months of age, when the infant learns responses (smiling response, negation, and anxiety) that act as "organizers" for developmental spurts. In a similar fashion Erikson (1959) writes of epigenesis where structure leads to further structure.

These descriptions and formulations have explanatory significance for many direct observations of infants, but they are not intended to explain how development occurs and how the psychic apparatus acquires structure and adaptive techniques; these questions require a microscopic scrutiny of the development of object relations (see pages 151–159).

As stated above, reconstructions made from studying the transference neurosis point to the plausibility of postulating a symbiotic phase. Psychopathology, although distorting, also emphasizes psychic features that might otherwise go unnoticed. Fixation upon the symbiotic phase broadens our understanding of structuralizing processes by highlighting those factors that impede emotional development.

Adult patients who demonstrate difficulties in resolving their infantile symbiosis suffer from serious psychopathology, as do Mahler's child patients. Many are psychotic; some are thought to be borderline or suffering from characterological defects. Others (for example, some psychoneurotics) may not have such severe developmental problems, but in the transference regression are able to recapitulate symbiotic elements (see pages 164–166).

CLINICAL CONSIDERATIONS

The following vignettes will illustrate the effects of fixation upon the symbiotic phase.

A middle-aged patient found that he was unable to work. He felt totally paralyzed and incapable of coping with the external world, which he felt had become inordinately complex. He had no perception of himself as having a separate identity and had absolutely no interest in relating to anyone. He felt sorry for his wife because he knew she wanted to be kind and helpful, but he could not respond or even acknowledge her efforts. At first he felt strange, but later he found that he didn't care about anything in the outside world; he was only interested in his relationship with me. Recently this patient had changed jobs: he left a position that offered financial comfort and status but no hope for further advancement, and accepted one where his horizons were unlimited. Recently he had also married a woman with whom he had been having an affair for two years.

He began suffering from an inability to concentrate, which was sometimes accompanied by anxiety of panic-like intensity. Curiously, he stopped referring to his wife as such and called her his "girl friend," as he had done before marriage. His associations were prominently oral; he was preoccupied with thoughts of swallowing and eating me or being eaten by me. He was also obsessed with the fear that I would kill him or that he would commit suicide. At first, the patient seemed to be expressing self-destructive guilt because of his vocational success and because of his marriage after so many years of bachelorhood; it was certainly a factor. However, he expressed very clearly that he was afraid of me in a way that went beyond the projection of his superego.

He believed that a job with upward mobility would lead to

his separation from me; he equated upward mobility with independence. His previous job, insofar as no advancement was possible, meant a fixated state that posed no threat of change. He explained that having a wife gave him definite status (identity) as a married man, whereas a girl friend made him feel that he was in an amorphous, ill-defined state. Although he was relatively comfortable in his niche, there were conflicts.

There were many facets to his fears. Thoughts of moving away from me (the symbiotic fusion) led him to be afraid of my anger. He believed that I wanted to maintain the status quo and would kill him if he showed any evidence of "growing away." He was also afraid that he would kill me if we separated. He fantasized that if he literally pulled away, he would tear some vital part out of me that would result in my death. He also wanted to kill me in order to get rid of the hated part of himself that had, to some extent, become projected into me through the symbiotic fusion. On the other hand, because of the fusion he believed that killing me would also constitute suicide.

In summary, all of his symptoms and transference reactions could be understood as the result of the dissolution of the mother-child symbiosis that was being reenacted in the transference regression. He was ambivalent: he wanted to feel autonomous and yet separated from me. Because such independence was frightening, in many fantasies he questioned whether he could survive without my "omnipotent support." Symbiotic fusion also meant annihilation of his psychic existence as an individual entity, and he experienced this with terror. Consequently, he was faced with the unbearable conflict of wanting an independent identity in the context of magical fusion.

A colleague (Borowitz, 1966) who has had considerable experience with children supplied me with the following material. He has obtained data from both the treatment of children and direct observation of the mother-child interaction that point to conclusions similar to those derived from the study of the transference neurosis in adults. For example, an institutionalized 11-year-old boy who was autistically withdrawn had to be forcefully taken to his first therapy session. Once inside the consultation room he no longer struggled. He saw a stove in the corner of the room. Without saying a word he walked up to it and lay down in front of it, basking in its warmth but completely ignoring the therapist. Subsequent sessions were similar in that the child said nothing, did not acknowledge the therapist's presence, and continued to curl up in front of the stove. In spite of his apparent indifference, others were impressed when they noticed the boy eagerly running to his sessions, slowing down only as he passed through the consultation room door. The patient needed to find a situation from which he could withdraw. The therapist respected this need by not intruding; finally, after several months, the patient started talking.

There are many direct observations of the mother-child relationship that have a meaning similar to the one described above. A toddler who could barely walk was playing very actively. His mother was sitting in the same room, one that had an ample supply of toys. He broke several of the toys and could not manage others, but he doggedly continued to play even though he obviously felt frustrated. The mother sat there quietly, but the child never turned to her for either help or comfort. The child displayed a remarkable independence which, in spite of the many frustrating toys, was characterized by determined calm. When the mother finally left the room, the child's reaction was rather surprising. Even though he had seemed to be nonchalant about her presence, he broke down completely when she left. His expression changed to terror and he had a temper tantrum. He looked miserable and began to engage in chaotic and purposeless screaming and kicking. Others entered the room to try to comfort him, but the tantrum only became worse. Nothing would pacify this child until his mother returned. She walked back into the room and he gave no sign that he even saw her; not once did he directly look at her, but his anguish vanished and he returned to his "autonomous" play.

These vignettes are examples of persons suffering from relatively severe psychopathology. Several psychic elements are particularly prominent. The adult patient at the beginning of analysis demonstrated a constricted development of drives. His needs were simple and minimal. To him, eating was a mechanical response to a feeling of hunger — a feeling that had no discriminating features. He had no appetite for any particular type of food. To him there was no distinction between oatmeal and caviar. His sexual drives were also poorly elaborated. He had no fantasies while masturbating; he described it as relieving himself of some ill-defined tension. In fact, he found the urge to defecate and urinate not particularly different from the sexual drive. In general he was not aware of any definitive sensations. He stated that at times he felt a vague uneasiness and then would have to "decide" whether he was hungry, needed to defecate, or was sexually aroused.

Such retarded development of drives is not infrequent in children (Furer, 1962), and I suspect that the two children just described also have incomplete drive differentiation with fixation on an early developmental phase and limited further structuralization. In such cases characterological development is distorted; both the drives and other psychic elements do not structuralize to a level that is characteristic of advanced development; this is illustrated by Spitz's (1957) dramatic and tragic examples.

In normal development the ego boundaries become consolidated after the dissolution of the symbiotic fusion. Consequently, a fixation on this stage also leads to a blurring of ego-non-ego boundaries, which has many manifestations. My patient often did not know what was not part of himself. He frequently demonstrated this during the transference regression, and he also spoke of other situations that could be explained by his inability to distinguish "me from not-me." For example, during his first week of analysis he often pounded the wall with his fist. In this way he would establish where his body (fist) ended and the outside world (wall) began. This patient had difficulty paying his bills, a not too unusual symptom. Paying money meant surrendering part of himself to me. Since his ego boundaries were so tenuous, he was sensitive to many situations that he believed threatened his integrity.

In other cases the blurring of ego boundaries is manifested by a lack of perceptual discrimination. What is, in fact, outside the self is perceived as belonging to the self. Consequently, the external object is only dimly perceived and its distinct qualities are not recognized. This frequently happens with obese and alcoholic patients. Often a markedly overweight patient does not really enjoy food. Bruch (1967) has described such phenomena. These patients rarely allow themselves to feel hungry and seldom have any appetite, a manifesting of a nondifferentiation of drives. But there is an added factor in that these patients do not distinguish between food and non-food; one patient actually did not know when she was eating. For her, eating had become a mechanical, automaton-like procedure; she did not cathect it sufficiently to be aware of what she was doing. Her basic pathology included a fluid ego boundary that encompassed the universe. If, by chance, she managed to perceive something outside of herself, it was only momentary because she was continually incorporating and maintaining a state similar to symbiotic fusion and infantile megalomania. This patient never had an organized meal where she sat down at the table at a prescribed time and ate a particular type of food appropriate to what is conventionally served at that time of day. Her eating habits reflected her general lack of structure; her ego was unable to relate to structured, distinct situations because her diffuse boundaries contained an amorphous, unorganized ego.

The same constellations can be found in many alcoholic patients. They do not enjoy liquor and are often unaware of what or whether they are drinking. One patient said that alcohol was one of her body secretions (see DeLevita, 1965). She could not buy anyone a drink because it would be equivalent to giving away part of herself, thereby establishing a distinction between herself and the surrounding world. When drunk she was very generous and wanted a drinking companion, but she said that at these times she was totally fused with her companion and so, emotionally speaking, she was giving nothing away. Through a vicarious identification, she was merely providing herself with drinks; thus, she was not forced to distinguish between herself and the outer world, that is, to disrupt her symbiotic fixation. This patient was not aware of her drinking (when she said that she never drank, she believed it) because she was drinking all the time. Alcohol had become so much a part of her that she did not perceive it as a separate entity, nor did she perceive it as a specific activity.

When an individual cannot distinguish an external object as separate from the self, there is a further problem in being able to perceive the self. When early object relations have not led to structuralization beyond the symbiotic phase, there are identity problems. The patients described above had difficulty knowing who and what they were and they questioned the purpose of their existence. The obese patient sometimes found that everything was hazy, including her body image, which seemed to "blend" with her surroundings. At such a time she "forgot" her name, profession, and other facts about herself that would identify her as an individual. Similarly other patients, especially when the transference regression recapitulated the symbiotic fusion, lost their precarious sense of personal identity. There is a relationship between the loss of identity and fixation upon the symbiotic phase.

Children demonstrate similar phenomena. Dramatic examples of the malformation of a sense of identity are found in autistic children. Bettelheim (1967) describes a young autistic girl who had no organized identity. Her behavior reflected her preoccupation with boundaries and borders, a manifestation of the diffuseness of her ego boundaries, which were the result of an incomplete differentiation from a traumatic symbiosis. Many less dramatic examples are associated with lesser degrees of psychopathology, demonstrating similar problems and emphasizing the correlation between diffuseness of the sense of identity and the degree of symbiotic fixation. Identity is discussed here only from a phenomenological perspective; to pursue the operational aspects of identity is beyond the scope of this chapter.

One aspect of identity, however, is related to exploring arrested development and object relations. A person's executive style is a significant aspect of his sense of identity (Giovacchini, 1966b). Techniques of mastery and control of inner impulses are an important aspect of the self-representation, and vicissitudes in this area are easily observed in children.

At one extreme are the tragic children described by Spitz (1957) who achieved practically no techniques of mastery or control. Because they were emotionally impoverished by the complete lack of object relations, these children never even progressed to the symbiotic level. In other instances, especially when the symbiotic fusion is traumatic, a peculiar kind of "autonomy" may develop. When the child's psychic integrity (his very existence) has been impinged upon (see Winnicott, 1952), a defensive type of insulation may occur. Winnicott (1949) described the development of a "false self" as a reaction to a traumatic, assaultive environment. This self cannot generally be integrated into the ego and is not synchronous with a cohesive, synthesized ego organization. It is a "false self" — a product of an incomplete differentiation from a constricting and threatening symbiotic fusion.

To relinquish control to others, to relax, and to trust external objects are impossible for these children. In cases of severe psychopathology, the child may shut out the external world completely. The extreme counterpart of this condition in the adult is the catatonic who, by his withdrawal, maintains megalomanic control. In children, usually under one year of age, there are stereotyped repetitive movements that constitute part of their autistic withdrawal. It is impressive how totally preoccupied body-rockers or head-bangers are with what they are doing and how utterly oblivious they are of their surroundings. It would appear that they are flamboyantly demonstrating that they do not require the environment, that they can maintain themselves without any outside help. Insofar as this is an infantile megalomanic orientation, their methods of control are primitive, rigid, and robot-like in nature. Older children sometimes show similar automaton-like, controlling behavior. If they mature physically (there may be retardation at the somatic level), this behavior becomes elaborated into an obsessional ritual. If there is sufficient involvement with reality so that the adult does not catatonically withdraw, complex obsessional systems may develop.

It is, of course, impossible to know from direct observation what automaton behavior, such as head-banging or body-rocking, means in a child under one year of age. Still, inferences can be drawn from the treatment of adults. For example, an adult patient sought treatment because his obsessional rituals had become so time consuming and constricting that he found it was almost impossible to carry on his routine activities. He reported he was told that, as a child, he had been a body-rocker and head-banger. Although these symptoms in other children may be sporadic, transient, and not necessarily a sign of severe psychopathology, this patient supposedly spent all his waking time from approximately seven to ten months of age either head-banging or body-rocking. After he began to walk at about the age of two, these symptoms vanished.

Several years later he had fantasies in which he constructed a complex city that was run by machines and robots; he was the only human there. He described the intricate details of how this city maintained itself. Equally complicated were its transactions with the rest of the world. They were handled in a mechanical, precise, mathematical fashion. This city did not directly recognize the existence of the surrounding environment, yet in some ways it operated in the context of something outside itself.

This patient currently seemed to demonstrate a need for omnipotent control that would be independent of external objects. Still, like the child who was oblivious to his mother's presence until she left the room, this patient seemed to need the framework of his environment to maintain himself. For example, he talked endlessly and without interruption about how crass and intrusive everyone was, never acknowledging that there may have been some redeeming features in the persons or situations he was describing. He spoke calmly and without bitterness and acted as if I were not in the room. If I interrupted him with a comment or interpretation, he would wait politely for me to finish and then continue where he had left off without acknowledging the gap created by my "intrusion." He seemed perfectly content to have me sit there saying nothing. He never asked a question or sought my opinion or advice.

This patient was a striking contrast to other patients who resent the analyst's silence. It is commonplace for patients to complain that the analyst gives them nothing. They feel that they might as well lie on their living room couch and free associate, thereby saving themselves considerable money and time. However, both the analyst and the patient know that this would not work. The resentful patient needs to have someone he can complain about and upon whom he can project his devaluated self-representation.

My patient did not complain, but he demonstrated a need to have someone around from whom he could withdraw and thereby establish his autonomy. He was similar to the young boy who eagerly came to his sessions in order to curl up in front of the stove and have the *opportunity* of ignoring his therapist. This was a primitive, omnipotent autonomy but one that was necessary in order to save him from being crushed, "dissolved," and destroyed by symbiotic fusion. Therefore, this patient needed to have someone around whom he could relegate to oblivion. His action represented mastery but he had to reassure himself continually that he could successfully shut out external objects. Without an external object to serve this purpose, he would lose a vantage point from which he could consolidate an identity, even though it might be a "false self" (Winnicott, 1954).

This patient had a history of head-banging and body-rocking during childhood, and it is possible that other cases of automaton-like behavior have similar histories. These symptoms are autistic and are frequently associated with similar behaviors. Head-banging, body-rocking, and trichotillomania sometimes occur together and can be explained in terms of defensive processes similar to those described for this patient. Spitz (1965) has discussed specific aspects of the mother-child interaction of head-bangers.

Control is needed, not only to separate the patient from the external world but to maintain some order within an otherwise chaotic intrapsychic world. This means that the patient has to control what goes out as well as what comes in. For example, a middle-aged woman who had had trichotillomania for as long as she could consciously remember, as well as a history of body-rocking, head-banging, and enuresis, showed tremendous conflict about relinquishing any part of herself. As in the case of many obese persons (this patient had been quite obese during adolescence), she did not clearly distinguish the boundary between herself and the external world. Eating her hair had many meanings; here it is pertinent to emphasize that she was incorporating something that could be separated from herself. Her action in detaching her hair was part of her need for omnipotent control.

To summarize briefly, various autistic, automaton phenomena that have been viewed as manifestations of developmental vicissitudes are described as examples of reactions to a traumatic symbiotic fixation. The analysis of adults with a history of such behavioral anomalies during childhood sheds light on certain characterological defenses that result from the symbiotic phase. Both the observation of children and the retrospective reconstructions made from the treatment of adults emphasize that difficulties in the symbiotic phase can have the following consequences: 1.) drive differentiation is impaired; 2.) ego-non-ego boundaries are blurred, leading to a defective sense of identity; and 3.) there is an exaggerated need for omnipotent control, leading to the interesting paradox of autonomy within the framework of symbiotic fusion.

DEVELOPMENTAL ASPECTS OF ADAPTATION

The neonate is helplessly dependent and requires a long period of mothering in order to maintain himself as well as to structuralize enough to achieve substantial autonomy. To understand more about the psychic processes required for progressive structuralization, the interaction among developmental phases, maturational sequences, and external objects must be scrutinized microscopically.

From the patients described above, one can make inferences about development in general; these patients can be understood in terms of object relations pertaining to disturbances of the symbiotic phase of development.

Pre-Object Phase

The matter of what precedes the symbiotic phase has been discussed by many psychoanalytic theoreticians. They stress neurophysiological factors because they perceive the neonate as biologically oriented. His sensorimotor apparatus is not sufficiently differentiated so that he can see the external world in a coherent, integrated fashion. Therefore, the neonate cannot distinguish between the inside and the outside; in fact, his psyche is not sufficiently mature so that the concepts "inside" and "outside" have any meaning. Instead, the infant presumably experiences only vague, visceral sensations of comfort or discomfort, which are determined by cyclical biological needs.

The neonate does not have a relationship with an external object since his psyche is not integrated to the point where it can coherently perceive or emotionally incorporate. In a sense the infant's earliest life can be considered prepsychological since mentation has not yet developed. The external object, of course, is important but mainly for sustenance. Bowlby (1951, 1960a, 1960b) believes that the individual qualities of the external object are not important during the early months. He states that the mothering person can be changed during the first 27 weeks of life without disrupting the child's development so long as the nurturing source is competent and nontraumatic. Just how interchangeable the mother is during that period is a debatable question. The ways in which the mother is needed beyond providing basic care require further study. One important function, however, has been established: *During the pre-object phase, the external object (mother) is responsible for preparing a setting in which object relationships can occur.*

There has been considerable controversy about the length of this stage. Some analysts, especially the Kleinian school, ignore this phase and discuss psychodynamic constellations within the infant from the moment he is born. Certain experiments (Reisen, 1947) suggest that perceptual discrimination and learning begin quite early — within a week or two. The timetable of development from a primarily biological orientation to significant mentation is still imperfectly understood. For our purpose it is important to recognize that nothing occurs abruptly; rather, there is a continuum from the biological to the psychological, a gradual progression from one stage to another while elements of a former stage continue to exist with decreasing prominence alongside greater structure.

Symbiotic Phase

As clinical examples illustrate, the symbiotic phase is a developmental one that can be studied in a psychotherapeutic framework.

There are incomplete mental representations that can later be activated and observed during the transference regression. At the time when mental representations occur and the external world is perceived coherently enough so that the psyche "wishes" to blend with it, denying its separate existence, this stage can be considered the first phase of *psychological* development.

It is not certain whether one should consider the symbiotic phase an object relation or pre-object relation stage. To a large extent this is a semantic question. If the requirement for object relations is to perceive someone else as distinctly separate from oneself, then the symbiotic union with the nurturing object does not constitute an object relationship. However, since the child is "engaged" in a relationship (even though he is fused with someone else), this has been considered a primitive form of an object or part-object relationship. One can argue that the process of fusion requires some concept (even though vague) of something outside the self in order to be able to fuse with it. The previous, so-called biological state, which has no mental representations, is not one of fusion or lack of distinction between ego and non-ego. Fusions and boundaries separating the self from the non-self are psychological constructs; they have not been established during the early neonatal period. In order to be one with the external world, there must be some dim percept of oneself and something apart from the self. The latter can be considered a primordial perception of an object or a primitive form of object relationship.

Maturational factors provide the stimuli for emotional development. In the pre-object phase, there are no mental representations because the neurological apparatus is not sufficiently differentiated to perceive, incorporate, and conceptualize. With the maturation of the perceptual apparatus and the central nervous system generally, the child begins to perceive in a more structured fashion. From another viewpoint the Nirvana (not necessarily blissful but pre-blissful) state of nondifferentiation is biological; with somatic differentiation it becomes impossible to maintain. Increased bological structure becomes an impetus for corresponding emotional development.

Consequently, the symbiotic phase can be conceptualized as a *transition* phase between a more-or-less biological orientation and one in which external objects are perceived in a somewhat structured fashion and can be used for adaptation. Winnicott's (1953) concept of the transitional object is compatible with this viewpoint since the transitional object is experienced as both outside the self and an omnipotently controlled part of the self. From this control the child can eventually let the object remain in the outside world while retaining its representation within the ego system. The symbiotic fusion is a phase in which an internal object representation begins to form, although it is not consolidated until there has been a partial resolution of the fusion. The child's perception of objects is of part-objects, as Winnicott emphasizes; the transitional object represents the breast.

In a sense, the symbiotic phase can be considered an attempt to maintain a biological orientation or to return to a pre-object level. It is difficult to assign a complex purpose to such early periods of life, but it may not be too teleological to believe that there is some form of inertia inherent in the living organism. As soon as the child's perceptual apparatus becomes structured to the point where he has some awareness of the external world, symbiotic fusion counteracts such a perception and tries to reestablish the earlier state of less differentiation.

On the other hand, fusion with the outside world is, in itself, a form of perceiving and relating that is appropriate to primitive levels of development and represents a *necessary* first stage. By analogy, the more primitive (embryonic and undifferentiated) an organ or organism is, the more global its reactions. Freud (1923) reminds us of Roux's experiment in which he stuck a pin in a group of embryonic cells; this had a profound effect, producing extensive malformation in the mature organism. At a later time, when the organism was more developed, a pinprick would have had only a minimal effect. Similarly, stimulating a neonate produces global effects — the whole body responds, as in the Moro reflex — whereas applying the same stimulus when the infant is older may only cause it to turn its head.

It has been postulated that the first visual perceptions are of shades of light and dark and stillness or motion. Auditory perceptions are believed to be equally undifferentiated in the neonate and to consist of only the recognition of different amplitudes. Certainly he cannot be aware of the subtle nuances and intonations of complex language, although he learns to react to affects quite early.

From a mentational viewpoint it is assumed that the first object relationships and perceptions are also global. It seems reasonable to believe that initially the mother, although a part-object, "fills" the perceptual apparatus whenever she is perceived at all. If one considers her to be introjected, the introject is massive and un-differentiated during the symbiotic phase. To form discrete intro-jects requires a structured perception and an ego that is able to maintain a well-formed introject. If the perceptual system is part of the ego, it is still operating at a primitive level; the rest of the ego, which is operating on a similar plane, can only maintain an introject that is similarly constructed. In the symbiotic phase, that which is introjected and that which is introjecting are indistinguish-able and constitute fusion.

The structuralizing process initiated by innate maturational forces is characterized by responses that move from the general and massive to the coherent and discrete; in psychological terms, these responses are conceptualized as secondary process. Consequently, to postulate a symbiotic phase as the beginning state in the develop-ment of the psyche is a logical extension of what has been observed in the structural development of the soma. As psychic differentiation proceeds, one would expect object relations to become more cir-cumscribed.

The attempt to achieve consistency within the theoretical framework can be exciting because it calls attention to phenomena that would otherwise not have been discovered. The latter in turn strengthens the validity of the conceptual framework. If our theory has general validity, then the formation of the psychic structure within the context of object relations *must* proceed from a symbiotic global fusion to complex object relations that are used for adapta-tion. From this viewpoint teleological considerations recede into the background; whether the child attempts to remain at early levels of development or wants to fuse with the mother's breast is no longer meaningful. There are wishes, of course, but the earlier they emerge, the less operative they are in determining the course of development. Volitional factors are minimal and they arise in inverse proportion to innate maturational factors. The child's development, although profoundly affected by the nature of his introjects, undergoes a sequential pattern in which there is a pre-determined method of incorporation based upon structural con-siderations. What is incorporated, of course, varies with the unique qualities of the environment; each introject in turn, will affect later ones, but the maturational sequence is not significantly influenced by the environment just before the symbiotic elaboration. Unusual environmental circumstances and intense trauma can upset the innate maturational pattern. Severe developmental arrests leading to little subsequent development may occur during these early stages and result in emotional malformations. These are, however, extreme exceptions that have been described by Spitz.

Resolution of the Symbiotic Phase

Resolution of the symbiotic phase generally leads to more sophisticated object relations; to the extent that the psyche becomes progressively more differentiated from the external world, the self-representation (for our purposes the sense of identity) becomes consolidated and increasingly distinct from object representations. As stated earlier, biological maturation contributes to this differentiation, but the influence of the external object requires further scrutiny as it becomes increasingly meaningful in the process of individuation.

Insofar as the mother is an adequate provider and does not unduly disrupt her child's homeostatic harmony, the symbiotic phase is relatively comfortable. This does not mean, however, that the child "wishes" to remain in what is becoming a pleasurable state. On the contrary, *the fact that the relationship is satisfying permits maturational forces to unfold without impediment.* The whole psychic apparatus structuralizes; as there is "more" ego, the global relationship (fusion) with an object representation changes and becomes more elaborate. Metaphorically it is as though differentiation were accompanied by a shrinkage of the ego from its previous vast amorphous, diffuse, amoeba-like state. What is perceived undergoes a similar shrinkage so that the external object is eventually "registered" within the ego system as a more discrete entity. It is more sharply delineated and there is more "space" between the object representation (later referred to as an introject) and the boundaries of the ego. In this sense, the ego has "expanded" from a mere involvement with the nurturing source.

Biological maturation and the emerging qualities of the external object are interrelated and should not be artificially isolated. For example, if the mother has been disruptive and assaultive, the infant will find it harder to integrate her into his ego system. In order to perceive trauma as a first step toward mastery and integration, one must have effective structure.

The infant is aware of his basic needs (hunger, thirst, warmth, etc.) and a competent mother provides for them in a nonthreatening fashion. Her smooth, synchronized responses are gratifying because they are appropriate to the child's needs and they are nonintrusive. Simply because a mother feeds, clothes, and holds her child does not mean that she is meeting his needs. To give the child something when he does not need it is felt to be an intrusion, sometimes an assault. Need tension disturbs the homeostatic balance and the nurturing substance reestablishes it. If there is no disturbance in the homeostatic balance, attempts at feeding, for example, will disrupt the child and he will react either defensively or chaotically.

A child cannot use gratuitous offerings. In order to incorporate an adaptive experience smoothly, the experience must be part of the process of reestablishing homeostasis. The ego expands by incorporating the tension-reducing qualities of the mothering interaction. If the relationship leads to a disruption of homeostasis the child will fend it off; whatever intrudes into his ego is traumatic. Any incorporation that occurs during a disturbed state leads to a similarly disturbing introject.

The period of symbiotic fusion, if satisfactory, is characterized by an ego that has smoothly incorporated the mothering experience. Because it is a fusion the mothering experience and the child's ego are indistinguishable; it is harmonious in the sense that it achieves intrapsychic balance. When the ego becomes more structured and the mothering experience is a more discrete part of the ego, the same harmony and balance are maintained.

Ferenczi (1909) introduced the word "introject" — a very useful concept. Some authors (for example, Sandler, 1956) distinguish between preoedipal incorporations and those that lead to the postoedipal superego. The latter are considered to be introjects. Introjects are formed by the process of introjection, although the terms "incorporation" and "assimilation" are often not distinguished from introjection. As used here, introjects will refer to experiences and objects that have become part of the ego but have a structure of their own that distinguishes them from the rest of the ego. Once they are integrated into ego systems (as adaptive techniques), they lose their introject status and become "assimilated." If the introject is traumatic or disruptive it is not assimilated into the ego.

To return to the progressive developmental sequence from the symbiotic phase: as the diffuse but harmonious mother-ego fusion undergoes differentiation, the internalized mothering experience becomes delineated and develops into what could be considered an introject. Within the ego, boundaries form around the maternal representation. These boundaries mark the beginning of the psychic

separation of the child from his mother. As the ego begins to differentiate itself from the maternal introject, the child sees himself as
separate and distinct. At this point he becomes aware of his dependency, not in a sophisticated sense, but in terms of needing his
mother's presence.

In an immature ego a mental representation has to be reinforced by a relationship with the external object that has been
introjected; it has to continue being cathected by repeated gratifying experiences with the mother. Later the ego will be able to
retain a mental construct even when the mother is not present. As
the maternal introject is increasingly consolidated, the child's behavior becomes organized and goal-directed. His play activity
usually includes a problem situation that he has to resolve; often
the problem is the actual or anticipated separation from the mother.
Freud (1923) illustrated this thesis by describing the behavior of his
nephew; he symbolized his mother's departure and return by alternately pulling an object at the end of a string into view and then
putting it out of sight, thereby controlling the separation. This child
demonstrated both his need for his mother and his need to be
autonomous.

The child "learns" the mother's adaptive techniques without
having her repeatedly demonstrate them to him. By making her
methods his own he achieves further separation and strengthens his
ego boundaries. The maternal introject thus becomes part of the
child's ego and is no longer a discrete entity like a foreign body.
Insofar as the maternal introject promotes psychic harmony rather
than disruption, the ego does not have to erect defenses against it.
Consequently, the introject loses its boundaries and becomes assimilated.

The object relationship with the mother is functional. That
which is introjected is operational. The mother represents nurture
and care, and the child's inner representation of her reflects her
adaptive significance. As the maternal introject is "absorbed," it
helps to structuralize various ego systems, such as the integrative and
executive systems. *The executive apparatus expands and acquires
further techniques of mastery by incorporating the functional
maternal introject. The latter is no longer a distinct entity but has
become a modality.*

This discussion has focused solely upon the object relationship
with the mother. Although this is a vital relationship during the
early months of life, other object relationships are also important

for emotional development. The father is a significant contributor to the child's maturation; later on, teachers and others will also be important. Because other object relationships add to the ego's dimensions, the psyche becomes multifaceted. Multiple identifications constitute the elements of a gestalt, accounting for the richness of personalities. However, the mechanisms by which individuating qualities are acquired resemble those that produced the maternal introject.

In summary, the resolution of the symbiotic phase is, in part, initiated by innate, biological, maturational forces. *If the maternal (part-object) imago and the ego are indistinguishable but harmoniously united, the symbiotic phase is a transitional, developmental stage between a pre-object (basically biological) orientation and one where object relationships are established and self-representation is consolidated.*

DISRUPTIVE INTROJECTS

Repetitive gratifying experiences cathect further functionally adaptive introjects, which are then incorporated into the ego. The above are theoretical constructs about relatively nonpathological developmental sequences. Insofar as these are microscopic descriptions, one can ask what type of data would be required in order to make such formulations plausible.

Again, we are confronted with the same methodological considerations discussed in the introduction. Direct observations of children, although helpful, are within a frame of reference that is not particularly appropriate to microscopic formulations about intra-ego processes. Rarely, if ever, is a person analyzed whose early relationships were devoid of trauma.

Still, the study of an adult's psychopathology in the context of the transference neurosis is a relevant approach to this type of conceptualization. Psychopathology is selective. Not all ego systems or object relationships are equally involved; some areas have not been significantly affected or traumatized. One can learn a lot about emotional development in general because the early stages are recapitulated in the transference regression. In spite of the defensive distortions of this regression, many observations can be made. Furthermore, impaired development yields inferences about the customary course of events. The effects of defensive distortions upon ego development relate to our concepts about psycho-pathology, which have been expanded considerably beyond psycho-dynamic factors with the inclusion of characterological elements in our formulations. Consequently, the study of cases suffering from severe psychopathology is valuable for our further understanding of clinical phenomena as well as of concepts of intra-ego processes that underlie emotional development.

Insofar as the main emphasis of this chapter is on object relationships and the internalization of the object as an introject, it is not necessary to discuss psychopathology at length. The influences of the external object will be recognized as traumatic and disruptive rather than cohesive and adaptive, as discussed earlier.

During the biological pre-object phase, the external object is already significant for later psychic development. Even though neurologically the neonate is poorly developed and may not retain potentially conscious memory traces, his mother's positive or negative influence will nevertheless affect his later development. The child's maturational impetus must be augmented and sustained by properly timed nurture. Although the neonate lacks mentation, the mother can set the stage for future psychological elaboration by giving appropriate care.

The symbiotic phase will reflect any improper care received earlier. The child will experience fusion with a traumatizing mother as dangerous. Although infants are not capable of sophisticated fear or subtle perceptions of danger, direct observations indicate that there are situations they find terrifying and noxious. Tantrums characterized by purposeless and chaotic screaming are often seen in children who find their mothers threatening. Mahler (1952) skill-fully describes two reactions that characterize disturbances of the symbiotic phase : 1. children who cling to the object in a tenacious state of fusion and will not tolerate separation — symbiotic psychosis, and 2. children who avoid external objects because of a fear of fusion — autistic psychosis.

Some of the clinical examples that were discussed here showed a markedly conflicted attitude about being fused with the external object. The two children had to assure themselves that the external object (mother and therapist) had no significance. One of them could not let his mother leave ; in order to maintain "independ-ence," he needed his mother nearby so he could withdraw from her. The adult patient demonstrated the same conflict in the transference. He was afraid of independence in part because he believed he would destroy me if he "tore" himself away from me. He was also afraid of being "dissolved" if he remained in a state of symbiotic fusion.

To reach a state of relative separation is exceedingly difficult; once there is some dissolution of the symbiosis, the ego has to react defensively or (in some instances) it may undergo a rigid fixation — a state of paralysis where further development is minimal.

If the environment is not in harmony with maturational drives, later structuralization will be distorted. If biological progression does not receive reinforcement from the outside world, the psychic structures will be functionally constricted. Reisen (1947) describes experiments with monkeys who have been blindfolded since birth; he reports that even though their retinas structuralize, their vision is markedly impaired. In the human infant there are many corresponding situations where environmental responses do not stimulate maturational progression.

Introjects become established after the partial dissolution of the symbiotic phase. A traumatic symbiotic phase will lead to the formation of threatening maternal introjects in later developmental stages, and there will be difficulties in "absorbing" such introjects into the general ego structure. The sense of identity will eventually incorporate the mother's hatred as self-hatred, with feelings of worthlessness and inadequacy. The child will feel unlovable and vulnerable; its self-representation will be tenuous because of its lack of self-esteem. Still, the ego attempts to defend itself against the devouring qualities[2] of the maternal introject. It cannot smoothly incorporate such an introject into integrative and executive systems.

To the extent that the external world is traumatic, its internal representation (disruptive introjects) is also felt to be threatening. The ego, therefore, has two monumental tasks. First, it must protect itself from the maternal introject. This means that it must be powerful enough so that it will no longer feel threatened. It must be able to handle any disruption created by the maternal introjects; this is achieved by a rent in the ego's unity. The ego requires complete control, but it is especially vulnerable because of the split;

---

[2] Granted that the horrendous, monstrous qualities of the archaic maternal imago as described in the transference regression are the outcome of projecting the child's hatred, symbiosis precedes projection, and hateful self-feeling is the residual of the partial dissolution of the symbiotic fusion.

one part maintains control over the other which contains the disruptive maternal introject. The second task of the ego is to master problems "autonomously." Since the maternal introject is split off and has to be "controlled," the child must deny that the mother has any influence whatsoever — either negative or positive. The child cannot turn to his mother to satisfy his inner needs, and he cannot rely on his own resources because he has acquired only a minimum of adaptive techniques from her.

To augment the defense of dissociation by regression is not entirely satisfactory since the next earlier stage is the symbiotic phase. Regressing to this phase would undo the defensive splitting; the child would again be faced with an intrusive and "swallowing" maternal imago. Because there has been further maturation and development, regression to the symbiotic phase is perceived more intensely. In the transference regression the patient describes this state in terms of fearing annihilation, that is, destruction of himself as a distinct entity. Regression to the symbiotic phase often occurs but, as illustrated during the transference, it is nonadaptive (see pages 164–166).

The patient or child must maintain a facade of control and autonomy within the framework of a helpless and vulnerable ego. In order to maintain this control the child has to be isolated from the threatening introject which he can achieve by defensive splitting. On the other hand, he must cling to an external object because of the intense helplessness he feels. He requires both nurture and rescue from inner assault by the frightening, disruptive introject. But insofar as his self-representation includes derivatives of the primitive symbiosis, an inner assault also seems to emanate from those hateful aspects of the self that are "precipitates" of the mother-child fusion. The child then turns to the outside world for anaclitic nurture and salvation from a raging, self-destructive self.

Anaclitic clinging is often observed in very disturbed children, but the psychotic transference of patients with characterological defects often emphasizes the need for and the cataclysmic fear of fusion. The need for isolation and control conflicts with the need for nurture and rescuing, as illustrated in all of the clinical examples presented earlier. If one can maintain a relationship with an external object while simultaneously ignoring and withdrawing from it, then one has achieved a tenuous degree of intrapsychic harmony; this is, however, a very precarious balance.

An adolescent patient spoke of the above conflict and its tragic consequences in students taking drugs. He described a young woman who paraded her independence and flaunted conventions by frequently using LSD. As was the custom she took the drug either in a group or in the presence of her boyfriend. The patient said that the various participants ignored each other during a "trip". The last time the young woman tried the drug she was with her boyfriend. For some unexplained reason he left her just when she was experiencing the effects of the drug most intensely. Suddenly she became panicky and incoherent, and was unable to gain control and reestablish normal perception and reality-testing. Eventually she was institutionalized, suffering from a psychosis. Her behavior highlighted her basic helplessness, which was hidden by her facade of control and independence.

In the clinical examples presented earlier there was little ego structure, and the patients needed a specific kind of object relationship for their survival. In contrast, the psychoneurotic patient has considerable autonomy and a variety of useful adaptive techniques.

As a child grows older the world of object relations expands. He comes into contact with more people, and he relates to many facets of different persons. For example, he no longer views his mother as just a source of nurture but as a whole person. Other significant maternal roles increase in importance as the personality expands. Every stage of psychosexual development is characterized by distinct parental functions. The oedipal conflicts that characterize the psychoneuroses, for example, are brought about by a disturbance of object relations in terms of a specific role. The child may find himself in a conflict with the sexual mother whereas earlier he may have had a harmonious relationship with the nurturing mother.

The distinction between suffering from characterological defects and the psychoneuroses is one of degree. Disturbances in object relations do not usually occur abruptly. If a particular facet of an object relation becomes a source of conflict during a later phase of psychosexual development, there was usually some difficulty during an earlier period when the external object was less differentiated. It may not have been a severe disturbance, but, to the extent that there was one, every psychoneurosis will have an underlying characterological problem, minimal though it may be. Since no phase of development can be completely harmonious, everyone has residuals of developmental disturbances. How significant these may be is another question, but the characterological distortion underlying the psychoneuroses is relevant for our therapeutic understanding.

THERAPEUTIC IMPLICATIONS

Infantile disturbances of object relations are reenacted in the transference regression of children and adults. The question has frequently been asked as to whether therapy can undo the effects of severe early trauma and deprivation. Once the personality has been consolidated, can a benign, helpful relationship be as influential as a damaging one was during the early formative months? Most therapists agree that in both children and adults the effects of severe disturbances in early object relations can never be totally eradicated. A defective psychic structure makes it difficult for the ego to profit from potentially constructive experiences.

The psychoanalytic setting stimulates regression, causing the ego to lose some of its cohesiveness. Previous developmental levels are re-created, not as exact replicas of earlier stages, but with enough elements of more mature functioning so that both the therapist and eventually the patient can understand the nature of the early trauma. For example, through the transference projection, the patient revives early traumatic experiences with his mother. He reacts to the analyst as if he were fused with him and reveals megalomaniac expectations or the fear of annihilation. There are, of course, many individual differences, depending upon specific aspects of early object relationships, but, in general, one is impressed by the threatening qualities inherent in the stage of symbiotic fusion in patients suffering from characterological problems.

This transference regression results in greater resiliency than was present in the formed personality before analysis. The rigidity of defective structuralization and the constrictions that prevented further development are not as operative during the transference regression. Consequently, even though object relationships do not have such an intense impact, either disruptive or constructive, upon later developmental stages, the analytic setting creates a situation that not only recapitulates early trauma but has some potential for nondefective development — an opportunity that was not available during infancy.

The resolution of the symbiotic fusion during the course of

psychoanalytic treatment can be of considerable benefit. Both children and adults can emerge from such a transference state with an ego that is better structured because it has overcome the forces that previously caused maldevelopment.

During infancy the dissolution of the symbiotic fusion was followed by defensive splitting and denial of the maternal introject. Since this meant the disavowal of significant portions of the psyche, development of the self-representation had to be constricted because parts of the self were "lost" (unavailable for integration into adaptational ego systems).[3]

There are significant differences between the symbiotic dissolution that occurs in the transference and the one that took place in infancy. These differences can constitute the essence of the therapeutic process in psychoanalytic treatment. The patient projects the traumatic aspects of early object imagos onto the therapist. Instead of reinforcing this projection the analyst can help the patient understand how his mind is working. He does not treat the patient as a helpless, vulnerable baby who needs omnipotent rescuing. (Instead, he views his psyche as a phenomenon worthy of study.) He does not respond to the patient's terror or helplessness, but, with analytic calm and interpretation, he brings his secondary-process organization to the patient's primary-process chaos. *The analyst's availability for projection and his nonparticipation at the level of the transference regression brings some security into the symbiotic fusion. The patient no longer experiences the fusion as threatening because the analyst displays interest (not the feeling of vulnerability due to the patient's destructiveness) and he does not accept the patient's helplessness as a tragic reality that he has to do something about above and beyond analysis.* As the analyst brings meaning into an apparently chaotic state, he is helping the patient achieve organization through self-understanding. By incorporating the analyst during the regression to the symbiotic level, the patient is also internalizing some elements of the analytic attitude.

When the patient achieves separation, or at least partial separation, his ego retains an introject of the interested, analyzing

---

[3] A patient described himself as being defective in that he was "missing many parts." At first he described methods of relating to problem situations. He believed that he simply never learned how to handle many situations that were routine for others. During therapy his fantasies indicated that he was worried about lost parts of the self, including both the psyche and soma.

analyst which counteracts the assaultive mother or omnipotent rescuer. The regression to the symbiotic phase during analysis can lead the patient to regain parts of the self that had been split off, and *the catalytic effect of the analytic introject causes them to be synthesized into various adaptive ego systems — not to be dissociated as they were in childhood.* The fusion with the analyst has a corrective potential; although the effects of early trauma can never be completely undone, the patient's ego can still develop sufficiently so that he can respect himself as a person.

Both the children and the adult cases presented earlier demonstrated an inability to profit from external objects because of ego distortions following a disruptive symbiotic phase. If the therapy proceeds in the direction of a recapitulation of this early stage, perhaps a purposeful introduction of extra-analytic procedures might blur the distinction between the helpful, nonanalyzing analyst and the omnipotent, rescuing introject. Strachey (1934) believed that active support can help to foster paranoid attitudes where the therapy is perceived as good and the outside world as bad. This may lead to the alleviation of symptoms but not to character improvement. Active support can encourage an ego split, perhaps a more comfortable one; but, in terms of structure-promoting potentials, such a split is similar to the ego dissociation of childhood. Activity designed to help the patient by education or environmental manipulation is often experienced as an intrusion by susceptible, sensitive, vulnerable egos, which characterize patients who are suffering from developmental arrest; this is true of adults and frequently of children (Anthony, 1964).

SUMMARY AND CONCLUSIONS

1. An ego-psychological model based primarily upon a hierarchy of all psychic elements (drives as well as structure) is particularly apt for the study of pathological and relatively non-pathological development in the context of object relations. This model does not require a hydrodynamic-energic-discharge hypothesis.

2. The study of psychopathology enables one to make inferences about non-pathological development. Here, clinical accounts of children and adults who have disturbed early object relations are presented in an abbreviated form. Data obtained from the

direct observation of children as well as from the transference regression can be conceptualized in terms of early object relations.

3. Both types of data can be understood as examples of a disturbance and fixation of the symbiotic phase of development, one in which the child does not yet distinguish between himself and the nurturing source.

4. The symbiotic stage, conceptualized as a psychic fusion between mother and child, is thought to be a transitional period between the early neonatal stage (which is biological and pre-object) and the one in which there is a dim awareness of objects as separate from the self. Biological maturational forces serve as the impetus for greater somatic structure and subsequent elaboration of the psyche.

5. The nurturing object can either augment the maturational potential or cause maldevelopment.

6. A disturbed symbiotic phase is followed by fixation. The subsequent maternal introject is perceived as dangerous and disappointing. The ego uses primitive defenses, such as denial and dissociation (splitting), to protect itself against the assaultive qualities of the introject.

7. During the transference regression, the symbiotic phase is relived in a modified form. The analyst's interpretive attitude serves as an impetus for resolution of the symbiotic phase, and the subsequent ego states reflect the corrective experience.   Whether corrective changes can be achieved if the therapist attempts to provide "support" (other than analytic) by education or environmental manipulation is conjectural. It is believed that, although such support may bring about considerable symptomatic improvement, especially in children, there will be no basic characterological changes. There are limits to what can be accomplished in severely traumatized patients. However, many therapists are hopeful about them ; some cases have been reported that were helped considerably.

REFERENCES

Anthony, E. J. (1964). Panel on child Analysis at different developmental stages. *J. Amer. Psychoanal. Assoc.* 12 : 86–99.

Benedek, T. (1938). Adaptation to reality in early infancy. *Psychoanal. Quart.* 7 : 200-215.

————. (1949). The psychosomatic implication of the primary unit : mother-child. *Amer. J. Orthopsychiat.* 19 : 642–654.

————. (1956). Psychobiological aspects of mothering. *Amer. J. Orthopsychiat.* 26 : 272–278.

————. (1959). Parenthood as a developmental phase. *J. Amer. Psychoanal. Assoc.* 7 : 389–417.

Bettelheim, B. (1967). *The empty fortress.* New York : Free Press.

Borowitz, G., and Giovacchini, P. L. (1966). Workshop on the psychotherapy of adolescents. *Society for Adolescent Psychiatry Bulletin* 1 : 4–6.

Bowlby, J. (1951). Maternal care and mental health. *World Health Organization* 2.

————. (1960a). Grief and mourning in infancy. *Psychoanal. Study Child* 15 : 9–52.

————. (1960b). Separation anxiety. *Int. J. Psycho-Anal.* 40 : 89–114.

Boyer, L. B., and Giovacchini, P. L. (1967). Psychoanalytic treatment of schizophrenic and characterological disorders. New York : Science House.

Bruch, H. (1962). Falsification of bodily needs and body image in schizophrenia. *Arch. Gen. Psychiat.* 6 : 18–24.

Colby, K. M. (1955). *Energy and structure in psychoanalysis.* New York : Ronald Press.

DeLevita, D. J. (1965). *The concept of identity.* New York : Basic Books.

Erikson, E. H. (1959). Identity and the life cycle. *Psychol. Issues* 1.

Ferenczi, S. (1909). Introjection and transference. In *First Contributions to psychoanalysis.* London : Hogarth, 1952.

Freud, S. (1900). *The interpretation of dreams.* Standard Edition, vols. 4 and 5. London : Hogarth Press.

————. (1905). *Three contributions to the theory of sex.* Standard Editions, vol. 7. London : Hogarth Press.

————. (1915). *The unconscious.* Standard Edition, vol. 14. London : Hogarth Press.

————. (1918). *The history of an infantile neurosis.* Standard Edition, vol. 17. London : Hogarth Press.

————. (1923). *The ego and the id.* Standard Edition, vol. 19. London : Hogarth Press.

————. (1926). *The problem of anxiety.* Standard Edition, vol. 24. London : Hogarth Press.

Furer, M. (1962). Discussion at the Spring Meetings, American Psychoanalytic Association, St. Louis, Mo.

Gill, M. (1963). Topography and systems in psychoanalytic theory. *Psychol. Issues* 3.

Giovacchini, P. L. (1966a). Workshop on structural theory. *Bull. Chicago Psychoanal. Soc.* 2 : 3–4.

————. (1966b). Psychopathological aspects of the identity sense. *Psychiat. Digest* 26 : 31–41.

————. (1967). Characterological aspects of marital interaction. *Psychoanal. Forum* 2 : 7–30.

Hartman, H.; Kris, E.; and Loewenstein, M. (1949). Notes on the theory of aggression. *Psychoanal. Study Child* 3 and 4 : 9–36.

Mahler, M. (1952). On child psychosis and schizophrenia — autistic and symbiotic infantile psychoses. *Psychoanal. Study Child* 7 : 286–305.

Mahler, M., and Elkisch, P. (1953). Some observations on disturbances of the ego in a case of infantile psychosis. *Psychoanal. Study Child* 8 : 252–261.

Rapaport, D. (1966). The structure of psychoanalytic theory. *Psychol. Issues.*

Rapaport, D., and Gill, M. (1959). The points of view and assumptions of metapsychology. *Int. J. Psycho-Anal.* 40 : 153–163.

Reisen, A. H. (1947). The development of visual perception in man and chimpanzee. *Science* 106 : 6–20.

Sandler, J., and Rosenblatt, B. (1962). The concept of the representational world. *Psychoanal. Study Child* 17 : 128–145.

Spitz, R. (1946). Hospitalism. *Psychoanal. Study Child* 2 : 53–74.

————. (1957). *No and yes.* New York : International Universities Press.

————. (1965). *The first year of life.* New York : International Universities Press.

Strachey, J. (1934). The nature of the therapeutic action of psychoanalysis. *Int. J. Psycho-Anal.* 15 : 127–160.

Winnicott, D. W. (1949). Mind and its relation to the psyche-soma. *Collected papers.* New York : Basic Books, 1958, 243–255.

————. (1952). Psychoses and child care. *Collected papers.* New York : Basic Books, 1958, 219–229.

————. (1953). Transitional objects and transitional phenomena. *Collected papers.* New York : Basic Books, 1958, 229–243.

8

Fusion States

GILBERT J. ROSE

AT THE turn of the century Ehrlich and Morgenroth recognized that the living animal refuses to form antibodies that could be harmful to its own tissues. They coined the term "horror auto-toxicus" to express the fear of the living body of poisoning itself. Biologists now attribute to the immunologic apparatus the capacity to distinguish between self and not-self and they call this "self-recognition." Certain diseases (hemolytic anemia and disseminated lupus erythematosus) may be caused by an abnormality of the patient's immunologic apparatus which affects its capacity for self-recognition and results in the formation of destructive auto-anti-bodies.

What is carried out by the immunologic apparatus is, on a psychological level, a function of the ego; impairments of psycho-logical self-recognition are ego disorders. "The ego," Freud (1925) wrote, "periodically sends out small amounts of cathexis into the perceptual system, by means of which it samples the external stimuli, and then after every such tentative advance it draws back again." In the language of the oral impulses, the first function of judgment is to decide what is inside and what outside, whether one wants to eat something or spit it out, whether it is good and inside or bad and outside. In these terms, testing reality is testing the constant stimulus nutriment that the organism requires[1] (Rapaport, 1960). Some infants, presumably neither autistic nor schizophrenic, appear unable to move beyond attempts to determine orally what is inside and what is outside. In the syndrome of rumination they stimulate regurgitation with their fingers in their mouth without retching and then reswallow. If their arms and jaws are immobilized, some manage to regurgitate by arching their backs, throwing their heads back, and working their tongues to gag themselves. The resulting mortality may reach 50 percent. The syndrome is not relieved by antispasmodic or sedative medication but may respond to a satisfactory contact with another individual (Lourie, 1955).

What is primitive reality-testing seeking? Freud suggested that perception seeks not to find an object but to refind the mother's breast (1895, 1925). We tend to perceive that which comes close to what is already inside in the form of a presentation; perception and thought aim at establishing an identity between outside and inside. One wonders whether the aim of establishing a fusion between inside and outside could be related to the fact that newborn infants cry less and gain significantly more weight when a normal heartbeat is played continuously in the nursery (Salk, 1965). Similarly, one recalls that severe rhythmical head-banging in infants may be stopped by a metronome that beats at the same or slightly greater frequency than that of the head-banging (Lourie, 1949).

From the perspective of the environment, what we perceive depends partly on what we have been taught to perceive. The native boy in the Andes is unable to recognize, unless he is taught, that the pattern of dots on the photographic paper constitutes his picture. Peterson (1963) has listed ten different ways the birdcall of the chiffchaff is heard by people in ten different language-speaking countries.

Recent experiments (Gerard, 1966) indicate that the quality of the environment has a critical influence on cortical structure as well as on perceptual capacity. The cortices of brains of rats exposed to an enriched environment (light, sound, fondling, companions, playthings) were 5 percent thicker than the cortices of litter mates who were raised without companions or playthings and had only routine care. Newborn chimpanzees raised for a few months in total darkness or in an environment where they could experience

---

[1] Peto (1959), studying archaic thinking, believes the sampling also involves thermal, tactile, vestibular, and kinesthetic elements.

only light and dark but no patterns were able to acquire pattern vision only with great difficulty or not at all after they were released from the controlled environment. The same reaction occurs in humans who are born with cloudy corneas that are later corrected.

Recently McLuhan (1964) has been emphasizing that the form of our electronic media of communication has more impact on our modes of thinking and perceiving than the content of the media. Putting it more psychologically, as part of the ongoing process of internalizing the institutions and instrumentalities of the social system (Parsons, 1964), there is a continuing internalization of aspects of our electronic milieu.

But the essential factor in the child's learning about reality is, of course, his dependent relationship with adults (Hartmann, 1956). Kestenberg (1965) has shown that the child may eventually demonstrate a permanent impairment of his ability to deal with reality if he is unable to modify a poor rhythmic "fit" between his mother and himself in the feeding situation. If, however, the parents' views of reality are distorted, the child who fits the demands of his environment too well may eventually hold similarly distorted views of reality. Lidz and coworkers (1965) have impressively documented that some adult schizophrenics have practically been trained in irrationality by their parents.

The environment thus provides a constant stimulus nutriment that leads to the development of cortical structure and the building of mental presentations. Certain ego functions, including perception and reality testing, search for these presentations in the external world. Perceptual scanning continues to provide more stimulus nutriment for the development of further mental presentations, and further scanning seeks to find them again in the external world. Ego strength may be estimated in part by the degree of discrepancy between the already present mental image and the external stimulus that the perceptual apparatus is able to perceive rather than deny. In the transference neurosis the patient projects what has been lost and thus is able to "refind" it. Reality testing is improved and the ego is strengthened in the analytic process of examining the omissions and distortions that have been introduced.

At best, however, only a fraction of the world is available to the perceptual apparatus of a particular organism. That part which is available has been termed our "Umwelt" (Von Uexküll, 1934). The part of reality that constitutes our Umwelt is learned in the form of shapes. Gestalt psychology has shown how stimuli are perceived in configurations according to certain formal principles. Psychoanalysis has shown that the configurations have meanings, often signifying the bodily parts, especially sexual. Schilder (1942) has remarked that Freud had little interest in the symbolization of nonsexual body parts and was rarely interested in the symbolism of the body as a whole. (This may not be strictly true.) It was Schilder more than anyone who taught the importance of the body image in constituting our Umwelt. He emphasized the continuing struggle of building the image of the body. "We build the picture of our body again and again. . . . There are forces of hatred scattering the picture of our own body and forces of love putting it together. . . ."

With increasing knowledge of early development, it is becoming clearer that the developing and dissolving images of the body are not the first forms with which we attempt to shape our reality. The individual must be treated and experienced as a whole by his early environment in order to be able to experience his own invariant identity, spatial wholeness, and the identity of others (Devereux, 1966). Otherwise, although he may build coherent configurations, they will be based on the first forms of the relatively undifferentiated states of symbiotic fusion with the mother. Relationships will be narcissistic-symbiotic, defensive adaptations (Limentani, 1956; Weiland, 1966) in which he and his partner externalize each other's ego-dystonic projections. Reality will be manipulated to conform with projections and validate prior conclusions (Brodey, 1965). At the cost of casting reality into a simplified mold based on some early pre-object symbiotic form, the individual will reinforce the sense of certainty that restricted reality is the whole world and buy mutual protection from perplexity and a fear of abandonment and dissolution.

Giovacchini (1965) and Pollock (1964) suggest that there are varying degrees of symbiosis along the developmental axis up to and including normal, health-promoting symbiosis. Whether or not one wishes to stretch the concept of symbiosis this far, insufficient attention has been given to the continuum of the transformations of narcissism (Kohut, 1966). There are a number of patients on various levels of narcissistic development, or of degrees of symbiotic attachments, whose sense of identity depends on the persistence of unconscious fantasies of fusion with objects. These patients might be said to have "narcissistic identity disorders" (Rose, 1966b.) They have preoedipal fixations with hazy boundaries between self and object representations within the ego (Hartmann and Loewenstein, 1962).

One such group of patients, primarily neurotic, shows deformations of the body ego and have been described in an earlier paper (Rose, 1966b). They may conceive of themselves as phallic extensions, anal products, breasts, or mouths, and their view of the world may bear corresponding imprints. If there are many of these unconscious bodily self-representations, their energetic cathexes are not pooled within the total frame of reference of the self (Spiegel, 1959). This leads to a weakness in the sense of the self and an impaired sense of reality. Their symptoms, based on body ego deformations, are charged with much narcissistic libido; the parts of the self may represent transitional objects and may be clung to with the intensity of an addiction.

Another group of patients with narcissistic identity disorders may have the same symptoms of body ego deformations but appear to have a psychotic core. To a large extent, they use external objects and reality for ego and superego functions to improve their reality testing. Because external agencies may substitute for ego or superego structures, it might be said that their symbiotic relationships are based on degrees of structural fusions. In addition, the boundaries between self and object representations are more fragile, there is a preponderance of aggression rather than libido, there is less striving for object cathexis, there is a subjective feeling of impoverishment rather than enrichment, and the shifts in empathy are more massive and less reversible (Jacobson, 1964). To illustrate these particular psychic mechanisms, I will present a clinical example. Fusion played a significant role in this patient's psychopathological adjustment.

Ariel was an attractive but carelessly groomed art student in her early twenties. Her manner conveyed something tentative, unsubstantial, and vaguely bewildering. The fleeting expressions on her face as well as her tiptoeing gait made her seem like a young Alice lost in a Wonderland. She sought treatment because, just as her formal training was nearing its end, she developed a work inhibition. She had black depressions, often felt suicidal, and sometimes slept for 16 hours at a time.

"Mommy" knew better than anyone, including Ariel, what Ariel was going through. She had never kept secrets from Mother, yet she would often follow Mother around tearfully beseeching, "Why won't you believe me?" Sometimes she had the feeling that

Mother was looking over her shoulder, and Ariel would try to hate Mother or pick a fight to hold her off, or she would try to make her mind blank so that Mother would not be able to read it. In childhood, Ariel had invented code words and a secret language to refer to the things that frightened her; if Mother guessed them correctly, Ariel would panic. She would jump "in pain" if Mother did her hair, but she could tolerate others doing it. If a comment made Ariel feel uncomfortable, she would cough; laughing or retching would enable her to hold something at an even greater distance. Compulsive yawning was Ariel's way of expressing her desire for greater closeness.

Ariel was closer to her Mother than to anyone else. They shared the same feelings, so that Ariel would feel responsible if her Mother had any pain. The Mother would tell Ariel what she (Ariel) was really thinking and what she (Ariel) really meant and felt. When Mother said, "You want to," it meant "You must." When Mother said, "You don't want to," it meant "You can't." Thus, when Ariel wanted to do something, she acted as if she had to do it right away; when she didn't want to do something, she acted as if she couldn't do it. These actions were often elaborated into paralyzing degrees of procrastination or alarming impulsivity. For example, the feeling "I don't want to" would be expressed as "I cannot do it on time." Often, too, when Ariel became interested in something, Mother would become depressed and would tell Ariel how immature she was. This could make Ariel go to sleep for 16 hours.

Where perception led to an awareness of something that Mother considered "negative," the perception would be repressed and reality denied. For example, Ariel thought she saw misery, hatred, and dishonesty in the world, but Mother said these views were "negative." When the new car would not start in the morning, Ariel pointed to the corroded battery terminals, suggesting that the local mechanic might have substituted an old battery for the new one, but Mother wouldn't even discuss the matter.

Mother systematically erased clues about external reality in order to keep Ariel bound to her. She refused to have the speedometer of the car or the gas gauge fixed; thus, the speedometer and the gas gauge always registered zero. Not being able to rely on these customary instruments, Ariel had to discover other visual or auditory cues in order to estimate the car's speed and to know if the tank needed gas: a special vibration told her the gas level was within five miles of being empty.

A dream indicated the extent to which Mother could dominate Ariel's perception: "There was an eerie, blue, beautiful, but threatening, luminescence over the landscape at night. It was vast, cold, and distant. When Mother looked out to see this light on the horizon, she said that it must be wrong and not real and that it should be put out. When she said that, it became pitch black again, and I lost the desire to look because she made me feel it was awfully evil." There could be light only to the extent that Mother controlled the switch.

An important part of Mother's superego must have been her ego-ideal to be a male. From the beginning Mother had wanted Ariel to be the boy she herself had wanted to be, dressed her as one, and told her she was like Mother's dead brother. Before the age of two, Ariel developed an infection of the external genitals. On medical advice the inflamed and adherent labia were repeatedly separated and hot compresses applied. Not surprisingly, perhaps, Ariel in adolescence developed the secret delusion of not having a vagina. This undoubtedly accorded with Mother's own ego-ideal, and one might speculate further that for Mother Ariel unconsciously represented the wished-for phallus.

In any event, there was an urgent need for forms, in the sense of formative experience, to reinforce ego boundaries and mold reality into systematic experience. These forms and the experience they shaped would have to be consonant with Ariel's psychological existence as a creature of Mother's mind. Psychopathology provided such neurotic forms; tastes and sublimations provided normal and socially valuable ones.

One of the most generalized forms was that of de-aggressivizing and de-sexualizing fantasy. In adolescence, Ariel had experienced a mystical, ecstatic illumination after reading Thomas Mann's *Dr. Faustus*. Her love affair with the hero, the gifted but insane musician, Adrian Leverkuhn, obsessed her. Almost everything came to her filtered through it; it channeled many of her sexual and aggressive tendencies, focused her life, and provided a defense against unneutralized aggression and sexuality. Without such a fanatical obsession Ariel said she felt gelatinous — like a jellyfish.

Fantasies not only channeled her feelings, but provided a passport to reality. Whatever could not be embroidered into a fantasy with self-reference simply did not exist for her; reality could be recognized only through personal fantasy. Thus, fantasy acted both as a connection with reality and as a buffer against it. Any strong, direct impingement of stimulation might be experienced as a sexualized assault which she feared might destroy her. This included the morning sunlight from which she often attempted to escape by sleeping till well into the afternoon. Various qualities of light stimulated her sexually. She would try to transform it into an aesthetic response, diffuse it over the whole inanimate world, and fragment it into fantasies to prevent her feelings from becoming so strong that she might not be able to stop them and thus have to remain forever in an orgastic trance-like state.

Sexual and aggressive instincts that could not be managed by a de-sexualizing and de-aggressivizing fantasy could be projected in the form of paranoid fears and avoided or counterphobically confronted. These phobic externalizations of instinct also helped to protect her fragile ego boundaries from dissolving in fantasies of fusion with her surroundings. For example, without phobias to keep people at a distance, Ariel was afraid she might become the passive instrument of their wishes, unable to resist them. She was compulsively permissive and hyperempathic. If she hit her sister, she would weep; if she stepped on someone else's toes, she would say "ouch." If she had an intense conversation with a friend and then looked into the mirror, she would be surprised to see her own face instead of her friend's.

Ariel's fears protected her somewhat from dangerous action by keeping her at a distance from people. But there was also counterphobic acting out. Sometimes she would wander off in the early morning hours and strike up conversations with strange men. Her air of unearthly innocence disarmed them of any sexual or hostile intentions and she was able to reduce them to tearful confessions of their own unhappiness. Her conviction that artificial divisions between people must be abolished led to a small amount of pleasureless sexual acting out.

The urge to return to some undifferentiated state of fusion was rationalized into various sociopolitical convictions with a sado-masochistic coloration. The chief of these was the civil rights movement. She left treatment for several months and worked in this cause at considerable sacrifice. She felt almost constant fear, but was able to act with courage and even heroism so long as she felt she was contributing to a real reconciliation between polarities. The intact part of her sense of reality showed her in time that there were many villains on both sides of the civil rights struggle. This insight, born of hard, firsthand experience, prevented her from further projections of sadomasochism in this framework.[2] It was reintrojected and she returned to treatment disillusioned and depressed. The last dream before she left treatment had to do with a perilous flight and rescue with Mother and Baby Sister, a theme suggestive of a birth fantasy. It is interesting, therefore, that she returned to treatment nine months and six days from the time she had first entered treatment (Rose, 1969).

Some of Ariel's tastes and sublimations helped provide external form for her feelings. When her ego boundaries felt particularly fragile, she would make an effort to walk stiffly, comb her hair straight, keep her throat tight, and adopt an aloof manner and an implacable expression. She loved winter because its strong, clearly outlined forms of snow and ice seemed to provide structure and thus be full of life. Contrary to the usual connotation, spring represented death for her, as it does in Eliot's "The Burial of the Dead," because melting and rotting led to the loss of rigid forms. Her preference in music depended on the current state of fragility of her ego boundaries. When she felt reasonably secure, she could enjoy classical music because it offered a wide range of possibilities for her to let herself feel. At such times, rock 'n' roll was merely a bore. On the other hand, when she was upset she would use rock 'n' roll as a tranquilizer. She said that it "centered" her. Its very predictability and repetitiveness seemed to signify reliability, consistency, and security — like the sound of a radio compass to a pilot in the fog. When she was especially upset she would listen to rock 'n' roll constantly. It seemed to me that she let herself be enveloped within its embrace like that of the good mother whose verbal language is not yet understood, but whose unchanging formal characteristics are recognized and trusted. Possibly its noisiness helped to create new anticathectic barriers, facilitating the differentiation of self from non-self.

Drawing pictures was Ariel's most highly developed skill. When she drew she felt "most really real." Her first serious drawing, like so much of her activity, was oriented toward Mother. It was an act of love and an attempt at apology and reconciliation. Aside from their content meanings, Ariel's drawings also had an important formal meaning: they represented the packaging of an intense emotion into an aesthetic form.

---

[2] Later she was able to remark with characteristic humor that if treatment changed her from being an ardent political integrationist to an archsegregationist, the cure might be worse than the disease.

When Ariel suddenly took a massive dose of LSD, all of the various forms that had helped to constitute her reality in accordance with Mother's requirements were fragmented or destroyed. She was flooded with repressed libidinal stimulation and her integrative and reality-testing functions were swept up in a regressive tide. At first she felt she had been reborn; she saw the world without the protective filters and restrictive blinders of obsessive fantasies and paranoid fears. The world seemed new with fresh and luminous color, and she was aware of a wide range of libidinal and aggressive feelings. She felt freed and euphorically eager to sample the world which had magically been opened to her in this LSD "cure."

But every night for months the LSD psychosis returned and brought recurrent terror. Although she felt sexually aroused and masturbated, the excitement would not subside. She was terrified to fall asleep and further lower the defenses of consciousness. Chronic sleeplessness increased her anxiety; she didn't want to fall asleep for fear that the LSD experience would persist and she would lose her mind permanently. Although she feared it, the LSD psychosis never recurred during daylight or without prior masturbation. Ariel never lost her awareness that what she was experiencing were the illusions and hallucinations of a waking dream. She could not be sure whether she was touching herself or being touched. Objects appeared variable and imbued with shifting and fluid qualities. At the same time she knew that they were real and solid. These states could alternate or oscillate rapidly with normal perception.

The nocturnally recurring LSD psychosis was characterized by an instinctualization of perception. All orifices appeared to be vaginal and undulating; all projections were phallic. While lying awake she would see vivid images of gigantic genitalia of both sexes, sometimes condensed into a bisexual symbol like a crocodile. Oral features, such as cannibalistic biting, sucking, or being devoured, would be prominent. Size, shape, and distance had no reliability; forms fell apart. As the elements of a visual gestalt disintegrated into sexual fragments, they appeared to fuse and copulate with each other. These abnormal perceptions served multiple functions, defensive and self-punitive; they may have also represented partial reactivations of the infantile traumata of having her adherent labia repeatedly separated and hot compresses applied. Aside from such content meanings, they represented the toxic dissolution of relatively autonomous forms of perception.

In an effort to protect herself from the intense anxiety of these experiences, she developed vivid fantasies of fusing with her surroundings. She imagined that she was part of the walls and of everything else, and she would hallucinate these fusions taking place. These hallucinations added to her terror but also reassured her. She explained that if everything were really herself, she could, by fusing with it, control the amount of hurt she administered or received. Merging with the walls was thus an attempt to defend herself against the massive aggressivization and sexualization of her visual field. Aggressivization paralleled the fragmentation of percepts, and sexualization (in the form of apparent copulation) paralleled the refusion of the fragments.

Ariel said that if she invested herself in everything she would have control and thus wouldn't need to be afraid of assaulting or of being assaulted by everything. To her, "real" meant separate, which meant that she would have no control over an object. Therefore, she had to obliterate any distance or separation between herself and an object, sacrifice reality, and retreat to the pre-object forms of narcissistic fusion.

In Ariel's treatment the interpretive work was, of course, important, but the quality of the treatment relationship was even more important. This relationship enabled her to get through the difficult period of recurrent LSD psychosis without the aid of drugs or hospitalization. The spirit of treatment was to see her as a person who had not been experienced as a whole person by her parents and thus had not experienced her own identity or that of others. The therapeutic alliance offered more realistic superego standards than Mother's and directly confronted and opposed pathogenic superego elements. Mother's superego had withheld permission to recognize the hostile and sexual aspects of reality as well as her own female identity. Without Mother's imprimatur, Ariel's sexual identity had not been accorded the sanction of being real, and her drives were largely split off and always threatening to destroy her tenuous differentiation from her Mother and the world.

In treatment, Ariel's right to exist extended to all of her thoughts and feelings; superego criticism would not preclude recognition of their reality. The doctor-patient relationship could sustain mutual disapproval and affection. Criticism of her destructive acting out did not impugn her integrity or compromise her right to her own behavior within the law. All of this helped to free Ariel's reality-testing from the restrictions imposed upon it by her mother's superego distortions. Humor (Rose, 1969) helped to bring thoughts and feelings into awareness and moderate self-criticism; it helped to maintain the affective tone of the treatment at an optimal balance between distance and closeness. It neither merged into hyperempathy nor became isolated by excessive aloofness.

As Ariel became more tolerant of her thoughts and feelings, her actual behavior became less lax. She learned that disapproval and affection could coexist and that reality continued apart from either one. Since she could have both an affective relationship and reliable ties to reality in the treatment relationship, she realized that perhaps she could exist in reality apart from Mother's approval. She might not have to exist divorced from reality or fused to Mother, in an attempt to recapture the form of a narcissistically perfect earlier union.

In one of her final sessions she recalled that, as a little girl, she had walked unsteadily for years. When her Mother finally consented to her demands to be dressed in girls' clothes, Ariel suddenly began to walk steadily. Having won from Mother some grudging recognition, if not approval, of her sexual identity, she could assume greater bodily and psychological separateness from her. She left treatment knowing that, although there was much growth still to be accomplished, she was more of a real person, as was the ground she walked on, since she was less united with Mother; she might perhaps rely upon these things to support the growing weight of her own identity.

Primary narcissism refers to the initial blurring between mother and child from which the sense of self begins to evolve. In the beginning there is always oneness — a coalescence of child with all that is, unbounded as to time, space, and sense of self. Little by little the idea that Mother is distinct from oneself begins to take shape and with it the idea of a self and one's separateness in the world. With individuation, primary narcissism gives way to progressive internalization.

Internalization is the establishment of inner regulations to replace reactions that originally occurred in relation to the external world (Hartmann, 1956). Loewald (1965) has pointed out that internalization of object relations transforms them into an intrapsychic relationship which increases and enriches psychic structure, renounces identity with objects for a heightened individuation and reinforced sense of one's own identity, and leads back to external reality with deepened perspective.

No matter how much internalization has been achieved, however, the capacity for effecting at least a fleeting oneness with objects is never completely lost. The boundaries between the self and object-representations within the ego may remain somewhat fluid and interchangeable even into adult life. Although they may achieve a relative stability, they are not static. In the actuality of experience, self and object are partly a matter of relative position; both satiation and deprivation may bring about a shifting of boundaries and an alternation of fusion and separation. In the fluid processes that make up our workable equilibria, projection and introjection oscillate, and activities and objects are invested with varying amounts of narcissistic libido. Through the rapid alternation of projection and introjection, there may be re-merging of the self and object-representations within the ego. The boundaries of our separateness and identity are repeatedly dissolved and re-created as we dip back and reemerge from looser and earlier arrangements of reality. Attention should be focused more on relative position, boundary shifts, and alternating patterns of fusion and separation rather than on stable structure in either the person or his environment. Such a model is more consonant with modern, scientific conceptions of reality that were made necessary by the advent of quantum theory.[3]

Because inner and outer, self and object are partly matters of fluid processes, we might say that there is an evershifting ration between externalization and internalization; psychic structures may be externalized, and external agencies may act as substitutes for psychic structures.

Both ego and superego structures may be externalized. In addition to psychotic problems, there are others involving severe separation and castration anxiety, interminable analysis, and neurotic problems of marriage (Stein, 1956; Giovacchini, 1965) where one finds that there has been a projection of the reality-testing function or of bodily self-representations. The superego

---

[3] Cf. Heisenberg (1958): "Natural science . . . is a part of the interplay between nature and ourselves; it describes nature as exposed to our method of questioning. This was a possibility of which Descartes could not have thought, but it makes the sharp separation between the world and the I impossible."

may likewise be projected (Cameron, 1961) in an attempt to externalize inner problems and defend against depression and dissolution. A superego projected onto a symbiotic partner has much to do with problems of acting out (Bird, 1957). A psychoanalytic examination of literature, of course, reveals many examples of psychic structure : for example, Iago as Othello's archaic superego (Orgel, 1966) and the Fool as King Lear's reality-testing function (Rose, 1969).

In psychotic conflict the therapist is often used as a substitute for ego or superego functions ; at times of danger it is essential that this should be permitted (Jacobson, 1965). The therapist is not the only one who serves at times as externalized psychic structure, nor does he do so only for the psychotic. Where a capacity for full object relations has not been attained or is not being exercised, other individuals may serve as need-satisfiers or partial objects as well as performers of intrapsychic functions. Social institutions may also serve this purpose ; hospitalization is often beneficial regardless of what, if any, treatment modality is used, perhaps because the hospital provides "structure." A more depth-analytic scrutiny might reveal what intrapsychic structure hospitalization supplies or reinforces, or whether it merely simplifies external reality.

In point of fact, many of the activities of daily living discharge both alloplastic and autoplastic processes; work may be the most significant of these. It is important to remember that projection is part of normal functioning as well as a pathogenic mechanism. Hartmann (1956) was alluding to this when he wrote, "In the grownup, a workable equilibrium is normally established between what we here call 'our world' and the objective knowledge of reality." In the fluid processes that make up our workable equilibria, projection and introjection oscillate, activities and objects are invested with varying amounts of narcissistic libido, and multiple microscopic acts of fusion take place.

Narcissistically invested objects are most exaggerated, perhaps, in the state of being in love, being creatively inspired, and being absorbed in mystical, religious experiences. A homosexual patient described an encounter in which an immediate and uncanny feeling sprang up between himself and a stranger. (An unconscious, oral, receptive fantasy may have been mobilized because the patient also felt nauseated.) The patient felt that another person wouldn't be able to walk between them, although they were sitting at opposite ends of the room. He was agitated for three days — pacing, wringing his hands, taking showers (cf. *Death in Venice* by Thomas Mann). But following this intrapsychic storm and rearrangement of his narcissistic equilibrium, he was able to perceive and to react to people more warmly and spontaneously than he thought he had ever done before.

Kris (1952) has described the state of creative inspiration as one in which id energies suddenly combine with ego energies, mobile with bound and neutralized cathexes, to produce the subjective experience of being in a passive-receptive attitude to meet forces that are felt to reach consciousness from the outside. At such times, a creative artist or scientist may dedicate himself to his work with great intensity. As Eissler (1962) and Kohut (1966) have pointed out, creative work takes on the character of a fetish or a transitional object and is invested with transitional, narcissistic libido.

William James (1902) has described a whole range of mystical states in which there is a progressive obliteration of space, time and sense of self to the point of dissolution. One's will feels as if it is passively held in abeyance and possessed by a superior power. There is a transient feeling of immediate unity with the object and a consciousness of an enlargement and union with the vastness of the universe. There seems to be a revelation of the depths of truth and lucidity, and the world appears new and luminous. The mystical state may have no specific intellectual content; James says that the experience can be described less by conceptual speech than in the language of music. He speaks of the entire state as a return from the solitude of individuation. Likewise, Freud perceived the "oceanic" feeling of belonging inseparably to the world as a whole as an attempt to reinstate limitless narcissism (1930). James, who apparently had had first-hand experience with this feeling, was more inclined to find it admirable than was Freud, who had not experienced it.

Modern ego psychology seeks to differentiate regression (which is a return to developmentally earlier structures or functions) from the normal reappearance of less advanced modes of functioning (which are omnipresent in the ego). *The Kris Study Group on Regressive Ego Phenomena* (Joseph, 1965) pointed out that though in earlier psychoanalytic writing it was considered regressive for primitive thinking to emerge in the course of analysis, the primary-process mode of functioning is, in fact, omnipresent and only overlaid by more advanced forms of various ego functions. An attempt was made to outline a conceptual framework that would accommodate a range of phenomena from the healthy ego regressions of free association or artistic production to the severe pathology of the most regressed psychoses. Ego functions may be able to regress to more primitive states — to reinstinctualization through involvement in specific conflicts — and specific ego functions may vary in their level of development and vulnerability to regression to earlier points of arrest. In the selective patterning of regressions of ego functioning, it was suggested that the nature of early object relations was especially important as was the possibility of reactivating early traumata.

Early object relations, together with other factors, protect the ego against being flooded by the activation of earlier ego states. If the integrative and reality-testing functions are firmly rooted in healthy early object relations, the ego is better able to perform its normal scanning and screening. The ego is ceaselessly scanning its world and screening the chief nodal points of its past (Rose, 1960). It seeks to simplify, shape, and control a world that, to a certain extent, is narcissistically experienced.

Throughout life the ego may temporarily suspend the distinction between self and others and thus momentarily experience a state of mind similar to the earlier unity with the mother. We observe the ego drawing on the early fluid boundaries between self and reality to create imaginative forms : in psychotic episodes and identity problems as well as in normal aspects of reality construction and artistic creation. The ego effects multiple trial fusions and separations as it establishes shifting, workable equilibria with the outside world.

Mastering something by "fusing" with it, temporarily obscuring the boundaries between the self and object representations, recalls the primary narcissism of the infant and the psychotic. But to merge in order to re-emerge, may be part of the fundamental process of psychological growth on all developmental levels. Although fusion may dominate the most primitive levels, it contributes a richness of texture and quality to the others. Such operations may result in nothing more remarkable than normally creative adaptation to circumstance. At the least, it affords what James (1902) called the "return from the solitude of individuation," refreshed to meet the moment. At the most, it may result in transcending the limitations of earlier stages of narcissism to simplify, unify anew, and recreate an expanded reality.

SUMMARY

Certain theoretical considerations are presented that pertain to the interaction between early ego states and the environment. The sense of identity of a group of patients with "narcissistic identity disorders" depends on the persistence of unconscious fantasies of fusion with objects. Some of these patients form a subgroup, characterized chiefly by the patients' use of external objects and reality for ego and superego functions in what is termed "structural fusion." A case example is cited in which a mother represented the daughter's superego and exerted a profound influence on her perception of reality. The daughter's perception of reality was also molded, as well as reflected, by various aspects of her psychopathology: fantasies, phobias, and counterphobic acting out. An LSD episode was followed by months of recurrent, nocturnal states of perceptual regression. In normal reality flow there is an ever shifting ratio between internalization and externalization of psychic structure. The workable, shifting equilibria between projection and introjection are thought to be states of partial fusion and levels of narcissistic development. A range of phenomena from healthy ego regressions to severe pathology is within the conceptual framework of modern ego psychology.

REFERENCES

Bird, B. (1957). A specific peculiarity of acting out. *J. Amer. Psycho-anal. Assoc.* 5 : 630–647.

Brody, W. M. (1965). On the dynamics of narcissism. *Psychoanal. Study Child* 20 : 165–193.

Cameron, N. (1961). Introjection, reprojection, and hallucination in the interaction between schizophrenic patient and therapist. *Int. J. Psycho-Anal.* 42 : 86–96.

Devereux, G. (1966). Loss of identity, impairment of relationships, reading disability. *Psychoanal. Quart.* 35 : 18–39.

Eissler, K. R. (1962). Goethe : a psychoanalytic study. Detroit : Wayne State University Press.

Eliot, T. S. (1930). The burial of the dead. In *Collected poems.* New York : Harcourt, Brace & Co.

Freud, S. (1895). Project for a scientific psychology. In *The origins of psychoanalysis.* New York : Basic Books, 1964.

———. (1925). *Negation.* Standard Edition, vol. 19. London : Hogarth Press, 1961.

————. (1930). *Civilization and its discontents.* Standard Edition, vol. 21. London : Hogarth Press, 1961.

Gerard, R. W. (1966). Paper presented at meeting of the Carl Neuberg Society for International Scientific Relations, New York, March 31, 1966.

Giovacchini, P. (1965). Treatment of marital disharmonies : classical approach. In *Treatment of marital disharmonies,* edited by B. Green. New York : Free Press.

Hartmann, H. (1956). Notes on the reality principle. In *Essays on ego psychology.* New York : International Universities Press, 1964.

Hartmann, H., and Loewenstein, R. M. (1962). Notes on the super-ego. *Psychoanal. Study Child* 17 : 42–81.

Heisenberg, W. (1958). *Physics and philosophy.* New York : Harper & Row.

Jacobson, E. (1964). *The self and the object world.* New York : International Universities Press.

————. (1965). Psychotic conflict and reality. Paper presented as the Fifteenth Freud Anniversary Lecture at The New York Psychoanalytic Institute, May 11, 1965.

James, W. (1902). *The varieties of religious experience.* New York : Modern Library.

Joseph, E. D., ed. (1965). Regressive ego phenomena in psychoanalysis. In *The Kris study group of the New York Psychoanalytic Institute.* Monograph 1. New York : International Universities Press.

Kestenberg, J. S. (1965). The role of movement patterns in development. *Psychoanal. Quart.* 34 : 1–26.

Kris, E. (1952). *Psychoanalytic explorations in art.* New York : International Universities Press.

Kohut, H. (1966). Forms and transformations of narcissism. *J. Amer. Psychoanal. Assoc.* 14 : 243–272.

Lidz, T.; Fleck, S.; and Cornelison, A. R. (1965). *Schizophrenia and the family.* New York : International Universities Press.

Limentani, D. (1956). Symbiotic identification in schizophrenia. *Psychiatry* 19 : 231–235.

Loewald, H. (1965). On internalization. Paper presented at meeting of The Western New England Psychoanalytic Society.

Lourie, R. S. (1949). The role of rhythmic patterns in childhood. *Amer. J. Psychiat.* 105 : 653–660.

————. (1955). Experience with therapy of psychosomatic problems in infants. In *Psychopathology of childhood,* edited by P. H. Hoch and J. Zubin. New York : Grune & Stratton.

McLuhan, M. (1964). *Understanding media: the extensions of man.* New York : New American Library.

Orgel, S. (1966). Iago : the vile analyst. Paper presented at the Fifty-third Annual Meeting of The American Psychoanalytic Association, Atlantic City, May.

Parsons, T. (1964). *Social structure and personality.* Glencoe, Ill. : Free Press.

Peterson, R. T. (1959). *The birds. Time,* p. 121.

Peto, A. (1959). Body image and archaic thinking. *Int. J. Psycho-Anal.* 40 : 223–231.

Pollock, G. H. (1964). On Symbiosis and symbiotic neurosis. *Int. J. Psycho-Anal.* 45 : 1–30.

Rapaport, D. (1960). On the psychoanalytic theory of motivation. In *Nebraska symposium on motivation,* edited by M. Jones. Lincoln : University of Nebraska Press.

Rose, G. J. (1960). Screen memories in homicidal acting out. *Psychoanal. Quart.* 29 : 328–343.

Rose, G. J. (1966a). Transference birth fantasies and narcissism. *J. Amer. Psychoanal. Assoc.*

———. (1966b). Body-ego and reality. *Int. J. Psycho-Anal.* 47 : 502–509.

———. (1969). "King Lear" and the use of humor in treatment. *J. Amer. Psychoanal Assoc.* 17 : 927–940.

Salk, L. (1965). Study abstracted in *SKF Psychiatric Reporter,* May-June, No. 20.

Schilder, P. (1930). The unity of body, sadism and dizziness. *Psychoanal. Rev.* 17 : 114–122.

———. (1942). The body image in dreams. *Psychoanal. Rev.* 29 : 113–126.

Spiegel, L. A. (1959). The self, the sense of self, and perception. *Psychoanal. Study Child* 14 : 81–109.

Stein, M. H. (1956). The marriage bond. *Psychoanal. Quart.* 25 : 238–259.

———. (1966). Self-observation, reality, and the superego. *Psychoanalysis — a general psychology.* New York : International Universities Press.

Von Uexküll, J. (1934). A stroll through the worlds of animals and men. In *Instinctive behavior,* translated and edited by C. H. Schiller. New York : International Universities Press, 1957.

Weiland, I. H. (1966). Considerations on the development of symbiosis, symbiotic psychosis, and the nature of separation anxiety. *Int. J. Psycho-Anal.* 47 : 1–5.

9

Regression as Progress

BRUNO BETTELHEIM

MOST CHILDREN are fascinated by the marsupial mother who carries her infant in a pouch. To normal children, knowledge of this form of development can help them to understand life before birth, to visualize how they grew in the mother's womb. Nearly all psychotic children we have worked with also engage in elaborate fantasies about kangaroos, but for another reason. What they feel they missed out on was not so much life inside the womb as the warmth, the total protection and indulgence after birth that they think the marsupial baby enjoys in the mother's pouch.

There is another reason why they prefer the lot of the marsupial baby to the uterine existence. The marsupial baby can enter and leave the pouch more or less at will, at least after reaching a certain age. This is even more attractive because it combines a measure of independence with the always available security of the pouch. The psychotic child wants the chance to venture out at his leisure, but is too fearful unless he knows that the protective walls of his defenses will not be closed to him because of it.

While some autistic children wish only to have another babyhood and infancy of this kind, most want to be reborn altogether. This second desire can often mean trouble since some of these chil-

189

dren, in order to make sure that they will have a new life, try to shed their present one first. They try to die in order to be reborn, and this may mean a period of suicidal danger. During such a time they need to be watched and protected most carefully.

Do these children somehow know that basic trust, on which we build satisfying relations with others, is best acquired during the infant's utter dependency on his mother through the good mothering he receives? It is hard to believe that they can know it, but something inside them must exert a powerful push in this direction since they all want it so much and go to such lengths to re-create the situation.

But when is the right time for the child and for us to rebuild his life on the deepest — and normally the earliest — level of experience? In encouraging a child to relive emotionally the very beginning of life, timing is of paramount importance. If not timed correctly, things may go wrong and irreversibly so. Only two dangers need be mentioned here. The first is that the child may find the experience of reliving his earliest life so comforting that he may never wish to change. This may be a serious problem because physiological developments no longer provide the push and support for the steps in personality growth. At a later age the chronology of physical and neural maturation is out of gear with the structuring of basic personality and personal relations. Thus, the task may seem beyond him, and the child may permanently settle for being dependently cared for. In the autistic child this may merely lead him to exchange a total and inhuman isolation for a more comfortable but nonetheless inhuman existence.

The other danger is that the child may be seduced into experimenting with emotional experience when he is not trusting enough to give up his defensive armor. Then the longing for infantile emotional experiences may still induce him to be like a baby, but with much of his armor intact. This armoring will prevent him from experiencing true mutuality, without which nothing he gets from us will produce the deep trust in some adult that he should have experienced in infancy. Armoring might even prevent him from truly enjoying the care itself. Although yearned for and hence partly accepted, the care will fail to humanize; worse, it may debilitate him further. There are ministrations at all age levels which, if they occur in a relation of deepest mutuality, are the most humanizing ones, but outside of such a context they can degrade and humiliate. Instead of leading to a sense of worth and hence to the development of a self, these ministrations have the opposite effect.

If a child has once had a difficult time trying to effect a new beginning, he is not likely to venture it again. By inducing total dependency too soon, we can lose forever the chance to induce it again at the right time. In order to be therapeutic, a "regression" does not merely bring id satisfaction but leads to ego development. In short, it has to be a regression in the service of a still nascent ego, which is in one sense no regression at all. It is a recapturing of early experience through a partial re-experience that will support a very different development.

Freud (1900) used the term "regression" to refer to the loss of psychic structure, normal or pathological, not just manifest infantile behavior. When I speak of "regression" I am using a term that is no longer restricted to the technical meaning Freud gave it, but which has entered the common language. Popular usage of the word has improved neither its precision nor our understanding of its meaning. Everyone, without too much thinking, is sure he understands the term, and even dictionaries do not particularly help to define it. The confusion arises because one seems to be able to return to a point in space but not in time. Of course, we may question whether there can be a return to the same place. As far back as Heraclitus men knew that one cannot step twice in the same place in a river, for, precisely because time has elapsed, each place is continuously changing. (I understand from some physicists that it is now possible to think of time as flowing in both directions, but I doubt that anyone has this in mind when he speaks of regression.)

If regression is defined even in a psychiatric dictionary as "the act of returning to some earlier level of adaptation" (Hinsie and Schatzky, 1953), we can only wonder at the superficiality of the view of human nature that assumes there can be such a retracing of steps in time. The following is a common use of the term in psychiatric literature: An infant wets because he has not yet achieved bladder control; the older child who has gained control and then wets again, perhaps because a sibling was born, is said to regress. However, the older child does not wet because he has again become an infant without bladder control; he has not "regressed" to wetting. He has progressed to a deliberate (albeit unconscious) wetting as a means of conveying a need to his parent, which is certainly a step forward in adaptation. Or he has done it to express specific feelings or to gain relief from new pressures, all of which are movements forward in time and adaptations to new needs.

As commonly used now, the term "regression" seems to suggest forms of behavior of which we as observers are unable or unwilling to see the adaptive purpose. Behind this lies a narrowly conceived idea of progress that interferes with our ability to recognize immense variations in how different people deal with new problems. It is a concept that, even in its most technical sense, harbors the connotation that certain behaviors are, or should be, restricted to a specific age level. So long as we feel that "going backward" is undesirable and "going forward" is desirable, no matter what the cost to the individual, the concept of "regression" will not be free of value overtones that should have no place in our efforts to view human behavior with empathy and objectivity.

If all this is so, why not dispense entirely with the term "regression"? Why is it even used in the psychoanalytic literature? The reason is that the term seems to have a cautionary value. For all of us there is a continuous struggle to maintain our socialized behavior against the asocial tendencies within us. It seems easier to avoid the problem of when, and to what degree, we should give these asocial tendencies their due. Thus, if giving in to them is always and forever "regression," then in our "forward"-oriented culture the term helps to maintain social control. But in taking this stance we avoid the real problem of when, and for what gains, we ought to strip away social adjustment for the sake of our personal development.

Why do *I* not refrain from using the term "regression"? Because the term is useful when it is clearly understood that we are discussing how a behavior looks to an observer who knows nothing about what it means to the person who enacts it. Thus, the dictionary definition would be quite acceptable if it stressed this important qualification. It might then read as follows: "Regression is behavior that simulates a return to some earlier level of adaptation."

As suggested earlier, there are as many reasons for what appears to be regressive behavior as there are persons and situations. Still, at least two of them should be differentiated. One of them is comparable to the following example: The crew of a ship in dire distress may jettison all, including valuable cargo, and set the ship adrift on the seas. This is preferable by far — and represents a much higher achievement — than to let men, ship, and cargo all sink. This action is like a "regression" in which an aged person stops investing his energy in socialized behavior in order to husband his depleted resources for sheer survival. This kind of regression is too often the only defense available to patients in our mental hospitals.

But there is an entirely different type of regression : that of the adolescent who has a deep inner need, or that which we try to help our autistic children achieve when the setting and the timing are right. An analogy here would be to the crew of a ship with a leak in its hull that throws overboard a cargo of little value, or one that could easily be replaced or retrieved later on. Their purpose may be to raise the hull so that the leak becomes accessible and repairs can be made, or to lighten the ship so that she can make her harbor in safety. In this case energy is required not just for survival, but to achieve a significant goal.

Precisely because socially acceptable behavior has been contrary to the autistic child's deeper needs, his "regressive" shedding of it is an important step in acquiring a true personality. Thus, when the child begins to soil again, this can mean tremendous progress if, previously, he had gone to the toilet mechanically, as he was told, without daring to question whether it tallied with his needs or made sense to him.

If such a development is viewed as "regression," I can only wonder what progress is! Too often children's progress is viewed not in terms of a move toward autonomy, but in terms of the convenience to society, which cares less about autonomy than about conformity, and in terms of parents who at all costs do not want to have to wash their children's underclothes.

It is a reflection of the progress we are slowly making that for adolescents the importance of some kind of so-called regressive behavior is beginning to be recognized. Erikson (1959) stressed that many adolescents need a psychosocial moratorium, pointing out that merely because they seek it against society's pressure for "progress" does not mean that they have regressed; rather, they are searching for autonomy. It would be nice if this insight could be extended to where it would do the most good — to the child in his earliest years of life.

Just because it is the most important progress the autistic child can make, the time, place, and conditions for a symbolic re-experience of earliest infancy, if not of life in the womb, must be his own spontaneous choice. This is the essential safeguard against his permanent fixation at this way of experiencing the world (because it proves too desirable) and against a premature effort at mastery (premature because the child is still so well defended that the experience is meaningless).

Here is only one of the many tragic contradictions in the treatment of autistic children. To rebuild their lives without danger, they must choose such a course on their own. To do what they must to gain autonomy, they have to exercise a capacity they barely possess.

Thus, we cannot tempt or induce the child to take such a course. All we can do is to create the most favorable conditions for so extreme an emotional venture. These conditions, more than anything else, can convince the child that if he should start life again from the beginning, should "rebear" himself, so to speak, the world will not disappoint his trust; that he will not be hurt though he has made himself utterly vulnerable; that all his needs will be answered in a way that will not peg him to a level of helpless dependency but help him to develop his own self. In short, he must be convinced that his rebirth is self-chosen and self-regulated; that his development as a person from there on will proceed autonomously, with us as helpers, not controllers.

I want to present some clinical material from a case to illustrate these processes. Joey[1] was an autistic child who felt and acted as though he and his whole world were quite literally dominated by overpowering machines. The delusional machines that powered, controlled, protected, and threatened Joey originated in his infantile experiences. Because of difficulties of their own, both psychopathological and environmental, Joey's parents had been unable to respond to him during his babyhood in alive, human ways adapted to the constantly changing needs of an infant. Further, there was evidence that these parents, like the parents of other autistic children we have studied, were unable to care if their child remained alive at all. It is our impression that an important factor in the development of autism generally is the parents' active (although more often than not unconscious) wish that the child not exist.

When he came to the school at the age of nine and a half, Joey ignored all human beings and preoccupied himself with impersonating the machines that dominated him. He had elaborate rituals by which he connected himself to delusional sources of electricity to power the machinery that he imagined operated his body. In addition, he had elaborate "preventions" to protect himself from

---

[1] The case Dr. Bettelheim calls "Joey" is described in detail in *The Empty Fortress,* by Bruno Bettelheim (New York: Free Press, 1967, pp. 233–342).

being destroyed by the machinery on which he felt utterly dependent.

He did not refer to other people by name, but said "small person" for children and "large person" for adults.

Even if we had had the capacity within us at the very beginning before Joey and we knew one another, to give Joey the infantile care he needed, he could not have accepted it; he would have felt that he was being overpowered by adults. Although our care would not have been hostile or for the convenience of adults (as his parents' care evidently had seemed to him), it would have been experienced as overpowering and hence not likely to further real trust.

As for ourselves, it took time before our staff felt they would be able to carry through day and night the emotional closeness that Joey needed. To accept another person as one's baby — to give him the warmth, the total care an infant needs and enjoys after birth — takes a particular emotional relatedness that Joey's counselors did not feel they could continue for an extended period of time. He was still too strange, too mechanical. Even our counselors find it difficult to take electrical tubes to their hearts, as it were. Although they are more than ready to give sincere babying care under difficult conditions, they were not ready at first to do this with Joey because they cannot mean it if the child does not respond a little humanly.

If the counselors had decided at that time to induce Joey to go all the way back, if need be, to a womb-like existence, their decision would have been based on theory and not on the conviction that "this is what he needs, and this is what I am eager to give him. Whatever he may think at first and however he may try to resist, soon we both will enjoy it very much, he the getting and I the giving." *We do not believe that total dependent care does any good unless it is given with this conviction, and we have seen some very bad results when a child gives up his defenses without it.*

For this and other reasons we had to wait until Joey was ready himself and could communicate this readiness to his counselor. But, in order for him to have the courage, he had first to believe that good human relations were possible for him here. He had to work out and humanize his machine life — his "preventions." Most important of all, he had to get rid of anal concerns and misconceptions so that his rebirth could be a human and not an anal one. He had the idea that the vagina was a source of explosions, a place too dangerous for a baby to emerge into the world. He had told us this himself.

Joey gave indications that he was not ready for much closeness, though he wanted it. At the end of his first year at the school, he told us he was living on Mars, and sometimes Jupiter, but always on another planet. Since he was emotionally drawn to his counselors, he had to defend himself against his feelings by putting planetary space between himself and others. If he got too close, he told us, the warmth would burn him up.[2] But though he warded off his budding attachment, he began to see us a bit more as persons. Eventually he began to call by name the three persons who worked most closely with him — his two counselors and his teacher. Since we did not overpower him, either by asking that he conform or by expecting more closeness than he could afford, he no longer had to see us as machines controlled by him and his gadgets. At certain times we appeared human to him, and hence he called us by our own names.

Still, Joey was not yet functioning as a person who had integrated the various steps in development. On the contrary, a mechanized elimination predominated over all other psychosexual urges and modalities (to use Erikson's conceptual structures), due in part to his failure to master the stages and modalities that precede and follow it. He was largely preoccupied with problems of elimination but was far from mastering them. He could not do this alone because mastery of each stage requires the appropriate social experience around it. He could not be helped with earlier stages so long as he remained beholden to a depersonalized and mechanized taking in (through motors and wires) and giving out (through anality).

Before he came to us most of Joey's "preventions" had to do with taking in, with acquiring vital energy. Only later did his anality begin to assert itself openly, first by his eliminating freely into wastebaskets and then by diarrhea that he felt engulfed the world. Although when he arrived at the school he had had some anal preoccupation, this had been minor compared with his overriding concern with ensuring his flow of "electrical" input by delusional connections with sources of electricity. I believe that the emergence of anality as a dominant issue had to do with two factors: first, that the autistic child needs at least a minimal amount

---

[2] Ekstein (1954) and Ekstein and Wright (1952) have discussed the psychotic use of space to ward off dangerous closeness.

of autonomy to start life anew, and second, that elimination is a much more assertive act than intake.

To be born does not require a decision, but in order to grow up successfully, the infant must become active very early in the process. If activity and autonomy have failed to develop or have withered, why can't the older child regain them around intake? It seems to be true that he cannot, despite the importance of the infant's activity in rooting for the nipple and in sucking. I believe the reason is that, however active the infant may be, eating cannot be as self-assertive as elimination because it depends upon what another person gives. This is true to an even greater degree of more passive pleasures, such as being stroked.

It is true that many of our children, autistic or not, try to assert themselves around intake by grabbing food away from us, though we offer it freely. The idiosyncratic way in which some autistic children eat only a limited and often strange diet and reject all else we may offer, together with their strange ways of eating, is due mainly to anxiety but is also a token striving for autonomy around intake. However, the small bit of autonomy that they win here has never, in our experience, equaled the autonomy they gain around elimination. Hence, the child who will eat only what he can grab from another person doesn't get quite the feeling that "it's me who did this, and nobody else" that he gets when his own body pushes out feces. My speculation seems to be borne out by the fact that Joey could dispense with the machines to run his elimination long before he felt there were things he could do to assure himself of the food he took in.

From the beginning we had offered Joey both dependent care and chances for self-assertion, but he seemed to be unable to assert himself in a dependent context. Where he did use it to advantage was by eliminating as he pleased. Although we encouraged him to soil, he knew quite well that this was not the way of the world. He took us up on our offer, but there was little doubt in his mind that it was he who decided to do so. We did not ask him to defecate in our wastebaskets or urinate on our floors; we readily accepted these acts, but that is quite a different matter. By soiling, he knew that he was defying the customs of the world. Moreover, his defiance was much more decisive than it ever could have been with regard to eating, no matter how deviant his eating behavior.

Although some autistic children have responded more quickly than others to infantile care of a tender, loving kind, they have all experienced it around intake, kinesthesia, or other physical or emotional satisfactions we could offer them. This is why the tender, loving care we offered Joey, which he indicated he wanted by asking to be carried in a pouch like a marsupial, could not be fruitful for him at first. It was only possible after he had achieved some autonomy around the function of elimination.

Some readers might wonder why I do not discuss phallic phenomena here since the phallic modality specifically characterizes aggressive self-assertion. The answer is that we have never worked with an autistic child who had progressed this far in his psychosocial development when our work with him began.

Joey's counselors tried to act in accordance with his needs rather than to impose their needs on to him. They made every effort to adapt to Joey's needs in such a way that he could, in effect, safely dominate them rather than feel dominated by them. This gave Joey his first inkling that human beings could be worth relating to. In Joey's case it was not simply that he lacked the experience of self-assertion, but that it had not yet become a shared experience. At first when we offered him our company, we were planets away as human beings, yet we could not join him as machines. We felt empathy, but that was as far as we could go. At first he was unable to join our human company. Only the very close adaptation by devoted counselors over an extended period of time kindled in him a longing for human company.

Through many small steps that cannot be described here (see *The Empty Fortress*), the care he received led Joey to begin to feel that he could control his machines and his life, rather than be controlled by them; eventually he began to substitute human relationships for the machines. After much experimenting to test our reliability, he finally relinquished, bit by bit, the rigid, defensive behavior that had blocked his development and isolated him from human contact, and began to accept care of a kind that is appropriate to a small infant.

Then he staged his own rebirth from an imaginary chicken egg. The shell of the egg seemed to represent his autistic isolation. This protective "shell" function was finally, bit by bit, over several years of treatment, given over to his counselors in the school. "Regressive" behavior, which included infantile modes of relating, was more of an adjustment to reality in terms of the protective environment of the school than was his earlier rigid, defensive, mechanistic behavior. He had *achieved* freedom from crippling defenses that had developed as adaptations to a pathological, infantile environment. Without the crippling defenses, his personality belatedly resumed its maturational processes, and developed in a healthy way toward independent functioning in relations with others rather than in autistic isolation.

In summary, what has been termed "regression" can be seen as the relinquishing of rigid, crippling defenses, thus making possible the beginning of progress in the development of the personality.

REFERENCES

Bettelheim, Bruno. *Empty Fortress,* Free Press, New York, 1967.

Ekstein, R. (1954). The space child's time machine. *Amer. J. Orthopsychiat.* 24 : 492–506.

Ekstein, R., and Wright, D. (1952). The space child. *Bull. Menn. Clin.* 16 : 211–223.

Erikson, E. H. (1959). *Identity and the life cycle.* New York : International Universities Press.

Freud, S. (1900). *Interpretation of dreams.* Standard Edition, vols. 4 and 5. London : Hogarth Press.

Hinsie, L. E., and Shatzky, J. (1954). *Psychiatric dictionary.* 2nd ed. New York : Oxford University Press.

10

Keeping Secrets

RUDOLF EKSTEIN AND ELAINE CARUTH

> *How can I tell the signals and the signs*
> *By which one heart another heart devines?*
> *How can I tell the many thousand ways*
> *By which it keeps the secret it betrays?*
> — Longfellow

FREUD ONCE explained[1] that the child's first lie, that is to say, his first secret, is one of the first signs of his beginning capacity for separation and individuation and also reflects a growing ego that is now able to put aside the infantile conception that, "having obtained its language from others, the infant has also received thoughts from them. . . . " Parenthetically, we might note here that the Latin root of the word "secret," *sécernere*, actually means "to put apart, to separate." It is a psychological "truth" that, in contrast to "all stealing [which] is rooted in the initial oneness of mine

---

[1] In a footnote, Tausk (1933) describes Freud's discussion of his paper at the Vienna Psychoanalytic Society. Tausk had himself pointed out that "until the child has been successful in its first lie, the parents are supposed to know everything, even its secret thoughts." Tausk, in this instance, goes on to describe the "first successful lie" — usually occurring very early in infancy — as related to the child's attempts to mislead the person who is training him about elimination of his bodily wastes and to the fact that "children learn to lie from parents and upbringers who, by misrepresentations and unkept promises, make the child obey and teach him to disguise his true purposes."

and thine, self and object" (Freud, A., 1965), all lying, all secreting, derives instead from the capacity to put apart, to separate me from thee, mine from thine, self from object. Similarly, the need to share one's secret can also be understood as rooted in the universal wish to return to that state where there is no separation, where mine and thine are again one, as in the earliest fusion states. Indeed, if one looks upon the Bible as a metaphor for describing the genesis of the human mind, one might even propose that the original sin was the newly developed capacity of Adam and Eve to keep their secret and to keep secret those acts whose secret, incidentally, is at the same time inevitably given away by their secretions. Indeed, one might suggest that out of the conflict arising from this original dialectic dilemma : between the wish to have secrets — the wish to become separate and independent — and the longing to share the secret with the love object — to confess the sin in order to restore the love object and thereby return to the maternal matrix and remain dependent — the vicissitudes of the subsequent development of character have evolved. For we are describing here the secret of the human condition, which is to seek constantly *for* the object, *with and through* whom one regresses and restores oneself, while also seeking incessantly for independence *from* the object, *apart from whom* one can and must progress and fulfill oneself.

Clinically, this universal conflict — *la condition humaine* — can be described along a number of parameters. Mahler and Furer (1968) explained that the clinical syndromes of autism and symbiosis are but pathological resolutions of a normal developmental progression from early symbiotic relationships to those that allow for separation and individuation; others, such as Ekstein (1966a), Balint (1968), Ronald and Fairbairn (1952), and Winnicott (1958), have discussed the alternating needs for passivity, regression, and fusion states, and the strivings for activity, progression, and autonomy. Freud's very definition of mental health as the capacity to love and to work perhaps best encapsulates these essential conditions of life : the ability to fulfill oneself with the object as well as to achieve mastery on one's own. Some writers have referred to this capacity as the human paradox ; that is, that man can both experience something uniquely and also share this experience with someone else under certain conditions, for example, he can share his emotional response to creative artistic and poetic expression. In fact, these writers have suggested that "the unique private experience and the shared experience are really only two parts of an identical unified process and . . . the shared aspect is the more mature aspect or the fulfillment of the beginning, which is the private experience. One might say that the private experience has reached its full growth in the shared experience" (Tauber and Green, 1959).

The issue of keeping and sharing secrets becomes, of course, paramount in psychoanalytic therapy whose techniques have traditionally been predicated upon the so-called basic rule, which directs patients not to withhold conscious secrets in order that their unconscious secrets may ultimately be revealed. For the patient is seen as bringing us his manifest symptoms and not being aware of their hidden meaning, which presumably must be uncovered in order to make him well. Thus, in asking us to make him well, he is apparently asking us to discover the secret meaning of his symptoms, even though more often he secretly wants us merely to make him feel well (that is, relieve him of his suffering) but leave their secret meaning undisturbed. (Parenthetically, he believes that we, too, have a secret : a magic formula that can make him well if we will only reveal it to him.) More recently, it has been recognized that even though the conscious secret is a form of deliberate, overt resistance, "it is something to be respected and not crushed, coerced or begged out of the patient" (Greenson, 1967). Nevertheless, Greenson goes on to insist that the secret is a significant psychic event that must be analyzed and that there can be no compromise on this point. The contents of the secret are seen as generally related to secretions and either regarded as something very shameful or very valuable, while "secrecy and confession are always involved with problems of exhibitionism, scoptophilia, and teasing." In addition he says that "Secrets also are connected to the parents' secret sexual activities, which now the patient repeats via identification and which the patient does in revenge in the transference situation."

The meaning of the secret, particularly as it obtrudes itself in psychoanalytic work, was first elaborated upon by Alfred Gross (1951) in a now-classic article which, although emphasizing the libidinal aspects of secrets and secreting, also implicitly highlighted the importance of object relations and ego functioning. Gross makes the important distinction between the content of a secret and the process of possessing it — secreting, as we use it here. He points out the unconscious identity between the secret and bodily excretions (or secretions), the ambivalence over surrendering or maintaining a secret, and the ambivalence around expulsion and retention.

Gross goes on to lay the groundwork for a kind of epigenetic scheme of secreting: "The phenomena of the secret undergo certain changes above the anal stage which are a function of the sexual regime." Specifically, he describes the following development: Under the domination of the anal phase, the person feels it is important not to give up the content of the secret as a possession; in therapy this retentiveness is often directly related to comparable bodily retentiveness that "acts out" or "somatizes out," so to speak, the secretiveness; if this is given up, there can be ego expression in the transference that directly relates to keeping the secret. At the phallic level, the *process* of secreting and exhibiting becomes paramount and is related to the seemingly universal need to hide "the first stirrings of sexuality" as well as to the accompanying and equally universal compulsion to communicate them in some form. At this stage, the bearer of secrets is no longer content to conceal his secret treasure but must exhibit the fact that he has a secret. Pathogenic, traumatic experiences pertaining to Oedipal secrets that are kept from the child may at this stage lead to disorders in character formation in which the child "identifies with the parents' secreting which he equates with their genitals and hopes by having secrets of his own to attain the desired possession and all its functions." Parenthetically, in this connection, Selma Fraiberg, in "Tales of the Discovery of the Secret Treasure" (1954), related the popularity of tales of buried treasure, which "are among the oldest daydreams of the race," to the "universal and perennial mystery which confounds the child in his first investigations of his origins." She writes: "In every life there is this momentous discovery of the secret through an accidental touching or an observation, a revelation of the 'magic' of the genitals. . . . And always there has been a magician with greater power and a secret knowledge which is denied to a poor boy . . . who . . . steals the magician's secret, the pirate's map, and outwits the powerful opponent who stands between him and the treasure." One might speculate that the perennial popularity of the detective story is also relevant here.

With subsequent development following this phallic phase, the secret, according to Gross, "gradually turns into a potential gift to be used as a means of initiating friendly relationships with the outer world (intimacy, sympathy) and finally as an aide to wooing," as the individual moves into a postambivalent genital primacy where he is capable of truly giving and sharing — the mythically perfect *homo psychoanalysens.*

Gross merely touches upon the aspect of secreting that manifests itself in psychotherapy, which interests us here. He suggests that full transference only develops after the patient finally succeeds in confiding one of his secrets to us. He notes that this is often accompanied by an emotional release that can manifest itself through bodily functions, such as a flood of tears or the urge to defecate and urinate; he points out that if this happens before the analytic hour, it can serve as a resistance by somatically releasing the psychic tension elicited by the urge to communicate.

Thus, both Greenson and Gross regard the secret as essentially a form of resistance in therapy,[2] whereas we would like to suggest that the very process of psychotherapy may be described in terms of the conflict over secreting, and that the mode of secreting — of withholding and of telling — not only dictates the technical issues in the treatment but also provides diagnostic cues as to the structural and adaptive, as well as genetic, dynamic, and economic aspects of the personality organization. For the transference neurosis must also be understood as a re-creation or re-edition of that original situation in which to grow up means, symbolically, to begin to withhold secrets — to develop a mind of one's own — whereas to retain the good will of the archaic maternal image means to withhold nothing. Thus the patient, in bringing us his secrets, is afraid of having to give up the "secret self" (Reik, 1952) which holds the essence of his individuality as well as the core of his illness. This latter point can be seen quite clearly in very disturbed patients, many of whom can withstand the pressure to regress to the safety (albeit an engulfing one) of the symbiotic stage only by retreating to the craziness of an autistic withdrawal. The therapeutic task of the patient, therefore, is to retain just enough of the secret self to remain separate and independent, and to become just enough of a "secret sharer" to relate to others. The resolution of these two tasks provides the two tracks of treatment: the analysis of resistance and of transference along which the therapeutic process unfolds. Viewed from this perspective, it is clear just how and why resistance is as essential to the therapeutic process as is transference. Interest-

---

[2] This conception is derived from constructions related predominantly to the topographical model which invites the technique of uncovering layer after layer until one penetrates to the Pandora's box of the "dynamic unconscious" — that primal core of all secrets — and the hideous, frightening furies escape, one by one, until, finally, there emerges the last secret: that soft but persistent voice of hope.

ingly enough, it often turns out that the very method by which the secret is defended is also the means by which it is given away. We are reminded here of Raskolnikov (in *Crime and Punishment*), who is endlessly driven to return to the scene of his crime to protest his innocence to the commissioner; the latter listens patiently and noncommitally, as a good transference figure should, while Raskolnikov gradually reveals through his repeated protestations (or, as Shakespeare has suggested, through "protesting too much") the very secret he has seemingly sought to conceal.   Dostoevski is intuitively describing the process whereby the gradual revelation of a secret is both a bond and a bondage that unites the penitent and confessor; for that which unites people so that they "join and act together in a common purpose and endeavor," also causes them "to be or become bound together by adhesion," that is, to become "unus" or one.[3] Paradoxically, as we have seen, the very struggle against such a union may also further it; indeed, the psychoanalytic contract is but the visible expression of a much deeper commitment that binds both patient and analyst terminably and interminably.

Translating this into issues that are more immediately relevant to the psychoanalytic situation, we have the paradox that one cannot reveal his secrets until there is a "closed door" (Bernfeld, 1941) — the unique analytic technique that permits a transference to develop; at the same time, revealing the secret heightens the transference and makes its development possible. In this connection, Stone (1962), in discussing the psychoanalytic encounter, refers to Menninger's quotation from *The Scarlet Letter* that "a man burdened with a secret should especially avoid the intimacy of his physician." Certainly, the psychoanalytic encounter is one that gets immediately to the core of the issues around secrets, for the analyst is, after all, a kind of professional secret-taker (or, more aptly, secret-receiver); he is often perceived as a confessor by both patient and therapist alike. Bernfeld (1941) has, in fact, described the "confession" as the *"observation fact"* of psychoanalysis — one that never needs verification (in the sense of proof or disproof), but that does need confirmation as to whether it is the "right" confession. By "right" Bernfeld meant those confessions that disposed of the "indications of resistance" that had served both to maintain and to proclaim the secret. However, such a confession

---

[3] *American Heritage Dictionary of the English Language.*   Boston: Houghton Mifflin, 1969.

of secrets may lead to fantastic dependency situations, which, in turn, may tremendously burden the doctor. Bearing in mind that "if to these qualifications of a confidant be joined the advantages afforded by his recognised character as a physician, then, at some inevitable moment, will the soul of the sufferer be dissolved, and flow forth in a dark, but transparent stream, bringing all its mysteries into the daylight,"[4] the *so-called rule of abstinence should be understood as referring to conditions that will protect both patient and doctor from possible transference and countertransference acting out, by requiring the doctor to abstain from gratifying his own needs, or revealing his own secrets.* Although the psychoanalytic situation must be predicated upon what Stone describes as "a palpable human relationship, incorporating an attitude intelligible and meaningful to the patient from the start," it should also have a quality of "intimate separation" or, as the senior author has suggested elsewhere (Ekstein, 1970), by a quality that permits distance from the person and intimacy with the material. Thus, we might alter Stone's concept of *"intimate separation"* to that of *"separate intimacy," thus acknowledging the fact that true closeness, as opposed to fusion, can only exist when there is separation, that is, two separate individuals.* Therefore, in a way secrets are inevitable — not in an infantile sense (of concealing something from the parent), but in the sense that there is a private core that doesn't need to be communicated to or withheld from the other person. We might postulate a kind of developmental line[5] to describe growth and development ranging from the secretless state of infantile fusion and communion, through secreting of the growing child who can only conceal *or* confess, through the secreting of the preadolescent who conceals and reveals, to the mature adult who can either maintain a private self without secretiveness or be intimate and confide without confessing — that is, who can give and take, enter into a truly mature relationship of mutuality and sharing that permits the distance necessary for individuality and allows for the closeness of object-relatedness. We might suggest that since the psychoanalytic situation demands a greater sharing of that which is ordinarily private, it probably guarantees a greater distance from that which is ordinarily shared; therefore, it is essential that the

---

[4] *The Scarlet Letter,* by Nathaniel Hawthorne. New York: Modern Library.

[5] Using Anna Freud's concepts for a meaningful, schematizing, normal development (1965).

therapist remain relatively anonymous and suspend his own needs. We might speculate that in the closest personal love relationships, where there is maximum physical contact and sharing even of bodily and preverbal experiences, that which is often kept private are certain thoughts and fantasies, while in analytic situations, where the innermost fantasies are revealed, that which is kept private are those preverbal experiences that cannot, rather than must not, be communicated — those alluded to by Wittgenstein (1922): "Whereof one cannot speak, thereof one must be silent."[6] Total intimacy — complete union — can only be achieved by giving up individuality and returning to that early Garden of Eden where mother and infant are one complete unit. Our sickest patients, who both seek and flee from a symbiotic state, reveal most clearly how their manner of concealing their secret also expresses their wish for such a fusion relationship. Thus, their secret is that they have no secret; they feel empty and want to be filled up — to regain fusion via a secret; their feeling of depersonalization is a demand for communion. We have in mind the silent schizophrenic patients for whom "speech becomes that which both *intrudes,* as when there is too much understanding and the patient experiences this as a kind of annihilating invasion, as well as that which *isolates,* which hopelessly confronts the patient with the inevitable distance that exists between separate objects" (Caruth, 1970). In working with these sicker schizophrenic patients, it has become clear that what is important is the process of secreting, not the content of the secret. This finding has both paralleled and been predicated upon the theoretical work arising from the structural model, such as hierarchical levels of psychic organization and development. Clinical work with these schizophrenic patients highlights their incapacity for secreting, so to speak; they cannot keep secret their innermost core, for there can be no secret without a secret self, nor can there be a sharing or a telling of secrets without the capacity to maintain object relations, for example, separate mental representations of self

---

[6] We are referring to *current preverbal* experiences, those that are associated with still-existing primitive structures that derive from the earliest stages of life. There are also, of course, "unrememberable memories of childhood" (Frank, 1969) that are not available for direct recovery because of the concomitant immaturity of the mental apparatus when they occurred. Frank (1969) has recently categorized their subsequent vicissitudes, for example, by way of "passive primal repression" or reorganization into "ego qualities, strengths and capacities," which indicate indirectly the existence of this core and, inevitably, secret self.

and object. Technically, therefore, we find that the analyst — that conventional secret-taker — must become a kind of secret-restorer, one who helps reconstitute the capacity to keep secrets — to withhold the primary process, so to speak. Silence then becomes an adaptive device that defends against the eruption into psychotic acting out or fantasying out of the archaic impulses; momentarily at least, they are expressed through such "acting in" (Zeligs, 1957) of the communication.

Thus, one silent schizophrenic adolescent, who had earlier complained that "words make things worse" and had spoken despairingly of how the therapist could never understand her, was able to tolerate a communionlike silence more easily than contactless, empty language (Caruth, 1970). Another somewhat more psychologically advanced borderline schizophrenic child, whose therapy has been described elsewhere in the literature (Ekstein and Wallerstein, 1966), would repeatedly play out the following game:

> The therapist was stationed by the child in the middle of the school yard and was instructed not to move while the child ran at breakneck speed from one end of the yard to the other. Ted told her that it was her task to guess his current secret fantasy (referred to as a "secret field") in the spilt second that the child crossed in front of her. The strict conditions of the interplay were that if the therapist guessed correctly the child would drop the ball that he was holding. If not, he would return at the same speed and each time provide her with a single chance, a single clue, and a single second in which to guess.

The authors point out that on those rare occasions when the therapist could meet such a test, "the child was vastly and pathetically relieved for the remainder of the hour." The secret revealed by this apparent withholding of secrets was, of course, his "feeling of being almost inaccessible to a relationship with another person and hence almost beyond help, except by what would appear to be magical intervention," for the essentially impossible external conditions that he set up for contact revealed the comparable hopelessness he felt internally about ever establishing contact.

The manner and style of maintaining the secret thus reveals not only its content, but the nature of the individual psychic organization with its generic as well as specific secrets. One might think of the symptom as the prototype of all secrets in psychotherapy, for the symptom contains both the forbidden impulse and the defense that seeks to keep it hidden or secret. Thus, the excessively clean compulsive reveals by his very preoccupation with eliminating dirt the underlying concern with "dirty" elimination; the phobic who must secrete away all knives tells us at the same time about his secret knifing fantasies; the exhibitionist who seems unable to keep secret his "private parts," simultaneously reveals his secret conviction that he — like a naked babe — does not, in fact, have anything to keep secret; the child with the functional learning disability indicates that he must keep secret his ability to know in order to be sure that he does not learn what he already knows he should not know; similarly, the screen or cover memory exemplifies how the method of concealing is simultaneously the mechanism of revealing.

However, we are interested here not merely in unconscious secrets but also in those that the patient consciously harbors and seeks to preserve; it is significant how a secret is kept and, in the process, revealed. It would appear that one of the most characteristic features of having a secret is the urge to reveal it. Most obvious, of course, are those instances where the secrets are guilty ones and thus there is a "compulsion to confess" (Reik, 1961) in order to alleviate the guilt. In other cases, however, the urge to tell can be understood as a desire to flaunt the "magic power over those who do not share in this possession" (Sulzberger, 1953); having a secret has somehow always been associated with having secret power. It is a historical fact, for example, that the magician Houdini, whose secrets could seldom be fathomed even by other magicians, had to fight against the public belief that he must indeed be the possessor of extra-human (secret) powers, such as those claimed by the clairvoyants, whom, ironically, he devoted such energy to exposing (Caruth, 1969). Secret codes, rites, gestures, and so forth have always been used as a means of binding friendships and societies whose very existence seems to depend upon sharing a secret among the "haves" and withholding it from the "have nots."

In psychoanalytic therapy, it is the patient and doctor who share a secret : the process that takes place during their time together, and is thought to be interfered with if there is a "leak." At the same time, they both keep secrets from each other; the interpretation, like free association, is a kind of secret that is withheld or given at the correct time. Paradoxically, both the doctor's and the patient's secret, when finally revealed to the other, seems at that moment not to have been a secret; the patient generally experiences the interpretation as if it were something he has known all along (which, of course, is true at some level if the interpretation is correct), while the doctor generally has a good idea about the patient's secret which sometimes proves to be irrelevant to the therapeutic situation. We are reminded here of an anecdote about an analyst who had suffered patiently with her patient's endless obsessive struggle to reveal his secret. Finally, and within the countertransference, she is lulled into a momentary lapse of consciousness just at the moment when the patient is able to reveal his secret. In this instance, the way in which he revealed his secret actually concealed it by provoking the therapist's lapse of attention at the crucial instant. Frequently, however, the buried secret turns out to be like the buried mummy that, when finally unearthed and exposed to the light of day, slowly crumbles and blows away. Thus Freud (1909) in describing the phenomenological experience of lifting a repression, writes:

> I then made some short observations upon the fact that everything conscious was subject to a process of wearing away while what was unconscious was relatively unchangeable; and I illustrated my remark by pointing to the antiques standing about my room. They were in fact, I said, objects found in a tomb and their burial had been their preservation; the destruction of Pompeii was only beginning now that it had been dug up.

For the basic rule and tool of psychoanalysis is neither a tool nor a condition of but rather a result of the process: he who can truly free associate — that is, fully share his secrets without losing his secret self — no longer needs to maintain that secret which is the illness. We might think of this illness — this secret — as a kind of alibi, or what Kris (1956) calls the "personal myth," referring to those autobiographical memories that serve as a protective screen. The senior author has suggested elsewhere (Ekstein, 1966b) that this personal or neurotic myth is replaced in the course of treatment by another, more adaptive, myth and that the very process of reconstruction during analysis is essentially the replacement of one myth with another. We call the later myth more adaptive since it is not based upon repression or isolation; it allows the patient to reunite memory and fantasy in a way that permits him to endow himself with a "continuous life history." The new myth is no longer tied to infantile fantasy but is viable and can change with the course of life to fit current experiences. It doesn't need to be kept secret because it enables the patient to adapt to his present experience rather than to defend himself against past memory.

But the new myth is adaptive to a present that can be described as the "average expectable environment," a concept that, parenthetically, is also a kind of scientific myth. Freud described the religious or cultural myth as one that is based on blind faith and also remains unmodified regardless of changes in the data. He contrasted this with the scientific myth, which is also based upon arbitrary basic assumptions but is given up and replaced when it no longer fits the data as well as a new set of hypotheses — a new myth that may also be based upon a kind of blind faith, that is, arbitrary presuppositions. Thus Freud (1932a) writes in a letter to Einstein:

> It may perhaps seem to you as though our theories are a kind of mythology, and in the present case, not even an agreeable one. But does not every science come in the end to a kind of mythology like this? Cannot the same be said today of your own physics?

For he had long recognized that

> The theory of the instincts is so to say our mythology. Instincts are mythical entities, magnificent in their indefiniteness. In our work we cannot for a moment disregard them, yet we are never sure that we are seeing them clearly. (Freud, 1932b).

No myth, be it personal or scientific, can ever be proved; it can only be disproved. But this disproof is of a peculiar kind: "it does not mean that the theory is invalid and useless within the context in which it was established" (Bondi, 1967). For example, Newtonian gravitational theory still fits as a perfect description of the way gravitation behaves, but only *within certain limits of accuracy*. Similarly, the neurotic myth — the personal alibi — also fits within the limits of accuracy imposed by a personality organization constricted and distorted by neurotic conflicts; it also serves the adaptive purpose of functioning as a kind of organizing principle.

The same is true for what might be called the psychotic myth : the delusions that incorporate hallucinations which have displaced a repressed infantile experience. Freud (1937) suggested that such a view of delusions, relating them, like dreams, to the upward drive of the unconscious and the return of the repressed, indicates that there is "not only *method* in madness, as the poet has already perceived, but also a fragment of historical truth." Freud also pointed out that those who suffer from delusions, like those who suffer from hysteria, are actually "suffering from their own reminiscences." He concluded, via analogy, that "the delusions of patients appear to me to be the equivalents of the constructions which we build up in the course of an analytic treatment — attempts at explanation and cure, though it is true that these, under the conditions of a psychosis, *can do no more than replace the fragment of reality that is being disavowed in the present by another fragment that had already been disavowed in the remote past* [italics added]."

Just as scientific theories can be refined and revised when advances in technology permit more accurate observation of data (Freud, 1932b), the neurotic myth (or alibi) can be replaced with a more adaptive one when advances in psychological technology — the participant observer and the psychoanalytic process — create new conditions of observation, for example, those in which the patient slowly looks inward with the analyst so that his need for defensive mechanisms aimed at "keeping the secret" are reduced. The revised myth is constructed from memories that are recovered after the infantile amnesia has been worked through. These memories are now integrated and enable the patient to adapt to the present, whereas the neurotic myth utilized current experience primarily as a defense and to repress the past by such maneuvers as preserving the secret with the screen memory. But even the so-called adaptive myth is just that : a myth that also provides an alibi but can, like the scientific myth, accommodate to itself an ever changing life situation. This myth is no longer dominated by the neurotic compulsion to repeat a past that must not be remembered but cannot be forgotten; it is capable of integrating both "unrememberable" experiences (those that are subject to the passive, primal repression of a primitive, prelogical, preverbal mental apparatus) and "unforgettable" ones which, unsynthesized, had constantly sought to return via neurotic conflicts, alibis, and symptom formation.

To consider secreting again in terms of an epigenetic schema, we might say that, in the beginning, there is no secreting because there is no self; there is only an optionless communion experience — the primal secret. With individuation, the first secret appears that must be repressed, as in latency. With separation, the secret must be betrayed, as in puberty, where the secret impulse must be acted out and betrayed. We might think here of typical adolescent behavior with respect to a diary — that "secret" container whose very lock is an invitation to be unlocked by those against whom it is allegedly locked. And finally, there is the mature individual, who neither needs to secret nor to secrete (that is, retain or expel), but who is capable of both intimacy and sharing, distance and privacy, autonomy and selective sharing with the love object — one who has discovered that a life of secreting dies with the discovery of the secret of living.

We therefore, suggest, that the need to keep secret as well as the inability to do so are both manifestations of fixations and/or regressions in the normal growth and development of a function that is related to the dialectic struggle between maintaining individuality and establishing interpersonal relations, between the cathexis of inner and outer reality, between autoplastic and alloplastic fantasies, between narcissistic and libidinal cathexes that, when fully synthesized, allow the individual to work and love, to individualize and socialize, to maintain privacy or share intimacy as the situation requires.

Now it is clear how our understanding of the nature of the secret is predicated upon the current status of psychoanalytic thinking. We might even say that the development of our theory of secreting recapitulates the development of psychoanalytic thinking regarding the growth of the psychic apparatus. Just as psychoanalytic theory started with the economic, dynamic, and genetic aspects of the unconscious and proceeded to structural and adaptive formulations about the organization and functioning of the psychic apparatus, our understanding of the meaning of the secret proceeded from its contents to the nature of secreting and the personality organization of the "secreter." For it is not the *philosophy* but *how* to philosophize that is crucial (to paraphrase Kant); it is not the thought or the judgment but the act of thinking and judging that is important; it is not the discovery but the search that we must prize (to paraphrase Bronowski); and it is not the secret but the process of secreting that we must analyze.

REFERENCES

Balint, M. (1968). *The basic fault: therapeutic aspects of regression.* London : Tavistock Publications.

Bernfeld, S. (1941). The facts of observation in psychoanalysis. *J. Psychol.* 12 : 289–305.

Bondi, H. (1967). *Assumption and myth in physical theory.* New York : Cambridge University Press.

Caruth, E. (1969). No exit : the dilemma of the escape artist and how it relates to the problems of the borderline and schizophrenic patient. Unpublished manuscript.

———. (1970). The sounds of silence and the silence of sound in the treatment of child and adolescent schizophrenia. Unpublished manuscript.

Ekstein, R. (1966a). *Children of time and space, of action and impulse.* New York : Appleton-Century-Crofts.

———. (1966b). The space child's time machine. In *Children of time and space, of action and impulse.* New York : Appleton-Century-Crofts.

———. (1970). Psychoanalytic reflections on the emergence of the teacher's professional identity. *Reiss-Davis Clin. Bull.* 7.

———, and Wallerstein, J. (1966). Choice of interpretation in the treatment of borderline and psychotic children. In *Children of time and space, of action and impulse.* New York : Appleton-Century-Crofts.

Fairbairn, W. and Ronald, D. (1952). *Psychoanalytic studies of the personality.* London : Tavistock Publications.

Fraiberg, S. (1954). Tales of discovery of the secret treasure. *Psychoanal. Study Child* 9.

Frank, A. (1969). The unrememberable and the unforgettable; passive primal repression. *Psychoanal. Study Child* 24 : 48–77.

Freud, A. (1965). *Normality and pathology in childhood: assessments of development.* New York : International Universities Press.

Freud, S. (1909). *A case of obsessional neurosis.* Standard Edition, vol. 10. London : Hogarth Press, 1955.

———. (1932a). *Why war?* Standard Edition, vol. 22. London : Hogarth Press, 1964.

———. (1932b). *New introductory lectures.* Standard Edition, vol. 22. London : Hogarth Press, 1964.

————. (1937). *Constructions in analysis.* Standard Edition, vol. 23. London : Hogarth Press, 1964.

Greenson, R. R. (1967). *The technique and practice of psychoanalysis,* vol. 1. New York : International Universities Press.

Gross, A. (1951). The secret. *Bull. Menn. Clin.* 15.

Kris, E. (1956). The personal myth : a problem in psychoanalytic technique. *J. Amer. Psychoanal. Assoc.* 4.

Mahler, M., and Furer, M. (1968). *On human symbiosis and the vicissitudes of individuation.* Infantile psychosis, vol. 1. New York : International Universities Press.

Reik, T. (1952). *The secret self.* New York : Grove Press.

————. (1961). *The compulsion to confess: on the psychoanalysis of crime and punishment.* New York : Grove Press.

Stone, L. (1962). *The psychoanalytic situation: an examination of its development and essential nature.* New York : International Universities Press.

Sulzberger, C. F. (1953). Why it is hard to keep secrets. *Psychoanal.* 2 : 37–43.

Tauber, E. S., and Green, M. R. (1959). *Prelogical experience: an inquiry into dreams and other creative processes.* New York : Basic Books.

Tausk, V. (1933). On the origin of the "influencing machine" in schizophrenia. Translated by Dorian Feigenbaum. *Psychoanal. Quart.* 2 : 519–556.

Winnicott, D. W. (1958). *Collected papers.* London : Tavistock Publications.

Wittgenstein, L. (1921). *Tractatus logico-philosophicus.* Translated by D. F. Pears and B. F. McGuiness. New York : Humanities Press.

Zeligs, M. A. (1957). Acting in. *J. Amer. Psychoanal. Assoc.* 5 : 685–707.

PART IV

Technical Factors and the Psychoanalytic Process

Editor's Introduction

Part III dealt with a variety of elements surrounding the psychoanalytic relationship — what might be called the "psychoanalytic ambience." The broad framework of the psychoanalytic interaction was discussed, and ubiquitous factors, such as regression in the context of psychic mechanisms associated with emotional development, were emphasized. This part discusses specific techniques and maneuvers within such a context.

Technique can be approached from many perspectives. Inevitably, the question arises whether there have been any innovations in technique that parallel theoretical extensions and further clinical understanding in characterological terms. Has anyone gone beyond Freud's basic tenets on treatment? This question, from a certain viewpoint, is peculiar. If one describes a modification of technique, many will believe that the modification is no longer psychoanalytic. Many analysts, in fact, define psychoanalytic technique as Freud wrote about it early in this century, and any differences are thought to be deviations rather than innovations. Although this position is rigid and static, it often seems that the proponents of such a view are correct. Accounts of modified therapeutic approaches show that they are often nonanalytic and sometimes antianalytic.

Thus, one ought to determine how to modify psychoanalytic technique (in the interest of progress) and still remain psychoanalytic. The fundamental constants that define psychoanalysis as a treatment modality should be made explicit; then other factors that might be considered variables can either be discarded or changed. First of all, however, it is important to ask whether

219

modifications are desirable or necessary since change is not synonymous with progress. Therefore, one should consider what clinical experiences or situations make it important to discuss technique.

As this book demonstrates, there is clinical interest in a wider range of patients than those described by Freud. Still, many of the authors do not want to and have not abandoned the psychoanalytic approach with their patients; furthermore, they have not attempted nonanalytic treatment.

Practically every analyst will agree that the essence (the fundamental constant) of psychoanalytic technique is interpreting the transference projections. Other factors can be discussed and perhaps modified.

One debatable aspect of psychoanalytic treatment is whether, in order to be considered psychoanalysis, it requires the achievement of conflict resolution through interpretation of the transference neurosis, specifically sexual transference at the oedipal level. Some practitioners would argue that this transference seldom occurs and that cases with a basic oedipal core (rather than pregenital fixations) are rare. By this definition, a real psychoanalysis is rare.

Another questionable element of psychoanalytic technique — in terms of its utility or feasibility — is whether to instruct the patient about the fundamental rule. It is generally agreed that no patient can really follow it; if he could, he would probably not be in analysis. Therefore, should the analyst insist on the patient doing something of which he isn't capable? On the other hand, if the patient tries but is not completely successful, he has at least approximated spontaneity. Other analysts, myself included, believe that the fundamental rule — instructing the patient to tell everything that comes to mind — should not be given to certain types of patients who suffer from severe psychopathology because they often perceive it as an intrusion, and so it does not foster either spontaneity or autonomy.

The following chapters highlight the need for reappraising psychoanalytic technique because of frequently encountered cases that, in a traditional sense, would be considered untreatable or, at least, very difficult. The so-called technical innovations presented here are, in my opinion, consistent with the fundamental principles of psychoanalysis. The transference interpretation is given central importance and may even be emphasized more than usual. Consequently, the discussion of technical factors is really an attempt to apply psychoanalytic principles more strictly in specific but com-

monly seen clinical situations. These chapters are presented within an ego-psychological frame of reference; those elements that are inherent in psychoanalytic treatment and those that can be considered variable become more discernible when our theoretical context emphasizes characterological factors. Furthermore, with this emphasis, the importance of and necessity for extra analytic communications in addition to the psychoanalytic perspective can also be evaluated.

Dr. Kernberg discusses the latter point specifically in treating patients whom he classified as suffering from narcissistic neuroses. His conclusions are the product of extensive clinical experience as well as an exhaustive developmental and characterological study. As stated in Chapter 1, the difference between extra-analytic and analytic is, in many cases, a semantic issue that can only be resolved by sharpening our theoretical focus.

Finally, very specific analytic interactions (such as interpretations) are examined. How much interpretation should be given depends upon the psychopathology in a particular case. Certain patients require an active demonstration of the psychoanalytic relationship through transference interpretation, even in the first interview, while others would feel that such interventions were intrusions. Some of the differences between these two types of patients are highlighted. The analyst often "defines" the analytic setting, and this type of communication is examined in this section in terms of its interpretative characteristics which may not be obvious. Such a discussion may blur the boundaries between the extra-analytic and the analytic but, in so doing, it helps to clarify another dimension (technical) of the psychoanalytic process.

11

The Analytic Setting and the Treatment of Psychoses

PETER L. GIOVACCHINI

As we move further into the matter of applying the psychoanalytic method, we must face the question of what type of case is analytically treatable and what modifications of technique are required because a patient cannot fulfill a "condition" that is believed to be necessary in order for him to be analyzed. Extending psychoanalysis to the treatment of schizophrenic patients has been a rather controversial matter. It is often felt that such patients can be treated psychotherapeutically but not psychoanalytically. The psychoanalytic clinician is obliged to decide which patients he will treat; the patients we encounter frequently do not fit the standard categories that we were led to believe were psychoanalytically treatable.

Freud (1915) said that schizoid patients had narcissistic neuroses and therefore could not form a transference. I will not discuss the matter of whether a transference occurs since many analysts (besides myself) believe that it does and that it can be managed therapeutically (Boyer, 1961; Boyer and Giovacchini, 1967; Little, 1966; Searles, 1961; Modell, 1963). Rather, I will focus on two topics: 1. the relevance of the analytic process to specific aspects of the psychopathology of the schizophrenic or other severely disturbed patient, and 2. whether there are special technical features and modifications required for the treatment of certain psychotic patients.   I am not speaking of modifications that represent a departure from analysis, but of techniques that are particularly relevant to characterological or schizophrenic pathology and constitute, in themselves, particular facets of the analytic process. As I hope to demonstrate, such maneuvers represent a stronger adherence to psychoanalytic technique and not a temporary abandonment. Both topics require us to consider whether and how contact is established with such patients, thereby making therapeutic engagement possible.

Besides the lack of transference, what special problems are presented by severely disturbed patients so that they are believed to be analytically inaccessible? Perhaps the most important and uniformly agreed upon problem is a high degree of reality distortion. These patients are thought to be so withdrawn and narcissistically fixated that the therapist and therapeutic situation has little meaning to them (Freud, 1924a, 1924b).

The lack of contact with reality also creates difficulties in the transference resolution. Some analysts who feel that psychoanalysis is not possible with such patients admit that there is a transference but, because of its psychotic delusional nature, believe that it cannot be resolved.

Undoubtedly, there are many patients who are so out of contact that it would be ludicrous to attempt a standard analytic approach with them. Let us consider, however, just what are the special characteristics of their withdrawal and whether it would be possible in cases that were not rigidly fixated to create an atmosphere where such obstacles could be overcome. Could some patients benefit from an analytic relationship if it were "offered" to them? Or must we make the a priori assumpton that other methods and parameters have to be employed?

THE ANALYTIC SETTING

Psychoanalytic treatment needs to be understood in terms of the psychic processes that take place in the context of interlocking frames of reference. There are, of course, two persons present, the patient and the analyst. The patient's orientation embodies the whole gamut of his developmental experiences and their psychopathological elaborations. The analyst, on the other hand, tries to maintain as much as possible an orientation based primarily upon his professional experience. Although all levels of his personality are to some extent involved, he still has a way of looking at things that differs fundamentally from the patient's experience. The therapist's ability to keep his frame of reference from becoming enmeshed and confused with the patient's will determine whether psychotherapy is possible.

For the purpose of this chapter patients can be divided into two groups — those who come for treatment more or less on their own and those who are forcefully brought for professional help (usually in a hospital). My experience has been almost exclusively with the former group. The differences between these two groups may perhaps determine their treatability. In the few instances in which I saw involuntary patients, I noted that some could become involved in an analytic relationship when I offered an analytic setting from the beginning. Often it became apparent that the patient had manipulated others to "force" him to do what he actually wanted because he was unable to do so himself. Patients are often unable to make spontaneous choices because of the constrictive qualities of their psychopathology.

Something happens to the patient's usual adjustment. His defensive balance becomes upset. His frame of reference, so to speak, loses some of its earlier integration. The paranoid, for example, constructs a world of persecutors. He lives in that world, perhaps not too comfortably, but he makes an adaptation. He becomes a patient because he is no longer able to hold his private world together. *The analyst seldom sees paranoids in his office; rather, he sees patients who are no longer able to be paranoid.*

The patient wants to repair the "rent" in his defensive adaptation; he wants treatment to reestablish his usual equilibrium. Generally speaking, he wants the therapist to enter his private world and supply what has been lost in his decompensation. He comes to treatment with a particular frame of reference and tries to put the therapist into it. The analyst's frame of reference has to be congruent with his. The patient, hoping to establish a relationship that will correspond to his level of psychopathology, attempts to blend the two frames of reference. These maneuvers vary in form, depending upon the specific psychopathology. Some patients want an omnipotent savior who will help both to maintain and to vanquish persecutors. Others are unable to continue projecting in their daily life and need a therapist to make up for the lack of external objects that can be used for defensive purposes.

Winnicott (1954) writes of how the mother may "impinge" upon her child because she is more concerned about her own narcissistic needs than with him. She reacts when the child is not needful and neglects him when he is. In his treatment of such children, Bettelheim (1966) carefully avoids repeating what the mother did.

What should be emphasized is that the patient wants the therapist to intrude. Intrusion may take many forms. It is analogous to Winnicott's "impingement" and consists of any behavior on the part of the therapist that is designed to gratify instinctual needs or to support or undo a defense. The patient uses various defenses to get the therapist to intrude, *including withdrawal*. This may at first seem paradoxical because if intrusion is as traumatic as the mother's early assaults, why should the patient seek to repeat a painful situation? Before decompensating, the patient was able to adjust in some way to a traumatic reality, and he finds that it is even more painful to have this adjustment disturbed (Giovacchini, 1967).

For example, a young, hospitalized schizophrenic man said almost nothing spontaneously and when he spoke his words were practically inaudible. The patient was being interviewed by me so that his case could be discussed in a class for psychiatric residents. His presenting illness was characterized by severe withdrawal, even though he had always been a shy person. I could either respond or not respond to the patient's withdrawal. Responding meant asking questions (for example, trying to take a history) in a fashion that would not let the patient get too far away. This is sometimes referred to as getting the patient engaged or helping him maintain his hold on reality. As his later behavior indicated, he was extremely ambivalent about effecting a symbiotic fusion with me. He wanted to get emotionally close but feared being swallowed up and thereby annihilated. Still, he wanted the megalomanic support he felt such a fusion would give him. As with all defenses, withdrawal protected him from merging with an external object but it also represented a wish to do so and a fantasy of having done so.

By responding to the patient's withdrawal, I would be intruding into his world, providing the patient with someone to withdraw from; thus, he could justify his defense. He could not withdraw from a vacuum. *A defense has to be in context with a segment of the environment; it requires some support from the outside world for the ego to be able to maintain it adaptively.*

In this case I tried not to intrude, but to some extent I had to. This may be a criterion of treatability. To the extent that a patient will not let the analyst *not intrude* he becomes decreasingly analyzable; there are schizophrenics who will not relate at all unless the therapist intrudes. Perhaps the regressed catatonic is an extreme example; by being mute and immobile he "forces" those around him to deal with him in a non-analytic fashion.

To repeat, the patient tries to reestablish his former equilibrium by incorporating the analyst into his defensive system. This results in a situation where the patient cannot separate the analyst, as analyst, and the analyst as an archaic object; he cannot distinguish between the therapeutic relationship and his general environment. Paralleling this is a blurring of ego boundaries to the extent that the patient cannot distinguish between behavior initiated within himself and his own reactions to external stimuli.

Because of the schizophrenic's primary-process orientation, the therapist's intrusion is experienced as similar to his mother's "impingements" during early childhood. Longitudinal studies (Spitz, 1965) demonstrate that this type of maternal behavior makes it difficult for the child to construct a coherent self-representation. The mother's motives are usually destructive, and she does not recognize the child as a separate entity; rather, she sees him as a hated, narcissistic extension of herself that she has to rescue from her destructiveness. The psychodynamics of the mother-child relationship vary, but it has been repeatedly demonstrated that the mother's impinging behavior brings about a defective character structure. Thus the child's identity sense is imperfectly formed and his autonomous potential is submerged (Giovacchini, 1964).

Schizophrenic patients have especially severe characterological problems and their autonomy is minimal. They do not see themselves as separate and distinct. Because of their extensive use of such primitive defenses as splitting, denial, and projection, they find it especially difficult to decide what feelings emanate from within and what behavior is motivated by the external world. The therapist's intrusion makes this distinction even more difficult.

The young schizophrenic man tried to provoke intrusion by withdrawing; there were long periods of silence, vagueness, and inaudibility. At times he was so incoherent that his speech was like a "word salad." Instead of responding to him by asking him to speak louder or questioning him for the sake of clarity, I eventually interpreted what I believed were the motives underlying his behavior:

to withdraw from me by both hiding from and confusing me. Of course, there were also many exhibitionistic elements, but these were not essential for understanding the general movement within our interaction. The patient then blamed his inanimate surroundings for his behavior. Since our interview was videotaped, he had much reinforcement from the environment: camera, lights, and the knowledge that eventually he would be seen by an audience. Still, it was obvious that he was trying to avoid expressing feelings about me; he emphasized what was *around me* and then became inaudible and talked about the past.

It became apparent that the patient did not want to acknowledge that he had any specific feelings about me at that time that originated within himself. Therefore, I asked him what he believed *I* felt about him, and he spoke relatively freely. I assume he felt free to speak because he was being asked about someone else's feelings. In any case, he indicated that I must hate him and find him an unworthy person. Then it became my task to show him that these feelings were the outcome of projections — that these were attitudes he had about himself but attributed to me. In other words, I was attempting to keep our frames of reference separate by attributing his feelings, defensive or otherwise, to intrapsychic sources.

When he asked me what I wanted from him, I said that I was there to listen to what he *chose* to tell me — that I would respect his decision either to reveal himself or to withdraw, if that was what he needed to do. Following this interchange, his previously detached and seemingly apathetic demeanor changed dramatically. He complained of stomach cramps, yawned, and showed considerable anxiety. I said nothing. Then he got up and agitatedly walked around the room. He asked about leaving and headed for the door. Again I did nothing to stop him, hoping to indicate that it was for him to decide whether to stay or leave. As a result, he was unable to make a decision; he reached for the doorknob and then walked back into the room, and then repeated this maneuver several times. Finally I pointed out that part of him was eager to reveal himself but that he also perceived this as dangerous. (I believed I was referring to his ambivalence about symbiotic fusion.) I also said that this was a problem that originated within himself and that it might be amenable to psychoanalysis. He visibly relaxed.

My aim was to keep the patient's feelings in the consultation room. If I had taken a family history, for example, he would have been able to escape into the past and the world outside. He could have avoided his current reactions which, because of their immediacy, were possible to examine. I wanted to indicate that his responses were intrapsychic in origin and, to some extent, had adaptive value. If I had asked this patient to free associate, I believe he would have interpreted it as another imposition he could resist. To order someone to be spontaneous (the fundamental rule) is in itself a contradiction. On the other hand, to let the patient "choose" what he will or will *not* say leads to an intrapsychic focus. Since I did not participate (intrude) in the patient's frame of reference, he found it increasingly difficult to blame the environment, that is, attribute his behavior to factors outside himself.

A schizophrenic patient does not defensively withdraw because of an inner problem; he uses outside circumstances to justify his behavior. In this way the patient is relieved of responsibility for his actions, and so he can successfully continue to project. To deny responsibility for his actions also means, however, that he is vulnerable. He avoids acknowledging his psychopathology by blaming others; on the negative side, this deception and relationship with the outer world submerges his potential autonomy. This submergence may result in a defensive stabilization but it also makes further development and ego structuralization difficult.

When I spoke of autonomy, the young schizophrenic man's equilibrium was upset. By stressing that it was up to him to decide whether our interview would take place and whether he would speak, I indicated that I was doing my best not to submerge his potential autonomy. Afterward the patient began to experience a glimmer of autonomy through an awareness that he was withdrawing because of something within himself rather than because the outside world was forcing him to do so. He paced back and forth when withdrawal was no longer an effective defense. He began to acknowledge that he had wishes of his own (for symbiotic fusion) that might destroy him; however, these were his *own* wishes and they were manifestations of a core autonomy.

I believe that to the extent that there is some manifestation of autonomy, a patient is treatable. This autonomy may be hidden at first, but if the therapist and the analytic setting can lead the patient to feel, even minimally, that he has decisions to make, analysis is possible. The analytic setting is designed to enable the patient to understand that there, at least, he has some freedom to choose.

INTERACTION BETWEEN THE ANALYTIC SESSION AND THE EXTERNAL WORLD

Stepping outside of the analytic situation by becoming part of the patient's life may lead to stability, but such therapeutic maneuvers by themselves are likely to produce fixations. The patient's primary-process orientation will be reinforced and there will be no movement in the direction of structuralization. Strachey (1934) referred to this psychotherapeutic situation as a mutual delusion of patient and analyst, although in some instances it may endure and be adaptive.

What is lacking in this blending of the frames of reference is the opportunity for the patient to achieve states of regression within the context of the analytic structure. The segment of time the patient spends in the analyst's office differs significantly from the time he spends elsewhere. Sometimes a patient isolates his psychosis to the office, while he behaves fairly rationally in his everyday activities. This occurs because the analyst has not participated in the patient's defensive struggles and can thus become the recipient of his transference projections. On the other hand, especially during the early phases of treatment, some patients behave sanely in the office and delusionally outside. Both of these examples illustrate the structuralizing qualities of a stable, reliable analytic environment (Winnicott, 1955). The consistency of the session and the fact that it has a beginning and an end help structure the experience so that it is unique and separate from the rest of life. When the patient's insanity is restricted to the analyst's office, there is considerable reassurance in the fact that at a specified time his regression will, to some extent, end.

A middle-aged schizophrenic woman spent most of her time during the hour crying, whining, and asking for nurture (sometimes literally). She emphasized how miserably helpless she felt and how totally paralyzed and incapable she was. Before treatment I had learned from the referring colleague that she lived a completely chaotic life. After six months of analysis this same colleague reported to me that this woman's behavior had changed to an extraordinary degree. Although she was still rather disorganized, she could conduct her life in a reasonably orderly fashion. Gradually she began to report episodes in which she had been able to master situations that previously would have been insurmountable. Then she revealed that she spent most of her time "talking to me."

Whenever she had a problem or began to experience anxious tension, she fantasied that she was talking to me as a *patient talks to an analyst*. This was always a calming and organizing experience. Apparently this patient had succeeded in taking the structuralizing element of the analytic session (even though her behavior was quite regressed during the hour) into her daily life and used it adaptively.

There are many kinds of behavior within the analytic session and outside, depending upon the dominant transference theme and projections. By keeping the analytic experience separate, patients can use its adaptive features either during the session or in their daily lives.

TECHNICAL CONSIDERATIONS

Regardless of the specific interaction between patient and analyst, the question still arises whether one should modify the analytic approach when treating psychotic or severely disturbed patients. Instead of discussing purposeful deviations from analysis, I will deal with modifications thought to be within the context of analysis. These are technical considerations that are part of the analytic approach; opening gambits and maneuvers, of course, vary according to the patient's psychopathology and the analyst's style. Do patients who suffer from severe psychopathology have to be approached differently from those whose ego is better synthesized?

One modification was impressed upon me some years ago when a colleague saw one of my patients in consultation. This female patient in her thirties had developed such an intense paranoid reaction toward me that it could not be used for therapeutic purposes. Initially she had been referred as a "classic" phobic. Her beginning sessions were characterized by both dependency and idealization. She responded to interpretations as if they were correct, but, as I learned later on, she was not particularly attentive to their content. Instead, she felt she was gaining omnipotent goodness by absorbing within herself the magic she attributed to these interpretations. During this period of analysis we seemed to have a good rapport. In spite of our apparently good relationship, she was unable to gain any insight that might lead to higher levels of integration.

As her primary-process-oriented demands were invariably frustrated, her friendly demeanor gradually changed. She stopped glorifying our relationship and idealizing me; she became aware of a mounting anger. Her rage was handled by projective mechanisms. At first she felt mildly paranoid about me, but later it increased to the point where she felt the only thing wrong in her life was my persecution of her. These feelings could have been utilized but the patient did not want to continue treatment. Leaving treatment could constitute an adjustment, but in order to justify herself she sought consultation with a colleague. Her reactions to the consultant were extremely interesting. She started the session by being extremely dependent and positive, but as the hour passed she gradually became suspicious and paranoid. In the span of one session she reenacted our entire three-year therapeutic interaction.

The young schizophrenic interviewed on videotape caused me to wonder whether I had altered my interviewing technique. Of course, the encounter was different from one that would take place in a private office because it was to be displayed for classroom purposes and there was no intention of initiating an ongoing relationship. In trying to overcome my own anxiety (which subsided surprisingly quickly), I was not particularly aware of how I was conducting the session. However, the patient tried to use the unique aspects of the setting for defensive purposes, and soon it became apparent that the source of his anxiety was somewhere else.

When I looked at the videotape later on, I concluded that I had been somewhat more active (intrusive) at the beginning of the interview than I would have been in my own office. To some extent I attributed this to my anxiety and my eagerness to impress the psychiatric residents favorably. Silence might not have been detrimental to analytic treatment but it would have been very dull for the class. I wondered if some other approach (regardless of the setting) would have encouraged the patient to speak more freely, and I wondered if ordinarily I would have made so many interpretations in a first session.

There were certain similarities between the videotaped interview and the consultant's report on my patient. The interview seemed to anticipate the probable course of treatment if it had been undertaken. The patient began by withdrawing and defending himself against acknowledging that he was attempting to withdraw from the interviewer. Later, after a few interpretations and questions, he acted out his ambivalence about symbiotic fusion. Because this acting out threatened to disrupt the interview, I offered a final

interpretation about his ambivalence. The consultant's report indicated a panoramic miniature recapitulation of what had occurred
in treatment. The patient's transference seemed to cover the same
ground in one session as it had in three years of treatment. This
reenactment occurred spontaneously since the consultant did not
probe nor was he aware of the details of the patient's difficulties in
treatment.

For some patients to enter analysis, they may need a replication at the outset of possible future therapeutic progression. In
reviewing case histories of schizophrenic and borderline patients it
was clear that some would not continue with the interview if the
therapist did not initiate some activity or indicate some direction.
Other patients, however, do not want the analyst to interfere with
their spontaneous streams of association. Among the former group
I have tried to modify my approach in the same fashion I did in the
videotaped interview. Of course, it is impossible to know how
therapy would have progressed with some other approach, but it
seems likely that the patients who appeared to need a panoramic
prevision of "things to come" could not otherwise have formed a
therapeutic alliance. It is also difficult to predict how the other
group would have reacted, but their associations and some of their
past therapeutic contacts indicate that they probably would not
have remained in treatment if the analyst had tried to guide them.

It is not easy to distinguish one group from the other. Generally, however, the patient with whom one has to anticipate the
future course of treatment is taciturn and sometimes visibly frightened and withdrawn. He seems to be less integrated or to have
less defensive stabilization than those in the other group (see Chapter 12).

In reviewing the data about both groups of patients, it was
interesting to note that a "panoramic" first dream was only reported by those patients who did not want the therapist to be active.
(A panoramic first dream is one that often occurs at the beginning
of analysis, outlining in a sweeping fashion the structure of the
neurosis and depicting the sequence of the unfolding of the transference neurosis or psychosis [Freud, 1900]). Five patients in the
seemingly better integrated group had such panoramic dreams,
three of them on the eve of the first interview; none in the other
group ever reported such a dream.

Fragmentation of the ego was, however, clear in the dreams of
those patients who did not have panoramic dreams. Frequently,

especially during the early phases of treatment, their dreams reflected specific defensive patterns. However, in the dream these patterns were not connected with other aspects of psychic functioning, such as other defenses or underlying conflicts. For example, the dreams of a patient whose initial defense was withdrawal (not too unlike the young schizophrenic man) consisted of hiding in holes and caves. His dreams seemed to be fragmented from the general associative stream; although they were quite revealing, they were not comprehensive, panoramic dreams.

Patients who want the therapist to take an active part seem to need a synthesizing experience. Although fragmentation represents a primitive defensive adjustment, there may be considerable anxiety if the patient feels there will be more uncontrolled fragmentation. He may perceive analysis as a force that will disrupt his precarious equilibrium. If an initial interview can, in a sense, outline the course of the unfolding of the transference, the patient may receive considerable reassurance. Just to have someone around who perceives him as a totality is a stabilizing experience. Even though the patient's self-understanding is distorted and fragmented, he is, at some primitive level, aware of his psychic organization. He can only perceive certain aspects of himself at a particular moment and cannot integrate them with the rest of his personality. By actively demonstrating the unfolding therapeutic drama, the analyst can show the patient that there is a fundamental unity to his psyche. He needs to know that the analytic setting will provide a structure. Although analysis may stimulate regression and further fragmentation, it will take place in the context of an observational frame of reference that is designed to promote synthesis and secondary-process organization. The panoramic interview will reassure the patient that the analyst is, to some extent, aware of the total picture and that there is more to the patient's psychic organization than the fragmented element he perceives at the moment.

Those patients who would react to the panoramic interview as an intrusion are also fragmented and use fragmentation as a defense, but they are able to view themselves as a synthesized whole. The fact that they have panoramic first dreams may indicate this capacity, but they are not *always* able to effect synthesis by viewing themselves as a whole or mastering problems with the external world. They hope to regain this diminished or failing capacity in analysis. The analyst does not need to supply specific integrative experiences directly, but the analytic setting may provide a context in which the patient can pursue cohesive individuation without hindrance.

SUMMARY

The analytic setting is discussed in terms of emphasizing whatever autonomy the patient possesses. Once the patient recognizes that there are two frames of reference — his psychopathologically distorted one and the analyst's nonintrusive, observational one — he can acknowledge that he is to some extent responsible for his nonadaptive or defensively adaptive behavior.

Some patients need an initial analytic experience where the course of the analysis in miniature, so to speak, is demonstrated. This type of interaction may be essential for severely fragmented patients whose capacity for synthesis is minimal, whereas for other patients who can function in a better integrated fashion such an approach might be considered an intrusion.

REFERENCES

Bettelheim, B. (1966). *The empty fortress.* New York : Free Press.

Boyer, L. B. (1961). Provisional evaluation of psycho-analysis with few parameters in the treatment of schizophrenia. *Int. J. Psycho-Anal.* 42 : 389–403.

————, and Giovacchini, P. L. (1967). *Psychoanalytic treatment of schizophrenic and characterological disorders.* New York : Science House.

Freud, S. (1900). *The interpretation of dreams.* Standard Edition, vols. 3 and 4. London : Hogarth Press.

————. (1924a). *Neuroses and psychoses.* Standard Edition, vol. 19. London : Hogarth Press.

————. (1924b). *Loss of reality in neuroses and psychoses.* Standard Edition, vol. 19. London : Hogarth Press.

Giovacchini, P. L. (1964). The submerged ego. *J. Acad. Child Psychiat.* 3 : 430–442.

————. (1967). Frustration and externalization. *Psychoanal. Quart.* 36 : 571–583.

Little, M. (1966). Transference in borderline states. *Int. J. Psycho-Anal.* 47 : 476–486.

Modell, A. (1963). Primitive object relations and the predisposition to schizophrenia. *Int. J. Psycho-Anal.* 44 : 282–293.

Searles, H. (1961). Phases of patient-therapist interaction in the psychotherapy of chronic schizophrenia. *Brit. J. Med. Psychol.* 34 : 169–193.

Spitz, R. (1965). *The first year of life.* New York : International Universities Press.

Strachey, J. (1934). The nature of the therapeutic action in psychoanalysis. *Int. J. Psycho-Anal.* 15 : 127–160.

Winnicott, D. W. (1954). Mind and its relation to the psyche soma. *Brit. J. Med.* 27 : 243–254.

———. (1955). Metapsychological and clinical aspects of regression within the psycho-analytical set-up. *Int. J. Psycho-Anal.* 36 : 16–27.

12

The Treatment of Characterological Disorders

PETER L. GIOVACCHINI

Opinions about the types of cases that can be psychoanalytically treated are constantly changing and the number is being enlarged. It is interesting to note that the contributors to this volume have chosen to present clinical material that, if diagnostic categorizations were attempted, could be included under the rubric of character disorders, borderline syndromes, and even psychoses. These are all experienced psychoanalysts and some of them were raised in the classic tradition among the original pioneers of psychoanalysis. The fact that the clinical material presented for the discussion of psychoanalytic treatment comes from what we could broadly refer to as sick patients, regardless of diagnostic category, obviously indicates that many analysts believe that these cases need not be abandoned to other treatment modalities.

Since the clinical material I am going to discuss is familiar to most clinicians, perhaps diagnostic considerations are superfluous. Still, for the sake of clarity and precision, although custom may be the more precise term, I will briefly outline some nosologic distinctions.

I have in mind a group of patients who have what we might call character disorders. In contrast to the usual psychoneurotic

236

patient, they do not present distinct symptoms; rather, they complain of general and vague dissatisfactions relating to who and what they are, where they fit in today's world, the purpose of their life, and the meaning of life in general. These are, of course, existential questions and they relate to the patients' identity. These patients may have symptoms, too — anxiety, depression, and paranoid preoccupations — but their primary concern is with difficulties in adapting to the world. Their maladjustment goes beyond social issues because they suffer substantially and feel truly miserable.

The question frequently arises as to how one distinguishes such patients from those diagnosed as borderline or psychotic. Once one understands the character structure and the underlying psychodynamics of this group, the problem is more difficult rather than easier. This is not particularly unusual since there are often differences that manifest themselves on the surface but fade away as epiphenomena when looked at more deeply (microscopically). Still, from a behavioral viewpoint, patients who suffer from characterological problems maintain an operational relationship to reality and, even though it may be constrictive, make an adaptation. They do not often become psychotic in the sense of suffering from florid delusions and hallucinations for protracted periods of time.

I am being purposely tentative because what I am calling character disorders can, at times, develop qualities that are phenomenologically indistinguishable from a psychosis. This happens most often during the course of therapy, but, as a rule, such episodes are transitory, and these patients seem to have considerable resiliency when compared with more traditional psychotic patients. It is equally difficult to distinguish the borderline patient. Unlike the character disorders, one usually thinks of this patient as one who can decompensate to a psychotic state rather readily. His ego state is never far from a schizoid disorganization and his adjustment is believed to be precarious. To repeat, these variations are imprecise and, in my opinion, not particularly useful except for statistical and classificatory purposes. When one wishes to study the therapeutic interaction — the main interest of the clinician — such diagnostic distinctions are of limited value.

Here, I would like to consider once more the question of specific therapeutic approaches that constitute variations of the psychoanalytic method but are not deviations or parameters. I plan to discuss in more detail the points made in Chapter 11 about initial strategy. As was stated, some patients do not want the therapist to interject himself into their associations. They feel his interpretations or comments are intrusions. In some instances these patients are willing to answer questions about their histories or provide other factual information in the interest of clarity, but they become disturbed when the therapist makes a statement about what is going on inside their minds. Other patients who may be more difficult to treat (see Chapter 16) behave in a completely different fashion, demanding that the therapist lead and manage them. Most patients can be placed somewhere between these two extremes, requiring specific therapeutic tactics. I will illustrate several types of psychopathology and various treatment maneuvers.

THE PATIENT AND THE NONINTRUSIVE THERAPIST

An example of a patient who resents any type of interpretative activity was a 35-year-old businessman who believed that he was a chronic failure and felt markedly depressed and generally worthless. He reviled himself for his emotional lability and what he thought were totally unjustified bouts of anger. During the initial interviews he presented, without being asked, a well-organized, complete history. If I asked a question he would gladly answer it in relevant detail. Otherwise, I had the distinct impression that he would resent any comment that I might make about him. He could gratify my curiosity and give me information; however, he seemed to be irritated by even my most casual impressions.

I do not usually make interpretative comments early in the therapeutic relationship, although there are exceptions. This patient signaled to me in many subtle ways not to make any comments. At times I felt tantalized since he brought material that was so easily understood, yet he did not seem to see its significance. I very much wanted to say something, but I rarely gave in to this feeling; when I did, he would frown and otherwise indicate his annoyance. During the initial interviews he ignored my comments, sometimes with forbearance.

As he continued treatment on the couch, he sometimes credited me with having taught him something important about his relationship with some significant figure in his past (for example, his mother); he thought that this type of insight indicated progress and demonstrated my analytic skill. These were essentially non-transference interpretations but, rather curiously, I had not made them. These interpretations were the products of the patient's ruminations that he attributed to me and then praised me for having made.

His reactions were quite different, however, when I made my first *transference* interpretation. I pointed out that he needed to maintain a certain distance between the two of us, which he accomplished by drawing a curtain of intellectualism between us. My comment was not intended as criticism nor did he take it as such. As a matter of fact, I was intrigued by both the form and the content of his associations, and I was just as interested in the specific details of his defense as I was in the underlying anxiety that made him keep us psychically apart. His responses were especially interesting. At first, he was confused. Even though my statement consisted of a simple declarative sentence, he claimed he did not understand what I had said. He asked me to repeat it several times and, since I felt that his response was puzzling and full of anguish, I did. As he painfully and slowly grasped the meaning of my interpretation, he became increasingly sad.

Although the subsequent material more than abundantly indicated that the patient was, indeed, maintaining distance through intellectual control, he felt that he had been completely misunderstood. He resented the idea that I would have anything to say about his feelings and motivations; he felt that no one could know anything about them except himself. He believed that what I said could only be a projection of myself and not a true understanding of him. This, oddly enough, was the way he felt about every transference interpretation I made. Although this patient's reactions struck me as being particularly bizarre, I have since noted other cases who behave in a similar fashion, and sometimes in an even more circumspect fashion. For example, another patient, a professional man, told me during our very first session that he wanted me to remain silent. He did not want me to "intrude" into his thoughts; the time was his alone and I was not to introduce parts of my psyche into it.

Inevitably, the question arises as to how to handle such cases psychoanalytically when the chief therapeutic tool avowedly is the transference interpretation. Must our technique be modified when a patient apparently resents or "forbids" such interpretations? Several factors should be clarified. Although it may not be apparent, these two patients (as well as others I have subsequently seen) had a highly idealized attitude toward me. In some instances this idealization developed quickly during the beginning interviews. In others, they had already formed an idealized concept of me before the first interview. The first patient was referred to me by a former patient, one who praised me "to the heavens," apparently because of an unresolved positive transference. The second patient had read some of my writings and found himself very much drawn to them. Both patients had formed rather exalted pictures long before they actually saw me.

These patients seemed to present a paradox. On the one hand, the therapist is idealized but then whatever he wishes to impart is summarily rejected. In any discussions of therapeutic handling, one must first understand the psychopathology. In these cases, there is a specific type of relationship that has transference significance. Understanding the nature of this relationship should reveal a lot about these patients' specific characterological difficulties, and these insights might indicate the most reasonable therapeutic course.

To understand more, let us return to the clinical material. I found it prudent to take a wait-and-see attitude, and both the patients and I felt more comfortable after I decided to remain silent. The subsequent material emphasizes several themes. First, both patients indicated that I was intruding parts of myself into them. They perceived this as an assault and an attempt to rob them of their precarious autonomy; consequently, they had to keep me "at arms' length." Next, there was an antithetical factor in that they felt very close to me. They were referring to a symbiotic fusion where the boundaries between us did not exist. They saw the relationship as consisting of total unity between patient and therapist.

If I made an observation about our relationship, it indicated that a relationship between *two* people existed. If I commented about situations that were outside of the transference — that did not involve the two of us — it was not threatening. However, any transference interpretations upset the symbiotic unity that seemed to be so vital. Furthermore, the atmosphere of magical omnipotence seemed to be disturbed by a transference interpretation. To remain a diety one must stay concealed; gods do not reveal themselves if they are to preserve their omnipotence. If I said anything I ran the risk of being wrong and of exposing my frailty. My remarks about situations outside the transference did not particularly matter because they could be made within the context of symbiotic unity

and so their validity didn't matter. Within the transference, however, my interpretations were intrinsically wrong.

When a patient laments that I do not understand him, from
his viewpoint, he is correct. By intruding, I do not understand his
need for symbiotic unity; therefore, his idealized view of me is
shaken.

In a witty moment, Dr. Winnicott said that he makes interpretations for two reasons: one is to let the patient know that he is
still alive and the other is to show the patient that he can be wrong.
Perhaps in this pithy statement, Dr. Winnicott was summarizing
the above points. To let the patient know he is alive points to the
fact that the analyst exists, separate and apart from the patient, and
the second reason indicates that he is not divinely infallible. These
formulations remind me of an unusual situation that I hesitate to
call clinical and yet may illustrate to an extreme degree the type of
interactions described.

A colleague referred the husband of one of his patients to me
for psychoanalysis. The wife gave her husband my name and he
promised to call me. About two years later my colleague compli-
mented me on the progress this man had made in his treatment.
His patient would, from time to time, report about her husband's
behavior which, at least descriptively, seemed to be much better
integrated than before; certain phobic symptoms had disappeared.
At times she would describe what happened during one of her husband's sessions, and the general movement seemed to be a gradual
resolution of an idealized transference. In this case, there could be
no question of my intrusion simply because the "patient" never
called me and so I never even saw him! I was astonished at my
colleague's remarks about a *proxy analysis* and an even more
remarkable *proxy transference*.

I do not believe that these patients require a specific approach
or basic alteration of the psychotherapeutic relationship. Once the
analyst becomes aware of the transference and adaptive significance
of the patients' reactions, they needn't hinder analysis. Even though
the aim of analysis is to achieve further ego integration by acquiring insight, these patients can reach self-understanding in a setting
where they do not feel intruded upon. Gradually, the analyst can
augment the patient's self-observations, and eventually the patient
will begin to view the analyst's interpretation as an extension of his
own.

To reach such a state of mutual cooperation requires considerable patience and respect for the patient's autonomy. It can be an especially difficult analytic relationship because the analyst has to "suspend" his analytic operations and seemingly relegate his professional identity to the background. Once he recognizes, however, that his so-called lack of activity is, in itself, an active demonstration of his analytic forbearance — which may eventually help to clarify the patient's symbiotic needs — the analyst can relax and allow the analysis to continue unhampered by any intrusion.

OTHER CHARACTEROLOGICAL TYPES

In contrast to the inactivity demanded by the patients just described, there is another group that requires the analyst's intervention. These patients were described in Chapter 11 as being in need of a panoramic prevision of the therapeutic course. Briefly, they need a unifying, cohesive experience during their first interview; without it, they seem to be unable to become engaged in treatment. The experience usually consists of interpretations of what will later be expanded into the main transference themes. Here I would like to discuss the manifestations of psychopathology that may help to determine our initial therapeutic approach.

Some patients do not want any intrusion; this is quite clear because of their reactions to our comments. Other patients may not resent interpretations and yet do not require an analytic demonstration "in miniature." Both types of patients will indicate, sometimes subtly and sometimes quite openly, that they want the analyst to participate in their psychopathological frames of reference; otherwise they will feel anxious.

A patient often seeks therapy not because he really wants to change; rather, he hopes to have his defenses reinforced in order to feel more comfortable with his psychopathologically determined adaptations. He doesn't want to give up his symptoms; he merely wants them to work better. However, when the therapist creates an analytic observational framework — a platform from which to view the psychic turmoil going on within the patient — instead of supporting the patient's defenses by educative or managerial activities, there is inevitably some tension. If the tension is very intense, analytic treatment may not be possible. The patient will indicate if he can tolerate the analyst's refusal to take sides with one or another aspect of his intrapsychic conflicts.

I believe that the occurrence of panoramic first dreams (see Chapter 11) is a positive indication for analysis without intervention; it signifies a unity and cohesion of the personality. These patients may suffer from severe psychopathology, and there may be defective and primitive functioning (even considerable asynchrony among various ego systems), but there is a relative degree of integration reflected in their behavior and manner of relating. In retrospect, it seems that this group of patients tends to view both situations and feelings in a holistic fashion; they do not deal with certain matters in an isolated way. Even when they are markedly obsessional, they can still place their preoccupations in a larger context. This capacity is not necessarily a sign of psychic health because the larger context may be delusionally constructed.

For example, a young scientist was quite dissatisfied with the way he was being treated at work, especially by his immediate superior. He believed that this man was jealous of his creativity and was doing everything possible to hinder his advancement. There was an obvious paranoid element in this patient's feelings, and it resulted in a florid, paranoid psychosis later on. Although he spent considerable time marshaling evidence to support his view that he was being persecuted by the senior scientist, he did not restrict his associations mainly to this area. He was able to think about his work in relation to the other areas of his life. He hoped to achieve fame from his scientific discoveries, as well as money, prestige, and admiration; then he hoped he would be successful and popular with girls.

His paranoia was not confined to his mentor; he had a rather paranoid attitude about everything but his attitudes were not exclusively paranoid. Although he tended to be generally suspicious and mistrustful, he could also be friendly and cheerful. Sometimes he used his suspiciousness productively: since he didn't trust the motives or reliability of a colleague's reported data, he might repeat the colleague's experiment. He often obtained different results, which then permitted him to carry the formulations further. In retrospect this patient seemed to be able to coordinate the different facets of his life. Perhaps his chief adjustive (characterological) modality was paranoid, but it had many themes and variations. It even had a certain flexibility because it varied according to the situation and was determined by many factors.

This patient's early dreams were panoramic in the sense that they depicted the structure of his personality in a sweeping fashion and were predictive of the course of the transference. His first dream, which took place the night before his initial appointment, was long and involved. He was taking an ocean voyage with a very skillful and highly respected captain. However, somewhere during the voyage the patient found himself in the midst of a storm; he described the ship's precarious balance and indicated that it was in serious danger of sinking. The captain then became the villain because the danger being faced was his responsibility. The captain was not basically irresponsible or careless, but he knew he could save himself and did not particularly care about the patient's welfare. For the rest of the dream, the patient worked with the captain (the period of animosity having passed) and together they weathered the storm.

The dream was not quite this coherent. Some of its meaning was obvious from the patient's associations, and in presenting it here I undoubtedly used some of my secondary process. Nevertheless, there was a remarkable coherence between this dream and most of his others. *I did not feel it was necessary to do anything in particular except allow the transference to develop* (see pages 246–251). As the dream predicted, after an initial idealization, the patient became quite paranoid about me and had to be hospitalized briefly. However, he reintegrated and the analysis continued without any unusual complications.

Other patients may require a different initial approach. For example, one patient — an attractive, single woman in her thirties — was referred to me as a "classic" hysteric with phobic symptoms. She vividly described these symptoms; the main one was agoraphobia and there were numerous lesser phobias. She was afraid of riding in trains, automobiles, airplanes, or other form of public transportation. These fears, however, were overshadowed by her fear of open spaces, which was equated with leaving home. As a consequence, she was virtually confined at home and continued to live with her parents.

In view of her crippling symptoms, it seemed remarkable that she had managed to come to my office. She, herself, complained about the great effort and then said that she could control her anxiety somewhat if her father were with her; he had driven her to the interview. This was the first time she had sought therapy although her symptoms first appeared after she graduated from high school. Because of her anxiety she did not go to college. The only change in her life that seemed to be associated with entering treatment was her father's illness. He had just recovered from a coronary, and it was fairly obvious that the patient was very much afraid of losing him.

The patient, although soft-spoken and demure, seemed to create an air of tension and urgency. At first, she appeared to be able to speak freely and to impart considerable information; her attitude was pleasantly cooperative. Nevertheless, I felt a vague sense of uneasiness and soon recognized that I knew very little about her. The patient went into considerable detail about her numerous phobias and gave an exact description of her house; however, she imparted no feeling about her relationship with her parents, siblings, and other significant persons. In fact, her descriptions of other people, which she never gave spontaneously, were mechanistic and wooden; although initially I believed I was learning something about her interpersonal relationships, later I realized that this was not so.

It seemed that her life consisted of only her phobias and being at home. She did not discuss the vocational, social, or sexual areas of life; I saw that she seemed to be isolated in these respects, but I was reluctant to make any inquiries. I may have been afraid of offending her or of upsetting a delicate balance, although she presented a picture of sophisticated poise. She seemed to have a delicate, porcelain veneer that appeared as if it could easily crack.

Although her symptoms were supposedly characteristic of a high-grade, hysterical neurosis, I came to believe that I was dealing with a fragmented person; I also saw her as a "difficult" patient. This feeling came to me toward the end of the interview. The patient finally reached a point where she had told me all she could and had nothing more to say. I would have preferred to let her continue talking or to remain silent if she chose. However, after she indicated that she had nothing more to say, I had the distinct impression that if I remained silent I would lose her as a patient.

She looked at me with both an imperious expectancy and a pleading helplessness. Her narcissism was manifested by her straight, regal posture. She was immaculately groomed, with not one hair out of place. Still, the picture she presented was incongruous. When she turned her head, her profile impressed me, perhaps because of a hypnagogic distortion of mine, as that of a six-month-old infant. I thought I saw two distinctly separate ego states, indicating a serious fragmentation. She also convinced me that I would have to "do something" if I were sincerely interested in treating her.

This patient never had what could be considered a panoramic dream; they all dealt with circumscribed themes and had very little, if any, action in them. In the first dream she reported, she simply sat in her living room with a strange man; there was no movement or conversation. Later she had dreams in which she was imprisoned in a cave behind an iron grill. Further on in her treatment she dreamed of storms and holocausts, but she was always standing off at a considerable distance.

TECHNICAL CONSIDERATIONS

The phobic patient impressed upon me the need to do something definite, therapeutically speaking. It is sometimes difficult to ascertain why one feels such a need and what exactly is signaled by the patient, but the feeling is unmistakable. With some patients it is possible to sit back, relax, and adopt a wait-and-see attitude, but with others this cannot be done. These two types of patients cannot be distinguished by the severity of their psychopathology. It is clear that the first patient described had many obvious psychotic features, whereas the second one presented an almost classical picture of an hysterical neurosis with phobic symptoms.

From an ego-psychological viewpoint, there were distinct differences between these two patients in the degree and kind of psychic organization. In spite of the predominant primary-process thinking in the first patient, his ego was fundamentally unified. On the other hand, the second patient was markedly fragmented. Her ego used the defense mechanism of splitting to keep various facets of her life separate from each other. The outside world was no longer part of her experience since she confined herself to her parental home, where her father, in particular represented a lifeline.

As treatment later indicated she had split off parts of herself — unacceptable, destructive fragments — and then phobically isolated herself from them. The paranoid scientist also projected parts of himself but he did not separate himself completely from them. He interacted with others actively, which required the maintenance of inner unity. The so-called hysterical patient withdrew from and, to some extent, even denied the outside world, which she equated with the unacceptable within her. Thus, she lived a highly constricted life with only part of her total ego. She sought treatment because the equilibrium of even that part was being threatened by her father's illness and possible death, and if she split off a painful part, this time she would have nothing left, so to speak, for herself.

One is reminded of a situation in organic medicine where a patient may not be able to function efficiently because he is missing a part of himself, perhaps a limb; the problem for that patient is rehabilitation. My phobic patient was missing parts of herself but, unlike a missing limb, they were potentially recoverable.

My patient wanted treatment so that she could continue to live with her constrictions. As her first dream indicated, she wanted to have me simply replace her father without establishing a relationship; the dream was set in her living room, and she and the stranger did not communicate.

These constructions are all retrospective; actually I understood very little during the first crucial interview except: 1. I could not wait for understanding to come, and 2. I was dealing with an ego with many split-off components.

In contrast to the first dream (which was reported at a later session), she felt uneasy with and did not seem to tolerate silence. I definitely felt she wanted me to talk *to her,* which is quite different from communicating with one another. I could feel an immense dependency when she expressed needs that are so primitive (and belong to preverbal developmental stages) that they cannot be articulated. Still she wanted something verbal from me; in this instance words would have concrete, magical powers. Her fragmentation seemed obvious in spite of the fact that such structural characteristics were part of a neurosis that is supposed to represent the highest order of psychosexual integration. Many psychoanalysts have noted the close proximity of a surface hysterical picture and an underlying, often malignant, schizophrenia.

As mentioned above, I did not know how to meet her expectations for silent, magical support. I wondered if such a part-ego could tolerate both a regression inherently stimulated by the psychoanalytic setting and an analyst who would not actively try to provide such elemental support. I knew that this patient would attribute (in fact she had already done so) omnipotent qualities to me, but how would she respond if I maintained an analytic stance and did not try to respond within her frame of reference?

From my theoretical understanding, although minimal, I surmised how a fragmented ego might respond to the psychoanalytic approach. This patient seemed to be able to generate considerable and disruptive anxiety if her needs for magical subsistence were not met. I soon realized that if I could give her what she wanted, she would probably have a fixation, perhaps a delusional one. However, the idea of giving her what she wanted was simply an academic conjecture for me because I would not have known where to begin if I had decided to respond to her at the level she herself presented.

I felt that it was not feasible just not to respond at all except with analytic expectancy. A fragmented ego, per se, does not exclude an analytic approach, but the analytic patient has to learn to see the outside world and his reactions in terms of what is going on within himself. In other words, there has to be some cohesion among the parts of the self and a recognition of the external world toward which he is responding. My phobic patient did not seem to be able to discriminate between different parts of herself and the qualitative and quantitative aspects of her environment. She did not understand how situations are related to one another and how one event determines another; it could be said that she had little concept of dynamic interrelationships.

Psychoanalysis as a procedure seemed to be incomprehensible to her. I now believe that this fairly common phenomenon among patients suffering from characterological problems is the product of the patients' fragmented view; they have no appreciation of deterministically related interactions. Psychoanalytic treatment requires an observational frame of reference where connections between parts of the self and feelings and behavior toward external objects are made. The analytic process has, in a sense, a unity of its own. My patient and many others have no feelings about analysis because they have none of the unity that is inherent in the analytic process. However, it is precisely this type of patient who needs the unity that analysis offers. Although they can only fragment (and this may prevent them from tolerating an analytic approach), they are in dire need of a unifying experience.

I became aware of an impasse in my thinking and had a strong desire to try analysis even though it might be beyond the patient's capacities. I also realized that I wanted to impress her with my wisdom in knowing what was best for her — in this case, analysis. Without being completely aware of what I was doing, I asked the patient why she put herself entirely in my care on such short acquaintance. The patient was not at all astonished to have me speculate about her trust in me; she simply wondered why I felt her trust was naïve and why I questioned her at all. To her it was perfectly natural to see me as a father substitute and she was incapable of questioning her own motivations or the defensive and adaptive functions of such an interaction.

After she replied, there was a period of silence. This time the silence didn't seem to bother her. On the other hand, I felt a need to collect my thoughts, and as I struggled with them, I became uncomfortable. Later that day, I recognized that the patient was displaying total dependence upon me and was making me responsible for her life; I felt uneasy because of the magnitude of that responsibility.

During later sessions I also felt inhibited about making interpretative comments if I had something to say. My reluctance to look for intrapsychic sources of behavior and attitudes became quite intense. I finally concluded that I was responding to her fragmentation and that if I continued doing so, analysis, at least with me, would not be possible. Consequently, I told her that she had an inhibiting effect upon me, which I believed she purposely, although unconsciously, created in order to keep me under control. At the same time I implied that she had to render me powerless because she was afraid I would attack her.

Again, she did not seem to be upset by my observations but was able to relax and speak freely. For the next ten minutes, she was warm and friendly and made many positive statements about me and my office. I had the distinct impression that she was in a state of starry-eyed idealization; I found this oppressive rather than narcissistically enhancing. Although I felt controlled by her idealization, I decided to wait and see what would happen.

The patient began to have periods of silence, and it became obvious that she was visibly struggling with certain feelings or thoughts. I said that maybe she had feelings about me that were difficult to express. I also indicated that I would respect her decision if she chose not to express them. Her affect changed immediately and she became increasingly angry. She confessed that she felt I had suddenly become unsympathetic and was not the least bit interested in either helping or understanding her; she believed that I actively disliked her and would do her harm if I could. Just then I felt much more relaxed and believed that analytic contact had finally been made, if the patient did not, in the meantime, walk out on me. I felt impelled to make an interpretation that would "pull together," that is, unify her fragmented behavior. Therefore, I told her that her reactions were understandable in view of her intense need to see me as a god-like protector, a need that would be disappointed as she became more aware of my limitations. To some extent, she perceived my ineptness as dangerous.

At this time the patient relaxed and seemed pleased; we had reached the end of the session and there was no doubt about further interviews. We both assumed that therapy had begun. In fact, I felt that she was a long-standing patient and that all we needed to do was to set up a schedule. I emphasize this point because initially she had asked many questions and raised objections about treatment hours and how to get to and from my office. She said nothing more about such difficulties and was quite flexible about fitting into my schedule.

The next session seemed to be a continuation of the material she had presented before she became angry; her associations repeatedly referred to her need to both idealize and control me. Although no treatment proceeds with predictable regularity, this woman's treatment went through various phases. For a long time she was extremely dependent and attributed omnipotent powers to me. There was often marked evidence of a symbiotic fusion. After this she displayed increasing anger which finally reached paranoid proportions. She became delusional about me and developed somatic delusions. She believed that a small freckle on her left forearm was a cancerous mole and sought verification from me and other physicians. Her paranoia increased tremendously and she bitterly reviled me. Strangely enough, however, these attacks were usually confined to my office. She talked of quitting treatment but never too seriously. She went only so far as to demand a consultation. In spite of my lack of understanding and competence she asked me to make the referral.

At first, the patient idealized the consultant but, during the course of the consultation, she developed a paranoid distrust. She finally considered him an ally of mine and, therefore, worthless. The consultant's description of their one-hour interview was an exact replica of the three years she had been in treatment with me. (He had had no previous information about my patient.) It was also remarkably similar to what I had experienced with her during our initial interview.

Although she was angry, she was impressed when I spoke of the similarity of her reactions toward me and the consultant and the similar movement in the two first interviews. Recalling our first interview made it easier for her to see that there was a preordained quality to her reactions. From this point on, there was nothing unusual in her treatment. She experienced regressive fluctuations but was consistently able to recognize them, often with considerable affect, as transference manifestations.

GENERAL COMMENTS

Patients who suffer from characterological problems bring into focus both diagnostic factors and technical considerations (see Chapters 5 and 6). My phobic patient illustrates the fact that symptoms alone do not provide an adequate understanding of the more subtle aspects of psychopathology. It is preferable to rely on the patient's reactions toward the therapist as they occur in the here-and-now of the consultation room. My patient presented an interesting sequence of reactions during our first interview that were identical with the later unfolding of the transference. The young scientist, however, reacted in a more conventional fashion. Each patient's reactions and the resultant technical approaches were attributed to certain structural qualities best described in terms their egos. Holistic unity, as compared with ego fragmentation, led to a different course of therapeutic events.

It can be asked whether all patients with fragmented egos will react in the same fashion as the woman described here; one can also examine the criteria for treatability. I can recall other patients whose egos were probably fragmented who reacted differently from this woman. In fact, it has been reported that these patients cannot tolerate an analytic relationship and that they require a modified therapeutic technique in order to derive any support from the relationship.

Patients' reactions are determined by many factors. My phobic patient might have responded quite differently if I had actively probed or tried to be reassuring. *Her reactions seemed to be a response to my nonintrusive approach.* I have also treated other patients with fragmented egos. *Maintaining an analytic attitude (which simply means relating the patient's attitudes and behavior to his feelings toward the analyst and analytic setting) seems to be the instrumental factor that produces a sequence of reactions that indicate the development of the transference. I have repeatedly noted such reactions whenever I was able to respond as I did with the patient discussed here.*

The criteria for treatability cannot be dealt with on an absolute basis. The qualities that make a patient treatable or nontreatable do not reside wholly within the patient. Rather, it is important to look at the reactions and counterreactions; the relationship itself between the patient and therapist may determine whether the patient is treatable. This perspective emphasizes the interpersonal factor. A patient may be nontreatable by one therapist but treatable by another. The responsibility for success or failure, from this viewpoint, resides in their interaction. This does not mean that technical issues and the structure of the patient's personality are not important. Nor does it mean that therapeutic failure is always due to some idiosyncratic countertransference element. Because of specific defenses or ego defects certain patients cannot respond to any approach that is designed to foster self-observation and introspection.

On the other hand, many patients who seem to be analytically inaccessible may respond very well to analysis. Therapists, of course, may abandon the analytic approach for a variety of reasons. *Some patients (and I believe those with fragmented egos can be included in this category) are especially skillful in stimulating the therapist's ambivalence about analysis.*

If a patient's ego is fragmented, the therapist tends to be protective toward him. The therapist senses his helplessness and his relative lack of adaptive techniques to cope with the exigencies of the external world. The patient may create further frustration by not being able to articulate his needs; if he can, the therapist may still not understand what he is seeking. Consequently, the therapist's wish to be protective and helpful while not knowing how, creates an impasse that is of greater urgency than conducting analysis. The therapist may be impressed with the patient's needfulness and, for some reason, believe that it is inconsistent with an analytic approach. Consequently, there is a tendency to want to offer the patient a constructive experience but not an analytic one; it may be experienced intensely as an urge to "do something," which dominates the entire treatment setting.

The primitive fixations of these fragmented patients involve preverbal ego states. The urge to "do something" for them cannot lead to constructive gratification in the sense that it will produce higher states of psychic integration. At best, the patient may achieve a defensive stabilization which may be reflected in greater comfort. However, this is usually a precarious and temporary adjustment.

I have found that once I become aware of my inability to respond to needs that neither the patient nor I understand, the easiest path to follow is that of analysis. I find it is an effective way out of a dilemma since the analytic viewpoint does not require me to become involved at the level of content. Instead, I can view the patient's overt and covert demands in terms of intrapsychic forces and their relationship to the defective functioning of various ego systems. The patient's material is not seen as a problem per se but his productions are viewed in a broader perspective. Using analysis the therapist is not faced with an impossible request; rather, he tries to understand what is happening in terms of psychic determinism. Engaging once again in a familiar frame of reference makes the analyst more comfortable, his comfort is transmitted to the patient; this, in itself, may be instrumental in making the patient analytically accessible.

13

Treatment of Borderline Patients

OTTO F. KERNBERG

THIS IS the third in a series of papers about borderline personality organization. In the first (1966), I suggested that there exist two levels of ego organization resulting from the degree of synthesis of "identification systems." The term "identification systems" was used to include introjections, identifications, and ego identity as a progressive sequence in the process of internalization of object relationships. The organization of identification systems first takes place at a basic level of ego functioning, at which primitive dissociation or "splitting" is the crucial mechanism for the defensive organization of the ego. Later, a second, more advanced level of defensive organization of the ego is reached, at which repression becomes the central mechanism replacing splitting. Splitting can be defined, in this restricted sense, as the active process of keeping apart identification systems of opposite quality.

254

I also suggested that patients with so-called borderline personality disorders present a pathological fixation at the lower level of ego organization, at which splitting and other related defensive mechanisms predominate. The persistence of the lower level of ego organization itself interferes with the normal development and integration of identification systems and, therefore, also with the normal development of the ego and superego.

In the second paper of this series (1967), the term "borderline personality organization" for these conditions rather than "borderline states," or other nomenclature was used because it appears that these patients present a rather specific, quite stable, pathological personality organization rather than transitory states on the road from neurosis to psychosis, or from psychosis to neurosis. The clinical syndromes that reflect such borderline personality organization seem to have in common : 1. typical symptomatic constellations, 2. typical constellations of defensive operations of the ego, 3. typical pathology of internalized object relations, and 4. characteristic instinctual vicissitudes. Under severe stress or under the effect of alcohol or drugs, transient psychotic episodes may develop in these patients; these psychotic episodes usually improve with relatively brief but well-structured treatment approaches. When psychoanalysis is attempted, these patients may develop a particular loss of reality-testing and even delusional ideas restricted to the transference situation — they develop a transference psychosis rather than a transference neurosis.

In the earlier papers the analysis of the structural characteristics of borderline personality organization was emphasized. Structural analysis referred to two issues : 1. ego strength and the characteristic defensive operations of the ego of these patients, and 2. the pathology of their internalized object relationships. In regard to the first issue, in the borderline personality organization there are nonspecific manifestations of ego weakness, represented especially by a lack of anxiety tolerance, a lack of impulse control, and a lack of developed sublimatory channels. In addition, there are specific aspects of ego weakness : particular defenses in these patients bring about distortions in ego functioning which clinically also manifest themselves as ego weakness. The implication of this observation is that the therapeutic undoing of these particular defenses may actually strengthen the ego, rather than create further ego weakness. Splitting, primitive idealization, early forms of projection, and especially projective identification, denial, and omnipotence constitute characteristic defense constellations in patients with borderline personality organization.

In regard to the second issue in the structural analysis of these patients, namely, the pathology of their internalized object relationships, I attempted to trace the origin of that pathology as well as its consequences for ego and superego development, with special stress on the syndrome of identity diffusion (Erikson, 1956).

Finally, I suggested that in borderline patients there is an excessive development of pregenital and, especially, oral aggression which tends to induce premature development of oedipal strivings; as a consequence, there is a particular pathological condensation of pregenital and genital aims under the overriding influence of aggressive needs. It is this constellation of instinctual conflicts which determines the peculiar characteristics of the transference paradigms of the patients that will be discussed below.

In the present paper I shall examine the difficulties of the treatment of these patients and present some general propositions about psychotherapeutic strategy with them. A general outline of these propositions follows.

Many patients with borderline personality organization do not tolerate the regression within a psychoanalytic treatment, not only because of their ego weakness and their proneness to develop transference psychosis, but also, and very predominantly, because the acting out of their instinctual conflicts within the transference gratifies their pathological needs and blocks further analytic progress. What appears on the surface as a process of repetitive "working through" is in reality a quite stable compromise formation centered in acting out of the transference within the therapeutic relationship.

Efforts to treat these patients with supportive psychotherapy frequently fail. Supportive psychotherapy aims at reinforcing the defensive organization of the patient, tries to prevent the emergence of primitive transference paradigms, and tries to build up a working relationship in order to help the patient achieve more adaptive patterns of living. Such an approach prevents regression within the transference; transference psychosis does not develop; and the kind of therapeutic stalemate previously mentioned is avoided. However, a supporting approach frequently fails because the characteristic defenses predominating in these patients interfere with the building up of a working relationship — the "therapeutic alliance" (Sterba, 1934; Zetzel, 1966). The negative transference aspects, especially the extremely severe latent negative transference dispositions, tend to mobilize even further the pathological defenses of these patients. The final outcome of such an approach is often the splitting up of the negative transference, much acting out outside the treatment hours, and emotional shallowness in the therapeutic situation. The "emptiness" of the therapeutic interaction over long periods of time may be a consequence of such a supportive approach, and this emptiness also tends in itself to produce therapeutic stalemates. In this case, instead of the turbulent, repetitive acting out of the transference within the hours, a situation develops in which the therapist attempts to provide support, which the patient seems incapable of integrating.

In most patients with borderline personality organization, a special form of modified analytic procedure or psychoanalytic psychotherapy may be indicated. This psychotherapy differs both from the classical psychoanalytic procedure and from the more usual forms of expressive and supportive psychoanalytically oriented psychotherapies. Following Eissler (1953), this psychotherapeutic procedure can be described as representing the introduction of several "parameters of technique" into the psychoanalytic situation, without expecting them to be fully resolved. The term "modification of technique" seems preferable to "parameter of technique" when a modification is introduced into a treatment situation that corresponds to a psychoanalytic psychotherapy rather than to a classical psychoanalysis (Frosch).

The main characteristics of this proposed modification in the psychoanalytic procedure are: 1. systematic elaboration of the manifest and latent negative transference without attempting to achieve full genetic reconstructions on the basis of it, followed by "deflection" of the manifest negative transference away from the therapeutic interaction through systematic examination of it in the patient's relations with others; 2. confrontation with and interpretation of those pathological defensive operations which characterize borderline patients, as they enter the negative transference; 3. definite structuring of the therapeutic situation with such active measures as are necessary to block the acting out of the transference within the therapy itself (for example, establishing limits under which the treatment is carried out and limiting the nonverbal aggression permitted in the hours); 4. utilization of environmental structuring conditions, such as hospital, day hospital, foster home, etc., if acting out outside of the treatment hours threatens to produce a chronically stable situation of pathological instinctual gratification; 5. selective focusing on all those areas within the transference and the patient's life that illustrate the expression of pathological defensive operations as they induce ego weakening and imply reduced reality testing; 6. utilization of the positive transference manifestations for maintenance of the therapeutic alliance, and only partial confrontation of the patient with those defenses that protect the positive transference; 7. fostering more appropriate expressions in reality for those sexual conflicts that, through the pathological condensation of pregenital aggression and genital needs, interfere with the patient's adaptation; in other terms, "freeing" the potential for more mature genital development from its entanglements with pregenital aggression.

REVIEW OF THE PERTINENT LITERATURE

A general review of the literature on borderline conditions is included in a previous article (Kernberg, 1967). From the point of view of the treatment of borderline conditions, Knight (1953a, 1953b) and Stone (1954) present the most comprehensive overview. The main question raised in the literature is whether these patients can be treated by psychoanalysis or whether they require some form of psychotherapy. Intimately linked with this question is the delimitation of what psychoanalysis is and is not. Thus, for example, Fromm-Reichmann (1950), who has contributed significantly to the treatment of borderline and psychotic patients, implies that the psychoanalytic procedure may be used for such patients, but she extends the concept of what is referred to as psychoanalysis to include what many other authors would definitely consider analytically oriented psychotherapy.

Gill (1951, 1954) has attempted to delimit classical psychoanalysis from analytically orientated psychotherapies, stating that psychoanalysis, in a strict sense, involves consistent adherence by the analyst to a position of neutrality (and neutrality, he rightly states, does not mean mechanical rigidity of behavior with suppression of any spontaneous responses). He believes that psychoanalysis requires the development of a full, regressive transference neurosis and that the transference must be resolved by techniques of interpretation alone. In contrast, Gill adds that analytically oriented psychotherapies imply less strict adherence to neutrality; they imply

recognition of transference phenomena and of transference resistance, but they use varying degrees of interpretation of these
phenomena without permitting the development of a full-fledged
transference neurosis, and they do not imply resolution of the transference on the basis of interpretation alone.

This delimitation is a useful one but exception can be taken
to Gill's (1954) implication that in psychoanalysis the analyst
"actively produces" the regressive transference neurosis. In agreement with Macalpine (1950), Gill (1954) says that "the analytic
situation is specifically designed to enforce a regressive transference
neurosis." However, an analytic situation permits development of
the regressive pull inherent in the emergence of repressed, pathogenic childhood conflicts. Macalpine's description of what she calls
the regressive, infantile setting of the analytic situation seriously
neglects the progressive elements in that situation, such as the
analyst's respect for the patient's material and independence, and
implicit trust and confidence in the patient's capacity to mature
and to develop his own solutions (G. Ticho).

To the return to the main point, Gill's definition is very helpful
in differentiating psychoanalysis proper from psychoanalytically
oriented or exploratory psychotherapies. Eissler (1953) has further
clarified this issue in his discussion of the "parameters of technique,"
which imply modifications of the analytic setting that are usually
necessary for patients with severe ego distortions. He suggests that
the treatment still remains psychoanalysis if such parameters are
introduced only when indispensable, not transgressing any unavoidable minimum, and if they are used only under circumstances
that permit their self-elimination — their resolution through interpretation before termination of the analysis itself. Actually, as Gill
(1954) points out, this involves the possibility of converting a psychotherapy into analysis. Additional clarifications of the differences
between psychoanalysis and other related psychotherapies can be
found in papers by Stone (1951), Bibring (1954), and Wallerstein
and Robbins (1956).

From the viewpoint of Gill's delimitation of psychoanalysis,
it appears that authors dealing with the problem of the treatment
of borderline conditions may be placed on a continuum ranging
from those who recommend psychoanalysis to those who believe
that psychotherapy (especially a supportive form of psychotherapy)
is the treatment of choice. Somewhere in the middle of this continuum are those who believe that certain patients presenting

borderline personality organization may still be analyzed while others would require expressive psychotherapy; and there are some authors who do not sharply differentiate between psychoanalysis and psychotherapy.

The first detailed references in the literature to the therapeutic problems with borderline patients were predominantly on the side of recommending modified psychotherapy with supportive implications, in contrast to classical psychoanalysis. Stern (1938, 1945) recommends an expressive approach, focusing on the transference rather than on historical material, with constant efforts to reduce the clinging, childlike dependency of the patient on the analyst. He feels that these patients need a new and realistic relationship, in contrast to the traumatic ones of their childhood; he believes that such patients can only gradually develop the capacity to establish a transference neurosis similar to that of the usual analytic patient. He concludes that analysis may and should be attempted only at later phases of their treatment. Schmideberg (1947) recommends an approach probably best designated as expressive psychotherapy and believes that these patients cannot be treated by classical analysis. Knight's (1953a, 1953b) important contributions to the psychotherapeutic strategy with borderline cases lean definitely in the direction of a purely supportive approach — at one extreme of the continuum. He stresses the importance of strengthening the ego of these patients and of respecting their neurotic defenses; he considers "deep interpretations" dangerous because of their regressive pull and because the weak ego of these patients makes it difficult for them to keep functioning on a secondary-process level. He stresses the importance of structure, both within the psychotherapeutic setting and in the utilization of the hospital and day hospital, as part of the total treatment program for such patients.

Somewhere toward the middle of the spectrum are the approaches recommended by Stone (1954) and Eissler (1953): Stone feels that borderline patients may need preparatory psychotherapy but that at least some of these patients may be treated with classical psychoanalysis either from the beginning of treatment or after some time to build up a working relationship with the therapist. Stone also agrees with Eissler that analysis can be attempted at later stages of treatment with such patients only if the previous psychotherapy has not created transference distortions of such magnitude that the parameters of technique cannot be resolved through interpretation. Eissler suggested that in some cases it might be necessary to change analysts for the second phase of the treatment. Glover (1955) implies that at least some of these cases are "moderately accessible" to psychoanalysis.

At the other end of the spectrum are a number of analysts influenced to varying degrees by the so-called British school of psychoanalysis (Bion, 1957; Heimann, 1955b; Little, 1951; Rosenfeld, 1958; Segal, 1964; Winnicott, 1949, 1960). These analysts believe that classical psychoanalytic treatment can indeed be attempted with many, if not all, borderline patients. Some of their contributions have been of crucial importance in understanding the defensive organization and the particular resistances of patients with borderline personality organization. Despite my disagreement with their general assumption about the possibility of treating most borderline patients with psychoanalysis, I believe that the findings of these analysts permit modifications of psychoanalytically oriented psychotherapies specifically adapted to the transference complications of borderline patients: I am referring especially to the work of Little (1958, 1960a, 1960b), Winnicott (1949), Heimann (1955b), Rosenfeld (1964), and Segal (1964).

My suggestions for treatment outlined in the present paper would appear in the middle zone of the continuum; I believe that, in most patients presenting borderline personality organization, a modified analytic procedure or special form of expressive psychoanalytic psychotherapy (rather than classical psychoanalysis) is indicated. This expressive approach should include consistent interpretive work with those defensive operations that reflect the negative transference and contribute directly or indirectly to maintaining the patient's ego weakness. There are some patients with borderline personality organization for whom psychoanalysis is definitely indicated, and I shall attempt to identify them.

TRANSFERENCE AND COUNTERTRANSFERENCE CHARACTERISTICS

An important feature of the therapeutic problems with borderline patients is the development of transference psychosis. Several authors have described the characteristics of this transference regression, and a general summary of them can be found in a paper by Wallerstein (1967).

Perhaps the most striking characteristic of the transference manifestations of patients with borderline personality organization is the premature activation in the transference of very early conflict-laden object relationships in the context of ego states that are dissociated from each other. It is as if each of these ego states represents a full-fledged transference paradigm — a highly developed, regressive transference reaction within which a specific internalized object relationship is activated in the transference. This contrasts with the more gradual unfolding of internalized object relationships as regression occurs in the typical neurotic patient. Clinical experience reveals that the higher levels of depersonified and abstracted superego structures are missing to an important extent, and the same is true for many autonomous ego structures — especially neutralized, secondarily autonomous character structures. Thus the premature activation of such regressed ego states represents the pathological persistence of "non-metabolized," internalized object relations of a primitive and conflict-laden kind.

The conflicts that typically emerge in connection with the reactivation of these early internalized object relations may be characterized as a particular pathological condensation of pregenital and genital aims under the overriding influence of pregenital aggression. Excessive pregenital, and especially oral, aggression tends to be projected and determines the paranoid distortion of the early parental images, particularly those of the mother. From a clinical point of view, whether this is a consequence of severe early frustration or actual aggression on the mother's part, whether it reflects excessive constitutional aggressive drive derivatives, or whether it reflects a lack of capacity to neutralize aggression or lack of constitutionally determined anxiety tolerance is not so important as the final result — the paranoid distortion of the early parental images. Through projection of predominantly oral-sadistic and also anal-sadistic impulses, the mother is seen as potentially dangerous, and hatred of the mother becomes a hatred of both parents when they are later experienced as a "united group" by the child. A "contamination" of the father image by aggression primarily projected onto mother and a lack of differentiation between mother and father tend to produce a combined, dangerous father-mother image and a later conceptualization of all sexual relationships as dangerous and infiltrated by aggression. Concurrently, in an effort to escape from oral rage and fears, a "flight" into genital strivings occurs; this flight often miscarries because of the intensity of the pregenital aggression that contaminates the genital striving (Heimann, 1955a).

The transference manifestations of patients with borderline personality organization may at first appear completely chaotic. Gradually, however, repetitive patterns emerge, reflecting primitive self-representations and related object-representations under the influence of the conflicts mentioned above, and appear in the treatment as strongly negative transference paradigms. The defensive operations characteristic of borderline patients (splitting, projective identification, denial, primitive idealization, omnipotence) become the vehicle of the transference resistances.   The fact that these defensive operations have, in themselves, ego-weakening effects (Kernberg, 1966, 1967) is suggested as a crucial factor in the severe regression that soon complicates the premature transference developments.

What is meant by "ego weakness" in borderline patients? To conceive of ego weakness as consisting of a rather frail ego barrier which, when assaulted by id derivatives, is unable to prevent them from "breaking through" or "flooding" the ego, appears insufficient. Hartmann and his colleagues' (1946) and Rapaport's (1957) analyses of the ego as an over-all structure within which sub-structures determine specific functions, and are determined by them, convincingly imply that ego weakness should be conceptualized not simply as the absence or weakness of such structures, but as the replacement of higher-level by lower-level ego structures. One aspect of ego weakness in patients with borderline personality organization is evidenced by the "lower" defensive organization of the ego in which the mechanism of splitting and other related defenses are used, in contrast to the defensive organization of the ego around the "higher" mechanism of repression and other related defenses in neuroses (Kernberg, 1966). Also, the failure of normal integration of the structures derived from internalized object relationships (integrated self-concept, realistic object representations, integration of ideal-self and ideal-object representations into the ego ideal, integration of superego forerunners with more realistic introjections of parental images into the superego, etc.) interferes with the process of identity formation and individualization, and with neutralization and abstraction of both ego and superego functions. All of this is reflected in the reduction of the conflict-free ego sphere, clinically revealed in the presence of "nonspecific" aspects of ego weakness, particularly a lack of anxiety tolerance, a lack of impulse control, and a lack of developed sublimatory channels (Kernberg, 1967).

In addition, and most importantly from the point of view of psychotherapeutic intervention with these patients, "nonspecific" ego weakness is also evident in the relative incapacity of patients with such a pathological ego organization to dissociate their ego tentatively into an experiencing and an observing part and in the related incapacity to establish a therapeutic alliance. The dynamics of borderline personality organization are much more complicated than what is conveyed by the metaphor of "flooding" the ego because of its "weak barriers" since beneath the "weaknesses" can be found extremely strong, rigid, primitive, and pathological ego structures.

Let us now return to the issue of transference regression in such a patient. Once he embarks upon treatment, the crucial decompensating force is his increased effort to defend himself against the emergence of the threatening primitive, especially negative, transference reactions by intensified utilization of the very defensive operations which have contributed to his ego weakness in the first place. One main "culprit" in this regard is probably the mechanism of projective identification, described by Klein (1946) and others (Heimann, 1955; Money-Kyrle, 1956; Rosenfeld, 1963; Segal, 1964). Projective identification is a primitive form of projection, used mainly to externalize aggressive self- and object-images; "empathy" is maintained with the real objects onto which the projection has occurred and is linked with an effort to control the object now feared because of this projection (Kernberg, 1965, 1967).

In the transference this is typically manifested as an intense distrust and fear of the therapist, who is experienced as attacking the patient, while the patient himself feels empathy with that projected, intense aggression and tries to control the therapist in a sadistic, overpowering way. The patient may be partially aware of his own hostility but may feel that he is simply responding to the therapist's aggression and that he is justified in being angry and aggressive. It is as if the patient's life depended on his keeping the therapist under control. The patient's aggressive behavior, at the same time tends to provoke from the therapist counteraggressive feelings and attitudes. It is as if the patient were pushing the aggressive part of his self onto the therapist and as if the counter-transference represented the emergence of this part of the patient from within the therapist (Money-Kyrle, 1956; Racker, 1957).

It has to be stressed that what is projected in a very inefficient and self-defeating way is not "pure aggression," but a self-representation or an object-representation linked with that drive derivative. Primitive self- and primitive object-representations are actually tied together as basic units of primitive object relationships (Kernberg, 1966), and what appears characteristic of borderline patients is that there is a rapid oscillation between moments of projection of a self-representation while the patient remains identified with the corresponding object-representation, and other moments in which it is the object-representation that is projected while the patient identifies with the corresponding self-representation. For example, a primitive, sadistic mother image may be projected onto the therapist while the patient experiences himself as the frightened, attacked, panic-stricken little child ; moments later, the patient may experience himself as the stern, prohibitive, moralistic (and extremely sadistic) primitive mother image, while the therapist is seen as the guilty, defensive, frightened, but rebellious little child. This situation is also an example of "complementary identification" (Racker, 1957).

The danger in this situation is that under the influence of the expression of intense aggression by the patient, the reality aspect of the transference-countertransference situation may be such that it comes dangerously close to reconstituting the originally projected interaction between internalized self- and object-images. Under these circumstances, vicious circles may be created in which the patient projects his aggression onto the therapist and reintrojects a severely distorted image of the therapist under the influence of the projected aggressive drive derivatives, thus perpetuating the pathological early object relationship. Heimann (1955b) illustrated these vicious circles of projective identification and distorted re-introjection of the therapist in discussing paranoid defenses. Strachey (1934) referred to the general issue of normal and pathological introjection of the analyst as an essential aspect of the effect of interpretation, especially in regard to modifying the superego. This brings us to the problem of the influence of "mutative interpretations" (Strachey) on the establishment and maintenance of the therapeutic alliance.

It was mentioned above that one aspect of ego weakness in patients with borderline personality organization is the relative absence of an observing ego. We may now add that this factor is compounded by the patient's distortion of the therapist which results from excessive projective operations because of the negative transference. Establishing a therapeutic alliance is equated with submitting to the therapist, a dangerous, powerful enemy, and this further reduces the capacity for activating the observing ego.

A repeated observation from the Psychotherapy Research Project at The Menninger Foundation about the psychotherapy of borderline patients is that a high price was paid when the therapist tried to avoid the latent negative transference and attempted to build a therapeutic relationship with the patient while denying the negative transference. Frequently, under these conditions, there was an emotionally shallow therapeutic relationship and a pseudo-submission by the patient to what he experienced as the therapist's demands. Serious acting out or even interruption of the treatment followed periods in which the therapist thought that the patient was "building up an identification" with him, or "introjecting his value systems," while the patient remained emotionally detached. The implication is that a consistent undoing of the manifest and latent negative transference is an important, probably indispensable, prerequisite for broadening the observing ego and solidifying a therapeutic alliance.

The gradual boadening of the conflict-free ego sphere together with a broadening of the observing ego throughout therapy facilitates the disruption of the vicious circle of projection and reintrojection of sadistic self- and object-images in the transference. Strachey (1934), in his description of mutative interpretations, identifies two phases of such interpretations: the first phase consists of a qualitative modification of the patient's superego; and the second consists of the patient's expressing his impulses more freely so that the analyst can call attention to the discrepancy between the patient's view of him as an archaic fantasy object and as a real external object. Strachey implies that, as his superego prohibitions decrease, the patient permits himself to express his aggression in a freer way; then he can become aware of the excessive, inappropriate nature of his aggressiveness toward the external object and be able to acquire insight into the origin of his reaction; therefore, the need to project such aggression once again onto the analyst gradually decreases. I would add that, both in the phase of superego modification and in the phase of differentiation between the patient's fantasied object and the analyst as a different object, an observing ego is needed. Thus, the observing ego and interpretation of projective-introjective cycles mutually reinforce each other.

This discussion of projective identification leads to the issue of how the intensity of projection and reintrojection of aggressive drive derivatives in the transference interferes with the observing functions of the ego and how this interference in itself contributes to the transference regression. Yet, the most important way in which projective identification contributes to the transference regression is through the rapid oscillation of projecting self- and object-images; this rapid oscillation undermines the stability of the patient's ego boundaries in his interactions with the therapist.

In earlier papers (1966, 1967) I commented on the differentiation between self- and object-representations that are part of early introjections and identifications. I stressed the organizing function of this differentiation of ego boundaries. In the psychosis, such differentiation between self- and object-images does not take place sufficiently; therefore, ego boundaries are largely missing. In contrast, in patients presenting borderline personality organization, this differentiation has taken place sufficiently so that their ego boundaries are more stable. The borderline patient is capable of distinguishing between the self and external objects, internal experience and external perception, and his reality testing is largely preserved. This capacity of the borderline patient is lost within the transference regression.

A rapidly alternating projection of self-images and object-images representing early pathological, internalized object relationships produces a confusion between what is "inside" and what is "outside" in the patient's interactions with the therapist. It is as if the patient maintained a sense of being different from the therapist at all times, but concurrently he and the therapist were interchanging their personalities. This is a frightening experience which reflects a breakdown of ego boundaries in that interaction; consequently, there is a loss of reality testing in the transference. This loss of reality testing in the transference significantly interferes with the patient's capacity to distinguish between fantasy and reality, between past and present in the transference, and between his projected transference objects and the therapist as a real person. Under such circumstances, it is not likely that a mutative interpretation will be effective. Clinically, the patient may experience something like : "Yes, you are right in thinking that I see you as I saw my mother, and that is because she and you are really identical." At this point what has been referred to above as a transference psychosis is reached.

Thus, the therapist and the transference object become identical, there is a loss of reality testing as reflected in the development of delusions, and hallucinations may complicate the transference reaction. The therapist may be identified with a parental image: one patient felt that the therapist had become her father and would rape her. At other times the therapist may be identified with a projected, dissociated self-representation: one patient became convinced that his analyst had carried on an affair with the patient's mother, and he threatened to kill him.

"Transference psychosis" is a term which should be reserved for the loss of reality testing and the appearance of delusional material within the transference that does not noticeably affect the patient's functioning outside the treatment setting. Some patients have a psychotic decompensation during treatment which is for all purposes indistinguishable from any other psychotic breakdown; it affects their life outside as well as in the therapeutic situation. It may be that regression in the transference contributed to the breakdown, but it is questionable whether the term "transference psychosis" is always warranted under these conditions. In contrast, patients with a typical transference psychosis may develop delusional ideas and what amounts to psychotic behavior within the treatment sessions, over a period of weeks or months, without showing these manifestations outside. On occasion, hospitalization may be necessary for such patients. Sometimes it is quite difficult to separate a transference-limited psychotic reaction from a broader one; nevertheless, in many borderline patients this delimitation is quite easy, and it is often possible to resolve the transference psychosis within the psychotherapy (Holzman and Ekstein, 1959; Little, 1958; Reider, 1957; Romm, 1957; Wallerstein, 1967). Control of transference acting out within the therapeutic relationship is of central importance.

Transference acting out within the therapeutic relationship refers to the acting out of the transference reaction during the sessions, within the treatment setting itself. As part of a transference regression, any patient may act toward the therapist rather than reflect on his feelings about him. For example, instead of verbally expressing strong feelings of anger and reflecting on the implications and sources of this anger, a patient may yell at the therapist, insult him, and express his emotions in direct actions (not verbally) over a period of weeks or months. This, of course, is not done exclusively by borderline patients, but in the typical analytic treatment of neurotic patients, such acting out during the session only occurs at points of severe regression — after many months of build-up — and can usually be resolved by interpretation alone. This is not so in the case of patients with borderline personality organization, and the therapist's efforts to deal with acting out within the therapeutic relationship by interpretation alone — especially when it is linked with a transference psychosis — frequently appears to fail. Part of this is due to loss of the observing ego by virtue of the projective-introjective cycles and part of it is due to loss of ego boundaries and the reality testing that goes with it. To a large extent, however, such unrelenting transference acting out is highly resistant to interpretation because it also gratifies these patients' instinctual needs, especially those linked with the characteristic severe, pre-oedipal aggressive drive derivatives. *This gratification of instinctual needs represents the major transference resistance;* two clinical examples will illustrate this point.

A hospitalized borderline patient literally yelled at her hospital physician during their early half-hour interviews, and her voice could be heard in all the offices of the building. After approximately two weeks of such behavior, which the hospital physician felt unable to change by any psychotherapeutic means, he saw her by chance shortly after leaving his office. Although he was still virtually trembling, he was struck by the fact that the patient seemed to be completely relaxed and smiled in a friendly way while talking to some other patients with whom she was acquainted. Before entering the hospital, the patient had engaged in bitter fights with her parents for many years. In the hospital, all her fighting centred on the physician, while the hospital staff was surprised by her relaxed manner with other personnel. Gradually it became clear that her angry outbursts at her physician reflected a gratification of her aggressive needs far beyond any available to her before she entered the hospital and that this gratification was functioning as the major transference resistance. When this was conveyed to her, and the physician limited the amount of yelling and insulting he would permit during the interviews, the patient's anxiety increased noticeably outside the sessions, her conflictual patterns became more apparent within the hospital, and shifting attitudes in the transference became apparent, indicating movement in the therapy.

Another patient who was seen in expressive psychotherapy demanded a larger number of sessions in an extremely angry, defiant way. Over a period of time it was interpreted to him that it was hard for him to tolerate his guilty feelings about his own greediness and that he was projecting that guilt onto the therapist in the form of fantasies of being hated and depreciated by him. It was also interpreted that his demands to see the therapist more often represented an effort to reassure himself of the therapist's love and interest in order to neutralize his distrust and suspiciousness of the therapist's fantasied hatred of him. The patient seemed to understand all this but was unable to change his behavior. The therapist concluded that the patient's oral aggression was being gratified in a direct way through these angry outbursts and that this development might contribute to a fixation of the transference. The therapist told the patient of his decision not to increase the number of sessions and also said that, as a condition for continuing the treatment, he would have to exercise some control over how and when he expressed his feelings during the sessions. With this modification of technique in effect, there was a noticeable change in the patient over the following few days. The patient became more reflective and finally could admit that he had obtained considerable satisfaction in being allowed to express intense anger at the therapist in such a direct way.

The acting out of the transference within the therapeutic relationship is the main resistance to further change in these patients, and parameters of technique required to control the acting out should be introduced in the treatment situation. There is a danger of the therapist entering the patient's vicious circle of projection and reintrojection of sadistic self- and object-images as he introduces parameters of technique. He may appear to the patient as prohibitive and sadistic. This danger can be counteracted if the therapist begins by interpreting the transference situation, then introduces structuring parameters of techniques as needed, and finally interprets the transference situation without abandoning the parameters. Some aspects of this technique were illustrated in a different context by Sharpe (1931), who demonstrated how to deal with acute episodes of anxiety.

In many cases, the consistent blocking of the transference acting out within the therapeutic relationship is sufficient in itself to reduce and delimit the transference psychosis to such an extent that further interpretive work may be able to dissolve it. The very fact that the therapist takes a firm stand and creates a structure within the therapeutic situation that he will not abandon tends to help the patient differentiate himself from the therapist and thus undo the confusion caused by his own frequent "exchange" of self- and object-representation projections. Also, such a structure may effectively prevent the therapist from acting out his countertransference, especially the very damaging chronic countertransference reactions that tend to develop in intensive psychotherapy with borderline patients (Sutherland).

Chronic countertransference fixations are to an important degree a consequence of the patient's success in destroying the analyst's stable and mature ego identity in their relationship (Kernberg, 1965). In order to keep in emotional contact with the patient, an analyst who works with patients who present borderline personality organization has to be able to tolerate a regression within himself, which on occasion may reactivate remnants of early, conflict-laden relationships in himself. Aggressive impulses tend to emerge in the analyst, which he has to control and utilize in gaining a better understanding of the patient. The extra effort needed for his work with countertransference and the very tolerance and neutrality toward the patient which is part of the analyst's effort to keep in emotional touch with him increase the stress within the therapist. At the same time, the aggressive behavior of patients with severe transference regression continuously undermines the analyst's self-esteem and self-concept in their interaction and thus also the integrating ego function of the analyst's ego identity. Therefore, the analyst may be struggling at the same time with an upsurge of primitive impulses in himself, with an urge to control the patient as part of his efforts to control these impulses, and with the temptation to submit in a masochistic way to the patient's active efforts to control (Money-Kyrle, 1956). Under these circumstances, pathological, previously abandoned defensive operations, especially neurotic character traits of the analyst, may become reactivated, and the patient's and the analyst's personality structures may appear as if they were "pre-matched" to each other, interlocked in a stable, insoluble transference-countertransference bind. *The establishment and maintenance of structuring parameters or modifications of technique are thus a fundamental, protective technical requirement and must often be maintained throughout a large part of the psychotherapy with borderline patients.*

The indications for hospitalization in order to provide this structure when it cannot otherwise be provided is beyond the scope of this paper. I would only stress that for many patients hospitalization is indispensable for creating and maintaining an environmental structure which effectively controls transference acting out.

Does the transference psychosis also represent the reproduction of unconscious, pathogenic object relationships of the past and thus provide further information about the patient's conflicts? Sometimes it appears difficult to find evidence in the patient's past of interactions with the parental figures that were characterized by the violence and primitiveness of the transference reaction at the level of a regressive transference psychosis. At other times, the transference indeed appears to reflect actual, very traumatic experiences that these patients underwent in their infancy and early childhood (Frosch; Holzman and Ekstein, 1959). It is probable that the transference in all of these patients originates, to a large extent, in the fantasy distortions which accompanied the early pathogenic object relationships, as well as in the relationships themselves, and in the pathological defensive operations mobilized by the small child to extricate himself from threatening interpersonal relationships. The transference psychosis represents a condensation of actual experiences — a gross elaboration of them in fantasy — and efforts to modify or turn away from them (Klein, 1952). This brings us to the technical problems of dealing with the pathological defensive operations characteristic of borderline patients that were mentioned above. Interpretive work attempting to undo these pathological operations as they enter the transference may help to resolve the transference psychosis and to increase ego strength.

Because the acting out of the transference within the therapeutic relationship itself appears to be such a meaningful reproduction of past conflicts, fantasies, defensive operations, and internalized object relationships of the patients, one is tempted to interpret the repetitive acting out as evidence of a working through of these conflicts. The repetition compulsion expressed through transference acting out cannot be considered working through so long as the transference relationship provides these patients with instinctual gratification of their pathological, especially their aggressive, needs. Some of these patients obtain much more gratification of their pathological, instinctual needs in the transference than would ever be possible in extratherapeutic interactions. The patient's acting out at the regressed level overruns the therapist's effort to maintain a climate of "abstinence." At the other extreme, to maintain such a rigid and controlled treatment structure so that the transference development is blocked altogether, especially so that the negative transference remains hidden, also appears to induce a stalemate of the therapeutic process, which is as negative in its effect as an unchecked transference acting out. A "purely supportive" relationship, calculated to avoid focusing on the transference, often brings about a chronically shallow therapeutic relationship, an acting out outside the treatment setting that is rigidly split off from the transference itself, a pseudosubmission to the therapist, and a lack of change despite years of treatment. There are patients who, in spite of all efforts, cannot tolerate transference regression nor the establishment of any meaningful relationship without breaking it off; nevertheless, the overall psychotherapeutic chances are much better when attempts are made to undo emotional shallowness and bring about a real emotional involvement in the therapy. The price is high and the danger of excessive transference regression is unavoidable, but with a careful and consistent structuring of the therapeutic relationship it should be possible in most cases to prevent the development of insoluble transference-countertransference binds.

How much of a "real person" does the therapist need to appear to be in the patient's eyes? Several authors have stressed the importance of the therapist appearing as a "real person," permitting the patient to use him as an object for identification and superego introjection. Gill (1954) has stated that "we have failed to carry over into our psychotherapy enough of the non-directive spirit of our analysis." If "real person" refers to the therapist's direct and open interventions, his provision of structure and limits, and his active refusal to be forced into regressive countertransference fixations, then the therapist would indeed be a real person. However, if "real person" means that the regressive transference reactions of borderline patients — their inordinate demands for love, attention, protection, and gifts — should be responded to by "giving" beyond what an objective, professional psychotherapist-patient relationship would warrant, objection must be made to the therapist being such a "real person." The so-called excessive dependency needs of these patients actually reflect their incapacity to depend upon anyone because of their severe distrust and hatred of themselves and of their past internalized object images that are reactivated in the transference. The working through of the negative transference, the confrontation of the patients with their distrust and hatred, as well as with the ways in which that distrust and hatred destroy their capacity to depend on what the psychotherapist can realistically provide better fulfill their needs. Clinical experience has repeatedly demonstrated that the intervention of the psychotherapist as a particular individual, opening his own life, values, interests, and emotions to the patient is of very little, if any, help.

The supposition that the patient may be able to identify himself with the therapist while severe, latent, negative transference dispositions are in the way, or are being acted out outside the treatment setting, appears highly questionable. The development of an observing ego appears to depend not on the therapist's offering himself as an unconditional friend, but, as a consequence of focusing on the pathological cycles of projective and introjective processes, on transference distortion and acting out, as well as on the observing part of the ego itself. In this connection, what Ekstein and Wallerstein (1956) have observed in regard to borderline children, holds true for adults also :

> This maintenance of the therapeutic relationship, often made possible by interpreting within the regression, thus lays the foundation for the new development of identificatory processes rather than the superimposition of an imitative façade. . . .

A systematic focus on and analysis of the manifest and latent negative transference are essential to undo the vicious cycle of projection and reintrojection of pathological, early self- and object-representations under the influence of aggressive drive derivatives. This systematic analysis, together with the blocking of transference acting out and a direct focusing on the observing function of the ego, represents a basic condition for change and growth in therapy. In addition, the interpretation of the negative transference should stop at the level of the "here and now" and should only partially be referred back to its genetic origins, to the original unconscious conflicts of the past. At the same time, the ventilation and interpretation of the negative transference should be completed by a systematic examination and analysis of the manifestations of these negative transference aspects in all areas of the patient's interpersonal interactions.

The rationale for this suggestion is that the regressive nature of the transference reaction makes it hard enough for the patient to differentiate between the therapist as a real person and the projected transference objects, and that genetic reconstructions, by opening up more regressive channels, may further reduce the reality-testing of the patient. This does not mean that the patient's past should not be drawn into the transference interpretation when that past is a conscious memory for him rather than a genetic reconstruction and when it reflects realistic aspects of his past and preconscious fantasy distortions of it. Sometimes referring to an experience from the past that relates to what the patient erroneously perceives in the therapist now may actually help him separate reality from transference. The secondary "deflection" of the negative transference by incorporating its interpretation into the broader area of the patient's interactions outside the treatment and his conscious past tends to foster his reality-testing and provide considerable support within an essentially expressive psychotherapeutic approach.

The question of "insight" in borderline patients should be discussed. Unfortunately, one frequently finds that what at first looks like insight into "deep" layers of the mind and into the unconscious dynamics of some borderline patients is actually an expression of the ready availability of primary-process functioning as part of the general regression of ego structures. Insight that comes without any effort, without being accompanied by a change in the patient's intrapsychic equilibrium, and, above all, without being accompanied by any concern of the patient for the pathological aspects of his behavior or experience is questionable "insight." Findings from the Psychotherapy Research Project at The Menninger Foundation indicate that the concept of insight, especially when applying it to the description of borderline patients, should be restricted. "Authentic" insight is a combination of the intellectual and emotional understanding of the deeper sources of one's psychic experience, accompanied by a concern for and an urge to change the pathological aspects of that experience.

The differentiation between "positive" and "negative" transference requires further scrutiny. To classify a transference as positive or negative is certainly a rather crude oversimplification. Transference is usually ambivalent and has multiple aspects within which it is often hard to say what is positive and what is negative, what is libidinally derived and what is aggressively derived. Patients with borderline personality organization often tend to dissociate the positive from the negative aspects of the transference and to produce an apparent "pure" positive or "pure" negative transference. It is important to undo this artificial separation, which is another example of the mechanism of splitting in these cases. It would be misleading to understand an emphasis on the consistent working through of the negative transference as implying a neglect of the positive aspects of the transference reactions. On the contrary, emphasizing the positive as well as the negative transference is essential in order to decrease the patient's distorted self- and object-images under the influence of aggressive drive derivatives and to reduce his fears of his own "absolute" badness. The positive aspects of the transference have to be highlighted, therefore, while ventilating the negative aspects. It is important to deal with the here-and-now of the positive as well as the negative aspects of the transference of borderline patients, without interpreting the genetic implications of their aggressive and libidinal drives (G. Ticho). At the same time, much of the positive transference disposition available to the patient may be left in its moderate, controlled expression as a further basis for development of a therapeutic alliance and for the ultimate growth of the observing ego (Schlesinger, 1966).

PSYCHOTHERAPEUTIC APPROACHES TO THE SPECIFIC DEFENSIVE OPERATIONS

I referred in earlier papers (1966, 1967) to the mechanism of splitting and others (primitive idealization, projective identification, denial, omnipotence), all of which characterize borderline patients. Here I will only state how these defensive operations appear from a clinical point of view and suggest some overall psychotherapeutic approaches for dealing with them.

Splitting

It should be stressed again that the term "splitting" is being used here in a restricted, limited sense to refer only to the process of active separation of introjections and identifications of opposite quality; this use of the term should be differentiated from its broader use by other authors. Manifestations of splitting can be illustrated with a clinical example.

The patient was a single woman in her late thirties, hospitalized because of alcoholism and drug addiction. She appeared to make remarkably steady progress in the hospital after an initial period of rebelliousness. She began psychotherapy several months before being discharged from the hospital and then continued in outpatient psychotherapy. In contrast to her previously disorganized life and work, she seemed to adjust well to work and social relations outside the hospital, but she established several relationships, each of a few months' duration, with men who appeared to exploit her and with whom she adopted quite masochistic attitudes. The therapeutic relationship was shallow; the patient was conventionally friendly. A general feeling of "emptiness" appeared to hide a strong suspiciousness, which she emphatically denied and only later admitted to her former hospital doctor, but not to her psychotherapist. After several months of complete abstinence, she got drunk, became quite depressed, had suicidal thoughts, and returned to the hospital. At no point did she let the therapist know what was going on, and he only learned about this development after she was back in the hospital. When she was released again, she denied all transference implications and indeed all emotional implications of the alcoholic episode. It must be emphasized that she could remember having strong emotions of anger and depression when she had been intoxicated, but she no longer felt connected with that part of herself and repeatedly said that this was simply not her and didn't see how such an episode could ever happen again.

This marked the beginning of a long effort by the therapist, over a period of several months, to bring the usual "empty," "friendly," detached attitude of the patient together with her emotional upheaval during the alcoholic crisis, and especially with her efforts to hide that crisis from him. After two more similar episodes, separated from each other by periods of apparently more adaptive behavior and good functioning over several months, it finally became evident that she was experiencing the therapist as the cold, distant, hostile father who had refused to rescue her from an even more rejecting, aggressive mother. At one point, the patient told the therapist with deep emotion how on one occasion in her childhood she had been abandoned in her home, suffering from what later turned out to be a severe and dangerous illness, by her mother who did not wish her own active social life to be interfered with. The patient felt that if she really told the psychotherapist-father how much she needed him and loved him, she would destroy him with the intensity of her anger over having been frustrated so much for so long. She solved this by trying to keep what she felt was the best possible relationship (detached friendliness) with the therapist, while splitting off her search for love, her submission to sadistic, father representatives in her masochistic submission to unloving men, and her protest against her father in alcoholic episodes during which her rage and depression were completely dissociated emotionally from both the therapist and her boyfriends.

Efforts to bring all this material into the transference greatly increased the patient's anxiety; she became more distrustful and angry with the psychotherapist, her drinking reverted to the old pattern of chaotic involvements with men that were associated with excessive intake of alcohol, and all efforts to deal with this acting out through psychotherapeutic means alone failed. It was decided to rehospitalize her. It should be stressed that from a superficial point of view the patient appeared to have done quite well earlier in the psychotherapy but now appeared to be much worse. Nevertheless, the psychotherapist felt that for the first time he was dealing with a "real" person. He hoped that psychotherapy combined with hospitalization for as long as necessary might help the patient to finally overcome the stable, basic transference paradigm outlined above.

This case illustrates the predominance of splitting, its defensive function against the emergence of a rather primitive, largely negative transference, and the consequent shallowness and artificiality of the therapeutic interaction. A therapeutic alliance could not be established with this patient before the mechanism of splitting had been sufficiently overcome. Only the consistent interpretation of the patient's active participation in maintaining herself "compartmentalized" finally changed the stable, pathological equilibrium. Consistent efforts had to be made to bridge the independently expressed, conflicting ego states, and the secondary defenses protecting this dissociation had to be sought out and ventilated in treatment. With these patients it is not a matter of searching for unconscious, repressed material, but of bridging and integrating what appears on the surface to be two or more emotionally independent, but alternately active, ego states.

Primitive idealization

Primitive idealization (Kernberg, 1967) manifests itself in therapy as an extremely unrealistic, archaic form of idealization. Its main function appears to be protection of the therapist from the patient's projection onto him of the negative transference disposition. There is a projection onto the therapist of a primitive, "all good," self- and object-representation, with a concomitant effort to prevent this "good" image from being contaminated by the patient's "bad" self- and object-representations.

One patient felt that he was extremely lucky to have a psychotherapist who represented, according to the patient, the best synthesis of the "intellectual superiority" of the country where the therapist was born and the "emotional freedom" of another country where the therapist had lived for many years. On the surface, the patient appeared to be reassured by a clinging relationship with such an "ideal" therapist; he felt protected against what he experienced as a cold, rejecting, hostile environment by a magical union with the therapist. It soon developed that the patient felt that only by a strenuous, ongoing effort of self-deception (and deception of the therapist about himself) could he keep his good relationship with the therapist. If the therapist really knew how the patient felt about himself, the therapist would never be able to accept him and would hate and depreciate him. This, by the way, illustrates the damaging effects of overidealization; it makes it impossible for the therapist to be utilized as a good superego introjection, in contrast to an overidealized, demanding one. It later turned out that the patient developed his idealization as a defense against devaluating and depreciating the therapist, whom he saw as an empty, pompous, and hypocritically conventional parental image.

It is hard to convey in a few words the unrealistic quality of the idealization these patients give the therapist; it makes the transference quite different from the less regressive idealization of the usual neurotic patient. This peculiar form of idealization has been described as an important defense in narcissistic personality structures (Kohut, 1966; Rosenfeld, 1964). Psychotherapists who themselves have strong narcissistic traits in their character structure may at times be easily drawn into a kind of magical, mutual admiration with a patient; they may learn through bitter disappointment how this defensive operation can effectively undermine the establishment of any realistic therapeutic alliance. To firmly undo the idealization, to confront the patient again and again with the unrealistic aspects of his transference distortion, while still acknowledging the positive feelings that are also part of this idealization, is a very difficult task because underneath that idealization there may be paranoid fears and quite direct, primitive, aggressive feelings toward the transference object.

Early forms of projection, especially projective identification

Projective identification is central in the manifestations of the transference of patients who present borderline personality organization. Heimann (1955b) and Rosenfeld (1963) describe how this defensive operation manifests itself clinically.

One patient, who had already interrupted psychotherapy with two therapists in the middle of massive, almost delusional, projections of her hostility, was finally able to settle down with a third therapist, but managed to keep him in a position of almost total immobility for many months. The therapist had to be extremely careful even in asking questions; the patient would indicate by simply raising her eyebrow that a question was unwelcome and that she wanted the therapist to change the subject. The patient felt that she had the right to be completely secretive and uncommunicative about most issues of her life. She used the therapy situation on the surface as a kind of magical ritual and, apparently on a deeper level, as an acting out of her needs to exert sadistic control over a transference object onto which she had projected her aggression.

The acting out within the therapy sessions of this patient's need to exert total, sadistic control over her transference object could not be modified. The therapist thought that any attempts to put limits on her acting out or to confront her with the implications of her behavior would only result in angry outbursts and interruption of the treatment.

This raises the question of how to cope with patients who begin psychotherapy with this kind of acting out and attempt to distort the therapeutic situation to such an extent that either their unrealistic demands are met by the therapist or the continuation of treatment is threatened. Some therapists believe that it may be an advantage to permit the patient to begin therapy without challenging his unrealistic demands, hoping that later on, as the therapeutic relationship is more established, the patient's acting out can gradually be brought under control. From the vantage point of a long-term observation of cases of this kind, it seems preferable not to attempt psychotherapy under unrealistic conditions. If the therapist fears that an attempt to control premature acting out would interrupt the psychotherapy, he should consider the possibility of hospitalization and discuss this with the patient. One indication for hospitalization is to protect the beginning psychotherapeutic relationship with a patient in whom regressive transference acting out cannot be handled by psychotherapeutic means alone, and where confronting the patient with his pathological defensive operations may induce excessive regression. Hospitalization under these circumstances may serve diagnostic as well as protective functions; it should be considered for patients who, even without psychotherapy, would probably be able to continue functioning outside a hospital. If psychotherapy is indicated, but if it is unrealistically limited by premature acting out, hospitalization, even though stressful for the patient, is preferable to psychotherapy where the necessary structuring is interfered with by the same pathology for which structuring is indicated.

Projective identification is mainly responsible for creating unrealistic patient-therapist relationships from the beginning of treatment. The direct consequences of the patient's hostile onslaught in the transference, his unrelenting efforts to push the therapist into a position in which he finally reacts with counteraggression, and the patient's sadistic efforts to control the therapist can produce a paralyzing effect on the therapy. It has already been suggested that these developments require a firm structure within the therapeutic setting, consistent blocking of the transference acting out, and, in simple terms, protection of the therapist from chronic and insoluble situations. To combine a firm structure with consistent clarifications and interpretations aimed at reducing projective mechanisms is an arduous task.

Denial

In the patients we are considering, denial may manifest itself as simple disregard for a sector of the patient's subjective experience or a sector of his external world. When pressed, the patient can acknowledge his awareness of the part that has been denied, but he cannot integrate it with the rest of his emotional experience. It is relatively easy to diagnose the operation of denial because of the glaring loss of reality testing that it produces. The patient acts as if he were completely unaware of a quite urgent, pressing aspect of his reality.

One patient, who had to meet a deadline for a thesis upon which his graduation and a possible job depended, simply avoided mentioning his thesis in the psychotherapy sessions during the last two weeks before the deadline. He had discussed with his psychotherapist his fear of and anger toward the members of the committee who would examine his paper; his denial primarily served the purpose of protecting him against his paranoid fears of being discriminated against and those teachers whom he supposed wished to humiliate him in public. The therapist repeatedly confronted the patient with his lack of concern about finishing the paper and with his lack of effort to do so. While interpreting the unconscious implications of this neglect, the therapist explored and confronted the patient with the many ways in which he was actually preventing himself from completing the paper in reality.

Denial can take quite complex forms in the transference, such as the defensive denial of reality aspects of the therapeutic situation in order to gratify transference needs.

One patient, in an attempt to overcome her anger about the analyst's unwillingness to respond to her seductive efforts, developed fantasies about the analyst's hidden intentions to seduce her as soon as she expressed her wishes for sexual intimacy with him in a submissive, defenceless way. At one point this fantasy changed to one in which she was actually enjoying being raped by her father and by the analyst; once she developed intense anxiety with a strong conviction that the analyst was actually her father and that he would sadistically rape her, bringing about disaster. Of several implications of this transference development, the need to deny the reality of the analyst's lack of response to her sexual overtures and her anger about this seemed to predominate. The analyst pointed out to her that one part of her knew very well that the analyst was not her father, that he was not going to rape her, and that, although these fantasies were frightening they still permitted her to deny her anger at the analyst for not responding to her sexual demands. All oedipal implications were excluded, for the time being, from his comment. The patient relaxed almost immediately and then the analyst commented on her reluctance to enter into an intimate relationship with her fiancé because of the fear that her unrealistic, angry demands on him would stand in the way of her sexual enjoyment and because of the fear that projecting her own anger onto her fiancé would turn the actual intimacy into a sadistic rape for her. This revelation opened the road to further insight about her denial of aggressive impulses as well as of reality.

This last example illustrates what the consistent working through of the pathological defenses that predominate in borderline patients attempts to accomplish. It helps to increase reality testing and brings about ego strengthening and does not induce further regression. This example also illustrates the partial nature of the transference interpretation and the deflection of the transference outside the therapeutic relationship.

At times the patient especially needs to deny the positive

aspects of the transference because of his fear that expressing positive feelings will bring him dangerously close to the therapist. He fears that such excessive closeness will free his aggression in the transference as well as the (projected) aggression of the therapist toward him. In illustrating this particular use of denial Schlesinger (1966), has suggested that in the area of positive transference reaction, denial should be respected because it may actually permit the patient to keep himself at an optimal distance from the therapist.

Omnipotence and devaluation

These two, intimately linked defensive operations — omnipotence and devaluation — refer to the patient's identification with an overidealized self- and object-representation, with the primitive form of ego-ideal, as a protection against threatening needs and involvement with others. Such "self-idealization" usually implies magical fantasies of omnipotence; the conviction that he, the patient, will eventually receive all the gratification that he is entitled to; and that he cannot be touched by frustrations, illness, death, or the passage of time. A corollary of this fantasy is the patient's devaluation of other people, his conviction that he is superior to them, including the therapist. Other forms of this defensive operation include the patient's projection of his magical omnipotence onto the therapist, and his feeling magically united with or submissive to that omnipotent therapist.

This defensive operation is actually related to the primitive idealization mentioned above. Fractionating the defensive operations that characterize borderline patients into completely separate forms may clarify their functioning, but it oversimplifies the issue. There are complex intertwinings of all these defensive operations, and they present themselves in various combinations.

A patient with severe obesity and feelings of intense insecurity in social interactions eventually became aware of her deep conviction that she had the right to eat whatever she wanted and to expect that, whatever her external form, she would still be admired, pampered, and loved. She paid only lip service to the acknowledgement that her obesity might reduce her attractiveness to men, and she became very angry with the therapist when he stressed the reality of this consideration. The patient began psychotherapy with the assumption that she could come for her appointment at any time, take home the magazines from his waiting room, and could leave cigarette ashes all over the furniture. When the implication of all this behavior was first pointed out to her, she smiled approvingly at the therapist's "perceptiveness," but there was no change. Only after the therapist made it very clear that there were definite limits to what he would tolerate, did she become quite angry, expressing more openly her derogatory thoughts about him that complemented her own feelings of greatness. This patient's conscious experience was that of social insecurity and feelings of inferiority. Her underlying feelings of omnipotence remained unconscious for a long time.

INSTINCTUAL VICISSITUDES AND PSYCHOTHERAPEUTIC STRATEGY

A predominant characteristic of the instinctual development of patients with borderline personality organization is their excessive development of pregenital drives, especially oral aggression, and of a particular pathological condensation of pregenital and genital aims under the influence of aggressive needs. This instinctual development has direct relevance for the therapeutic approach to these patients. The therapist should remember that in the midst of the destructive and self-destructive instinctual manifestations are hidden potentials for growth and development; what appears on the surface to be destructive and self-destructive sexual behavior may contain the roots of further libidinal development and deepening interpersonal relationships.

There was a time when a typical misunderstanding of the implications of psychoanalytic theory and practice was the assumption that sexual activity in itself was therapeutic. We have advanced a long way from such misunderstandings and have learned that often what appears on the surface to be genital activity is actually serving aggressive, pregenital aims. With patients presenting borderline personality organization, there is the opposite danger of seeing only their pregenital, destructive aims and of neglecting their efforts to overcome their inhibited sexual orientation.

A promiscuous, divorced, young woman, hospitalized after a psychotic regression following years of disorganized behavior, was secluded from male patients in the hospital. On several occasions a few minutes of unobserved time had been enough for her to have intercourse in an impulsive way with other patients, practically strangers. During many months this patient was regularly controlled, and in the sessions with her hospital doctor, the implications of her behavior were discussed only in terms of her "lack of impulse control" and her "inappropriate behavior." When a new hospital doctor tried to evaluate further the implications of her sexual behavior, it turned out that her sexual activity had deep, masochistic implications and represented the acting out of her fantasy of being a prostitute. The hospital doctor took the position that not all sexual freedom implied prostitution; in discussing these issues, the patient became very angry with the doctor stating that he was "immoral," and she became very anxious and very angry with him when he eliminated the restrictions. Then she became sexually involved with several other patients in a provocative manner, all of which the hospital doctor used to confront her with the masochistic fantasies and the pattern of becoming a prostitute, implying that she was submitting to a primitive, sadistic superego that represented a prohibitive, combined father-mother image. Eventually the patient was able to establish a good relationship with one patient, with whom she fell in love, went steady for a two-year period, and whom she planned to marry. During the latter part of these two years they had sexual intercourse and for the first time in her life the patient was able to have tender as well as sexual feelings toward just one man and to take precautions not to get pregnant, which she had been unable to do before.

To dissociate the normal, progressive trends within pathological sexual behavior from its pregenital aims is easier said than done. This must be a continuous concern of the psychotherapist working with such patients.

FURTHER COMMENTS ON THE MODALITY OF TREATMENT

This particular form of expressive, psychoanalytically oriented psychotherapy differs from classical psychoanalysis in that a complete transference neurosis is not permitted to develop, nor is transference resolved through interpretation alone. It is an expressive psychotherapeutic approach in that unconscious factors are considered and focused upon, especially the negative transference and the pathological defenses of these patients. Parameters of technique or modifications of technique are used when necessary to control transference acting out, and, although some of these parameters may be resolved during the course of the treatment itself, this is not necessarily possible nor desirable with all of them. There are also clearly supportive elements implicit in this approach, first, in manipulating the treatment situation, which the therapist has to undertake as part of the need to structure it. The frequency of the hours, the permissiveness or restriction regarding out-of-hour contacts, the limits to which the patient may express himself are examples of factors that may be changed as the treatment demands. Second, clarifications of reality take up an important segment of the therapist's communications, and direct suggestions and implicit advice-giving are difficult to avoid under these circumstances.

The therapist should try to remain as neutral as possible, but neutrality does not mean inactivity; beyond a certain degree of activity, the issue of whether the therapist is neutral or not becomes academic. In general, it appears preferable to keep this kind of therapy on a face-to-face basis in order to stress the reality aspects of it, but there is nothing intrinsically magical in either lying on the couch or sitting in front of the therapist. Some treatments carried out on the couch are in effect psychoanalytic psychotherapy rather than psychoanalysis.

The goal of ego strengthening is ever present in this expressive, psychoanalytically oriented treatment. The working through of the pathological defenses of the borderline personality organization permits repression and other related defenses of a higher level of ego organization to replace the ego-weakening, pathological defenses of the lower level: this in itself strengthens the ego. Conflict resolution is necessarily partial, but sometimes a great deal can be achieved with this kind of treatment approach.

One final and very important question remains. Are some of these patients analyzable, either from the beginning of the treatment or after a period of preparatory psychotherapy of the type suggested? Differences of opinion on this question were discussed above in the review of the literature. There are specific patients within the large group presenting borderline personality organization who appear to benefit very little from the expressive, psychoanalytically oriented treatment approach I propose and for whom nonmodified psychoanalysis is the treatment of choice from the beginning. This is particularly true for patients presenting the most typical forms of narcissistic personality organization.

Such patients show an unusual degree of self-reference in their interactions with other people, a great need to be loved (and especially admired) by others, and an apparent contradiction between a very inflated concept of themselves and an inordinate need for tributes from others. Superficially, these patients do not appear to be severely regressed and some of them may function very well socially; they usually have much better impulse control than the average patient presenting borderline personality organization. They may be quite successful and efficient. It is only their emotional life which, on sharper focus, appears to be shallow and reflects an absence of normal empathy for others; a relative absence of enjoyment of life except for the tributes they receive; and a combination of grandiose fantasies, envy, and a tendency to depreciate and manipulate others in an exploitative way.

These patients usually have such solidified, functioning, pathological character structures that it is very difficult to mobilize their conflicts in the transference using the therapeutic approach proposed in this paper. Many of these patients appear to tolerate classical psychoanalysis without undue regression. Some of them, unfortunately, not only tolerate the analytic situation but are extremely resistant to any effort to mobilize their rigid characterological defenses in the transference. Ernst Ticho (1966) has suggested that there is one group of indications for psychoanalysis that may be called "heroic indications." They are for patients in whom, although it seems more or less doubtful whether psychoanalysis would help, it seems reasonably certain that any other treatment would not help. Narcissistic personalities are part of this group. Other authors also feel that psychoanalysis is the treatment of choice for these patients, and they have contributed decisively to our understanding of the dynamics of these patients and the technical difficulties in their analyses (Kohut, 1966; Rosenfeld, 1964). During the diagnostic examination of every patient presenting a borderline personality organization, the question of analyzability should be considered and psychoanalysis rejected only after all the contraindications have been carefully evaluated.

This paper attempts to outline a general psychotherapeutic strategy with patients presenting borderline personality organization. The danger of such an outline is that it may be misinterpreted as a set of fixed rules, or that, because of its necessarily comprehensive nature, it may appear too general. It is hoped that this outline may contribute to the overall frame of reference for therapists who are working with these patients and who are, therefore, well acquainted with the complex, tactical, therapeutic issues that each patient presents.

REFERENCES

Bibring, E. (1954). Psychoanalysis and the dynamic psychotherapies. *J. Amer. Psychoanal. Assoc.* 2.

Bion, W. R. (1957). Differentiation of the psychotic from the non-psychotic personalities. *Int. J. Psycho-Anal.* 38.

Eissler, K. R. (1953). The effect of the structure of the ego on psycho-analytic technique. *J. Amer. Psychoanal. Assoc.* 1.

Ekstein, R., and Wallerstein, J. (1956). Observations on the psycho-therapy of borderline and psychotic children. *Psychoanal. Study Child* 11.

Erikson, E. H. (1956). The problem of ego identity. *J. Amer. Psychoanal. Assoc.* 4.

Fromm-Reichmann, F. (1950). *Principles of intensive psychotherapy.* Chicago : University of Chicago Press.

Frosch, J. Personal communication.

Gill, M. M. (1951). Ego psychology and psychotherapy. *Psychoanal. Quart.* 20.

———. (1954). Psychoanalysis and exploratory psychotherapy. *J. Amer. Psychoanal. Assoc.* 2.

Glover, E. (1955). The analyst's case list (2). In *The technique of psycho-analysis.* London : Ballière, Tindall & Cox; New York : International Universities Press.

Hartmann, H.; Kris, E.; and Loewenstein, R. M. (1946). Comments on the formation of psychic structure. *Psychoanal. Study Child* 2.

Heimann, P. (1955a). A contribution to the reevaluation of the Oedipus complex : the early stages. In *New directions in psycho-analysis,* edited by M. Klein et al. London : Tavistock Publications; New York : Basic Books.

———. (1955b). A combination of defence mechanisms in paranoid states. In *New directions in psycho-analysis,* edited by M. Klein et al. London : Tavistock Publications; New York : Basic Books.

Holzman, P. S., and Ekstein, R. (1959). Repetition-functions of tran-sitory regressive thinking. *Psychoanal. Quart.* 28.

Kernberg, O. (1965). Notes on countertransference. *J. Amer. Psychoanal. Assoc.* 13.

————. (1966). Structural derivatives of object relationships. *Int. J. Psycho-Anal.* 47.

————. (1967). Borderline personality organization. *J. Amer. Psychoanal. Assoc.* 15.

Klein, M. (1946). Notes on some schizoid mechanisms. In *Developments in psycho-analysis,* edited by J. Riviere. London : Hogarth Press, 1952.

————. (1952). The origins of transference. *Int. J. Psycho-Anal.* 33.

Knight, R. P. (1953a). Borderline states. In *Psychoanalytic psychiatry and psychology,* edited by R. P. Knight and C. R. Friedman. New York : International Universities Press, 1954.

————. (1953b). Management and psychotherapy of the borderline schizophrenic patient. In *Psychoanalytic psychiatry and psychology,* edited by R. P. Knight and C. R. Friedman. New York : International Universities Press, 1954.

Kohut, H. (1966). Transference and countertransference in the analysis of narcissistic personalities. Paper presented at the Second Pan-American Congress for Psychoanalysis, Buenos Aires, Argentina, August.

Little, M. (1951). Countertransference and the patient's response to it. *Int. J. Psycho-Anal.* 32.

————. (1958). On delusional transference (transference psychosis). *Int. J. Psycho-Anal.* 39.

————. (1960a). Countertransference. *Brit. J. Med. Psychol.* 33.

————. (1960b). On basic unity. *Int. J. Psycho-Anal.* 41.

MacAlpine, I. (1950). The development of the transference. *Psychoanal. Quart.* 19.

Money-Kyrle, R. E. (1956). Normal countertransference and some of its deviations. *Int. J. Psycho-Anal.* 37.

Racker, H. (1957). The meanings and uses of countertransference. *Psychoanal. Quart.* 26.

Rapaport, D. (1957). Cognitive structures. In *Contemporary approaches to cognition,* by J. S. Bruner et al. Cambridge : Harvard University Press, 1957.

Reider, N. (1957). Transference psychosis. *J. Hillside Hosp.* 6.

Romm, M. E. (1957). Transient psychotic episodes during psychoanalysis. *J. Amer. Psychoanal. Assoc.* 39.

Rosenfeld, H. (1958). Contribution to the discussion on "Variations in classical technique." *Int. J. Psycho-Anal.* 39.

————. (1963). Notes on the psychopathology and psychoanalytic treatment of schizophrenia. In *Psychotherapy of schizophrenic and manic-depressive states,* edited by H. Azima and B. Glueck, Jr. Washington : American Psychiatric Association.

————. (1964). On the psychopathology of narcissism : a clinical approach. *Int. J. Psycho-Anal.* 45

Schlesinger, H. (1966). In defense of denial. Paper presented at meeting of the Topeka Psychoanalytic Society, June.

Schmideberg, M. (1947). The treatment of psychopaths and borderline patients. *Amer. J. Psychother.* 1.

Segal, H. (1964). *Introduction to the work of Melanie Klein.* London : Heinemann; New York : Basic Books.

Sharpe, E. F. (1931). Anxiety, outbreak and resolution. In *Collected papers on psycho-analysis,* edited by M. Brierly. New York : Humanities Press, 1969.

Sterba, R. (1934). The fate of the ego in analytic therapy. *Int. J. Psycho-Anal.* 15.

Stern, A. (1938). Psychoanalytic investigation of and therapy in the borderline group of neuroses. *Psychoanal. Quart.* 7.

———. (1945). Psychoanalytic therapy in the borderline neuroses. *Psychoanal. Quart.* 14.

Stone (1951). Psychoanalysis and brief psychotherapy. *Psychoanal. Quart.* 20.

———. (1954). The widening scope of indications for psychoanalysis. *J. Amer. Psychoanal. Assoc.* 2.

Strachey, J. (1934). The nature of the therapeutic action of psycho-analysis. *Int. J. Psycho-Anal.* 15.

Sutherland, J. D. Personal communication.

Ticho, E. (1966). Selection of patients for psychoanalysis or psychotherapy. Paper presented at the Twentieth Anniversary Meeting of the Menninger School of Psychiatry Alumni Association, Topeka, Kansas, May.

Ticho, G. Personal communication.

Wallerstein, R. S., and Robbins, L. L. (1965). The psychotherapy research project of The Menninger Foundation : IV. Concepts. *Bull. Menninger Clin.* 20.

Wallerstein, R. S. (1967). Reconstruction and mastery in the transference psychosis. *J. Amer. Psychoanal. Assoc.* 15.

Winnicott, D. W. (1949). Hate in the countertransference. *Int. J. Psycho-Anal.* 30.

———. (1960). Countertransference. *Brit. J. Med. Psychol.* 33.

Zetzel, E. R. (1966). The analytic situation. In *Psychoanalysis in the Americas,* edited by R. Litman. New York : International Universities Press, 1966.

14

Interpretation and Definition of the Analytic Setting

PETER L. GIOVACCHINI

INTERPRETATIONS AIMED at overcoming resistance are believed to be the essence of psychoanalytic technique. The setting in which insights are communicated to the patient is one where regression and transference projections predominate. Within this framework, interactions between the patient and analyst can be scrutinized in detail. Working with patients who suffer from severe psychopathology makes such an examination mandatory, and certain technical concepts we take for granted may be seen in a different perspective.

For example, the *goal* of undoing resistances, one that most analysts accept unquestioningly, may not be as feasible as Freud had initially thought. The concept of resistance as something to be "overcome" creates an atmosphere, a moral tone, that is antithetical to the analysis of many patients, especially those suffering from severe psychopathology. True, looking at the personality in terms of layers and strata of opposing forces that should be dealt with from the surface downward is a useful and orderly approach. Analysis of resistance, however, is not the same as overcoming resistance, and what may seem to be only a trivial distinction can, in fact, be that which distinguishes analysis from an exhortative struggle to make the patient give up something in the interest of analysis. The latter is really a managerial intrusion, which does not help the patient acquire insight nor foster autonomy.

Freud made rules about such things as patient decision-making, free association (the fundamental rule), and abstinence. Such rules were believed to be necessary in order to make the patient recall events rather than translate his feelings into behavior that would dissipate tension which might otherwise be amenable for analysis. No matter how well motivated the therapist may be, I have found that such rules are, to some degree, always felt as an intrusion by the patient; they signify to him a need to dominate his life and suppress whatever residual autonomy he might have. True, there are always a few intrusions — paying the fee, using the couch, even coming to the analyst's office — but the rules of abstinence (including the withholding of secrets from the analyst) constitute an added burden on the patient's symptomatic adjustment; the few intrusions mentioned are usually related to the needs of the analyst and are not, as a rule, a significant aspect of the patient's adjustive modalities. By "forbidding" certain behavior, no matter how analytically rational it may seem to be, the analyst is trying to do away with something that, in itself, demands analytic scrutiny. I have found that a number of British analysts sympathize with this viewpoint, and some of them even approve of the recommendation that we delete the word *"resistance"* from our technical vocabulary because of the opprobrium that is now attached to it, even though Freud used the word in a more benign sense and did not view resistance in moral tones.

Restrictions, in general, are difficult to impose. Even though patients want to cooperate and seem to comply with the doctor's instructions, they still behave, by and large, as their inner needs dictate. More often than not, both the analyst and the patient deceive themselves when they believe that they have agreed upon the conditions necessary to establish an "analytic contract." The very word *"contract"* seems inappropriate to me when an analyst is discussing a relationship that is designed to achieve states of higher ego integration in the patient and to release his autonomous potential.

Student therapists usually find it difficult to impose any kind of restrictions upon their patients, or, if they do, they grossly caricature an analytic stance. The student therapist's behavior is mechanistic and robot-like, and soon it is readily apparent to the patient that he is following some prescribed technique. When supervising residents, especially beginners, I have often heard them admit that they feel foolish and presumptuous in authoritatively telling another person, sometimes of comparable education and often older, how to live his life. The resident's practice of forcing himself to do something that he finds uncomfortable, or of caricaturing without integration, cannot be therapeutically successful.

Beginning therapists also may find it difficult to tell another person how to live his life or set conditions in the analysis because of certain social and cultural factors. First of all, it is difficult to impose rules when the patient population frequently changes. Also our culture differs in many respects from Freud's. Although the matter of sociocultural differences is beyond the scope of this chapter and the competence of this author, some of these are obvious. For example, freedom, although a vague concept, is cherished today far beyond anything known in Freud's mid-Victorian milieu. In the Western world of the nineteenth century and up to World War I, dependence upon the family, even to the extreme of obliterating individuality, was part of the social structure. Today, the emphasis is on autonomy and "liberation" from the values of the "establishment." Many adolescents even insist on the right to make their own mistakes rather than accept the values of their elders unconditionally. The rule of abstinence — telling a patient what is best for him, even analytically — is fundamentally at variance with the ideals of the younger generation, and even older patients have developed somewhat similar values.

The traditional approach has often precluded consideration of such social factors. It has also precluded the treatment of a wider group of patients, such as those suffering from characterological disorders and schizophrenia. Since many analysts adhere to a rigid diagnostic distinction of what is treatable and what is not (and consequently consider some psychic states as "good" for analysis and others "bad"), they obviously do not accept patients with a traditionally untreatable disorder. Some analysts, however, will modify their treatment in view of their belief that the more standard analytical approach is contraindicated. This usually means that they do more than merely interpret transference projections; for example, they may give advice, try to educate the patient, and set up conditions for his conduct at the beginning of treatment.

Other analysts (for example, Greenson, 1967) believe that the optimal conditions for analysis will come about once there is a good "working alliance." This expression is somewhat similar to Zetzel's (1956) "therapeutic alliance," although she points out that hers does not emphasize activity and purposeful work as much as Greenson's. In any case, Greenson believes that the positive feelings that a patient develops towards his analyst motivate him to look at and work on his problems. He feels that an alliance based on confidence and trust in the therapist is preferable to one where the patient tacitly follows the analyst's edicts.

In a working alliance there is only a minimum of transference in the patient's reactions, that is, the bulk of the alliance is based upon rational, realistic factors and not upon primitive, unconscious, infantile feelings. Technically, a negative transference should not develop until a working alliance has been firmly established, and such an alliance is an indispensable condition for analysis.

Concepts such as working alliance and therapeutic alliance are enjoying widespread acceptance today. Because psychoanalysts are commonly using these terms, one may assume that they are saying something significant about how psychoanalysis occurs. Words evoke images, and the concept of an alliance between a patient and his analyst has an inherent appeal. To me, this concept is much more attractive than that of contract. But does the combination of this particular adjective and noun actually introduce a new idea? Is such a combination part of the modern analytic theme, that is, does it have technical implications about how and what to treat? For example, does it implicitly advise the psychoanalyst to tone down the initial development of negative transference and warn that such alliances do not (or are less apt to) develop in cases described by Freud as narcissistic neuroses?

Both Sterba (1934) and Strachey (1934) developed concepts about ego functions and introjects in the analytic process. Sterba wrote of the ego's self-observing function and said that such a function was a prerequisite for analysis. Strachey emphasized that gradual changes occur in the introjects after a "mutative" interpretation has been made; these changes, in turn, facilitate the assimilation of further insight, and thus there is a positive feedback. Psychopathology, on the other hand, is characterized by a vicious circle — a cycle of projections and introjections. Since interpretation focuses on the distortion created by the transference projection, it interrupts the process of re-introjecting an ever increasing number of primitive, disruptive, and, of course, constrictive elements.

Both authors explore the therapeutic process in a detailed fashion, especially in terms of ego subsystems.

Strachey's formulations would not, of necessity, lead clinicians to reject patients who suffer from characterological defects for analysis. It is also conceivable that negative transference could be utilized at the very beginning of treatment. Still, the idea that the patient must have some positive feelings toward the therapist in order to be able to start treatment is valid. The analytic setting has to engender some feeling of comfort and trust, and the analyst's relaxed attitude can help to bring this about. If the patient felt nothing but hatred for the analyst at the outset, and even if he could recognize that this was an irrational response, it is not likely that he would remain in treatment. Something else has to be present — something positive — which can coexist with an intensely negative transference so that it can be analyzed.

Many therapists, past and present, have written about this positive factor. The majority cannot describe it precisely, but they agree that this element affects the analyst's ability to create an appropriate setting — one in which the patient will not feel overwhelmed by anxiety. The analyst can communicate security and calmness as well as his effort to understand the patient's psychic processes; his aim is to foster a setting in which both regression and insight can occur. Gitelson (1962) said that the analyst feels less anxious and depressed than the patient, and Spitz (1956) spoke of the diatrophic attitude; such factors must be recognized as part of the working alliance.

All descriptions of what the analyst does to engage a patient in treatment remain vague. This may be due to the fact that there are many variables and that each analyst has a different, but perhaps equally effective, style. On the other hand, if one tries to explain the analytic process in terms of ego concepts (as did Sterba and Strachey), there may be some common conceptual denominators that have diverse manifestations at the behavioral level.

I have often heard analysts speak of patients being "in analysis." This presumably occurs either after a trial period or after certain resistances have been overcome. What happens prior to being in analysis is considered undesirable and antianalytic and something that should be dispensed with as quickly as possible. I believe, however, that a patient is in analysis from the first moment he enters the office. Actually, the concept of being in analysis is, in my opinion, antianalytic. If the therapist views the patient analytically from the beginning and does not convey to him the idea that he has to "achieve" a particular point of view in order to be in analysis, the atmosphere is likely to be relaxed and the patient has more of an opportunity to become interested in what is going on inside himself. I also believe that the theoretical foundation of this type of interaction can be elaborated by focusing on those exchanges between the therapist and patient that are the essence of psychoanalytic treatment.

Although interpretation of the transference is believed to be the chief mode of communication in analysis, there is disagreement about what aspects of the transference should be interpreted, and when. It is not even clear whether the content of the interpretation is particularly important. Many analysts who adhere to the classical position may permit themselves other forms of communication, but they believe that only the transference interpretation is analytically relevant.

I believe there is considerable merit in the classical position and have usually found that my difficulties in treating patients occurred when I abandoned the interpretative approach. However, from time to time, I have found myself saying something to a patient that did not seem to be a transference interpretation, and yet I had the conviction that I was analytically "correct" and the patient's subsequent behavior seemed to bear out that conviction.

Dr. D. W. Winnicott illustrates this point splendidly. One of his patients became inspired after accomplishing something that previously, because of inner constrictions, had been beyond his capabilities. He then chided his analyst by asking him why he was not equally excited. Dr. Winnicott replied that although he was not *as* excited, he had not despaired as much either. Later, he added that he was, indeed, excited but not elated; presumably he was referring to the patient's hypomania (this clinical material is described more fully in Chapter 23 (page 455).

On the surface, this interchange does not seem to be a transference interpretation. Dr. Winnicott is responding to the content and apparently not exploring the patient's motivations for wanting him to be excited nor their transference implications. Still, I (and others with whom I discussed this interchange) had the firm conviction that Dr. Winnicott responded to his patient in a "correct" analytic fashion. In fact, some of my colleagues (who did not know my purpose in presenting the material to them) never even suggested that there was anything unusual about this interchange.

The patient's subsequent behavior in the consultation room also indicated that the flow of the analysis had not been disturbed at all; in fact, it seemed to have been enhanced.

In the interchange Dr. Winnicott was telling his patient that he was capable of reacting and having feelings about what the patient did in his daily life; on the other hand, he spelled out the limits of his reactions — indicating the boundaries and stressing his control. He did not become either as excited or as desperate as the patient; he was only moderately excited, not elated or hypomanic. In essence, Dr. Winnicott's reactions retained considerable secondary process and were not enmeshed with the patient's psychopathological extension of his feelings. In effect, Dr. Winnicott explained that he saw himself reacting as a reasonable human being who has emphatic feelings toward his patient and who is pleased by his patient's progress and further ego integration. In this way, Dr. Winnicott was, in a subtle fashion, also defining the realistic limits of his patient's reactions and indicating the quality and extent of his own counterreactions. He was, in fact, defining the *analytic setting*.

I have learned that patients suffering from characterological problems (a group that Freud felt was unsuitable for analysis) require definitions of the analytic setting at various stages of their analyses. The content of the definition varies, depending upon the dominant material and affect, but the definition always tries to clarify the same element. The analyst emphasizes his function, indicating that he reacts to the patient's feelings as intrapsychic phenomena that are interesting and worthy of understanding. He specifies that he is not reacting to the content per se; rather, his frame of reference is primarily an observational one in which he does not feel elated or despairing or, in other instances, seduced or threatened by what he observes. His purpose is to understand both the intrapsychic sources and the depth and significance of the patient's productions. This is equivalent to maintaining an *analytic* attitude; by defining the *analytic setting* he is conveying this attitude to the patient.

Defining the setting is often a useful "intervention" when the patient feels threatened by uncontrollable regression. It is understandable that the analyst will do what he can to make the analysis less painful, for if it should become too disruptive, it could no longer continue. Many therapists have explained how they handle such situations; they frequently write about clinical situations similar to the one presented here by Dr. Winnicott. As mentioned earlier, the content of the interaction will vary but the communication received by the patient will indicate how much protective stability there is in the analytic setting. Dr. Winnicott makes this point explicit when he speaks of the reliability of the analytic hour and says that the analytic setting also defines the limits of regression.

I believe it is also useful to define the analytic setting when the patient is not particularly disturbed. (This procedure need not be limited to patients suffering from disruptive psychopathology or to moments of decompensation.) There are specific indications for this technical maneuver regardless of the category of patient or phase of treatment. Defining the analytic setting often facilitates analysis, even if the patient responds with silence or "resistance." The transference aspects of the patient's feelings can become clearer, and he may find himself capable of understanding their significance. Since defining the analytic setting is another technical factor (in addition to transference interpretation) that seems to be necessary for analyses, it appears that we are dealing with two closely related but nevertheless *distinct* factors. Defining (and thereby creating) an analytic setting could be considered supportive. Because the patient receives reassurance, he is better able to investigate the transference further. Moreover, defining the setting could lead to the formation of a working alliance.

Here is another example of how the analyst's attitude and orientation help create a setting that may be conducive to analysis. When the analyst conveys to the patient what he expects the "ambience" to be, he is explicitly indicating that he will behave in a specific fashion; no matter how much the patient may wish to introduce another level of interaction, he will not succeed. The analyst will confine himself to psychological realities, thereby enabling the patient to see his productions in terms of their intrapsychic origins. The supportive and reassuring aspects of the definition help to make integration of the transference interpretations possible.

Furthermore, distinctions between support, definition of the analytic setting, and interpretation, I believe, are to a large extent metapsychologically inconsistent. I hope to demonstrate that *the definition of the analytic setting is itself a variety of transference interpretation*. If this is true, there is no distinction between this kind of support and analysis, and it would no longer be necessary to separate the working alliance from the activity of analysis. I realize that such a separation has never been made, but these points can be pursued further and help us to better understand the therapeutic process in general.

If an analyst says that he will not respond in the same way as the patient, either the analyst or the patient is reacting idiosyncratically. Analysis always assumes that in certain respects the analyst is more integrated than the patient. The patient accepts this assumption; otherwise he would not seek analysis with that particular analyst. Dr. Winnicott said that he would not let his feelings develop beyond a certain point. The fact that his patient's feelings went beyond that point was unique to that patient and an outcome of his psychopathology. His expectation that Dr. Winnicott would feel as he did represented a *transference expectation.* In this case the patient projected his feelings and expectations onto the analyst. This constituted a projection of infantile responses; even though the patient continued to attribute such feelings to himself as well, the portion that he projected was transference. By keeping his observational frame of reference separate from the patient's, an analyst thereby indicates that his reactions are different and that some of the analysand's reactions are due to transference expectations. When an analyst tells a patient that many of his feelings are the result of transference, he is taking a step in making a transference interpretation. Dr. Winnicott, in replying to his patient, was correcting the transference distortion, thus emphasizing that the patient's reactions were idiosyncratic, or at least different from his own. This "difference" can become a subject for further investigation. Dr. Winnicott was not simply telling his patient that he was not his father or mother (a type of confrontation that I have seldom found effective), but was actively demonstrating transference distinctions in the current affective setting. Defining the setting leads to recognition of transference. It distinguishes the frame of reference in which material is to be scrutinized and also tells something about what is being projected.

Thus, the patient finds himself — together with all of his archaic introjects and infantile orientations — in an environment that does not "blend" with these distorting and psychopathological elements. Defenses, in order to be integrated into the psyche and to be adaptive, have to be supported by the environment. There must be a congruence between the intrapsychic structure and the external world so that defensive interactions can maintain their adaptive qualities. To some extent congruence always fails and the degree of failure will determine whether the patient seeks treatment. Still, the patient attempts to create a setting where his projections need not be viewed as projections. Insofar as the analyst specifies what the frame of reference will be, he is introducing an element of order and is creating an environment in which the patient's reactions and attitudes will be highlighted — clarifying which reactions and sources emanate from within and which from without.

In such a setting, time distinctions become blurred. The past is the present; the patient can more vividly perceive his experiences if they are not confused with external realities. Analytically speaking, the only reality is the here-and-now of the consultation room. The patient cannot remove himself from his feelings by retreating into the past. It is not significant if the patient views the analyst as his father; what is important is the content of the projection itself in terms of its adaptive or maladaptive qualities.

Every analyst recognizes the unique features of the analytic frame of reference; what has not been sufficiently emphasized is that the setting itself *helps the patient to consolidate his ego boundaries and to see himself as a separate, discrete individual.* The analyst, by affirming this setting, communicates that he is different than the patient. Thus, there are three combinations of people in the consultation room : 1. the patient-analyst combination, a transference fusion; 2. the analyst as analyst; and 3. the patient as a person. An explicit reference to the analytic setting indicates transference, specifically an acknowledgment of the symbiotic fusion. Defining the analytic setting is intended to resolve the fusion; it represents a reliving in the present of an early developmental phase. Although defining the analytic setting seems, on the surface, to be different from the usual interpretative activity, when viewed in terms of clinical theory, it has all the ingredients of a transference interpretation.

The value of analytical activity whose aim is to resolve the symbiotic fusion is apparent in patients who are suffering from severe psychopathology, such as borderline cases and schizophrenia. However, even with patients whose egos are relatively integrated, explicit statements about the analytic setting help to create a favorable environment. Although such patients probably have fewer developmental defects and less fixation upon the symbiotic state, *every transference, insofar as the patient retains within him some portion of what he projects onto the analyst, represents a fusion; and to the extent that it does, it is a replication of the symbiotic phase.* The difference between the so-called healthier and the more disturbed patient is one of degree. Insofar as the patient has a capacity for transference projection, he also has an element of symbiotic fixation. True, the better integrated patient develops transference displacements on objects that are thought to be more whole than part objects, and he may use displacement mechanisms in addition to projection. To some extent elements of projection and fusion become apparent during the analytic regression. In a healthier patient such elements are often displayed in a less stormy or disruptive fashion than may occur with more disturbed patients; nevertheless, they have to be resolved in order for analysis to be effective in creating a developmental progression as higher states of ego integration are achieved. Even analyses of so-called classical patients are directed at characterological factors as well as at resolution of the oedipal complex.

Certain characterological modalities, such as fusion, are believed to be specific for primitive ego states. Nevertheless, even among patients with relatively well-integrated egos, one finds evidence of fusion during the transference regression. This should not be surprising because if one accepts the existence of a symbiotic fusion as a beginning developmental phase, one should expect its persistence in the context of more integrated superstructures. During regression it can become activated once again. Consequently, when the patient's expectations of the analyst are similar to his own, he is, at some level, demonstrating a fusion mechanism. Depending upon the principal ego orientation, there may be other psychic mechanisms as well. However, viewing any psychic interaction in terms of a hierarchical continuum enables us to detect the more primitive elements of this continuum as they become energized, or at least partially energized.

Definition of the analytic setting refers (sometimes indirectly) to the patient's attempted fusion with the analyst or to his defense against such a fusion, as, for example, when he wants to keep secrets (see Chapter 10 and the example below). Precisely, how does one define the analytic setting? As mentioned earlier, such definitions vary and can occur in many different analytic circumstances. Perhaps a few brief examples can indicate at least minimally what is meant by defining the analytic setting. In many instances, it is far from apparent (even to the analyst) that he is engaged in such activity. Referring again to Dr. Winnicott's clinical material, he interpreted to his patient that "satisfaction annihilates the object for him. He had obtained some satisfaction last week and now I, as the object, had become annihilated." This is, from any viewpoint, a transference interpretation. Later, Dr. Winnicott said, "I made an *interpretation* concerning the continuation of my interest during the period in which I seemed to be annihilated" (italics added). I was fascinated by Dr. Winnicott's comment — "I made an interpretation" — because it refers to his interest and does not say anything explicit about the patient. Unlike his reference to satisfaction and annihilation, this comment was not an obvious transference interpretation. Still, I believe he was quite correct in his assertion that he had made an interpretation, and the subsequent material flowed smoothly. In my opinion, Dr. Winnicott was showing his interest in being a transference object. His comment also emphasized that he didn't feel threatened by the patient's wish to annihilate him; rather, he implicitly stated that he was available for transference projection — an important attribute of the analytic setting. The fact that he was interested meant that there was a phenomenon that interested him — the patient's feelings — and the specific use of himself in regard to these feelings communicated to the patient that there were two separate persons in the transference context. This is a type of transference interpretation; in this instance, the patient continued to unfold the transference and began to understand how he had used frustration (a symptom) to protect the object — in this case, the analyst — from being annihilated.

Another example comes from my own practice. During the course of free association, a patient confronted himself with a situation that he could not understand. He remained silent for several minutes and then, by his expression and exclamation, indicated that he had had a sudden insight and now understood what had previously puzzled him. Quite spontaneously he stated that he was not going to tell me what he had discovered, and he seemed very pleased. Equally spontaneously I said that all that mattered was that he knew; it wasn't necessary for me to know. Both the patient and I felt very strongly that my statement was correct; it had a tremendous impact on him and facilitated meaningful, reversible regression. Clearly, the patient understood that I was not envious of his autonomy. The analytic setting produced an environment where he could withdraw from an object who, he believed, wanted to engulf him yet also respected his need to withdraw. The setting enabled the patient to feel that the analyst (or analytic situation) might rob him of his individuality and that he was free to react to that feeling. On the other hand, he realized that I would do nothing to reinforce those feelings. The patient could permit himself further regression and fusion because the analytic setting, by affirming his "right" to withhold (a transference defense) made it unnecessary for him to continue defending himself so rigidly. Since I would not be destroyed by his withholding, he could continue to use me as a transference figure and eventually reach the implicit recognition that he was defending himself from an engulfing imago that he had projected onto me. Defining the analytic setting as a place where he could keep secrets from me was a way of interpreting a transference defense (see Chapter 10).

These interpretations of the setting eventually lead to the formation of what I have described as a solid *analytic introject*. The patient incorporates the setting, thus enabling the analytical attitude to become a characterological modality. The therapeutic (or working) alliance is similar in many ways to the concept of the analytic introject, but my formulation does not require a distinction to be made among the generally healthy parts of the ego or feelings that are relatively free of transference. The analytic introject is a specific introject that undergoes constant revision and, hopefully, gradually gains more secondary-process qualities.

During the initial stages of introject-formation, the introject may react as if it were a foreign body. Gradually, however, the introject becomes integrated until it is finally incorporated (amalgamated) as an aspect of the ego's executive system. The development of the analytic introject is basically the same as the development of any introject. However, insofar as it is formed in the context of an analytic relationship, it has certain unique qualities, particularly self-observing and autonomous elements. The transference interpretation is an integral factor in the formation of such an introject, but the concept of transference now includes the definition of the setting. Such concepts lead logically to a further extension of the range of applicability of the psychoanalytic method.

REFERENCES

Gitelson, M. (1962). The curative factors in psychoanalysis. *Int. J. Psycho-Anal.* 43 : 194–234.

Greenson, R. (1967). *The technique and practice of psychoanalysis.* New York : International Universities Press.

Spitz, R. (1956). Transference : the analytic setting and its prototype. *Int. J. Psycho-Anal.* 37 : 380–385.

Sterba, R. (1934). The fate of the ego in analytic therapy. *Int. J. Psycho-Anal.* 15 : 117–126.

Strachey, J. (1934). The nature of the therapeutic action of psycho-analysis. *Int. J. Psycho-Anal.* 15 : 127–159.

Zetzel, E. (1956). Current concepts of transference. *J. Amer. Psycho-anal. Assoc.* 1 : 526–537.

PART V

Specific Clinical Situations: Theoretical Viewpoints

Editor's Introduction

A logical extension of Parts III and IV brings us to the examination of clinical material per se. The psychoanalytic process cannot be described in a vacuum; eventually, technical maneuvers have to be discussed in the context of specific pathology.

The patient-analyst interaction needs to be understood in terms of the patient's reactions. To be intelligible, the latter should be systemically conceptualized, that is, understood in terms of psychic mechanisms. A patient's reaction to psychoanalytic treatment will, of course, depend upon his general characterological organization. Specific psychopathological configurations will respond in a typical fashion, although there may be large variations due to innumerable factors, including, to a significant extent, the analyst's own character structure. Still, in a broad, conceptual sense, there are significant common denominators in certain groups of patients so that it is meaningful to discuss particular characterological types.

For didactic purposes, the "classical" psychoneurotic patient is often presented as having a predictable therapeutic course if analysis is properly conducted. Allowing for some variation because of the analyst's personality, he generally expects to analyze defensively regressive ego states until he finally reaches a transference neurosis based upon an oedipal configuration. The latter is then analyzed and worked through; even though there is a back-and-forth movement — a further defensive regression against the oedipal conflict — the over-all movement is in the direction of analyzing pregenital defenses to a resolution of phallic-genital conflicts.

As has been mentioned elsewhere in this book, the sequence described above is not often encountered. If it were, then con-

307

ducting a psychoanalysis would be relatively simple and predictable. Treatment would probably be a dull and routine experience, and there would be no need for books on psychoanalytic therapy. It can be said with almost dogmatic certitude that analysis is not a dull or routine affair, and is by no means simple. In many instances analysis is baffling and exhausting; sometimes there are surprising consequences, especially when an analyst initially believed he was dealing with a fairly routine problem.

Setting aside for the moment the question of the efficacy of psychoanalytic technique, it might be well to investigate to a greater extent the clinical data presented here. Our formulations of psychopathology should be further scrutinized. The contributors to this volume, as mentioned in Chapter 1, chose to present cases that have very little in common with the hysterical models described by Freud. In many instances, however, these patients do well in psychoanalytic therapy. If these cases are conceptually understood in the context of a constant analytic setting, it is possible to discern a modicum of predictability so that one can make organized formulations.

In this part, various clinical examples are discussed in theoretical terms, and in some instances insights are presented in the context of treatment. Each discussion could be thought of as a conceptual exposition of a particular clinical syndrome. Sometimes the "syndrome" (such as the borderline or the borderline psychotic) is discussed in terms of various ego subsystems, such as the self-representation (the identity system or the maternal introject), or in terms of the dominant adaptive modality, such as fusion. Once patients are understood in such terms, which essentially represent a characterological and adaptive viewpoint, the analyst often does not need to be pessimistic about certain patients who seem to be untouched by the psychoanalytic experience. In many instances, what may appear to be noninvolvement or lack of transference is actually a manifestation of basic psychopathology and is an important aspect of the inevitable sequence of analytic interactions.

The concept of transference in analysis is extended beyond that of the transference neurosis at the oedipal level, which deals mainly with whole objects. Projection of parts of the self (rather than libidinal impulses) is stressed. However, in spite of differences in content, the mechanism of projection continues to operate and therapeutic engagement becomes possible. Emphasis is placed on the conditions that constitute a workable (potentially resolvable) transference, and these are related to the interactions among various ego systems.

My colleagues have been eager to discuss these topics because, in so doing, they are sharing clinical examples with one another; and by sharpening their theoretical focus, they find their work less baffling and more rewarding.

15

Early Mothering Care and Borderline Psychotic States

MARGARET LITTLE AND ALFRED FLARSHEIM

AN INCREASING proportion of patients suffering from borderline psychosis or severe characterological disorder are being seen in psychoanalytic practice. " 'Borderline state' is an imprecise descriptive term used to label any mental illness which is neither clearly neurotic nor so obviously psychotic that the patient concerned has to be treated as insane" (Little, 1966). We want to review some features of early mothering care and infant development and relate these to the etiology, special clinical characteristics, diagnosis, treatment, and possible prevention of borderline psychotic states.

We are starting with a pregnant mother, an ordinary woman, with an ordinary husband, living in an ordinary world. Within her body is a growing organism which will in time become separate from her. She and the fetus constitute a physical entity whose oneness is broken up by the birth process. But, up to that time, although the fetal circulation is distinct from hers, the mother's respiratory, digestive, and excretory systems are working for both. The fetus could not exist without her. Without the fetus, she could, of course, go on living as a person, but she is dependent on the fetus for her status as a mother. The needs of the fetus are met by the mother without the fetus being aware either of needs or of an object who meets those needs. The mother's needs are met by people and things that are seen by her to exist separately and independently of her.

At birth comes the infant's first major contact with the outside world. For the first time he breathes, feeds, digests, absorbs his food, and excretes waste products. His body has weight for the first time. He is bathed and dressed, handled and pushed around. He is still dependent on mothering for a considerable time, but to a gradually lessening degree. Freud (1926) points out :

> Just as the mother originally satisfied all the needs of the foetus through the apparatus of her own body, so now, after its birth, she continues to do so, partly by other means. There is much more continuity between intra-uterine life and earliest infancy than the impressive caesura of the act of birth would have us believe. What happens is that the child's biological situation as a foetus is replaced for it by a psychical object-relation to its mother.

It is the thesis of this study that psychotic and borderline disorders are related to disturbances of processes that characterize the infant's progression from the biological situation as a fetus, to a psychical object-relation to its mother.

To preserve stability for the neonate there is an urgent need for reestablishing and maintaining for a time conditions that are as much like those of prenatal life as is humanly possible. Conditions closely simulating intrauterine existence are as much a life-and-death matter for the infant *psychically* as was the continued existence of the mother and his *physical* relationship to her when he was *in utero*. Without these conditions, the massive total experience of being born cannot be assimilated, that is, joined up with prenatal experience ; thus, the incident of birth would remain a disturbance of the order of a world catastrophe, and all later experiences would tend to join up with the body memory of birth, rather than with prenatal ones. The effect of the birth experience upon later development thus depends not only on events during the birth process but also on subsequent events in the life of the neonate, which determine the way in which the memory traces of the birth experience are assimilated. Infant care that facilitates the assimilation of the memory traces of the birth experience restores and preserves continuity with the prenatal oneness between mother and infant.

When this restoration is brought about, a sense of continuity can be found; survival of the entity mother-infant can be taken for granted; and out of this a sense of identity and true independence can, during the process of growing up, develop. Without it, survival cannnot become axiomatic; annihilation or catastrophe always seems imminent; all energy is used in the fight to live; and nothing else can acquire any meaning. Annihilation anxiety characterizes psychotic disorders, just as anxiety about injury (castration) or loss of a separate object characterizes neurotic disorders.

We have been talking of two extremes, neither of which perhaps ever totally happens. Usually there is something between the extremes; according to which end of the scale the infant's experiences can be placed and according to later experiences (which can modify things either way), development of greater or smaller areas of independence will be helped or hindered. Freud (1938) said :

> The damage inflicted on the ego by its first experience gives us the appearance of being disproportionally great, but [this becomes understandable when we] take as an analogy the differences in the results produced by the prick of a needle into a mass of cells in the act of cell division . . . and into the fully grown animal which eventually develops out of them.

The implications of Freud's analogy are far-reaching. On the basis of it we should expect the smallest details of infant care to be of the greatest importance in subsequent development, and this premise underlies this study.

The entity of mother-infant is at the beginning a *physical* reality. This entity persists psychically for some time after birth, in both mother and infant. This basic unity is an illustration of the application of Freud's concept of early stages of ego development as expressed in his frequently quoted remark : "At the very beginning in the individual's primitive oral phase, object-cathexis and identification are . . . indistinguishable from each other" (Freud, 1923).

The term "basic unity" refers to the primal state of lack of differentiation between psyche and soma, ego and id, self and object which throughout life underlies all states of development and differentiation (Little, 1960). In the primary undifferentiated state, there is absolute consistency of a monistic view and total identification of everything with everything else. Specifically there is total identification of all opposites or polarities (I am you, I am not you, you are me, you are not me, you are you, you are not you, black is white, good is bad, east is west — affirmation is denial and denial is assertion) without extent or limit in time or space. Therefore, paradox, either in maintaining or in denying the monistic view, is inevitable.

Our ordinary mother has, during her pregnancy, developed what Winnicott (1956) called "primary maternal preoccupation." That is to say, throughout her pregancy she has become progressively more and more centered on the coming child. She has been dreaming, planning, arranging for the care of herself as herself; of herself in relation to him; of him as an individual; and of him in relation to the home, the rest of the family, and the outside world. By the time he is born she is deeply committed to him and experiences him not only as a part of her own body, but as part of her very self in such a way that his needs are hers.

During the pregnancy she has been slowly preparing, both physically and emotionally, for the puerperium and the care of her baby. The puerperium is the time of maximal dependence in the infant and maximal infant-centeredness in the mother; hence, her vulnerability, both during pregnancy and the puerperium. From the time of birth there is a gradual and progressive separation out from him in order to allow him to be a person in his own right, a separate individual with whom, nevertheless, there is a deeply felt closeness rooted in the shared, albeit differently felt, experiences of prenatal and early postnatal life. Common language refers to the stages of infant development: We speak of "an infant in arms," a "lap-baby," a "knee-baby," and later a "toddler," showing the progression of his changing relationship to himself, to his mother, and to the outer world, as well as his growing independence.

In the newly born infant, bodily life and body happenings are all important, and psychic life, as we come to know it later, is practically nonexistent. There is no distinction between the psyche and the soma, any more than there is *for the infant* any distinction between himself and his mother or between any two parts of his own body. At one moment he *is* all mouth, fist, breast, scream, rage, or calm. Before the development of a sense of personal identity, he is a "state of being" rather than a person *in* such a state.

Freud (1930) pointed out that "originally the ego includes everything; later it separates off an external world from itself." Considerable ego development must take place before the identity of an experiencing self, continuous in time, is formed. Before that the experiencing person is the mother part of the infant-mother unit. This has practical clinical application in the treatment of patients who need to regress in analysis. It is not necessarily hostility that causes a regressed patient to behave in a fashion that makes the analyst uncomfortable. The patient is subjectively merged with the analyst during regression. When the patient seeks feelings of his own, he must find them in the analyst part of the patient-analyst unit before he can experience them himself and know that they are his own (Searles, 1961). This is because the "analyst part" is the more organized part of the unit, able to experience feelings without disintegration. During regression the patient can reach a state of oneness with the analyst such that the ego boundary is effaced and the total ego of the patient is undifferentiated from that of the analyst. The complex ego mechanism of projection is not then responsible for the patient's feeling that the analyst literally is the patient's illness. Under these circumstances the patient treats the analyst as his illness.

Because of early undifferentiatedness, the earliest memories are body memories, and the earliest form of remembering will not be "recalling" but reproducing or reenacting in a very concrete bodily way. Winnicott (1954) points out that in analysis "the regressed patient is near to a re-living of dream and memory situations. An acting out of a dream may be the way the patient discovers what is urgent, and talking about what was acted out follows the action but cannot precede it." Action has a similar significance in the repetitive play of young children when they need to assimilate a painful or frightening experience by reliving it in a safe setting, joining it with memories of good and reassuring experiences. Transference itself, in its positive reassuring and negative frightening aspects, represents a repetition that has an integrative significance in the psychoanalytic situation.

As her child grows, our ordinary mother actively separates herself out from her infant while also remaining close to him. His growth, maturation, and lessening dependence on her, as well as the other realities of her life, foster this process. She may experience his birth as a loss within herself which she can only deal with by caring for him. Pediatricians and mothers have observed that where there is too great a separation early in the puerperium the mother loses the sense of contact with her baby, and difficulty in reestablishing emotional contact creates problems in the early feeding situation. Social workers who place children for adoption find that the baby must be separated from the mother either at birth or after she and the child have grown away from one another to some extent. In between there is a period of varying length during which a mother who is anywhere near emotional health cannot stand the pain of separation from her infant.

For the infant there is a corresponding process. Alongside progressive separation it is important that there be imaginative or psychic continuity from prenatal life through infancy, childhood, and adolescence up to adult life. Breaks in this continuity are damaging to emotional life and development. Winnicott (1960) states that in the developing child there are two opposing tendencies:

> The first is the tendency . . . to get away from the mother and . . . away from the family, each step giving increased freedom of ideas and of functioning. The other tendency works in the opposite direction and it is the need to retain or to be able to regain the relationship with [one's own infancy and one's parents]. It is this second tendency which makes the first tendency a part of growth instead of a disruption of the individual's personality. . . . In the healthy development of the individual, at whatever stage, what is needed is a steady progression [of steps toward independence, each step] being compatible with the retention of an unconscious bond with . . . the mother.

Out of the stability of this continuity new things can safely emerge. This continuity constitutes the "basic unity," a state of the essential self, the basis of all communication and relationships, and a *sine qua non* for the healthy emotional life and development of every individual.

It is here that understanding of the conditions necessary for healthy early development can help to prevent psychotic disorders. For example, in some maternity hospitals mothers are not allowed to have their infants with them, to pick them up or feed them when they cry. After a few days of such separation, long enough to break the continuity, mother and infant are sent home in the resulting disrupted state. The mother must start running the home again while also trying to repair the disruption in her relationship with her baby.

We would like to digress for a moment to apply this understanding of the conditions necessary for ego development to the treatment of patients in the mental hospital, where a similar disruption is often seen. The continuity of experience of the mentally sick patient can be disrupted by ill-advised efforts to change his behavior. It is supposedly "for their own good" that mental patients are coerced and regimented into O.T. groups or therapy groups *against their wishes and their need to have their illness, which is a necessary precondition for recovering from it.* They are made to feel unwelcome if they don't cooperate. At its worst, such so-called cooperation can exploit such pathological defenses as, for example, manic denial of depressive effect and the psychodynamic reasons for depression. It is necessary to relinquish such pathological defenses before the ego can master the underlying reasons for depression. Therefore, the patient using manic or hypomanic defenses must usually go through periods of depression on the way to health. Under optimal circumstances, depressive (or paranoid) episodes can be contained in the analytic sessions. But this, at best, is a delicate and precarious therapeutic situation. The additional strain of putting on an act of healthy behavior for the benefit of a zealous occupational therapist can make it impossible for the patient to experience regression and dedifferentiation, including, for example, the depression that he may need to reach if he is to achieve real recovery, characterized by integration of destructive and constructive impulses and fantasies, and not simply a reinforcement of denial mechanisms.

To return to infant care, perhaps only a mother who has been able to care for her baby as *she* felt can really know how important their relationship is. All of the child's future relationships can be made or marred in this earliest relationship.

A newborn infant, totally inexperienced, totally dependent, and unconscious of either himself or his environment starts on the journey toward becoming an adult. He faces a whole range of experience in the stages between, and what these may bring in the way of understanding and development, relationship and concern until he is able to take responsibility for himself and others. Within the space of 21 (or perhaps 18) years, the individual must pass through the history of the race, just as in the nine months of intra-uterine life the fetus recapitulates the stages of man's evolution from a "primordial protoplasmic globule." From a biological standpoint, each of us originates from a single cell. That cell was formed by the fusion of two nonidentical cells, each of which in turn came from a single cell by the mitotic division of chromosomes. The biological rhythm of repeated division and fusion has its psychic counterpart in differentiation and integration. These things ordinarily happen automatically if the setting is right. The changes come about from within the child, as they have come from within the race, and interference or prompting from outside cannot produce or even hurry them, except at the cost of disturbing a finely balanced organism with built-in patterns of development.

The foundations of a child's mental health are there from the beginning, and the building is furthered and emotionally financed, so to speak, by parents who have the courage and patience to watch and wait, can make adaptations, can provide the right setting, can respond to outward movement or withdrawal; are sensitive to individual needs, and do not try to mold the child into a pattern — whether their own or that of society. The parents themselves need to be firmly rooted, for it is their stability and maturity that provide the milieu in which the child can find himself and develop his individual adaptational modalities.

An important element in the parents' integrity is their willingness to enlarge their own boundaries and to take full responsibility for their child from the time of conception (whether consciously intended or not), acknowledging that he did not ask to be conceived or to be born, and that therefore he has the right to live without demands being made on him to pay emotionally for his keep or to be grateful. If they can then accept what he gives in his own time, they may find that his body movements — biting, hitting, excreting — can become loving things, and if they can allow him to be his age, to be himself and nothing more (abrogating their own rights long enough and bearing guilt and anxiety for him), he will in time be able and willing to take over for himself. In time he will perceive his parents as separate from himself and be aware of what they are doing as he develops the capacity to accord them rights, to feel concern for them, and to recognize that a shared event is experienced differently by the partners in it.

Every relationship has elements of dependence and independence, and each has meaning only in relation to the other, as is true with all opposites. The development of any relationship — including that between analyst and patient, and that between partners in marriage — follows the *reverse pattern* of the mother-infant relationship. At first there is separateness, then a gradually increasing confluence (which progresses from ambivalence to its resolution), and finally a merging into some kind of oneness (Searles, 1966). The sequence may be repeated many times, and of course in psychotherapy it has to end in actual separation, but each repetition brings new mutuality in both dependence and independence, new personal maturation in each partner, and mutual creation.

The idea that "normal" or "mature" people are free from hate, anxiety, guilt, inhibition, or sadness dies very hard. Everything found in pathological states exists also in normality. The essential normality of such mechanisms as projection, repression, and identification is only too often overlooked. Each person's continual need to resolve internal conflicts and his continual interaction with others who have conflicting individual needs and claims and an equal right to exist, make life a precarious and difficult thing at best.

It is rare for an infant *not* to be born "normal" in the sense of having the potentiality to develop all ordinary bodily functions as well as form relationships and take responsibility. A "normal" baby is potentially a *person* from the start, and he begins to become that person as he moves in response to impulses within himself, relating both to his own body and to his environment. There is a continual interchange, to and fro, between him and his environment, and the response of the environment to his expressive movement will largely determine his next movement or feeling.

Here we would like to look at what happens when an infant moves, remembering that it looks different to the infant from the inside than it does to an adult from the outside. For the infant, or for a regressed patient of any age, there is no differentiation between the aim and the object of an instinctual impulse. Some kind of urge turns up — perhaps hunger or mother. The awkward phrasing is deliberate, because, although the observer knows that hunger comes from inside and that mother comes from outside the infant, to the infant hunger and mother are at first the same. Neither seems to belong to the infant; both are felt as alien and may be experienced as exactly the same thing. They come to be felt as good or bad according to how the mother responds to the expressive movements of the hungry infant. The mother interprets these movements as indicating hunger, and hunger is felt to be good if it is promptly met by the mother's feeding response but bad if there is delay or other interference.

The mother's empathic response to the infant's uncoordinated signs of discomfort leads to psychosomatic integration. Without such empathy there may be a failure of psychosomatic integration, leading to functional gastrointestinal disorders. Progressively remote signals: part-objects and part-functions; visceral hunger sensations; proprioceptive and motor reactions such as crying and reaching out; and tactile, olfactory, visual, and auditory perception of the mother and her techniques of infant care are integrated in the interaction between infant and mother around feeding. The infant's mouth, his whole body, or his whole self (again experienced as one and the same) is excited and is impelled violently toward the stimulus — subjectively pulled by it — meets it, fuses with it, and destroys it (or is destroyed by it — again the same thing in this undifferentiated state), as the urge itself is destroyed and is no longer there once it is satisfied.

Satisfaction of an instinctual need leads to temporary decathexis of the providing object. This is equivalent to temporary annihilation of the object until the instinctual tension returns. When the climax of satisfaction has been reached and the urge vanishes, there is a turning away from the object and from the satisfying experience — a losing and forgetting — although the body memory remains. The term "body memory" refers to memory traces formed during the preverbal era before psychosomatic differentiation. This memory provides confidence that when instinctual tension recurs there will be a recathexis of the perceptual and executive apparatus and of the object, and that the instinctual need will be satisfied. Instinctual inhibition can result from failure to establish a body memory that can survive both instinctual tension and its satisfaction. The fantasy of destroying the mother in an orgy of eating leads to guilt and to grief at the loss, and these are resolved in health by the repeated discovery that the mother is not destroyed in fact nor does she destroy in retaliation. This is where discovery of the difference between imaginative and factual reality can begin.

Searles (1961) says that in the stage of therapy of the schizophrenic that corresponds to the "pre-ambivalent mother-infant symbiosis," the therapist and the regressed patient oscillate between infantile and maternal roles in relation to one another. In the undifferentiated state these two roles are experienced simultaneously by both therapist and patient. "At this level of dedifferentiation [undifferentiatedness] 'love' and 'hate' are one and . . . any intense and overt relatedness is, in effect, love." In the primal undifferentiated state, destruction by separation is the same as destruction by fusion, and these are the same as creation by separation and by fusion.

The body experiences of infancy form the pattern of later sexual orgasm. They *are* orgasm, and the whole infant is involved. Repeated experiences where the infant's expressive movements, motivated for instance by hunger, are met satisfactorily by the mother lead to the establishment of a pattern of movements that is object-directed and valuable. These movements come to have meaning, to be emotionally enriched as loving movements, to be imaginatively elaborated, and to be repeated or not at will.

At first, the elaboration can be as simple as a headline: "I am," "I eat that." Later, ideas of what "I" is, what "eat" can mean, and what "that" may be, lead to ideas of what happens afterward. When teeth come, "that" is torn to pieces, the pieces are swallowed, and end products come out. Other products are absorbed and built into the child himself, or, altered by the child's subjective feelings of love and hate, act again from within as stimuli. All this is the stuff of the child's inner imaginative life and world.

It is important to emphasize the significance of the child's discovery, first, of his own body, sensation, and movement; then of the sense of being a person-who-has-felt-and-moved that is found in the identity "I am." Later, there is the discovery of the "not I," the outside world, repudiated as part of the self. Eventually the child understands that the "not I" also feels and moves in response to something or spontaneously, separately and differently. Both insight and relationship begin here with the discovery of ego boundaries.

At this point it is appropriate to consider again the infant's motility. "At origin aggressiveness is almost synonymous with activity; it is a matter of part-function. It is these part-functions that are organized by the child gradually . . . into aggression." In health, the environment is "discovered because of motility" (Winnicott, 1950). The mother's response to the spontaneous movements of the infant enables these movements, in healthy development, to contribute to individuation and to the creation and re-creation of the infant's subjective world.

If, instead, the environment repeatedly "impinges" and the neonate must react to these external stimuli, healthy development is disrupted. At an early time, of course, an infant's movements are not effective but are uncontrollable reactions, involuntary and uncoordinated. Induced reflex response, such as automatic bladder or bowel control, is only too easy to establish by premature training, and has to break down before the control can become voluntary. The development of deliberate and intentional movements depends, as stated earlier, upon the response of the environment to the movements made by the kicking foot, waving fist, clutching fingers, and yelling or sucking mouth. When deliberate, emotionally motivated movements have been established, the infant is able to choose between immediate and delayed expression of emotion.

If, when the infant moves (while hallucinating the mother who will satisfy hunger), the mother is not there, or she begins by diaper-changing, or wiping away saliva from the excited mouth, the movement becomes useless. It falls in a vacuum ; discovery is minimal or misleading, and something potentially valuable — that could develop into a capacity to make assertions or form relationships — is lost. If a movement is met with pain, if an excited hand hits the bars of a crib or is slapped, or if the child's excited body is grabbed and hugged by an excited mother, the movement becomes positively dangerous, annihilating, and hateful. The sense of self then is only of a hating self, living in an unfriendly, uncomfortable, not-self world — a world that threatens the child's existence and denies him personhood.

An individual's later ability to experience and recognize emotion depends upon the appropriateness of the responses of the mothering person to his first gestures as an infant. These responses form the basis for the individual's later ability to express emotion in ways appropriate to complex social situations. His capacity to observe and evaluate increasingly complex social situations depends upon the critical faculties of his parents ; their ability to distinguish between real and imagined dangers ; their scale of values ; their degree of insight ; and their ability to tolerate anxiety and to bear separateness and fusion. The building of the child's inner world accompanies his body maturation and his expanding awareness of the outer world, which result from his increasing integration of perception, memory traces, and motility.

Processes of differentiation and integration take place in the child ; as a result of his increased awareness of "self" and "not-self" and his sorting out of the various people around him, personalization (or individuation) becomes a rhythmic and continuing process throughout life. Repetition brings about stability, and when there is enough stability, variation can help achieve an increasing capacity to bear surprise and even shock. Anxiety and emotion, which are initially found and expressed somatically, are later translated into psychic phenomena, largely separated off from body things and expressed in words or in substitute symbolic ways.

Along with his actual smallness and total helplessness (and as a defense against recognizing it), the infant feels magically powerful, and the mother's size and her abilities lend a quality of omnipotence to the mother-infant entity. Separation from this entity entails the gradual giving up and destruction of this omnipotence and the growing recognition and acceptance of human limitations. If the mother has to keep her own infantile omnipotence, she cannot allow the child to separate, for she has to feel superior to him. She feels that his development would threaten her own existence, and she depends on him. The child will then remain dependent on her, developing the kind of false independence (based on pathological omnipotence) we see in mentally ill patients — often delusional in its intensity and fixedness — which manifests itself as arrogance and superiority. This "independence" is maintained to avoid both loss and awareness of separation-annihilation.

If the mother has been able to accept the loss of her own imagined omnipotence and retained it only as part of her phantasy world — psychically real, but not actual — she can bear her own ambivalence and the child's, and therefore she can help him to bear his. Without this assistance, the child is caught in an impossible situation in that he cannot *but* develop biologically and yet must remain part of an entity that cannot be dissolved. To become a person then, literally means to destroy the mother and bear both loss and guilt; to remain dependent is to be destroyed himself.

Analysis of patients with such a background frequently reveals two states, which are dissociated and experienced alternately.

The first state is a feeling of fusion and undifferentiation in the transference. This is delusional and may manifest itself in the patient's belief that he can read the thoughts of the analyst and that the analyst can read his thoughts, while the patient is helpless to conceal them.

The second state is a feeling of absolute separateness and isolation. This may first manifest itself in a partial way, for example, in the patient's need to keep secrets from the analyst. This can be the patient's way of bringing under control a feeling of absolute and total aloneness, isolation, and inability to establish meaningful object contact.

The destruction of self and object that accompanies differentiation requires further examination. A hallucinated object does not, of course, satisfy a libidinal need, and the libidinal impulse (such as hunger) requires an external object for gratification, which can never be complete. However, Freud felt that instincts are dualistic from the beginning of life, and he regarded aggression as a primary instinct, rather than only as a reaction to frustration.

Winnicott (1969) says that the recognition of an object as separate from the self coincides with the subjective destruction of the object. This is consistent with Freud's views about the origin of object relatedness, during the phase of infantile omnipotence. Freud (1915) wrote:

> Hate, as a relation to objects, is older than love. It derives from the narcissistic ego's primordial repudiation of the external world with its outpouring of stimuli.

We also find that "Masochism is older than sadism. . . . [S]adism is the destructive instinct directed outwards" (Freud, 1933). This was not settled in Freud's mind, as we can see from the following:

> The turning inwards of the aggressive instinct is the counterpart to the turning outward of the libido when it passes over from the ego to objects. . . . [A]t the beginnings of life, all libido was directed to the inside and all aggressiveness to the outside [Freud, 1937].

Freud (1920) discussed the consequences of the destructiveness of the earlier instinctual drives:

> During the oral stage of organization of the libido, the act of obtaining erotic mastery over an object coincides with that object's destruction. . . . [T]he sadistic instinct separates off. . . . [T]he sadism which has been forced out of the ego has pointed the way for the libidinal components of the sexual instinct, and . . . these follow after it to the object.

Thus the primitive instinctual impulse destroys its object as the ego cathects the object.

Winnicott (1969) postulates that destructiveness accompanies recognition of the object as 1.) separate from the self, and 2.)

needed by the self. He approaches Klein's concept of early "envy," but Klein (1957) traces destructiveness to: 1.) the need for an external object into which to project inner destructiveness (the "death instinct" [Freud, 1920]), and 2.) the frustrations inevitable in any relationship with real objects. Klein's formulations presuppose self-object differentiation, while Winnicott focuses on the process of ego structuralization by which ego boundaries are established. For Winnicott, as for Freud, destructiveness is inherent in the initiation of cathexis of objects separate from the self and is independent of frustration. The destructive drive contributes to the subject's perception of the object as external and separate from the self. This process depends upon the object's survival of the subject's destructiveness. Both Winnicott and Klein stress the lifelong struggle to find actual constructive and creative activities that can replace the need for a magical re-creation of the world that corresponds to the infantile omnipotent (magical) destruction of the world.

The mothering person who provides continuity of care and who survives the infant's fantasied destruction of her is essential in order for the infant to link external reality with instinctual impulses, memory traces, and creative and re-creative fantasy. Successful maternal care, that which Winnicott (1952) calls "active adaptation" to the infant's needs, enables the infant to use the actual mother and her techniques of infant care to build up the imaginative basis of his personality. The failure of maternal care here, failure to maintain the psychic inseparableness of creativity and destructiveness, leaves the infant with an autistic, self-created, delusional object world superimposed on a world of destroyed objects.

Destruction as part of individuation as well as the temporary loss of object cathexis and the corresponding annihilation of the object that accompanies instinctual gratification are more primitive than the fantasied destruction of the object from aggression resulting from the instinct frustration that is inevitable in any object relationship because of the reality principle.

So far we have only considered differentiation from the maternal object. When we look at differentiation from the basic unity of earliest infancy, we find that it is not only the object, but also the self that is destroyed (or lost) and re-created (or found). Infantile ego states are assimilated in subsequent higher states of ego integration. This process characterizes healthy development but is never complete. Partially unassimilated, archaic ego states, including total undifferentiatedness, are always present and valuable. Freud (1930) said :

> [I]n mental life nothing which has once been formed can perish. . . . [T]he unconscious is quite timeless. . . .[A]ll impressions are preserved, not only in the same form in which they were first received, but also in all the forms which they have adopted in their further developments. . . . Theoretically every earlier state of mnemonic content could . . . be restored to memory . . . even if its elements have long ago exchanged all their original connections for more recent ones.

To become a person with his own separate identity means largely to lose the original infant-mother undifferentiated unit and the associated primal omnipotence. At the most primitive levels of the ego, this is equivalent to omnipotent destruction of the infant-mother unit, which, however, still remains as an unconscious psychic structure. Steps in developing one's own independent identity are experienced as a destruction, but *not only* as destruction. They are also experienced as a rebirth and re-creation of the self and of the world. *Birth fantasies and memories in analysis are not traceable only to the actual birth experience. They can come from memory traces of the individual's emergence from the early state of subjective oneness with the mother and entrance into the state of relatedness with separate persons.* In contrast to the single event of physical birth this psychological "birth experience" can occur repeatedly. In the process, the infant (as well as the analytic patient) must bear both loss and guilt over the unconscious destruction. If he cannot bear the loss and guilt, he will remain in an undifferentiated union with the mother (and the patient will remain in an interminable analysis, a parasite of his analyst). This represents another kind of destruction, that of one's own potential individuality. After ego structuralization has reached the level at which introjection and identification are established, internal objects with which the self is to some extent identified can be maintained while external objects are recognized as separate. This is another way of conceptualizing the linking of inner and outer reality that Winnicott (1951) clarified in his work on transitional objects and phenomena. The first task of the mother is to fit into the infant's needs sufficiently to ensure that he will not be prematurely forced to perceive her as someone real and external and separate from himself until his ego has become strengthened and structuralized by natural processes to the point where introjected details of maternal care can be maintained during times when the mother is seen as separate and, therefore, destroyed.

Pleasure-seeking and the pleasure principle can only begin to have meaning after survival can be taken for granted. They require a continuity between the earliest body memories and later experience. The survival principle is replaced by the pleasure principle, which in turn gives way to the reality principle. Eventually it becomes possible to distinguish between personal, inner, imaginative reality and shared, outer, factual reality, and to live by both — no longer demanding that truth be absolute or unchanging. Lost omnipotence and omniscience, both the child's own and that personified in the mother, can be mourned so that guilt and anger are replaced by sadness, and the pain of ambivalence can become pleasure through the experience of contrast. Actual oneness with the mother can become an imagined oneness with other people, and acceptance of their real separateness can form the basis of empathy and understanding. The child's discovery of the father and other members of the household as separate and whole people is important, apart from the father's importance all the while as a background figure supporting the mother and the home. The father's importance as an individual increases as time goes on, until eventually it comes, intermittently at least, to supplant the mother's.

In stressing the importance of the early transactions between infant and mother, we have traced events that foster the *innate tendency* to mature. Of course, other factors need to be remembered, such as differences in heredity and environment, that can show up throughout life. Only uniovular twins are genetically identical, but even they will never have identical environmental experiences. Often the external events that are important to the child go unnoticed by anyone else. A child's reaction to an external event is based on his perception of it, and this perception depends not so much upon the actual shared reality of the external event as upon the suitability of that event for projecting onto it significant parts of the child's inner world. The same kind of maternal behavior will be experienced differently by different infants. A particular sample of maternal behavior will be experienced as successful mothering by one infant and as unsuccessful mothering by another infant.

Psychotic and severe characterological disorders have their

roots in the failure of maternal care in early life. These disorders are characterized by the prevalence of survival anxiety (psychotic anxiety) and areas of delusional persistence of the primary undifferentiated state. The earliest experiences set a pattern for later events of a fairly consistent kind.

The essence of the "borderline" state is partial fixation in the undifferentiated phase. There is not enough differentiation between psyche and soma, and failure of fusion between ego and id, making adequate development to the depressive position and the early oedipal situation impossible. Failure in the early oedipal situation leads to interference with development of the later (classical) oedipal situation, and hence ordinary psychoneurosis is not developed.

At the same time the degree of differentiation and fusion are sufficient for the condition not to be psychosis. The determining factors are both quantitative, i.e., the size of the areas affected, and qualitative, i.e., the localization; whether *all* excitement becomes a threat of annihilation, or only some; and, if the latter, whether oral, kinaesthetic, visual, etc.

Nevertheless, certain characteristics which distinguish neurosis from psychosis have to be considered in greater detail because of their bearing on the question of the suitability of any patient for analysis, and the kind of transference phenomena one may expect to find.

A person who has been able to build up a body of experience that enables him to take survival for granted may yet suffer from castration anxiety, and fear the loss of a part of his own body; in defence against this he may regress and show separation anxiety, fearing the loss of love objects which he recognises as whole, real, and distinct from himself. Anxieties of this kind (neurotic anxieties) are different from those of a person who is *not* able to take survival for granted. Separation anxiety in such a person involves fear of loss of objects which are not recognized either as whole or as distinct from himself, but which are regarded as *identical* with himself, i.e., he fears annihilation. Anything which comes to be perceived as separate or different from himself is perceived as dangerous, threatening to annihilate him by virtue of its very separateness, and therefore as something to be destroyed by him [i.e., to be made not-separate]. Yet his own destructiveness is feared as soon as it attaches to something other than himself, and hence loss, i.e., separateness [or fusion] must be avoided at all costs. Such a person's anxieties are psychotic in type, and there will always be a tendency to regress towards anxiety about survival.

Where annihilation anxiety predominates, only one idea can have any meaning, and it is presumably this that *brings about* a state in which everything relates to survival or non-survival, and where the patient's ideas are found to be fixed, with an intensity which must be recognized as delusional (Little, 1966).

A child who has been fortunate in the early experiences of complete dependence on his mother and of increasing separation out from her will enter the later stages of childhood and adolescence and eventual adulthood with the ability to take survival for granted; he will also have a growing sense of personal and sexual identity and be able to see life with meaning and value. Thus, he will find that he is able to enjoy relationships with himself, with others, and with things. His path will not be free from difficulty, for difficulty is inherent in life itself, but he will have an inner resource with which to meet problems.

The following clinical material is intended to illustrate ways in which these developmental processes affect psychoanalytic practice. The ego defects of a "borderline" patient, whose sense of identity included archaic introjects, coexisted with areas of good ego development. First we will describe the relevant details from her early history that led to the areas of undifferentiatedness and to psychotic anxiety. Then we will describe how these were manifested in her treatment.

Jean, who was seen for over six years (by Margaret Little), was 46 when she first sought treatment. She was the second of four children. Elizabeth, the eldest, was mongoloid. Two years after the birth of Elizabeth, the mother found herself pregnant again but had "lost all of her maternal feelings." She hardly attempted to breast-feed Jean. Jean and her sister Phoebe, three years younger, are both highly intelligent and sensitive people. John, the youngest, the longed-for son and heir, spent the first year of his life in a hospital during which his parents visited him only about three times. Since adolescence he has spent most of his life in expensive mental hospitals because he is unable to live without support although his parents regarded him as only neurotic. (He has been labeled an "inadequate psychopath.") Elizabeth, having become unmanageable at home, was placed in a "home" at the age of seven; she had died (at age 37) before Jean started treatment. Jean had not been allowed to visit her at the "home" or to attend her funeral.

Jean and her siblings were put into the care of nannies; they only saw their parents for a short time each day, when they were expected to behave prettily and to be a credit to the parents. At least one of the nannies was actively sadistic, though she had curiously inconsistent patches of kindness. When she was an adolescent Jean tried to tell her mother about the sadism, but the mother hotly denied it as "impossible," since she "would of course have known and dismissed her, if it had been true."

Shortly after Jean had divorced her first husband and returned with an infant son to her parents' home, her mother died after a long and distressing cardiac illness, incorrectly diagnosed at first. Jean nursed her mother during her terminal illness and took care of her father until her second marriage, eight years later.

Her father was still alive, though very old and completely deaf, with the paranoid reactions that so often accompany deafness. He was the son of a well-known musician and had been ambitious professionally and socially. The relationship between her father and mother was still idealized. They were devoted and inseparable, and the children were not allowed to disturb this. Diaries of both parents confirmed Jean's story.

Jean was referred by Phoebe's psychotherapist (a woman). She was depressed at the start of treatment and expected to be told that no treatment was necessary and that all she had to do was to "pull herself together;" at the same time she expected a "miracle cure in six sessions." The kind of help she consciously wanted was to make her marriage succeed, not by changing herself but by altering her husband. Her depression had been precipitated when a much-loved dog "had to be destroyed" because her husband had been promoted and they had to move to London. We found that much of her unconscious sexual feeling had been centered on this dog.

Barry, her husband, saw her relationship with Phoebe as the cause of the trouble. The two had hour-long telephone conversations daily, and if either one bought or received anything, the other would compulsively get the identical thing. Their only acknowledged differences were that Jean had remarried after her divorce and Phoebe had not, and Jean had one child and Phoebe two. These facts were cited as showing how completely different and separate they really were. After her divorce, Jean became first a receptionist, then a patient, and finally mistress of a gynecologist. She sent Phoebe to him as a patient, and he seduced her, too.

Patients who have an history of a *folie à deux,* like that beween Jean and Phoebe, often manifest a psychotic transference in analysis, accompanied by delusional identity with the analyst (Little, 1966). This turned out to be true in Jean's case. In addition, "A regressive illness during the course of analysis is often inevitable in cases in which an existing *folie à deux* has to be destroyed for the analysis to be carried out" (Little, 1958). To anticipate, Jean manifested a delusional transference, characterized alternately by feeling one with the analyst and feeling absolutely separate and alone. She was able to work through and overcome much of the delusional nature of the transference within the context of the analysis without a severe regressive illness requiring hospitalization.

At the first interview, Jean attributed her difficulties to the fact that she had been sent to a progressive ("crank") school where she became involved with one boy after another. Later she revealed that, before the "crank" school, she had been sent (at the age of eight) to a girls' boarding school, where she was deeply unhappy. Then she attended another school where she was less unhappy, but she was expelled for "necking" with the garden boy and sent to the "crank" school in the hope of "dealing with this tendency." Actually she had been happy there and had loved and respected the headmaster, as she had never been able to love or respect her father. In reality, we found that her father had been warmer to Jean than to either her mother or Phoebe, but guilt had prevented Jean from loving him. It was her repressed oedipal fantasies that were directed toward the headmaster.

Barry wanted her to enter treatment in order to force her to separate from Phoebe and become one with him instead. At the start of treatment Jean unconsciously equated the analyst with Barry. She insisted that Barry also be seen and could not imagine why neither he nor the analyst suggested or wanted this. Jean was unable to continue treatment until the analyst agreed to see Barry, but when Barry finally was seen, Jean became acutely paranoid until she found by opening the bill sent to him for the interview that her suspicions were unfounded. Her discovery that Barry had received a bill and not a letter from the analyst turned out to have been important and valuable because it meant that she had to recognize the reality of the professional relationship between Barry and the analyst, thus making her delusional expectations (that Barry and the analyst were allied and equated) available for interpretation.

The analytic work consisted largely of finding and establishing her identity, personal and sexual; this required, first, the perception of her own body and its separateness. At the outset it was quite unreal to her; she had not subjectively differentiated herself from either parent. For example, she was either dying of the cardiac condition from which her mother had died, or she was going deaf, like her father. She had no confidence in day-to-day survival but felt it would be useless to see a doctor about the bronchitis from which she actually suffered because he would surely misdiagnose her, despise her, hurt her, and seduce her. She expected, and to some extent sought or provoked, pain and humiliation, believing that the whole world thought of women as inferior to men; she was incensed when a male friend jokingly referred to her as "Colonel Jean."

She had delusions of identity not only with her parents, but with both her sisters, her brother, and her son. She considered herself defective, insane, or infantile. There were also delusions of identity between Elizabeth and Jean's dog. She regarded Elizabeth, the mongoloid, as nonhuman like the dog; and both Elizabeth and the dog were dead, as was her mother. Later, Barry sustained a fractured skull with extensive frontal lobe damage; after that she had similar delusions of identity among Barry, Elizabeth, and the dog, as well as between the analyst and the sadistic nannie, the seducing gynecologist, and the uncaring parents. It was necessary to accept the absolute reality *for her* of her belief in her identity with the analyst, while at the same time recognizing its delusional nature. There were two realities for Jean: 1.) The awareness of herself as an autonomous person related to other autonomous persons. This was the basis for her self-observing function, enabling her to perceive the reality of her analyst and the analytic relationship and to maintain herself between sessions. During the sessions she occasionally lost this differentiated identity and at those times depended on the analyst and the analytic setting to sustain her while she was aware of only: 2.) The delusional identity among the various parts of her experience and her personality and between herself and other persons. Without ego boundaries her ego included everything. Thus there was no separate person with whom she could have a relationship, and she was in effect absolutely alone. Her delusion of absolute and total oneness therefore coexisted with her delusion of absolute and total isolation. She experienced this delusional state as having absolute reality in the present; consequently, she needed the analyst to acknowledge the subjective reality of it for her, while all the time remembering that it was a reality from Jean's past, deriving from her unity with her mother in earliest infancy and unresolved during that infantile relationship with her mother. In addition, Jean alternated between awareness of the delusion of oneness with the analyst and the delusion of absolute isolation and aloneness. At any one time she was aware of one or the other as her total reality and needed the analyst to link the two states with one another by transference interpretation.

The transference delusion displaced other delusions in importance for her and led to more structured defenses, such as projection. Delusions of omnipotence both in herself and projected onto the analyst and others (especially all psychiatrists) were gradually resolved.

Progressively Jean found the analyst to be a real autonomous person, who was able to let her exist as a real autonomous person. She discovered that the analyst was fallible, limited, often helpless, and subject to all human emotions, conflict, anxiety, and ambivalence. She found that the analyst was not destroyed by separateness or closeness and did not expect Jean to be destroyed by them. Together with this Jean discovered that she is a person and that she can survive self-assertion. Her ego strength, which was always perceivable, began to be real for her, and her capacity to organize her life in a realistic way increased steadily.

All of her family and acquaintances were obsessed with money, and this was an obstacle in forming relationships. This obsession had also been an obstacle in developing her imaginative life, but she learned how to use it appropriately and how to symbolize it.

The delusion of oneness and the delusion of total separateness are linked conceptually but experienced alternately, as previously mentioned. Such dissociation is sometimes illustrated by the fact that patients who feel one with and inseparable from the analyst may simultaneously have secrets that must be withheld from the analyst. These "secrets" are kept in a carefully guarded inner world which has little contact with the outer world of shared reality. The patient's relationship with the analyst in the inner world is an idealized and denigrated double of his actual relationship with the analyst.

Links between the inner world and the outer world depend upon development of the patient's capacity to utilize symbols. In Jean's case such symbolic links began to form, and thus we could anticipate the development of one element that was still missing from her personality — her ability to use her creative imagination, to be playful, and with this the ability to develop latent artistic talent. The real external circumstances of Jean's life since her husband's accident, although they served as a powerful stimulus to her ego development, were an obstacle in the area of play. But working through her mourning over Barry by caring for him and mourning for her other losses helped to build up her inner reality. She needed to find that her creativeness was inseparable from destructiveness, rather than try to keep them apart, as she did before analysis. There is no doubt that she has the ability to play and that it will develop, as will her capacity for artistic creativeness.

SUMMARY

1.) A fundamental aspect of early mothering that promotes mental health is the mother's adaptation to the infant's needs so that the infant is not prematurely obliged to recognize the separateness of objects. This recognition arrives naturally when his ego develops the capacity to form structured introjects and identify with them. This aspect of ego development is a precondition for stable identity and for relating to objectively perceived separate persons without either loss of contact with or destruction of the central self-object unity.

2.) The psychotic and borderline ego states differ from the neurotic ego state. The latter is characterized by organized defenses that maintain repression of organized introjects, that manifest themselves in transference — positive and negative. Psychotic and borderline patients must achieve considerable ego structuralization before they can conceptualize a truly separate internal or external object to love and to hate.

During the process of differentiation and individuation, the conscious link with the original self-object unit is lost, while it is unconsciously maintained. Good enough early mothering care can restore continuity with the original self-mother unit and facilitate a natural, spontaneous development toward identity, independence, and object relatedness. Failures of early maternal care can interfere with continuous development and lead on the one hand to premature awareness of separateness from the mother and on the other hand to fixation on delusional identity with her.

3.) Failures of early mothering can produce continuous and pervasive anxiety about survival, which is more primitive than paranoid anxiety involving organized projective mechanisms. Chronic anxiety about annihilation, with avoidance of pain rather than seeking of pleasure, characterizes borderline states as well as psychoses. With such anxieties the energies of the ego are totally employed as defenses against the expected annihilation; pleasure-seeking and object relatedness must be totally subordinated to this defensive task. Successful early mothering care helps to modify annihilation anxiety, which can then be experienced as anxiety about partial destruction (for example, castration anxiety) or about object loss (for example, depressive anxiety). Anxiety about partial destruction elicits localized (neurotic) ego defenses, whereas anxiety about annihilation elicits pervasive ego defects.

4.) Differentiation from the mother figure has not taken place in borderline states; in analysis, regression in the transference reveals a delusion of identity between patient and analyst, who is perceived as identical with archaic parental imagos and as functioning in accord with infantile ego states.

5.) In order for maturation to take place and for the split in the ego to heal, the analyst must accept the fact that for the patient there are two parallel realities: first, he is aware of his identity as an autonomous individual and may be able to manage his practical affairs quite well, but his personal relationships will be unsuccessful; and secondly, he feels that he or parts of himself are either actually and literally one with the analyst or absolutely isolated and out of contact. Both the self and the analyst are equated with infantile imagos. This psychic oneness is commonly denied and only revealed during analysis.

6.) The parallel existence of two realities, often dissociated, characterizes borderline states. During regressive phases in analysis the borderline patient often experiences the delusional state as his only reality. This is a primary-process reality, and at these times he depends upon the analyst to provide secondary-process orientation.

We use the term "borderline state" in referring to patients who retain *some* capacity for object relatedness, however painful it may be to recognize their own identity and that of separate persons toward whom they feel close or remote. In a frank psychotic there is no capacity for a relationship with a separate object; there is *nothing* between absolute oneness and total isolation. The borderline psychotic patient may regress temporarily to this state during analysis; at such times an interpretation of the dichotomy — inseparable oneness versus absolute isolation — is itself an activity that links the two states. Insofar as the patient can recognize this linking interpretation, he is a borderline rather than a frankly psychotic case.

7.) If there is only one reality — delusional — we diagnose a frank psychosis rather than a borderline psychotic state. A diagnostic distinction between borderline state and frank psychosis often cannot be made on phenomenological grounds when the patient is first seen in consultation; the state of the ego can often be assessed only on the basis of the patient's response to analysis.

REFERENCES

Freud, S. (1915). *Instincts and their vicissitudes.* Standard Edition, vol. 14. London : Hogarth Press.

———. (1920). *Beyond the pleasure principle.* Standard Edition, vol. 18. London : Hogarth Press.

———. (1923). *The ego and the id.* Standard Edition, vol. 19. London : Hogarth Press.

———. (1926). *Inhibitions, symptoms, and anxiety.* Standard Edition, vol. 20. London : Hogarth Press.

———. (1930). *Civilization and its discontents.* Standard Edition, vol. 21. London : Hogarth Press.

———. (1933). *New introductory lectures.* Standard Edition, vol. 22. London : Hogarth Press.

———. (1937). *Letter to Princess Marie Bonaparte.* Standard Edition, vol. 21. London : Hogarth Press.

———. (1938). *An outline of psycho-analysis.* Standard Edition, vol. 23. London : Hogarth Press.

Klein, M. (1957). *Envy and gratitude.* New York : Basic Books.

Little, M. (1958). On delusional transference (transference psychosis). *Int. J. Psycho-Anal.* 39 : 134–138.

———. (1960). On basic unity. *Int. J. Psycho-Anal.* 41 : 377–384.

———. (1966). Transference in borderline states. *Int. J. Psycho-Anal.* 47 : 476–485.

Searles, H. F. (1961). Phases of patient-therapist interaction in the psychotherapy of chronic schizophrenia. *Brit. J. Med. Psychol.* 34 : 169–192.

————. (1965). *Collected papers on schizophrenia and related subjects.* New York : International Universities Press.

Winnicott, D. W. (1950). Aggression in relation to emotional development. In *Collected papers.* New York : Basic Books, 1958.

————. (1951). Transitional objects and phenomena. In *Collected papers.* New York : Basic Books, 1958.

————. (1952). Psychoses and child care. In *Collected papers.* New York : Basic Books, 1958.

————. (1954). Metapsychological and clinical aspects of regression within the psycho-analytical set-up. In *Collected papers.* New York : Basic Books, 1958.

————. (1956). Primary maternal preoccupation. In *Collected papers.* New York : Basic Books, 1958.

————. (1960). The family and emotional maturity. In *The family and individual development.* London : Tavistock Publications, 1965.

————. (1969). The use of an object. *Int. J. Psycho-Anal.* 50 : 711–716.

16

Identity Problems

PETER L. GIOVACCHINI

THIS BOOK emphasizes that in recent years the study of patients has compelled us to adopt a more ego-psychological orientation (focusing on structural factors) rather than maintain a predominantly psychodynamic orientation. It is apparent that various ego functions and systems are significant. As a source of psychopathology, it is important to understand the structure of the ego as well as clashing and opposing forces. I would like to mention the first case I treated that convinced me of the necessity of expanding our theoretical etiological explanations and concepts regarding treatable psychopathology.

This patient was a married woman in her middle twenties who complained of free-floating anxiety. Previous therapists thought that she had a type of classical anxiety neurosis with innumerable phobias, and they tried to uncover and resolve the oedipal struggle. I discussed this case with two of her former analysts who consistently described her in terms of an hysterical neurotic. What interested me, even at that time, was the fact that these generally calm and experienced analysts appeared to be excited and, to some extent, disturbed. They did not seem to care about the fact that they had lost the patient (because of a "stalemate"); they maintained an intense interest in her welfare, even though both analysts had been solely responsible for the termination of treatment. After

I started treatment, these analysts frequently asked me (to an unusual degree) how she was getting along. I felt that they were genuinely concerned and not primarily motivated by therapeutic rivalry; they seemed to me to be confused and frustrated about their approach to this patient.

Agreeing with my colleagues, I believed that she was primarily an hysterical woman with regressive oral defenses. I waited for the usual dependent transference to develop and, putting the erotic components to one side, began to deal interpretatively with her dependency. Instead of resisting or accepting my interpretations, the patient remained friendly and responded to my "insights" as if they were correct but incidental and irrelevant. She was not disparaging but, nevertheless, succeeded in creating a state of anxious confusion in me which, somehow, reminded me of my colleagues' reactions.

Eventually I learned that this patient's anxiety was unique and different from that which is usually described. Even though her anxiety had a signal function (to a minor extent), its pervasive omnipresence indicated a more elemental, primitive meaning. The patient informed me that she had constantly suffered from anxiety for as long as she could remember. It was not associated with any particular class of incidents, nor was it ameliorated by any specific conditions. She claimed that she could "create" anxiety (she could consciously produce it) and could also "turn it off," but never completely. During a particularly memorable session she illustrated this affective control, and I could see the spontaneous generation and subsidence of the vasomotor and physiological components of anxiety.

This startling material (I do not believe we would be amazed at such events today) emphasized my lack of psychoanalytic understanding, and I gradually become aware that my professional identity, which, to a large extent, was based upon standard clinical psychodynamic constructs, was being threatened. Insofar as my technical background was inadequate to understand this patient, my role as a therapist was threatened; this accounted for the vague, uneasy confusion I experienced. I must confess that it was only later that I finally understood my identity crisis, and this patient was instrumental in helping me arrive at this understanding.

To summarize her background, this patient had a sister — an identical twin — who, because of frequent physical illnesses, received all of the parents' attention. The patient felt as if she were a Cinderella-like nonentity without an existence of her own. She experienced periods of blankness and described herself as hollow and amorphous (see Giovacchini, 1956). Since these feelings and attitudes about herself seemed to be fundamental, her psyche constructed what might be called superstructures to defend itself against intolerable emptiness and nonexistence. Her generation of anxiety was related to maintaining organization of the psyche; otherwise, she might have experienced "apathetic terror" or complete psychic collapse.

Thus, anxiety represented feeling, although it was painful. Any kind of feeling at least assured the patient that she was alive, that she was capable of feeling, and that she existed as a separate entity in a real world. As one pinches himself to determine whether he is awake, this patient, by feeling anxious, knew that she belonged to the outer world and was not a shadowy phantom of the inner world. The importance of self-representation (which is being used here as a synonym for identity sense) becomes increasingly clear when one is confronted with patients like this young woman. As we have learned throughout the years, there are many patients who suffer from similar characterological problems. Their identity system, as well as other ego-subsystems, is always involved.

The concept of identity should be clarified and elaborated because we learn from our patients that psychopathology frequently affects that part of the psyche that has been conceptualized as the self-representation. How the patient views himself, his self-esteem, and his security in various roles are all aspects of his sense of identity. Many analysts, particularly Erikson (1959) and Federn (1952), have written about different facets of identity and have distinguished among the identity system, the sense of identity, and other aspects that are important in development and have pathological vicissitudes. I do not wish to review the literature or deal with the development of the concept of identity. From Freud's (1895) discussion of identification as both a developmental and defense mechanism that promote ego stability to Erikson's (1959) graphic description of the identity disorders of adolescence (the identity diffusion syndrome), our focus has become increasingly clinical within a structural context.

I find it theoretically convenient to perceive the ego as containing, among its numerous introjects, a system known as the self-representation whose function is to define the person's feelings about himself that will become integrated into his identity. Thus, the sense of one's identity can be explained by operational concepts and viewed as a function of the self-representation. Furthermore, insofar as it is a function, it is not static; it fluctuates and changes depending on the general ego state which always affects every ego system. The self-representation is a complex, multifaceted structure that encompasses many levels that are related to the various stages of psychosexual development. Our hierarchically stratified psychic model shows that earlier stages of development leave their imprint upon later, better integrated stages. Similarly, the structure of any aspect of the ego, such as the self-representation, contains all of its developmental antecedents. The general ego state of progression or regression will be paralleled in the self-representation and the identity sense will be correspondingly affected.

A secure, well-balanced identity sense is one in which the self-representation is harmoniously integrated with the rest of the ego. Integration refers to a situation in which all ego systems can function well and efficiently; it also includes a sense of time continuity as the psyche relates to the external world. With a general ego balance, one can differentiate and integrate concepts of past, present, and future. The self-representation is an ego system that belongs in this time continuum; its ability to utilize its past as well as its anticipated future provides an integration that makes the self-representation especially relevant to the present. Percepts of the external world in the present can be placed in a differentiated context that is arranged in a fashion that preserves the continuity from the past to the future. Therefore, a person's identity will depend upon his present frame of reference and whether it is in context with that frame of reference. His current ego state naturally includes his environment and the interaction of his psyche with it. There is another continuum here — at one end the ego is completely absorbed with the inner world, and at the other end it is completely absorbed with the external world.

Disturbances of an individual's identity equilibrium are often found when there has been a precipitous change of environment. One is reminded of Jacobson's (1959) description of political prisoners and their experiences in a concentration camp. Eissler (1953) mentioned the phenomenon of depersonalization when he described the reactions of a stranger who had moved to a foreign country. A more common occurrence is when an individual experiences a momentary confusion and a slight degree of identity diffusion just when he begins his vacation or returns to work. In all of these instances, the usual adaptive techniques are not effective in the changed environment, and so the individual has to reorient himself in order to reestablish equilibrium. Adaptive techniques, as part of the ego's executive system, must be included in the concept of identity. The ego's reactions to an id impulse, an affect, or disturbed homeostasis are not sufficient to form a concept of identity, but the techniques used by the ego to establish and maintain homeostasis are what distinguish one person from another, convincing each person of his existence.

The feeling of emptiness against which my patient had to defend herself indicated a lack of structure, and it was intensified by her inability to satisfy her inner needs. Consequently, she always had a low self-esteem and had to constantly seek reassurance that others could relate to her. She required acknowledgment.

The establishment of homeostasis depends upon successful mastery and reflects general ego organization. The balance and harmony among the various ego systems will determine whether the individual feels a sense of confidence and integration or a sense of misery and emptiness. However, his self-awareness may not be a direct representation of his basic ego integration since it may contain many defensive elements to compensate for its lack of integration (as was true with my patient).

What one feels, as with any psychic element, should be viewed as part of a hierarchical continuum ranging from early primary-process id aspects to reality-oriented, conscious, secondary-process elements. The self-image contains, as previously mentioned, all levels of the psychic apparatus. The uppermost layers consist of identifying characteristics that are operationally elaborated, for example: "My name is —————— and I am ——— years old, of a particular race and nationality, and I have the following physical characteristics. . . . I am a —————— by profession, and I earn my living by ——————. This enables me to live in a certain fashion and to satisfy a variety of needs." Thus, the range extends from identifying characteristics to executive techniques and needs, which can be subdivided into their basic elements. As a need becomes elaborated from its physiologic substrate, different levels of the psychic apparatus are set in motion to handle this need so that it may eventually be gratified. Once the higher techniques of mastery are activated, the preconscious identifying characteristics become more elaborated and sophisticated. For example: "I am a man who has certain rights as a citizen; I am skilled in my work and am sufficiently competent to secure those things that I require to fulfill my responsibilities and to gratify what I feel I need." True, this individual may not be competent and his self-image may hide his helplessness and lack of the techniques of mastery, but his identity sense will be determined by what he believes he is.

The discrepancy between the way the world views a given individual and the way he views himself is often a significant factor in determining the quality and extent of his psychopathology. Those who suffer from severe characterological defects do not have a smooth and harmonious frame of reference that is integrated with the world in general. Consequently, they often have to create their own world; if their world is sufficiently elaborated, it may constitute a delusional system.

In any case, one's self-appraisal only deals with a small portion of his total identity at a given time. This is consistent with the view that only a fraction of the self-representation can be conscious because, according to Freud (1900), the range of consciousness is a narrow one. One's identity sense is determined by the particular conscious element that is experienced at any given moment. If an individual's drives are strong, they will be experienced as the dominant aspect of his identity. Or one may think of himself only in terms of eating — as a hungry mouth and an empty stomach — or as being otherwise needful. If, on the other hand, an individual is engaged in problem solving, then the executive factor — his profession, for example — will probably be the predominant identity.

Once again, the concept of a hierarchical continuum is indispensable. To begin with, one feels alive because he experiences needs that are initially physiological. The experiencing of such needs is reflected in the soma, where formation of the body image begins; at first this image is diffuse, its sensory components consisting of feelings of hungry tension. Then needs become elaborated — from primitive orality to aggressive heterosexual strivings. Experiencing different body parts is paralleled by the progressive structuralization of various drives, and the body image changes from an amorphous, undifferentiated one to one where different appendages and structures are associated with specific feelings. These, in turn, are associated with greater psychic structure, leading to a wider range of self-awareness and a variety of goals that satisfy inner needs and promote self-esteem.

It is conceptually consistent to equate the self-image and the perceptual systems' self-observations with the identity sense. What an individual observes about his total integration is basically the way he perceives himself. Although integrative mechanisms do not have mental representations, their operations are associated with affects that do; it is these affects that are felt and related to the ego integration. Although conscious awareness of the self is finitely limited and dependent on the activity of the moment, the individual still views himself as a totality at a preconscious level. To summarize briefly, the various images he has of himself are in context with each other — the present, together with the past and future realities. His various self-representations can also be seen as ranging from somatic representations (his body image) to complex, abstract conceptualizations. The integration of all of these levels of self-representation gives the individual a feeling of continuity and relevance.

In psychopathological states these various self-images are not integrated into a harmonious whole. Patients who suffer from characterological problems experience a multiplicity of affective states and symptoms that are explained most economically by assuming some disturbance in the way they view themselves. During treatment, the phenomenon of a disturbed identity has been noted in a variety of behavioral states. Patients who regress because of a disruption of their defenses or an upsurge of conflictual impulses often have difficulty achieving a consistent picture of themselves. The above-mentioned continuity is disturbed.

Adolescence is characterized by doubts and obsessional ruminations about the meaning and purpose of life and is associated with many instinctual upheavals. Dr. Rose presented clinical material describing the vicissitudes of the self-representation as they are related to genetic factors (see Chapter 8). Both Dr. Rose's patient and mine developed specific techniques to deal with their inner oppression and barrenness. These techniques helped them to maintain equilibrium; to the extent that they were adjustive reactions to a psychopathological orientation, they could be considered defensive techniques. However, unlike the customary defense mechanisms which consist of aberrant, disruptive id impulses and the ego's attempts to achieve repression, these adjustive reactions were not responses to intrapsychic conflicts; they were attempts to keep the ego from regressing to a state of helpless vulnerability where the self-representation would lose its previous organization, and all ego systems would function less efficiently. Reality-testing and the ability to relate to the demands of a given environment (executive ego systems) are markedly impaired when these patients, who have only a precarious identity sense, decompensate.

Both Dr. Rose's patient and my own emphasized how they protected themselves against the painful feeling of their loss of identity. Before dealing with their adjustive modalities, I would like to discuss why an amorphous self-representation should be experienced so painfully, sometimes with feelings approaching panic and terror. At first, it might seem self-evident that the loss of individual boundaries is intrinsically disruptive. However, most clinicians can readily recall situations where patients have regressed to very primitive developmental stages — preceding any demarcation of ego boundaries — and have not been anxious or disturbed. In fact, many of these patients have experienced a blissful, calm, Nirvana-like state. Such states are not restricted to the therapeutic setting; those who have taken drugs have frequently described similar states, and they seem to place a high value on such seemingly regressive experiences.

FUSION

Those who do not become anxious or disturbed at the loss of their ego boundaries differ significantly from those who do. Those who remain undisturbed tend to feel a unity with others — persons, causes, or ideals. They experience a symbiotic fusion with something that transcends their own identity; they are uniting themselves with a force that represents omnipotence and invulnerability. Consequently, even though they are sacrificing their own identity, they do not feel helpless because of a loss of control and lack of structure; rather, the symbiotic union gives them stability and security, which, in some instances, may be delusional. This fusion state can aso be precarious, as illustrated by a female college student who often took LSD either with a group or with her boyfriend. One evening while on a "trip" with her boyfriend, he deserted her for some unexplained reason. Once alone, she psychotically decompensated; a year after this episode she was still in the hospital suffering from a severe catatonic schizophrenia (see Chapter 6).

Patients who are threatened by the loss of their ego boundaries thus reveal their intense loneliness and feelings of vulnerability. If the regressive process should continue unchecked (get out of control), they may experience a state of psychic collapse, which could take the form of a psychosis, as happened to the young lady mentioned above. In such cases, there is an almost total lack of object relations that could be integrated and used to maintain some contact with the outer world, leading to the development of adaptive techniques for handling both inner and outer turmoil. *The capacity to relate to some external object, even though in a primitive fashion, seems to be crucial in determining whether a regression to an amorphous ego state with its corresponding lack of identity will result in bliss or in terror.*

The capacity to fuse with a person or certain aspects of the environment was one of the defensive techniques frequently used by my patient. I believe this type of fusion happens quite often in the psychoanalytic situation, especially in patients who suffer from characterological problems and identity disorders. Although such patients may regress to very primitive developmental stages, there is no risk of an intractable psychosis if the transference is allowed to evolve naturally and is not hindered by the therapist's intrusion or his desire to manage the patient's life. Eventually the transference regression will reach back to the level of symbiotic fusion, a level that will become, to some extent, stabilized. This ego state will then be utilized as an adaptive defense against disruption, which would manifest itself as an existential crisis. Thus, analysis contains an intrinsic adaptive technique against intractable regression. References to the structuralizing and stabilizing effects of analysis and its intrinsic supportive elements often mean this state of symbiotic stability. To the extent that the analyst is not intrusive, the symbiotic fusion will not recapitulate the destructive assaults of the patient's early development to the same extent. It is this difference between the benign analytic introject and the devouring internalized primitive object relationships that make the regressive fusion bearable and analyzable.

My patient also used fusion to protect herself against psychic dissolution, but to secure her identity she used the mechanism of spontaneous-generating anxiety. Unlike many patients who suffer from characterological defects, she was able to control her affects, although occasionally she lost this control.

As discussed elsewhere (Giovacchini, 1964), some patients who suffer from a defective self-representation also have poorly developed drives. Consequently, they cannot discriminate among their inner feelings; one such patient couldn't tell whether he needed to defecate, whether he was hungry, or whether he had sexual feelings. His inability to identify his feelings made him even more confused about who and what he was, and, in this instance, made him more bewildered about what he wanted and needed. His inability to discriminate was also reflected in a vaguely constructed and poorly defined body image.

PERCEPTUAL HYPERDEVELOPMENT

For imperfectly understood reasons, my young woman patient had well-developed senses and she seemed to have a superior ability to distinguish nuances of feeling. Although she had not had much experience listening to music, she could hear a selection and readily identify the various instruments in the symphony orchestra. She could recognize a work, the conductor, and certain players (for example, the soloist or the first violinist). She became an excellent photographer after very little training, indicating her inherent visual skills; she also had an unusual taste sensitivity as evidenced by the fact that she could tell whether certain sauces had been properly prepared and, more impressively, could identify different wines and their vintage years. Apparently she was also sensitive to smell and had an unusual ability to recognize various perfumes. Her sense of touch was also thought to be very sensitive, and she could easily detect small temperature changes. This patient's unusual sensitivity was quantitative as well as qualitative. Her hearing and sight were much better than average, as determined by testing. Intense stimuli, however, did not disturb her; she probably had a better than average tolerance of loud noises.

At a later time I learned from colleagues about other patients with unusual sensitivities. Although they are not particularly common, they seem to be found among those who have a special variety of characterological disorders with identity problems. Greenacre (1957) described similar patients but in the context of a study of creativity; although my patient appeared to be creative, my focus here is on structural psychopathology.

The generation of affect in order to maintain a sense of identity indicates another unusual aspect of this patient's perceptual system. An affective experience involves various psychic systems (including the id), but the experiencing of feeling, by definition, is a function of the perceptual system. This patient had an unusual ability to generate, experience, and discriminate among feelings — she had what might be considered a hyperdevelopment of the perceptual system (and her history showed that these qualities had been present since early childhood, indicating a precocious development).

Patients who suffer from characterological problems have a defective development and fixation of various ego systems. However, the ego is not totally affected; some ego systems are more constricted than others. Children who have been intrusively hyperstimulated (Boyer, 1956; Giovacchini, 1971) often show premature ego development, especially with respect to the intellect. Of course, they have to have the innate capacity, but intellectualism can be used adaptively as a characterological defense.

Instead of being subjected to the impact of intrusive, non-adaptive stimuli, my patient felt abandoned and isolated. Rather than feeling that her existence was assaultively threatened, she felt as if she did not exist at all; in relation to her sister, no one acknowledged her. This seemed to be an instance of lack of stimulation; an extreme form of this — perceptual isolation — leads to the generation of certain feelings that can become hallucinations. Such feelings often seem to be self-generated.

Still, the distinction between assaultive hyperstimulation and the feeling of abandonment (with a corresponding lack of parental interaction and confirmation) is more a matter of form than of polarized extremes. The intrusive mother is not relating to her child as a separate and distinct person; rather, she is relating to a narcissistic extension of herself and what she does usually has very little relevance to the child's needs. Consequently, the child feels misunderstood and abandoned since he cannot get his parents to respond to his needs. This situation is quite similar to that of my patient whose parents did not really relate at all. This lack of early nurturing care leads to certain ego defects, such as an imperfectly formed and inadequate identity sense, which necessitate special defensive reactions and often involve the perceptual system.

SPLITTING MECHANISMS

A common way to achieve some measure of adjustment with an unstructured self-representation is to use splitting mechanisms. This defence is especially prevalent among adolescents, who reject segments of the outside world as bad, thus throwing away their potential for future identifications. Regardless of the reality of certain issues, it is the categorical rejection and the extreme con- cretization of values that betray some adolescents' psychopatho- logical struggles. They also have an obvious identity struggle.

Splitting of the ego here refers to the projection of unaccept- able or disruptive aspects of the self-representation into the outer world. Patients who suffer from identity disorders have a very low self-esteem and considerable self-hatred. My patient felt that since she had been ignored she had also been abandoned. She believed that she had been rejected because she was bad and hateful, where- as her sister, although delicate and frail, embodied goodness. Therefore, she had both an amorphous sense of nonexistence and a self-representation of a hateful, unlovable person. Her self-repre- sentation made her even more tense. She generated affect in order to feel less vulnerable and nonexistent. However, the affect did not protect her from the pain of self-hatred which threatened to over- whelm her ego and often led her to contemplate suicide. In fact, she had taken overdoses of barbiturates on two occasions and was considered a definite suicidal risk.

This patient used defensive splitting to protect herself against self-destructive manifestations of her inner hatred. Like many patients who have ego defects, she had a somewhat paranoid out- look and regarded herself in a fragmented fashion. For example, she sometimes blamed her husband for all her difficulties and could not perceive herself in any role other than a housewife in the most constricted sense. She would maintain this orientation although she fully understood the importance of the traumatic events in her background. At such times she believed that all of her troubles emanated from outside, and she refused to take any responsibility for her condition. These attitudes, however, were not fixed.

Another patient who did not know if he was "fish or fowl" split his ego in a very graphic fashion with very little paranoia. This young man gradually accumulated about a dozen apartments, each one representing a different facet of his identity. For example, he had one apartment for study, one for relaxation, one for making love, and so forth. No single dwelling could serve more than one function (see Giovacchini, 1964). This patient's ego-splitting was typical of primitive fixated egos with narcissistic character disorders. His self-representation reflected his ego-splitting and could function only in a fragmented fashion. This patient's identity sense was defective because it had never developed to the level where there was an integrated synthesis of introjects pertaining to his self-representation. The concept of synthesizing seemingly isolated ego elements is, of course, a restatement of Glover's (1930) formulation about the coalescence of ego nuclei.

Whether a defective identity sense will lead to splitting defenses or whether splitting defenses are responsible for a defective identity sense is not a very useful question; these things usually happen simultaneously. In its formative stages the ego is not very well differentiated, and all systems are, to some extent, involved in every aspect of general adaptation. Consequently, when the early environment is traumatic, the imperfectly formed identity sense, together with the rest of the ego, utilizes splitting mechanisms; these, in turn, will determine what direction the self-representation will take in further growth.

Ego defects involving the identity system are seen quite often in patients, and such defects lead us to raise certain questions about psychoanalytic technique. Many prospective patients are painfully aware of their identity struggle and urgently seek analytic help. I can recall several who had such characterological problems and wanted analysis; they could distinguish to an unusual degree an analytic from a nonanalytic approach. Even though such patients are difficult to treat analytically, it is clear that it would be impossible to treat them with any other method. They understand enough about the analytic process to know that they probably could not gain further structure and integration unless permitted the freedom to regress within the transference framework.

SUMMARY

Clinical experience highlights the need to understand many patients from a theoretical frame of reference that goes beyond an id-oriented psychodynamic model. Clinicians constantly encounter patients who can best be understood as having structural defects within an ego-psychological frame of reference — defects in particular subsystems. By viewing the ego in terms of such subsystems, we can conceptualize much of the material presented by the patient as defects of his self-representation. It is apparent that he has disturbances of his identity sense as well as defenses against the pain caused by such existential problems. Three specific defenses against an amorphous and defective self-representation were discussed : fusion (symbiotic), the generation of affect in the context of a hypersensitive perceptual system, and splitting. These important psychic mechanisms are designed to maintain equilibrium in an environment that might otherwise threaten an ego that feels vulnerable, unloved, and — in extreme states of regression — nonexistent.

REFERENCES

Boyer, L. B. (1956). On maternal overstimulation and ego defects. *Psychoanal. Study Child* 11 :236–256.

Breuer, J., and Freud, S. (1895). *Studies on hysteria.* Standard Edition, vol. 2. London : Hogarth Press, 1955.

Erikson, E. (1959). *Identity and the life cycle.* New York : International Universities Press.

Eissler, K. (1953). Notes upon the emotionality of a schizophrenic patient. *Psychoanal. Study Child* 8 : 199–251.

Federn, P. (1952). *Ego psychology and the psychoses.* New York : Basic Books.

Freud, S. (1900). *The interpretation of dreams.* Standard Edition, vols. 4 and 5. London : Hogarth Press.

Giovacchini, P. (1956). Defensive meaning of a specific anxiety syndrome. *Psycho-Anal. Rev.* 43 : 373–380.

———. (1964). The submerged ego. *J. Amer. Acad. Child Psychiat.* 3 : 430–442.

———. (1971). Fantasy formation and ego defect. *Annals Adoles. Psychiat.* 1.

Glover, E. (1930). Grades of ego differentiation. *Int. J. Psycho-Anal.* 11 : 1–12.

Greenacre, P. (1957). The childhood of the artist. *Psychoanal. Study Child* 12 : 47–72.

Jacobson, E. (1959). Depersonalization. *J. Amer. Psychoanal. Assoc.* 7 : 591–610.

17

The Concrete and Difficult Patient

PETER L. GIOVACCHINI

QUESTIONS REGARDING the applicability of the psychoanalytic method eventually become focused upon two basic issues : 1.) What types of case are amenable to analysis (what are the indications for this specialized type of treatment)? and 2.) Assuming that the psychoanalytic method can be extended beyond Freud's use (which was limited to the transference neuroses), what modifications of the classical technique are required in order to be able to engage these more difficult patients in a treatment relationship? These questions have been argued from many viewpoints (see Chapter 1); only the first one will be specifically discussed here, although inferences pertaining to the second one can undoubtedly be drawn (see Chapters 14 and 18).

Freud's main argument against analysis for certain patients was that they could not experience transference. Thus, he distinguished between the transference and the narcissistic neuroses. In recent years other analysts have challenged Freud's belief that there is no transference in the narcissistic neuroses (see Little, 1958; Modell, 1963; Searles, 1963). Psychotic patients, as well as the so-called borderlines, seem to be able to form intense reactions toward the analyst, reactions that are directed at infantile archaic

351

objects (part-objects endowed with considerable primary-process qualities). If transference, as suggested by Anna Freud (1946), consists of an exclusive projection upon the analyst viewed as a whole object (presumably at the oedipal level of psychosexual development), then these intense reactions do not constitute transference. Patients who suffer from severe character pathology often project parts of themselves onto the analyst — a narcissistic transference. Still, it is probably too restrictive to think that transference belongs only to a particular level of psychosexual development, and probably the transference mentioned by Anna Freud is clinically rare. Freud (1895, 1901) initially postulated that transference was a projection of the same infantile feelings that characterize primitive object relationships. As ego psychology emphasizes, such relationships are part-object relationships, and feelings toward such part-objects are often split between one part-object and another. Such egos are frequently fragmented.

Regardless of how one defines a patient's irrational reactions toward the therapist, the important question is whether these reactions can be used for therapeutic benefit. Exactly what type of regressive phenomena are we encountering? How can they contribute to our understanding of fundamental pathology as well as determine our treatment approach? It has jokingly been said that psychoanalysts will only treat patients who are not sick. After reviewing the characteristics that analysts usually require of prospective patients (for example, considerable ego strength, relatively little resistance, a minimum of acting out, good motivation, ability to free associate), one has the distinct impression that the only patients who are suitable for psychoanalysis are those who don't need it; "difficult" patients are not believed to be suitable.

"Difficult" patients should be defined in terms of intrapsychic processes, and this can be done by studying the types of transferences they form. At the outset a therapist usually has a quick impression about the patient's potential for treatment. This appraisal is usually based on the patient's ease in becoming engaged in the treatment relationship. At times this ease may be accompanied by considerable anxiety; nevertheless, there is a kind of relaxation that indicates an ability to communicate. The therapist feels secure if he believes the patient can become aware of the irrational nature of his transference projections. "Difficult" patients often give the impression that there will be difficulties in forming or resolving the transference. Frequently they seem to be rigid and inflexible. An analyst may be reluctant to treat a patient because he is afraid that analysis will bring about a dangerous decompensation, perhaps an unmanageable regression.

There are certain patients who appear to be so "tightly held together" that they do not seem to have the freedom to regress; their concreteness might preclude analysis. It is difficult to describe the concrete quality of the mental operations of these patients. Nevertheless it creates an unpleasant and tense atmosphere; regardless of the patient's avowed willingness — sometimes eagerness — to enter into a therapeutic relationship, the therapist has misgivings about the final outcome. One can quickly sense the underlying hostility and the unmanageable dependency of these "concrete" patients.

I am using the term "concrete" to describe a mind that is either unwilling or unable to deal with both inner and outer experiences in psychological terms. In fact, it is difficult for concrete patients to acknowledge inner experiences. These patients can only deal with very simple cause-and-effect relationships, and they do not have the capacity for free-flowing spontaneity that would enable them to capture the emotional nuances of subtle intrapersonal and interpersonal relationships.

To repeat, although it is difficult to characterize a concrete patient, I have found that my colleagues know precisely what type of patient I am talking about and can quickly supply me with clinical examples of their own. Their exasperation with such patients is evident, and, regardless of their unique countertransference attitudes, it is apparent that they are responding to possible ego defects as well as to a controlling manipulativeness designed to defeat any therapeutic effort in spite of these patients' apparent cooperative attitude.

For example, an unmarried man in his middle thirties sought psychotherapy because of impotence. He didn't seem to have any real understanding of psychotherapy; he was simply following his internist's suggestion that psychiatry might help since all of the clinical tests pointed to the functional nature of his disturbance. Since psychotherapy had been recommended, that was what he was going to "get." He showed his enthusiasm and a willingness to cooperate, as exemplified by the following statement: "Tell me what to do, Doc, and I'll certainly do whatever you say." It seemed ridiculous to talk about spontaneity, and the most we ever achieved was a travesty of free association. At best, this patient went through the motions of analysis. He lay down on the couch and usually waited for me to ask a question to "guide" him. I explained that I didn't want to choose his topic or theme for him; he expressed his gratitude to me for this and then totally ignored it. He would turn and look at me and then say something to the effect that he wanted to choose something I would find useful.

He frequently brought me dreams because he understood that dreams were important. His dreams had some unique and interesting qualities. From his viewpoint they were full of "Freudian symbols." He dreamed of snakes, cigars, chandeliers, holes, and caves; he would often be running up or downstairs. His dreams seemed to be caricatures of those reported in *Interpretation of Dreams* or the *Introductory Lectures to Psychoanalysis*. He also had other dreams that were quite different. These were equally interesting but impossible to work with, *for they were exact replicas of reality*. It was often difficult to ascertain whether he was talking of an actual experience or of a dream. The themes were vivid and organized, the action was sequential and logical, and the id forces seemed to be under complete control of reality-testing.

Some concrete patients seem to be naïve, and of limited intellectual and cultural endowment. Therapists often encounter these characterological types in low fee or free clinics. I do not believe, however, that such patients are a product of any particular socio-economic group, for my impotent patient came from a socially prominent, wealthy family. He was a business executive and was reputed to be quite talented in his area of specialization. He belonged to the "right" clubs and had been graduated from a sophisticated preparatory school and an ivy league college. His background, therefore, contrasted sharply with his naïve approach to psychotherapy and his inability to relate emotionally.

Analysts sometimes categorize difficult patients by their inability to become "engaged" in the analytic relationship. Some schizoid patients and many adolescents, although they may faithfully keep their appointments, seem to be unable to develop meaningful and deep feelings toward the therapist. They are often reserved and do not spontaneously express themselves. When they do speak, their words tend to be monosyllabic; if the analyst feels frustrated and asks questions in order to "force" them out of their withdrawal and isolation (see Chapter 11), their answers are cryptic and terse.

Are these clinical situations psychotherapeutically hopeless? In view of the large number of patients who suffer from characterological problems, including the concrete patients described here, I believe that we should muster all of our clinical experience and understanding in order to learn to utilize, as much as possible, whatever inherent therapeutic potential there may be. True, many patients discontinue treatment early in the relationship, but there are some, such as my impotent patient, who, after facing certain fundamental conflicts, lose their need to withdraw and eventually their concreteness.

Perhaps there are important differences among patients who have the same characterological manifestations. Some patients may use concreteness as a defense to protect themselves against intolerable ego states, while others use this type of thinking because of a faulty organization (ego defect). The latter patients have a rigidity to their secondary process, the result of a fairly primitive ego organization that has not developed to any great extent the integrative capacity for abstraction and symbolization, the tolerance of inner disorganization and ambiguity, and the autonomy of self-observation and spontaneity.

These distinctions between a defensive reaction and one due to faulty structure are, of course, the same that are so often encountered in our diagnostic conceptualizations of defensive regression and fixation. However, when patients are viewed from a characterological perspective, differences between regression and fixation have less clinical relevance (see Giovacchini, 1969). Whenever the ego adopts a certain modality to maintain cohesion and homeostasis, it is still utilizing a characterological stance. This stance may have a defensive function, but not in the traditional sense of a unilateral, unacceptable inner situation (such as an id impulse) and an ego response that is designed to preserve organization by repression. In patients with characterological problems, the ego resorts to a characteristic mode of functioning, determined by its structure and designed to maintain a degree of harmony between the inner psychic world and the environment. In the case of concrete patients, concreteness is both a perceptual response and an executive technique; it is a method used by the psyche to preserve itself. Thus, concreteness can be considered defensive, but it is also typical of a particular type of ego organization. Whether these patients are amenable to therapy, therefore, cannot be answered simply on the basis of a quantitive fixation; other factors must be considered.

It is natural to wonder whether these patients have similar underlying conflicts — conflicts of such magnitude that demand an inflexible noninvolvement in the therapeutic setting. Furthermore, should the analyst try to break through such a needed defensive barrier since he will probably not be successful and could cause irreversible disruption? The analyst almost always thinks about these questions when he considers treating concrete patients; he usually declines treatment if it will involve deeper layers of the personality. It is generally believed that the patients' characterological fragility and withdrawal are insurmountable obstacles.

Before saying anything definitive about therapy it is necessary to understand more about a patient's underlying psychopathology. Since my frame of reference is purposely ego psychological, other character traits should be considered. When a therapist is able to obtain enough information, he often learns that concrete patients have only a vague idea as to who and what they are and what their . purpose in life is. They feel a vague dissatisfaction about not belonging, and they do not see themselves as distinct individuals. As they describe themselves, their identity sense lacks organization. In ego-psychological terms, these patients can be viewed as having defective, poorly developed self-representations. Perhaps all who suffer from severe pathology have disturbances of their self-representation; the differences among patients may be just a matter of degree.

Clinically, not all patients with severe psychopathology have difficulty becoming engaged in a therapeutic, even a psychoanalytic, relationship. *Potential difficulties can be foreseen by determining how much disturbance there is of the identity sense. It is possible that there is a direct relationship between the amount of disturbance of the identity sense and the patient's tendency to isolate himself from the therapist.* The existence of such a relationship is only conjectural, but the subject can be explored further in terms of developmental and characterological factors. I hope to demonstrate that many of these psychopathological patients can be treated. Rather than simply citing cases that were successfully conducted as empirical proof, I want to formulate concepts based on the therapy of such patients to indicate the feasibility of treatment. Therefore, I will present conclusions drawn from material obtained during the transference regression of such patients (more specific clinical material is abundant elsewhere in this book) — a regression that followed the relaxation of their initial withdrawing defenses.

During relatively deep transference regressions, these patients may have intense antithetical reactions. For example, they may experience blissful calm and have omnipotent feelings of transcendental unity. They may feel that they are harmoniously fused with the analyst and they may no longer recognize the boundaries between themselves and the therapist. They may still say that they have no identity, but, whereas previously such an awareness might have reached the proportions of an existential crisis, now, during the transference regression, they show an almost magical degree of comfort. Instead of feeling amorphous, empty, and chaotic, as they had at times prior to treament, they see themselves as having a kind of "super-identity" (as reported by one patient) — a transcendental identity based upon the patient-analyst fusion. To stabilize this fusion state, practically every other aspect of their lives loses its previous meaning. Although they go through the motions of relating to people and situations, their meaningful, affective ties are restricted to the analytic situation. Whereas at the beginning of treatment they were maintaining a state of non-involvement with the therapist, now their relationship with the outer world is largely one of withdrawal. Thus, there is a dramatic and striking change in these patients as treatment progresses.

As with most phenomena that occur during treatment, these changes are not sudden, nor do they stand out clearly. These patients showed shifts from one transference state to another; their transference projections and defenses against such projections sometimes underwent rapid alterations. Following periods of tranquil fusion, these patients returned often to their previous aloofness. They might interrupt a long period of silence to say that they were disappointed in the treatment relationship and that they found it meaningless and hopeless. Sometimes they would blame me, although just as often they would blame themselves for being too unworthy or lacking the resources to avail themselves of the potential benefits of analysis. Although they found treatment to be "meaningless," they still kept their appointments and were disappointed and angry if, for some extraneous reason, a session had to be canceled. Then gradually their mood tended to change and once again they would establish a state of fusion. We can establish a sequence from the initial distressing symptom of non-involvement to a specific transference regression. I believe we can postulate certain psychic processes that will help explain these back-and-forth shifts and enable us to understand that what might initially have been interpreted as the patient's therapeutic inaccessibility is actually analytically meaningful.

Before proceeding with this discussion, I would like to describe another path taken by the transference projection that seems to be almost inevitable when treating these patients. Although clinical events do not occur in an orderly or predictable sequence, the phase I am going to describe usually follows the patient's fusion with the therapist but sometimes precedes it. When the latter occurs, the therapist is more likely to become discouraged; therefore, it should be understood in the proper context.

The patient may reject everything interpreted by the therapist. He will hold steadfastly to a position of invulnerability — a psychic state that seems to be almost a psychotic exaggeration of his previous reserve and apathy. However, instead of apathy, the analyst observes an intense amount of affect (sometimes anxiety) that may approach panic. Since the patient is actively trying to keep himself separate from the analyst, he may demonstrate a hateful rejection (rather than a passive awareness) of him.

An obvious connection can frequently be observed between the regression characterized by blissful fusion and this phase of hostile rejection. The patient often begins by complaining that the analyst is not meeting his megalomanic expectations. A blissful state cannot survive without some magical reinforcement, which the analyst is unable to provide. The patient's resentment builds up until he finally tries to separate himself entirely from the analyst. The fusion is no longer harmonious, but threatening, and the analyst is perceived as dangerous and engulfing. At this point the patient may have dreams of being inundated or swallowed up and he may complain that the analyst is trying to manipulate or smother him. He fights hard to maintain a distinct boundary between himself and the analyst, one that he needs to sustain a precarious self-representation.

This defense against fusion does not necessarily occur after a period of harmonious symbiosis; it may appear as an extension of the patient's initial nonengagement. This defense seems more apt to come about if the therapist does not actively try to get the patient involved (if he doesn't probe or otherwise try to make the patient respond or talk). In any case, the patient's initial defense seems to gather momentum and to acquire content. The patient will indicate that *his noninvolvement is based upon his relationship with the analyst; the analyst is significant to the extent that the patient has to withdraw from him.* The patient will specifically defend himself against the analyst, clearly indicating that he means something very special to him, even though it is threatening. *Thus, the patient assigns a particular significance to the therapist and this constitutes a transference projection.*

Even though the patient's behavior and affect in a state of blissful fusion seem to differ significantly from the state just described, basically they are quite similar. During fusion, of course, the patient shows his admiration for the therapist and finds the relationship vital and life sustaining, yet, on closer examination, *the therapist can see that his presence is not really acknowledged; the patient is only reacting to an internalized imago of him.* The patient has introjected the imago and discusses the relationship between two parts of his own self in the hope of effecting a synthesis. Since he basically ignores the external object, from a psychodynamic viewpoint, fusion brings about the same result as an initial state of passive withdrawal or a defense against fusion.

During periods of contentment and fusion with the analyst, the analyst as a person is simply ignored, whereas during periods of disruptive regressions, the analyst is feared. The differences can be explained in terms of the content of the projections : in the former case, megalomanic expectations are projected and then incorporated (Klein [1946] would call this projective-identification), and the external world is ignored ; in the latter case, the hateful, chaotic parts of the self are projected and then pushed away or violently withdrawn from.

Bleger (1967) makes an interesting distinction between symbiotic and autistic mechanisms that operate during narcissistic transference states. In the Kleinian tradition, he elaborates the concept of projective-identification, specifying the position of objects, inside or outside. The symbiotic state is mainly one of projection : the external object becomes a depository of the patient's projections, and then the patient effects a fusion with it. He usually does this in order to defend himself against his own aggression and greed. Autism represents the other side of the coin : the analyst is internalized and then the patient reacts to his imago.

In accord with Bleger's distinctions, the clinical phenomena described in this chapter could be categorized as symbiosis (the blissful state) and autism (the hostile, rejecting state). However, I would like to emphasize the advantage of considering everything manifested by the patient as occurring in his mind. In regressed states the distinctions between external and internal object *representations* are blurred. In both the blissful and the hostile states, the integrity of the self-representation is a central issue. As mentioned earlier, concrete patients have unusually severe disturbances of their identity sense which reflect their general ego organization; consequently, whatever vestige of structure their self-image has must be zealously protected. The transference regressions of these patients help to protect their autonomy, in the one case by defensively withdrawing, and in the other (in a seemingly paradoxical fashion) by introjecting projected, idealized, structured parts of the self and then denying the significance or the dangers inherent in external objects. Both states utilize splitting mechanisms, a general characteristic of schizoid patients.

Whether patients who do not seem to be able to become engaged in therapy are treatable can now be viewed from another perspective. Granted that these patients are difficult to treat, they are not impossible. What may appear to be noninvolvement is really a symptom of their psychopathology; in itself, it represents a type of involvement, that is, a transference manifestation.

Thus, it is apparent that the more amorphous and hateful the self-representation is initially, the more painful and threatening the symbiotic fusion will be. In some instances, the prospective patient will not allow himself to become engaged in analysis because the anticipated symbiotic regression is too threatening due to the intensity of his inner hatred. His precariously constructed identity sense cannot withstand the threat of having his anger turned toward the self as would inevitably occur during a fusion state where distinctions between the inner and outer world are obliterated.

Some analysts believe that it is important to make a distinction between transference and a defense against transference. They do not believe that a defense is a transference; they feel that if it is too intense, it may be a deterrent to analysis. I do not believe that one can make absolute distinctions; patients who suffer from severe psychopathology, especially, develop transference states where the content of the projection and the defense against the disruptive aspects of the projected material are so imbricated that they are virtually inseparable. As in the case of symptoms, there is inherent in the transference projection a relatively primitive defense against the anticipated consequences of that projection.

One could conceptualize a situation in which the patient would muster his resources so that he would not project infantile elements into the analyst. This, of course, would mean that their relationship would be influenced less by primitive factors and more by the better-organized, mature parts of the patient's psyche. The patient would be oriented more at a secondary-process level. Any other type of defense (if the above can be considered a defense and not an adaptation) on the part of the patient against his relationship with the therapist would be more primitive. Certainly, a passive withdrawal reaction clearly demonstrates primary-process factors. Consequently, a patient with this reaction must have already projected infantile elements into the analyst and then defensively retreated. He would not have to withdraw from someone he perceived at a secondary-process level; this person would not be threatening because nothing had been projected into him (there was no transference).

Perhaps because patients suffering from severe psychopathology have a primitive ego organization (their perceptual and integrative ego systems have not achieved much secondary-process organization and their reality-testing is somewhat defective), they are more apt to perceive the analyst as an archaic object. *Others who have a better ego organization can relate to the analyst in a realistic fashion and, in contrast with those who suffer from severe psychopathology, do not develop transference reactions as readily. This view contradicts the usual distinctions between the transference neuroses and the narcissistic neuroses. Stated somewhat differently, the patient with severe psychopathology develops transference reactions more easily than the one who is better integrated.*

Since the content of transference projections differs, one can also consider treatability from the perspective of whether a patient can recognize that he is projecting (confusing reality with events that are going on in his mind). Although this is another issue completely, the analyst's ability to perceive and react to behavior in terms of its transference aspects will enable the patient to adopt a similar viewpoint.

Even with the constricted concrete patients described earlier, one is dealing with a transference phenomenon. The defense that characterizes a secondary-process organization is still a reaction to an imago of the analyst. Not intruding into the defense but letting it develop has, in my experience, led to two diametrically opposed reactions. Either the patient will establish an analytic relationship (as happened with my concrete patient) or he will spontaneously terminate. One might ask whether it is feasible to let the patient terminate, especially if he is suffering. If the analyst takes a nonanalytical approach initially, there is no way of knowing whether analysis might be possible. However, I believe it is better for the patient to seek help elsewhere if analysis is not, *at the moment,* possible. If the analyst preserves the analytic setting, the patient can always return to it sometime in the future. I can recall three patients who fled from my analytic stance but then came back months or years later. In the interval one had had psychotherapy and the other two had had no further professional contacts. There are many types of noninvolved patients. I believe that the diagnostic types who are called "as-if" or "pseudo as-if" should also be categorized as noninvolved (see Chapter 18).

In summary, a group of patients thought to be difficult cases because of their apparent inability to become engaged in a therapeutic relationship is discussed in terms of their ego processes that are relevant to the analytic interaction. These patients are viewed in terms of characterological pathology (particularly their defective self-representation) and in terms of the transference implications of their recalcitrant behavior.

Even though one can generalize about the defective self-representation and say that it is an intrinsic part of the psychopathology of patients who suffer from characterological problems, noninvolved patients are probably more disturbed in this area than those who do not have any difficulty forming a therapeutic relationship. *I believe that the more defective a patient's self-representation is, the more he will be inclined to withdraw from analytic involvement.* There is a logical reason for this; it becomes apparent if one looks closely at the various transference regressions these patients undergo, if they continue in analysis. A patient's initial noninvolvement is, in itself, a manifestation of transference; he withdraws from an imago of the analyst upon which he has projected hateful and destructive parts of the self. After reviewing the distinctions between a transference and a defense against transference, it was concluded that they are not particularly meaningful for the group of "difficult patients."

REFERENCES

Bleger, J. (1967). *Simbiosis y ambigüedad.* Buenos Aires : Paidos.
Breuer, J., and Freud, S. (1895). *Studies on hysteria.* Standard Edition, vol. 2. London : Hogarth Press, 1955.

Freud, A. (1946). *The psychoanalytic treatment of children*. London : Imago Publishing Co.

Freud, S. (1901). *Fragments of an analysis of a case of hysteria*. Standard Edition, vol. 7. London : Hogarth Press.

Giovacchini, P. (1969). The role of interpretation in the treatment of schizophrenia. *Int. J. Psycho-Anal.* 50 : 179–186.

Klein, M. (1946). Notes on some schizoid mechanisms. *Int. J. Psycho-Anal.* 27 : 99–110.

Little, M. (1958). On delusional transference. *Int. J. Psycho-Anal.* 39 : 134–138.

Modell, A. (1963). Primitive object relationships and the predisposition to schizophrenia. *Int. J. Psycho-Anal.* 44 :282–293.

Searles, H. (1963). Transference psychosis in the psychotherapy of chronic schizophrenia. *Int. J. Psycho-Anal.* 44 : 654–716.

18

The Blank Self

PETER L. GIOVACCHINI

IN CHAPTER 17 I discussed certain characterological types who are believed to be difficult patients because they maintain a protective distance from the analyst. Here, I would like to discuss a particular subgroup in detail — those with the syndrome that Helene Deutsch (1942) designated "as-if." Although this syndrome is reputedly rare, these patients, because of their flamboyant ego defects, highlight a variety of psychopathological processes; therefore, they may help us understand a larger segment of the patient population and, in turn, improve our therapeutic attitude. We will focus on the significance of early environmental factors and their bearing upon the developmental process and the structuring of various ego systems. Viewing the as-if patient we have an opportunity to learn more about such ego subsystems as the self-representation as well as early mother-infant symbiosis and the consequences of both its pathological formation and its resolution as reflected in the treatment setting.

Many discussions of the as-if personality begin with defining the syndrome; Helene Deutsch, herself, distinguished between as-if and pseudo as-if. I do not wish to repeat what has already been said; rather, I will describe the ego mechanisms and processes underlying a specific phenomenological entity which is an aspect of wider, more heterogeneous behavioral responses. The patients who will be discussed here lack the identity sense and organization that have generally been believed to characterize pseudo as-if patients. Of course, quantitative assessments cannot be precise because the psyche can never be viewed unilaterally; a multiplicity of variables is responsible for psychic functioning and for varying degrees of integration and organization of different levels of the mental apparatus.

Behaviorally, both as-if and pseudo as-if patients lack individuality; like chameleons, they blend in with their surroundings. Supposedly they adopt the characteristics, styles, and in some instances, even the standards and ideals of others. However, such "identifications" are transient and easily exchangeable with others. The pseudo as-if personality is not phenomenologically different from the as-if personality. From the viewpoint of psychic structure, however, the self-representation of the pseudo as-if patients is thought to have a modicum of organization; relatively speaking, the as-if aspects of his personality (the incorporation of significant external objects) are supposedly defensive superstructures, whereas those of the as-if patient himself are basic.

Ross (1967) pointed out that the as-if reaction can be described in terms of a continuum: at one end is the as-if behavior which is associated with varying degrees of pathology; in the middle are pseudo as-if states; and at the other end are the as-if responses found in fairly well-functioning persons. Greenson (1958) discussed the specific behavioral characteristics that result from the need for object contact (screen hunger), and Gitelson (1958) stressed the rigid but adaptive ego features that maintain adjustment and prevent psychic dissolution in patients with as-if qualities. Reich (1953) referred to transient as-if reactions as regressive defensive reactions to specific traumatic situations. Various analysts have stressed such behavioral distinctions as the lack of real engagement in object relationships and the paucity of true affect.

CLINICAL MATERIAL

Two clinical vignettes will emphasize the early object relations of an as-if patient from different perspectives. The first patient, a woman, seemed to have the characteristics of an as-if personality as she discussed her behavior and demonstrated it in the transference. The second patient (also a woman) has a son who has been seen by several psychoanalysts, all of whom have been impressed with the as-if qualities of his behavior. Therefore, the first patient will illustrate the impact of the maternal introject upon later personality functioning and the second patient will illustrate specific projections onto the child. Even though there is no relationship between these patients, material obtained from the one complements that obtained from the other. The first patient provides us with a microscopic view of various ego subsystems, permitting inferences to be made about her maternal motivations, whereas the second patient gives us a cross section of her maternal behavior, permitting inferences to be made about its effects upon the development of her son's as-if character structure. Furthermore, the first patient is also a mother, and the second patient has aspects to her behavior that could be considered as-if.

The first patient's husband called to arrange for her initial appointment. He was extremely concerned about his wife's welfare and, even during our brief telephone conversation, expressed bitterness about the fact that her mother had neglected her. He stressed that his wife was helpless, almost to the point of being unable to function. The patient, a pale woman in her twenties, was brought to the office by her husband; she appeared hesitant and timorous. In spite of her apparent fragility — almost bordering upon dissolution and panic — she was able to give me a surprising amount of information. As the session progressed she seemed to anticipate what I wanted to know, and so I found it unnecessary to ask questions to satisfy my curiosity. At the time, I was aware of an uneasy feeling within me which I could not explain; there was an uncanny quality to what I was experiencing.

This patient reported that she had always been shy and withdrawn but, paradoxically, had always felt a need to be with people. Whenever she was alone, she would panic for fear that her loneliness would "swallow" her up. She had difficulty "anchoring" herself and knowing who and what she was and what the purpose of her existence was. She had had these attitudes and reactions since early childhood and they dominated her earliest memories. She had had some psychotherapy in college but didn't feel that she had ever been deeply involved in it. This didn't surprise her because she didn't feel that she was capable of involvement. Her husband had insisted on treatment because she had become totally incapable of doing anything (taking care of the house and her daughter, shopping, and the usual routines of everyday life — including personal grooming). This regression occurred precipitously after the husband's job required that they move to Chicago; for the first time in her life, the patient was separated from her mother. During college she had lived in a dormitory, but the school was located in the same city fairly near her parent's home.

Of course, I became extremely interested in the patient's relationship with her mother as she was telling me about herself. Again, without any overt requests from me, she described in detail her relationship with her mother, which was remarkably similar to one described by James (1960). The patient is an only child. Her mother is still an extremely beautiful woman, with an imperious aristocratic demeanor. Her mother had a rather set routine, one that did not include the patient and included her husband only in a superficial, social sense. The patient believes that her mother's only interest in life has been clothes, for which she still spends an enormous amount of money.

The patient was brought up by a succession of indifferent maids; the mother habitually stayed in her bedroom until noon and, consequently, did not speak to either her husband or daughter in the morning. She would have breakfast brought to her in bed and then would take care of her correspondence, which apparently was voluminous and often required a personal secretary. She would spend the afternoon either at fittings or at some rather "high level" social function. Around five o'clock in the afternoon she would return home, presumably for a nap, and then would remain in her room for the rest of the evening. If her parents were entertaining or were invited to some important social function, her mother would appear sparkling and exuberant. Gradually, the patient became aware of how brittle her mother was underneath this facade. For example, she learned that her mother was an alcoholic and that she spent many of her long hours in her boudoir drinking. Once when the patient was nine years old and was sent home from school unexpectedly because she had developed some flu symptoms, she found her mother completely intoxicated, whimpering, and generally disheveled — a startling contrast to her usual proper, impenetrable aplomb.

The patient's father also had very little contact with her since he was away on business trips during the week and usually busy with showy social functions with his wife on the weekend. When the patient was an adolescent it became apparent to her that her father's apparent passivity was actually a contemptuously patronizing attitude toward his wife's alcoholic weakness and vulnerability. He used her as a showpiece and tried to play the role of a protector, but whenever the patient overheard her parent's rare conversations, she was surprised at his cutting and sneering sarcasm; it also had a whining quality. In the vague relationship she had with her father, she felt that he also used her as a show-piece, "a china doll." Her relationship with her husband was similarly patterned, and during his telephone conversation with me, I could sense both a patronizing attitude and a whining quality in his voice.

The patient reported that she never had any ideas of her own — that nothing came from within herself. She saw herself as a "sponge," soaking up the personality and the identity of the person she was with. She could not bear to be alone, for it made her feel that she did not exist. With another person, she felt that she was part of him or that he was part of her. For example, in high school when she was dating a boy who wanted to be a lawyer, she became convinced that law was also her calling. Then he went away to school, and she had an affair with a premedical student; she became persuaded that nothing else mattered but the practice of medicine. When this relationship ended, so, too, did her interest in medicine. Others noticed her tendency to imitate and to incorporate both their ideals and mannerisms. One of her friends suggested that she consider a stage career, but the patient had no interest whatsoever in being an actress.

Interestingly enough, the man she married has no distinct vocational or professional identity. He is an officer in a family-owned business, but it is clear to the patient that he is only going through the motions of having a position. A job was created for him, one that involves considerable busywork, but it has no real significance in the operation of the business, which is completely dominated by his father. All of his earlier pursuits had failed to materialize.

Before discussing this patient's psychic processes that relate to her particular characterological problems, I will introduce the second patient. This woman, in her early forties, also did not seek the initial consultation for herself. Although she made the first appointment, it was because she wanted help for her eight-year-old son. As she described him, he appeared to be shy and withdrawn and could not be left alone. He seemed to be very unhappy although he never complained; consequently, she had not sought professional help before. She changed her mind, however, when her son's teachers strongly suggested psychiatric consultation. They believed that his almost total reading block was due to emotional factors and that some of his mannerisms and gestures might indicate autistism. I referred him to a colleague. Later, the boy's analyst said that he was not autistic but had an as-if personality. The boy reported that he generally incorporated the characteristics of anyone who related to him, and the therapist noted such reactions in the consultation room.

Returning to the mother, she soon revealed she had a number of problems and wanted help for herself as well. She described a lifetime of continual self-sacrifice; she had dedicated herself to others at the expense of her own autonomy and self-esteem. Her parents had lived in genteel poverty; apparently they had lost a large amount of wealth during the Depression. Her mother seemed to be an aristocratic woman who could never quite accept her impoverished condition; the whole family treated her as inadequate and incompetent. Since her mother had never learned to do anything but instruct servants, the patient, the oldest of three children, assumed the responsibility for taking care of the family and the house. The patient's father was an invalid; he had been bedridden with arthritis since the patient's early childhood.

In spite of all her family responsibilities, she managed to finish high school. Immediately afterward she obtained a position as a secretary to the head of a small firm. Her employer was 25 years her senior and she admired his distinguished, sophisticated manner. She dedicated herself to her work and in five years she became manager. She worked many evenings and weekends and became indispensable to the business; in effect, she had no life of her own outside of work. She would receive telephone calls at home anytime, and might have to interrupt a holiday or vacation in order to return to the office, but she never complained. As time went by the patient became more and more intimate with her employer. At first, he told her about his personal life, and then there was physical intimacy and she became his mistress.

She didn't make any demands on him. However, he felt sufficiently guilty about the relationship and unhappy about his marriage so that he wanted to marry her. His invalid wife, though, would not give him a divorce, and his two sons (one of whom was a year older than the patient) disapproved vehemently of the liaison. This impasse continued for about 12 years, when the wife died. Then he married the patient, and she felt more secure and wanted. However, shortly after the marriage, she recognized that her husband was a totally dependent, helpless hypochrondiac, and that he need the care and attention of a young infant.

Therefore, the patient began to take care of both her husband and the business. She saw herself as a business women who had no investment in the household. Her life remained pretty much as it had before marriage, except that she went home with her husband and continued the relationship there — a mixed business and nursing one that could not include anyone else. She scarcely mentioned her son at all after she began her own analysis, even though he had been the focus of her first interview. She spoke of her pregnancy and delivery in such a casual, off-hand fashion that it was difficult to realize that she was speaking about herself.

The patient described herself as a bland, dull person without any specific individual characteristics. In her eyes her husband seemed to be a strong personality and so she clung to him as a savior. It didn't seem to make any difference that, after the marriage, she had described him as a weak and ineffectual person; she still saw him as an idealized, exalted person. It was clear that she had a well-developed ability to tolerate contradictions. Another example is the fact that during her childhood and adolescence she seemed to have been unaware of her family's poverty-stricken circumstances, even though it was this that led her to assume so many household responsibilities.

The patient often went into what apparently were fugue states; her companions would find her "lost in a fog" — staring in a fixedly blank fashion and unresponsive to them. During analysis she continued to experience such spells, although they were not as frequent as in childhood. Repeated EEG's had always been normal.

DISCUSSION

Freud's first description of the actual neuroses (1898) was of a nosologic entity based primarily upon physiologic tension or depletion states that bypassed "higher" mentational systems. Extending these ideas logically would lead us to believe that if patients with actual neuroses entered a psychoanalytic relationship, there would be no transference relevant to their area of conflict.

However, there is considerable controversy over this matter. I mention it here only because both of my patients developed a relationship with me that (on the surface, at any rate) seemed to be devoid of transference projections. I hope to demonstrate that this was not actually the case; rather, these patients developed a unique type of transference that was the specific product of their peculiar characterological difficulties. Their transference was similar in principle but different in content from that of the patient's described in Chapter 17.

It was particularly noteworthy that during our early sessions neither of these patients made any reference to me, either in their dreams or in their associations. As a person upon whom they attached some specific emotional significance, I did not seem to exist. They talked freely and gave detailed descriptions of events in their present and past lives, but these "travelogue" narratives (as Freud [1909] called them) were without substance; they told me nothing about their feelings and gave me no clue about the qualitative or quantitative aspects of their object relationships. Similarly, the primary-process factors that are ordinarily associated with primitive affects were so elusive that I couldn't find an anchor upon which to organize my understanding of the intrapsychic pathology of these patients. I felt that there was nothing I could "grab hold off" — that there was nothing to analyze. I felt a void within myself when I tried to view each patient in terms of unconscious processes and defensive mechanism, but even more when I attempted formulations in terms of the dominant transference theme.

An elusive transference is not particularly rare, especially when one is treating patients who suffer from severe characterological pathology. Such patients are often afraid of the dissolution of the symbiotic fusion with the analyst, or else they have to maintain a rigid control against intense disruptive regression. One can easily discern the defensive nature of their withdrawal manifested in rigidity and tension. My patients, however, were perfectly composed and relaxed and (on the surface, at least) did not appear defensive. Although there seemed to be a paucity of analytic material (transference projections), my patients were not boring. I had the distinct impression that I was being confronted with a baffling phenomenon, but one that might eventually be understood in analytic terms.

Gradually both of my patients developed mannerisms that puzzled me, until eventually I realized that they were imitating my gestures, inflections, and favorite expressions. Their behavior was not clearly obvious, and they had no awareness of what they were doing. It seemed that even though they apparently projected nothing onto me, they were especially adept at incorporating parts of me at some level. This did not constitute a solid identification, though, because I learned later on that my patients imitated me only in my presence; once they left the consultation room, they reverted to their usual behavior. When I confronted them with their capacity to imitate many of my mannerisms, neither of them was surprised. However, the subsequent course of events was different for each patient; I believe these differences reflected the unique aspects of their characterological pathology and indicated two distinct types of as-if reactions.

The first patient soon became benignly dependent. She expected me to know what was going on inside of her and to anticipate her needs, as she had anticipated my curiosity during our first interview. She became docile and submissive, and there were many periods of comfortable silence during her analytic sessions. However, unlike patients who project megalomanic expectations upon the analyst, she indicated no melodramatic wish to be omnipotently rescued; nor did she manifest the subsequent inevitable disappointment of such expectations. On the contrary, intrinsic to her dependent expectations was the conviction that they would not be met. Thus, there was a contradiction: she wanted me to anticipate and to respond to her unexpressed needs, yet she knew that I would fail her. *Failure was inevitable in this situation, not because I could not fulfill her omnipotent needs but because I didn't really exist;* what she saw was a phantom — a hollow "ectoplasm" that would evaporate if she touched it.

This patient's vision of me was obviously a projection of her self-representation and the principal aspect of her maternal imago. After I pointed out her projection, she brought up material that dealt with her amorphous imago of her mother and her mother's amorphous image of her. She saw herself as a robot with no soul or identity; she alternated between having this view of herself and having a similar view of me, the analyst-mother. The patient's father also contributed to her self-image of nonexistence, but her mother's role was more crucial.

The patient often described ours as a "tape-recorder" relationship. She was completely blank and she projected "blankness" onto me. The only way she could fill the void was to incorporate others into it, but they could not be "held." This was an extremely interesting phase of her analysis because, as her existential anxiety mounted, she was able to obtain some relief by incorporating me. Then she would ignore me again but, as could be seen, this represented a transference fluctuation rather than a lack of transference.

The second patient reacted quite differently after I confronted her with her imitative behavior. This patient idealized me and analysis became her exclusive preoccupation. She transformed me into an omnipotent savior. Unlike the first patient, this one had a certain melodramatic attitude and she fully expected her needs (which she could not verbalize) to be met. She did not see the rest of the world as hostile or persecutory (as happens with patients who use dissociative defenses); it simply did not exist for her. From this patient's point of view, rescuing and being rescued were equivalent. She converted our relationship into an alliance; we would take care of each other. She, of course, knew of my other patients, but through dissociation she believed that I was exclusively attached to her; in a similar fashion, she also had no "life" between analytic sessions. This patient was not delusional; she was fully aware of reality, but these fantasies were vivid and powerful.

A significant aspect of this woman's analysis was the inevitable disappointment of her megalomaniac expectations. Later she experienced states of disruptive rage, which contrasted sharply with her usual tightly controlled self. As with all patients who suffer from ego defects, this patient reacted with anger to two common feelings: frustration, which usually followed her awareness of guiltily denying her anaclitic dependence through self-sacrifice, and a sense of vulnerability, which led her to revile herself (sometimes she even appeared to convulse on the couch), indicating how uncontrollably helpless she felt. Her maternal transference helped us to understand the genesis of her depreciated self-representation. She was terrified at the thought of being completely "swallowed up" by an engulfing, powerful, demanding mother, one whom she believed was intolerant of any individuation. She attributed such qualities to me; I wanted to rob her of all autonomy. During this time she had many nightmares of drowning.

Periods of panic and rage alternated with periods of calm, which were characterized by the fragmentation I noted at the beginning of the analysis. Her ego dissociation (in which everything outside of the analysis ceased to exist) was a defense against her fears of losing her autonomy. During her stabilized defensive states against a threatening maternal fusion, this patient focused upon certain maternal aspects of her self-representation. The patient's need to negate the existence of the outer world was also reflected in her attitude toward her son: she projected her feelings of non-existence onto him. Her concept of him was one of "blankness" — an important aspect of her self-representation. Her description of blankness resembled Lewin's (1946) dream screen, and I believe it had the same structural and functional meaning.

Blankness was also an important factor in helping this patient maintain a defensive balance. During regressed, disruptive states, she would speak of her son, indicating that she hated him and would like to annihilate and repudiate him. These feelings were, in part, a replication of the murderous rage she had repressed toward her siblings. More pertinent, however, was the projection of her hateful, destructive, vulnerable self. She reported several dreams in which she had given birth to a deformed monster, thereby indicating that her son represented a narcissistic extension of the intolerable parts of her self-representation. Blankness, therefore, served as a defense against this dangerous and guilt-laden projection. Having a non-existent son protected her from these death wishes; through projection it also relieved her of the oppressive burden of her inner void.

Both patients had specific structural defects and characteristic methods of dealing with them that were reflected in their general behavior as well as in their as-if behavior. Their as-if reactions, including the second patient's behavior during the initial phases of treatment, exemplify neither imitation nor identification. Imitation is believed to be consciously contrived, whereas identification is an unconscious process. These patients, like others who have been called as-if or pseudo as-if, were not conscious of what they were doing or of its significance. Still, they could not form a solid core identification that would endure without the external object. It seems that the as-if patient utilizes an incorporative mechanism that is somewhere between imitation and identification (a point that other analysts have also made).

The capacity of these patients for what might be called a partial or transient identification seems to enable them to sense others' feelings and subtle reactions. During the initial interview with the first patient, I felt that she was particularly sensitive to my feelings and could anticipate what I wanted to know. However (as others have also noted), the sensitivity of these patients seems to be restricted to superficial feelings; when I have experienced deep reactions, including countertransference, these patients show no awareness of them; they seem to have little capacity for true empathy, as might be expected in view of their psychic impoverishment. In fact, my early feelings of bewilderment, I believe, were evoked by their projection of emptiness onto me, a projection that precludes understanding. Patients who suffer from characterological problems have a defective self-representation. Both of my patients considered themselves empty, thin, hollow shells. They always seemed to be trying to fill this void by incorporating significant external objects.

Examining the genesis of this type of identity or lack of identity highlights important aspects of early mothering. Apparently the mother of the first patient was an extremely brittle woman who had little capacity to relate to anyone. She had to preserve whatever libido she possessed in order to maintain a shaky narcissistic balance. Her daughter's early concept of her was vague, remote, and distant. The mother was practically nonexistent, and that which the patient eventually incorporated — the maternal introject — was of a nonexistent (blank) entity. To the extent that the maternal introject contributes to the formation of the self-representation, the patient constructed an identity sense based upon blankness. Another reason for the patient's blank identity sense may have been her mother's projection of blankness onto her. A woman, such as her mother, cannot relate to her child in any substantial fashion except as a narcissistic extension of herself. Probably the fact that this patient's mother had no definition of her self-representation affected her perception of and relationship with her daughter; she saw her daughter merely as an extension of the amorphous (blank) part of herself.

This description of the patient's mother is, of course, speculative, but it gains plausibility if we recall the sequence of the patient's transference reactions. Of particular interest (and what makes this type of characterological defect unique) is the fact that hatred and self-hatred were *not* prominent in the patient's self-representation or transference projection; feelings of nonexistence and blankness predominated. Usually the mothers of such patients project the hateful parts of their selves onto their children, who then incorporate these parts into their own self-representation. In treatment the hatred manifests itself in deeper transference projections. However, in the case of my patient, her projections indicated that blankness constituted a primary level of her self-image; it was not a superstructure designed to defend her against self-hatred and disruptive rage.

It is important to be aware of such psychic processes for technical reasons. What may appear to be a lack of engagement in some cases is actually a necessary transference projection. A patient will establish a relationship with the analyst in terms of his own character structure (the product of early object relationships); his adaptation to the analytic setting constitutes transference. My patient's projection of a blank self-image was, at times, the dominant transference theme. This often made her appear to be dull and uninteresting, too afraid or incapable of analysis, but this projection belied her intense interactions with the analyst below the surface.

My second patient's reactions did not remain dormant very long; she showed hatred and self-hatred and projected them both on the analyst and on her son. This woman differed significantly from the first one in that the blankness she initially projected on me represented a defensive superstructure; it also characterized the way in which she perceived her son. Underneath this blankness, however, was a murderous rage that she later expressed eloquently. She defended herself by feeling blank and empty. Many patients who suffer from characterological disorders have similar problems and reactions. However, my second patient was unique in that she used blankness as a defense against her underlying rage and self-hatred (as well as to demand magical salvation). Her projection of blankness onto her son was probably important in determining his as-if orientation.

The defensive use of blankness is not particularly rare; Kalina (1969) has encountered it in adolescents who were struggling to achieve identity. Using blankness as a defense may also indicate that there is some blankness in the underlying self-representation. I believe that patients who use blankness as a defense exemplify pseudo as-if personalities and not true as-if personalities (my patient's son is probably also a pseudo as-if). However, if there are amorphous elements in the underlying self-representation, the distinction between my first and second patients (that is, between as-if and pseudo as-if) becomes blurred, and their differences are then a matter of degree and not of kind. The capacity to introject and make solid identifications is generally impaired in both as-if and pseudo as-if patients. They cannot make clear distinctions between themselves and the outer world; they tend to fuse with external objects instead of making selective identifications. Although their superego development would ordinarily be affected, both of my patients were able to withhold their aberrant impulses by conforming to the repressive aspects of the outer world. Their affectlessness resulted from their lack of distinct structuralization (Zetzel, 1949; Zilboorg, 1933).

In conclusion, as-if and pseudo as-if patients illustrate the interactions among various ego systems that lead to distinct transference manifestations. In discussing patients with schizoid personalities, Khan (1960) suggested that their passivity is the result of specific relationships among their various ego systems. Although this chapter has not dealt with libidinal conflicts, it doesn't mean that there are no such conflicts; it only means that during earlier phases of treatment they are poorly developed and not particularly meaningful.

SUMMARY

Patients who display as-if behavior help us to understand a larger group of patients who suffer from characterological problems. Specific character defects are the result of unique early object relationships. The way in which some of these defects manifest themselves in the treatment relationship may make it appear that there is no therapeutic engagement. However, such appearances are actually the outcome of an important transference projection — the projection of the patient's "blank" self-image.

I believe that the two patients discussed here exemplify as-if and pseudo as-if personalities, respectively. The essential difference was their self-representation. The first patient's blankness and emptiness were primary and resulted from her relationship with her fragile, narcissistic mother who treated the patient as if she didn't exist. The second patient felt the same way about herself (that she was a void), and she projected this aspect of herself onto her son, who had as-if symptoms. She exemplifies a pseudo as-if character structure because her blankness represents, in part, a defensive superstructure to protect her against self-hatred and disduptive rage.

The pathological relationships among the various ego systems have important technical implications. The transference projections of these two patients, especially during their initial phases of treatment, involved parts of the self (rather than libidinal feelings) that are typical of this nosologic group.

REFERENCES

Deutsch, H. (1942). Some forms of emotional disturbances and their relationship to schizophrenia. *Psychoanal. Quart.* 11 : 301–321.

Freud, S. (1898). *Sexuality in the aetiology of the neuroses.* Standard Edition, vol. 3. London : Hogarth Press.

———. (1909). Note upon a case of obsessional neurosis. Standard Edition, vol. 10. London : Hogarth Press.

Gitelson, M. (1958). Panel discussion. Curative factors in psychoanalysis. *Int. J. Psycho-Anal.* 39 : 243–275.

Greenson, R. (1958). On screen defenses, screen hunger and screen identity. *J. Amer. Psychoanal. Assoc.* 6 : 242–262.

James, M. (1960). Premature ego development : some observations on disturbances in the first three months of life. *Int. J. Psycho-Anal.* 41 : 288–294.

Kalina, E. (1969). El proceso analitico de un adolescente con un estado "como si." Paper presented to the Argentinian Psychoanalytic Association, November, 1969.

Khan, M. M. R. (1960). Clinical aspects of the schizoid personality : affects and technique. *Int. J. Psycho-Anal.* 41 : 430–437.

Lewin, B. (1946). Sleep, the mouth and the dream screen. *Psychoanal. Quart.* 15 : 419–443.

Reich, A. (1953). Narcissistic object choice in women. *J. Amer. Psychoanal. Assoc.* 1 : 218–238.

Ross, N. (1967). The "as if" concept. *J. Amer. Psychoanal. Assoc.* 15 : 58–83.

Zetzel, E. (1949). Anxiety and the capacity to bear it. *Int. J. Psycho-Anal.* 30 : 1–12.

Zilboorg, G. (1933). Anxiety without affect. *Psychoanal. Quart.* 2 : 48–67.

PART VI

Specific clinical situations: Clinical Viewpoint

EDITOR'S INTRODUCTION

*A forum provides an opportunity to share one's experiences
and to learn how others may have handled situations that we have
found difficult. It is often reassuring simply to know that colleagues
have been confronted with problems similar to one's own.*

*Since the focus of this part is primarily clinical, emphasizing
the individual case, the chapters here will discuss different types of
patients and their management — from children with difficult home
situations to adults with a variety of characterological problems.*

*Discussing the treatment of such a wide variety of conditions
will, of course, bring the analyst's therapeutic style into focus. I
believe that such revelations are a significant learning experience;
such frankness will also help to dispel the mystique that has for
years been associated with psychoanalytic treatment. Many of
the authors do not hesitate to reveal countertransference elements;
indeed, they feel it is essential in order to discuss rationally the
treatment relationship. Countertransference has both rational and
irrational elements; the former directly augment our understanding
of clinical data, and the latter do so indirectly by helping us to
learn what has impeded and distorted our understanding. Countertransference is discussed in a casual and relaxed fashion, thus
putting it into proper perspective, that is, as a legitimate and
significant factor in the therapeutic interaction that is always
present, and must be taken into account and not ignored or treated
as if it shouldn't be there.*

*Although Part VI places more emphasis on clinical detail than
earlier parts, there is considerable overlapping; this is inevitable
since theory and practice cannot and should not be separated. It is*

inevitable that the opinions of different clinicians will often conflict. One author may advocate strict adherence to analytic principles, while another (who is dealing with an apparently identical situation) may recommend an environmental change in preparation for treatment. Fortunately, each author describes his experiences and reasoning in detail so that the reader can select that which can best be integrated into his professional self-representation.

19

Exorcism of the Intrusive Ego-alien Factors in the Analytic Situation and Process

M. MASUD R. KHAN

PSYCHOANALYSIS TODAY is facing a crisis from within : a crisis of stasis. There is an irrefutable disparity between its theories and its clinical practice. The ever increasing complexity and assurance of the first does not match the recurrent failures of the second. As Giovacchini (1967) points out, everyone has "eagerly awaited the 'analyzable' patient," and such a patient is getting very hard to find. Hence the preoccupation of an analyst of Greenson's acumen and dedication with the causes of "the unexpected failures" in our practice. We expect our patients to be able to tell us their truth so that we can interpret to them the meta-truth. All too often they fail to oblige our goodwill (Balint, 1968); Lacan (1966), in a foot-note in his huge tome *Ecrits,* has very pertinently stated :

> *On reconnaîtra là formule par où nous introduisons dans les débuts de notre enseignement ce dont il s'agit ici. Le sujet, disions-nous, commence l'analyse en parlant de lui sans vous parler à vous, ou en parlant à vous sans parler de lui. Quand il pourra vous parler de lui, l'analyse sera terminée.*[1]

---

[1] One will recognize the formula there which we introduced at the beginning of our teaching which is being considered here. The subject begins the analysis by speaking of himself without speaking directly to you, or by speaking to you without speaking of himself. When he can speak to you of himself, the analysis will be terminated.

But nowhere, to my knowledge, does he indicate how to bridge the gap between the analyst's omniscient rhetoric and the patient's incapacity to speak his truth. The prophylactic evangelism of Bowlby (1969) and the psychic nihilism of Laing (1967) are reflections of this crisis in contemporary psychoanalysis. It is to Anna Freud (1969) that we owe a sober and positive diagnosis of this crisis:

> Nevertheless, in our times, the term metapsychology has assumed a very different meaning. What it denotes now is largely theory building, distant from the area of clinical material, an activity which demands and is reserved for a specific, speculative quality of mind. As such it has become the bugbear of the clinically oriented analyst who feels wholly divorced from it. This brings about a division which, in the long run, threatens both areas with sterility: the theoretical field due to the absence of clinical data, the clinical field due to a diminution in their theoretical evaluation and exploration. What is lost, finally, is what used to be considered as a *sine qua non* in psycho-analysis: the essential unity between clinical and theoretical thinking.

THE CLINICAL FRAME AND ITS FUNCTIONS

Jean Pouillon (1940), the French anthropologist, in his paper, *"Malade et Médecin: le même et/ou l'autre,"* gives a very lucid account of the doctor-patient-illness relationship in its social frame in three primitive African societies, and from this context asks the analyst to define his own position *vis à vis* his patient and the patient's illness. Pouillon christened this relationship between the doctor, the patient, and the illness: *le triangle thérapeutique.* The three apices of *le triangle thérapeutique* being the malady, the patient, and the doctor — and it is the interrelatedness, or the lack of it, among these three that constitutes the dynamism of *le triangle thérapeutique.* From Pouillon's examples, it is obvious that this dynamism changes as the social *frame* of each given society changes. In other words, one particular style and distribution of dynamism in *le triangle thérapeutique* which is valid in one social frame would not be valid for another social frame. To state it in its extreme form: the shaman of one culture who is effective in one social frame with its established symbolic cultural code and significations will not be effective in another social frame. In the schematic diagrams that Pouillon so neatly delineates of the distribution of relationship between the malady, the patient, and the doctor, he takes for granted the circumscribing omnipresence of the social frame. For us, what is important here is to see how this social frame in primitive societies has been transformed by Freud into the therapeutic frame of the analytic situation. It is an accepted fact in recent psychoanalytic discussions that an integrated theory of psychoanalytic technique, as yet, does not exist. Of course, there are the rules and procedures of conduct in the analytic situation which we inherited from Freud's practice, like placing the patient on a couch, more often than not, sitting behind the patient, regulating the length of the session to 50 minutes or so, and keeping a certain amount of frequency of sessions, and inviting the patient to use verbal behavior as the preferential vehicle for expressing his problems and inner conflicts (Freud, 1911–1915).

What, however, has not been discussed sufficiently is the therapeutic frame which Freud invented in which the analytic process and work materialize. In Freud's own writings as well there is very little discussion of what one might call the metapsychology of the therapeutic frame (Stone, 1961; Khan, 1962; Winnicott, 1963a). In Pouillon's material and examples, one thing strikes one vividly : in each society discussed there is no ambiguity or confusion as to the nature of the illness, the mode of its operation in the patient, and the doctor's attitude to it. This is indeed a most happy state of affairs for everyone concerned because the important question here is not whether the notions operating in any given social *frame* are true or not true, but that they are believed in and shared by everyone concerned. Lévi-Strauss (1963) expresses this situation very neatly in his statement :

> The efficacy of magic implies a belief in magic. The latter has three complementary aspects : first, the sorcerer's belief in the effectiveness of his techniques ; second, the patient's or victim's belief in the sorcerer's powers ; and, finally, the faith and expectations of the group, which constantly act as a sort of gravitational field within which the relationship between sorcerer and bewitched is located and defined.

The first thing that strikes one when one looks at Freud's undertaking in isolating the patient from his social *frame* and putting him in the therapeutic *frame* of the analytic situation is not that the analyst is necessarily more objectively knowledgeable and scientific, and hence less "magical," but that in the new therapeutic *frame* there is no tradition between the patient and his therapist of a shared belief in the etiology of his ailment or, for that matter, a shared agreement about the potential therapeutic efficacy of the frame and the psychological processes entailed. One could argue that the therapeutic frame of Freud facilitates processes which, though they have all the attributes of magical practices, entail that willing suspension of disbelief by both the parties concerned which makes the participation and nonparticipation by each a valid and creative experience leading to an increment in the self-awareness and insight of both. Freud had conceptualized an aspect of this by theorizing that one works best in the analytic situation when one works with the resistances of the patient (Winnicott, 1963b).

Pouillon rightly demands that we evaluate our own role and function in its social frame. Today, it would be impossible for anyone to deny the fact that psychoanalysis is a logical and inevitable result of a very long sociological process of the evolution and alienation of the individual in the matrix of Judo-Christian, European cultures. At a very fateful and historical moment, Freud arrived and had the genius to evaluate the situation and give it a new frame in which this alienated individual could find his symbolic, therapeutic speech and expression. There is no gainsaying the fact, of course, that mental illness and disturbance are universal human phenomena that have been the attribute of human experience since time immemorial. But it is equally true to say that the psychiatric patient, and specifically the analytic patient, is a by-product of the European civilization and cultures.

Foucault (1965), who is perhaps the one scholar who has tried to define the crystalization of the psychiatric patient from the changing social frame across many centuries of cultural developments in Europe, states the whole issue of the new status of man in Western cultures very succinctly when he says in *The Order of Things* (1970):

> One thing in any case is certain: man is neither the oldest nor the most constant problem that has been posed for human knowledge. Taking a relatively short chronological sample within a restricted geographical area — European culture

since the sixteenth century — one can be certain that man is a recent invention within it. It is not around him and his secrets that knowledge prowled for so long in the darkness. In fact, among all the mutations that have affected the knowledge of things and their order, the knowledge of identities, differences, characters, equivalences, words — in short, in the midst of all the episodes of that profound history of the *Same* — only one, that which began a century and a half ago, and is now perhaps drawing to a close, has made it possible for the figure of man to appear.

Toward the tail end of the nineteenth century when Freud arrived on the psychiatric scene, he found the psychiatric patient being treated largely either as a bizarre social fetish or endured as a familial nuisance. When he isolated this potential patient into his therapeutic frame, what emerged was a therapeutic situation, unique in the history of human experience. Within the frame of the analytic situation, the analyst and the patient were unknown phenomena to each other, with no tradition of reliable shared symbols that could help them to negotiate with each other, and Freud soon discovered that the patient was as suspicious of the analyst as the analyst was unbelieving of the overt rationale that the patient offered of his own ailment. From this ambience of mutual unknowing alone could be discovered that symbolic discourse which constitutes the analytic process and dialogue.

The classical psychoanalytic patient can be described as a person who has evolved enough maturity of psychic functioning and emotional development to be able to relate to another and to sustain a minimum of trust and faith in the face of discouraging failure of communication; and who has, across his own development, internalized the significant, experiential, interpersonal relationships with his familial environment; and who, when helped, can give them symbolic expression. Those who did not fit in with these requirements Freud considered unsuitable, and they were the cases of madness or psychoses or those highly introverted, self-absorbed individuals whom we call narcissistic character disorders (Guntrip, 1968). Of course, in the past four decades the situation has radically changed, and the refinement of Freud's therapeutic frame and understanding of how it functions have enabled us to take on cases in which much more demand is put on the analyst to *participate* in the patient's illness than was in the original, classical, analytic situation. This development in psychoanalysis is perhaps reflected in two distinct traditions of pedagogic analysis that one meets in the profession. One considers that having a pedagogic analysis is a definitive experience which starts at a point X and ends at a point Y in time, and after it the "analyzed analyst" is in the know of his own unconscious and therefore can use himself quite objectively as an instrument to help the patient decipher his own problems, but he himself is not necessarily any further in need of being influenced or enlarged from the reciprocity of dialogue with the patient. The second regards personal analysis as little more than crystallizing a capacity to keep on growing in oneself and that all future growth and enlargement of self in the analyst is dependent as much on his private experience as on his being able to assimilate whatever new elements he comes across through his empathy and involvement with the patients' psychic situations and experiences, which would otherwise have been, in terms of his own style of sensibility and living, outside his range of experience (Greenson and Wexler, 1969 ; Khan, 1969a ; Milner, 1969 ; Searles, 1962 ; Winnicott, 1963a).

Pouillon quotes Lévi-Strauss to the effect that societies have two ways of treating the malady in the psychiatrically ill, namely, either as something unique and remarkable — outside the range of most people — and therefore to be coveted and included into social experience, or as something negative and destructive that should be isolated and eliminated from the patient's experience. One sees that in Freud's frame of reference both these attitudes operate according to the temperament and sensibility of the analyst concerned.

Perhaps one of the inexhaustible advantages of Freud's invention of the therapeutic frame is that in it all three styles of *le triangle thérapeutique,* as described by Pouillon, can be crystallized and worked with in the service of the patient. The analyst can in a given case operate as an exorcist of an illness that the patient feels is alien to him, and/or he can know a patient's potential illness of which the patient is as yet unaware in his own experience and thus, through his own sensibility and symbolic behavior, help the patient to be ill in order to recover from it. And lastly, there is a third and perhaps the ideal of therapeutic endeavor, which Pouillon christens *adorcisme,* where the task is not so much to eliminate an illness or to render it innocuous but to put a person in the total possession of his affectivity and sensibility, both in its positive and negative aspects, so that he can live to the maximum of his potential and in terms of the full awareness of the handicap and the illness that it entails for him.

Merely objective observation of the analytic patient (the so-called neutral stance of the analyst) at best leads to arid confirmation of established dogma and does not engender any new discovery or extension of psychoanalytic theory or skill. In this context, one would be quite justified in saying that the growth of psychoanalytic theory and technique is inherently dependent on the analyst's dual capacity to be both involved with the patient's illness and to be able to distance himself from it in order to know it both for himself and for the patient.

It is also necessary for analysts to realize that for *le triangle thérapeutique* to work in the analytic frame, we are dependent on the patient's talent and/or capacity to metaphorize his malady to some extent in terms of our symbolic logic and expectancy of behavior and thinking (Khan, 1969b). Hence, in Freud's therapeutic frame, the emphasis is not only on the understanding of the meaning and resolution of the malady but, even more importantly and essentially, on the discovery by the analyst and the patient together of a symbolic language which is larger and richer than the individual effort and tradition of each alone (Pontalis, 1969; Smirnoff, 1969).

It is precisely when we are faced today with the task of finding a symbolic language in the analytic situation with patients who cannot communicate that we find we have to enlarge our use of the potentiality of the analytic situation as invented by Freud in order to meet the *needs* of our patients. Marion Milner, in her book *The Hands of the Living God* (1969), has given a most vivid account of a treatment of 20 years' duration in which she endeavored with a patient to help the patient find a symbolic language that would communicate her illness and predicament. Winnicott's account of his consultations with children in his book *Therapeutic Consultations* (1970), also gives us a profound discussion of these issues. Freud had taken for granted with his patients a coherent, ongoing, familial environment and organized social values that could be internalized (Freud, 1918). The urgent need of the patients that Freud was dealing with was to be able to speak of what was pressing upon them from within (the repressed unconscious). They had a more or less coherent internal psychic reality with all its conflicts and confusions. What they were seeking was a person who would help them speak about and understand it. Today, most of the patients that we are encountering come from a milieu where the family system itself has, to a large measure, disintegrated, and hence the intimacy between mother and child has taken on a more intense proportion and dynamism.

I shall detail a case history of a boy of 12 to show how an intrusive, pathogenic maternal relationship and a very disturbed familial environment became organized in the child's ego and personality as a manic state, and outline the route the clinical process had to take to arrive at the discovery of that which the patient in himself was utterly unable to communicate in a symbolic way in terms of transference, language, or play (Khan, 1964; Winnicott, 1959–1964).

THE CASE OF TONY, AGED 12

I shall try to present my clinical material as near to the events that were precipitated by the analytic situation and process as possible, with as little intrusion from hindsight as I can manage. There will be a certain amount of repetition, but that cannot be avoided. I am sacrificing elegance of style for the sake of the veracity of the narrative of the process itself. The case that I am describing here was treated by me more than 15 years ago, and the reason why I can detail it with such accuracy is that it was part of my training as a child analyst, so I had to keep very accurate notes. The case was supervised by Dr. Winnicott; he was also the pediatrician-consultant who had referred the case as eminently suitable for analysis. Dr. Winnicott had been in touch with the boy almost since birth and had seen him on two earlier occasions. My total account will consist of the first interview with the mother; then the first phase of the treatment of the child, followed by the next phase of the treatment, ending up with the critical session; and then my interviews with both the father and the mother, which led to some very momentous discoveries, resulting in our decision that Tony should be put in the care of a family other than his parents.

The First Interview with the Mother and the Child

I saw Tony with his mother. He was a delicate, bashful, and girlishly petite boy. The mother was in her early thirties and was a rather tense, fragile, excitable, and petite woman who talked very articulately and confidently. She was used to discussing her son with physicians and psychiatrists. I noticed that while the mother kept up her spate of information about him, Tony sat very docily and preoccupied himself with some magazines that were in the consultation room. The mother gave me a finely focused and organized account of Tony.

The mother was ill at labor, and there was some irregularity in the neonate's behavior for which he had to be sent to hospital at the age of four months, and he was hospitalized for a period of three months. He had developed well on his return from the hospital. At the age of three, he had to be sent to a residential nursery because the family home had been bombed during the war. He was there till he was seven years of age, and, according to his mother, he had done very well and been a happy child at the residential nursery.

When he returned home, the mother had to go to hospital for an appendectomy and was there for 12 weeks. Tony had made a very good relation with his aunt (his mother's sister, who was some five years younger) and his own father during this period. He had a tendency to overeat, particularly sweets, and he developed worms for which he had to be treated at the hospital at the age of seven. When Tony was ten, according to his mother, she had to go into hospital again for a tubercular, ulcerated area on the cecum and was in hospital for a period of five months, during which time Tony was looked after again by his aunt and father. It was after this that his "habits" had started. She had sought advice because of these "habits," which consisted of a compulsion to touch his face and other persons as well as objects, which made him, in his own words, "look silly at school." Also, since her return from hospital, Tony had been somewhat depressed and at one time was heard saying that he wished he were dead. Furthermore, he had a very low toleration of any sort of frustration in his life and had to be spoiled the whole time or he would collapse into tears and be helpless.

The mother gave the whole account in a rather breezy, impersonal way, though with true concern. She jokingly remarked that she often teased Tony that it would have been much better had he been born a girl because he was always too eager to help her in the kitchen. He also often sneaked into her bed at night, and then she had to go and sleep with her sister, who had lived with them since her last operation (which was some two years before the date of the present interview). The mother's reference to her husband was very brief. She said he was an affectionate person and a good father, though he was beginning to lose his patience with Tony's "habits." They had an elder son, two years older than Tony, who was evidently quite normal and ordinary. She stressed the fact that Tony was a very intelligent and sensitive boy and much loved at school. What had struck me particularly at the end of the consultation was that she was also worried that Tony might have a brain disease and asked me whether he was mentally defective. This seemed rather contradictory to what was otherwise a highly rationalized psychiatric case history of emotional disturbance in a child. The parents came from a lower-middle-class Jewish family. I was also impressed by how psychiatrically orientated the mother was for someone coming from that class. Tony's "habits" and present restlessness as well as depression had been worsening progressively over the past two years — that is, since her return from hospital after her last operation. The mother was very eager to seek help for Tony, and so was he.

The First Phase of Tony's Treatment

Tony started his treatment in February in a very regular, classical way. Because of his age, it was thought expedient that both pencil and paper and painting materials should be made available to him, as well as the possibility of lying on the couch and communicating by speech and free association, should he so wish. Tony always arrived punctually and was most cooperative. He was eager to draw and paint and, as I look through his drawings, I find that one of the first was of a house being bombed by airplanes — to which his associations were not that of his own house being bombed, but that his residential nursery school when he was five had also suffered damage from bombs. It was also noticeable that he was very restless and could not settle down to any one thing for long. He also had a compulsion to go and urinate, over which he took a long time. It was quite obvious that the boy was trying to cope with the whole problem of reaching an age where he could possibly have an ejaculation but could not manage it as yet. Most of his drawings showed specifically urethral and urinary elements with vivid, aggressive, and destructive fantasies. We were able to go on working on these lines for some considerable time. He also had a tendency to get tired too quickly and would have to lie down and rest. Then he would sometimes pretend that he was dead. I had associated it, of course, to his whole concern about his mother and her health, but he refused to listen to that and said that she was very well and it was Daddy who was lazy and that his mother was the active one in the family.

As the treatment progressed, Tony's behavior began to take on a distinctly disturbed character during the sessions. He became more noisy and disorganized and stopped altogether being able to play with crayons and painting materials. Instead, he would sing loudly and impersonate different characters that he saw in the films. His extreme need to seek reassurance by touching me or his own face or other objects was continuously interpreted to him in terms of his hypochondriacal anxieties and fantasies of body damage deriving from internal conflict. The extraordinary fact was that he rarely ever seemed to register what one said to him, and every now and then he introduced something bizarre; for example, if he knocked against the leg of a chair, he would immediately lie down and say he had been hurt badly and was dying and would insist that I pick him up and put him on the couch. He was a rather petite child for his age. The passive homosexual elements, as well as the anal messy components of his whole behavior were continuously interpreted, but with not very much effect. He seemed to disregard everything. As I read through my notes, I am embarrassingly impressed by the fact of how relentlessly I kept on interpreting to him from his material, which was flagrantly vivid, all the polymorph, perverse sexual components in his play and behavior; it seemed a bit too easy and facile, but it seemed to have no effect on him whatsoever. During the first six months, there was a definite improvement in his "habits," and he was happier at school and was able to work well, as well as being less agitated and restless at home. He had a good summer vacation with his family.

When he returned after the summer vacation, which was the first big break in his analysis, his behavior changed completely in the sessions. He became totally violent and uncooperative; he would shout, shriek, sing loudly, mess around with everything, and disregard me completely: He was like a child possessed. At home, he became totally unruly and extremely rageful. His mother rang me once or twice to say that, though Tony was behaving very well at school, he was really being extremely difficult at home.

I found that though he came punctually and left in a very docile manner, during the sessions one could only describe his behavior as a manic, berserk mess, and all attempts at interpretation merely aggravated his condition. Also, he always came now eating an apple, and he would spit a lot all over the place. My attempts to interpret his behavior as regression to infantile patterns were completely disregarded by him. He felt as if he had no anxieties whatsoever, and all attempts to create some insight in him about his latent dread of depression and anxiety were utterly useless. During this term of some four months, his behavior was extremely chaotic and unmanageable, and often I had to use force to restrain him from throwing the furniture around in the consultation room. I was also afraid that in his manic thrashing around he would hurt himself. The peculiarity of this period was that every now and then he would bang against something ever so slightly and fall down and pretend he was dead, and had to be lifted and put on the couch. All attempts to interpret this to him in terms of internal anxiety situations were also utterly useless. He now gave absolutely no account of his life outside, and if I talked to him he would block his ears with his fingers. Alongside, he made incessant demands for gifts and things and threatened to break off treatment if he was not indulged. I was reduced to complete bewilderment and helplessness by him. One could manage him physically because he was a tender, fragile boy, and every now and then there was a look of such anguish on his face that one could not but register that all his behavior was one huge manic defense against some awesome reality which he could not communicate. This brought us to the Christmas break.

The Next Phase of His Treatment

When Tony returned in the New Year for his analysis, I decided to completely change my tactics. Instead of interpreting the content of the material presented, behaviorally and otherwise, in the sessions, I decided merely to observe and control him only when his behavior got physically out of hand.

He would thrash around and then fall down or lie down for long periods rocking on the bed or on the floor and singing loudly. One could not make out whether he was crying, shrieking, or howling. The little that I said to him made him more frenzied. Just before the Christmas holidays, when I was interpreting to him his spitting and mess-making in terms of its aggressive anal implications, he had remarked in a desperate way, "Everything you say drives me crazy." I had felt as if my interpretations had taken on the same value for this child as something in his life experience which I could not identify, nor could he name. Hence, I decided to provide more of a holding environment to him in my person and watch him. This phase was really very taxing because, for the four or five weeks before the critical session, which I shall report shortly, he behaved totally madly during the sessions, and yet at the end of the sessions he was quite capable of walking out in a quiet, docile way. He was frenzied and at times looked bewildered. From the little I could gather from him by asking here and there, he had to clutter his whole day with some activity or another and therefore looked pale and exhausted all the time. I was afraid that he would compel some sort of an accident on himself in order to find respite from this relentless hypomanic inner tension. It seemed an endurance test between him and me as to which of us would crack up first : whether I would despair and give up his treatment because he was certainly pushing the process to its very limits, and yet I felt that this was his only way of showing and exteriorizing something that was happening to him the whole time and that I must keep faith with him and persist ; or whether he would run amok, which he sometimes threatened to do, and take total flight from everything. I had remembered, of course, his mother saying in the first interview with her how Tony had recently been saying that he would run away from home. It was in this climate that the critical session happened.

The Critical Session

Tony had come in in a very manic mood. He had declared that he was perfectly healthy and all right, and that he was going to stop his treatment and had told his mother that after this session he was not coming again. I did not comment at all. He rushed up and stood on the table. He messed around with water and spat his apple pips all over the place, but I kept sitting adamantly in my chair. Suddenly, he shouted at me from one corner of the room in his manic voice : "Look, look, Khan ; there is a bump on the floor ! Come, look at it." I refused to look at it and said, "You describe it to me." It is impossible to detail with what rapidity his whole behavior disintegrated, and he went into complete panic. He came over to me and said, "If you do not look, I will give you a bump." And before I could stop him, he had kicked me hard and truly given me a bump on the shin. Then, for the first time, he burst into howling tears and collapsed on the floor and begged me to look at the bump. At this point I decided to look at the bump because I felt that he could not take the trauma of it anymore. It was just a bit of the linoleum that had warped, but I was so impressed by the chaotic panic that it had created in him that I decided to give a reconstruction. I started to say to him that today, for the first time, he had managed to tell me that he knew perfectly well how gravely ill his mother had been and that it had all been hidden from him, but he had information about it which he himself was helpless to decipher and turn into information and was entirely dependent on what we could tell him about it. Furthermore, I added that these ungraspable, unrecognizable "perceptions" in him were at the root of all his "habits" and manic behavior, and he was helpless to tell us anything about it. He went absolutely wild and said that I must never mention to his mother that she had been seriously ill or he would kill me and that he would go and tell his father. Then he suddenly collapsed again on the couch and sobbed and sobbed for some quarter of an hour. I told him that I would talk to his parents myself.

He was in too distressed a state for me to let him go home alone, and because he was also the last patient of the evening, I drove him home myself. Unfortunately, his parents were not at home, so I left him in the care of his aunt. Later that evening, around midnight, I had a telephone call from his father who was absolutely enraged, abusive, and said that I must never tell his wife or hint to her that she was suffering from cancer. This was the first time I had heard anything about cancer. I placated and quieted him as much as I could and asked him to see me the next day.

Interview with the Father

Tony's father was very different from what I had expected from the mother's account. He was a huge, uncouth, uneducated man. He talked aggressively to me at first and then suddenly burst into tears. He said that the last operation his wife had undergone was for cancer, but the hospital had told him not to let his wife know that she was suffering from cancer. The operation was successful, but she had not continued with the X-ray treatment after coming home from the hospital. She had visited the radiotherapy clinic only for two or three weeks, and she took Tony with her every time. He said that his wife often threatened that if she was suffering from cancer, she would kill herself because her own mother had died in great pain and suffering from cancer only a few years earlier, and she had nursed her. He was also aware that Tony's "habits" had started in their more severe form since the mother's return from the hospital after her operation. One very significant bit of data that the father imparted was that the hospital had specially instructed her to take life very easily and convalesce gently for a period of at least a year after the operation. Instead, his wife had gone out and bought herself a bicycle and had manically cycled all over the place. She had been in the hospital for four months and the operation had been four years ago, when Tony was eight years of age, not two years ago, as the mother had indicated to me. The father insisted that under no circumstances was I to tell his wife that she suffered from cancer and that he was not going to allow Tony to come back for treatment, and he left with this threat.

Later that day, I was rung by his wife who wanted to see me urgently. Meantime, I had also rung the hospital where she had undergone the treatment, and was given the information that it was four years earlier that she had an ovariectomy done and a malignant pseudo-mucinous cyst had been found. The operation had been quite successful, but she had not kept up the radiotherapy treatment that had been recommended afterwards. From a medical examination of her three years later, they found there were no signs of any recurrence. I had this information available to me when I saw the mother that very evening.

Interview with the Mother

The mother arrived without Tony and was in a very distressed state. She cried almost the whole time and said she was very ashamed to have to tell me the truth. In fact, what had happened was as follows: She had developed a very big stomach and thought she was pregnant. Her G.P. had also thought the same, but then it was discovered that she had a huge cyst, for which she had to have an operation. The operation was done four years ago, and she had called in her younger sister to look after Tony and her husband. She was quite comfortable in hospital, and Tony went to see her regularly. When she came out of hospital, she discovered that her husband had got her sister pregnant, and the mother had to arrange for an abortion. According to her, it was after her return from hospital that Tony had this incessant compulsion to come into her bed unexpectedly at night. During her absence, Tony had slept in the same room as her sister, so there was some evidence there that her husband had perhaps come into the room at night and made love to her sister, thinking the child was asleep. In fact, she was quite sure of it. She then went on to say how her husband was a very oversexed man, and, though after her operation the doctors had said that there should be no sex life for a period of at least three months, the very night she arrived home he could not do without sex. She said that he had to have sex at least twice every day — otherwise, he would go mad with rage, and the only way she had of avoiding being pestered by him was to find things to do outside the house. One technique for this was to take to cycling.

She knew that she had cancer of the ovaries, but had hidden it from her husband because she felt that he would panic and maybe desert her because he had absolutely no capacity or toleration for any sort of anxiety or stress. She said she had forgiven him the whole affair with her sister, and the sister was still living with them. I had the distinct feeling, from oblique hints here and there, that she knew that her husband was still carrying on with her sister, and she was using her sister to spare her some of his excessive sexual demands. She asked me what I was going to tell Tony, and I said that I thought he should be given the minimum of factual information about her serious illness and be told that the operation was successful and that she was better since he had visited with her the radiotherapy clinic for two months twice a week, where he had heard from all the other patients there that they were suffering from cancer, and the mother's myth to him had been that she was suffering from a minor stomach ailment. She said that Tony was very adamant that he was not going to come and see me again. I requested her to let me talk to him that evening on the telephone, and she agreed. As she was leaving, she remarked, "We are all in such a mess, aren't we? Can you do anything about it?"

Interview with Tony

When I talked to Tony on the telephone that night, he was very evasive, but I could hear in his voice a distinctly depressed and sad note. He agreed to come for one more session, so I saw him the next day. The boy who came was strangely changed. He was in a state of collapsed apathy and kept crying. I told him very briefly that he had been worried all this time about his mother's health and the goings-on in his family, about which he knew a very great deal more than he permitted himself to know. He suddenly said to me, "Can you please arrange for me to go and live in a school? I don't want to live at home." I said I would discuss it with Dr. Winnicott and see if we could find a place for him with a family where he could rest for a little while. He thanked me and left quietly. I did not give him any more information at this point.

CONCLUSION

Thanks to Dr. Winnicott's efforts, we were able to find a family that took disturbed children, and Tony went there immediately, and the parents agreed to this. It was some 30 miles from London, and I promised Tony that I would see him once every weekend. The Tony I saw in this home during these visits was a completely transformed being. He was extremely sad, deeply depressed, and *dispossessed*. The routine was that I would go and call on him on a Saturday or Sunday afternoon, and we would go for a walk. He was very gentle and began to talk about how much his mother had suffered and at one point explicitly said that "Daddy was a bastard" and that he hated his father. He also volunteered the information that he knew his father had given a baby to his aunt, so the boy had really an enormous amount of information available to him, but, because of his loyalty as well as developmental immaturity, he could not divulge or communicate this. These were the ego-alien factors which his manic hyperactivity was desperately trying to deny as well as cope with. He was in that residential home only for a month and then had to return to his own home, where he was very miserable indeed. He did not want to have regular treatment, and I agreed to see him only once a week. I felt very strongly that the treatment had served its purpose of *dispossessing* him of the ego-alien factors which were making him mad and which he could exteriorize only with continuous restlessness and manic messing. His excitable hypomanic state had distinctly abated, and in my judgment it would have been cruel to pry into his privacy at this point. I felt it was best to leave him to his own resources of development and inner capacities once one had removed from him the awesome burden of the foreign body of his environmental intrusion on his psyche and his inner reality.

What was most important at this point was to find a new setting for him to live in, and this is precisely what we achieved by his going to a grammar school. Once Tony went to the grammar school, I only saw him one more time, and this petite, girlish boy had suddenly shot up into a very tall youth. He still had some of his "habits" and was a distinctly withdrawn and schizoid person.

He was coping well with his studies and enjoying his school. Dr. Winnicott saw him some five years later again, and I understand that he has maintained his growth satisfactorily. It is worth mentioning here that during this period the aunt also left the house and the mother went back and had the proper course of radiotherapy from which she had taken flight. She had accepted her own illness and the possibility of its recurrence and was willing to do something toward her own health.

DISCUSSION OF CLINICAL MATERIAL

The treatment of this child has preoccupied me off and on through all the years of my clinical work because it compelled me to try and integrate in my own work the researches into early mother-child relationship and all the knowledge that has accrued about the differentiation of the ego from its beginnings with its attendant object-relationships (Khan, 1964; Winnicott, 1960).

During the first phase of this patient's treatment, it was possible to interpret most of his products in drawing and verbal behavior, as well as physical behavior, in terms of intrapsychic conflict and instinctual tensions. However, it had absolutely no impact on him. And at the end, when I had all the facts available to me of the environmental intrusion on him throughout his development, what strikes me most is how the mad muddle that this child eventually enacted in the analytic situation carried in a bizarre way all the symbolic, distorted derivatives of the events in his family to which he had been exposed and which had been extensively interpreted to him, though not, of course, as actual facts but as his fantasy. The crucial fact, however, is that none of this material was under his ego control or in his ego experience. It was a foreign body in him from which he could either seek respite by his wish to die, or which, once he had found a suitable setting that he could trust, he could unburden in an orgiastic, abreactive way (Khan, 1969a).

We are all only too familiar with how Freud at the beginning of his career had thought that the hysterics suffered from actual traumata of seduction which they had repressed and that the symptoms were a symbolic expression of the repressed memories. It is a strange irony that today one has to return to Freud's hypothesis of *actual traumata* but in a different frame of reference (Khan, 1964).

We have to accept the fact of our current theories of early development that the vulnerable emergent ego of a child, particularly if it is well endowed, can suffer actual traumata which it has no way of coping with, and this leads to a very deep dissociation in the person (James, 1960; Rycroft, 1962). Winnicott (1960) has tried to express this state of affairs in terms of his theory of True and False Self. I have no doubt that if this boy had not come to analysis at this point in his life, gradually he would have either turned to homosexuality as one way of solving his problem (since he had already been seen, according to his mother, lurking around lavatories) or his "habits" would have so alienated him from his environment that he would have collapsed into a psychotic-type illness (Winnicott, 1959–1964). Had that happened, what one would see would be a vast pathological organization from which it would be almost impossible to reconstruct the real events.

As I look back on my material, I find that if I had this boy in treatment today, I would not have waited a year because a certain concept would have been available to me to guide my clinical judgment, namely, the concept of muddle. The concept of muddle has been offered by Winnicott in his paper "Ego Distortion in Terms of True and False Self" (1960). I shall give a lengthy quotation from it :

> In the extreme examples of False Self development, the True Self is so well hidden that spontaneity is not a feature in the infant's living experiences. Compliance is then the main feature, with imitation as a specialty. When the degree of the split in the infant's person is not too great there may be some almost personal living through imitation, and it may even be possible for the child to act a special role, that of the True Self *as it would be if it had had existence.* In this way it is possible to trace the point of origin of the False Self, which can now be seen to be a defence, a defence against that which is unthinkable, the exploitation of the True Self, which would result in its annihilation. (If the True Self ever gets exploited

and annihilated this belongs to the life of an infant whose mother was not only "not good enough" in the sense set out above, but was good and bad in a tantalizingly irregular manner. The mother here has as part of her illness a need to cause and to maintain a muddle in those who are in contact with her. This may appear in a transference situation in which the patient tries to make the analyst mad. There may be a degree of this which can destroy the last vestiges of an infant's capacity to defend the True Self).

Searles, in his paper, "The Effort to Drive the Other Person Crazy — an Element in the Aetiology and Psychotherapy of Schizophrenia" (1959), has discussed this problem from another angle, which is most pertinent to my discussion. One of the dangers when we enter this area of clinical work is the precariousness of our knowledge. Our theories are most tentative and our clinical practice is entirely experimental, and yet we cannot, I feel, abnegate our responsibility towards work in this area and hide behind treating the so-called classical patient with the classical technique. Freud had the indomitable integrity to face clinical facts for what they were and accepted them as such first, and only then tried to find theories that would give some sort of a rationale of explanation toward the understanding of these facts. Today we are in danger of being smugly cocooned in those of our theories that make good sense and not letting our clinical experience question them. Unless this stasis is broken by vital new questioning from within ourselves in terms of our clinical experience, psychoanalysis is threatened with paralysis by its dogma. The way out of this paralysis, so far as I can see, is to try and integrate the researches into the infant-mother relationship with our daily clinical work. I would also like to add that the processes of infancy in such an interaction between mother and infant do not come to an end when the infant grows to be a child because the family environment perpetuates and reverberates them throughout childhood. Hence, it is not a simple question of the preverbal versus the verbal, but the continuous impingement of one tradition of relating on the newer, emergent capacities of the ego and the id and their distortion from it in the child. The deciphering and disentanglement through the analytic process and situation of this interplay between the environmental impingement and the growing, innate capacities constitute the true clinical task that we have to deal within these patients. Thus exorcism, insight, and *adorcisme* achieve a coherent and dynamic totality in the experience of the patient.

REFERENCES

Balint, M. (1968). *The basic fault: therapeutic aspects of regression.* London : Tavistock Publications.

Bowlby, J. (1969). *Attachment and loss.* Vol. 1 : Attachment. London : Hogarth Press.

Foucault, M. (1965). *Madness and civilization: a history of insanity in the age of reason.* New York : Pantheon Books.

———. (1970). *The order of things.* London : Tavistock Publications.

Freud, A. (1969). *Difficulties in the path of psycho-analysis.* New York : International Universities Press.

Freud, S. (1911–1915). *Papers on technique.* Standard Edition, vol. 12. London : Hogarth Press.

———. (1918). From the history of an infantile neurosis. Standard Edition, vol. 17. London : Hogarth Press.

Giovacchini, P. L. (1967). Preface No. 2. In *Psychoanalytic treatment of characterological and schizophrenic disorders,* by L. B. Boyer and P. L. Giovacchini. New York : Science House.

Greenson, R. R., and Wexler, M. (1969). The non-transference relationship in the psychoanalytic situation. *Int. J. Psycho-Anal.* 50.

Guntrip, H. (1968). *Schizoid phenomena, object relations and the self.* London : Hogarth Press.

James, M. (1960). Premature ego development. *Int. J. Psycho-Anal.* 41.

Khan, M. M. R. (1962). Dream psychology and the evolution of the psycho-analytic situation. *Int. J. Psycho-Anal.* 46.

———. (1964). Ego distortion, cumulative trauma, and the role of reconstruction in the analytic situation. *Int. J. Psycho-Anal.* 45.

———. (1969a). On symbiotic omnipotence. In *The psychoanalytic forum,* vol. 3. New York : Science House.

———. (1969b). Vicissitudes of being, knowing, and experiencing in the therapeutic situation. *Brit. J. Med. Psychol.* 42.

Lacan, J. (1966). *Ecrits.* Paris : Editions du Seuil.

Laing, R. D. (1967). *The politics of experience and the bird of paradise.* Baltimore, Md. : Penguin Books.

Lévi-Strauss, C. (1963). *Structural anthropology.* New York : Basic Books.

Milner, M. (1969). *The hands of the living god.* London : Hogarth Press.

Pontalis, J. B. (1969). Interpréter en analyse. *Bulletin de l'Association Psychanalytique de France,* No. 5.

Pouillon, J. (1970). Malade et médecin : le même et/ou l'autre? *Nouvelle Revue de Psychanalyse,* No. 1.

Rycroft, C. (1962). Beyond the reality principle. In *Imagination and reality.* London : Hogarth Press.

Searles, H. F. (1959). The effort to drive the other person crazy — an element in the aetiology and psychotherapy of schizophrenia. In *Collected papers on schizophrenia and related subjects.* London : Hogarth Press, 1965.

————. (1962). Scorn, disillusionment and adoration in the psychotherapy of schizophrenia. In *Collected papers on schizophrenia and related subjects.* London : Hogarth Press, 1965.

Smirnoff, V. N. (1969). Du style dans l'interprétation. *Bulletin de l'Association Psychanalytique de France,* No. 5.

Stone, L. (1961). *The psychoanalytic situation.* New York : International Universities Press.

Winnicott, D. W. (1959–1964). Classification : is there a psychoanalytic contribution to psychiatric classification? In *The Maturational processes and the facilitating environment.* London : Hogarth Press, 1965.

————. (1960). Ego distortion in terms of true and false self. In *The maturational processes and the facilitating environment.* London : Hogarth Press, 1965.

————. (1963a). Communicating and not communicating leading to a study of certain opposites. In *The maturational processes and the facilitating environment.* London : Hogarth Press, 1965.

————. (1963b). Psychiatric disorder in terms of infantile maturational processes. In *The maturational processes and the facilitating environment.* London : Hogarth Press, 1965.

————. (1970). *Therapeutic consultations.* London : Hogarth Press.

20

Mother's Madness Appearing in the Clinical Material as an Ego-alien Factor

DONALD W. WINNICOTT

THE CHAPTER presented by Masud Khan reminds me of a recent case of mine in which the sudden intrusion of "foreign" material needed to be noticed, understood, and interpreted. The patient was a boy of six years who was referred to me on account of his being unable to make use of his good intelligence; instead, he would bite holes in his gloves, coat, tie, and jersey, and he would only defecate in a chamber pot near one of the parents. Further, he demanded routine that was strict in many details, and he was restricted in the foods he could eat.

There is no need for a detailed description of the case here, where I have the limited aim to describe the psychotherapeutic interview that he had with me on the only occasion that I saw him. The interview had a good effect because I was able to sort out the muddle in the boy's mind from the muddle introduced into his life by certain characteristics of the mother. It can be taken for granted by the reader that this only child was loved by his parents and that the family was in no danger of breaking up. The father was of professional class, and the mother had had her own training as a teacher.

In order to give a useful picture of the session I must ask the reader to follow many details which need to be reported simply because they give continuity to the material.

He and I played "the squiggle game" together, and it was easy for me to find his capacity to enjoy playing and to play along with him. This is what happened alongside the drawings: After a

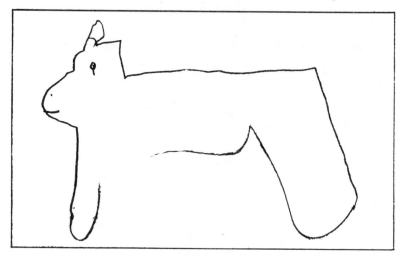

Figure 1.

Figure 2.

desultory discussion of his home and his family situation, we prepared the paper and two pencils, and I started with the first squiggle.

Figure 3.

Figure 1. is mine, which he made into a donkey, giving alternatives: pig, cow, horse, dog. "It has a funny eye." Here in the "funny eye," we already had a reference to the unpredictable. *Figure 2.* is his, which he said was a head, and I gave it a girl's body. *Figure 3.* is mine, which he turned into a funny head. Note the recurrence of the theme of "funny," indicating its significance. He made a reference to me which belonged to the mother's assessment of me. Apparently she possesses a book by me and he had seen this, and he said: "You do good head writing." I think the elaborate scribble on the forehead referred to brains, as if it were a portrait of me seen through the mother's eyes. "The man has a funny nose with three nostrils. His ears are behind so that you do not see them."

He told me about other things he could draw, including a bus, and he was very keen to get colored crayons. He had already used me to talk to about the idea of something funny about the mind. I, of course, made no interpretations. The three nostrils could be thought of as mad, but within the area of the boy's play activities.

Figure 4.

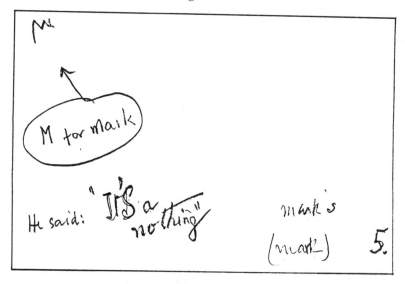

Figure 5.

In *Figure 4.* the paper got torn in the process of vigorous drawing. He did not manage to draw anything at first. *Figure 5.*

has some sort of mystery to it. It was his and up in the corner he made a mark. This mark was also part of an M. There is a pun on his name here. He said, "It's a nothing." He had reached an extreme defense, for if he is a nothing then he cannot be killed or hurt by the worst trauma imaginable.

I followed up the theme in talking to him here of drawing as a way of getting something out of his head onto the paper. He talked about the way in which the train sometimes has to stop to allow an express train to come through. He said, "Our train gets blocked because they have to change the points and then we can come back again."

Here he just saved the pencil from falling onto the floor, and these and other small things seemed significant, indicating that there was chaos rather than order in his immediate experiences. Now the pencil slipped off onto the floor. Nevertheless he was not in a frightened state, and it could be said that he had found a position from which to look at the express train coming through.

We had an interlude here. I used the pause to ask him about dreams. He said, "I don't know." Now he was back doing *Figure 4*. "It is an engine. That is a good window. It is like a real engine's window, a steam train."

He was getting towards the traumatic express train, which evidently reminded him of Mother. "In Battersea Park there is a train that looks like a steam train but really it is a diesel. Mummy thinks it is a steam train!" He went on about steam trains that he sees on the underground. He watches real shunting and he has seen one lots of times on various trips to Victoria Station; backwards and forwards. "I have seen in the paper something on the other side of the world that was on fire. People weren't killed; well, not while it was a little fire."

The immense potentialities for danger are indicated — a comment on the fire in the steam engine. "Oh we forgot the coal tender." And he started to try to add it onto the back of the engine; many other small details got lost at this point, and then he suddenly manifested something quite new and out of the general trend of the material.

The traumatic agent arrives

At this point he started to behave quite out of character. I could hardly recognize him as the same boy. A new thing had come and had taken hold of him. This that was new had to do with hearing a funny noise; it was a booming sound. It might come from the gasfire, a sort of sound when it is leaking. He went over to examine the gasfire, but there was no smell to it, so it wasn't leaking.

It was not possible to be sure whether he was hallucinating or remembering in auditory terms. I fished around by making an interpretation about hearing the parents in the other room, to which he gave a strong "No," and he said: "It was very high up on the hills or perhaps right away at the source of the Thames."

I continued with my theme saying, "Like it might be the beginning of Mark, something happening between mother and father."

He followed up my theme in an effort to comply by saying, "I started inside Mummy and I ended up out of Mummy at the hospital. There was no noise, babies crying."

I said, "I wonder if there was a noise inside Mummy," and he said he had his eyes closed so that he could not hear. I, myself, was bewildered and I seem to have persevered with this primal scene interpretation as if at a loss.

It was difficult to take notes of the chaotic way in which material was appearing. He made noises illustrative of the sort of noises that he was hearing or remembering, and they seemed to include the word "no," and this sort of thing repeated itself many times. It was all frenzied or hectic. He interrupted this by saying, "What are you doing — writing more books?" referring to the notes that I was taking. So I wrote "Mark" very big and in several different ways. He said, "It's not good writing; it's scribbling."

I think it was here that *Figure 4* got torn by Mark making his mark more and more vigorously. Here he found he had completely lost his pencil. This seemed significant, although for a time he went over to an interest in an old penknife in the pencil box. Together we explored this and he said, "I am allowed a knife." With the knife he jabbed the paper and sometimes jabbed the table, and it was at this point that most of the damage to *Figure 4*. was done. Several times the sheet got new damage, and I think he was showing why he had to be nothing if he was to let the traumatic "thing" arrive. Here, too, was the penetration theme that we had already obtained of the origin of Mark.

He was then exploring the tin containing pencils and crayons.

Have I got a "rubber"? (I haven't.) "My goodness!" And so on. The game was now at an end and he began walking around starting some new theme. He took something from his right and left pockets and stuffed them in his right and left ears, and it seemed legitimate to suppose that he was dealing with the hallucinated sounds and moreover that he had come prepared to deal with them, and had brought right and left bits of paper for use in this respect.

He was manifesting a confused state, but he quickly changed the subject and referred to my roof garden which he could see from the window. He referred to a story in a comic and he wondered where the comic might be. Probably Mother had it in the waiting room, he thought. In this way the actual Mother came back into his mind, and I was able to see that *the express train had been a mad Mother.* I was still unsure of my ground, however, and postponed making the main interpretation.

Anxiety showed still further by his saying, "I might be going home soon, or now." He referred to fear of the noises, and there was some fun about the chair walking away and behaving as if it would kick Mother or get knocked over.

I made a reference to the madness that this represented. Either he or I said, "Everything's gone mad," and there was some laughing. I said, about the head, "It's got eyes but no ears," and he said, "Yes it has, but it fell over and now it's upside down."

There was a moment of a mad world and some kind of sound like "Woof, woof" inside the mad chair, and then this noise went out on the other side of the chair. I made a remark about a mad place inside his head or possibly inside his mother, and I began to have a conviction that this boy was bringing me a picture of his mother as an ill person.

Continuing the primal scene theme, I said, "And then Mummy did a big noise and it was called Mark." Eventually I definitely stated. *"Mummy sometimes goes mad when you are there. This is what you are showing me."*

He was distracting himself by talking about the care that you have to take with electric gadgets. He said, "I was born a boy."

I said, "You were born a big noise!" And he said, "I didn't!"

He was now wanting to go but saying that he was not scared, simply that he wanted to see his mother, so we went together to collect her.

COMMENT

When I had a new look at the mother, I realized that she does carry with her a severe personal problem, and when I spoke to her about this she was very willing to admit that she was often an ill person.

Later the mother said she was so very glad that I had seen in the way the boy behaved that she does go mad in front of the child, and she knew that it was this that was disturbing him. She is herself having treatment for her mental condition.

In this example of a therapeutic consultation, it is possible to watch a boy of six years communicating a complex and dynamic personality pattern, not a profile but a representation in depth, integrated in a space-time continuum.

He quickly senses the special conditions of the professional situation and develops the necessary trust in myself. On this premise he plays around with personal madness, testing out whether I can stand the "funny" eye and the triple nostrils. Then he shows the way he has learned to adopt the extreme defenses of nothingness or invulnerability. He is no more than a mark, a mark that can be easily unnoticed. He happens to have the name Mark and he uses this in a playful way.

Now the stage is set. He is there playing with me, and all is well. He warns me of the trains that have to go into a sideline to let through the express. In terms of the details of the steam train, he tells me about an immense potentiality for destruction : fire on the other side of the world.

Then suddenly he goes mad, but it is more true to say that he is *possessed by madness*. It is no longer him, but it is a mad person that I watch — one who is completely unpredictable. The express train is rushing through the station while the local train is standing still in a sliding. "Nothing" is not being destroyed by the mad "something."

Then the mother's madness passes and the boy begins to want to use his mother as a mother who cares for him and whom he needs in order to get home. The boy leaves my house in a happy state. He is confident in this mother whose going mad has now been shown to me, whose going mad has become objectified and limited by its own boundaries. Mark has now become something instead of nothing, and he can play again, even play at absurdities which, being part of his own madness, are not traumatic so much as comical and laughable.

I think that I was needed in my special role as someone who could see him, think about him (clever brains in head), experience contact with him (communication through playing), recognize and respect his defense organizations (and the extreme defense of his being "nothing"), and then witness his states of being possessed by a mother's madness when his own mother goes mad in front of him. He also needed my other contact with his mother by which I could know that when not insane she is a good and responsible parent and wife to the boy's father.

Where is he when he is nothing? I think that in the consultation he relied on my having a mental image of him in my head which he could recall after the express train had gone through and the local train could come out of the siding.

Added Note

Although this is not the purpose of this paper, I wish to add that there was considerable clinical improvement following this one psychotherapeutic consultation. This showed in a clearing up of the scholastic block of which the boy's teachers complained; it also showed in the boy's general attitude at home, in his progress towards independence, and in his new ability to function normally in regard to excretions.

21

Treatment of Psychoses

GUSTAV BYCHOWSKI

Since 1952, when I first discussed the principles of the psycho-analytic therapy of psychosis, the number of psychoanalysts who are interested in these problems has increased considerably. They have discussed their experiences and ideas in a large number of papers and books. Thus, our knowledge of this new chapter of psychoanalytic psychiatry has grown impressively. I, myself, have continued to follow these problems in my office practice as well as in the hospital setting. I have recorded some of my experiences and ideas in a number of papers, but I have hesitated to expand them. I feel strongly that our knowledge is still limited and in flux since our experience grows with every new patient who is thoroughly analyzed and, if possible, followed up.

In this chapter I propose to deal mainly with my own observations, specifically the following problems: regression, symbiosis, acting out, and reversibility and irreversibility.

Due to the widening scope of psychoanalysis (or psychoanalytic psychotherapy), we have the opportunity to deal with highly regressed patients, not only in the hospital but also in our office practice. For this, two factors are responsible: first, a regressed patient may be able to remain in certain environmental settings, for a long period of time without hospitalization; second, the condition of various mental functions in schizophrenia is so unequal that in many instances, despite the intense regression of some functions, others remain on a level that makes ambulatory existence possible (even if not always easy and pleasant) for the patient and those in his environment.

I wish to describe certain forms of regression and their dynamics and outline the therapeutic interventions that, in my experience, have proved useful. In my opinion, regression in various forms occurs with a specific aim; the ego is firmly and passionately bent on preserving and protecting the original state of symbiosis with one or both parents, and less frequently with other family members or parental substitutes. Every step forward in the direction of rehabilitating the ego or its various functions endangers the symbiotic state and, as a rule, is countermanded by a new bout of regressive movement, either of the same or other ego functions. In such cases the general rule followed by the psychotic ego seems to be: "Do not abandon your state of helplessness because, when you show some sign of competence, Mother (or parents) will abandon you." Since Mother (or parents) is supposed to be the sole source of strength, abandonment may prove catastrophic. Consequently, this anticipation is met by the ego with considerable anxiety verging on panic. Upon receiving this signal there is a general withdrawal from the threatening reality situation and a regression of some specific ego functions. In keeping with the general rules of regression, some of the ego functions are replaced or contaminated by primitive drives, and primary processes substitute in part for the higher organized affective responses and ideations.

In certain cases, when some reality-testing is preserved and encouraged by the environment and the therapeutic situation, the ego tries to recapture lost parts of reality and mobilizes some of its remaining resources. With some experience, we can distinguish patients who are capable of such moves toward restoration from those where regression seems to prevail and where, as one of my patients put it, "One step forward is followed by two steps backward."

In another group of patients restorative steps have a definite defensive character and lead to new symptoms. The latter serve to protect the regressed ego from the dangers that threaten it from primitive id impulses. In addition, the primitive punitive superego interferes and voices its own destructive threats. The regressive moves bring about a diffusion of both basic drives;

consequently, the released destructive hostility turns against the original love-hate objects and ultimately against the self. Hence, in analysis we can observe in some cases an alternation of bouts of aggression with depressive and self-destructive moods, and in other cases an alternation between spurts of rather frantic and chaotic activity and paralyzing apathy. Naturally, all of these trends become prominent in the transference, but more will be said about this later.

A clinical vignette will illustrate these trends and aspects of regression. "A," a woman in her early thirties who had graduated from the best schools and colleges, eventually began to show signs of progressive deterioration. In hopes of earning a doctoral degree, "A," had passed her oral examination, but she couldn't get started with her thesis. After one brief attempt, she abandoned any hope of gainful employment. She could not live alone since she was engulfed in chaos and disorder, which seriously interfered with her daily existence.

The following points are relevant for this discussion: This woman was able to live at her parents' home since they had the economic means to support her, but they only tolerated her behavior grudgingly. Both her mother and domestic help did what they could to keep "A" from getting lost in her own disorder.

However, there were other factors that enabled "A" to live outside the hospital. Her intelligence was intact, and on occasion she could be brilliant, especially when she was dealing with her own particular interests and area of study; here, her memory served her with perfection. She read profusely and could discuss whatever she had read with perfect lucidity and coherence. However, she couldn't organize the material she needed for her thesis; she couldn't get beyond the introduction and innumerable notes and footnotes. The latter were her veritable undoing: it required months of analysis for her to learn to avoid interminable digressions and to develop a topic or idea. Obviously, the synthetic, integrative function of the ego was severely impaired; so, too, were other functions of the ego. For instance, "A" had a striking inability to perceive the passage of time; it was impossible for her to be on time and she sabotaged all attempts at reeducation. Her numerous watches were inevitably out of commission; she didn't know how to wind them, and she often lost, broke, or forgot to wear them.

"A" displayed a severe deficiency in motor functioning. This weakness, which started in early childhood, was characterized by clumsiness, poor muscular control and coordination, and ineptness in performing simple, everyday tasks and movements. Thus, an important element of the executive apparatus of the ego was highly deficient. During puberty and early adulthood, "A" 's deficiency was greatly enhanced by a heavy layer of fat that covered her body and distorted her otherwise pleasant appearance (her fat was confirmed by photographs taken at that time). All these traits contributed to "A" 's rapidly increasing social isolation and withdrawal. She rationalized this attitude by saying that she was shy, "ugly," inept, and had achieved nothing.

The dynamics and origin of various elements of her regression emerged clearly in the course of psychoanalysis. Regressive behavior offered an obvious and formidable secondary aim. The more helpless she was, the more she could rely on the help of her parents, especially her mother. She turned to her for help with almost every simple task. According to "A" 's private mythology, her mother was omnipotent and omniscient. Since "A" seemed to be unable to accept time as an aspect of existence and was constantly late, she had to rely on her mother to remind her of the hour.

Moreover, it became clear that by disregarding time, she was protesting and opposing the unfailing (perhaps even compulsive) punctuality of her parents. Another source of tardiness was her wish to avoid everyday tasks that reminded her of bleak reality. Moreover, "A" 's increasing tardiness and procrastination caused her considerable anxiety, although she was relieved once a task was accomplished or an appointment was kept and there was no penalty. Her masochistic savoring of anxiety was an important factor. "A" 's hidden primary gain was to prevent her parents' anticipated punishment and to masochistically enjoy anxiety and final relief.

Closer analysis of certain clinical symptoms will permit a better insight into the metapsychology of regression. In reviewing the history of regressive processes in this patient, we come to the conclusion that regression was initiated at an early age by the ego, which was alarmed at the danger that threatened it from various sources. The alleged initial inefficiency of the executive (mainly motor) apparatus, coupled with intense anxiety and provoked by an exposure to social situations, caused the ego to seek withdrawal, retreat, and special compensation. We have to ask: What was the source of this anxiety and what was the nature of these compensations?

Playing with other children made "A" anxious since she did not feel equal to them, especially in physical skills and agility. Thus, at an early age, she was extremely sensitive to and afraid of mockery and criticism. She felt threatened by the former when it came from her playmates and by the latter when it was expressed by her parents. Anxiety as a twofold threat thus disrupted the young ego : there was the threat of the parental introject (loss of love represented by the superego) and later the threat of abandonment. It should be pointed out that "A" was the oldest of three children and the only daughter.

Since she was intellectually superior to her brothers and for five years was the repository of her parents' ambitions and neurotic trends, she incorporated their imagos as cornerstones of her primitive and ever demanding superego. Consequently, her superego made unrelenting demands; at an early age her ego felt desperately driven as well as frightened by the prospect of failure. "A" felt that she had to fail since a daughter could never equal, let alone outshine, a son ; also, a daughter could never meet the demands of her parents and thus secure their love and approval.

In a previous publication, (Bychowski, 1953) I described how "A," to defend herself against her destructive drives and to protect familiar introjects, incorporated the imagos of her parents (and, to a lesser degree, those of her brothers) in the form of omnipotent and omniscient mythological beings. However, the advantages of these mechanisms were overshadowed by their impact as a source of superego anxiety. In the course of all these ongoing conflicts and struggles, the ego developed crippling obsessive symptoms that contributed significantly to general regression. These symptoms countermanded the superego drives and made it impossible to attain superior cultural goals. "A" 's examinations were accompanied by intense anxiety; her preparations and regular work were endlessly delayed. Her goal of earning a doctorate and working in her chosen field couldn't be realized because of her incessant tardiness and interminable digression.

"A" 's regressive processes had led to an increasing divorce between an adequate perception of her existential reality and the preservation of fantasy images of her parents, herself, and her role in life. "Double bookkeeping," so characteristic of the schizophrenic ego (as described and named by Eugene Bleuler, 1952), allowed "A" to function to a limited extent, despite her fantastic concepts and ideas. She could, for instance, think of herself as a delicate princess who was entitled to the greatest luxuries and all kinds of special considerations and also view herself as a scholar and aesthete; at the same time, she could also see herself as a miserable wretch — a weak little girl who was unable to function without the constant support and protection of her mother.

Thus, the goals of regression in this patient are fairly clear. Regression served to assuage and protect the ego from anxiety when facing the demands of external and internal reality so far, (this term refers only to superego anxiety). Furthermore, by creating the image of helpless weakness, regression tends to secure unceasing love, succor, and protection from parental figures who assume the proportions of mythological beings — omnipotent and omniscient Olympians. When faced with such creatures, the ego inevitably reduces its self-image and retreats even further into abject weakness. The ego is always faced with the following question, even though it may not be conscious: "How can I live up to the demands of these superior creatures?" The urge and appeal of regression thus become stronger; an element of hostile competition in the ambitious superego motivates an unconscious wish to outmatch these prototypes of greatness — to beat them literally as well as metaphorically. The increasing helplesness assumed by the ego serves as a most effective camouflage for this wish, which finally appears and becomes impossible to attain. We must ask: "What happens to the mental apparatus in the course of such prolonged regressive processes, especially when they are allowed to run their course without therapeutic interference?"

We must bear in mind that the third source of danger threatening the ego and causing anxiety lies in the instinctual demands that brew in the id. The ego tries to avoid these demands by replacing them with infantile urges that meet with less condemnation from the punitive superego. At the same time these infantile urges reaffirm the demand for parental protection, even if these urges are met with parental disapproval. In the course of all of these processes, there takes place what one might call "the reciprocal contamination of mental systems," and the outcome is structural confusion.

"A," who sees herself as a refined aesthete with aristocratic and sometimes esoteric tastes, manages to transform her environment into filth and chaos. She can do it with incredible, almost uncanny, rapidity. She throws books and papers onto the floor and mixes old newspapers and magazines with her clothing. When she moved out of her parents' home and started to live alone, she left her dishes unwashed for days and did not dispose of her garbage. In brief, "A" gives way to her anal urges while she also tries to maintain a facade of obsessive cleanliness by ablutions and superfluous visits to the beauty parlor. An illuminating memory goes back to her third or fourth year of life, when "A" vomited on the toys in her nursery and then called to her mother, squealing with delight: "What a mess!" The counterpoint of primitive anal drives breaking through and being countermanded by crippling defenses created a bizarre and confusing picture. "A" bathed with religious regularity, yet refused to wash her own stockings or touch her body because it was filthy and repulsive. She also spent the little money she had foolishly but refused to throw away old newspapers and magazine clippings.

Even more striking are examples of contamination proceeding in the opposite direction — from the id to the superego — especially examples of oral contamination. Generally speaking, "A"'s oral regression was impressive: she frequently overate yet despaired about her "ugliness" and obesity, which did distort her otherwise shapely form. These oral symptoms represented the general goal of regression since they offered "A" justification for avoiding the company of other human beings and limiting her social contacts to her family. While this oral regression could also be described as desublimation, another aspect of her behavior showed certain contamination of both other mental systems by the id.

We have remarked that from early childhood "A" sought refuge in books and avoided the company of other children. She became more and more fascinated and obsessed with books and with all printed matter in general. She literally bought and devoured them even if she didn't have the money to pay for them. She repeatedly confessed that she was suffering from an irresistible impulse, an insight that she gained in analysis which filled her with horror. This urge to buy books bore a striking resemblance to direct and irresistible oral urges. Anal contamination was manifested by "A"'s inability to part with the many books she compulsively borrowed from the public library. She would accumulate them just like newspaper clippings and notebooks. These accumulations served (like most other symptoms and regressive patterns) to ward off anxiety: a clipping might be useful or a piece of information might be needed at some indefinite future time.

As I have remarked, "A"'s regressive processes and the ego-crippling symptoms began during the early, prelatency period. However, at the onset of puberty, new dangers to the ego emerged and, accordingly, new impulses toward regression. "A" looked upon sex as an important source of danger that she experienced at various levels. First of all, she thought that participation in the sexual act required special skill, and she was convinced that she would be as inept in this performance as in any other. As she got older, this fear was enhanced by her apprehension about her clumsiness. Secondly, she was afraid of penetration and of possible damage that might be inflicted upon her delicate, flower-like body. In the third place, she refused to abandon the object of incestuous mythological fixation for the sake of some exogamous and, by the same token, inferior love object.

"A" was stunned when she discovered in her analysis her erotic and symbiotic attachments to her parents and brothers, especially to her mother. "A" 's symbiotic urges toward her mother proved the most powerful and resistant; the mother was also caught in a symbiotic and neurotic bond with her daughter. This complex situation was expressed most poignantly in a dream that had a powerful impact on "A." In this dream she was in a plane where she was both kissing and biting a baby. "A" was appalled at what she was doing, yet she could not resist it. She felt both very tender and cruel toward the baby. She felt that the baby was frightened but also liked being bitten so cruelly. Here it was clear that she identified with a cruel, biting mother on the one hand, and with a tender child who lends itself eagerly and yet with terror to this sadistic ministration of the mother on the other hand.

A new thrust of regression could easily occur if "A" s mother telephoned to suggest that they do something together. "A" felt guided and controlled by her mother, who was obviously stronger and more competent. At one time, while this situation was being worked through in analysis, "A" gained new hope and vigor. However, after hearing of her mother's success in a business venture, "A" 's newly gained vigor ebbed away; she felt "paralyzed" and had to lie down to rest. "How can I do anything worthwhile, when my mother is so great?"

In an earlier publication (Bychowski, 1953) I described a symbiotic relationship as a system of communicating vessels. With the rise of the level of liquid in one vessel (one member of the symbiotic bond), the other vessel is depleted and experiences the feeling of abject weakness; it sends out an SOS and throws itself at the mercy of the first member of the symbiotic bond, who then becomes a tower of strength. Unfortunately, the first member too often takes advantage of its privileged position. When "A" feels encouraged by progress made in her analysis and the first signs of success, she quickly loses it if her mother questions her closely : such questioning implies present and (even worse) future criticism. In anticipation, she yields to this terrifying maternal (and paternal) superego and abdicates; this results time and again in paralyzing weakness and crippling regression.

Thrusts of destructive hostility toward parents and parental introjects result in increased anxiety, guilt feelings, and compensatory strengthening of the symbiotic ties. In addition, reaffirmation of the symbiotic bond with one parent is used to the detriment of the other — a mechanism that is made possible by the highly ambivalent situation prevailing between the parents. In yielding to the magnetic pull toward the maternal love-hate object, "A" tries to infantilize the image of herself and to eliminate her father as an unwelcome, hostile rival. On the other hand, in identifying with her father, she enhances the masculine image of herself, turns against her mother and, finally, directs her hostility against both parents. The danger of these actions to "A" 's own security is counteracted by the unconscious ego commanding her to act out infantile weakness and thus eliminate herself from any contest. She can accomplish this quite well if she sabotages her own efforts to be effective and competent. Here again infantile regression triumphs when it is put in the role of the symbiotic bind. By ruling itself incompetent, the ego puts itself, as it were, in the position of a legal incompetent whose family is obliged to take over.

The general regressive behavior, with ensuing instinctual primitivization and desublimation, creates therapeutic difficulties and poses special technical problems. My remarks refer mainly to patients who, though with difficulty, can be treated without hospitalization. Generally speaking, we must note that a certain degree of instinctual regression and desublimation not only creates difficulties for the family and society, but also leads to the problem of reversibility of the process of degradation of instinctual drives. We shall return to this problem later when discussing the reversibility of symptoms. When dealing with desublimation in our analytic work, we meet with resistance that originates in the power of the initial drives and the immediate direct pleasure that their gratification offers to the ego. Since the ego has to some extent

regressed in the course of psychotic regression, the delay in gratification required by psychoanalytic treatment may be difficult (if
not impossible) to obtain. As I have noted elsewhere, this resistance may be encouraged by the environment. On the whole, it may
prove easier for the regressed ego to cling to primitive gratification
instead of exerting the effort required to sublimate.

Such nonanalytical methods as persuasion, encouragement,
and emphasis on existential and moral values may prove necessary.
To quote Freud, (1919) we have to "alloy the pure gold of analysis
plentifully with the copper of direct suggestion." Instinctual
regression in our patients is often accompanied by obsessive-compulsive symptomatology in keeping with the repetition-compulsion
and the typical defenses against the desublimated and sadistic
drives.

Active intervention may be necessary with obsessive-compulsive
symptomatology even if it is not always successful. However, as
is well known from clinical experience, even a slight inroad into
the obsessive-compulsive armor is beneficial and augurs well for
the future. The reduction of symptoms brings relief to the patient's
ego and fosters hope and feelings of competence and self-esteem.
Such active intervention is especially necessary whenever new
obsessive-compulsive symptoms emerge with the implicit secondary
gain of blocking the progress of analysis.

Returning to "A," one day she seized an old scrapbook in
order to patch it up and "correct" it by "improvements" and additions. She put this scrapbook together with the laudable intention
of helping her brother in one of his classes. This scrapbook "behaved" like a colony of cancerous cells; it took over her free time,
kept her up long hours at night, and interfered with the elementary
activities of her small household. The primary gain of this particular digression was transparent. While it satisfied her anally derived
tendency to smear and mess, it also gave "A" the illusion of producing something artistic and nonpractical; this pseudosublimation
offered some consolation for her drab and utterly nonproductive
existence. The complete uselessness of this activity could be looked
upon as a true parody of the principle of *l'art pour l'art* and as a
total contrast to the highly efficient and productive activity of her
industrious and energetic parents. The structure of this compulsive
act is another clear illustration of the reciprocal contamination of
various systems of the mental apparatus.

Minute interpretation of regressive symptoms is an invaluable tool. I find that focusing on the deepest layer of the symbiotic fixation is an all-important part of the interpretive work. I follow such interpretations with praise for the patient's competence whether prospective or already partially achieved. This praise encourages the ego and helps to counteract the destructive criticism of the punitive superego which occasionally gets support from parental authorities. The recurrence of symbiotic impulses requires a thorough and systematic working through of the innumerable attempts of the ego at sabotage and abdication. Frequently, bouts of depression necessitate encouragement as well as repeated interpretations of the destructive impulses that are being released in the course of analysis and turned against the self.

Special problems are presented by the environment. The ego of these patients, because of its weakness and primitive organization, is subject to parental magnetism somewhat like the ego of the child. This impact may take two directions: critical and punitive interventions via the medium of the superego or magnetic — almost hypnotic — seduction via appeal to infantile symbiotic and anaclitic needs and desires. In view of this situation, it may be important to exert our influence upon parental authorities.

I hardly need to emphasize that we must observe tact and caution in these interventions. Inadmissible though they are in the setting of the analytic treatment of an individual with no ego damage, interventions may be essential when dealing with patients with psychotic regression. In hospital settings interventions are usually entrusted to the social service department, whereas in office practice we must bear the total responsibility. A great deal could be said about the difficulties and resistances offered by the family. In some instances it may be necessary to try to impart some insight to the family into the dynamics of psychotic regression; this is especially true when dealing with symbiotic ties. In "A" 's case, treatment would have been unrealistic and impossible if her parents — especially her mother — had not been made aware of their contribution to the psychotic regression. The powerful, magnetic pull exercised by "A" 's mother whenever she tried to invade what little remained of her daughter's privacy and independence had to be brought to her attention by personal conferences or brief telephone conversations.

While we can only rarely count on the parents' reasonable help and assistance, we can at least try to countermand the impact of their punitive and seductive interventions. I have found that occasional, brief telephone calls are valuable when dealing with these patients. In certain cases I may call a patient as well as permit him to call me. To hear the doctor's voice may help to reassure the patient in moments of anxiety and loneliness as well as during depressive-regressive episodes. Naturally, one must be careful not to encourage compulsive telephoning and gratify anaclitic needs. I may call a patient at certain specific times of the day or at some critical point in his treatment or daily life. For example, I would telephone "A" in the morning when she was struggling to get up and experiencing deep anxiety and resistance against having to face the day and go to work. Obviously, these interventions must be measured in their frequency and duration.

We often encounter cases in which psychoanalysis has been able to effect a significant improvement or even an apparently complete remission in a relatively short time. A deeper analysis of these clinical data leads to the conclusion that improvement has been due in part to what may be called a "transference cure" and also to the interpretative work of the analyst. We know only too well that such rapid cures are often deceptive and of short duration. Further analytic work with these patients sometimes reveals a psychotic core, which then becomes the main object of our endeavors. In a number of cases prolonged analysis of the psychotic core and of the secondary characterological and neurotic defenses results in the abolition of the former and dissolution of the latter; the outcome meets our criteria for a psychoanalytic cure.

When I reflect upon some of my blatant therapeutic failures, two examples come to mind. In both cases the initial therapeutic result seemed most encouraging; however, further observations and a prolonged follow-up proved highly disappointing. My first case (Geraldine) is discussed in "Psychotherapy of Psychosis" (1952). Geraldine was the only child of a highly disturbed, borderline (perhaps even psychotic) mother and an anxious, neurotic father. The latter reacted to his wife's psychopathology by separating himself for long periods of time from his little family, and by isolating himself and immersing himself in his work during the brief periods when they lived together.

The atmosphere at home was tense with strife and conflict. Geraldine had shown the first symptoms of disturbance at the onset of puberty but did not come for treatment until she was 20 years of age. She displayed the clinical picture of a florid, paranoid psychosis; her symptoms consisted of wild fantasies, illusions, and hallucinations. I have described at some length the intricate patterns of regression and restitution. I have also emphasized the obsessive-compulsive personality structure operating at a primitive, regressed level and manifesting itself, among other symptoms, in unsurmountable bulimia and an exasperating trichotillomania.

Classical psychoanalytic therapy brought about a dissolution of symptoms. Finally, this deeply regressed young woman, who lived in a completely autistic, psychotic world, regained her sense of reality; she graduated from college and earned a master's degree; eventually she became a teacher, married, and had a child. This result, after several years of psychoanalysis conducted entirely on an ambulatory basis (without even a brief hospitalization) seemed extremely gratifying. However, her later life was disappointing. Although six years after terminating treatment, she remained free from secondary schizophrenic symptoms and did not return to her autistic world, she was also emotionally unstable, couldn't get along with her husband or other people, and couldn't hold a job for any significant length of time. Even though she did not hallucinate, occasionally she felt that someone was watching or observing her. She imagined that her schoolmates were looking at her critically, and she associated this with the image of her mother nagging her incessantly during her childhood.

Geraldine's obsessive-compulsive personality structure remained intact. Although the psychotic symptoms derived from her orality disappeared, her greed remained and led to occasional relapses into bulimia — one of the horrors of her psychotic past — or it became displaced to a burning envy of other people's possessions. During her marriage she had a psychotic relapse, which led to hospitalization and electroshock therapy, but this episode occurred in another city. Her marriage finally ended in divorce. Yet such was Geraldine's and her husband's pathology that she had a second child by him after their divorce.

Geraldine appeared again in my office seven years after her last visit, that is, 13 years after termination. This time she was agitated; she wanted to sue the judge, whom she felt was responsible for her hospitalization, and to sue me for having published her case history. Despite the compulsive repetition of her accusations, she was persuaded to calm down and to desist from litigation when I promised that I would never recommend hospitalization. She continued to remain free from delusions and hallucinations, yet she had vivid fantasies in which she imagined, for instance, a handsome young man falling in love with her and rescuing her. These fantasies never reached the conviction character of reality. Unfortunately this patient, who owed so much of her pathology to her mother, continued to live with her. This close, largely symbiotic relationship gained momentum after the death of the father, who apparently served as a mitigating influence and as a buffer between the two women.

The devastating impact of the disturbed milieu on the early development of this patient could be observed even during analysis. In retrospect, it seems that the effects of severe traumatization and emotional deprivation could not be eradicated, even though secondary psychotic symptomatology yielded to psychoanalytic ministrations; here, the irreversibility of the scaffolding of the personality could be traced to both genetic and psychogenetic factors, and it would obviously be futile to try to isolate the two.

If we apply our recently acquired knowledge of infantile psychoses, the early symbiosis and the separation — the individuation phase elucidated by Margaret Mahler (1968) — we can, in general terms, conclude that Geraldine did not develop an entirely separate ego and self-image. She could not find sufficient compensation or protection from her father for the trauma inflicted upon her by her semipsychotic mother. Thus, she was thrown back upon the maternal love-hate object which prevented her from ever achieving complete separation — individuation. Consequently, the mother continued to exert her corrosive influence, preventing Geraldine's from developing a good sense of reality, intensifying the punitive aspects of the superego, and encouraging regressive trends in libidinal and ego development. Continued emotional deprivation fostered infantile fixation, which then became the anchor point for regression and symptom formation. General emotional deprivation encouraged compensatory fantasy patterns and, lacking a reality sense, the formation and maintenance of hallucinations and delusions. The ego could never assimilate the original love-hate object. The latter persisted in the form of a split introject, which then became the source of persecutory ideation.

The impact of the disturbing milieu, especially the corrosive interaction with the semi-psychotic mother, had wrought indelible and irreversible damage to the personality of the child. Subsequent education and therapeutic efforts influenced only the secondary derivatives of these basic ravages but couldn't undo them in order to establish a sound personality scaffolding. Speaking theoretically, this case presents the well-known interaction of factors that function as a complementary series, such as the constitutional endowment of the infantile personality, the intensity and chronicity of trauma, and, last but not least, the time element, that is, the onset of damage (in this case it started in earliest infancy).

My second case, "B," is discussed at some length in "Congealment and Fluidity" (1971). I shall briefly recapitulate the relevant points of his history, which appears to be like an unfortunate experiment with an infantile ego.

"B" was the only son of middle-class parents. At the age of 20, when he started analysis, his parents had attained economic prosperity. However, during his infancy and early childhood, they were struggling hard and were thoroughly absorbed in building up their business. Thus, "B" was left in the care of a succession of maids; each one stayed only a short time partly because of "B"'s growing rebellion and her difficulty in handling him. (One of these maids turned out to be a Negro prostitute.) There were constant scenes of despair and agitation, fights between the little boy and his inadequate substitute mothers. His psychopathology manifested itself at an early age. At ten he became withdrawn, took his meals alone, and spent hours masturbating, daydreaming, and playing with chains. In his fantasies he saw himself beaten by a man or a woman or else he saw one woman beating another. These fantasies evolved considerably over time; for instance, at 18, when he learned about segregation and the civil-rights struggle, he adopted the white Southerners' viewpoint and fantasied Negro men raping white women. These fantasies gave him both pain and pleasure; he liked these women, yet he destroyed them in his fantasies.

In the course of analysis we could observe various complex solutions to the Oedipus situation and the clear emergence of highly ambivalent bipolar introjects of the original love-hate objects. The self-image, as well, oscillated between femininity viewed as masochistically passive and masculinity represented as aggressive brutality; the introjects became externalised, giving rise to transient hallucinations. With a few interruptions, the analytic work lasted for seven years and resulted in considerable improvement. Social contacts, object relationships, and working ability reached truly astonishing levels.

However, in spite of treatment, "B"'s attitude toward women as libidinal objects did not change significantly. Hoping to improve this situation, I referred him to a young woman analyst; I felt that he needed an opportunity for a heterosexual transference. Unfortunately, my expectations proved futile. Although he developed both positive and negative transference feelings, his basic attitude toward female libidinal objects remained the same. His defense pattern was a repetition of his infantile struggle with the original introject.

> In summary, "B" presents us with a picture of a general regression of ego functions which we must consider as a defense against the dangerous impact of heterosexual libido. In the course of these regressions the ego moves with great rapidity toward early points of fixation. Not only were such positions revived as a far-going maternal identification, but the boundaries between introjects lost their sharpness so that there occurred an exchange of sexual characteristics between both parental introjects, extending to both sexually differentiated classes of human beings. The concreteness with which were revived old cross identifications reflected on the perception of the entire animated and non-animated world. Consequently, the confusion extended from the image of the self to the basic introjects and, finally, to the perceptual world at large. In the world of perception the regression proceeded toward dedifferentiation and partial alienation of the boundaries between animated and non-animated world. We have here a striking illustration of perception and object constancy as ego functions being subjected to regressive processes which destroy the integrity of the object world (Bychowski, 1971).

As of now "B" has still not achieved heterosexual libidinal object cathexis, even though his perceptual system shows considerable improvement. Upon superficial observation, "B"'s parents did not reveal any manifest psychopathology. During his long treatment they showed undiminished patience, tolerance, and love for their son, whom they learned to regard as a hapless victim of their past ignorance.

In evaluating this clinical material, the conclusion is rather clear. The handling (or rather mishandling) of the young child in the formative stages of mental development leads to irreversible distortions of personality. The role of traumatization and emotional deprivation in bringing about destructive hostility and thus interfering with the sublimation of aggression emerges clearly in our brief clinical vignette.

Seitz's (1952) experiments with young kittens who were separated from their mother two weeks after their birth represent a uniquely eloquent analogy from the experimental viewpoint. Here, too, the distortion of personality and behavior proved irreversible. Seitz mentions an obvious biological analogy derived from experimental embryology: "Spitz, Bowlby and Benedek . . . spoke of the development of confidence in the human child predicated upon repeated experiences of satisfaction from the mother."

It has been my experience that, despite the progress made in analysis, the basic symptoms of depersonalization and depression can at best be altered only slightly. The lack of full self and object cathexis (poor engagement and commitment) lead us directly back to the unhappy mother of the patient's early childhood.

Now, I wish to deal with the concept of symbiosis and its importance for the psychoanalytic treatment of severely disturbed individuals. Although my observations do not include children, I could fully confirm the validity of Mahler's (1968) conceptualizations in my work with adults. With increasing experience and insight, I have learned to perceive some of the intricate and subtle defenses and action patterns that the ego resorts to when it wants to camouflage or to act out symbiotic tendencies. I shall outline these mechanisms and conclude with some remarks on therapy.

We do not always have to rely on psychoanalytic reconstructions since, unfortunately, many of our patients remain entangled in a symbiotic bondage throughout their adult life. Such was the case, for instance, with "A." Discussing the dynamics of her regressive symptomatology, I mentioned that, among other goals, regression preserved the bliss of symbiotic unity between herself and her mother. To recapitulate, at times when "A" became aware of her mother's superior ability, she felt paralyzed and thoroughly drained of strength. She felt reduced to the status of an infant who might jeopardize maternal support by any show of competence. Thus, we may say that these attacks of apathetic weakness represented the acting out of infantile symbiotic tendencies; so, too, were "A"'s compulsive appeals for help, amounting at times to an SOS for immediate assistance in performing the simplest tasks of daily life. It could clearly be seen that this attitude had permeated and determined entire areas of "A"'s life and had served as a blueprint for the totality of her existence. It had started with her motor ineptness, proceeded to her growing social awkwardness, extended to the sphere of sexuality, and eventually made her utterly incapable of earning a living. "A" succeeded in making herself utterly dependent upon her parents.

A paradoxical combination of the symbiotic urge and the defensive wall led to rather bizarre behavior; for example, "A" would yield to a slight cue from her mother while provoking her by ineptness, distortions of her requests, and violent outbursts of unmitigated hostility. Or, if she met her mother or father unexpectedly in a public place, she might experience ineffable joy such as that of a faithful believer who had a surprise encounter with a guru or a charismatic leader.

The combination of the repressed symbiotic urge and defensive hostility could be so intricate that it might elude us, but, when finally revealed, its impact upon the patient's conscious ego could result in genuine surprise, if not amazement. Hostility serves to camouflage the symbiotic urge that was masked originally as ardent love. We can observe this confusion in analyzing a husband or wife, one partner in a pair of lovers (Giovacchini, 1958), or a parent or an adult child who have a close relationship with one another.

"A" 's infantile relationship with her mother brought about increasing incapacitation and invalidism before her analysis. During analysis, every new insight and move toward independence led to bouts of regression. "A" 's mother blamed her for her invalidism or, in the transference, she accused me of trapping her. The latter accusation, at times a bustling paranoid ideation, emerged with great vehemence after "A" was helped to find a job and started working again after years of complete parasitic inactivity. She rationalized her accusation by the exigencies of schedules that required her to come for her sessions directly from her place of work. "A" 's outbursts of violent hostility against her mother or the analyst could be seen and interpreted as a protest against and denial of dependency needs and symbiotic urges. While these protests were explosive and short lived, a more effective protest consisted of passive sabotage using regressive patterns (these patterns were described earlier).

Another patient, a married woman in her early forties, engaged in passive sabotage, outbursts of hostility, and sexual rebuffing in her marriage. She pretended that her husband interfered with any move she might make toward independent thinking and acting. She believed that he was like her father in having a low opinion of women. In the transference she accused the analyst of conspiring with her father and husband to maintain the marriage and thus interfere with her striving for autonomy. Analysis revealed that, in reality, she had abdicated her own autonomy — first in favor of her father and then of her husband. It became clear that in her marriage she continued the semiconscious game of pretending to strive for autonomy while still maintaining the fantasy of a knight who would come to relieve her of her symbiotic bond with her omnipotent father and lead her away to some romantic life.

In this situation hostility enabled this woman to deny her unconscious needs for dependency and symbiotic love, to proclaim and reaffirm her conscious desire for autonomy, and, by the same token, to delineate the image of her independent self. Since unconscious patterns of passive sabotage did not allow for manifestations and strivings toward individuation (initiative, sublimation in constructive work, and consistent cultural interests), hostility seemed to be the only reaction left for the anguished ego.

Fear of abandonment may be triggered by any separation; of course, it is infinitely enhanced by the death or real loss of a loved person. The woman in her early forties had suffered two such losses in her childhood and adolescence: the untimely death of her young mother and the tragic death of her brother in an automobile accident. As a consequence of her mother's death, this woman transferred her ardent desire for love to her father, who, for various reasons within himself as well as in the demands of his little daughter, could not gratify it.

It is unavoidable that in the course of psychoanalytic therapy, some of the firmly and regressively established bonds have to be loosened and finally disrupted. This eventuality poses a formidable threat to an ego that has just begun, as it were, to find itself and to struggle for individuation.

"A" experienced repeated crises of despair after she finally moved into an apartment of her own. At such moments she forgot her years of symbiotic living with her parents, punctuated by bitter fighting and acrimonious recriminations; she longed for the comforts of her parents' well-established household and for the care and unfailing competence of her sweet "Mammy."

In the treatment of such patients we have to be prepared for crises of despair, moments of melancholic depression and resigned apathy, and occasional outbursts of fury against the analyst as the cause of their misery. The analyst has to summon all his resources, not only of his training but also of his personality, including warm interest, conviction, and potential for understanding and empathy without sentimentality. If he is in full command of all these reactions (which are not adequately covered by the term "countertransference"), he can play an active role in ferreting out the patient's resistances at all levels, in bringing out (if necessary) his aggression, and in impeding its deflection against the self. While discouraging physical assaultiveness, the analyst must be sufficiently unperturbed to deal with verbal aggression and multiple forms of noncooperation.

At times I find it extremely useful to take a firm stand against repetitive, regressive maneuvers and passive sabotage. It pays to show anger at conscious and deliberate sabotage; obviously, we can only afford such demonstrations when the positive transference is firmly established and when we can point to previous experiences in the analysis when the patient was able to cope with situations that at present seem to exceed his potential. Destructive hostility, which I have called the first line of defense, may cause the ego to shield itself from the pain of separation or from the destruction of the love-hate object by phobic symptoms; the latter should be called the second line of defense.

The analysis of particularly irrational and intense phobias often reveals violently hostile impulses directed against the original love-hate object. Since I theorize that the ego of these patients is filled with primitive, unassimilated introjects that represent the archaic love-hate objects, I must conclude that this hostility quite naturally turns against the patient's self. This pattern obviously contributes to bouts of self-hate, lowering of self-esteem, and melancholic depression.

On the other hand — and this is another vicissitude of regression which is either spontaneous or released in the course of analysis — the ego defensively reinforces its passivity and dependence upon the parental objects. In so doing it denies its hostility, but especially its striving for autonomy. The message to the patient's family is as follows: "Please, I beg you to ignore my misbehavior and all my protestations. Don't you see that I cannot do without you? I am lost and helpless and, of course, I still adore you." Thus, in constant oscillation between forward and backward movement, the ego is compelled to reaffirm and reinforce regressive positions; it is afraid of progressing toward individuation.

"Z," a professional woman in her early forties, harbored overt hostility toward her parents and her husband. Yet the phobic defenses, which she mustered in her attempts to deny and neutralize, did not prevent her from experiencing and manifesting hostility; for months she had rejected her husband's sexual advances, and for many years she had refused to address her mother either by her first name or as Mother.

Yet "Z" experienced her most absurd phobias in her relationship with her most beloved and "gorgeous" children; she was truly frightened when, after considerable and prolonged efforts, analysis exposed her intense hostility. Much to her dismay, she realized to what extent her overconcern and solicitude for her children camouflaged her hostility. She was appalled when she became aware of the direct relationship between her wish for complete mutual absorption and violent hate. This tendency to turn every relationship into an all-absorbing symbiosis extended to persons outside her family. In this patient, as in many others, insane hostility turned against the self and produced bouts of depression and hypochondriasis. "Z" 's wish to compensate for the introject "torn out of her insides" by psychoanalytic intervention resulted in bouts of bulimia. She tried to fill the ensuing vacuum by eating excess amounts of food at inappropriate times of the day and night.

CLINICAL CONCLUSIONS

Special problems are presented by psychotic patients when they engage in compulsive acting out. Unless we are able to gain a quick insight into the dynamics of their behavior and time our active interventions quite well, the treatment may proceed in a vacuum, so to speak; there will be no modification of behavior, and the treatment will seem to be a purely intellectual exercise. I have seen this happen in consultation with many colleagues who were treating schizophrenics, latent psychotics, and active homosexuals. Sharp perception of the frequent role of symbiotic urges and defensive countermeasures in various forms of acting out is of considerable help in establishing a basis for the conduct of analysis. Thus, analysis is significant in handling such patients. Therapeutic maneuvers derived from an understanding of the basic symbiotic pathology and the resultant regression and defenses can lead to considerable improvement and integration.

REFERENCES

Benedek, T. (1939). Adaptation to reality in early infancy. *Psychoanal. Quart.* 7 : 200–215.

Bleuler, E. (1952). *Dementia praecox or the group of schizophrenias.* New York : International Universities Press, 1966.

Bychowski, G. (1952). *Psychotherapy of psychosis.* New York : Grune & Stratton.

——. (1953). Some aspects of masochistic involvement. *Amer. J. Psychoanal.* 7 : 248–273.

——. (1971). Congealment and fluidity. *Psychoanal. Forum.*

Freud, S. (1919). Turning in the ways of psychoanalytic therapy. In *Collected papers,* vol. 2. New York : Basic Books, 1959.

Giovacchini, P. (1958). Mutual adaptation in various object relations. *Int. J. Psycho-Anal.* 39 : 1–8.

Mahler, M. (1968). *On human symbiosis and the vicissitudes of individuation,* vol. 1. New York : International Universities Press.

Seitz, P. D. (1952). Infantile experience and adult behavior. *Psychosom. Med.* 21 : 353–378.

22

Preverbal Communications

MARTIN JAMES

At a certain point in an analyst's career two things can happen that complement one another: he can become sure of his ability to do defense analysis at the oedipal level and, in the light of experience and follow-ups, he can question his handling of preverbal experiences.

During 20 years of full-time practice of private psychoanalysis, I have steadily come to take the technique of defense analysis for granted. However, whenever I do any type of psychotherapy or therapeutic consultation with the young, I am especially glad that classical technique is the backbone of my work. Outside analysis proper there is no check on the use of constructions and of the projections that these require of us. In modified analytic cases the classical analyses of other patients provide the confirmations that are missing in the rest of the practice.

From talking with colleagues and from reading between the lines of papers, I infer that the fate of preverbal experiences preoccupies analysts all over the world. In clinical work there are many practical and good reasons for ignoring this territory. It is easier to select "well-chosen cases": such cases are less bother; they do not need relatives; they respect consulting hours and do not

436

sprout borderline phenomena; they have short and successful analyses.

What is needed now, however, is description of work with borderline and atypical or nonclassical cases. Admittedly this exposes the analyst, but so many papers are published about theory that merely discuss other papers. Often these papers refer only tangentially to what happens in the consulting room. Of course, such abstracted material can be used in teaching and does not invite interpretations or constructions about the writer from analytic colleagues; in this respect the writers show good political sense. Moreover, they seem to be objective, not subjective, and this means that sister sciences can consider them respectable.

Nevertheless, psychoanalysis does rely on subjectivity. The personal training in analysis does not abolish subjectivity; it merely helps to regulate and tame our intuitions. For the sake of abstract "objectivity," it is sad to say that intuitions proceed from our basic character; but our character will ultimately determine whether our skill and technique stand or fail. Nor is this problem confined to analysts. T. S. Eliot (1948) discusses the matter of cultural distance and assimilation :

> To understand the culture is to understand the people, and this means an imaginative understanding. Such understanding can never be complete : either it is abstract — and the essence escapes — or else it is lived; and in so far as it is lived, the student will tend to identify himself so completely with the people whom he studies, that he will lose the point of view from which it was worthwhile to study it. Understanding involves an area more extensive than that of which one can be conscious . . . . [but] the man who, in order to understand the inner world of a cannibal tribe, has partaken of the practise of cannibalism, has probably gone too far.

It is especially true of psychoanalysts that "By their fruits shall ye know them," but how shall we know them if their clinical work is not fully presented? So, there are good reasons for documenting the nonclassical experiences of our consulting rooms, our work with borderline ego areas associated with otherwise "sound" parts, our atypical clinical issues, and even our failures (as well as our successes) in understanding later defenses.

THE ROLE OF GENETIC PREVERBAL
COMMUNICATIONS IN CLINICAL PSYCHOANALYSIS

Because the preverbal experiences of our patients affect their behavior in later life and constitute residual difficulties in otherwise well-analyzed cases, they can affect the quality of therapeutic success. Preverbal communications are also important because the genetic basis of preverbal trauma dates from a time when, because of the individual's immaturity, the environment was essential for life. Therefore, when preverbal material is revived in the analytic situation, the analyst becomes a feature of the environment together with historical and genetic factors. This means that the analyst becomes, imaginatively or actually by acting out, included in the patient's ego boundaries. The analyst's counter-affects then become those of the patient, and progress can only be made if he verbalizes them. Admittedly, the analyst is only doing what parents, schoolteachers, aunts, foster parents, ministers of religion, and others do; however, he is also participating in preventive mental health work, which is done unsung. For there are many caring figures who constitute the environment of the child during his preverbal life and treat his preverbal ego with the habitual dependency and fusion of older age groups.

It would be traditional and proper to hold that psychoanalysts should take care that they not be confused with such untrained people. Certainly, it is safe to say that the analyst's job is to take for granted a good enough infancy and to trace back the current misuse of reality to the genetic situation that is being transferred and can be remembered and named. We can safely argue (many do, and they may be right) that the integrity of psychoanalysis as a body of knowledge is threatened by attempts to reconstruct preverbal experience, for this can only be remembered by reliving it in affects, physical sensations, and somatizations, which can lead both the analyst and the patient into a wilderness of wild analysis. Eliot wavers over the cannibals. However, the two points I have mentioned could be important: that analysis might theoretically be more complete and effective if it also included preverbal experience, and that infant-rearing techniques (and all techniques practiced by those who use devotion at any age) might be more critically understood.

I would like to sketch out some actual clinical situations that arise when the lessons of infant development are combined with the lessons of psychoanalytical work with children, preadolescents, and nonclassical parts of adult work. Analysts are keen, and properly so, to record what is unique in their work, but they have neglected to record the part that dependency and preverbal fusion fantasies play in the positive transference. For good reasons we do not analyze the positive transference until it becomes a resistance, but I believe we should understand the preverbal elements in it better. The personality of the analyst is quite important — the kind of person he is matters more in countertransference than it does in a detached classical role. For example, undoubtedly, for both patient and analyst, important fantasies play a part in the "transference at first sight." This is evident in many ways and can make it difficult to pass a patient to a colleague after an initial consultation; part of this unconscious transference stems from the preverbal period of development.

If in life there is a stage when there is no such thing as a baby, only a baby and its mothering environment, then in analysis there is no such thing as analysis of the preverbal baby in our patients without the analyst appearing in the patient's experience as its transferred environment. Naturally such transference cannot be linked to historical word representations; there can only be thing representations. But when they are verbalized they move from the level of drives (or constitutional forces) and become subject to secondary process. So, as Winnicott says of the ordinary mother, it is her devotion, not her cleverness, that counts; the same applies to the analyst in the area of preverbal communications.

There is an important theoretical point here. Acquired constitution is not a foolish, paradoxical idea. Certain experiences in early life have the quality of ethological imprinting. We cannot analyze, for example, oral impulsiveness and anal procrastination; we can only learn to live with them — to handle their consequences better than before we had insight. Later disturbances of development induced by inappropriate environmental handling — experiences falling in the verbal period, perhaps after one and a half or two years of age — can be dissolved; these can cease to be a serious issue and no longer require anticathexes. The antisocial tendency (Winnicott, 1956) arises during this period, while the core of autistic and severe isolating obsessional mechanisms and thought disorders perhaps belong to an earlier time with some oral and anal character traits that are commonly thought to be constitutional by inheritance — something I rather question. Such traits can only be lived with and handled by ego restriction and learning one's limitations. The preverbal areas I am interested in are post-constitutional and preoedipal; they can be dissolved but, as in development and psychoanalysis, only by environmental means.

I would like to give some clinical examples of how the environment, in the form of response from the analyst, has entered into particular analyses in my own work. I have generally chosen examples where *adults have required verbalization of their loss of ego boundary and where management, in the ordinary sense of direct or indirect physical intervention, has been unnecessary and indeed had to be avoided because it would have constituted mutual acting out of an hysterical residue.*

Personally, I became interested in the preverbal aspects of patients through child analysis, especially from work with pre-adolescents — those who are in puberty but who remain dependent socially on the adults who were once their infantile objects. This approach was the easier one for me because I had had a lot of experience in raising my own children, and I had also helped their friends when they needed a secure figure at times of crisis.

First Case /

I served as a security figure for a six-year-old girl who wet herself at a party. I had not met her before, but she trusted me as her host to help her out of an awkward social fix without loss of face. I asked myself, "If a social situation can require this of an adult who will never see the little girl again, should not the crises of child patients one sees every day also be recorded? Do we not bury assumptions by taking for granted all the environmental facilitations we practice in child analysis, such as drinks, biscuits, aspirins, Band-Aids, and accompanied visits to the lavatory? And if this happens in child analysis, should we not also record as significant the support given in adult work?"

The technical departure in this case is that, instead of saying something, the security figure *did* something; thus, an impending crisis was avoided. The little girl will give no further thought to what happened than she would think about or be grateful for food she received when she was hungry or air she inhaled when she wanted to breathe; my service was merely a part of the environmental support system, and our preverbal baby-selves only notice such support when it fails us. So it is, no doubt, with what we might call analytic tact or good manners. Patients merely notice that things are going well, and we ourselves forget how laboriously we had to learn what eventually comes so naturally — the setup in which they thrive.

Second Case

This example is from the analysis of a nine-and-a-half-year-old girl. In hospital she was diagnosed as suffering from an obscure myopathy affecting all her limbs and her speech. Before committing her to a Long-Stay Hospital, her parents insisted on having a psychoanalyst's opinion. After seeing her daily for a month in hospital, I believed her paralysis was unconsciously motivated and so I decided to see her in Harley Street.

To make this possible I departed from classical technique, suggesting that she could walk with support for very short distances; this was virtual hypnosis. In this way she could come every day by car, not ambulance, and walk through the hall to the lift. I introduced a further technical deviation: when she got to my floor, I would carry her to my room. I did so intuitively, but later I supposed that my reason was to avoid a direct confrontation with the symptom and to reduce the noise for other doctors. Perhaps I also did it because her mother had rheumatoid arthritis and had never been able to lift her even as a baby; I reasoned that perhaps she needed it in some way and was conveying this need. I had been influenced by my work with adolescents, where it is necessary to do what is appropriate and then discover retrospectively what phase (schizoid withdrawal, delinquency, and so forth) the young person is in; with preadolescents phases change so rapidly and require different techniques from hour to hour or even within the same hour.

I assumed that carrying the girl would bring responses on many levels. The significant one was preverbal, certainly not genital. In time we found that walking was genitalized (stepping on little men — phallic stamping); thus, by carrying her I saved her from genitality at that time. It seems to me that this type of intervention is similar to that imposed by lying on the couch in adult classical analysis. The couch is used by patients in different ways: by some to increase schizoid or paranoid organizations, by others to feed hysterical ones or enhance obsessional isolating, and so on. The classical analytic situation of necessity causes management; by its very nature it provides support and its reliability invites dependence; the successful interpretation is profoundly gratifying and it can be both caretaking and ego building.

Third Case

A withdrawn, gesturing, schizoid boy of nearly 14 began analysis with a tic of looking at the ceiling. He sat as far from the analyst as possible and, after a week or two, began to play with an ashtray. For several hours it was clearly on the verge of falling to the floor. When eventually he let it fall and break, he looked for the first time directly and with fright at the analyst who did not react. The eye movements could then be linked to averting his gaze when he was told off by his father. This, in turn, ended a phobia of red petrol tankers and led to an understanding of other tics and compulsions.

The analyst's tolerance of the acting out was both a route to understanding and an encouragement (by unacknowledged suggestion) of a new or reevoked capacity for dependence on an adult. This second unverbalized trust was vital. In a ten-year-long analysis, much of which was classical because he was obsessional, he had to work his way through classification — first of cricket scores, then of railway lines, of types of engine, and finally of details of the Japanese navy (ships' names, armament, battle order, and so on). After seven years of analysis five times a week, he complained that I had taken away "the words" and left him defenseless so that, as was literally true, only the analyst could save him in moments of vulnerability. From then on, in principle, I had to let him telephone me whenever panic threatened.

This panic was always a schizoid annihilation, as when a friend let him down or loneliness overwhelmed him. Even when it became genitalized later on in the analysis, it had the same core. For example, at 7:30 one evening we ended his analytic hour as a torrent of rain was coming down outside. I offered him a lift in my car, as he always arranged to live only 200 – 300 yards from my home. This was the first car journey in five or six years of analysis; it was only given because of the exceptional weather. Within an hour after I left him at his house, the telephone rang and he began a long, obsessional worry about the end of the world. It was completely unrelated to the material of the hour just finished, and I cut him short by saying, "I only gave you a lift. You are not pregnant; there is nothing to worry about." He responded by saying, "Oh yes, of course, I am so sorry to have been a nuisance. I shall be quite all right now."

For ten years I have remained a real object for this young man, now 24. In reality, no other object was easy for him because his father and sisters were inaccessible and his mother was dead. In his own inner processes he could not, of course, have used an object for dependency if it had been less available. Although he has had sexual intercourse with girls, he was very often disappointed in them because he is still so remote. Nevertheless he has advanced from using me as a real adviser on his social life to autonomy by true internalization. In most respects he can now function fairly well.

I don't recommend such a demanding relationship except to learn the importance of environment in the life and development of patients. Technically this young man could not have been helped without such a relationship; it could be argued that his therapeutic gain was minimal compared with what could have been done for other cases in the same time. However, in this case of an ungainly, unlovable bore, I learned that environment was all-important to him in his preverbal needs and that his excellent intellect and attainments would have taken him only into a false-self *cul de sac* if I had not offered more than interpretation.

What I offered was symbolized, not actual. It could be seen in the incident with the ashtray and the lift in the car : a prepared-ness to help — a sort of blank cheque that has, in fact, never been cashed. This is what parents offer children and what was missing for him developmentally, mainly because his mother suffered patho-logical withdrawal early in his life and died of a brain tumor when he was 17. At no time has he needed more than symbolic lifting. Certainly I have touched his feelings, but there was never any physical contact. I have given him tea, cigarettes, a fill for his pipe (even the loan of a pipe), but eventually it was possible to stop everything except his right to telephone in an emergency. The other interventions became a resistance by arousing real expecta-tions that I would accept him into my family. I think, however, that he could not have been wooed out of his withdrawal without them; they were only possible because of his schizoid, obsessional character, and they only became a reistance when they evoked the hysterical residue that Freud suggested may lie behind the obsessional defense.

I have not the space here to compare this analysis with that of Frankie, described so clearly and brilliantly by Berta Bornstein (1949). Looking back on Frankie's story and hearing the sequel reported at the Amsterdam congress, I have often wondered whether encouraging verbalization in this four- to five-year-old did not aggravate the capacity for isolating that was such a feature of his pathology, as reported of his later experience as an adult. In school consultations one is often faced with the fact that what a particular child needs is environmental aid. Of course, the environment cannot always be manipulated, analytically or otherwise. But to alter the environment in order to increase verbal defenses in such a case may help the child repress the sense of need he knows. It might be kind in some cases, but when I see it I always remember the biblical saying, "If your son asked for bread, would you give him a stone?"

These three examples have been drawn from analyses of young people. They raise an aspect of regression concerning which I would like to make two points. First, each patient undoubtedly received gratification in the interventions I have described, but this was not regression for gratification but regression for recognition (Balint, 1968). Moreover, it was not regression to id chaos but regression to a primitive but ordered ego state.

I see these three patients as being in a situation that, once stabilized, will allow them to deploy their ego attainments and to test and improve them with the help of the psychoanalyst. This is where the caring of untrained people is not enough; in Bettelheim's (1950) words: "love is not enough." Still, if someone in a little boat is threatened, storm-tossed, and seasick, it is no time to judge his ego or expect him to use it. In this situation the analyst merely helps the person to dry land where the work of insight can begin; only an analyst could have done it in the three cases described.

I would now like to present examples of similar situations in two adults, where the analyst's support was entirely figurative and not even remotely physical. In these cases it would have been unthinkable, technically wrong, and indeed fatal to have any kind of touching or practical intervention. The figurative intervention, however, was real enough, for transference is subjectively real and not an "as-if" situation. In both, acting out was minimal, but if it had occurred it would have been pure resistance and not really communication at all. Constructions and the projections on which they are based are needed, but they would be impossible without adult analysis to provide the knowledge. These two cases show how it is possible, for they illustrate how analysis of children can give developmental force and conviction in practice to the constructions we are taught by adult work by showing how the genetic situation (in this case, preverbal contributions to the infantile neurosis) was a historic one rediscovered in an actual situation once real for the child.

Fourth Case

Mr. C, aged 24, had every adult asset of endowment: physique, brains, money, family background, and technical training as an architect. He came to analysis because of his inability to sit at his final professional examination and because he suffered from speech blocking. Both symptoms expressed his inability to feel real. He had the kind of controlling mother who was described by Winnicott (1948) in his paper "Reparation in Respect of the Mother's Organized Defence Against Depression." The father was killed in the war when the patient was four. What was recovered through transference acting out was the patient's internalization of the mother's depression and sense of futility, her emptiness which he felt to be his fault, and his need to consider her developmental needs (and not his own) because he was afraid of her unconscious murderous and suicidal ideas.

On 12 September 1966, at the start of his second year of psychoanalysis, he returned for his first hour after a four-week break. His blocking was not apparent while, with affect, he described his experiences, but then he dried up. To save the patient from the pain of blocking, the analyst at an appropriate moment asked about times for future appointments. The patient reacted with a preverbal physical response: intense pallor, shock, a sense of annihilation, and nausea almost to the point of vomiting. The visible effect was such that the analyst apologized, offered him a glass of water, and suggested sitting or walking about. This restored some of his physical composure, and then the analyst made a construction while the patient was mute and unable to associate.

The interpretation suggested that the analyst was responsible for breaking the mood; that the analyst—as the environment— could fail and that he had impinged (instead of supporting), as had happened in infancy. This event recalled a similar experience the patient had had with his mother a year before. She had met

him at the station for a weekend visit and had denied the affect
of their reunion after a long separation by talking about the best
route through Ipswich. This experience had produced a similar
shock. The preceding year he had also witnessed his mother
humoring his old nannie by saying what the latter believed, but
what the patient knew his mother did not believe. The analyst
said that the present crisis recalled to the patient a time when the
analyst had looked up a quotation during the hour and the patient
had suffered an impingement, recalling his dread of being manipulated and interfered with; he had always refused the pot at
the age of 18 months, only to dirty his clean diaper at his own
volition when it was put on.

It was interpreted that the blocking was seen as putting
distance between the patient and the aggressor. In addition to
understanding the preverbal and unverbalized double bind situations mentioned above in his early relationship with his mother,
the interpretation led to understanding that anal procrastination
was a factor in the speech difficulty of a fluent man with a wide
vocabulary.

The key to the whole analysis and to the way in which
preverbal transference elements constituted such a large part of
the first two to three years' work lay in the first consultation
interview. At this first meeting, a highly verbal, intelligent, sophisticated, and ostensibly successful adult of 24 confronted an analyst
whose occupational problem could lie in exactly the same qualities
—especially the capacity to isolate affect. Quite intuitively and
from the analyst's trained first sight of the patient when he came
for consultation, the metapsychology was clear. Intuitively, the
analyst was able to help this dignified and composed young man
to cry. Such an outcome was possible because the analyst reported countertransference projections. He expressed sympathy
for the "teeny," inarticulate, helpless little Christopher hidden in
the big, composed, capable Christopher who had brought him
along. Tiny Christopher wanted someone to take him on his knee
and explain the world to him. Without some such affective experience, I do not think he would have agreed to have analysis
at all.

The proof of the pudding is in the eating, they say. In this
case the parameter did not prove to be an obstacle; on the
contrary, it has had tremendous potentiality. Although it had
been forgotten behind a year of ordinary classical analysis, it was

used as the point of departure to demonstrate all the false-self techniques of sophistication that create distance and thus protect the vulnerable true self. These distancing techniques included mocking, facetiousness, irony, and cynicism ; they were accompanied by compulsive daydreams. For example, the patient fantasized about being outside the window of the consulting rooms and climbing up the wall 50 feet above the ground. When he left the hour, he was beset by fearful fantasies : machine guns on top of the houses in Harley Street, meetings with acquaintances whom he felt were terrifying threats, and certain areas of the town which were terrifying for symbolic reasons. A whole paranoid way of life was verbalized and gradually connected with actual genetic incidents—cover-memories for a complementary series of preverbal memories expressed in somatic experiences relived and acted out, like the 12 September impingement, in the transference. Outside the hour this ideal analytic case barely acted out, if at all.

This man's regression was started, facilitated, or made possible by the active offering of symbolic environmental support at the diagnostic consultation ; by the third year of work his regression often found expression in contented silence, where he enjoyed waiting for the analyst to speak. For three years it was necessary for the analyst to verbalize repeatedly his sense of concern, care, and dependability. This need arose from the patient's symbiotic loss of ego boundaries, which could be undone by interpretation. Therefore, it was necessary to demonstrate that he weakened his own capacities by endowing the analyst with them. In a similar way he had weakened his developing ego years before out of fear that he would damage his mother by his autonomy and independence. The mechanism he used depended on his unconscious fantasy—based on earlier reality—that if he were self-reliant and went his own way, she could not survive and her death would thereby annihilate him.

He had two problems : 1. A self-imposed ego restriction that began for good genetic reasons—the mother's depression and withdrawal, first, because of threats to her controlling, and later her exaggerated controlling because of loss of her husband. 2. The need for substitution (or replacement) therapy of a developmental experience, also of genetic origin. This substitution was the fantasy working out of the analyst as a real father. It enabled the patient to accept his own autonomy and his right to let his mother go her own way without his feeling responsible. Aided by the analyst, the patient did not let his mother stay at his flat when she came up from the country; he refused to design her new house; and he accepted her severe depression that developed, no doubt, in part because of his withdrawal of support. On his own he told her that she should consult a psychiatrist. In all this the analyst protected the patient's ego autonomy and put professional know-how at his disposal. This experience led the patient to recall that at the age of three or four, he compulsively sought the company of the male gardener and preferred the rubbish dump as his safe place—his Tom Tiddler's ground—where, at the price of feeling like rubbish, he was immune from impingements and, to a lesser extent, the castration fears that can be their developmental sequel.

I use Winnicott's word "impingement" to mean a breach of the preverbal true self. The sort of actual genetic cover-situation I have in mind is a breach of the protective barrier against stimuli. To be called an "impingement," the breach has to occur basically at the physiological level, where there are no fantasy or thought defenses.

Physically, Ribble (1943) described how the affect of impingements appear in the nursling. I myself tried to describe their metapsychology in my paper "Premature Ego Development" (James, 1960); I described genetic causes and their immediate consequences, illustrating the etiology and dynamics of Bergman and Escalona's (1949) descriptive category "the baby with unusual sensitivities."

My clinical handling of this case, then, was based upon reification of analytic theory. From my knowledge of infant development, care, and observation, I was aware of the indispensability of environment up to, say, the beginning of walking. From the concept of the protective barrier, I saw the analyst's caretaker role for the vulnerable "teeny" self (the "true self," in Winnicott's terms). I judged this role to be that of interpreting the world to this preverbal area so that it could reach out and join up with the split-off part of the personality. None of this would, of course, be of any ultimate use without the ordinary defense analysis that begins with verbal and roughly phallic-genital genetic material at the three-person level.

In other words, recognition of the one-person and two-person relationship was critical. Balint (1932) prefers to use the metaphor of primary love and the idea that from the very beginning every impulse has its object. I prefer to think of a period of one-person need-satisfaction before object-satisfaction because, although I understand the political value of the idea, I can see no fantasy at the first-need levels, even though the observer realizes that an object is required. Omnipotence is the need of "His Majesty, the baby," and Balint has brilliantly described how since "the work of conquest" has not arisen, "there is no feeling of power, in fact no need for either power or effort as all things are in harmony." This harmony is as necessary for survival at this age as is air, and when harmony is threatened it leads to just as much disruption and desperate behavior as does choking. "Omnipotence," then, is our adult word for "everything going my way," without which the baby's proper developmental tasks cannot be undertaken. In this analysis, the supportive ambience restored the patient's sense of harmony by making sense of the world. Analysis at the three-person oedipal level could then allow healing of the split between primitive preverbal true self and a reality-adjusted false self.

This man had no manifest problem at the genital level : he was interested in girls and slept with them. His problem lay in his fear of their power over him — an expression at the oedipal level of an earlier, preverbal, double-bind controlling experience, which made him dread his mother's power. The only way in which the preverbal contribution could be understood was to accept and respond to it. The analyst's awareness at the diagnostic consultation that "this patient needs help and I will try to give it" was what set the stage. In all except the most obsessional patients, I think this type of positive acceptance and feeling by the analyst reaches the two-person aspect of the patient and eventually makes analysis at the three-person oedipal level possible.

Fifth Case

Mr. N. at 36 began analysis at the same time as Mr. C. I will use Mr. N. to point out the differences in recognition and technique in the two cases. Mr. C. was autoplastic in the way he acted out withdrawal, while Mr. N. withdrew from psychoanalysis by alloplastic acting out. He did this with girls sexually; in character equivalents such as feminine gesturing; in passive social relations with men (especially superiors); in antisocial character compensation through appersonation with clothes, possessions, his house, and car.

The countertransference in the two cases was interestingly different. Mr. C. required, for his reality sense, to be reminded of the countertransference concern he provoked at times of loss of ego boundaries. Mr. N. would have exploited this and needed strictly abstinent interpretation of his hysterical exploitation and defense. Mr. C. was aware of dependent needs as a problem from the start. Mr. N. was only aware of such needs after three years of work, for at the diagnostic interview he had to be managed out of a journalist's job into a steady job. Clearly he would have used hypomanic job excuses at moments of resistance to deny his need for analysis. He required gravity and strict abstinence on the part of the analyst until the end of his analysis.

Mr. N.'s character distortion lay in performing feats. He had done this originally to impress his mother. Having performed a feat, he always had to prompt her to praise him. Ostensibly his school prizes and his scholarship to public school, like his athletic successes, were aimed at his mother. In fact, they were a despairing recognition from his earliest life that he had to look after himself because his mother would leave him at any time it suited her. All this, of course, became clear in the transference, but it took a long time to acquire insight.

What was convincing was the primary reliance that Mr. N. eventually placed on analysis. This contrasted with his history of not trusting his mother because he felt that his achievements enhanced her, and not himself. Because it seemed that his mother had so appersonated him, it became important for the analyst not to give credence to a historical double bind; while interpreting the fantasy that the patient's gain was not his own but the analyst's, it was also suggested that the little child had *not* got it wrong : that there really *had* been a double bind with his mother, that she had stolen his glory, and that she believed he should be grateful to her for humiliating him. Although this was a breach of abstinence, it made Mr. N.'s idealization of his mother conscious and simultaneously served as a replacement therapy for his picture of his father. Mr. N. felt that his father had not been an ally or a source of security. The substitutive fantasy role of the analyst as a "good" parent clearly had both varieties of oedipal meaning at the genital-phallic level, but what is important here is the environmental support from the analyst, of a symbiotic type, which derived from preverbal needs.

Another interesting aspect is that both men, by their negative therapeutic reactions and their alternating indifference and anxiety in relation to success, show how a preverbal element contributes to this clinical state. They both became consciously aware of the oedipal and verbally derived elements in the linked reactions to the missing father and the fear of success, but to relieve the symptom, both men needed someone they could do things for and someone who could be pleased. So, for example, Mr. N. was always ambitious and successful, but his ambition arose from a prephallic dread; he was indifferent or even irritated by success because it inevitably brought a new challenge — something else in which, failing, he could be annihilated.

Mr. C. had a different response to success. The members of his family were so famous and successful that he used irony in asserting himself. Thus, for example, he once wrote an essay at school about his great-great-grandfather without mentioning the man's name, which was the same as his own. This whole mechanism, based on the preverbal double bind, could be expressed in terms of appersonating something as follows: "What I do is of no importance to my mother: If I do anything successfully she will take the credit and it will be considered part of the mechanics of pedigree — 'just like great-great-grandfather' or 'it's his family qualities coming out' — as though I were only an entry in the stud book or *Ruff's Guide to the Turf* or a piece of furniture in the ancestral mansion, not an individual who mattered to anybody."

By contrast, Mr. N. needed the continuity of the analyst to avoid becoming panicky. From the beginning of his analysis he would write down certain things the analyst said, and these words were a talisman to him, however trivial and undynamic they may have seemed to the analyst. Holiday breaks were particularly difficult for him; afterward he would say that he had forgotten everything and then revert to old defenses. His use of the analyst as an external superego was only temporary. At first, although he was aware of his own ability, it was affectively meaningless unless he could use it for the analyst.

Mr. N. could distinguish between what belonged to himself and what belonged to somebody else, but only if he could look forward to analysis. In general (even during analysis) he was subject to what he called "terrific extrusion and intrusion." By this he meant that he had a compulsion to appersonate and that he fantasized being appersonated. For example, when he began analysis he idealized and thought of marrying a particular rich and titled girl whom he realized was inappropriate; his wish to marry her was viewed as the symptom for which he had been referred. When he gave her up, he still attended grand parties compulsively, often escorting two beautiful "head-turning" models in order to attract attention to himself; in this way, he hoped to win whichever girl had the fashionable name of the moment and could serve as his entrée to some magic circle of wealth or social importance. Once he would arrive there with her he would feel disenchanted and thus begin the cycle again.

The mechanisms were those of obsessional isolating and denial of affect. When he experienced vulnerability it was mainly sexualized in masochistic character acting out or in fantasies of a homosexual nature where he unconsciously fantasized his rival's potency to replace his own diminished potency. But by using the analyst as a real person, he eventually used the word "cheating" to mean "borrowing." He knew that if he borrowed money, prestige, social standing, the right clothes, a good address, or a flashy car he would be denying his own skills and his real self. It took time for him to bring this into the transference, but when he did, as he said, by thinking and concentrating on his own thing, he could hang onto his own life: "Maybe something of my own has grown in analysis and has enough self-sufficiency to withstand the other. Previously it was locked in the false interdependence of a false diagram. Now I can distinguish which are someone else's and which are my own." For several years he could only adhere to this distinction when the analyst was present — not on weekends or during holiday breaks.

Naturally his passive wishes toward men were a problem, but only intellectually: he never actually acted out with his own sex at any age, but these oedipal aspects are not relevant here. Interestingly, he avoided the core of his potential homosexuality by borrowing everything except a penis. Once he had a row with his boss and suffered panic, not at a real castration level but more primitively; as a result, he recalled his feelings from the age of three or four when his father was not there to support him. He had actively longed for a real father who would support and embrace him and who would prevent his mother from curling his hair and egging him on to win prizes so that she could boast about them as if they were her own. He felt he could have tolerated his mother if his father had supported him as he was, without alteration.

Mr. N.'s dependability fantasy was acted out by insisting that the analyst be punctual even if he himself was late. If he had to wait a few minutes he would suffer a setback; therefore, he preferred to be regularly late and thus be sure that he would not be kept waiting. Once the analyst apologized for not understanding something, and this made a lasting impression. At no time would the analyst tolerate the hysterical claims that Mr. N. would have made with even the slightest encouragement. As he became aware of the cheating mechanism, he became abstinent, especially when he understood that his girl friends were female versions of himself. He felt lonely, lost, and in need of affection; he was on the verge of despair. He felt deprived in infantile terms. Throughout the analysis his conscious fantasies of the analyst were of a functional father. Thus, the analyst was a superego — a vital, transitional phenomenon that enabled the patient to cope realistically until the analyst could be discarded. Real aspects, then, of the analyst's personality were essential to control this patient's fantasies and to form a treatment alliance with a man who used "flight into reality" as an important defense mechanism.

REFERENCES

Balint, M. (1932). Character analysis and new beginning. In *Primary love and psychoanalytic technique*. London : Tavistock Publications, 1965.

Bergman, P. and Escalona, S. (1949). Unusual sensitivities in very young children. *Psychoanal. Study Child* 3 and 4 : 333–353.

Bettelheim, B. (1950). *Love is not enough*. New York : Free Press.

Bornstein, B. (1949). The analysis of a phobic child. *Psychoanal. Study Child* 3 and 4 : 181–227.

Eliot, T. S. (1948). *Notes towards the definition of culture*. London : Faber & Faber.

Fries, M. (1968). Problems of communication between therapists and patients with archaic ego functions. *J. Hillside Hospital* 17 : 213–229.

Goldstein, K. (1959). Abnormal mental conditions in infancy. *J. New Mental Disorders* 12 : 128–146.

James, M. (1960). Premature ego development : some observations upon disturbances in the first three months of life. *Int. J. Psycho-Anal.* 41 : 288–295.

———. (1964). Interpretation and management in the treatment of preadolescents. *Int. J. Psycho-Anal.* 45 : 499–512.

Ribble, M. (1943). *The rights of infants*. New York : Columbia Univ. Press.

Winnicott, D. W. (1948). Reparation in respect of the mother's organized defence against development. In *Collected papers*. London : Tavistock Publications, 1958.

——. (1956). The anti-social tendency. In *Collected papers*. London : Tavistock Publications, 1958.

23

Fragment of an Analysis

DONALD W. WINNICOTT

Annotated by ALFRED FLARSHEIM

Introductory Note

In "Withdrawal and Regression" (1954), Collected papers, (1958), Dr. Winnicott described an early period of the analysis of a schizoid young man. Among other symptoms, the patient suffered from emotional rigidity, being unable to express himself spontaneously in social situations. He withdrew in the analytic sessions and Dr. Winnicott described how he was able to convert futile withdrawn states into analytically profitable structured and controlled regressed states by interpreting certain aspects of the patient's dependence upon the analyst and the analytic setting.

In the present "Fragment of an Analysis" Dr. Winnicott reports in detail his subsequent work with this man.

During the six-month period reported here the patient progressed from rather empty compliance with the external forms both of analysis and of his professional life to deep emotional participation in both areas. We are able to follow the way this change came about by relating it to the evolution of the transference.

The benefits derived from the detailed presentation of an analytic case are emphasized by this example. Not only do we learn about Dr. Winnicott's clinical-theoretical orientation which has had and will continue to have, in our opinion, considerable impact on psychoanalytic theory and practice, but we are also made aware of how really exciting and rewarding the actual treatment of a patient can be. We particularly want to call the reader's attention to the way in which Dr. Winnicott has integrated fantasy and dream material with reports of routine daily activities, in the service of the analysis.

The form of the following presentation is that of the analyst's verbatim notes of the patient's associations and of his own interpretations, as well as some of his ongoing reflections about the analytic process. The condensation necessary for presentation gives an impression of more activity on the part of the analyst than was actually the case. In particular, periods of quiet occupied more time during the sessions than one might gather from the notes. In order to preserve authenticity of the free associative material, the text has been subjected to very little editing for syntax and punctuation. The index to this chapter is presented separately to assist the reader in locating passages dealing with various concepts that are particularly significant in the work of Dr. Winnicott. The italicized annotations may be comments about certain aspects of the clinical material, or they may be references to an article where the point made or illustrated by Dr. Winnicott has received extended treatment. Other annotations reflect upon the technical significance of what Dr. Winnicott has done. Still further comments consist of putting the therapeutic interaction in a theoretical frame.

There may be moments when Dr. Winnicott may not at the time have been aware of what he was doing in the terms we have described. Many such constructions have to be retrospective, and we do not know whether Dr. Winnicott would always agree with our formulations. However, with the generosity, that characterized him, which comes through so clearly in his interaction with the patient, he gave us a free hand.

We had hoped that Dr. Winnicott would be able to go over the manuscript before it was published. But Dr. Winnicott died in January 1971 and was not able to see the completed manuscript. Mrs. Clare Winnicott and Mr. M. M. R. Khan, Dr. Winnicott's literary executor, graciously gave us permission to proceed with publication.

Alfred Flarsheim
Peter L. Giovacchini

This fragment of an analysis is given in illustration of the oedipus complex as it can appear in the course of an analysis.

The patient is a man of thirty, married and with two children. He had a period of analysis with me during the war, and this had to be broken off because of war conditions as soon as he became clinically well enough to work. In this first phase he came in a state of depression with a strong homosexual coloring, but without manifest homosexuality. He was in a bemused state and rather unreal. He developed little insight although he improved clinically so that he could do war work. His very good brain enabled him to juggle with concepts and to philosophize, and in serious conversation he was generally thought of as an interesting man with ideas.

He qualified in his father's profession, but this did not satisfy him and he soon became a medical student, probably (unconsciously) retaining thereby his use of myself as a father figure displacing his real father, who had died.

He married, and in doing so offered a girl who needed it a chance for therapy through dependence. He hoped (unconsciously) that in his marriage he was laying down a basis for a therapy through dependence for himself, but (as so often happens) when he in turn claimed special tolerance from his wife he failed to get it. She fortunately refused to be his therapist, and it was partly his recognition of this fact that led him to a new phase of illness. He broke down at work (as a doctor in a hospital) and was admitted into an institution himself because of unreality feelings, and a general inability to cope with work and with life.

He was not aware at that time that he was seeking out his former analyst, and was quite incapable of asking even for analysis, although as it turned out later this is what he was precisely doing and nothing else would have been of value.

After about a month of the new analysis he was able to resume work as a hospital officer.

He was by this time a schizoid case. His sister had had a schizophrenic illness treated (with considerable success) by psychoanalysis. He came to analysis saying that he could not talk freely, that he had no small talk or imaginative or play capacity, and that he could not make a spontaneous gesture or get excited.

At first it can be said that he came to analysis and talked. His speech was deliberate and rhetorical. Gradually it became clear that he was listening to conversations that were going on within, and reporting any parts of these conversations that he thought might interest me. In time it could be said that he brought himself to analysis and talked about himself, as a mother or father might bring a child to me and talk about him. In these early phases (lasting six months) I had no chance of direct conversation with the child (himself).

> For further discussion of this kind of fragmentation see Dr. Winnicott's papers "Clinical varieties of transference" (1956); Collected papers, 1958, and his "Ego distortion in terms of true and false self" (1960), The maturational processes and the facilitating environment, 1965.

The evolution of the analysis at this stage is described elsewhere. (See: Winnicott, "Withdrawal and regression," Collected papers, 1958.)

By a very special route the analysis changed in quality, so that I became able to deal directly with the child, which was the patient.

There was a rather definite end to this phase, and the patient himself said that he *now came himself* for treatment, and for the first time *felt hopeful*. He was more than ever conscious of being unexcitable and lacking in spontaneity. He could scarcely blame his wife for finding him a dull companion, unalive except in serious discussion on a topic set by someone else. Actual potency was not disturbed, but he could not make love, and he could not get generally excited about sex. He had one child, and has since had a second.

In this new phase the material gradually led up to a transference neurosis of classical type. There came a short phase leading obviously to excitement, oral in quality. This excitement was not experienced, but it led to the work described in detail in the case-notes that follow. The case notes refer to the work done between the excitement that arrived in the transference but which was not felt, and the *experience* of the excitement.

The first sign of the new development was reported as a feeling, quite new, of love for his daughter. This he felt on the way home from a cinema where he had actually cried. He had cried tears twice in that week, and this seemed to him to be a good omen, as he had been unable either to cry or to laugh, just as he had been unable to love.

By force of circumstances this man could attend only three times a week, but I have allowed this, since the analysis has obviously gone with a swing and has even been a rapid one.

The whole of this material leads up to the *oedipus complex* which comes to blossom in the last session.

Thursday, 27 January

Patient	The patient said that he had nothing much to report except that he had had a cough. Probably this was an ordinary cold. It did occur to him, however, to think in terms of T.B., and he had been going over in his mind the use he could make of it if it should turn out that he should have to go to a hospital. He could say to his wife: "Now here I am . . ."
Analyst	Various interpretations were possible here and I chose the following: I said that what was ignored was the relationship of this illness to the analysis. I was thinking in terms of the break it would make in the treatment. I said that I was not at all sure that this rather superficial working out of the consequences was the most important part of the anxiety. At the same time I dealt with the reality aspect and said that I was going to leave it to him. He was conscious of the fact that he wanted me to deal with this as material for analysis and he did not want me to take part in actual diagnosing.

When the patient reported a somatic symptom and considered its effect on his relation with his wife. Dr. Winnicott responded by pointing out the transference aspects of the illness. He defined the setting of the analysis when he differentiated the reality aspect of the illness, which belongs outside of the analysis, from the fantasy associated with it, which belongs to the analysis.

Patient	After my interpretation he said that in fact the idea came at him not as T.B., but as cancer of the lung.
Analyst	I now had more powerful material to work with and I made the interpretation that he was telling me about suicide. It was as if there was what I called a five percent suicide. I said: "I think you have not really had

Patient   to deal with a suicidal urge in your life, have you?"
He said this was only partially true. He had threatened suicide with his wife but he had not meant it. This was not important. On the other hand he had at times felt that suicide was part of the makeup; in any case he said there was the fact of his sister's two suicide attempts; they were partial suicides and not designed to succeed. Nevertheless they showed him how real suicide could be even when not an urge involving the whole personality.

He now linked this up with the barrier that he felt he had to get through to get further.

Analyst   I reminded him (and he had forgotten) that he felt that there was a person preventing him from getting through the barrier.

Patient   He said he felt the barrier as a wall that he must break down or hit himself against; and he had the sensation of having to be carried bodily over the difficult patch.

Analyst   I said that we therefore had evidence that between him and health was suicide and that I must know about this as I must see that he did not die.

Many analysts would question the analyst's offering to assume responsibility for the patient's suicide. In a practical sense, of course, the analyst cannot control the patient's behavior to the extent of guaranteeing that the patient will not die. In discussing a similar situation involving another patient Dr. Winnicott said that he told the patient that if he and she together could not find a reason for her to live, then suicide would be inevitable. In both cases he was offering to help the patient understand the reasons for suicidal impulses, with confidence that the analytic process would release positive feelings and make life worth living.

Patient   He had the idea of various forms of starting life again with things different. *Pause.* He spoke about his lateness which had become a feature recently. This was due to the fact that something new had happened; he could have come, setting aside all his work and hanging around for a quarter of an hour so as to be on time. Instead of that his work had become more important and he now finished things off before coming; with luck he might have been on time. He put it that the analysis had now become less important than his work in some sense.

Analyst   I made an interpretation here gathering together the material of the past and pointing out that I could see this more easily than he could : first he could only contribute into himself, then he could contribute into the analysis; and now he could contribute to the analysis in his work. I joined this up with the guilt which underlies the whole of this phase including the suicide. I reminded him that the thing that the analysis was leading up to was excitement with instinct including eating. The guilt about the ruthless destruction here was too great except insofar as constructive urges and capacities reveal themselves.

In "The development of the capacity for concern" (1963), Dr. Winnicott elaborated on this idea. The patient is able to get to the experience of his destructiveness when it is balanced by simultaneous constructive and creative experiences. Constructive effort only becomes meaningful to the patient when destructiveness has been reached. Otherwise constructive effort is based on reaction formation against unconscious hostility, and is sentimental and unstable.

Patient   The effect of these interpretations was revealed in the next remark when he said in a much more easy way : "I now think of the illness in amusing terms; it might be measles, a childhood thing."

Analyst   I pointed out that a change had come over him since I had taken away the suicide communication which was hidden in the fantasies about the illness.

Patient   Following this he said that for the first time he felt if opportunity occurred he could use an affair and balance this with his wife's infidelity.

Analyst   I pointed out that this indicated a lessening of the dependence elements of his relationship to his wife, these having been gathered into the analysis.

Analyst   The report of the next three sessions is condensed into the following statement.

Patient   The patient reported that before the last session he had in fact slept with the girl friend. This was after a party. All feeling was damped down. He said that it might have happened at any time apart from analysis. He felt no love (potency was not disturbed).

The whole of this session was toneless and unconsciously designed to make the analyst feel that nothing important was happening.

Following this he reported that he had expected a great result. He had expected me to know without being told that he had had an experience with excitement in it.

The information came indirectly at first.

Analyst   I pointed out to him that he had so damped down the report of what had happened that I had been unable to make use of it. I was now able to interpret the transference significance of the incident and at first I said that the girl represented himself so that in the affair he as a female had had intercourse with me as a male.

Patient   He half accepted this interpretation but he was disappointed because there was no natural evolution belonging to the interpretation.

Analyst   The following day he was depressed and I made a new interpretation stating that my previous one had obviously been wrong. I said that the girl was the analyst (in the transference neurosis).

Patient   There followed an immediate release of feeling. The interpretation led to the theme not of erotic experience but of dependence.

The analysis now came out of the difficult phase which had lasted throughout the week and a powerful relationship to me developed which frightened the patient.

His question was: "Can you stand it?" He spoke about his father in particular among the people from whom he had sought the right to be dependent. His father could take it up to a certain stage but then always he would hand him over to his mother. His mother was of no use, having already failed (i.e. in the patient's infancy).

From this standpoint the relation to the girl could be regarded as a defense against dependency on the analyst. This is borne out in the next sequence by the association with thumb-sucking which recurred momentarily at the moment of interpretation of the thumb as representing a relationship characterized by infantile dependence.

Analyst   I made another interpretation which I had to withdraw because I could tell from the effect that it was wrong. I reminded him of the female version of himself that hovered around his male self throughout his childhood,

This had been an important feature in the earlier part of his analysis.

and I equated my new position in the transference neurosis with this female shadow self. After withdrawing this I saw the correct interpretation. I said that now at last his thumb had come to mean something again. He had been a persistent thumb-sucker till eleven, and it would seem likely now that he gave it up because he had no one for it to stand for.

This interpretation of the thumb was clearly correct and incidentally it produced an alteration in his very stereotyped hand-movements. For the first time in the whole of his analysis without being aware of doing so he put his left thumb up into the air and brought it towards his mouth.

Rudolph Ekstein traced the ego integrative effect of the psychoanalytic interpretation to the mother's empathic "interpretation" of the infant's unintentional expression of tension-need. ("The acquisition of speech in the autistic child," in Children of time and space, of action and impulse, *Meredith Publishing Co., N.Y., 1966, pp. 231-248.)*

Tuesday, 8 February

	The doorbell being out of order he was kept waiting three minutes on the doorstep.
Patient	He reported having a formula for starting, and compared it with history-taking. Patients assume that you know more than you do.
Analyst	"I have to bear in mind that you may have been upset by the waiting." Very unusual in the case of this patient.
Patient	He went on with the description of how one gets stuck in history-taking between going into great detail or simply satisfying the patient, presumably pretending that one knows as much as one is expected to know. Somewhere in the middle of this he had a withdrawal.

See previous communication dealing with an earlier phase in this man's analysis.

("Withdrawal and regression," Collected papers, 1958)

Recovering from the momentary withdrawal he managed to report the fantasy belonging to the withdrawal, in which he was very annoyed with a surgeon who stopped midway in an operation. It was not so much that the surgeon was angry with the patient as that the patient was just out of luck; he was being operated on when the surgeon went on strike.

Masochism as well as the degree of dependence are shown by the fantasy of a patient being operated upon. The weekend break is then represented by the striking surgeon. The momentary withdrawal was a defense against awareness of the dependence. It is important to remember that at this point considerable analysis had already taken place.

Analyst	I linked this with the reaction to the weekend following my acceptance of the dependence role. I brought in the bell failure, but this was relatively unimportant; whereas the long breaks linked up directly with his statement at the end of the previous hour that I might not be able to stand his need for an extreme dependence, such as

his living with me. The effect of this interpretation was very marked, the analysis came alive and remained alive throughout the hour.

Patient   The patient spoke of his negativity, how it bores him and makes him depressed. It leaves him high and dry. When he gets sleepy he gets annoyed with himself. This negativity is a challenge. Sometimes speech is not worth the effort. He feels literally dried up. Sleep means lack of emotion. Nothing presents itself. He then described the contrast between his wife's attitude and his own. His wife feels things and cannot stand his own intellectual approach to everything and his absence of feelings. He began to discuss the word love, not its sexual aspect.

He then spoke about Jones' in *The Observer*, mentioning especially the child with the button and the way Jones linked this up with cannibalism.

In "The dawn of conscience," London observer, 6 Feb. 1955, Ernest Jones discussed primitive id impulses that stimulate anxiety and a search for external authority to mitigate the uncompromising threats and demands of primitive introjects. Dr. Jones pointed out that when an infant sucks a button on his father's coat, this act may be associated with an unconscious fantasy of cannibalistically swallowing and incorporating the whole father.

I made no interpretation, knowing that he was coming the next day, and that the theme would reappear.

Wednesday, 9 February

Analyst   The patient came excited.
Patient   "I feel better." (Elation.) He reported having laughed with people. There was something new about all this. It was natural.
Analyst   I found that he could not remember what happened last time and I gave a summary. In giving this I was unable to remember the content of the withdrawal fantasy and said so. (It always helps this man if I am able to remind him of the material of the last hour.)

This could be regarded as integrative activity on the part of the analyst. On the other hand we can also wonder whether reminding the patient of previous material bypasses the adaptive meaning of the defensive withdrawal.

Patient He said that this liberation brought about by his feeling better made him independent of his wife. He now had a bargaining weapon with her which he could use although he felt no vindictiveness against her. He did not need to beg for sympathy any longer. It used to be nothing but himself, hopeless.

Analyst I said that it seemed to have strengthened his whole personality, his getting a little bit nearer to cannibalism and to instincts.

Patient He said that to make matters better he had had a discussion with a surgeon, very friendly, very satisfactory in result.

Analyst Here I remembered his withdrawal fantasy and reminded him of it.

Patient He continued that the surgeon had argued against the idea of an operation in regard to a certain treatment of a patient. The surgeon understood, but in a sense he had downed tools. *Pause.*

Analyst I interpreted that excitement was present but well under control because it brings its own anxieties.

Patient He reported other minor incidents. "I can afford to be excited. A year ago the same things happened but as I could not afford to be excited they passed over me. I allowed an intellectual appreciation only. I could not afford to do without my depression. In fact I could not understand how anyone could get excited and I had no conception of feeling competent. Now because of the progress that seems to be maintained here in this treatment I can let things go." *Pause.*

"I do not want to talk about excitement."

Analyst "The point of excitement is being excited."

Patient "There is a risk involved. You look silly. People might laugh if you prattle." (This word belongs in the analysis to a phase of his early childhood in which it was said that he prattled before he became sullen and withdrawn.) "And then you are left holding the baby." (Meaning excitement.)

The link between prattling and the holding of a baby is that the prattling constitutes the use of speech as playful motor activity rather than as a communication of content. Playful motor activity is safe only in a protected environment. It can lead to instinctual excitement, which requires the presence of someone else, originally the "holding" mother, to be the object of the instinctual aim.

Analyst	I made an interpretation joining together the prattling and the holding of the baby.
Patient	"People despise adult prattling. I have always been serious-minded. Now I feel that I could prattle naturally outside the analysis. In the analysis I can only be serious even now or I can be excited about something. There is something different about excitement in its own right. The danger is that if you are excited you lose it. You have it taken away or undermined."
Analyst	"If you show excitement it gets bagged." (I might have interpreted the castration anxiety here but refrained.)
Patient	"Yes. You are light-hearted and then you become heavy if the excitement is claimed and considered to be attached to something.

In a discussion of this case Dr. Winnicott mentioned another episode of this kind. At one point the patient was "twiddling" with his fingers during an analytic session. He did not want this activity to be interpreted, because if it were subject to any interpretation the patient felt that he would have to discontinue the activity. The reason for this was not that the analyst was experienced as a restraining or criticizing super-ego figure, but rather that any interpretation would link the activity with external reality, and break the patient's relationship with the inner sources of feeling and spontaneous motility. The activity could only be continued in a way that felt satisfying if it were not thought about as something linked to an external object relation. (Compare Note pp. 550.)

"It is important to be fancy free but this can only happen in the absence of a love relationship. I was thinking of this last night. The relationship to the girl is a fancy free affair. The relationship to my wife cannot be so."

Analyst   I reminded him that he was also talking about masturbation and he developed the theme as he already was on the point of doing so.

Patient   "The advantage is that there is no risk taken; no social complications." He was struck by the unexpected fact that when he was married the need continued even though this jeopardized his potency.

At this point there were bell noises; a man was mending the bell. This caused an interruption and the patient was surprised to find that he minded.

"It is usually the other way. You seem to be over-worried when there are interruptions and I cannot see that they matter. Just now, however, with such intimate matters under discussion I see for the first time the truth of what you have said about the setting of analysis and its importance."

Analyst   I linked this up with the theme of dependence.

Thursday, 10 February

Patient   He continued to report excitement, although this was at a low level compared with the elation.

Analyst   "It appears that you have lived most of your life at a level below par in regard to excitement, and now when you come even to ordinary excitability you feel conscious of it.

See article by P. Giovacchini in Psychiatry *and Social Science Review,* March 31, 1970, *partially quoted in Note pp. 474-476.*

Patient   "Yes, I find I am able to be gay and lighthearted with less effort. I used to be able at times but it was always an act. Something happened today which made me realize, however, that caution is needed. There are still unanswered questions to do with work and family. I feel apprehensiveness and guilt at feeling well, and of course at having a secret affair. It would be dangerous to get too excited, that is to say at the expense of the future. I cannot afford to ignore what remains to be done. But there is a difference. I can now look forward to a future. In the past it seemed that I had difficulties in the present with no solution, as well as no prospect for the future. There was no hope of living an ordinary life ever. My depression was something to do with looking for dependence. I could say that in the dependence and therefore in the depression I was claiming my birth-right."

Analyst   "The hopelessness about the future and the present therefore turns out to be a hopelessness in the past which you did not know about. What you are looking for is your capacity to love and without our knowing all the details, we can say that some failure in your early life made you doubt your capacity to love."

A question regarding genetics could be looked upon as a movement away from the transference and the patient's next response could be considered a confirmation of this. However regardless of its current precipitating causes, depression in the present activates depressive mechanisms which were formed during infantile development.

Patient   After agreeing with all this, he said : "There is the task still to be done."

Analyst   I made a rather wide interpretation linking up the reality that belonged to his discovering his love of his daughter and reminding him that this followed tears at the cinema.

Patient   "I have always had an intellectual idea of pleasure associated with pain. Similarly I associate love with sadness. I told somebody this once. It was at a Youth Club talk on sex. I said that there was an association between love and sadness and I was forcibly rebuked and called sadistic."

Analyst   I remarked that nevertheless he knew that he was right and that the speaker was wrong.

The capacity to love and the capacity to experience depression can be linked. The experience of depression includes sadness and grief about ambivalence, the sadistic component of object love. A precondition for depression would thus be a degree of ego integration such that there is both self and object constancy. By this is meant an integration rather than a dissociation of the loving and hating self, and the loved and hated object.

Patient   "Perhaps she (the speaker) knew but she found it inconvenient to agree with this point in the setting."

Analyst   "There is no need for me to try to answer this because the answer is evolving in your analysis."

Patient   "I was not being sadistic and this comment was therefore not true."

Analyst   Here I started making a rather more comprehensive interpretation, bringing in the word cannibalism which came from Ernest Jones' article in *The Observer*. (*See Note p. 465.*)

Patient   He filled out my remark by saying that he had always recognized that biting was important in lovemaking.

Analyst   In the comprehensive interpretation I spoke of this infancy situation which he had missed in some way and which he was needing me to provide in the analysis, speaking of the holding of a situation in time so that the dependence phenomena could be tested in relation to the instinctual moments and ideas. I happened to say in illustration that an infant might have three nurses in the course of a day in an institution, thus presenting a difficulty in regard to reparation.

The integration of hate and love in relation to objects is facilitated by survival of the object love and of the loved object during periods of frustration, hate, and aggression. The opportunity to make reparation for one's own hatred, and to gain reassurance against the destructive fantasies associated with hatred, depends on continuity of maternal care. If there is a discontinuity of maternal care and no opportunity to make reparation for the aggressive component of the primitive love impulse, one consequence can be an inhibition of the primitive love impulse, and an inhibition of all instinctual excitement. The continuity of maternal care which frees the development of spontaneous object related instinctual impulse, is one aspect of the "holding environment."

Patient   He picked up the idea of my interpretation quickly and said: "In my case there seemed to be four, because of my four lives — hospital, home, analysis, and the girl. Everything depends on my being able to describe in the analysis what happens in the other phases." He then said: "But adversely what is happening is that this split in the total situation is giving me more to talk about. In any one of the four places I have a lot to say, whereas usually I feel exhausted if I say anything and have nothing more to say."

Analyst   I spoke first about his need to feel that he was contributing in this analysis and that if he has nothing to say he has often felt awkward and deficient.

I said: "We are also talking about one of the origins of conversation in which each individual is integrating all the material of the spilt-off experiences by talking in one situation about another, there being in health a basic unified pattern."

This illustrates two functions of the patient's speech. One is a gift to the analyst, one which can serve to alleviate guilt over unconscious aggression. Secondly, speech is an integrative activity in terms of content. Both of these functions of speech depend upon integration of memory traces of the past with the perception of current experiences.

Previously all he had been able to find was various examples of the original pattern which he was all the time seeking. Now in the analysis he had found the pattern and could benefit from being able to split it up.

Patient   "There is a danger of going too far. One could get confused."

Analyst   At first I thought that he meant that my interpretation had been too complex. He was referring, however, to the innumerable odd things that he could bring into the analysis, and I was reminded of his having been noted for prattling until a certain age in early childhood when he changed over into being unable to talk except seriously.

Patient   He now told me about the fear of a hopeless jumble of bits and pieces, something that he called being too widely split. He chose to speak about the ward round that he does on Thursdays with Dr. X., especially as this always affects the Thursday evening session. I had never been told this fact before. Dr. X's round is never simple. It is always a series of challenges. He is full of ideas and demands. At present there is a new development in that the patient has innumerable ideas of his own and he now stands up to his chief and they both enjoy the contact. There was also the matter of a rather difficult surgeon. He had written a history of a patient and had received an amusing letter back thanking him for his very detailed and comprehensive report. This letter was praise and it came just when the patient was in a mood to receive praise, perhaps for the first time for many years. He certainly welcomed it. Just now there seemed to be too much of everything. He became worried always when there were innumerable bits and for this reason had developed a technique of generalizing and thereby simplifying issues.

Analyst   The alternative to an ordering of the material was getting lost in innumerable fragments. It would seem that the patient here was describing his growing ability to tolerate disintegration or unintegration.

The patient's growing ability to tolerate disintegration and unintegration is an aspect of his dependence on the stability of the analytic setting. In such a stable analytic setting, or "holding environment," the patient is able to "prattle," that is to say to relinquish his defenses

against free association. He is then relinquishing patho-
logical ego defenses, depending upon the integrative
stability of the analytic setting, or, to put it differently,
he is regressing in the analytic setting.

Patient   He said that these ideas felt like too many children.

Analyst   My job as analyst was to help deal with these children
and to sort them out and get some sort of order into the
management of them. I pointed out that he was cluttered
up with reparation capacity when he had not yet found
the sadism that would indicate the use of the reparation
phenomenon. The excitement in relation to me had only
been indicated and had not appeared.

The link with sadism was suggested by the patient's
previous associations (See p. 465) and also because
mechanisms belonging to early infancy, the oral-sadistic
stage, are being experienced. In the Kleinian concept
of the depressive position, the capacity for reparation
depends for its development upon the link between
sadism and reparation in the ego, and between their
consequences in the relation to real and fantasied
objects.   When such a link has not formed, as, for
example, because of discontinuity in maternal care, or
when it has been broken, as by a dissociative defense,
constructive activity loses some of its meaning and value
for the individual.

Patient   He then described the analytic situation as a difficult
one for the excited patient. Analysts are well protected.
They avoid violation by special mechanisms for protection. This was especially evident at the Institution where
patients and doctors do not meet except professionally,
and appointments are arranged indirectly. The doctors
also are having analysis. It is only possible to hurt them
by actual physical violence. Once some men tried to
break through and succeeded in annoying some of the
doctors by deliberate rudeness and were rebuked. An
analyst ought not to act that way. Or why do they?
"There are two ideas," he added here. "One, I am
annoyed that the analysts were not immune to verbal

	trauma. At the same time I am annoyed at their invulnerability. You can only annoy an analyst by not turning up, but that's foolish."
Analyst	I said that he had omitted talking about not turning up (I ought to have said playing at, but I left this out). It was as if he had told me a dream in which he had not turned up and we could now look into the meaning of this dream. We could see that it contains sadism for him at the moment and that the sadism leads us to cannibalism.

As an additional interpretation I said that in joining together all the different phases of his life there was one which was the surgeon's praise. I had been likened to the surgeon in the material of the previous hour and it was important to him that I should be able to see that I have praised him through the surgeon.

Patient	His response to this was that he thought that I ought to be able to show excitement along with his excitement. Why could I not be proud of his achievement.
Analyst	I replied to this that I was indeed excited although perhaps not as excited as he would be since I was also not so much in despair during his despair periods. I was in a position to see the thing as a whole.
Patient	He continued on the theme of the analyst's ability to be excited at progress in patients and I said :
Analyst	"You can take it from me that I do this kind of work because I think it is the most exciting thing a doctor can do and it is certainly better from my point of view when patients are doing well than when they are not."

Interpretation of the transference is considered the chief mode of communication in the analytic setting. What aspects of the transference are interpreted, and when, has been debated. Whether the content of the interpretation is particularly important is not a settled issue. Still, there are many analysts who retain the "classical" position, and even though they permit themselves some other forms of communication, they believe that only the transference interpretation is analytically relevant.

I believe there is considerable truth in the "classical position." However, from time to time I have found myself saying something to a patient that did not seem to be a transference interpretation, and yet I had the conviction that I was analytically "correct," and the patient's subsequent behavior seemed to bear out that conviction.

Dr. Winnicott illustrates this point splendidly. A patient of his became excited after accomplishing something which previously, because of inner constrictions, was beyond his capabilities. He then chided his analyst by asking him why he was not as excited as himself. Dr. Winnicott replied that he was not as excited but then again he did not despair as much either. Later, he added that he was, indeed, excited but not elated (presumably he was referring to the patient's hypomania).

On the surface, this interchange does not have the appearance of a transference interpretation. Dr. Winnicott is responding to content and seemingly not exploring the patient's motivations for wanting him to be excited nor their transference implications. Still, I and some colleagues with whom I discussed this clinical exchange had the firm conviction that Dr. Winnicott responded to his patient in a "correct analytic" fashion. In fact, some colleagues who did not know my purpose in presenting this material to them never even considered whether this interchange had anything unusual about it. The patient's subsequent behavior in the consultation room also indicated that the flow of the analysis had in no way been disturbed; in fact, it seemed to have been enhanced.

Dr. Winnicott is, in fact, telling his patient that he is capable of reacting and having feelings about what the patient does in his daily life; on the other hand, he delineates the limits of his reactions. He does not become as excited or as desperate as the patient. He only becomes excited, not elated or hypomanic. In essence, Dr. Winnicott's reactions retain considerable secondary process and do not become enmeshed with the patient's psychopathological extensions of his feelings. In effect, Dr. Winnicott explains that he sees himself reacting as a reasonable human being, who has empathic feelings toward his patient and who can share in the pleasure that the patient's progress and further ego integration produces. The analyst is, in a subtle fashion, defining the realistic limits of the patient's reactions and indicating the quality and extent of his counterreactions. In essence he is defining the analytic setting.

(Reprinted from an article in Psychiatry and Social Science Review, *March 31, 1970, by P. L. Giovacchini.)*

Monday, 14 February

Patient	He reported that the phase of excitement had subsided. The novelty of it was lost. There were three factors. One of these was that he was tired; another was that the excitement could not solve all his problems. (I noted the end of a phase of elation.) While he was excited he had expected that his difficulties with his wife, etc., would automatically solve themselves, but he realized now that they were as before.
Analyst	I brought in the end of the last hour when he hoped that I would be excited too. I pointed out that we were dealing with elation and that it was important to him that I had not shared his elation although I had shared his excitement.
Patient	He said that the change had persisted to some extent; for instance, he noticed a lessened need for putting on an act — living in itself had become less of a heavy burden and deliberate activity. His talking, although still difficult, was now not a permanent problem; it often seemed unimportant that he was not talking like others.
Patient	"That took the lid off. It showed that all I had been saying was of no value whatever. I feel exposed." *Pause.* He reported definitely not wanting to speak.
Analyst	Here I made a comprehensive interpretation bringing in a previous one in which I linked up the present analysis with the first phase which was completed in the war without his having achieved much insight. I said that satisfaction annihilates the object for him. He had obtained some satisfaction last week and now I, as the object, had become annihilated.

This is an example of the importance of continuity of care, originally maternal care and now continuity of the psychoanalytic relationship. The experience of satisfaction can temporarily reduce object cathexis and therefore "annihilates the object." The patient is then dependent on the continued interest of the mother figure, or the analyst, until he achieves sufficient ego integration to maintain object cathexis after instinctual gratification. This object cathexis includes concern about the results of one's instinctually motivated behavior on the object of the instinctual impulse. (See pp. 499, 625.)

Patient   "That makes me think, because I was concerned that the girl friend was no more of interest to me."
He then made a review of his relationship to his wife in the light of this interpretation of mine. He observed how satisfactions had to some extent always led to anxiety associated with annihilation of the object.

Analyst   I made an interpretation concerning the continuation of my interest in the period in which I seemed to be annihilated *(see pp. 302-303)*.

Patient   He reported that intellectually he could understand my interest continuing and the continuation of the object, but there had been an effort required to get to the feeling of the reality of these things.

Analyst   I drew attention to his use of frustration which keeps satisfaction incomplete and preserves the object from annihilation.

Pause.

Patient   "I now feel we have got down to important things. Looking back I am able to recognize the reality of this problem.
     "I wonder if this sort of reaction is unusual or uncommon or whether I am like other people."

Analyst   I discussed with him the two aspects of this question, firstly he was talking about a universal phenomenon, and secondly he was dealing with something which is more important to him that to some people.

Patient   "How does this affect the baby having a breast feed."
(Here he was getting very closely back to the essential features of the first analysis.)

Analyst   I now gave him a longer and more detailed description of the two possible reactions, the schizoid and the depressive (without using those terms). I spoke in terms of the button of the coat pulled at by the child which was associated in the patient's mind with the word cannibalism. I said that for him when he had got the button the important thing was that he was satisfied and therefore the button became unimportant (deca-thected). "There is another possible reaction which I mention because it is there in your analysis but you are not yet able to see it. This would be concerned about the coat that was now devoid of a button and also concerned about the fate of the button."

Patient   He obviously understood what I was saying. *Pause.* He said that he had been thinking a great deal over the weekend about which of two extremes to follow in his career. On the one hand there is the intellect and the highbrow line of development, with pleasures despised. Alternatively there is pleasure which he could make the most important pursuit. In practice the first meant following the advice of his chief, writing up case histories and starting off on a career in medicine based on intellectual attitude. His chief's whole life is in medicine and on an intellectual plane. He was tempted to follow this spartan regime but, he said, this would leave himself out of the picture, and the alternative would also be unsatisfactory as he would go out purely for pleasure. He could drift into some line between the two extremes but drifting would not be satisfactory either.

Analyst   I related this to the material at hand. I said that if his analysis got no further than it had got at present he was left with exactly the problem that he had described which belongs to the first of the two reactions (the schizoid). I said that it would be possible to talk about the future and to say that his analysis already did show that he was on the brink of the alternative line of development with concern about the object. Should his analysis cover this issue, then a new solution would automatically appear to the main problem of the management of his career.

Patient   He said that he wondered how there could be hope of getting at something here in the analysis which had never been before. "Is it possible to get at something in one's nature that does not yet exist? How can one achieve concern when it has never been there before? Can something be created out of nothing? Alternatively is there something buried which can be discovered?

See pp. 660, 665.

Analyst	I said that to some extent we might find that he had achieved concern and had lost this capacity through hopelessness in some infantile situation. Nevertheless it would not seem impossible to make a step in analysis that had never been made before. These things depended not only on himself but also on his analyst.
Patient	"Well of course the baby has to get at these things for the first time with the mother."
Analyst	"In the last few minutes we have been talking intellectually and talking about your analysis, and this is rather different from doing analysis."
Patient	"I do feel, however, that it is of positive value to talk about things intellectually."
Analyst	(I could not help comparing this state of affairs with that which obtained at the end of the first analysis when very big changes had occurred in the man's personality and external relationships, but insight was not a feature.)

Tuesday, 15 February

Patient	"I was thinking about the end of yesterday. You said we were talking around the subject. For some reason or other this made me laugh. It was really a very marked reaction. I could not help feeling that it was very funny. It was as if we had said, 'We are only pretending to be serious.' We were playing round in a light-hearted way. There was a break in our serious attention to matters and I laughed and felt very excited."
Analyst	"Your word 'playing' reminds me that I might have brought in this word 'play' in connection with the idea around your phrase 'fancy-free' in the previous session. At the end of last hour you and I were playing together

	talking round the subject and you enjoyed it, and felt the contrast with the usual hard work."
Patient	"That reminds me of something from Molière. Someone told a man that he had been speaking prose all his life. He was amazed. He had been unaware of this fact and it excited him."
Analyst	"I think there is a feeling that we were caught playing together."
Patient	"The same thing in medicine generally. I can see now how important it is when something lighthearted turns up in the middle of a serious subject. It can be bad taste, but occasionally it is very helpful in the middle of a serious medical discussion to have a little game, a wise-crack or a play on words. I spoke about the two extremes: should I undertake very serious work like a hermit or an ascetic or should I go out for pleasure and avoid everything serious? There seems now the possibility of a blend which is different from seeking a midway path. The blend includes both extremes at the same time."
Analyst	"This is the same subject as that of the thumb and your interest in it and your having me for it to stand for."

See Dr. Winnicott's paper, "Transitional objects and transitional phenomena" (1951), in Collected papers, *1958.*

Patient	"A new subject cropped up today. It had to do with the girl friend. I saw her just now. My attitude to her is changing. Originally I was only attracted intellectually. Firstly there was a demonstration of bravado in relation to my wife and secondly there was a physical excitement but this made me worried because I knew that boredom and exhaustion were bound to appear. Today there was a change. I actually experienced warmth of feeling and an interest in what she was doing and saying. I wonder if I might be starting to be in love. This would be absolutely new. I cannot judge. It never happened before. I don't want to pin a label onto it. There is a sharp contrast between my ease with this girl today and my general difficulty which continues with my wife.

It is the same with work. There seems to have arrived a bridge. In relation to the girl when there is a hiatus she continues with ideas from her end which my wife can no longer manage. Probably she used to but she has given up hope. A striking example would be that I phoned this girl for half an hour. This is absolutely new. I have never phoned anyone for more than three minutes as there was never anything to say except business arrangements.   At home there is a great easing of tension because it no longer matters about my wife and her boy friend."

Analyst   I asked about his wife and about how much she knows.

Patient   "Probably she knows pretty well but I prefer to make a mystery of it. It would be too cold-blooded to open up a frank discussion on the subject. Whoever starts the subject is in a weak position."

(Incidentally the patient is showing that he knows that this episode with the girl is part of the analysis and not an attempt to break up the marriage. He is always hoping that he can get well and that the marriage will mend.)

Analyst   I attempted to show that the various separated episodes in his life all came together in the transference.

Patient   He went on to speak about the way his wife expects him to be dominant, while she likes to be in the dependent position. With the girl neither is dominant. It occurred to him to say that this relationship with the girl is like that of a brother and sister, whereas with his wife the relationship is of father and daughter. Occasionally he had this relationship with his younger sister but they have drifted apart. The advantage with the girl is that while providing a relationship of this kind there is an absence of incest toboo. They can help each other. This provides an exciting novelty, discovering the possibilities. *Pause.* He reported that he was stuck.

Analyst   I continued with the theme of the bringing together of all the attitudes in relation to the analyst and the experiencing of conflicts which are avoided through the acting out in compartments. In speaking of this I referred to masturbation.

Patient   "I was thinking that you were sure to say that this relationship to this girl is something to do with masturbation, partly because masturbation has become very much less compulsive since the relationship started. I thought: 'He will say you are only acting out a fantasy.' "

Analyst   I pointed out that the introduction of the word "only" was important, a word that I had not used.

Patient   "Yes, you would pour cold water over it."

Analyst   I dealt with the reality of the masturbation fantasies which formerly we could not find, but which he has discovered in relation to the girl and particularly in the interplay which has turned up and which follows developments in his relation to myself.

Friday, 18 February

Patient   "The first thing that occurs to me to say is that it was three days ago when I came last. It seems a much longer time. There was a part of a dream which I had in the morning which I remembered. When I woke I was still in it and then as I gradually woke further I just remembered it, by which time I became worried because I felt I ought to be horrified, whereas it seemed quite natural. The dream was that I had seduced my daughter. For a time I lost the memory of this dream and then it came back."

Analyst   I pointed out that this dream followed on his having felt love for her after crying. I asked what he meant by seduced.

Patient   "Probably I simply mean that I had intercourse with her. I remember now that recently when she was on my lap I had some sexual excitement, something needing suppression. This occurred last week during a period of excitement and during the time when I was having occasional intercourse with the girl friend. It was all part of this same thing and in this period I was not masturbating. I did not want to. Also I was able to suppress it by conscious effort, in preparation for potency."

    All this reminded the patient of the problem belonging to several years ago, at home, with his wife. He reported for the first time difficulties in getting excited and premature ejaculation. At that time he would masturbate to relieve tension in order to get better control.

Analyst I reminded him that he had likened his relationship to his wife to a father-daughter relationship, and that the dream therefore indicated something happening in his relation to his wife.

Patient "That links up with what I was going to say. I have been depressed because I have been seeing the girl friend since the dream and I have been getting fond of her, but I now have found that she has become cold."

An earlier partner had turned up, so my patient was being pushed out. She herself had been seduced by her father at sixteen and therefore she hated him. There is the point that society does not frown on such a seduction as much as it does on incest between son and mother. In anthropology a father-daughter relationship may develop but not that of mother and son.

He said that in several relationships girls tend to lean on him because he is sympathetic and the relationship tends to end in a father-daughter way. He feels this as a defect of his personality. He is not able to be aggressive.

Analyst "What you are leading up to is that you have not been able to get to your hate of the man in the triangular relationship."

Patient "This only comes afterwards. It is not spontaneous. It is an academic point."

Now there had been an advance and there was danger of it all getting out of hand. How would it all end? He knew the rival with the girl friend.

Analyst Here I made a sweeping integration of the four elements which only joined together in the transference: dependence, instinctual gratification, incestuous dream, the marriage relationship.

Patient After this he said that he just remembered that many years ago he dreamed of intercourse with a woman and it now seemed that she could have been his mother. There was certainly some element of his mother in the woman of the dream. All this came on top of the practical dilemma in regard to the girl. There are unsatisfactory alternatives :

    1.) compete with the man

    2.) retreat

    3.) terminate the relationship.

He recognized all three as unsatisfactory and was angry. Such ends would only be convenient. Also he had been thinking on the way to analysis today, "A life without sex must be unsatisfactory, even although worries could be avoided in that way. If there were no expectations it would not be a life." He said that from early, somehow or other he had acquired the idea that intercourse is desirable; something he knew he would want even if he did not need it.

Analyst	I pointed out the absence of the father in the dreams.
Patient	It was here that he told me more of the rival with the girl friend, also a married man with two children. He felt that it was unsatisfactory in this relationship that these two men were treading in each other's footsteps (identified).
Analyst	I pointed out that the dream about his daughter and the relationship to the girl avoided the strong feelings and the conflicts that would belong to the dream about his mother.
Patient	He said that I must remember that for the last few years he had had no feelings at all about his father. They were buried and distorted except that they turned up at one stage of the analysis. (He associated the loss of feelings about his father with the absence of the father in the dream.)

      Also he said, "You must remember that what was happening with this girl is an act. It felt natural but it was an act and the act had come to an abrupt end. Naturally I am in a temporary depression; I feel there is gloom ahead."

Analyst	"In regard to this act, what has happened is that you have informed yourself as to the hidden meaning in the masturbation."

Pause.

Patient	"Also in the depression."

      He then went on to say that he wanted someone

to talk to about all these things, not the girl nor his wife. He had no friends close enough and has had none for many years and in the analysis everything is taken seriously. He needed someone for jokes and games. Some men would drink and feel jilted and others would work excessively hard or talk around it with someone.

Analyst   "The lack of a close friend is what you are reporting and it would have to be a man."

Patient   "Yes, perhaps."

Analyst   "Also it would be necessary for him to give you his confidences also."

Patient   "Yes, because only in that way would we avoid one leaning on the other."

Analyst   I asked if he ever had had a friend and he told me about one at college.

Patient   He said that he had in fact had no one to be best man and his wife constantly taunted him with the fact that they had to employ a relation of hers. He said he felt the hour was near the end. He would get dismissed, which meant jilted. So it was important not to let anything come up near the end.

Analyst   I brought out the full meaning of this word "jilted" which linked me so closely with the girl. I said : "There are only two of us here and if I jilt you, you have no one to be angry with."

This illustrates one of the functions of the oedipal triangle. The third person can be used as an object for hatred, thus preserving the love relationship between two persons. The oedipal triangle can thus be thought of as a defense against a more primitive anxiety, that of destructiveness in a two-person relationship. This in turn can be thought of as a defense against a still more primitive anxiety, namely that of the narcissistic state in which one's aggression threatens to destroy the universe.

Patient   At that point the bell rang and he said, "I'm not so sure ; there's someone at the door."

It happened that I had to let in the next patient, who was a man, and as I let my patient out he implied with his looks that he was enjoying playing a triangular game, hating a man who was responsible for his being jilted by a girl.

Tuesday, 22 February

Patient   (Five minutes late.) "It occurred to me to say that there is an article in *The Lancet* on enuresis in which emotional diuresis is recognized." He reported that at one time I had pleaded ignorance on this subject. (This seems unlikely.) He noticed that his own diuresis had disappeared along with the recent progress in his analysis.

Analyst   I spoke about my ignorance which he was pleased about. (I did not defend myself.)

Patient   He felt himself drawn between two attitudes, triumph over the analyst and also showing up the physical doctors. There was also in the article, however, a tendency to show that enuresis is frequently caused by a minor organic disability. Probably therefore many disorders which are called psychological are organic.

He spoke of himself as rescuing children from the psychotherapist. He reported this as if reporting a dream which had surprised him. He said it was like saving them from the surgeon's knife. He compared this with his desire for a more rapid approach than psychoanalysis.

It gradually became clear in this hour that he was in a state of resistance; this took the form of sleepiness.

He said he was in a dilemma, whether to be pleased at the attack on psychology or the contrary. The neurologist also implied that cases are labeled functional without evidence. All this implied that there might be a way of dealing after all with the vast flood of psychological cases. *Pause.* He said that he had a curious feeling : there was nothing. It was like any session when he was dealing with his own patients when nothing happens and he passes on to the next case. Here, however, the analyst is stuck for an hour. He cannot pass on. He felt guilty at the way he passes over difficult patients simply because they are not interesting. "It is rare in medical practice to get a situation like that in analysis."

Analyst   I reminded him of the surgeon "downing tools."

Patient	"You cannot get away. The logical sequence is that you must resent this sort of hour when nothing happens."
Analyst	I made an interpretation regarding the neglect of his patients, also drawing in the fact that in some respects I do neglect him, that is to say, between hours.
Patient	He said that the analyst puts up with the patient for an hour. He compared it with the claims his daughter makes on him. She really must not assume that because he is at home his two hours are at her disposal. *Pause.* He reported that he was stuck, and claimed that he was tired.
Analyst	*(Lost.)*
Patient	"I discovered with the girl that she is shocked by something different from what shocks me." Any sign of homosexuality shocks her and it appears that she had a homosexual tendency for which she has had something like analysis. "What shocks me is incest, not homosexuality." He feared as a child to be kissed by his mother and still dislikes it. Perhaps he had "abnormal incest ideas." This filled him with horror.
Analyst	I asked him what the horror was associated with.
Patient	"It is not enough to say that it is socially unacceptable. It is not frowned on when a boy kisses his mother." There was an episode at seven or eight which he reminded me about and which he had reported earlier in the analysis. It had to do with a walk; the whole family was present. The father pushed him over to the mother. There was a scene.

Pause.

Analyst	I made an interpretation covering a fair amount of ground, showing his development recently towards a triangular situation and linking up the sleepiness with anxiety that he is not able to feel but which concerns the new position. I said that I knew that he was really tired but that he would not like me to let this be the total explanation.

Pause.

Patient	"My mind seems to be wandering; it is difficult to concentrate, or to get at thoughts that I want to say."
Analyst	"My rather long interpretation squashed out these thoughts of yours."

Patient	"No, I could easily produce nothing at all today."
Analyst	I picked up the subject of undermining and the interpretation which was appropriate at the time and showed that it had a present equivalent in castration anxiety, father having turned up at least in theory in the triangular situation which was new. I also linked the end of the last hour with the word "jilt" and with the fact that he heard a man's voice when I let in the next patient after "jilting" him.
Patient	He reported that he was tired.
Analyst	"I think I may have talked too much."
Patient	"No, I would only sleep."
Analyst	(I was of course influenced by the fact that he had started the hour with a wish that there was a quicker treatment and I knew that he would prefer me to go ahead in so far as I had material to work on.)
Patient	He was concerned at my "awkward embarrassment;" he said he felt irritated. It was as if he were not accepted. Something was turned down. He felt he ought not to be so put out by his sleepiness. He ought to be able to take it in his stride. He was tired but there was something else in it.
Analyst	"The sleep therefore is dealing with something opposite, such as aggression, hate, or simply an unknown fear."
Patient	He reported himself to be drifting, very tired, sleepy.

Wednesday, 23 February

Patient	He came twenty minutes late. The lateness today was due to an emergency in hospital.
	He spoke about yesterday. His tiredness was only part of the story. Afterwards he was only just rather tired, which was quite different. (He recognized tiredness as a resistance.) "How often I do not remember what happened yesterday. I cannot remember yesterday's session and I feel I ought to be able to." He was concerned at his amnesia. Even at the time he was not taking anything in.
Analyst	I made an interpretation and linked up yesterday's hour and reminded him of the suggestion of anxiety underlying the tiredness.

Patient   He then reported a fragment of a dream which he had had the night before. He found himself saying, "It's probably not important but. . . ." In the fragment of the dream the girl friend had M.D., M.R.C.P. She took them without effort; hardly knew that she had been in for them; this is really just what she is not like. She is not intellectual or academic and she is even thought incompetent. She rather makes a point of not thinking clearly. The point about the real relationship with this girl is that she goes to the patient for support. He had anxiety at the idea of not automatically being superior, that is to say medically. She appeals to him for help. In other words, again he has become the father figure.

Analyst   "This ties up with the girl's dislike of homosexuality."

Patient   "Yes."

Analyst   "It's a question, who has the penis?"

Patient   "She is very much criticized by Dr. X, unmercifully, and I always defend her."

Analyst   "But one must defend a colleague, and this seems to imply that she is a male."

Patient   "There is also a difficulty which I can foresee. We only talk around the medical subjects. If we had not this subject to talk about we might be left with no conversation."

Analyst   "The dream gives the clue, it seems. The girl has a fear of homosexuality and artificially assumes incompetence in a tremendous attempt not to be masculine and this fits in in some way with your needs. The dream gives the other half of the total situation."

Patient   "From this I can see all the difficulties that men have with women colleagues. Till now for me girls have always had equal status and I have been keen on this. Firstly I was angry with men if they called girls incompetent and secondly it was satisfactory to think of a girl doing equal work with men."

Analyst   I made an interpretation concerning his attempt to deal with the differences between the sexes on a basis which applies more to two men or brothers competing.

Patient   "For the first time I can accept the idea of dominating. Remember that this is one of the chief complaints my wife makes of me that I will never dominate, make an

                arrangement for a holiday or anything. I have always felt it necessary as I see it now to make sure that she is equally capable."

Analyst   I made an interpretation here.

Patient   He commented, "What you said was just repeating what you said before."

Analyst   I agreed.

                I made a further interpretation about his inability to think of a girl as different from a man because it raised his own fears of loss of penis.

Patient   "She is very apprehensive about being masculine. For her, orderliness of thought is masculine."

Analyst   I interpreted that with regard to the psychology of the girl we were not just dealing with this problem of his but we were dealing also with her identification, what her father was like, and so on.

Patient   "But we are not concerned with her psychology. She only comes in so far as it throws light on my difficulties."

Analyst   I reminded him that the orderly thinking of which he was specially capable was masculine for the girl and also for him.

Patient   "The trouble is that for her, being impetuous, which is what I am trying to become through analysis, is a female characteristic, undesirable in men."

Analyst   I said that he was unable to tell immediately whether I would hold this girl's view or a personal one on this subject. I was sure that for him this subject of becoming able to be spontaneous concerned men and women alike. In making an interpretation about girls according to his fantasy I said, "It is as if their heads are cut off for you."

Patient   "Well, that's your fantasy and rather drastic."

Analyst   I tried to link up the orderliness of thought with the special characteristics of his father, but he reminded me that his father was capable of considerable spontaneity and that this did not make him unmasculine.

                I then asked him about the female version of himself that went about with him when he was a child.

Patient   "It's very difficult to know because although I remember telling you about this I do not get at it very easily. I think, however, that it had a penis.

"In adolescence I noticed that in my dreams about girls the girls all had penises. I was not dismayed in the dream but I was dismayed on waking. On the contrary, in daydreaming which required effort of thinking, I was able to produce girls as they really are."

Analyst   I said that it was a pity we had to have a short hour but I could not avoid this. Nevertheless we had arrived at his adolescent dream in which girls appear with penises and that we had therefore got to the place that the dream was leading to.

I had given him ten minutes extra and now terminated the session.

Thursday, 24 February

Analyst   (I had to keep him waiting for ten minutes.)

Patient   "Firstly I am aware that we were in the middle of something important. I broke off with reluctance. I have only a hazy idea what it was about, but perhaps I could think of it.

"Secondly I am aware of this matter of speed. How long will the treatment be? How does one know about the end of a treatment? It would help if one could have a target. What about the summer for instance? How does one know how far to go? Naturally treatment produces a disturbance so that one would not expect the good effects to show till some time after the end. There are difficulties to do with the arrangement of my future program, but I won't force the issue. I don't like an indefinite prospect.

Analyst   (I gave details about my summer holiday.)

"I am aware of your real difficulties." (Here I recapitulated yesterday's analysis, which ended abruptly on the note of the adolescent dreams of girls with a penis.)

"Your relationship with the girl friend is therefore part of this analysis, valuable just as a dream is."

Patient   "The girl is firstly not stable herself, and secondly not intellectually a companion for the future. I'm not sure of this. It sounds rather snobbish. We only have in common:

1.) A desire for intercourse, for pleasure, and we both use it for the restoration of confidence.

2.) As doctors we discuss medical matters, and

3.) She has had some analysis.

But there is really no future in the relationship. I don't feel justified in leaving my wife on her account. But the relationship is very valuable. I have found a much greater capacity for pleasure without tension with the girl friend. This is in part due to the analysis. With my wife I make a conscious effort to enjoy things, and it's more like a technique than an instinct. With the girl there is no romance, but it's all so natural. We are relaxed and take things as they come. There are and will be other men in her life, but I don't have to deal with that kind of complication. I have no wish to lean on her and it would be dangerous to do so. She has served me as an object for me to sharpen my claws on, and it doesn't matter because she herself starts off as unfaithful and unstable (though sincere in her way) and blunt. I also can be blunt and hard without awkward guilt feelings. I contrast this with what happened with the girl I met in hospital at the beginning, when I was ill. She wanted me to lean on, and if I had gone further I could not have let her down without disaster to her."

Analyst   "It is important all the time here that you feel you can count on me not to lean on you, so that here the only thing is your own benefit."

Patient   "When I left you before I thought I had completely left you, and was surprised to learn that you had kept up an interest in me. It occurs to me to wonder whether the same would happen again, whether you would remember me if I left off and whether you would expect me to come back."

Analyst   "Yes, I should, if like last time I knew you had left off before ready to do so."

I also reminded him of war conditions, which hampered me at the time.

Patient   "It's the same again with the domestic struggle."

Analyst   I continued with the theme of being ready for the end.

"There is still the fantasy of the girl with the penis, and if you left off now you would be evading that issue."

Patient   "Yes. With girls I don't hate other men, I just get annoyed to think of them. My present attitude to women depends on whether or not they take some action indicating interest in me, so that I don't have to be initiating everything. This is partly colored by knowing my wife's hostility to me, especially on account of my inability to initiate. I am driven into a pleading situation. So I don't allow this again, I don't want to let another girl become a necessity. I don't want to find myself pleading and begging again." *Pause.* "Now I am no longer the suppliant with my wife; also I have less urge to be trying to please her all the time. So she gets fed up. She isn't fond of me in any case and now she has less grounds than ever for keeping things going."

Pause.

"It's difficult to say any more now. There's nothing fruitful — only filling in time, talking for the sake of talking, not getting places."

Pause.

"I had no dream that I remember; that would set things going."

Pause.

"I am aware that there is something to be done. I am reminded here that you used to say that my mother had constant anxiety, when I was a small child, so that she had a need to be perfect. It's similar to my anxiety here. I expect this is in contrast to what other patients are like; they perhaps have less of a conscious need to get on, and are able to enjoy a healthy contentment. They might adopt the attitude: 'Why say whatever comes into your head to that silly old man.'"

Analyst   "You might feel just that."

Patient   "I think I have, but I must reassure myself by going ahead."

Analyst   "You have found out your feelings by indirect means."

Patient   "It's the same with my chief. I have anxiety about not getting to grips with a case, awkward about criticism. I feel I shall be disowned, and I have to take on responsibility; it's like destiny, to be perfect."

Analyst   I made an interpretation which included the following: "You can only meet your mother's perfect care by similar anxiety-driven perfection. Behind this is hopelessness about loving and being loved, and this applies now and here, in your relationship to me."

Patient   "I feel conscious of dislike and disgust."

Monday, 28 February

Patient   "On the way here I was thinking, it's not really useful talking about reality, about actual things. These things seem less real than dreams. I am thinking of actual things. Is it worth trying to bring them into the analysis? They seem less useful than dreams. I was depressed today, mainly or on the surface, because of home. It's more difficult at home now. Up till recently I've accepted the situation, been sad, but felt it would change through the analysis. Now I am faced with having to make a decision. Logically I should give up the girl friend. But I'm unwilling to give up this relationship to go back to the old conditions."

Analyst   "This feels real and it is real. You really are in a dilemma."

Patient   "I told the girl about home. It is difficult to get to the girl in actual practice. I was just planning a summer holiday with the girl — but here there would be a real need to tell my wife. This would raise the issue, and either she would understand or else it would bring about a break. But what have I to offer my wife? Only income and some loyalty, and if not even loyalty, well I'm useless. And I have no wish to be spiteful. Not that I've much sympathy for her, for she won't discuss my problems, only her problems with her boy friend. There is no place for talk about me and the girl. I'd like to be able to say it's all her fault. She might break up and I couldn't repair the damage. Perhaps she knows but does not believe, or she doesn't know but all the time suspects. I'm hoping that there will be some way that I will be able to start and talk with her. But then, I would only talk to gain a certain end, and I don't know what that end is so I don't risk it.

"I might put leading questions, but she knows that trick. There is also the complication of my wife's difficulty, etcetera, etcetera. So I opposed seeing the girl last night, as I don't like to see her too often. But after I felt — (detail lost).

Analyst   "You and the girl have some overlap of interests, so that when there is overlap you can play, whereas there is no play with your wife."

Patient   "There is a story of a man whose wife was unfaithful, written by an American author. Eventually this man traveled to Europe and in the end turned round and found himself a girl. Then his wife was no longer able to tolerate herself, gave up her loose life, and went to live with her daughter and became fixed to her and went to pieces. There is the risk that my wife is kept together by my loyalty, and that if I went off she would lose her ability to have a boy friend, and would break up. Do I hate her enough to do this to her? Could I stand it if she is either well and happy or if she breaks up? My wife once said : 'I'll never leave you.' I feel she meant she could not tolerate the disgrace, etcetera. She would throw this in my face. At the start she wanted to see you herself and I thought this was because she wanted to know if I'd commit suicide. Now I think she may have wanted to ask whether it would be worthwhile her waiting or whether I'd be likely to go off from her if the analysis succeeds. Remembering this makes me think her lack of interest may not be so genuine; she perhaps had to withdraw interest. She couldn't face the situation otherwise. Her disinterestedness may be a defense. I find I have less interest in my work. Work is not a substitute for life. Dr. X's pressure would lead me to a life of devotion to work. Here I'm wasting time, just thinking aloud, using the time to clarify my thoughts."

Pause.

Analyst   I said that these real things had not altered the fact that there is very important fantasy in the offing, and anxiety connected with it. There is the fantasy of the girls of adolescent dreams who had a penis. Perhaps the reality situation had sorted itself out according to the fantasy, so that his wife had a penis and presented a problem on that account whereas his girl friend was being used as the girl of daydreams, who is ordinarily female.

Patient "Here there is a difficulty in reality. There is an area of play with the girl. I need play in the real situation. Here we have a professional relationship and the only play is through dreams and the work we do with them."

Analyst "Yes, I see that. And you feel me as reluctant to play, as you have said before in other settings. The question is, where is the penis? As there is no man rival yet, there is no one to have the penis, and you expect the girl to have it. In the intercourse dream in which mother was to some extent the woman, you nearly reached the idea of a man — father."

Tuesday, 1 March

Patient "The depression about the dilemma has continued. I had hoped to argue the matter out with my wife, but I did not, and I'm pleased, but at the same time annoyed at having once again shelved it."

Analyst "The point is that you do not know what outcome you wish for, and therefore you feel that shelving it is more appropriate."

Patient "What step would make things better? I expect to gain two things by delay: I might get my mind clearer, and something else might turn up. It boils down to the fact that my marriage is a failure, and although I see this intellectually I cannot accept it. Also, I'm depressed because of the excitement phase, which proved to be short-lived."

Analyst "When hopeful you feel there ought to be changes in your wife as well as in yourself."

Patient "I tried that — but my wife was not interested. I'm also depressed because although with the girl friend it's less of an act than with my wife, still it's unreal. There is some strain and tension. What I really want is a relationship without pretenses. Also, though I've changed a lot there is still the talking difficulty."

Analyst "You are using the pattern of your defenses as a stable factor, something to catch on to when there's nothing else."

Patient "I expected because of the girl to feel colder towards my wife, but that's not the effect. I want her as much.

Before, the remedy was to sit at home and be in a depression. I told her I would not be home this evening on account of the fact that I plan to meet the girl friend. Before I told my wife we had a row over something else. I was annoyed. Here was an opportunity to inform her fully, but I was dishonest — I didn't want to be apologizing; it is better to be firm." *Pause.* "Also my wife perhaps sensed what is going on. There are pointers. For the first time for years she put out my pyjamas to warm. There were other details. This was after the row, and before I told her about not coming back. I want to avoid missing these opportunities.

"This confuses my relationship with the girl friend. My wife also talked about the holidays — this is new, she has always pooh-pooh'd this sort of discussion. It would be ideal if I had dropped the bomb at this dramatic moment, that I was planning to go away with the girl friend. But I'm not that sort. I don't enjoy cruelty. That reminds me, on a previous occasion, before I met my wife, I had planned a holiday with a girl friend. Before the day came we had found we didn't like each other. Here was a dilemma — cancel or carry through the arrangements? I was weak and carried on, thinking we might just possibly enjoy the holiday, but of course it was not a success. It will be — my wife will not accept my letting things go through weakness."

Analyst "The weakness seems to indicate a fear of your wife, a fear which you do not understand yet, and which you hardly feel as fear."

Patient "It is like eating without being hungry. Weakness means not taking the risk of being abandoned. Heroic people take this risk.

"It's like this with diving, which for me meant breaking from my mother. I was tied to her apron strings."

Analyst "It is a question of having no one to go back to. As if you were walking for the first time and there was no father present for you to go to when you ventured to leave mother. Leaving her simply meant going away from her with nowhere to go."

Patient	"That seems valid, but it is like a new subject. My daughter suddenly stood and walked."
Analyst	"Your daughter had got further than you, and had already at that time been seen through a stage of development that you are now at."
Patient	"I learned to ride a bike only by father holding and letting go without my knowing. If I found I was on my own I fell off. It was the same with swimming. I had to float first; then I could make movements, and at length I could swim. It is the idea of not being held that is important. The feeling is that there is nowhere to go to, or to come back to. Diving was the same. I always tried to cover my anxiety — I just shut my eyes and deliberately dived, but really I remained too anxious to dive. In my work I do find some anxiety when I work on my own. It happens to all, I say, but I fear abandonment — there I am floundering in a state of panic."
Analyst	"In your series of dreams soon after the withdrawal moment (the 'medium' interpretation), you had one about going for a holiday abroad. It was a weekend, and you came back." (I made a point of this as it was in the series — "medium," "lap," and then the idea of somewhere to come back to.)

See "Withdrawal and regression," Collected papers.

He gradually recalled this dream which he had forgotten. There was a girl in this dream, a hospital doctor.

Patient	"As a matter of fact it was this very girl, before I developed the special relationship to her. This is the the same as the end of the analysis — at the end what happens, does it just stop? I feel I would be floundering."
Analyst	"You feel that the end would be letting go and having nowhere to go to and no one to come back to. This applies especially to the end as a bite — which we have had before. In fact the present phase of the analysis is a long digression from the subject of eating me at the end of the hour, or at the end of the analysis. You would be left with me destroyed, and with anxieties about your inside."

Here we have a more specific content of the fantasy of annihilation of the object with instinctual gratification. (See pp. 477, 625.)

Patient   "Well, there seems to be nothing. Perhaps because I have a sore throat. Perhaps because it is Friday, which means a gap before and after. Friday seems detached from the general run of the analysis." *Pause.* "There's a difficulty on account of the break in continuity, etcetera. I might join it up with what we were saying last time. It's like letting go. A child walks, which means he lets go. But he must be able to hold on. Starting again means letting go again. There seems to be an obstacle here. . . ."

Analyst   "One way would be to say you are thirty and then two and then thirty years old again, and the goings to and fro are painful because of the dependence-independence. Or we could say that I have shown I let you down, because of the breaks, that I don't justify confidence for holding on."

Patient   "I could just lie still (without going to sleep) for the whole hour. I don't feel any tremendous urge today. It may be just that I'm physically under the weather."

Analyst   "If you are physically ill you know from experience it is more easy to get properly cared for." *Pause.*

One result of physical illness can be that it enables the patient to obtain care which meets dependent needs which have been stimulated by the transference regression. In the event of intercurrent illness with nursing care, the care can often be linked with transference expectations by interpretation. (See Note p. 658.)

Patient   "I'm just planning the weekend; I forgot I was here. I just filled in the time planning and thinking of trivial details of work. It seems I'm lazy; I feel someone else ought to do it for me, talk for me, just as when I'm not well I let the work go and someone else does it. It would really have to be you I suppose."

Analyst   "What trivial things, for instance?"
Pause.
Patient   "There's really nothing, only I can't accept the waste.
It's unproductive. Why come for just wasting time?"
Pause. "There's nothing to get a grip on. I was just
thinking about hospital then, and what I'll do this
evening."

Analyst   "What do you plan to do?"
Patient   "Well, I shall meet the girl friend. But what happens
depends on how I feel. But that wasn't the thing. I was
thinking of my home too, and hospital. It was really
a strange coincidence last night, I thought; since I was
ill before restarting analysis I haven't taken sleeping
drugs although I have had access to them, though while
at hospital as a patient I was sleepless and very much
needed sedative. That's a whole year ago now. And
then I got this sore throat and had rather a sleepless
night. But firstly I had had a very difficult and unusual
case, and had stayed up till twelve-thirty to get the notes
written up, having to concentrate, and secondly I had
this sore throat. I was awake two hours and then went
and got some tablets.

Analyst   "Perhaps not such a coincidence; you were already
feeling not so sure of yourself?"
Patient   "Well, yes, that's true. In the afternoon before the case
came in I was not feeling well and I remembered I
hadn't slept quite so well for a few nights. Of course
it's not like when I was ill. It was simply that I felt
that if I went to bed early I would not benefit because
I would lie awake a little. As a matter of fact I've not
felt so stable generally, the last few days. I've had a
lack of desire to do the job well, although I have actually
done it just as well. There's a paradox here. I was
concerned at not having concern. Since I've been with
this girl I've had less ambition, or perhaps less time for
work, and in the dilemma, work or life, I have chosen
life."

Analyst   "Perhaps there have been dreams during this phase?"
Patient   "No, it's more that I had prolonged consciousness."
Analyst   "There may be a relationship between the present phase
and the break up of a dissociation — you were not

disturbed in your home affairs by the affair with the girl, and then (as appeared in the last session) you began to feel the two matters at the same time and so to suffer the pain of conflict."

This is an example of the way in which integration of previously dissociated intrapsychic elements leads to conflict. (See Note p. 517.)

Patient   "Yes. (Here he went over the ground again confirming the interpretation.) It's the same thing as holding on. I don't want to let go of something till I know I have something else to hold onto that is reliable. Last night I felt perhaps I would cancel today's session."

Analyst   "But you did manage to come, which means that the meaning of canceling the session can be talked about and you can find out the effect of letting me know . . ." (Here the patient said "Yes" in a forced way and I saw he was asleep. After a few minutes I made a slight noise by mistake and this woke him.)

Patient   "I have a reluctance to talk today."

Analyst   "While I was talking you went to sleep."

Patient   "I think I said the last thing."

Analyst   "No." (I repeated the interpretation and he remembered forcing the "Yes" just before going off.)

Patient   "Yes, it's better that I came, even if I don't talk so that we can understand it. Not coming would be really wasting it all.

"Also I was reluctant to make the break bigger still by not coming. That would be not taking the analysis seriously. It would be unprofessional."

Analyst   "But what you seek is the impulse, and by not coming you would be making coming more real. If it is a professional matter, you come for other than reasons of impulse."

Patient   "Yes. With the girl most of the talk is professional jargon. It is very important to me when I can talk with her in a way that has nothing to do with our common profession. Sometimes I feel that rows at home are better than the smooth times, in which I am thrown back on myself. With the girl friend talk is in technical terms and there is some tension, but — this reminds me of one very difficult thing in my relationship with my wife. After intercourse, when we were having it pretty regularly, she wouldn't talk, she seemed awkward or wanted to sleep. It is just then that I feel free from tension, and with the girl friend it is just then that we talk naturally and without use of technical language."

Analyst   "This period after intercourse is very important to you, for here at last you reach a capacity to love naturally. This difficulty in your wife is therefore a very real one for you. This suggests that there is always some anxiety in your relationship with women, based on an unconscious fear of impotence, a fear of a demand that might be made on you by the woman. For a brief spell, after intercourse, you feel free from this threat, and you are free to love and be loved, which is what you are always looking for."

Dr. Winnicott has developed this theme in "The Capacity to be Alone." This contrasts with the annihilation of the object resulting from instinctual gratification and loss of object cathexis, when the object is "created by the subject's desire." (See, for example, p. 625.)

"There is also the matter of your having been given a short time twice during the past week; this may have affected your attitude here."

Patient   "I don't think so, because each time it was due to my being late and also I realize that I get a full hour where as the usual period for analysis is fifty minutes."

Analyst   "But what about illogical feelings?"

Patient   "Funnily enough I think I feel resentment more at the loss at the beginning when I am late."

Analyst   I did not go further, but I could see the relationship between this and the demands that may be made by the analyst, and also the lateness was a token "not coming" which was brought for analysis, and indicated the patient's need to be able to have me on impulse, which is the positive aspect of the anxiety about demands from my end.

Tuesday, 8 March

Patient   "I am wondering whether today won't be able to produce anything, like yesterday. I came to the conclusion
that Friday is different because it has a gap before and
after. But today there is no gap after. The only thing I
find to say is about home, continuing on the subject of
my dilemma. Shall I tell my wife about the girl? The
situation at home seems beyond repair. Logically I
should recognize this fact and not try to bring about a
reconciliation. Now I see I'll have to decide something
soon. The girl has hinted she would like us to live together, etcetera, etcetera. Last night at home when half
asleep I must have put my hand on my wife, she quickly
pushed it away. I woke and she was furious. I felt rejected but I said nothing and turned angrily away. A few
moment later she tried to cuddle up to me and then I
was puzzled. What does she mean? This was very awkward for it meant she was concerned at having rejected
me. Again, when I phoned today her tone was warmer
than it has been for a long time."

Analyst   "It was easier to deal with her rejection, but when she
seemed concerned you were thrown back onto the
dilemma and the conflict in your feelings."

Patient   "The girl friend has said now that she wants a baby
and she would like me to be the father. Since her
abortion she has been sterile, and now she feels she is
getting on in years and ought to have a baby soon if
at all. My feeling more hopeless about home has perhaps
made the girl optimistic but I think my wife is guessing
and is beginning to fight back."

Analyst   "The underlying problem is your two ideas of women,
with the girl friend as the woman without a penis and
your wife perhaps as the woman with one."

Patient   "Perhaps the same goes for my wife, too. She has always
hated being thrown over into the position of wearing
the trousers, yet that is what I have done to her. She
has always wanted to be the female."

Analyst   "The question does arise, what will the girl friend be
like in ten years' time should you marry her?"

Patient   "She fears dominating. In the past I feel I would have gradually become dominated by her, but I feel that wouldn't happen now. I used to be so easily dominated. I think I wanted to be dominated. With my wife I find it very difficult to change round to dominating."

Analyst   "It is always difficult to change a pattern in which someone else is involved."

Patient   "It's funny that being good-natured as I am supposed to be is linked with a willingness to be dominated."

Analyst   "Somewhere in all this is a relation to one or both of your sisters, with a reluctance on your part to be the one with the penis."

Patient   "Two things come to my mind here. One, how do you come into this? Are you to dominate me or what? I sometimes fear that I dominate the session."

Analyst   "Here I am the girl, who has or has not a penis. You wonder what I will feel like being the girl with no penis, when you have one."

Patient   "True. Then there is the difficulty about the girl friend who regards me as a male to make love to her, and has no very real interest in me as a person."

Analyst   "From what you say it might be that she could make use of any man, for the man is to represent her male self in her effort to avoid her homosexuality. She may be more interested in your male orgasm than in her own."

The girl reaches her own masculine identification in projected form, thus defending herself against her homosexuality while indirectly experiencing it through identification with the patient. She is therefore highly motivated to help him reach male potency, but is also potentially envious of him. The importance of her own feminine sexual experience is diminished by the emotional investment she has in her projected masculine identity.

One could question the technical advisability of making interpretations to the patient about another person, the girl friend. But the analyst's picture of the girl friend comes entirely from what the patient has told about her. Therefore the analyst can be confident that the patient can assimilate interpretations which consist of pulling together various fragments of the

*personality of the girl friend as the patient has presented
her to the analyst. This need not correspond exactly
with the objective reality of the personality of the girl
friend. Essentially the same thinking applies to the
analyst's formulations about others in the patient's life,
for example, his parents or siblings. This is one great
advantage of the analyst having no knowledge of the
patient except that which evolves naturally in the course
of the analysis. (See Note p. 545.)*

Patient "Yes, she is especially concerned with my orgasm. It's
rather curious I often think, since she is a selfish person
fundamentally."

Analyst "Her drive would be especially valuable to you now as
she needs to make you regain confidence in your
potency."

Patient "The idea occurs to me that her present interest in
having a baby is an attempt to establish herself as a
woman." (Add: implying, in spite of no very strong
female orgasm.)

Analyst "The future is therefore a separate issue from that of
the value that you and she are to each other at the
moment."

Patient "It's funny but I think I welcome the pregnancy idea
out of naughtiness. It would be a challenge to the world,
and to my wife. Also there is this, that I feel it would
be nice if it turned out to be a boy. I now see that I
wish I had had a son. My wife won't want any more
children, and so I had lost all hope of having a
boy."

Analyst "There is also the point that a son for the girl or for your
wife is rather like giving them a penis, which relieves
you of the delusion about the penis. The important thing
in all this is that you have discovered your sadness at
not having had a son for your second child."

*The fantasy of the phallic woman leads the patient to
expect a woman to take his penis. This anxiety can be
temporarily alleviated by giving the woman a child,
representing the penis, and this is particularly true if
the child happens to be a male.*

Patient   "Yes, I was pleased it was a girl, which was partly a simple denial, and also it made me feel it would be easier to get away from my wife. But I felt I don't deserve to have a son, so I would be glad to give the girl an illegitimate baby. This would be perverse, and this perverseness is important. The only way to make the world acceptable is to challenge it. Somehow the idea is naughty and therefore exciting. That makes it appeal to me."

Analyst   "Earlier you spoke of your compliant self and this can be said to be hiding your true self. The true self is in great danger because it is just quite simply a boy child with a penis and important in the family because of this penis. The false compliant self hides and protects the true self from expected danger. However, the true self can be allowed to show if actively antisocial, defiant, naughty."

Patient   "And what helps is that this antisocial behavior is unreal."

Analyst   "Yes, but it is very nearly your true self."

Patient   "That reminds me that the present trouble started up when I found myself qualified, and for the first time in a position of responsibility, having to make decisions as a doctor. It was just this that I couldn't accept, and my wife complained of the same in me, that I would never decide anything."

Analyst   "This applies to yourself as an infant and a young boy with your sisters. There is a complication that must be looked into — this question of your mother's attitude. It could be that as a boy you dreamed of a sexual relationship with your mother and so feared your father. But that is not how you are putting it. Father has not yet appeared in this setting. This makes me think that when you became a boy with sexual excitement and incest dreams you found mother evaluating you in a special way, so that you were in danger of getting your maleness bagged. Your mother too may have wanted you to be her penis. From this you retreated, and so you did not get on to the next stage of conflict with father."

Patient   "I do not remember ever having been conscious of being a boy with a penis, but it would be logical I

suppose for me to have forgotten all this. Myself as a
boy seems remote."

Analyst   "Your dressing up as a girl would come in too, as a
denial of your maleness. It would seem you couldn't
stand the plight of your sisters who had no penis, since
you knew of nothing else that they had. I also want to
remind you of your thumb-sucking and your need for
something to catch hold of. By sucking instead of catch-
ing hold of your penis you avoided the issue of penis or
no penis, and what you did made no distinction between
you and your sisters.

Wednesday, 9 March

Patient   "It's not about myself today; something has happened
that confuses the issue. Last night I had arranged to sit
in at home, with the idea of going to a party tonight with
the girl friend, which I very likely will still go to. But
my wife came back early, crying. She had called in on
her boy friend, and he had taken ill — had gone blind,
and had a fit. He is dying (this was inevitable sometime;
he has a heart, mitral stenosis and endocarditis). This
complicates matters for me. It seems mean for me to
enjoy myself, but on the other hand, I can't be of much
help to my wife since she won't talk. What point is
there in my sacrificing myself for her when I cannot
expect thanks? In the past I would have, as a symbol
of martyrdom, but now I'm less willing to devote myself
to her cause. But I was upset at the news, and she asked
me why I should be upset. This was difficult to answer.
It was partly seeing her upset about this man. I was
annoyed because she was never upset about me when,
in a different way, I was myself ill. Partly I felt all this
would interfere with my life. Partly too I was moved
by meeting grief in the abstract. I couldn't help being
affected and this was the most potent cause."

Analyst   "Yes."

Patient   "After that I was speculating about the future, the
probable outcome. On the one hand our relationship
might improve. On the other hand it is more likely to
deteriorate. My wife will have nothing to occupy her

and to keep her happy and so will tend to resent me more intensely than before when she could hide possible and probable resentment in guilt over her own behavior. She will be more critical and less sympathetic. Why do I say this? I am only conjecturing."

Analyst   "You do not know which alteration would be better or worse."

Patient   "It all depends on the degree to which there might be improvement. If things improve a great deal between us then I would know which alteration to prefer. I would be thrown back on having to say that it is her lack of affection that drives me away, since there would no longer be the boy friend. This is quite logical but difficult to justify to her. I would so much like to be able to talk it all over with her, as man to man so to speak, or dispassionately, but that's impossible (apart from this crisis). I want her to challenge me so that I can justify myself. It is upsetting to find that she says nothing about my unfaithfulness." *Pause.* "Did I interrupt? You were going to say something."

Analyst   "Perhaps you sensed that I was wondering whether or not to say something. It was this, that there might also be direct grief about this man's death, since you knew him."

Patient   "That is possible but I had dismissed this. I think it was grief of a more vicarious kind. In hospital I find I am not grieved at the death of a patient but what worries me is telling the relatives. Is it perhaps watching them react? It was very difficult to tell a mother and a a girl of a man's serious illness and especially to tell the mother of her son's death, though this man's death had seemed no more than a technical matter."

Analyst   "There is the locked-up grief, about your father's death. Perhaps your indirect reaction belongs to this?"

Patient   "Yes. It is significant that I felt no grief at the time of my father's death. Perhaps I have not felt grief on this account yet."

Analyst   "There are two things happening at once because of the man's illness. On the one hand you are brought up against grief for which you are not ready, and on the other hand your dilemma is intensified in the way you have described."

Patient	"Once again outside things have come along and have obliterated the underneath things, and it's not helpful; but it can't be avoided, they have to be gone over."
Analyst	"There remains the fantasy of the girl with the penis, and it seems likely that your girl friend is felt to have a need for men while your wife is self-contained and has a penis."
Patient	"I see the first part but not the part about my wife."
Analyst	I admitted muddle, and said I was not clear enough to continue with this interpretation.
Patient	"I have noticed for one or two weeks that I felt a rather greater wish for intercourse with my wife. What is thought and what is felt are evidently different things. I thought now that I have a sex outlet I would feel colder, but I find in fact that when in bed with my wife I have a desire for her, though my intellect says 'No, there's no need to pester her now.' Because I haven't any need now to demand it when I know it's unacceptable, it seems that my desire is less intellectual and more instinctive. In the past I was reduced to saying that if there is to be sex at all it should be with my wife, that's logical, so I approached it as a matter of rights. Now I can ignore my rights, and I find a new and natural feeling comes instead. Of course I could say that there is another explanation. Before I started to have intercourse with the girl I had feelings of impotence. Because I couldn't satisfy my wife I had no proof of my own powers and I had doubts; would it be wise to risk impotence, or to risk not being able fully to satisfy her? After finding I could rely on giving the girl full satisfaction I could afford to wipe aside doubts."
Analyst	"It used to be always a test, and now it is more of a natural thing."
Patient	"Also I'm no longer in a supplicant position. Now I know I'm able, it's not so much need as that it would be nice. Here I am in a more dominant position."
Analyst	"This links with being a male in the family."
Patient	"Yes. For the first time I begin to discover I am a male. That felt like boasting, boasting of sexual prowess, to the exclusion of everything else; here, to the exclusion of progress in analysis."

Analyst   "The question is, who am I, to whom you are boasting?
I might be sisters, or father, or mother or a brother —
I think I'm mother just now."

Patient   "Yes, you're mother. As a small boy I would prove my
progress in walking, reading, and then I'd say to my
mother: 'Look, mummy, I can do it now,' She would
notice. But this is what happens in my work. If I have an
exciting and difficult unusual case instead of getting
the investigation completed and the notes written up,
I call in a colleague and I simply must show it off, and
can't wait. It's exciting to show it off."

Analyst   "To mother."

Patient   "Yes, I'm sure it's mother because I come at it indirectly
through a schoolboy story. A boy had a wet dream and
rushed into his parents' room shouting 'Look, mummy,
no hands.' You see my direct approach to my mother
is buried."

Analyst   "You could be talking too about motions. First there
is excitement about the fact of shitting, and then there
comes the pleasure that belongs to saving the stuff up,
so that the result is a big motion. If training is imposed
the child has no time to make the natural progression,
and there remains a certain degree of need to go back to
the excitement over shitting. I could say the same in
terms of money, etcetera."

Patient   "You may be right, but I still think it's illogical for me
to show off a half-finished picture instead of waiting till
I can present the whole. I run the risk of looking foolish,
and in my work, of putting forward a wrong diagnosis.
I jump to conclusions and then try to make everything
else fit in.

This reminds me most of the childhood dilemma
of meals. When there was a tid-bit, should I eat it,
and then find the rest of the meal dull, or retain it till
the end, and usually I ate it up first." (n.b. This was the
theme of the first period of the analysis.)

Thursday, 10 March

Patient   "I find it surprising that I remember so little. I expected
or anticipated this at the start when I was in a very

disturbed and confused condition and when I was not talking much. Now I thought that I would begin to be able to know where I am in the analysis, etcetera. It is rather like a dream which may be very clear at the time, etcetera.

Analyst   "It certainly is very much like a dream. In the analysis to some extent you become withdrawn. We could say that the analysis operates at a layer which is nearer to dreaming than to being awake, especially when you are not talking about actual life and also after the hour has been started for some time." *Pause.* "I could of course remind you."

See Note p. 466.

Patient   "No, I can see that that's not the point just now. Last time I felt that it was not fundamental. I left with a vague dissatisfaction. I think vaguely that there were some ideas of domination. If I forget what went on last time I might start up a new subject and this would make it difficult for you. I often feel that I give you a very difficult task. Either you would need to take detailed notes all along or else you would do as I do with my cases, which is to wait until the end and then write a shorter note after I have integrated the material within myself." (I did not risk taking notes at this point; obviously the question arose as to whether he had heard.) He went on to say that this made him very conscious of dependence on me.

Analyst   I referred to the matter in the following way: "It doesn't fundamentally make any difference whether I am taking detailed notes or not; the fact is that I must hear and take in all that you say and all that happens and have a technique for sorting things out and integrating the material and this is true apart from note-taking."

Patient   He said that he hoped that one day he would be able to go through his material and to see how the changes had taken place; especially he felt this now that he was all the time so much better and he was unable to understand what was happening.

Analyst   I went over the material of the last hour. I said it ended with the idea of the tid-bit at meals and he remembered this. I went back further with the schoolboy story and the idea of myself as the mother to whom he could show off in all sorts of developments. I reminded him also that he had said that for the first time he was beginning to feel himself to be a male."

Patient   "When I got married I was very keen to show the world that my wife really was a woman, and took great trouble over this."

Analyst   "This would fit in with the idea that you had a fantasy of a woman with a penis." (I noticed that he was starting to go to sleep and it was unlikely that he heard the interpretation.)

Patient   "These things are tied to this idea and I was thinking this before I came. I get from this girl friend the feeling of being able to take a real interest in work. It is not always true enough. The relation to her makes me feel real, more interested in work, and more masculine. This is also related to the fact that the girl is a doctor interested in the things I do and so on, so there is not an absolute break and, as I have said, this all belongs to the fact that I hate to keep things to myself."

Analyst   "The positive side of that is that you proudly show off if you can find the right person to show off to. I wonder whether you are not suppressing something about hospital now which you might be telling me."

Patient   "Yes, in fact I am. In the first place there is a very interesting case and in the second place I decided to do something today absolutely on my own without exactly knowing why and I was very pleased with myself. In fact the Registrar would have disapproved but it turned out good. I let some air into a chest after drawing off fluid and this made a very good X-ray possible."

Analyst   "So that made a better diagnosis."

Patient   "Yes, we were making a diagnosis by default, and now we can make it more definitely."

Analyst   "And the case?"

Patient   "Yes." He then told me about an elderly man who had so much fluid that the diagnosis was obscure, probably cancer. There was no proof. Again he had put in air and so had made the contour of the lung show for the first time on the X-ray. "I did it without anybody suggesting anything."

Analyst   "You need me to be able to do this sort of thing here."

Patient   "Yes, I require you to have a technique for making things clear even perhaps using a stunt."

Analyst   "There is an identification with me here; you in your job are like me in mine. Or shall I put it the other way round?"

Patient   "I missed some of what you were saying. The fact is that I was getting excited about that case. It may be that as a result the cancer will be found to be operable."

Analyst   "Have you a good surgeon?" (I did this deliberately, in view of the fact that he had raised the matter of the half-dream state and also he had mentioned the word stunt.)

Patient   "I had a curious thought then. Your questions like that about work; it happened before; they always surprise me. Do you do it out of interest? In the case? Or what is it? Are you pointing out that I have missed something? I might be resenting this. In any case it is a great surprise when you do things like that. To some extent I am glad, to some extent resenting it. I feel it is wrong to talk about hospital."

Analyst   "The question is, who am I standing for? Perhaps your wife who does not know about hospital things?"

Patient   "Yes, or more likely my father, a kind of examiner."

Analyst   "I knew, of course, that my remark was outside analysis; not within good analytic technique, but you were dealing with the matter of being half asleep."

Patient   "I welcome it really. I really want anything that could be called a shortcut to psychoanalysis."

Analyst   "The fact is that I woke you." (I took account of this warning that he was wanting a stunt but I did not believe that this was the main reaction to what I had done.)

Patient   "Yes, there is the annoying thing. It is like working in hospital when I get woken up at night. It is not so much the loss of sleep. The irritation comes from having one's dreamlife broken into. That rather reminds me of a story of the Chinese of a previous generation. The idea which was taught that the spirit goes away during sleep and that there is an actual danger if someone is suddenly awakened; the spirit never gets back into the awakened body." (Other material here was lost.)

Analyst   I went again over the ground that the analysis has been done somewhat on the dream side of the borderline between sleeping and waking and that he is evidently just arriving at a position from which he can feel the call to be asleep and the call to be awake at the same time. (He sensed the end of the hour.)

Patient   "It is the same with not bringing up new material at the end and feeling rejected. If new material is brought forward and there is no time for it to be dealt with, there is a risk and it feels as if there is actual danger."

Analyst   "I did get the feeling in the last session that you were not expecting the end and that therefore my stopping was traumatic as if I were waking you suddenly."

Monday, 14 March

Analyst   The patient came late, and had to go on time because of an appointment with the dentist.

Patient   "Well, I feel there must be a pause. There is something to be said about reality, and if I started right away it would seem wrong, like eagerness. When there are real things happening there is no time for dreams and the discussion of them. A dream needs leisure. There is a new development in that I arranged last night to see the girl friend while I was on duty at hospital. She was to come over and see me by ten, but she did not come on time and I started speculating, feeling disturbed, and I was surprised because I did not expect to be upset, for she does not mean much emotionally, just rather useful. Perhaps she did not want to come or had become casual. She arrived at eleven-thirty. So I made love immediately and then was impotent. It was partly her lack of enthusiasm, and also the crudeness of my approach. It is like suddenly starting in when I get here, which I said I couldn't do at the beginning of this hour — it would be crude. I began to have anxiety. Was her usefulness coming to an end? I had enjoyed her because she had restored my confidence, and now it seemed like a new thing. Will the impotence continue?

"It is difficult to talk freely with her till after intercourse, so here again I missed the value of our meeting."

Analyst   "You were already angry, and that complicated the issue?"

Patient   "I was not concerned about her, I thought, except when she was there, because she was always available. Now I had to face the prospect of her not wanting to be available at a particular moment. Before I had no worry about competition with men. If she is not available, however, it can only seem as if she has other interests." *Pause.* "There is a dilemma here. Firstly, I find sex very important indeed; secondly, other things seem much more important."

Analyst   "You did need the experience which gave you sexual confidence before you could come to a 'balance' (his word)." *Pause.* "You needed confidence in your own sexual potency before you could consider the matter of balance."

Pause.

"Here you have me impotent, in the sense of being unable to make the interpretation you want, because I do not know what it is."

Patient   "I want to make sure this is not wasted before I go on to something else and forget it."

Analyst   "You would have to rely on me to remember it and to meet it at the right moment."

Patient   "I did not want to be crude, taking the girl before warming her up to it."

Analyst   "Here you have your analyst standing for the girl who ought to be warmed up. A more positive thing would be to say that your experience last night showed up the fact that usually you do trouble to warm up the girl. If she were excited at the start this excitement would belong to an experience that she had already had before coming to you." *Pause.* "This introduces the idea of the other men."

Patient   "I was thinking of something else." *Pause.* "It's odd. I was really wide awake when I came. I suddenly get sleepy. It seems that after talking to you about immediate affairs I was waiting for you to do something."

Long Pause.

"I want to start again but I feel sleepy. What I have said would be wasted if I were to start on something else. It must be dealt with first. If I restart it will all get forgotten. I have the feeling that you do not want to say anything. It is as if you were withholding something."

Analyst   (I was not at all clear what to interpret.) "The question arises since I am identified with this girl, what did the girl say? or, alternatively, what might she have said?"

Patient   "I am in a dilemma here and I can more easily say what she might have said. I was anxious that she did not want me personally. I thought I was involved in a lighthearted way, enjoying a relationship without there being any place for demands either way. I told her that I was upset at her not coming and this I felt made it sound like a protest. I sounded miserable. I also told her about my wife and her complete unresponsiveness at the present time since the relapse of the boy friend. She cannot be talked to at all. The girl friend said: 'What you want is to be loved.' 'I did not want her to know about my emotional demands, my wife being a mother-figure in this respect. I did not want the girl to be like that. The relationship will degenerate into dependence. A satisfactory relationship means equality."

Analyst   "It appears then that the relationship with the girl has undergone a development. It is now more than bio-logically satisfactory. The girl has turned up as a person and you have turned up as a person for the girl and the impotence came as a sign of this change."

Patient   "I seem up to now to have shelved the question of her needs. She in fact wants to get out of her casualness. She is wanting a permanent relationship and I am not sure about her, nor she about me. She would like me to throw in my lot with her completely and set up on a permanent basis. It really is improbable that it would work. I almost lied to her saying things about the holiday, etcetera, and I felt that this was just an act. Last night's discovery of a dependence in the relationship sharpened her concern about a permanent relationship. She is twenty-eight and she wants children, but I cannot just let my wife go like that."

Analyst   I continued with the theme of his impotence as a part of a widening of his relationship and his former potency as something closely associated with a limited type of relationship. The same can be said in terms of feeding and infancy. At a theoretical start there is only instinct, but in the course of time there appears a relationship after which the full satisfaction of instinct is impossible.

This is another reference to instinctual inhibition resulting from integration of part objects into whole objects, and corresponding integration of the self-representation.

As long as such integration is sustained, instinctual freedom depends upon concurrent constructive capacity.

A consequence of this is that there is a basis for morality in spontaneous personality development, not requiring indoctrination from the outside.

See Dr. Winnicott's paper, "Morals and education" (1963), Maturational processes and the facilitating environment.

Patient   "I feel that a stage has been reached. I cannot now keep up any longer the artificial situation and must consider the doubts as to whether she can offer me more. She has really a shallow personality. The consequence is that I feel hopeless about a further development of the relationship."

Tuesday, 15 March

Patient   "I can't remember yesterday. I seem to remember that yesterday I wanted you to say something and the hour stopped short."

Pause.

Analyst   "Shall I remind you or not?"
Patient   "I don't really know."
Analyst   "We did in fact stop early as you had to go to the dentist. You had wanted me to make an interpretation on your report of real happenings."

Patient   "Yes, I was trying to help you to interpret. It all hinged round the feelings of impotence which unexpectedly occurred. The question was whether this emotional experience could be productive."

Analyst   "The anxiety you felt had to do with your feeling that a phase had ended, since the impotence indicated a widening of your relationship with the girl."

Patient   "These feelings carried on after I had left. After the dentist I went home and I was depressed, thinking that my wife would be inert, and I had nothing to look forward to. Then I had a feeling of generalized impotence, with a total lack of interest in women, which was in great contrast to the excitement of a few days ago. To my surprise my wife wanted to go out to the pictures (the patient acts as sitter on these occasions), and this gave me pleasure; at any rate this would lessen tension at home, etcetera, etcetera. At her request I phoned up the hospital and found her boy friend was not quite as ill as she had thought, and immediately I felt more cheerful. The dilemma would be shelved. When she came back and I told her she was relieved and then I became depressed again, more than I had been before, I don't really know why, except that this threw into relief that conflict about the girl. A stage of decision would soon arrive, and I'm not awfully happy about the girl. I hinted to my wife about the possibility of taking a holiday separately and she was more ready to accept this idea than I had expected, so I am up against the dilemma. So I realize I am still attached to my wife, more so than I am prepared to admit.

Pause.

"It seems the same as yesterday. Will you take up the story, I wonder? I haven't offered you much I'm afraid."

Analyst   "I am wondering why it is that I have nothing to say." (I then passed yesterday's session in review and spoke about the dilemma; how to continue to make use of the girl without getting involved in complications that belong to the idea of a wider relationship and interdependence.)

Pause.

Patient   "There is something else, but I delayed telling you about it because I wanted to know if there would be a sequel to what we were doing yesterday. The question has come up, what job to do after this one? The idea has been suggested that I should be Registrar in the autumn in the same group. The advantages would be increased pay, and that the treatment could be continued. This has to be decided. I think I could tackle the job. This is what I was thinking about coming along; I found it exciting and so I put it into the background."

The Registrar in a British hospital corresponds approximately to the resident physician in a United States hospital. The Registrar usually aims toward becoming a hospital consultant rather than a general practitioner.

Analyst   "This idea indicates real changes in you, especially as the first sign of your illness came when you had to take responsibility."

Patient   "Also it means not taking more junior jobs, and that it's safe now to aim higher."

Analyst   "The job comes in as part of the analysis, and you would expect me to be excited too."

Patient   "It's easier now for me to be offering advice than to do the job myself, because after two years the routine work has become rather boring."

Analyst   "There will be teaching too?"

Patient   "Yes. The question is, am I mature enough to teach? I was not mature enough before or confident enough to tell people what to do."

Analyst   "Is it Junior Registrar?"

Patient   "Yes. The man doing it now is not as well qualified to do it as I am, and has had less experience."

Analyst   "You are saying that a general potency is not annulled by a specific localized impotence."

Patient   "Yesterday you said about my jealousy of men, that this was hardly showing at all. But it began to become present the night before last when I was impotent, even if it is in the background only. But I have a distaste for it. I don't like competition with men."

Analyst   "It seems all right to compete when you know you are superior."

Patient   "On the other hand I do not like to compete when on unequal terms."

Analyst   "In the analytic room it is important to you that either we are only two — as when you were a small child with mother — or else when we are three the third is excluded."

At the most primitive narcissistic level the patient and the environment are one. At a higher level of self and object differentiation, the infant and the mother are separate, and at a still higher level the infant can conceptualize a third person, and progresses toward oedipal rivalry. Exclusion of the rival and exclusion of affects associated with the rival begin to be possible.

Patient   "Now I see that with my wife I did not admit the possibility of a rival. With the girl even though I knew of the other men in her life I did not take them seriously. I was amused at the idea of them. I would play at competing. Here in analysis I take the great liberty of assuming that there is no one else, and refuse to recognize there is anyone before and after. I dodge people at the door but only see them by accident and they exist in the abstract. I deny their existence."

Analyst   (Rather off the mark.) "When you can admit three people you can get the relief that the third can have the rival penis, so you do not need the idea of the woman with a penis. (Rather loud now, patient going to sleep.) Last time you were either angry with me for stopping or else angry with the dentist for coming between us." *Pause.* (He woke after three to four minutes.) "You slept I think?" (He agreed. I repeated the interpretation, and he lost all the sleep tendency as he began to understand what I was interpreting.)

Patient   "It's odd, I thought yesterday, that the dentist has a lower status than an analyst, but I have to be more careful to be on time for him than for analysis. The dentist is impertinent, I thought, to expect me to be punctual."

Analyst	"It is sensible to be on time for the dentist, since you only go occasionally . . . though you probably had to wait."
Patient	"Yes."
Analyst	"But the main thing is that our relationship was stopped by a dentist who is imaginatively a dangerous man, who might take out teeth to punish you for biting, for your cannibalistic impulses and ideas — a form of castration."
Patient	"Yes."

Friday, 18 March

Patient	"Coming along I had the feeling that I did not want to say anything, it would be better for you to start off, to ask questions."
Analyst	"Yes, it's odd this way of throwing all the responsibility on you. Do you in fact remember yesterday? Was the idea related to yesterday's events?"
Patient	"No, I just had this attitude. The last few times I think I have not been productive. I haven't had much to say. So if you accept responsibility you couldn't say I was the cause of nothing happening. Perhaps there's a lot more to it, though. It's a lot to accept responsibility for the way the hour goes, to decide what's of interest, and also what not to say. What a lot has to be turned down as not important! Some things I don't want to talk about. Earlier I assumed that I ought to talk about everything, but with the arrival of more ideas I had to find reasons for suppression. I feel excitement here. It's a question : 'Who's to be father?' "
Analyst	"You mean you want to hand me the father role?"
Patient	"I feel anxious about being in the father role, concerned what you feel about this. A change is happening, and you are less impersonal, less of a pure analyst. This change is happening in general, too. I have become more aware of the effect of what I say on people quite apart from analysis. Also there is the difficulty about talking with my wife, when I select carefully because of a fear that I may be just saying something because of its expected effect on her."

Analyst   "You are just beginning to see that the choice of what to say can be part of anxiety (resistance)."

Patient   "At the start there was no problem of suppression, there was much to say, and then I forgot or went to sleep. These methods are now wearing a bit thin, and so a new method is needed if a subject has unpleasant features."

Analyst   "I am rather closely linked with your wife here." (Doubtful as an interpretation here.)

Pause.

Patient   "One more thing, there is the other technique, that there are many details, each obvious, too trivial for singling out."

Analyst   "Can you think of one?"

Patient   "Well, there was just the idea, a fleeting one, something about counting buttons. The idea came to me as essentially trivial."

Analyst   "Are there any associations to these two words?"

Patient   "No, nothing here, only that I was discussing with my wife and her mother the number of buttons on a guardsman's uniform. I had no idea that each guards' regiment has a specific number of buttons."

Analyst   "And to counting?"

Patient   "Well, my daughter is just learning to count and is very fond of games with counting in them, counting objects, and so on. There is also the idea of counting sheep, a practice I have never used when sleepless."

Analyst   "The idea of buttons has come into the analysis recently, do you remember?"

Patient   "No."

Analyst   "You spoke of Ernest Jones' reference to a button and this belongs to the idea of cannibalism."

See Note p. *465*

Patient   "Oh yes!"

Analyst   "And it happens that at the end of last hour there was the dentist who easily gets mixed up imaginatively with the idea of a man who punishes for biting by knocking out teeth. So the counting of buttons can either be reassuring yourself that all the buttons are present, or else accounting for the buttons inside after a cannibalistic orgy."

Patient   "Oh yes! and then there is also the idea in my mind of the 'belly-button,' so-called, which means undressed. At that moment I thought of the nipples. The idea of the nipples came to me before the idea of the umbilicus."

Analyst   "The question arises, are there two nipples, or is there one twice?"

Patient   "Here is the dilemma. It is difficult for a baby to decide which breast to start to get milk from." (At this point the patient seemed to be a baby actually reliving his experiences, and he had his right finger at his mouth. His thumb-sucking was left-handed.)

Analyst   "Here surely is the beginning of arithmetic."

Patient   "Two could mean mother and me."

Analyst   "There is the problem too, at sometime or other the baby knows of two nipples, but at an earlier date (no matter what date) there was only one nipple, reduplicated so to speak."

Splitting of the object of oral love is associated with splitting of the primitive ego, and of the affects associated with the instinctual object. An awareness of the concept of unity, the number "one," depends upon continuity of object representation and continuity of self-representation.

Patient   "With my daughter, I've always taken the trouble to bathe her and to come in early in her life, and this was my father's idea as I remember it. He said he took part in the care of his infants as early as possible so as to be recognized and accepted as the father, so as to establish his claim as father. I feel guilty that I have done this less with the second baby for various reasons. I wonder: will she recognize me as father, as the older one does?" *Pause.* "I have an urge to punish you by not talking, by not saying my thoughts."

Analyst   "The first thing about that is that you need to establish your power to withhold ideas, to find that I don't know your thoughts magically."

The patient's ego boundary, represented by his differentiation from the analyst, can be demonstrated by his

capacity to withhold his thoughts. The same pheno-
menon, the patient's wish to be silent, has different
meanings in different contexts.

Patient	"In psychoanalysis if I punish you, you may punish me by being ill or not coming; you have the means for extreme punishment." (The direct reversal of an impulse.)
Analyst	"This power of psychoanalysis to punish in a crude, talion, way —— are you asleep?"
Patient	"I expect to be dominated, so go out of my way to avoid punishment, to avoid withholding. I don't want to punish anyone, except that recently I have become able to some extent to lose my temper a little. There is a kind of acknowledgment of rivalry in this."
Analyst	"You are dealing with the transition from talion to the humanized conception of a father punishing."

Actual punishment can serve to mitigate the harshness
of the talion principle that characterizes the most primi-
tive superego. Introjection of an actual strict parent can
thus relieve primitive superego anxiety which metes out
not restraint or mild punishment, but the kind of sadistic
retaliation found in nightmares, delusions, and children's
fantasies, and also in the fairy stories written for children.
(See Notes p. 548.)

Patient	"Yes . . . yes . . . " (Sleeps and awakes, probably not aware of having slept.) "Punishment can take so many different forms. In an ordinary hospital ward, it can be part of a scheme of punishment to keep a patient a long while in one ward. It's like doing lines."
Analyst	"You have thought of school punishment?"
Patient	"Yes, but I avoided punishment there too. It was a rare feature at the school chosen for me."
Analyst	"Not finding a rival outside mother in the form of a separate person, father; and having father as an alternative version of mother, you had to find the rival in mother herself; this would sometimes simply be her refusal to play her part, as it would seem to you."

The patient had said that his father behaved in maternal ways toward him and that he now does the same toward his own children. This is linked in this interpretation with the adaptive meaning of the development of the oedipus complex. When a father is absent or is insufficiently differentiated from the mother, the patient is denied opportunity to divert hostile feelings away from one parent and toward the other. This forces the child to find other defenses against ambivalence, such as instinctual inhibition. In the extreme this can contribute to disorders of consciousness, such as epilepsy or, as in this case, compulsive sleeping. (See note p. 539.)

Patient   "These words 'refusal to play her part' apply exactly to what I feel my wife does. This is her attitude, to refuse interest and sympathy. I got to that idea in a roundabout way." (The patient always feels more convinced when he gets to an idea indirectly.) "With the girl friend I find it difficult to use her first name, especially at the time of intercourse when I forget her name and usually think of my wife's name. And in general I've gone off Christian names, the use of which I tried to introduce a little while ago at hospital. This could be said to be a denial of intimacy."

Analyst   "I think you are referring indirectly to your mother and what you called her. Did you perhaps not use her Christian name?"

Patient   "I may have occasionally, but only because of a difficulty over saying 'mummy' which is horrifyingly intimate. So I glossed over the difficulty by an avoidance of using any name at all. I gloss over similar difficulties in the same way by avoiding using a name."

Analyst   " 'Mummy' is a particularly 'mouthy' word. Let me see, what is your mother's name? Is that of any importance?"

Patient   (He gave the name.) "No, probably that's not significant."

Analyst   "Your father called her by that name?"

Patient   "Well, very occasionally — usually 'mummy.' With my wife after two or three years I tended to call her 'mummy,' and rebuked myself for doing so; she would resent it, I felt. It's only logical if the children are there to give her a label describing a special function; it's not recognizing her as a wife. I make an effort to use her Christian name, and I feel she prefers this. She hasn't actually said so. It's a question of function or person. In contrast to call my own mother 'mummy' would be all right, but to call her by her Christian name would be cold, or remote."

Analyst   "You remember how we started; am I an analyst or a person? You have never actually used my name in talking to me."

Patient   "It is more convenient to use the nonspecific title."

Analyst   "There is a danger that you sense behind all this. I will put it this way: if you lose the breast you are in danger of losing your mouth as well, unless you keep your mouth free from intimate contact with the breast."

At a stage before self-object differentiation, loss of an object, for example, the breast, includes subjective loss of those parts of the self that are functionally associated with the object, for example, the mouth and oral impulses. This is referred to as schizoid object loss in contrast to depressive object loss. The latter occurs later, after self-object differentiation, when the subject can lose an object while the ego remains intact. As a result, the ego can react to object loss by mourning and grief work, including introjection of the lost object. In depression grief work can be accomplished, although it may have to be repeated with subsequent losses. In schizoid object loss introjection also occurs, but the resulting introject includes primitive affects and parts of the self, and not only results in a feeling of having lost part of the self, but also evokes more primitive defenses such as fragmentation and projection. Schizoid object loss results in an ego defect which does not have a tendency to heal by natural process of grief work. Regression in analysis or fortuitous regressive experiences in life situations are needed to restore the maturational capacity in the defective ego that was traumatized at an earlier stage of development.

Patient   "I don't follow that. . . ."

Analyst "Perhaps I have gone a jump ahead — but (Here I repeated the interpretation and connected the conflict with the tendency to solve matters by sleeping).

Patient "Before I came in I thought : 'If I can change my attitude to wanting you to start the talking this will be like the changes that have come through the relationship with the girl friend.' Some while ago you were speaking of my acting out masturbation fantasy and I was horrified at the idea. I want things to be real, not acting. I was alternating from pure fantasy to talking about it. I reached an acting out of fantasy that was still unreal. It's now no longer just talking, it's doing."

Analyst "In the matter of the use of the mouth you have come to a point where talking, and acting, and fantasy all meet. It seems that your father came into your life very early, before you could count two, or when you could just count two but were still loving by mouth and loving the breast. If he is a separate person he therefore became linked with the crude talion fears about mouth activity. This means that he is linked with the loss of a breast mouth, which is so serious a danger that you must avoid intimacy between mouth and breast by sleeping and other measures. This interfered with your use of father at a later stage as a human being who could punish and who could become a castrator in your fantasy associated with erection of the penis in your love of your mother."

Castration anxiety is limited, in contrast to the global world destruction threatened by the most primitive superego. Castration anxiety, anxiety about partial destruction, is thus associated with more advanced states of ego development than is anxiety about total destruction. Compare, for example, castration and the world destruction fantasies of the schizophrenic patient.

Tuesday, 22 March

Patient "Well, I'll begin by talking about what happened this evening. I had arranged to go out with the girl friend and I did not want to tell my wife. I wanted to, but I knew it would not help. It would only lead to friction. I knew that she rather looked forward to going out this evening (the patient would be baby-sitting), but I phoned and told her I would not be home. My wife became cross and hung up, refusing to discuss the matter in any way. I found myself in a trembling rage, or was it an upset, and this is still there after three hours. I definitely do not want to precipitate a crisis at the present time. The alternatives are extreme : peace means giving up the girl friend ; so there is a dilemma now — carry on with endless crises or return meekly although existence at home can only be cold. The relationship with the girl friend is not ideal but at the moment it is very satisfactory in its own way." *Pause.* "The problem is like the one we had before. What can you do about this sort of material ?"

Analyst   "For one thing, you are relying on me to integrate two aspects of your life which for the moment you cannot integrate. The relationship with your wife with all its potential, good and bad, and the immediately satisfactory relationship with the girl."

Patient   "It seems that I am nearer to forcing a break at the present moment than I have been before, so it is more disturbing." *Pause.* "There are the two alternatives : one is home which only functions on the basis of complete unreality — no friendship, that is to say, shut off from relationships — or with the girl friend, though with her there is a big imaginative element. I can see it is peppered with romance. It has more reality to it. There is a stalemate in my relationship to my wife but I do not want to throw it all up. Somehow or other I still cherish a hope though I have no belief that it can come to anything. I can understand my wife's point of view, but I cannot accept her attitude that lacks feeling and also there is the fact that I can never discuss anything with her. She has laid down conditions. Undoubtedly I am terribly irritated by her hanging up, that is to say her refusal to discuss." (This took up about one-third of the hour.) *Pause.* "I have a reason for not saying any more. I do not want this to continue throughout the hour but I cannot go on to something else without a gap. The affair has cast too big a shadow."

Analyst "You are still affected by your reaction to the hanging-up. Possibly rage, you said."

Patient "Yes, the hanging up — I was thrown into a state of impotence. There was nothing I could do. I ought to be neutral or amused and say it's her fault but the rage has to do with anger with myself. Perhaps I am angry at being annoyed."

Analyst "You will remember that the antagonism used to be between your wife's attitude and the analysis, and now this takes the form of her antagonism that you feel towards your relation to the girl."

Patient "Yes, there is an interference with more fundamental issues." *Pause.* "I expected you somehow to be able to find a way of dealing with these things so as to get them out of the way, but of course you can't."

Analyst "One point is that here you have a triangular relationship with no other man in it. The potential hate is between two women."

Patient "Initially the girl was not concerned with my wife. The affair was not intended to get anywhere. Now, however, she wants more out of it, and she is afraid of being disappointed once again. But we both have misgivings about a permanent relationship. . . . I find her demands exciting and her dependence on me and her direct expression of need so we get deeper and deeper into a blind alley for which there is no resolution. I am thrown back on the choice between two blind alleys." *Pause.* "Also there is something new with my dealing with her side of the relationship. The fact is that she has other men and one in particular. I am beginning to find it exciting, competing and trying to eliminate another man. This is certainly new about men. First, the rivalry is new, part of my development, and secondly there is the immediate excitement about a fight with a man over a girl. I have never been able to cope with this before."

Analyst "In a sense you are all the time looking for the man that you hate on account of the love of a woman. In the long run this is father, a new aspect of father that you hardly encountered, especially as he came into

your life deliberately at a very early stage and established himself as an alternative mother to you as an infant."
(At this point the patient put his foot on the floor.)
Pause.

Patient   "There is another factor which I have not really discussed here. There is the aspect of the sexual relationship with the girl friend. There is much more real excitement and satisfaction than with my wife even when things were going well with her. This is partly due to the change in me because of the analysis. The difficulty is that the idea has been introduced that if I enjoy the results of the treatment, how can my wife keep pace or is it all to be wasted? I was not originally prepared for this. Before, I thought, if I get better I can deal with my wife. Now I have to cope with the feeling that she may become depressed as the result of the changes in me; she may possibly deteriorate. There is so much that cannot be explored directly with my wife. She does not even expect an orgasm, so sex is not desirable from her point of view. But the trouble is that this may be my fault. She may have developed this as a way of dealing with my original clumsiness and inability to be exciting. It would be better if one could talk this over with her. I cannot accept the idea that a sex relationship has to be brushed aside if I get better. My wife has said that I am not to look forward to sexual experience with her, but this is largely due to its having been so unsatisfactory in the past. She has hinted at feeling superior to sex. It is beneath her. I think that her relationship to her boy friend has been what she would call spiritual. I have a pity for her but she must reject what I am beginning to be able to give in regard to pleasure and excitement. If I get well what may happen is that I shall find that there is something wrong with her and nothing can be done about that as she would be horrified at the idea. All her difficulties up to now have hidden behind the fact that I have been ill, and before that unsatisfactory."

The mutual adaptation in a marital relationship can be disrupted by analysis of one partner. At this point there

must be a new interaction if the marriage is to persist.
Under such circumstances the partner who had earlier
refused treatment and was not known to be ill may break
down and seek treatment (See Giovacchini, P., "Mutual
adaptation in various object relationships," Inter. J. of
Psychoanal., XXXIV, (1958), 1-8.

Wednesday, 23 March

Patient   (Re-arrangement in regard to times.) "The next thing
that comes into my mind is that there has begun a
curious change in the nature of my problem. At first I
was not aware of specific symptoms, and it was just
a question of not being able to work or to take responsibility. Now work is not in fact a difficulty though I don't
feel I am yet at maximum capacity — perhaps because
of the nature of the job. The issue now hinges round
personal and sexual problems. It would be difficult for
my wife to understand the sexual and personal as a major
problem, that would be a frivolous approach. But at the
moment it's far more important. It comes to me to mention my wife's attitude. I don't know why, but it seems
to fit in. Till recently I have refused to recognize the
central position of sex but it was probably dormant all
the time. Lately I have been more willing to see that
the personal are the only real issues. I am reminded
that in regard to my inability to accept responsibility, the
key was my sexual immaturity."

Analyst   "You couldn't show a more specific symptom at the
start because you weren't there as a person to be having
sexual difficulties. It is a part of your emergence as a
person that you can now come with personal symptoms."

Before individual identity began to be firmly established
the patient primarily complained about external
demands, to which he reacted with withdrawal, com-
pliance, or defiance. As his identity emerges, he becomes
more aware of inner needs.

Patient   "The sexual with my wife seemed all right at one time,
but now I see that at the actual moment of intercourse

I was aware of impersonality, I would think of banal things, indulge in masturbation fantasy in order to stimulate myself in order to produce an ejaculation. With the girl friend that's no longer so. I accept intercourse in its own right. My wife must have been aware (perhaps unconsciously) of the incompleteness. Now I am faced with a dilemma, now I know of the possibilities of intercourse. Intellectually and socially I still want my wife. Nevertheless with the girl sex is good, but there are the social complications."

Analyst   "Yes, you certainly have a big problem."

Patient   "My wife is not likely to accept a divided relationship — it would be unworkable. The girl would not be willing for this either; she reacted to the same problem by promiscuity, but is not finding the solution satisfactory."

Analyst   "There are changes in yourself, for instance you are only just starting to meet the idea of men as rivals; also there is the matter of becoming conscious of the fantasy of the girl with the penis."

The patient reverted to considering external factors, the contradictory demands placed upon him by his wife and the girl friend, and in this interpretation Dr. Winnicott takes him back to the area of intrapsychic conflict. As the patient becomes aware of the fantasy of the phallic woman, progress of his development is indicated by the gradual replacement of that fantasy by rivalry with men.

Patient   "It seems likely that I will become promiscuous unless my wife improves or unless the girl friend relationship matures in the direction of stability."

Analyst   "If it were not for the ruthlessness implied, what you have needed is just your wife, then the girl friend, and then a new girl to be found for the permanent solution, but you are worried at the prospect of the two women lying around hurt."

Patient   "I found the girl friend crying and I had a feeling of responsibility — but this may be vanity — though she said she had been helped by my talking."

Analyst	"There is a value to you in feeling that a girl loves you and so could be hurt by you."
Patient	"Yes, so I am disturbed about my wife hanging up on the phone. It was not purely annoyance, but also I felt her jealousy. I am only guessing but I think she knew about the girl and she may have been hurt."
Analyst	"So she loves you."
Patient	"I had visions of getting home late and finding the door locked — it was just fantasy. I went home and found her already asleep — this was the same as a stony silence, for she certainly knew when I came in. I feel much has happened to flatter my vanity and I must be careful. I have always been able to help and have been known as sympathetic. The girl said I was the first person she had met who could be promiscuous and yet kind and considerate at the same time. . . . Have I perhaps been too soft and considerate? It occurs to me I have had a feeling of hating to be rejected, as at a dance, upset at not being acceptable."
Analyst	"In the extreme, you are loved, and so you must hurt if you choose one person. This could be a picture of your early childhood."
Patient	"It's more that I couldn't choose because I didn't want to miss anything; in fact, it was last night that I was thinking that I recognized that I have little difficulty in making decisions about little things. I believe neurotic people are like that. As I said to the girl, I only have difficulty in making major decisions; where there are genuine difficulties in a situation, and now for the first time in my life I feel I can cope with the future. No doubt there will be a lot of worry and misery and so on, but I can cope. I feel this is the result of two years of psychoanalysis."
Analyst	"You are saying that you feel you can make decisions, but these decisions involve hurting people."
Patient	"With me it seems that if I hurt other people that is the same as hurting myself."
	(He implied in his tone of voice that he was concerned in hurting people not so much with hurting them as with hurting himself.)
	"I suppose I project myself on to other people."

Analyst   "It is possible that when the girl friend talked about un-concern of exciting lovers, she meant that they did not identify with her. It would be interesting to know whether they were able to produce satisfaction in her or whether they were chiefly concerned with their own gratification."

Patient   "Yes, I think that they did include an interest in her sexual gratification but nothing more."

Analyst   "There is a point that you hurt yourself by choosing any one person. As you have said, you may miss something by eliminating the others."

Patient   "Masturbation turned out now to have been my need for promiscuity which was solved in that way without social and other complications. The difficulty in stopping was to do with not wanting to miss anything by choosing."

Analyst   "This seems to me to join up with what we were saying about sums and the beginning of arithmetic." (I recapitulated about his daughter learning sums and the whole of the interpretation about the one breast reduplicated or the idea of two breasts or a mother and child and so on, going into detail because it was clear that it was news to him.)

Patient   "Funny! I had completely forgotten all that, and yet it was quite clear three days ago. I had no impression left. It was completely blocked out."

Analyst   "Added to all this was father coming in your life very early, as you perhaps remember telling me, and so joining up with the woman and this being used by you eventually in your difficulty in dealing with him as a man."

Pause.

Patient   "I was thinking that I feel guilty at bringing too many problems. Why should I feel this to be wrong? I suppose in this I am encouraged by the frequent observation that facts are less productive in the analysis, I wonder whether this is actually true, and whether it need be."

Analyst   "I can see no reason why it should be true."

Patient   "Except in so far as real happenings — (at this point he put his foot on the floor) — have less bearing on the personality development than things in the mind. Perhaps they are all impersonal. Immediate things do not get past the impersonal barrier like dreams."

Analyst "You are using me in the analysis in various different ways. Today we have the idea of my integrating material for you and so on, but there are more specific ways in which you use me. At one time you will remember I was closely identified with your wife. Later I was identified with the girl friend, and there was an important moment when I made this interpretation after having made a wrong one."(I reminded him of the details.) "Now it seems that there is a new phase and I have become the man that you are concerned with in your relation to the girl."

Patient "So what I have been saying is boasting. It's curious, for a few days I have been feeling 'I think I would like to meet the man,' meaning the other man who is most important in the girl's life. I could score him off. Beforehand when I was not aware of sex problems there was not much point in meeting the man behind the scenes and I did not want to talk about you as the man simply because I ought to, but now the whole thing has become more to the point because I can boast and show off."

Analyst "In this analysis there has been extremely little negative transference but we are just coming up to it and the analysis has to be able to contain it. There is the fight between the two men who both love a girl. You are coming up to it in a very strong position of the triumphant man who can meet the other man on the basis of boasting of success."

Patient "I seem to have been aware of all this in a vague way for a long time but I felt you would be jealous. It has been there the whole time."

Analyst "It is not only that you were concerned about me in this way but also you had some work to do about the mouth excitements and the idea of a dentist punishing in a direct way. Only gradually have you come to be able to deal with me as a human being rival. It would seem at first that you are in a position to triumph but this is only true if we consider the girl. I suggest that in regard to the wife it is different. I know that there are real difficulties here which cannot be solved by analysis and which have to do with her ability to change and to recover from the past. Nevertheless in the imaginative situation while you are triumphant over me in regard to the girl you have accepted in regard to your wife the complete absence of a sexual future. In other words you have accepted a one hundred percent ban on sex as if giving me the triumph."

There are two aspects of the transference. The patient pays for flaunting his symbolic triumph over the analyst as a rival by simultaneously accepting defeat, again symbolically by the analyst.

Patient   "Yes, but there is also an idea here that you are the rival of my wife for my favor, hence her hostility. There is that way round which seems important to me at the moment. I can only come to analysis at the expense of her not allowing it. In this case, you are a woman, a mother-figure, from my wife's point of view."

Analyst   "Here your mother claims you, and so your wife has no chance."

Patient   "That reminds me that at the hospital when I was ill a doctor said that I was not in love with my wife and it was as if he had said, 'You belong to me,' although it did not strike me that way at the time. All I knew then was that I felt very disturbed and in fact insulted but there seem to be several things all at once here."

Analyst   "Yes, there are several things all at once, and the relationship between your wife and yourself and me contains many different meanings. It is a kind of portmanteau situation."

Thursday, 24 March

Patient   "I was thinking on the way that there are no immediate issues so the way is open for deeper things. But there was something I thought of last night. It's a bit hazy now, I may have given you a wrong idea of the position with my wife. I've done it several times because when here I have a different attitude from my attitude when at home. Here and at work I feel the difference springs from her, and I get a feeling of mastery, that I can afford to crack the whip. She is dependent on me, not I on her. I can tell her to pull her socks up — but when I am at home it's all different. I can't make the start of a show-down. The difficulty appears as I enter the door, and I become paralyzed. So there is a contrast in all this with my initial statement; when I was in a dependent state this didn't matter. I just went home to be miserable. Now when there is an alternative I wonder why I should go home to be a martyr (etcetera). With my wife I only talk about what she initiates, whereas with the girl it's altogether different, and never before have I been free to talk. On the phone I spend even an hour talking to the girl."

Analyst   "As we said before, there is no play area between you and your wife."

Patient   "Perhaps an awareness of the existence of a rival would stimulate my wife to be more considerate, but I don't let her know, and I don't really know what I want. A change would only be valuable if it were fairly complete." *Pause.* "I'm still not prepared to take the responsibility for a showdown."

Analyst   (I took up the interpretation of the end of the last session.) "Last time I spoke of my position as the man prohibiting sexuality with your wife." *Pause.* "Did you go to sleep?" (Probably he did sleep.)

Patient   "No. I felt then an unusual state of tension. This relates partly to my difficulty at home, where I deliberately avoid the decision which must be made fairly soon now. There is a kind of extended triangular situation, a pentagonal one, two women and three men. The job expires in two months and so I must orientate now· towards seeing the girl. Also there is the holiday. I don't want a repetition of the Christmas holiday in which I sat at home. I feel this is actually coming to a head, here and now, at this very minute."

Pause.

Analyst   "You are showing me how urgent the matter is, and how you want me to do everything I can do in the analysis before you bring about a showdown. The thing is that if I ignore your wife's difficulties and the

question of her ability to change and to recover from
the effect of your earlier treatment of her, I can say that
you are using her as the nearest you can get to the
mother with whom sex is prohibited by father. If I go
to your adolescent dream of intercourse with mother, or
to your early childhood, I can say that you needed father
to say 'I know you love mother and want intercourse
with her, but I love her and I do not allow it.' In that
way father would have freed you to love other women.
If this thing doesn't get cleared up mother will continue to turn up in your women, and if you were to
marry the girl friend the difficulties would appear in
that new marriage. Moreover, you have missed rivalry
with men and the friendships that come with such
rivalry."

Patient   "This is a new idea for me, that I have missed friendship with men, though I'm prepared to believe it's true.
It has struck me that I have no use for games of skill.
Cards are more a technical exercise for me, and I have
never wanted to watch football. Recently it has struck
me, in fact this week, that there are very few things I get
excitement out of except sexual intercourse, though
occasionally I feel some excitement in reading stories
or a few months ago at the pictures. Occasionally music
and in fact it was last week I was excited by a talk on
Elgar and the Enigma Variations. Two variations were
played. This was the first time for a long while that
music has excited me. There was a bit more to it since
the variations were written about friends of Elgar, and
so represented his friendships, etcetera."

Analyst   "So Elgar was capable of love and of warm friendships."

Patient   "It worries me about the girl friend that her interest
is almost exclusively in sexual excitement, though she
can be personal, lonely for instance. I could grow out of
her limited scope. She finds nothing in music — it's either
medicine or sex. Here I feel one thing I might be worried
about is that you might not only ban sex with my wife
but also advise against further relations with the girl
friend. You would be my guardian of moral welfare,
so I don't tell you all my proposals for the future. You

Analyst

might become less academic and advise. I like your advice but should not like it if you advised against the relationship."

Analyst   "So by not prohibiting I am permitting. You can only think of me as in one or other position."

Permitting and prohibiting are in the same frame of reference, and represent a projection of the patient's superego onto the analyst. The analytic position involves neither prohibiting nor permitting, but rather operates in a totally different frame of reference, namely that of interpreting the meaning of the patient's expectations, including those of prohibition and permission. (See Note p. 583.)

Patient   "With the girl friend I feel enthusiastic; it's like a wild leap into dangerous waters and I have never been able to do this before. It is of the nature of a good thing, an achievement."

Analyst   "You never met your father as a man to hate, a rival, someone you feared. Whether because of him or yourself or both you missed this, and so you never felt mature."

Patient   "If I never got to father's prohibition then I was left having to find it in myself."

The failure to get superego prohibition from his father led the patient to have to deal with his superego anxiety by 1.) Projecting it onto a mother figure, such as his wife; and 2.) "Finding it in himself," with a resulting instinctual inhibition.

Analyst   "Exactly, that is what I was meaning."

Patient   "So that would account for my failure to get excited throughout my marriage."

Analyst   "It would even have affected your choice of woman to marry."

Patient   "I married her because of her severity; this appealed to me. She was unfeminine, well-groomed, with a frown, and she has severe features with a narrow face and glasses. She can easily scold, and domineer. Also it is likely that her boy friend was attracted for this same reason. He is rather irresponsible, and he wanted someone who could and would dominate him. He allowed her to make major decisions — whether to leave his wife, and also to start to take care of his health which he had neglected. I was thinking today — what kind of girl do I find attractive? Certainly not gentle or cherubic, but a severe dominating type, and the girl friend is tall and angular and loses her temper readily. It's the very opposite of sweet and unspoilt. (Here the patient put his foot on the ground.)

Analyst "Then also there is the girl with the penis of adolescent dreams."

Patient "I thought that was coming. I feel worried. I might be looking for a man, which would be a kind of homosexuality, which would imply that I'm an effeminate type of man."

Analyst "No, I don't think so. The fact is you are looking for father, the man who prohibits intercourse with mother. Remember the dream in which the girl friend originally appeared and this was about a man, one who was ill."

Patient "This would account for my lack of grief or of feeling when my father died. He had not met me as a rival and so left me with the awful burden of making the prohibitions myself."

Analyst "Yes, on the one hand he never did you the honor of recognizing your maturity by banning intercourse with mother, but also he deprived you of the enjoyment of rivalry and of the friendship that comes out of rivalry with men. So you had to develop a general inhibition, and you could not mourn a father you have never 'killed.' "

Patricide is part of the total fantasy of oedipal rivalry. If the patient reaches this stage of development, and the father figure survives despite the patient's fantasy of killing him, this provides reassurance against anxiety about omnipotent destructive fantasies, and frees the patient for friendship with men who are potential rivals.

Tuesday, 29 March

Analyst	(The Monday session had been missed. He had notified me by phone.)
Patient	"Well, I find it difficult to start. Firstly there are no immediate problems, and secondly, it is curious, but the fact that I have got a bad cold seems to interfere. It clouds things over. It's as if free association and relaxation are a strain like physical exercise."
Analyst	"I can well understand that if you have a cold you do not feel like the work of analysis which really is a strain."
Patient	"It's happened before; having a cold tends to mask the main issues. I feel more like curling up and going to sleep and making no mental effort."
Analyst	"It would be more appropriate for you to withdraw."
Patient	"I feel that if I am here I ought to relax and that ought to be easy but it seems like work."
Analyst	"Yes, so that the limitation of the work to one hour is not only for the benefit of the analyst."
Patient	"It makes me wonder what is the ideal time for the session and what is the ideal interval. Would daily sessions be too frequent and a less effective use of analysis?"
Analyst	"Perhaps the cold was what kept you away yesterday."
Patient	"No, it wasn't that; it was just that there was a special case which had to be attended to. The cold hadn't started. I feel that we have talked about immediate problems and it is difficult to go back to the deeper issues. I cannot switch. This reminds me of children being wakened from a dream and being annoyed because it is so difficult to get back to the dream."
Analyst	"There is something here which does link up with your analysis which is done in a state which is towards the dream state. It would seem as if gradually in recent months there has been an emergence from the dream state towards last time when one could almost say that the analysis was being done with you awake, that is to say as a part of waking reality."
Patient	"I noticed today visiting a hospital because of work that I was able to talk more freely than ever before,

even with strange Residents of the other hospital, and I could take the lead in conversation. I thought this would never happen to me and it represents a big change not having to wait till I know people intimately before leading off with ideas." *Pause.* "Also a few nights ago I dreamed something and I felt I did not have to remember this; it's an ordinary dream."

Analyst   "Yes, a dream is an ordinary bridge between inner reality and external reality and to that extent you were well and not needing analysis because you have your own bridge as represented in the dream."

The process of dreaming has some integrative function in itself, independent of interpreting the dream, and independent even of remembering it. (See p. 668.)

Patient   "This is wrapped up with the idea of not coming here. There seems to be a lessening of the need to come."

Analyst   "That is to say, not needing psychoanalysis since the main symptom was that you had a dissociation between the sleeping and waking states and you had partially solved this on the basis of never being really awake."

Integration of the ego includes links between the sleeping and waking states, of which dreaming is an important indication. Analysis fosters ego integration, and when the patient feels that he has achieved some degree of it his need for analysis is reduced.

Patient   "I wish to make a break here with what we are talking about. I was discussing my future with a friend. The various alternatives to medical or specialization and general practice and I mentioned psychiatry. It occurred to me there is one great difficulty here that I am not ripe for at present because I am not yet sure of an ability to avoid identification. I definitely dislike long-winded people with no organized disease and I neglect them. Perhaps I go over a patient hoping to find something wrong because I know I am not interested in the patient as a person. Now in psychiatry I would be deal-

	ing with exactly those people. I would have to treat each on his or her own merits."
Analyst	"You find a relief when there is physical illness."
Patient	"For a psychiatrist a whole hour of a patient may be an intolerable burden."
Analyst	"I think you are thinking of me and yourself."
Patient	"Well, I suppose so. I have sometimes avoided going into this or it has come up but I have not liked to talk to you about my concern as to what you are feeling."
Analyst	"There is of course the psychiatrist's basic care but within all this there is love and hate."
Patient	"It's odd, I was just thinking then of two or three other matters. One was what shall I do this evening? The other was almost a dream of a confused kind about a patient in hospital. There were several people concerned. It was a reproduction in miniature of a worrying case that occupied the weekend. I was discussing the case with other people."
Analyst	"It is important to you therefore that in psychoanalysis there is one person, myself in your case, and no consultation."
Patient	"That is what I was talking about with the girl friend. Whether it is safe to discuss matters with a psychoanalyst. She said that psychoanalysts are not safe to tell everything to, and yet you must. I took the view that it would be quite possible to withhold an unpleasant detail. She said this would ruin the analysis."
Analyst	At this point it seemed to me to be important that I should stop taking notes. It was of course possible that the patient knew and needed me to inform him openly. On the other hand he may not have known and it would be important not to interrupt the course of the analysis at the present time by falsely introducing this idea. I could tell that the patient was very much under the influence of the main interpretation of the last session and I must therefore sacrifice the note-taking to the work in hand.

I realized that this man was giving me material supplied by his girl friend, and that I could only make indirect use of it. At the same time I must not waste it.

	[*See Note pp. 504-505.*] I spoke of the discussions around clinical material which analysts certainly do have.
Patient	"I was really only referring to gossip."
Analyst	I pointed out that this matter is of definite concern to his girl friend as idle gossip by me would give away details of the private life of the girl and might reach people she knew.
Patient	He spoke about doctors at the hospital where he was ill who gossiped with him about cases assuming that as he was a doctor it would be safe, but this worried him a great deal because he was a patient and the fact was that he was having to cope with a doctor gossiping and not with a scientific discussion of cases between doctors.
Analyst	I said that psychoanalysts, like other people, do gossip, being imperfect human beings. But in psychoanalytic practice this gossiping was recognized as something to be avoided.
Patient	He said that his girl friend had discussed the question of malpractice. Would the analyst act if a patient reported antisocial behavior? In her case she is afraid to go to another analyst because she would have to tell the second analyst about the behavior of her first psychotherapist which evidently she considers was unprofessional.
Analyst	I agreed that she would have to speak of this freely or otherwise not take up a new analysis.

It appeared that she felt that she would be able to talk freely if she could assume that the second analyst would not act on her accusations.

I pointed out that within an analysis a patient must be able to speak freely, which means not always confining observations to that which is strictly objective. There must be room for delusions and there is no room for these if the analyst is to act, since all the material brought into the analysis is for one purpose only, namely the analysis of the patient.

I followed up another clue by saying that it was important for me to recognize that what he was saying came from his girl friend. He might want to say something similar on another occasion and then it would be material to be brought into his analysis. It might happen in the course of time that we should look back and find that the reason why he did not come on the previous day was to do with his suspicion of me but at the present time the clear issue was that he had work which kept him away.

There was more than one reason for the patient's behavior; it was overdetermined. While interpreting motivation deriving from an unconscious transference reaction the analyst does not deny the validity of other motives, for example, the patient's conscious reason for his behavior.

Patient   He said that there might be some truth in it in the sense that earlier in the analysis he would definitely have come. This would have meant leaving his work aside.

Analyst   "It is possible then to state that earlier you had a fear of me which you knew nothing about and which you could only deal with by being good."

I said that now he was a little bit in touch with his fear of me and therefore could defy me under the cover of using or exaggerating a need for his services at hospital.

I then pointed out to him that he had a reason for the first time in the analysis to be suspicious of me since in the previous session I had come in in the role of the father who prohibits incest. In the previous session he had thought of the father, I reminded him, as avoiding the main issue in which there was hate between him and his son, and therefore the son had no fear of the father. It was this new thing turning up in his relation to me which made him able to bring suspicion as expressed by his friend. It can be said that he was not ready to bring it directly himself.

Previous interpretations of negative transference were based more on inference than was this one, although here the interpretation is based on attitudes of another person, reported by the patient. The analyst can regard this as the patient's analytic material, particularly because the patient reports having had and suppressed such thoughts during sessions in the past. Even without this confirmation, however, the analyst can regard the patient's reports of statements made by other people as analytic material of the patient, as long as the analyst actually is not in contact with others about the patient. (See Note pp. 504-505.)

Friday, 1 April

Analyst	The note on this session was made four days later. There had been some degree of a resumption of note-taking during the session.
Patient	"Well, I have been put off by something — very much upset by the girl. She has to be in hospital and I am not allowed to visit her for fear of upsetting another boy friend. I am very angry with her and with my wife. The question is whether the man knows about me. She obviously wants both of us but she cannot tell him about me. It's like with my wife: she didn't like to upset her boy friend and expected me to be able to stand everything. . . . Of course I don't really want an exclusive love affair; I'm alarmed at the idea of this."
Analyst	I made an interpretation about the setting repeating itself in which he is angry with the girl for frustrating him and not with the man.
Patient	"It would seem to be all right if I found yet another girl, but that obviously is not the solution."
Analyst	"It would always come round the same way with you as you are at present, and the reason is that you are all the time looking for your mother and your father has not played his part in coming between you and your mother. Had he done so he would have been a frustrating person; you would have come to terms with him and he would have freed you for all other women."

The process of working through is illustrated by the way in which this material recurs in different contexts.

(Patient sleeps.) "Were you asleep?"

Patient   "No, I don't think so." (It became clear that he had been.) "I can't see where immediately to go forward. Lately I have been taking it out of others in hospital, losing my temper. In the past I found I have been too lenient, too inoffensive, tolerating everybody; but now I find myself flaring up. I wanted to flare up with the girl but I thought how much I could have lost my temper to a better purpose at home."

Analyst   "You can see that you did just lose your temper here with me, and to some extent in the imaginative situation I am the person who has prohibited you from visiting the girl. In the previous session you said that you were half expecting me to tell you to keep off her."

The momentary sleeping can be interpreted as a defense against anger in the transference.

Patient   "I had thought of that, that you might be jealous. I didn't like the girl using the word 'ducky.' It's what prostitutes use — impersonal. She is probably more intimate with the other man, knowing him earlier than she knew me. I prefer 'darling' if it's said right. It all depends. It may be artificial or genuine. . . . Also I tend to forget her name when making love."

Analyst   "You told me that you sometimes think of your wife's name at that moment."

Patient   "Oh yes, I had forgotten. I forget things so easily, especially names. I might call people by their Christian names if I know them well."

Analyst   "What did father call mother?"

Patient   Here he gave his mother's Christian name. "Or he might have used the word 'mummy' talking about her. . . . With the girl I felt that I ought to use her Christian name but I was unable to, or forgot it. On the telephone I say, 'Hullo dear,' thus avoiding the issue. It's the same with my wife. The use of a Christian name except when adults are talking about children is a bit of an affectation. It's rather a predicament for children at adolescence to know what to call their parents. Their Christian names or 'mummy' and 'daddy?' Dependence

	or independence in the relationship? There are stilted words like 'mater,' but that is clumsy."
Analyst	"But there are difficulties in your relationship at adolescence with your parents which are reflected in these considerations of names."
Patient	"Yes, it's all right for a girl to say 'daddy,' but for a boy to say 'mummy' is rather like incest. Society seems to tolerate the idea of incest between a girl and her father more easily than that of a boy with his mother. I think anthropology supports this."
Analyst	"Are you talking about ideas or about actual intercourse?"
Patient	"I think I mean everything including intercourse. Mother and son is very objectionable. The word 'darling' belongs to this intimate relationship. The question is, what is meant by incest? I could have said 'love' or an emotional relationship. With the girl, intercourse is acceptable, but love is more doubtful. Today she said, 'Of course I'd be annoyed if you weren't upset.' "
Analyst	"You are using society's prohibition of incest between son and mother because you cannot find the man who will get in between you and your mother, which means that father did not play his part here, and so you have no hate and no fear of man and you are back in the old position of either being frustrated by the woman or else developing an internal inhibition."

This is an illustration of the way a social taboo can be used to avoid awareness of intrapsychic conflict. (See Note p. 465.)

Patient	"It is the girl who prohibits."
Analyst	"You are all the time looking for a man who will say 'No' at the right moment; someone you could hate or defy and with whom you could come to terms, and you are just a little bit allowing me to be in that position insofar as you got a little bit angry with me."
Patient	"It just occurred to me that it must be the end of the time and that in a way that is saying 'No.' "
Analyst	At this moment, as it was time, I said, "In that case I am saying 'No' which means no more analysis today.

I am coming in between you and analysis and sending you off."

Tuesday, 5 April

Patient   "Nothing seems to come except to repeat that contemporary problems don't seem to produce much, but there are two things about this: one is that this provides an easy way of starting, and the other is that recently contemporary problems have seemed to be much more useful. I am wondering why this should have been so."

Analyst   "I consider that the reason is that you have been less dissociated, if I may use that word."

Patient   "Yes."

Analyst   "It has been less a question of either external phenomena or inner phenomena and I have been able to stand at the borderline and speak about both because of the changes in yourself."

This is a way of conceptualizing the role of the analyst, interpreting the interaction between intrapsychic processes and the patient's perceptions of the external world. The principal way in which this is accomplished is by means of transference interpretation.

Other links between the inner and the outer world can be interpreted, as illustrated by the projection of an internal prohibition onto a social taboo. (See p. 465.)

Patient   "Oh, I see. Every now and again I seem to want to stand still and take stock. I find that I am much more in the world in my management of patients and the discussion of them. A year ago I felt as if I was two people and now these two seem to mesh in with each other.

"It may be a coincidence but it has been since I started with the girl friend that I have had less need for withdrawal. Also I am less worried altogether about making decisions. Another thing, I am able to take a genuine pride if things go well with a patient, whereas I used to be just pleased feeling that I had struck lucky. Now it seems that I can realize when I have done something well."

Analyst   "Going with this will be an ability to allow that I may do well with you."

More realistic perception of the analyst, with reduction of idealization and denigration, permits assimilation of the analytic introject. This is part of the process of identification that expands the ego capacities of the patient.

Patient   "Yes, you are less of a magician. I had to assume that you were professionally perfect, and now I can see you as a person trying your best to apply skill." *Pause.* "I have noticed an ability to get more feeling out of surroundings. Listening to gramophone records last night I found myself excited and at one time sentimental. I have known these records for a long time but have never had this sort of feeling about music. Another thing is a real capacity now to be jealous, emotionally rather than academically. I am definitely jealous of this other man who is in the life of the girl friend. I used to act as if I were jealous but now I really am."

Analyst   "It is very uncomfortable being jealous but you prefer the discomfort to the former lack of feeling."

Patient   "Yes, in the past there was a general lack of emotional reaction." (The patient put his foot on the floor.) *Pause.* "Sometimes I put my foot on the floor and it occurs to me that it might be important. It is as if I am getting my feet on the ground and just then there was a feeling of mild protest. Why should I stay on this couch? It was symbolic of something."

Analyst   "In the last few weeks you have put your foot on the floor half a dozen times and on each occasion I think I have been able to see that it was related to some kind of new relationship to external reality."

This behavior was not used for interpretation until the patient noticed it and spontaneously spoke of it. (See Note p. 467.)

Patient   "I did not know that I had done it before. It's got something to do with what turned up earlier as jumping up or somersaulting backwards off the couch."

In "Withdrawal and Regression," Dr. Winnicott reported a fantasy of somersaulting backwards off of the couch which led to discovery of a feeling of being supported by a medium in which the patient felt suspended. This was a way of experiencing and expressing the patient's dependence upon the analyst and the analytic setting.

Analyst   "In a way it is the very first step to ending the analysis and in another way to establishing an equality with me which is the opposite of dependence."

Pause.

Patient   "Recently I have become less stable, more easily upset, and I feel this to be a development in the analysis. It is a new phase."

Analyst   (Patient sleepy.) I made an interpretation linking my bringing about the end of the hour with the idea of the end of analysis.

Patient   "I was sleepy then. It is difficult to get at ideas. I can get at ideas in a dreamlike condition, but as I begin to wake they seem to be inappropriate. In any case the fantasy is not describable in words. It is more of a kind of action. I seem to be going on drifting."

Analyst   "It is true that the sleepiness can have two sides to it. On the one hand you are searching for ideas which are not available by direct intellectual effort. On the other hand you are defending yourself against an anxiety when you do not know what it is about."

The patient's sleepiness and sleeping during the analytic sessions is here interpreted in several ways. One, that during sleep the patient becomes in touch with derivatives of the unconscious, such as dreams, which are not available to him in full waking consciousness. Two, sleep also serves a defensive function, frequently in relation to warding off perception of the external world. Quite frequently the patient becomes sleepy in reaction to interpretations which stimulate transference, positive or negative.

> *These meanings of sleep, related to the borderline between internal and external perception, can be compared with the previous interpretation of the role of the analyst, intermediate between the patient's subjective and objective perception. (See pp. 549, 555.)*

Patient   "The things that go on when I am sleeping are not complete facts. It is difficult to make them coherent for reporting. There is less effort in talking about hospital than in talking about thoughts." (At this point he became lost and he could just say so. He yawned.) "The trouble is that I have to wake in order to say what is going on."

Analyst   "Behind the sleepiness at the present time I think is fear of me which belongs to hate of me which derives from my ending the hour as I did."

Patient   "I feel I ought to be more alarmed. It is more rich to be alarmed; nearer home than just having the idea of a frightening situation. Recently I have been surprised at having the confidence to be alarmed, feeling I could cope. Also I cannot get a definite answer out of you. At the time of being in hospital ill I had no conception of what was going on and I could not be alarmed."

Analyst   I made an interpretation referring to my saying "No" in terms of ending the hour, getting between him and analysis and his anger with me and his fear of me.

Patient   "I went to sleep then. I have forgotten what was said. There is something about going to sleep in this position. On one hand I can relax here and also I can deal with things when I am asleep."

Short sleep.

"There is one bit I just remembered. I had told you about a patient and someone else was criticizing me for telling you."

Analyst   "This reminds me of the idea expressed recently that I might tell about you."

Pause.

Patient   "While dreaming I was aware of waking but I felt before I woke that waking is less urgent. The treatment of this patient is more important. It occurs to me that this is very strange that I said to you that there is nothing in the immediate situation to discuss today, when actually (he was awake now) I had a bigger row with my wife than ever before, at the weekend. It was very upsetting, as it affected my daughter. I had been definitely alarmed. The thing is that my wife can and does exploit this situation, knowing that I must protect my daughter. She makes certain that we are never alone together and then at night refuses to speak so that there is nothing whatever that can be done about the matter in hand and I am left fuming. This time I was limp with anger, but I can see that I had hoped to make her start a row. But what I have to remember is that with my wife there is nothing that can be said."

Analyst   "In some way or other in the imaginative situation I am there — (I withdrew this interpretation as I realized that I had no clear understanding of the transference significance of the row.).

Patient   "My wife and I have no common language."

Analyst   "You have something in common, which is that on your part there is your difficulty associated with a lack of prohibiting father and with your wife there is a difficulty in relation to her own parents, and her attempt to achieve independence which seems to be breaking down."

Patient   "I feel depressed when I recognize that my wife really does not want intercourse; she despises the idea of it and despises me for suggesting it, but I have to remind myself all the time that I may be responsible for putting her in that position because of my original failure with her. The difficulty about quarreling with my wife is that I do not know what we are quarreling about. Do I want intercourse with her; Yes, but only if she wants it. It would not be of any value to me if I have to compel her to yield and I know that I cannot make her want it. In this respect she is like her mother."

Wednesday, 6 April

Patient   "I seem to remember that I was excited about something that arose at the end of yesterday's hour but I can't remember what it was."

Analyst   After some beating round the bush in an attempt to get at the significant detail: "There was the relationship of your wife to her mother."

Patient   "Oh yes, that was it. I felt great anger with my wife because of her contempt of sex which she shares with her boy friend, and despises intercourse and this is exactly her mother's attitude. This puts me in a dilemma because I am not prepared to accept a life in which intercourse is suppressed."

Analyst   "The attitude of your wife which you describe gives her an identification with her mother, that is to say, of child with adult, but at the price of a renunciation of actual intercourse."

Patient   "I deprived her of intercourse, or failed to satisfy her, and so she came to disapprove of it and to despise it."

Analyst   "If your wife were to become independent of her mother and able to bear the idea of defiance of her mother, you had to make it worth her while, and you feel you failed. So she has reverted to dependence on her mother and a kind of identification. This compares with your own lack of a relationship with your father of rivalry and defiance, which was partly due, it seems, to his attitude."

Patient   "There is a new difficulty on account of this. She does not want intercourse and is therefore incapable of jealousy. She rebuked me for being late. I said, 'You can't complain if I sink to your level,' and she (instead of becoming jealous) said, 'Oh, you'll never reach my level,' (probably meaning high level of idyllic love). And it's true that I have not a really deep feeling for the girl friend and I might get bored with her quite soon."

Analyst   "You feel doubtful about the girl's ability to create a home."

Patient   "My wife does not understand this comparison of attitudes — romance with contempt for intercourse, or opposition to intercourse. It's all right in theory but not in practice, and brings unhappiness. Actually what I do really want is to be loyal and faithful to one woman." *Pause. Pause Renewed.* "I'm trying to remember a dream I had this morning. I did remember it and I felt it was one of those dreams that are not significant in themselves. The dreaming of it was the thing. Mother was in it, driving me in her car. My wife was there too. It's gone."

Analyst   "What kind of car has your mother?" (I deliberately did not ask about the car in the dream.)

The patient had said that the dream is not significant in itself but that "dreaming it was the thing." Previously (p. 549) the analyst's position on the borderline between subjective and objective perception, dream and external reality, had been interpreted. At this point the analyst started his investigation of the dream from the side of external reality.

Patient   "Oh, she has a Hillman, but it wasn't exactly her car in the dream; it was older, and decrepit. That wasn't the point of the dream. The point was that it was dangerous, and I had to be exerting control in order to keep it straight. Mother doesn't in fact drive well. But I wouldn't be willing to admit that she could be a good driver. My wife doesn't drive. In the past I would have liked her to drive but now I don't like the idea. I don't like to think she might drive better than I do. I prefer to be superior. At the start I assumed that she was perfect, and now I'm pleased when she can't do things."

Analyst   "This reminds me of the girl-with-the-penis idea."

Patient   "My wife started off with a penis, and now she is in process of being deprived of it. At first I wanted her to be equal, but now I want to dominate. I want to make her jealous." (Some description of interplay along these lines.)

Analyst   "There is a kind of sex play between you in all this?"

Patient   "Yes, but she has this contempt for sex. She may be jealous, but hiding it."

                              Pause.

Analyst   "I am not clear what you mean because she might be jealous of you as a male, when you are with your girl friend — as well as the other way round."

Patient   "Oh, I see. I hadn't thought of that. There is a contrast here with what happened a year and a half ago when I was ill in hospital, and I told my wife of an affair that seemed to be on at the time. She said, 'Well, a good thing for you, it may help to solve your problems.' Now she's just annoyed. I'm reminded that, her boy friend having been ill, she no longer looks for any quality — " (Abrupt break — pause — sleep) "It was something out of a film I went to last night, which is appropriate. A man who hated to be made a fool of. I don't want to be made a fool of."

Analyst   "There is the problem all the time, that you have to be frustrated by your mother (your wife) or else develop internal inhibitions, because there is no man to come between you."

Patient   "There was the ending of the hour recently."

Analyst   "Today there is more than this since this is the last session before the Easter gap. I am soon going to come between you and analysis by saying it's time."

Patient   "Yes. I was really pleased at the idea of a holiday from you, but at the same time I am annoyed."

Analyst   "There is room for both feelings at once."

Patient   "The trouble with psychoanalysis is that so much depends on it."

Analyst   "So that while you are in analysis I do in fact remain a parent figure."

Pause.

Patient   "I was talking with my girl friend. She has had some psychoanalysis (I don't know with whom), and she was speculating vaguely about restarting. I ought to say yes, but I couldn't advise her to. It interferes with life, and is difficult to fit in with work. But also it would interfere with her usefulness to me. I felt some of my wife's attitude, that it would be frivolous."

Analyst   "In the *imaginary* situation I am the analyst the girl will go to, and in that respect you and I are rivals, and you prevent her from coming to me."

Patient   "Yes, although I know she did not go to you and she would not be coming to you. I feel jealous because analysis would make her want me less, as dependence develops in her analysis."

BREAK FOR EASTER

Tuesday, 3 May

AFTER THREE WEEKS' BREAK.

Patient "The first thing I want to say is that it seems much longer than three weeks. Mentally there has been a real break. For the first time I feel that I know what it would be like to have ended analysis. For one week I was depressed because of not coming, and then I dismissed the whole idea. The question now arises whether I should stop analysis or come less frequently. I cannot say that the result is perfect but I have come to a workable state. In regard to work I now feel that I can definitely cope. It is now a question, do I want analysis? And I find myself making plans for a holiday in a month's time which I must take if I am to get a holiday with pay. I would never have dreamed before of planning for a holiday at a time when analysis was available. In regard to home life, I have come to an understanding with my wife. There is a relative stalemate. I have come to accept the fact that there is no future in the marriage and so I plan accordingly; there is nothing to be expected."

Analyst "In saying this I know you are taking into consideration your wife's difficulties and also the history of the difficulty between yourself and your wife which you have told me about."

Patient "Yes, I can see now that it was a mistake our getting married. I feel that it was destined to failure from the beginning and we were never suited. I now find I feel resentment against coming here. It is an illogical thing. I have the idea that you are keeping me against my will. I find I am expecting you to say, 'You cannot go,' and I will be fighting for my right to go."

Analyst "If I have a definite attitude of this kind then at any rate there is something there to defy."

If the analyst has a definite attitude in favor or in opposition to some impulse of the patient, the patient can defy the analyst and avoid becoming aware of his own ambivalence. In this way the analyst's position can have a temporary organizing effect on the patient's ego. This is an important element in what is commonly known as supportive psychotherapy. Such so-called supportive psychotherapy fails to foster the autonomy of the patient's ego, in contrast to Dr. Winnicott's interpretive reaction to the patient's expectation that the analyst would intrude with his own values into the patient's conflict.

Patient   "Yes, the decision then is not just simply entirely mine." (That is, the decision is not based on abstract thinking but on feelings and reactions.) "I feel I am being hypochondriacal about myself in order to carry on on a basis of need. I have to plead ill-health."

Analyst   "There seems to be a changeover from needing to wanting, and along with wanting goes not wanting."

As the patient achieves greater symthesis, and greater freedom of affective responses, he also comes to be aware of his instinctual aims and objects. This leads to a change from relatively inchoate biological needs to more organized wanting and not wanting, increasingly linked with actual situations and objects in the external world rather than restricted to more or less unconscious and unstructured fantasy objects and situations. (See Note pp. 673-674.)

Patient   "And therefore I have come to a position in which I can weigh things up."

Analyst   "In accordance with this I am changing over from being a therapist to a person, and here the fact of your father's death comes in and my being alive, a human being. You have spoken of the way in which father's illness and death, as well as his general attitude, left you with a burden of personal decisions at a time when you needed a father to identify with and to react against."

Patient   "Yes, it is also important to remember how my whole attitude has changed since the girl came on the scene. It is this that gave purpose to my life although this seems rather pompous. I have of course considerable anxiety as to what will happen if the relationship to the girl breaks down. Will I come crawling back to analysis? In a way the girl takes your place, because there is an element of bravado both in not coming for more analysis and in continuing with the girl. I wonder how much of life is real."

Analyst   "The relationship to the girl is related also to the analysis and became possible as you began to exist and to have a capacity therefore for feeling real."

Patient   "Yes. For instance, coming along today I went to the Academy to look at pictures. I could almost say this is the first time I have enjoyed such an experience. Certainly for the two years I have not been able to manage this. I would always have pretended but it would have been a fraud and a waste of time. I enjoyed the pictures without a frantic search for feeling real. I would always have had to try to think up something to say. I might have been able to manage the cinema or the theatre where there are people to identify with but not going to see a picture exhibition. Pictures require of one a much greater degree of personal stability and independence."

Analyst   "Pictures do not come to meet you so much. You have to put something into them."

Patient   "All this makes me wonder, as I see the great progress that has been made in this analysis, whether it is foolish to stop here, because there might be further progress. The trouble is that the decision to leave off might be quite arbitrary. When I first came to you in the war it was an arbitrary decision, and I stopped simply because it was inconvenient. This was unsatisfactory. When I came to you this time there was a definite reason. I was ill and had need of analysis. Now I have gone back to the first state in the sense that as I no longer need analysis it has become like a game and I keep on wondering, is it necessary?"

Analyst   "If you are able to play in this way that is also a change brought about through the analysis."

"Playing" involves an integration of internal and external reality. In this way it is contrasted with dreaming which focuses more on internal reality, and with serious

working in which the focus is more on external reality.

Patient   "Yes, I had a great difficulty about playing and always if I played I wondered, 'Is it permissible? Is it not too frivolous? Dare I play?' I had to take deliberate responsibility whenever I was unserious. It always seemed like just playing, meaning that something more serious ought to be going on. I wonder whether my education was too serious and play may have been given too small a part. I was discussing with someone whether play ought to be constructive. I found myself saying, under the influence, I feel, of what we have found in the analysis, that there ought not to be too obvious a constructive element. The Montessori principle can destroy the idea of the value of play. It is as if one is inculcating the idea that play is naughty or immoral. I see that play has a value in its own right and I am aware of having missed something throughout childhood. I played in spite of my parents and also in play was always alone and lonely. With my wife if there is any play it is always serious, whereas with the girl play is spontaneous, and valuable for itself."

Analyst   "The pictures also have a value in their own right, I think you are saying, and are not part of the management of external reality or of a direct kind like work."

Patient   "I would like to go home and tell my wife about the pictures but the very fact of telling her would turn it again into something with a purpose. I would be talking in order to show her that I got somewhere. It would be only valuable if talking about pictures came quite spontaneously."

Analyst   "I am not quite sure what you feel about your wife; whether she would have been originally able to play or whether she has developed a seriousness in relation to the marriage with you."

Patient   "She has the same sort of attitude but it is quite a lot of fitting-in with me. She probably could be spontaneous. My wife must undoubtedly have found me very tedious in my inability to play. I am getting away really from the urgent problem which must be solved within a few days. The question of a new job has to be settled. Shall I plan to fit in my job with psychoanalysis, or can I afford now to think of the future and of a career and fit in psychoanalysis with these plans? This might involve coming less frequently or even leaving off for a time. There was a pointer when I was discussing things with my wife and she said about a job, 'Don't you think you would find it too worrying?' I am definitely not any longer concerned about work as something that might worry me. I know I can cope. The trouble in the hospital appointment when I broke down was partly that I could not tell what to do next."

Analyst   "Did you ever feel drawn towards any line of development?"

Patient   "Mostly the answer would be in negatives. I considered general practice, but felt that after the decision the whole of my life is determined. I have the possibility of becoming a casualty officer, which previously would have made me feel anxious. I would now find it exciting. The horizon is clouded by practical considerations. I have considered pathology and anaesthetics, but in these specialities I must get stuck in a small niche. I feel I am no longer in need of the security afforded by the limited niche."

Wednesday, 4 May

Patient   "I felt yesterday as a challenge. I really wanted an opinion out of you and did not get it." (Here followed a long discussion on a reality basis of the general situation, work, private life, and analysis.)

Analyst   I included in this discussion an interpretation about the idea of leaving off analysis as a defence against anxiety and spoke about his need to get more clear on the subject of male and female as compared with the combined figure. (During this time the patient put his foot on the floor.)

   I then brought in the idea of taking up psychoanalysis, making it clear that although this had been discussed before I had no definite evidence from him that he had it in mind. Nevertheless the subject was there as something being omitted.

Patient   He said that he considered psychiatry and psychoanalysis only in a negative way. His mother and others had suggested to him that he might use the value of his own analysis by taking up psychiatry. He had three objections to this. Firstly, it was a difficult subject. Secondly, the snag is that it involves too much sitting and talking and little activity. Thirdly, there is the amount of work that has to be done with long hours and comparatively little result. Also he had a definite hostility towards psychiatry, knowing that he was always clumsy about this branch of medicine, could not understand it and knew no basic terminology. Only today he had, he said, a patient who needed psychiatry and who ought to have been classified. "I had no ideas as to an approach. If I used the word 'mania' this was simply to impress officials. There is no question of a clinical entity and to have been honest I should have written 'off his rocker.' This, however, would not have impressed the D.A.O. I would like to add that the resistance to any understanding of psychological medicine is very widespread. I find it amongst all my colleagues. Further, I now have to consider how much importance to attach to the social aspects in determining my career. With such an unsatisfactory home it would seem that there are certain branches of medicine that it would not be right to enter." *Pause.* "I sort of feel I ought to have a more definite objective, but nothing appears. I seem to be waiting for some job to turn up and feel this is a sign of weakness."

Analyst   "It might be helpful to look once more at your change-over to doctoring from engineering."

Patient   "Well, that arose out of the fact that firstly I did not like the engineering students; secondly, I was not good at engineering as such; and thirdly, I hated the idea of an office job. I felt I must deal with people. It would be more satisfactory and offer more scope. I was in despair about factory work, dealing all the time with inanimate objects. Taking up medicine got me out of this gloomy prospect. There are also other circumstances such as the fact of my father's illness and something carried over from my father of a political nature. I suppose there is a missionary spirit somewhere and I must find a worthy occupation. In this way I got tremendous relief at leaving engineering. Here at last I felt I could look forward with pleasure for the first time. It occurs to me now, and I do not think I have ever thought of this before, that my father did not want to be an engineer. He wanted a university career but his father died and he had to run his father's business. He was always dissatisfied as an engineer. He might have been a barrister or a teacher; his subject was math. Unfortunately he had poor handwriting and was no good at spelling, and I seem to have inherited these characteristics. He longed for something more erudite than what is called for in engineering. He ought to have been a professor. At the start I took up medicine therefore because I needed something to justify myself, but now this motive has faded and I feel more that I want to look after my own happiness and this involves not getting stuck in a narrow groove. I feel now that almost any branch of medicine would do. If someone were to talk convincingly along any line I could probably be led, but not into business or engineering."

Analyst "Probably with everyone to some extent there is a dependence on what turns up."

Patient "Yes, but I don't like to feel that it is so." *Pause.* "Here I feel I want to come back to the question of my wife and her responsibility for placing me in this dilemma so that I have to consider social factors in my career since they are not satisfactory in my home life. How much can I blame on to her? It is probably wrong to accuse her. It is certainly to some extent my fault. I know I cannot blame her but in my marriage I cannot achieve anything." (Foot on floor.) "Will it ever be possible or will there always be an incompleteness? In my marriage I looked for friendship without effort but it did not work. Shall I continue the tremendous struggle? Or settle down to life without bother and without friends and without sex? I feel that my wife makes everything seem my fault, and so I react and make it hers." *Pause.* (It was time for the end of the session, but I had started late.) "I do not feel I want to say any more; I might say too much and overstep the time limit. My last remarks evoked no response. I feel they did not go down well."

Analyst　"Firstly, there is myself in the role of a person who is alive with whom you can discuss things on a reality basis, and this puts me in the position of your father. Secondly, there is something left over from yesterday where you had the feeling of myself holding onto you, not wanting you to go. I think that this is the point that you are wanting me to bring into the analysis, and you have been waiting for it and felt dissatisfied when it did not come. You were expressing by having this idea a wish I would hold onto you. From this position you could get away, but you cannot get away from someone who does not hold you."

In "The family and emotional maturity" (1960), and in The family and individual development, *Tavistock Publications, 1965, Dr. Winnicott says: "In the conscious life the child may have got away from the mother and father and may have gained great relief from doing so. Nevertheless the way back to the father and mother is always retained in the unconscious. . . . We can see two tendencies. The first is the tendency in the individual to get away from the mother and away from the father and mother, and away from the family, each step giving increased freedom of ideas and of functioning. The other tendency works in the opposite direction, and it is the need to retain or be able to regain the relationship with the actual father and mother. It is this second tendency which makes the first tendency a part of growth instead of a disruption of the individual's personality."*

Thursday, 5 May

Analyst　(This note was written after some delay.)
Patient　"I will begin by saying that after last time it is difficult to produce further material. If there is only one month more before a new break and possibly an ending, will it be worth while producing new things? I am comparing it with the difficulty that I experienced before the Easter break. This seems to be a potent barrier. I have a feeling that ideas need not come. Perhaps the idea of an ending is based on an unrealistic assessment

of the present position. Before I looked forward to an ability in the future to overcome difficulties." *Pause.* "I am reminding myself that in the past two sessions we spent a lot of time discussing practical details. There was little actual material of a more personal nature."

Analyst "You will remember that sometimes you have complained that real things did not seem important in the analysis, and you are comparing them now with the other kind of material."

Patient "Sometimes it seems that the deeper material is not so productive. It might be considered too frivolous, too conscious or something. I seem to be trying to produce the right thing. I often feel guilty that I may be wasting the time or fabricating in a way that is elaborate and meaningless."

Analyst "All the time there is myself holding you, and further there are the various methods; on the one hand my general management and on the other hand the interpretations of material."

In this interpretation the setting of the analysis, the "holding" environment, is compared to the patient's discussion of external reality. Within the "holding environment," derivatives of the unconscious become manifest, and are interpreted.

Patient "I am thinking of my father. Possibly father seemed to reject while mother would hold back. I feel hostile to the idea of mother holding me back, that is to say instead of father." *Pause.* "It is just possible that father failed me when I was an infant or a child. It's indefinite. It is an idea suggested some years ago. The idea is there of a child finding his father and being let down but I do not think this is true for me."

Analyst "I think that something may come in here which I have derived to some extent from your mother and I have spoken to you before about it. When your mother first spoke about your father before I saw you in the first treatment, she told me that your father was perfect. She obviously idolized him. I think she recovered from this afterwards in her own analysis. I think that you are trying to get to a statement of your feelings about this."

Patient   "Yes, there is something here. It is true that my father seems to have become less and less perfect as seen in retrospect. His attitude to child education was too theoretical; also in other ways his imperfections and inadequacies have always been shattering discoveries. There is a new idea here of his perfection, that it was mother's idea of him and that it had been accepted by me as self-evident truth. I was amazed in childhood to find imperfections. I can think of an instance when he played cricket at school — fathers versus boys. His movements were clumsy as compared with those of other fathers. On the one hand I assumed perfection and found it very difficult when discovering imperfection. On the other hand there were some difficulties arising out of this idea of perfection. On the whole I suppressed the imperfections that I noticed."

Analyst   "The important thing would be that this idea of his perfection coming from mother would mean that she did not love him; not being concerned with a real person she emphasized the quality of perfection. I think that you felt the whole thing as an absence of love between mother and father."

Patient   "It's really just exactly like this with me and my wife. I had the idea that she was perfect and built her up that way though I was aware of its illogicality. When I found that she did not want me the whole structure broke down, and was no use."

Analyst   "There is something like this about me too."

Patient   "Well, yes, at the start I assumed perfection. And again I brushed aside all the little evidence of imperfection. I suppose one has to in this position. I would have to think that if you were imperfect you were not an expert. In the analytic situation if you are not perfect then I have to be doing it myself. I suppose situations arise in which we can discuss things on the basis of equality, jokes for instance. I find myself excited and amused. I feel that you are disappointed or annoyed. The idea of perfection is unsatisfactory."

Analyst   "The idea of my perfection could be used as a defense when you have an anxiety about a relationship in which there is feeling and all sorts of imaginary possible outcomes."

Patient   "The alarming thing about equality is that we are then both children, and the question is, where is father? We know where we are if one of us is the father."

Analyst   "You are hovering here between the idea of your relation to mother alone and your relation to father and mother as a triangle. If father is perfect then there is nothing you can do except be perfect too, and then you and father are identified with each other. There is no clash. If on the other hand you are two human beings who are fond of mother then there is a clash. I think you would have discovered this in your own family if it had not been for the fact that you have two daughters. A boy would have brought out this point of the rivalry between him and his father in relation to mother."

Patient   "I feel that you are introducing a big problem. I never became human. I have missed it."

Analyst   "I am reminded that you did not consider psychiatry or psychoanalysis as a career on the grounds that you would not be perfect almost immediately."

Patient   "I have never really accepted not being good at something."

Analyst   "Your life was founded on a basis of perfection-imperfection which had to turn up and came along as illness."

Patient   "Imperfect for me means being rejected."

Analyst   "When I think of what you have told me of your wife I realize that I know nothing at all about her except her perfections and imperfections. I have no picture of her as a woman. I think this is not my fault."

Patient   "I do not know if I could describe her. I have tended to assume that you are not interested in her as a woman. Also I always have a difficulty in describing people. I never can describe a personality, the color of people's hair, and all that sort of thing. It occurs to me that others perhaps do describe people in their analyses and so therefore I felt immediately that you have made a criticism of me. I am always reluctant to use Christian names and I noticed the other day that I used a masculine name that sounds like my wife's Christian name, and behind the mistake was a description of my wife who for me has masculine qualities."

Monday, 9 May

Patient   "Last time I left here with a feeling of impotence; I mean sexual impotence. I can't think exactly what happened. There was a definite change in what I was like as compared with before I came. The change definitely had a relationship to the session. I had arranged to meet the girl friend and it was the same with her. I was very disturbed. There is the complication that her behavior has changed. She is cooling off, getting more out of her previous boy friend. He excites her more than I do so I am becoming somewhat of a nuisance. This produces a dilemma, to fight or to walk out? But to walk out means that I am left with nothing, yet that is not a good reason for hanging on. I explained to her that I did not like acting second fiddle, but I do not know how genuine it all was. Coming here it occurred to me that perhaps I have more need for analysis, that I had been too optimistic about the idea of the end; on the other hand it must be wrong to use coming here as a direct help out of a difficult situation. This is the sort of thing my wife accuses me of doing, and it is a general criticism leveled against psychoanalysis. It is a lazy way out of difficulties."

Analyst   "You can look at it as if there are two of my roles here as analyst covering this subject. In one I am as if your father had come alive, or an uncle, and you have a person to talk things over with. This is not my main function, however, although an important one. There is myself as psychoanalyst in relation to whom changes occur in yourself which affect you in a more general way, and which do not concern the actual solution of problems at hand."

Patient   "I feel it is wrong to use you the first way; an extravagant thing."

Analyst   "One does not exclude the other, and it is important for you to find out that I am not rigidly set in one or other role."

Patient   "The old difficulties have come back like waking up in the early morning. Has the benefit of analysis been lost? What was it that did happen in the last session? I know it was something to do with father and mother." *Pause.* "It was something to do with mother idolizing father and so I could not compete. Why did this produce impotence?"

Analyst   "The first thing we have to consider is this: was I right in what I said?"

Patient   "Well, if it was not right it was reasonable. And I feel the fact that it produced a reaction means that it probably was right. When you say something wrong the test usually is that it has no effect. Right or not, I am worried about the discovery of mother looking at father as a symbol of perfection." *Pause.* "I have tended always to expect others to look at me in the same light and I had no hope of being regarded as perfect. As soon as there was any criticism or evidence that I was second-rate I became depressed or unduly concerned. There is only one way to achieve anything and that is by perfection."

Analyst   "All the time you are saying that you have no hope whatever of being loved."

Patient   "Yes, with other people and especially with girls it is all right at the beginning when there is a prospect of being perfect, then gradually as it becomes obvious that there is imperfection the thing gets out of control and I have no confidence. With this girl for the first time I struggled against this and achieved a more normal relationship; at any rate sexually I seem to be perfect, but after last time I feel I can no longer cope. She did not regard me as ideal but as a satisfactory lover. An illusion is shattered so I go back to the ordinary position of competing with others, a position I never like. If I am second-rate, then I run away."

Analyst   "The difficulty seems to be in thinking of men as human beings fighting for a position on account of love for a third person. In that position men have to consider, 'Is the third person worth while?' "

Patient   "I think that I only fight if I am sure I will win."

Analyst   "You are not fighting for the girl but to establish who it is that is perfect."

Patient   "An important word carries over from last time, which is rejection. Imperfection means rejection."

Analyst   "You spoke of a reason for ending the analysis being its perfection or your having reached a stage of perfection."

Patient   "Rejection comes in again here. Do I go ahead to perfection and stop because of obviously having reached this aim, or do we work on a basis in which perfection is not important? In which case I am either rejected at some point or else I decide not to want to come any more. The danger is of adopting the idea of not coming in order to avoid rejection." *Pause.* "Just then I was avoiding thinking about here. I was thinking of a minor thing — shall I have a bath tonight? What about washing my hair? The whole point is that I was not being here."

Analyst   "From my point of view you did achieve going away from me. You walked out and you were able to tell me about it, on account of what we had been saying."

Patient   "The idea occurs to me, and this is quite new to me, would you follow or not if I walked out? If I walked out I have to turn round and come back which means tell you about it. The whole thing is if one walks out, will anybody be upset? Will anybody want to bring one back? It is a very uncomfortable thought to walk out and not to be asked to come back. It makes me think of the differences in child education. What do you do when a child is naughty? My father, for instance — only I think I am not really describing my father accurately — would deal with a child's temper tantrum by ignoring it. No, it's not especially father. It is said to produce results; if a child discovers he is ignored he stops. From the child's point of view I can see that this is an insult."

Analyst   "It leaves him with the thought that if he goes off he is abandoned."

Patient   "As a matter of fact I remember father was the opposite. If his children were naughty he said 'They are unhappy and need sympathy' and he acted on that principle." (n.b. Analyst remembers having been told about this in the first part of the analysis). "He neither scolded nor ignored."

Analyst   "This would surely produce a kind of paralysis in regard to ordinary rivalry. I can see the value in saying that a child with tempers is unhappy but I think that your father avoided the ordinary clashes that belong to the father-son relationship."

Patient   "I think he was like me. A clash was allowed by him only if he knew that he would win. In this context about fighting it seems senseless to fight if one knows one will lose. I fail to see how in the old-time dueling, honor could be satisfied by being killed. It seems pointless."

Analyst   "The subject is from your point of view one which can only be spoken of in terms of actual fights. You are not at the present time able to employ fantasy or playing or the easing of the situation which is shown in the touché of the duellist. You can only think in terms at the moment of actual death of one of you if you and your father were to fight, and therefore you have to make quite certain that the prize is worthwhile.

This interpretation illustrates the value of play, employing symbols. At the point at which the patient is unable to employ symbols in play, he can only think in terms of actual destruction or immunity to destruction. Inhibition of action, or in other instances acting out of a destructive nature, can derive from failure to develop a play area ("transitional area") in which symbols are meaningful.

See Dr. Winnicott's paper, "Transitional objects and transitional phenomena" (1951), in Collected papers, *1958.*

Patient   "This is connected with my wondering whether the hour is near its end. It is part of the same thing. If I go on I may get stopped and that means losing or being thrown out. If I am lying on the couch and it is time I feel that you order me out. (This occurred seven minutes before the end of the hour.) We effect a compromise in that I gradually come to an end and have no more to say and then you say it's time. I am prepared in advance but even so get an unpleasant surprise."

Analyst "It is not usual for you to deal with this matter several minutes before the end."

Patient "I usually keep quiet about it but I feel uncomfortable. It is very difficult to be stopped in midstream."

Analyst "I know that the expression 'stopped in midstream' is a metaphor but it is the nearest you have come to the idea of castration. I would say that it was as if you were stopped passing water in the middle of doing so and it brings to mind three degrees of rivalry; one in which there is perfection and the only thing you can do is to be perfect, too. The second is that you and your rival kill each other, and the third, which has now been introduced, is that one of the two is maimed."

Patient "I accept the idea here of being stopped in the middle of passing water; it is also very much as if one were stopped in the middle of intercourse."

Analyst "We thus come around to your using the word impotence in describing your feelings after the end of yesterday's session. I would like to join up the idea of your being interrupted in intercourse with your own impulses as a child to interrupt your parents when they were together."

Tuesday, 10 May

Patient "I was agitated last night. I suppose there were several reasons. One was the deterioration of the relationship with the girl friend which has rendered home less tolerable. There was also what happened here. I cannot quite make out why. Is it something real or is it just wishful thinking? There is certainly an element of wanting to feel disturbed by the analytic sessions. I feel that it is the only evidence I have of something happening. I feel very disappointed if there is no disturbance which to me means no progress. The distress of the last two sessions has been satisfactory from this point of view."

Analyst "Shall I speak about what has been happening?"

Patient "Well, yes, (doubtful) I think it would be a good idea."

Analyst   "The idea of rivalry with a man which has been so difficult for you to arrive at seems to have turned up in the relationship to me. You felt impotent after the session before last, and in the last session you came round to the idea of being cut off in midstream so that in fantasy the idea had been introduced of two men, one of whom maims the other. Previously there had only been killing and this meant that the rivalry situation was not worth taking up."

Patient   "I cannot quite explain why with girls I have a special difficulty in regard to flattery, which after all is part of the technique of love-making. It feels unreal. About girls I do not seem to be able to build up words in praise. Is this stretching things too far? It seems to me that there is a link here with the avoidance of rivalry."

Analyst   "One link would be that the girl must claim you without being won."

Patient   "Yes, so that has been the experience — that the girl must come and get me."

Analyst   "You are referring to rivalry in the process of love-making."

Patient   "It seems to me intolerable that there should be rivalry over love-making about a girl."

Analyst   "If the girl does not choose you then you feel abandoned."

Patient   "It has happened with regard to my wife and also with the girl. Now that I have become a nuisance she can only pity me."

Analyst   "There is something of this kind that could be spoken of in terms of yourself as a small child with your parents and rivalry with father in regard to gaining mother's affections."

Pause.

Patient   "I do not think there is any connection of that kind."

Analyst   "Perhaps you had something else in mind."

Patient   "Yes, I was thinking out what to do in the future. It was suggested by the girl friend that I should do a Casualty job as there was one available in her hospital. I had never thought of it till then. Now there is a Casualty job available in 'X,' nonresident. I am wondering whether to apply. There are some advantages.

For instance, I could come here and manage to keep on with the analysis if evening times are available; also there are practical things, I would not have to pay a resident fee and I would save a pound a week. It would be strenuous; mean getting up early in the mornings; also I should be home more and would have to face up to home difficulties but I feel attracted by the idea. The Casualty job would not be leading on immediately to a career but it would be a satisfactory way of postponing a decision."

Analyst   "Included in all this is the idea of wanting to continue the analysis."

Patient   "Yes, psychoanalysis bites into free time and makes it difficult to have time for friendships, but I am wanting to continue with it."

Analyst   "How far will it interfere with your relationship with the girl friend?"

Patient   "That has now become unimportant. It has gone by the board. I cannot seriously weigh it in with the other factors."

Analyst   "What are your prospects if you apply?"

Patient   "I have already telephoned the present Casualty officer and discussed the job with him and there appears to be a good prospect except that I have done no surgery before. At any rate I can apply and see. This means psychoanalysis for another year."

Analyst   "This gives you time to come round in your own way to your idea of the final aim."

Patient   "Yes." (Theme developed.) "Also there are perquisites in the job. There is a further point which is very curious. I am attracted geographically; it is on the other side of London and I know 'X' of course on account of the hospital. Perhaps this is not very important but it makes the job more attractive. It probably is nearer to here."

Pause.

Analyst   "Something has happened. You have walked off and you found that I have not abandoned you. You walked off by definitely considering stopping analysis and also a few months ago by having thoughts that were not obviously in the line of what was going on here in this room."

Pause.

Patient   "I feel a certain amount of general excitement. The idea of a new job partly, and this providing a way of getting round difficulties about stopping analysis, but this excitement makes it difficult for me to get down to anything else just now. Is not this rather common, that one comes round to something absorbing and for a limited time it is difficult to get on to a different subject? Now I want to get up and take action immediately. I feel a strain as if I were on a leash. I want to deal with it."

Analyst   "How much easier it is to have something like this that you can actively deal with than this business of psychoanalysis where you have to wait for things to happen."

Patient   "I feel guilty about the way I have got jobs during the last two years. They have come without my taking any active steps except going once to the British Medical Association. Everything else follows. I do not want to drift on any more. It is disgraceful. I am ashamed. I have a feeling of weakness, drifting with the tide, and in any case I am not decided on a career. Even with getting a girl I cannot go out of the way to start but drift along. When I went to college after school I hardly applied but drifted into it and even doing medicine the decision was to some extent mother's. She pushed me into it a bit. I feel very much sympathy with my wife who complains when I am shopping I can never decide on anything. I can never choose a present. My wife despises me. So I am excited at the idea of going and getting which has now come my way. My wife also criticizes me that if I go out with her she has to choose where to go."

Analyst   (The important thing in this session was the recovery from hopelessness shown in a general change of mood as compared with the previous hour.)

Friday, 13 May

Analyst   (He arrived ten minutes late which was unusual; this meant that at the end of the hour there would inevitably be a sense of "being cut off in midstream.")

Patient   "There is really nothing to say, except that I've continued to feel slightly better. The tension and the anxiety seem to have passed. This is in part related to the ending of the affair with the girl. The end has brought relief. I'm aware that there was a good deal of pretense in the whole thing."

Analyst   "Intellectually you have all the time been prepared for this ending, but emotionally it is a matter of experiencing. Perhaps you are sad?"

Patient   "Not so much sadness. It's more like desolation, despair, a feeling of 'never again.' As I look back I see I was aware that I was playing a game, and the game was to keep up the illusion, that in itself is a positive thing for me since formerly I could not play."

Analyst   "Playing with enjoyment."

Patient.   "Yes." *Pause.* "Something has happened over the last few months; I have certainly more ability to be frivolous, or lighthearted, though still self-conscious about it. But the game was to be frivolous, and it is as if all the time I disowned this being frivolous even while it was on. I was lighthearted in disguise. Of course there are times when I get tired or depressed and when tension returns, as if it's too much effort to create this other person that is me being lighthearted. So I'm not really quite spontaneous."

Pause.

Analyst   "What about you here, with me?"

Patient   "Well, that's different. There's no point in having an artificial self here, nor in being frivolous either. I can discard all that here and be my own self. Sometimes I have to drift away from here to get deep, and so I'm somewhere else, as if I leave my body and wander in my mind." *Pause.* "This drifting is hard to put into words." (Compare previous withdrawals.) "I have an image, and part of me wants to say it but another part says 'No you can't,' and the result is silence. Just now I'm in that mood, and in danger of going to sleep because there is nothing pressing to be said. So I wander, and forget I'm here." *Pause.* "There's a curious analogy that occurs to me. Those men clearing the wall opposite in painters' cradles *(scaffolds)*. I pictured myself doing the same, lazily swaying in and out of here as if in a painter's cradle. I can't help feeling there's something I want to say but fear to say. Last time felt satisfactory, because of the anxiety of the tension — now however I feel better and I don't seem to want to risk something fresh. Also it's a curious idea but I feel just now that I'm an assistant in here to help advise about someone else."

"Drifting" is a regressive phenomenon in contrast to withdrawal. The patient is just able to maintain contact with the analyst in the "drifting" state, depending on the analytic setting as the painters depend on the cradle. In this setting the patient is able to include primary process material, permitting the analyst to provide the secondary process integration, while the patient temporarily suspends his own secondary process organization. (See Note p. 608.)

Analyst   "That's true in a way, as you often can be said to bring yourself and at one time we used to talk about you, and you yourself hardly came at all."

The ego splitting in which the patient talks about himself rather than being himself, has been referred to as the "false self holding the true self." In the "drifting" state, the patient can rely upon the protective environment of the analysis and become "unintegrated," relinquishing the defensive "false self." At such a moment the patient can feel as though he is "being himself" rather than only talking about himself (See p. 479).

"You are wanting me to help you to see the way in which your present difficulties are related to the idea of rivalry that has come up recently. You first arrived at a recognition that there could be rivalry with one or two males getting killed, and the fight was not then worthwhile. Then you felt near the idea of two males in a clash, and one could be maimed and survive, and then there is the other theme of being abandoned."

Patient   "I can say about that, that if I bring myself the part that is due to be brought is reluctant to come. I have to keep on bringing it back."

Analyst   "This self cannot stand the idea of possibly being abandoned."

Patient   "Yes." (Unconvincingly.) (Immediate sleep.)

Analyst   "You did actually sleep then."

Patient   "I can't think why because I'm not tired."

Analyst   "There is something really dangerous about me and it was the word impotent that you used and meant to use a few days ago to describe the state I brought about in you. The affair with the girl friend happened to end at the same time, and I now wonder whether it was not as much brought about that evening by the situation here as by the change in the girl."

Patient   "Yes." (Sleep, momentary.) "I have a difficult task avoiding sleep. If I keep awake I keep back my thoughts; if I release control I go to sleep."

Analyst   "So that on the whole sleep is the more productive of the two alternatives."

Patient   "I feel that for the first time for some weeks there is no immediate problem, no distraction, and therefore my reluctance is shown up. I would like to know what it is that I fear."

Analyst   "That if you yourself come, and get into contact with me here, you will be maimed."

Patient   "Who will be maimed, me or the other?"

Analyst   "You." (Sleep, momentary.)

Patient   "There's an analogy between leaving the girl and leaving here. I fight to go on here, and run away from the idea of being maimed."

Analyst   "Soon the end of the hour will come and then I shall be quite literally in the position of someone who is maiming you. I say this while you are still here and before the moment for stopping has arrived. I think that the holiday was experienced by you as a serious maiming of you by me."

Patient   "Today is exceptional in this matter of going to sleep. It must have something to do with the topic of father being perfect, and my not being able to compete, and all that." (As if the patient had not really heard my interpretation in spite of his just managing to say yes before going to sleep each time.)

Analyst   "Yes, father and you in rivalry brings dangers, especially if you include actively making love. I am not sure if you feel father could make love?"

Pause.

Patient   "I've nothing to add, only to say the same in different words. It needs much more work to adapt oneself to diverting a woman's attention. The phrase 'I'm not ready for it' occurs to me. It's all very vague."

Analyst   "It seems you kept your penis and your physical potency partly by giving up all making love and active diverting of attention."

Patient   "And I would add to these negative things like not being at ease, or lighthearted, because it's curious how I'm lighthearted heavily, with great effort."

Analyst   "There seem to be these two alternatives, and if you now begin to be able to make love actively instead of being passively chosen, you find you have a new fear — impotence."

Patient   "I had a curious idea then. This all seems futile because father is dead. I've never come up against this before. If it's a matter of rivalry, well that's academic, since father's dead. I feel his death affects things in two ways: one, I recognize he's dead, and the other, the matter has now been talked out."

Analyst   "It seems a funny thing to say, but at this moment I think you are forgetting that in fact I am alive. And it's now time."

Tuesday, 17 May

Patient   "Really there is a lot to say today but I will start with what you said last time. You said you were alive. It had struck me that in the last session you were not doing any good and it seems to me now that it already symbolized that you were not alive. Your being alive is the same as your doing things, making a difference. It had occurred to me that I had no feelings about you at all, neither admiration, love, nor hate. It is as if I felt that you were not alive."

Analyst   "So when I said I was alive it did not cut much ice."

Patient   "No, I don't mean that, because it brought the subject to the fore. It brought something into sharper relief which arose out of a discussion that I had with my wife. I forced her to talk and forced admissions. I got her to talk about the idea of her seeing yourself at an earlier date when she decided not to do so. She has always refused to say why she decided not. She even said, 'I never will tell.' At the same time I guessed that she was thinking about my liability to commit suicide if she left me. She has now admitted that she wanted to ask you what would be the effect of her leaving me. She did not take the matter up, however, because in her own way she decided not to leave me at that time, in spite of having a boy friend. Also a few times ago you said you did not know what my wife was like because I never described her as a person. I felt that you implied that you had wanted to and that you deliberately did not see her. At the same time I had an idea that you had been in communication with her behind my back."

Analyst   "What would you feel if you found that I had been in communication with her?"

Patient   "I should be shaken, whereas earlier I did not mind the idea that mother spoke to you without my knowing it, because that was reasonable. I was incapable of managing my own affairs, but now I would be very annoyed. My wife tried to persuade me not to go to the hospital, not to give up work, and not to go to psychoanalysis. She has given a new reason now for not wanting me to go into hospital as a patient. She feared that because of her boy friend she might not be able to resist the temptation to leave me. At that time I was powerless. About not going to psychoanalysis her hostility was partly based on the fact that I had always told her that I was opposed to psychoanalysis and she was horrified at my weakness. She regards psychoanalysis as an expensive form of quackery. This raises the question, how much progress really has been made here? Would I not have made just as much progress if I had not come at all? I certainly have some sympathy with her point of view. I am now continually reminding myself of my illness three times a week, and this is what my wife says, and the implication is that I had better not come and that I had better go on developing normally. I suppose you can't provide an answer. Naturally you would not say, 'Yes I am a quack,' and if you were honest you would have left off the treatment if you thought it was not doing good. If my wife had concluded with a promise that she would stand by me if I left off analysis, I might try not to come any more, but she didn't. Moreover if she did promise, would she be able to keep it up? I wonder what has been done here. The trouble is that I always try to force others to make decisions for me. I would like to make you say something, but on the other hand if you make a decision that makes me feel childish."

Analyst   "I think that in talking about these matters you are leaving out of account the whole matter of unconscious cooperation. If you were to be coming here and I were to be failing you, I think you would have reacted by leaving off before now."

The term "unconscious cooperation" in this context refers to the patient's autonomy. The patient had been wanting the analyst to make the decision as to whether it was worthwhile or not worthwhile for him to continue analysis, and the analyst pointed out that the fact of the patient's continuing is sufficient evidence that the analysis is meeting some need of the patient.

Patient   "I am always expecting a stage at which you will say that although there is more to be done we have come to the end of what you can do."

Analyst   "Yes, that could be."

Patient   "Last time I certainly had doubts during the hour, 'Can Winnicott cope?' "

Analyst   "There are two ways of looking at this. One is the rational, which you have talked about. There is also the fact that there are certain very big anxieties in the offing. These have to do with the new developments belonging to recognition that there can be rivalry between men, and the further point that in the clash between two men one could get maimed instead of killed. Incidentally, last time you came late, which is unusual, and this meant that I knew all through the hour that the end of the hour was going to feel to you like a cutting off in midstream."

Patient   "Lately I notice I am much less fussy about arriving on time. This is Tuesday when you often keep me waiting. Previously I would have run the risk and been on time. Today I was a few minutes late and it was my own fault. It is just a matter of altered emphasis."

Analyst   "There certainly seems to be a lessening of fear in regard to this business of being on time."

Patient   "I feel I have gone as far as to dare to be very late. A few minutes today that I was late really symbolizes being incredibly late. It was a silent protest. I do not seem to have dealt with this before, that I never let myself know the exact time during the hour. I never look at my watch. I feel I must not. The fact that there is no clock visible must be part of the technique inducing relaxation. Occasionally recently I have looked at my watch surreptitiously but felt I was being rude, but I cannot see any reason for all this."

Analyst   "Incidentally by this means you avoid checking up on me to see whether you get your money's worth."

Patient   "Well, by the present arrangement I sometimes get overtime and then I feel you have given me a present. If I were to look at the watch I would feel I ought to remind you that it is time."

Analyst   "In these different ways you are engaging in rivalry situations with me in token form."

Patient   "I would like to go back to where I was about my wife. I certainly do not know what I want and I don't know what I ought to want. It seems it would be unrealistic to make her go back on her decisions, to drive a bargain with her. It would not be worth it."

Pause.

Analyst   "Your wife is still against psychoanalysis?"

Patient   "Yes, probably, but she does not say so openly. If she did she would have to offer something in exchange. What she would say is that she would like me to be standing on my own feet. The trouble is that she has never believed that I was ill or needing help and the consequence is that whatever happens now from her point of view is the fault of the psychoanalytic treatment. Also I have just been offered the job of Registrar. This excited me very much. It means increased status and pay, but then I came to realize that it was very dangerous. The question is, can I do it? And also, am I burning my boats making an academic career inevitable?"

Analyst   "Which would mean, of course, never doing a surgical job."

Patient   "No, that's not important. The important thing is that this job would give me too much opportunity to be undisciplined. In my present job I am kept at it by the patients, and their needs. As a Registrar I could get slack. In many ways I demonstrate to myself a lack of self-discipline. For instance, I decide not to smoke but then I smoke and this is in part weakness, but also it is being naughty. I have to smoke in order to defy my own discipline."

Analyst   "Something that controls you from within is so strong that you feel liable to be paralyzed by it and must defy it to retain freedom."

This links with the previous material about defiantly being late for the appointments. Internal superego forces are projected onto the analyst, who can then be defied. In this way the patient can achieve a momentary feeling of freedom from domination by an oppressive superego. (See Notes on pp. 465, 539.)

Patient   "When I have time to spare I cannot make myself work sometimes. Otherwise this inner drive would make me unhuman. Always there is the feeling that I do not want to miss something, and everything may be missed if I get into the power of this which disciplines me from within."

Analyst   "When you can wait until you actually want to do whatever it is, you feel in a better position about it."

Patient   "But I want so many things. For instance, there is the desire at the moment but I also feel a need to be good. The primitive desire is not the main thing. There is this feeling of a need to be good which is based on fear. Also

I do not wish to be good from fear as this makes me more lonely. In this job as Registrar if I do it well I become remote and the prospect is terrifying. At the end of the day I will just go home and life stops. I notice that I do not want to be alone with my wife because in this way I feel cut off and she has practically no friends. In a way this is an opposition to growing up, to being a parent. If we are children we are all children together, but parents are lonely. Also it is the same thing in regard to my difficulty over talking to people. I fear that I would dominate from above and so as a subterfuge I have nothing to say and then they start the conversation and I come in amongst them and thus avoid loneliness."

Wednesday, 18 May

Analyst	(On this day I personally was very tired and it was with the greatest difficulty that I could keep going. Evidence of this is clear. On this occasion the patient was not sleepy.)
Patient	"Yesterday we left off in the middle of something. I can't think what it was. I know that I said something about looking at my watch and the techniques to avoid being interrupted."
Analyst	"I cannot for the moment say what happened at the end of the last hour, but I will let you know when I remember it."
Patient	"I can't think what it was. I feel that my forgetting is a definite protest against something. There was something about my wife's attitude and you spoke about unconscious forms of cooperation." *Pause.* "There seems to be nothing in the bag today."
Analyst	"It is coming back to me now that we spoke at the end about your feeling that if you were to be in the parent position you would be lonely and if you are in the child position you have others with you."
Patient	"Oh yes, this fits in with my wife's criticism that I am childish and complaining in my talk. I feel that unconsciously, so to speak, I do this deliberately."
Analyst	"This is a kind of playing. There seems to be a very sharp distinction in your mind between being in the

parent position and being in the child position, as if the two were mutually exclusive."

Patient   "Also there is a fear of talking things out. The question is, will what I say go down well? I feel my talking is artificial and stilted."

Analyst   "In the two extremes you either tell and direct or else you are told."

Patient   "No, it's more the feeling that others will lean on me. It's not quite the same. It's the same idea said in another way. I ought to say that the anxiety about the new job is not only from the deep unconscious; it's also a conscious wondering, have I the ability? Something happened pictorially at that moment; someone came in from outside the house. There are unknown factors outside but inside anxiety is dealt with so I shut the door to prevent outside factors interfering." *Pause.* "I seem to be getting away. I thought for instance of a film I went to last night. It seems that I am choosing to run away. I could make the observation that if I produce ideas, that is work, but relaxation which seems to be demanded of me here is the opposite and no ideas come or I wander off."

Analyst   "Where in fact did your getting away get you? What film?"

Patient   "Well, I went to *Carmen Jones.*"

Analyst   I remarked that I had seen the film.

Patient   "A caricature of *Carmen.* This has to do with the hospital problem where the negro nurses are gradually replacing the whites. The film features all negroes and this in itself is abnormal. Even in the U.S.A. you would never find nothing but negroes. So the film was remote because it was different from real, so that the negroes and the negro nurses did not fulfill the role of friendship."

Analyst   "You went away expecting to find children to play with but there were no brothers and sisters suitable."

Pause.

Patient   "One thing comes in here. I went to the cinema with the girl friend and she told me that she had had an Egyptian man as an experiment, so the idea occurs, have I just been another experiment? It all becomes very impersonal. Also could I bring myself to try the experiment of a negress woman? There is a contrast here to do with my wife who in spite of the fact of her boy friend still has a horror of infidelity. She would never discuss infidelity even in the abstract. She feels very uncomfortable about her boy friend because in her mind she cannot allow the idea of two at once. The idea of aboslute fidelity seems to me too abstract and therefore not important. My infidelity does not matter as long as one is faithful ideologically. I think this was a reason why my wife thought she would leave me because she could not stand the idea of infidelity." (Notes not clear at this point.) *Pause.* "I cannot think why I cling to a hopeless situation in regard to my wife, leaving out for a moment the matter of the children. One reason is perhaps that I look at my wife as a parent. It is as if I were clinging to a mother-figure." *Pause.* "I seem stuck."

Analyst   "You seem to be able to be a child in relation to mother but if you become a child there are no other children."

Patient   "About that there are four things to be said. Firstly in clinging to my wife I am an only child. Secondly clinging to one's wife in this way is abnormal; society does not accept it even if my wife were willing which she certainly is not. Thirdly I know my wife has contempt for this attitude. Fourthly, I despise it myself. So I leave her to carry the weight of decisions about coming here. It was all right when I was ill. I could ignore her judgment then but now I feel that her ideas offer a real challenge. By coming here I degrade myself. I am looking through my wife's eyes and she can see that my mother and sister who have had a great deal of analysis are not normal and each in fact has gone back for more analysis. Mother is still extremely inconsistent and this emphasizes the idea of psychoanalysis as a quackery."

Analyst   Here I tried to give the two sides of the idea of leaving off analysis. One, the rational, which he was describing clearly, and the other, his fears belonging to the development in the analysis of a triangular situation and a rivalry and castration. My interpretation was not given clearly because I was tired and also because I was not certain before I started exactly the intepretation that was called for.

Patient   "I have been off again thinking about hospital." (At this point I myself was finding it very difficult to pay attention.)

Analyst   (This interpretation was given more to keep my own attention going than for any other reason.)

Dr. Winnicott has listed the following reasons for giving interpretations:

1.) To let the patient know the limits of the analyst's understanding of the patient. If the analyst says nothing, the patient may get the impression that the analyst understands everything. The limits of verbal communication show the patient that the analyst cannot read the patient's mind magically.

2.) To apply the analyst's secondary process organization to the patient's primary process material.

3.) To enable the analyst to be attentive and to remember the content of the session.

(See "The Aims of Psycho-Analytical Treatment," 1962, *in* The Maturational Processes and the Facilitating Environment, *1965.)*

"When we come to ideas of rivalry between yourself and myself you find yourself in difficulties. For instance, you have never referred to our relationship in the sense that you employ me."

Patient   "My wife despises me and I share her feelings. If I depend on you and on her for a decision, as I do, I cannot decide myself about staying in analysis or stopping. Two nights ago she said about her boy friend that the thing that was important to her about him was that he decided to leave his own wife. This was the first time that she had made this clear. She was then in a position to decide what to do about him. He certainly did not say to her, as I feel I am doing, that if she would live with him he would leave his wife. He made the decision on his own first. My wife would need me to make a decision about psychoanalysis and not drive a bargain by saying that I will leave it off if she decides to stick by me."

Patient   "I have forgotten again what happened yesterday. I always do tend to forget but this has been especially true the last two times and again I feel sleepy although there is no cause for it in the sense of my having a right to be tired."

Analyst   "I think it may be best today for me not to try to remind you but to let things come. I would, however, like to say that yesterday I was very tired and this may have affected you. I will mention the fact that at the end you managed to make a criticism on the subject of there being too much white around here when I pointed out that the house opposite was being painted."

The patient's self-criticism is linked to the analyst's fatigue of the previous hour, of which the patient presumably was at some level aware, and to the patient's criticism of the building as being "too white," implying "too lifeless."

Patient   "I should like to take the last of those points. I really had liked the yellow of the house opposite and I had thought that it was the natural color of the stone but I see now that it was painted. The point is that I feel you have a deliberate policy to make everything colorless to provide a neutral atmosphere."

Analyst   "Yes, there might be some truth in that. My pictures, for instance, are not very striking."

Patient   "The question is, is it a policy or is Winnicott really like that? Is that your outlook? For instance, sometimes you have a small vase with one flower in it. It seems to me mean or impotent, as if you can't produce, as if you are barren. I have a fear that I should be left at the end of analysis with a barren outlook. For instance, I have no photos in my room. Nothing of my family. I don't want this to be true for ever. I read a novel, the significant part of which was that a nurse on a ship had no feelings. In order to convey the fact that she was hard it said that in her cabin there was no ornament and no photos. I don't want to find this is really me."

Analyst "So there is a risk if I am like that, that the analysis will leave you as you are."

Patient "Yes, in a sense depersonalized. When I was in Switzerland I noticed how clean it was but characterless. The Swiss people seem to me to be an uninteresting sort of people. There is no evidence there of great culture. There is another aspect of the same subject. I noticed in a recent Italian documentary film — it showed electric trains, no soot or dirt. Efficient but nevertheless there was a lack of the powerful engine, which is a romantic symbol. There will be a loss of the dramatic if steam engines are to be abolished."

Analyst "This reminds me of something which happened last time which was to do with my having said 'I am alive.'"

Patient "That was two times ago. Also I am discovering the the things about you which cut across the idea of the perfect psychoanalyst. I used to think of the psychoanalyst as always in command. I wonder if you can carry on if you are tired. I must be boring, and all that sort of thing."

Analyst "By thinking of yourself as boring just there you are bringing back my tiredness to something coming from yourself and getting away from the idea of my having a private life."

The patient's taking responsibility for the analyst's fatigue is interpreted in two ways:

1.) If the patient caused it, he can control and predict it, rather than to have to be passively subjected to it; and

2.) If the patient caused it, the analyst has no family or private life to compete with his interest in the patient.

Patient "For the first time I recognize jealousy here, that you are seeing others."

Analyst "This reminds me that you said that if your wife is in the maternal role you think of yourself as the only child. Last time there was also this about your wife that she talked about her boy friend's attitude, how he had not tried to strike a bargain."

Patient   "Oh yes, I remember all about that; certainly I feel I must be cautious; there must be something available before I give anything up." *Pause.* "I seem stuck here." *Pause.* "I remember about last week that I said I could not stand on my own feet and you said that I had to stand on my own feet too early. This seems to fit in with the idea that I have to make sure that there is something there before I let go."

Analyst   "The phrase 'standing on your own' reminds me of the actual picture you gave me once of finding a baby on mother's lap and straining to stand on your own which produced pains in the lower limbs."

Patient   "It's all really a part of the picture of a child walking and holding on to things."

Analyst   "If people fail to hold a child in the early stages then the child has to take over holding himself up."

The "self-holding" here is referred to as the premature development of an ego function, due to failure of the environment to provide adequate "holding" during infancy. Masturbation in this context, as the next association illustrates, can be viewed as a derivative of the original infantile need to provide for one's self when the environment fails. Patricidal fantasies and castration anxiety have at this point in the analysis led to temporary abandonment of rivalry in the transference and an emphasis on the dependent maternal transference. This includes fear of abandonment and a need to defend himself against the dependent transference by "self-holding." (See Note pp. 661-662.)

Patient   "After last time I was thinking that masturbation fits in as a buffer against not having sex relationships. It is something to hold on to. I cannot tolerate the idea of no sex relationships and one of the ways of overcoming that difficulty is to pretend that there is no need. And it's literally holding on to something too."

Analyst   "You might also be speaking about thumb-sucking." (I was aware at this point that the patient and I were communicating without direction. Almost for the first time I felt that I as the analyst was floundering, simply dealing with the immediate points raised and I was wondering how to get back to the patient's own process which I felt I had interfered with at some point not exactly known.) "I suppose you are telling me that masturbation has come back."

Patient "Yes, and it never went altogether. Somehow I used it as a yardstick of progress. Failure to get away from it feels like a symbol of uncompleted progress. The idea was that a relationship with a girl would make masturbation unnecessary but this was not true and in fact it ought not to be since it would mean that the point in the relationship was simply to get away from masturbation and not something positive in regard to relationships. In any case I regard masturbation as a harmless addiction."

(I noted here in my own mind that there would be found a relationship between the masturbation and castration fears and that it was important that he had now told me about the return of masturbation. I thought this was not the right interpretation to make at this point.)

"I recognize here a contradiction. I am trying to achieve independence and yet by coming here I am more dependent. My wife does not understand this and in fact I don't either."

Analyst (I thought that this was the moment to try to gather the whole thing together and I made a long interpretation which was possible because he was very much awake.)

I said that at the present time there had been a return to the type of relationship which belonged to two people, himself as an infant and his mother, the sort of thing that started with the word medium and which went right on until there appeared a third person.

Patient "My wife's criticism of psychoanalysis has to do with the dependence."

Analyst "It is very painful to you yourself to be dependent, especially now that you are getting better. You run the risk of being abandoned and in any case developing dependence just for this analytic hour when you are independent in everyday life is a strain on you."

Patient "I certainly feel abandoned when you do not say anything after I have made a remark."

Analyst   "There is also to be taken into consideration your girl friend's attitude which must be felt by you as a rejection not only by her but by me since she represented some aspect of me. I mentioned that I was tired last time because I felt that you would feel it to be a rejection as you are sensitive on this point."

Patient   "As a matter of fact I didn't notice it. I was not fully there."

Analyst   "Yes, I think it possible that you didn't notice it but I could not tell. There was also the matter of the negroes in the film and at hospital and the experiment. The question arises as to whether analysis is an experiment and the neutrality of the psycho-analytic atmosphere seems to link up with the feeling you had that the negroes could not provide a relationship for you."

Patient   "I recognize the fact that psychoanalysis cannot guarantee success. At the start I had to assume that the analyst's failures which I recognized intellectually could not apply in the case of my analyst. I see it is a great gamble, this assumption that great progress is bound to be made."

Analyst   "I think that when you came to me it was essential that I had to look for you and therefore to take all responsibility. You were ill and you easily accepted this, but now that you are comparatively well you find yourself having to make the decision to come to me and to take all the risks and this is very painful."

Patient   "It is a difficult question to decide. When is it safe to try letting go? I cannot tell till I try. It's like learning to skate; as long as you hang on to the side you can't skate. So I see that one day it won't be a transition, but a sudden breakaway. There must be a dramatic decision by me unless you suddenly tell me to stop coming. It was the same learning to swim or to ride a bike. Father's attitude was to give support and then suddenly to let go, so I'd find that I thought I was supported but actually I was not. It worked, but I fear the same thing here. You might suddenly say : 'Well, you *are* on your own now.' Although it worked with the bike it would be a shock to me here."

Analyst   I said that there have been certain difficulties since the appearance of the third person and the course of the analysis was affected by a retreat from anxieties belonging to rivalry. Incidentally relief provided by a triangular situation was something that he could not obtain because of his retreat from it. The question therefore was at the moment one of dependence and independence or alternatively the fear of being abandoned.

"If you were to leave off at this moment you would be establishing independence or avoiding being abandoned but this would be breaking off in the two-person relationship and in your case would be avoiding the new features that belong to the triangular situation. In the triangular situation you have the chance to win or lose in the dream of a fight with father, and the fear changes from one of being rejected to one of being killed, or maimed. The important session was the one which made you go away feeling impotent, and it was as if I had damaged your potency and ended your relationship with the girl."

Monday, 23 May

Patient	"Again I haven't any clear idea except that I can say that since last time I have been more in the frame of mind in which I feel I could do without coming here though I can see that there is more to be gained by coming. I mean I could manage. This ability to manage depends partly on external factors but I have to consider what would happen if external difficulties recur. I have a greater ability, however, to cope with adversity. The main bit of adversity is loneliness, and this I find less worrying than it was. About loneliness I am mostly lonely when there is the smallest number of useful people and now I feel a gradually expanding number of people I can use."
Analyst	"If you can stand loneliness then you are in a better position to make contacts because if you fear loneliness each contact is spoiled at the beginning by the way you go at it."
Patient	"People only enjoy your company when you are not particularly concerned whether you meet them or not. But I am making less demand now on others. And also

I am very much less tense. Talking to people is not altogether easy; it requires effort and I am all the time conscious of the feeling that I must be boring them." *Pause.* "There is something I thought of at the beginning of the session about not talking. That is something that happens here. I am almost obsessed with the idea that I must produce something interesting. I remember in the Queen Anne Street days (the first treatment), that I kept on saying: 'I have nothing worthwhile saying.' If I talked of ordinary things it was silly, frivolous, but here I do not say things sometimes because I feel they are not worthwhile saying. Outside I find other people talk about minor things so I have to assume that that is the normal, so I make an effort to learn how to chatter. Here I do not feel self-conscious about it. Perhaps I could talk about what I see and odd things like that; if you take these things seriously, then it is as if you are patronizing, like dealing with a rambling delirious child — 'There, there, that's all right, dear,' etcetera. Only apparently taking the thing seriously. There is an inherent difficulty in psychoanalytic situations. You put up an atmosphere of formality. You pretend to be serious and so on. Perhaps you are avoiding laughing. I feel that all my prattle is immensely valuable but you might be laughing. If you were to say that something was rubbish I would feel very crushed."

Analyst "There are two elements then in your talking, the prattle element and then the content. There is the prattle which is apart from talking and which is derived from babbling, just something a small child does as part of being alive."

Dr Winnicott has developed this in his Playing and Reality, *London: Tavistock, 1971. In Chapter 4 of that book he says that trust of the analyst enables the patient to reach moments of free association in which there need be no significant links between the various components of the patient's associations. He refers to Marion Milner* (On not being able to paint, *New York: Int. Univ. Press, 1957, 148–165*) *in relating this state of undifferentiation to the substrate of creative origin-*

ality. Milner pursued this under the heading of "Creative Surrender" in her book, The hands of the living god, *New York: Inter. Univ. Press, 1969, 257-264.*

Patient	"But I sort of feel that I need convincing that the unserious is acceptable although I know perfectly well theoretically that for the analyst it is acceptable. The only way left me is to force myself to be frivolous and then to disown it quickly, especially if it misfires." *Pause.* "I seem to be casting around for a place to start. How can I express the difficulty I have in regard to prattling or talking lightheartedly? I can come to a sudden stop. There are no more words. It is an absurd situation. Stopping means that I am showing that I am ashamed." *Pause.* "Again I have the idea of waiting, hoping others will talk. It is a method of avoiding responsibility. If the other starts he cannot object. And at any rate one can avoid that way being laughed at."
Analyst	"It seems very likely that once or perhaps several times in a certain period you were prattling and then laughed at and that this was traumatic and you made a mental note 'never again.' "
Patient	"There might of course have been a specific instance. It's like a lack of achievement here that there are no specific instances discovered — it gives it lack of drama."
Analyst	"In this instance there may be a specific point. This thing relates to the question of whether you are loved or whether you are loved under certain conditions. The second is only any good to you if the first has had an inning. I am reminded also of the words 'cut off in midstream.' The idea is there of damage having been done to you."

The expression "cut off in midstream" was interpreted as symbolizing castration, and then as the patient's reaction to the end of the session. (p. 572). Here it is interpreted as representing an ego split resulting from a premature break in the continuity of maternal care. "Being loved under certain conditions" refers to frustration of id strivings to which the ego can adapt if sufficient ego supportive infant care has first "had an inning." Defective ego development, "damage," follows premature loss of environmental support for ego functions. Later the sudden loss of his mother's attention emerges as an illustration of a situation of loss of support. In the next association the patient makes a slip of the tongue, saying that he "attacked" mother's attention. In this way he implies that he had control over mother's preoccupation, rather than having been helplessly exposed to it.

Patient   "The idea came that it is intolerable to think of talking to someone and then they are not there and one is talking into an empty space."

Analyst   "There is always the problem for me whether to take up what you say or to concern myself with the fact of your talking."

Patient   "The question is whether you bother to listen or not."

Analyst   "There are two possibilities. One is that the other person goes away in fact, and the other is that the other person is preoccupied."

Patient   "I meant the second of these."

Analyst   "There can easily have been times when if you prattled the other person went off but if you talked in an interesting way they would stay."

Patient   "That must happen very often in childhood."

Analyst   "Perhaps it is the first time it happened that we are concerned with; someone who was preoccupied with you suddenly became preoccupied with something else, and to illustrate this I can take you to your own preoccupations that occur every now and again and which you sometimes describe now as going away from me here."

Patient   "Perhaps I tried to *attack*, I mean *attract*, mother's attention and got snubbed and felt ignored. So I decided to give no more opportunity for snubbing."

Analyst   "Probably you felt that you had snubbed me by going off."

Patient   "No, it doesn't strike me that way. When I come back I am not concerned about that. I can come back to continue the analysis. At times it would be nice here to be able to talk trivialities, not having to work hard."

Analyst   "You hardly believe that I could find you childish and still allow it and in fact you have never been able to do this here."

Patient   "A patient at the hospital described an interview with his analyst in which he had nothing to say so he talked about the opera. He did not believe it was right to do so and did it out of contempt for the analyst. 'You are no good so I will take you literally,' but he was surprised to find that what he said was taken seriously and something came of it."

Analyst   "As far as you bring yourself to analysis it cannot be expected that you will prattle because when you come to report as you do you can report content 'in the other aspect of talking.' "

Patient   "In a sense it is an absurd position because I come here to be able to do the thing that I cannot do in order to be able to do this very thing which in a way you are expecting me to do."

Analyst   "We are talking about your inability to hand over to me the care of the infant so that you could be the infant." *(See note p. 608.)*

Pause.

Patient   "It is rather difficult to go forward. I have got to make use of any absurd situation but that is the only way. I feel as if I have tried to be spontaneous but it has misfired."

Analyst   "I would like to remind you of the mistake you made earlier when you said *attack* instead of *attract*."

Patient   "Oh yes, I remember."

Analyst   "Possibly this is the one significant word of the session, the word 'attack.' "

Patient   "Yes. Also if I am spontaneous I feel as if I will not be accepted so I attack in order to restore the situation. This implies the idea that my temper attacks represent the destructive impulse directed at my mother because she would not listen to my prattling."

Analyst   "You may be speaking about a very high degree of anger."

Patient   "Again there is the risk of the end of this session here; this reproduces a situation in which mother or someone is not prepared to listen any longer."

Analyst   "By thinking things out in advance you protect yourself from intolerable situations. Intolerable partly because they produce rage."

Patient   "It is the same thing as plunging into water. If I am
not heard it is as if I jumped in in vain and I drown.
Self-control is necessary unless I am held."

Analyst   "It is as if you were speaking about actually jumping
onto someone's body and finding that they were not
really ready for you because they were thinking of
someone else. It would be no good if father let go the
bicycle not because he intended to help you to learn to ride
but because he became preoccupied with someone else."

Patient   "This reminds me of a game of hide and seek. As a
child I found the game of hide and seek very dangerous.
If a child is not found the people are preoccupied.
There is an intolerable sense of being abandoned."

Tuesday, 24 May

Patient   "Again I have nothing in my head. There might be
an hour when nothing comes. If I were to talk nothing
but trivialities that would be the same as nothing. I am
reminded that you said yesterday that perhaps there was
one significant word in the whole session so everything
else might just as well not have been said."

Analyst   "In a sense I fell into my own trap here by dealing
with content and for the time being ignoring the prattle
element."

Patient   "It is very rarely that things occur which are valuable
and they are more important than hours of discussion.
Dreams and mistakes are so rare."

Analyst   "The mistake was evidence that you exist apart from
yourself reporting. It was evidence of conflict within
yourself and of there being a contact somewhere.

_Prattling and the parapraxis are interpreted as deriva-
tives of the spontaneous "true self" in contrast to the
defensive "false self" talking about himself as about
another person. Contact with the "true self" implies
contact with unconscious conflict, manifested by the
parapraxis._

Patient	"I feel I ought to be trying to avoid the censorship but it is too difficult."
Analyst	"One thing we know is that you have a tremendous fear of being laughed at and of being cut off in the middle and you protect yourself from these dangers. Something that I note is that we are again talking about your direct relationship to your mother or to one other person who may frustrate you. Somewhere or other you are near the idea of being stopped in your relation to mother by father."
Patient	"In that connection I remember that father was in the habit of teasing. He would leave me inwardly very cross and out of that I think came a destructive wish so that I wanted to kill him. I was so annoyed that he would go on teasing."
Analyst	"We have to deal here with something in your father who avoided the direct clash with you and yet his antagonism came through in the indirect form of teasing. There is a magic in teasing which has an effect beyond the meaning of the words."
Patient	"There is something here appeals to me very much. It is like satire or sarcasm which I use to counter teasing. It can have a withering effect. It is a powerful weapon. Satire appeals to me much more than a direct assault. If annoyed I express myself through sarcasm which may be very subtle and which need not be recognized by the victim."
Analyst	"So through sarcasm and satire you have the power to wither your opponent and it is very important to you that you take for granted that I will not be sarcastic."
Patient	"It occurs to me that when I wonder whether you are effective or not, fully alive, it is because you are never angry; you never tease; you never are sarcastic, and never dogmatic; you will even be apologetic and ready to withdraw, to fold up in a profuse apology. If you are alive you must dominate more. On the whole you wait before making an interpretation. To come alive you would not wait. Also you never direct me. It is all negative."
Analyst	"This means that I am dead."

Patient   "This is in complete contrast with my father. When alive he did all these things that I have mentioned; took a strong line; so you are always mother who was not the sarcastic one, etcetera, etcetera.

Analyst   "So it is easy for you to have a relationship to mother here."

Patient   "It occurs to me that if you are going to be my mother that is no use because I have got one. It is father I have not got."

Analyst   "You will see that always I am either father or mother so that there is never more than two of us. You are therefore concerned with mother becoming preoccupied so that you feel abandoned or else with father who is dead. The idea of father interfering between you and mother does not occur unless we think of father being carried around alive inside you somewhere stopping you from prattling."

Patient   "Yes, father plays the role of censor. I only succeed by the game of pretending that what I say does not come from me." *Pause.* "One of the things about sarcasm and satire is that there can be a double meaning which the other person does not see; I visualize people hurt, actually wounded by sarcasm. It is more effective than a direct assault so I try to hurt that way."

Analyst   "It is important that it can be all done in a hidden manner."

Pause.

Patient   "One thing which is difficult to express is that if I want to praise because of love it is more hard to find a way to do it indirectly. I cannot find the equivalent of satire. When I cannot give presents it is because I am not there when I go to get a present in the shop. If I could do it in a veiled way it might work. For instance if I want to buy my wife flowers, in part that means that I want to show affection in a hidden way but there is a danger of being laughed at. The offer may be turned down. Somehow or other I have the picture of a small boy proud to present his mother a motion and then it is ignored and he suffers a crushing blow. This situation comes to my mind as an idea of what psychoanalysis expects and says: The child presents his mother with a motion and is very proud and it is ignored and disdained or disliked. That is my interpretation in psychoanalytic terms."

Analyst   "I do not want to lose the importance of the same thing in terms of babbling, prattling, and talking. Possibly also passing water."

Patient   "Passing water does not occur to me in the present context. All the things that I am saying could be expressed in the word 'lazy.' I know that psychoanalysis does not accept laziness as something existing in its own right and that laziness is an expression of hidden objections, etcetera, but a lot of my difficulties can be explained on a superficial basis as laziness. Playing tennis the other day, for instance, and not doing well. One reason was that I was lazy. I did not run towards where I knew the ball would come. Instead I substituted the idea of being in the right place. But then I would find that I must do and not only know."

Analyst   "In some way or other this avoids the risk of failure."

Patient   "I thought : 'If I go to hit the ball, that is all right if I succeed, but if not, that is silly. If I think the idea that I ought to be more to the left but I don't actually move, then I can explain the failure.' The end result is ridiculous when I hit nowhere near where the ball is, but I avoid in this way a more subtle danger and avoid some kind of blaming of myself. Also in serving, if I throw up the ball in the wrong place and I know that it is wrong, I do nevertheless hit it. After all, it might be all right. The alternative is to show that I cannot even throw the ball up."

Analyst   "You could be saying all this in terms of talking, couldn't you? So that you avoid making the mistake like the word 'attack.' "

Patient   "It is back to the same thing. I don't want to let go. I don't want to move to where the ball will be. Moving means letting go. Standing still with the idea of movement is safe. Moving means letting go the place where I was. Talking freely means taking a risk. Everything is out of control." (At this time he was playing with a rubber band and started flicking it, making a noise, and this kind of behavior is very unusual with him during the sessions.)

Analyst   "There seems to be a live father who dominates and who prevents you from being a child with spontaneous movements."

Patient   "The idea of carrying around father seems to me to be just about right. He is always ready to pounce if I make a false move or an indiscretion."

Analyst   "Which means that you cannot be your real self."

Patient   "It's odd. It's as if I have a father instead of a superego. Or perhaps that's what a superego means."

Analyst   "Well, there can be a pathological superego."

Patient   "At times I do feel almost aware of carrying father round with me. When I say I am angry with myself, I mean that this father is angry with me. When I say I am discussing something with myself, it is this father and I who are discussing. Sometimes I feel almost as if I am father."

Analyst   "The difficulty is that in your memories of your father you are not able to think of him as entering into your world."

Patient   "That is certainly a valid criticism of father. He could never enter into anyone else's world at all. People simply had to go into his world."

Friday, 27 May

Patient   "The question is where to start. How far can I get by conscious effort? At first here in analysis was the hope. Now too little happens here."

Analyst   "I think you are wondering whether to get up and walk around while here."

Patient   "That would make what goes on here less important. The ideal is when the subject is about sex — sometimes I feel like not bothering about sex, to wipe out all that. But shelving is not solving." *Pause.* "This is incidental. I might talk about abstract ideas and aims but that is unproductive. It is especially difficult at home when I talk and my wife does not answer and I get angry."

Analyst   "There is a contrast between talking about things and discussing problems."

Patient   "There is a barrier somewhere. I need to have some way of tearing down the barrier. After the break the barrier seems to be bigger."

Analyst   "You were, I know, disappointed last time at the end. You expected something suddenly to happen. We are looking for the reason for the barrier."

Pause

Patient   "I had an idea then. I was in a dream world and I was presenting a written abstract or report. If I had to write everything down that would be very difficult because I dislike this sort of thing. I was to leave the report on your desk. The report was illegible. I am in a dilemma here. If I do not talk I feel frustrated in the treatment. This is a matter for rage. The abstract idea occurs to me that a perfect sexual relationship depends on someone else entering into my world. I need not talk then or wake. It is the same here. You ought to know what is in my mind, and what I am feeling." (Probably asleep.) "I am toying with the idea of sleep to see how far you can get without my saying anything. In practice this is silly." (Material not recorded.)

Analyst   "I am reminding you here of your father's inability to enter into your imaginative world."

Patient   "Oh yes, I had forgotten. He talked a great deal. It was his pet hobby."

Analyst   "Which means that you all listened."

Patient   "I am trying to get away from my father's intellectual approach. The ideal is to be able to play. This is still unattainable for me. Tension in myself is part of the effort to get away from the intellectual talking about play. The more I try the less playful I become. I know I am boring because I talk instead of playing. I am not able to effect the use of substitutes for the actual. I had an idea then that talking about hitting you is like hitting you. I am not certain what I am hitting you for."

Analyst   "This is an example of the sort of sudden action that you fear."

Patient   "It is as if you are the obstruction. You are not lifting the barrier. Hitting you would be to force you to do something."

Analyst   "In that case you had the fear that you would find you had suddenly hit your father."

Patient   "I cannot recollect having actually done it. I certainly wanted to. He was difficult to hit because he showed no resistance."

Analyst   "He was opposed to the idea of opposition."

Patient   "If you hit father he would fold up. He would just not be there. It is different in playing where aggression might enter in.

Analyst   "In the playing with me that you describe we were bashing without aim."

Patient   "I am tempted to remember a discussion at the hospital about relief of tension by finding ways of expressing aggression. It is of no use. Aggression is not there."

Analyst   "That is about father I think."

Patient   "Yes, he really was a pacifist."

Analyst   "And at the same time you had no brothers for mutual loving and hating and pushing around."

Patient   "I feel that that is what I am doing to you, pushing and pushing. I feel though that you would be damnably peaceful, limp like cotton wool; nothing firm. If I hit you my arm would be left there; it would not come back, but I had a respect for my father's strength. With you hitting would be out of place."

Analyst   "You never seen to be able to find anyone to match your strength against."

Tuesday, 31 May

Patient   "Two things occur to me. The first has to do with realizing more what you mean about my true self not coming so that I censor everything before speaking. This makes it all impersonal and there is no excitement or anger or elation and I do not want to get up and hit you. It is only what we talk about, and nothing is felt or demonstrated. Others are personal, angry, and avoid getting worked up. This is a shortcoming but it cannot be manipulated. The second thing is about last night — well, it's hardly worth talking about. It doesn't add anything to the situation, but reproduces the present state of affairs. It has to do with my wife and her boy friend. In a dream my wife's mother was to blame for everything. I refused to see her. I have felt like that sometimes. In the dream she was all remote and impersonal. I have not much feeling of dislike of my mother-in-law — just annoyance."

Analyst   "In the dream you and your mother-in-law come into a clash. Here is someone real and external, playing the part which you cannot easily give to your father."

Patient   "I am thinking of my feelings here. The only emotional expression seems to be sleep, which is going away — negative expression."

Analyst   "You remember that once you had the idea of brushing past me and rushing out."

Patient   "My attitude then was the same as my wife's. I don't want to get involved. Here I am dependent and I find I need to come."

Analyst   "One part of you is in the way between your true self and me."

Patient   "I often wish I could add something to psychoanalysis so as to get dramatic responses. The idea is to break through the barrier of lack of feeling. My mother-in-law tries to be friendly but this makes me shudder and I keep her distant. She irritates me. I keep picturing the idea of breaking down the barrier. It is like breaking a dam; there is a flood pent up behind; a flood of water. When I first came back I said I would like to be able to cry. It is all part of it. I need something outside to break it down. I have no courage to do it on my own. There is a need for dynamics. For emotional situations. To bring on the crying. But it only happens occasionally and always away from here. We ought to plan to break down the barriers. I picture you either unwilling to do something to unleash the forces or not able to do it." *Pause.* "I am still thinking the same, like walking on the edge of a wall exploring the perimeter."

Analyst   "You have always said that you dislike the idea of the transference."

Patient   "I am not quite sure how genuine that was. Or was it just a phase? The girl friend had some influence over me then when I said that. She despised homosexuality.

So my hostility to the transference was part of a need to demonstrate to her that I was a man not needing a positive transference to a man. You see I had to take her point of view into account."

Pause.

Analyst "You have described a great deal of pent up feeling and that behind the dam are tears of grief."

Patient "And also love. My wife would not be able to help. She can only patch up the wall which leaks. My wife would try to oppose the idea of breaking down a barrier. She would rather have me bury what is difficult to get at. She is not concerned with getting it out. The question is, will it happen and also is it necessary?"

Analyst "The barrier is between you and me and one of the things that it avoids is the idea of my loving you."

Patient (Sleepiness.) "Only odd fragments which are difficult to bring out. A feature was that there was less control and so things were much faster."

Analyst "We must assume that the lessening of control produces water, peeing, and crying."

Patient "Also slowness of speech belongs to the control. This explains my causing everyone to be bored."

Analyst "It causes an even rate of talk because no impulse comes through."

Pause. (Probably asleep.)

Patient "Thought there is completely lost. Something was dramatized. Something to do with the attitude that the talking has to babbling. My mother-in-law is the opposite to myself in this controlled thinking. She talks fast all the time without worrying what she says. A lot of it is obvious nonsense. She says the first thing that comes to her head and so I dislike it because I envy her. It is stupid but people stop and listen whereas with me they get bored."

Analyst "I suppose what she does comes straight from herself like your prattling that you described as a feature of your early childhood."

Patient "I feel restless as if I have something to break through or is it that I want to be restless? Or is it just the idea of wanting to be restless?"

Analyst "By this time everything is impersonal and this has

been a feature all your life." (Here I referred to Wordsworth's "Ode on the Intimations of Immortality from Recollections of Early Childhood" — "Shades of the prison house," etcetera, but to my surprise he was not acquainted with this.)

Wordsworth's poem refers to the memories of carefree spontaneous happiness of infancy and childhood. In practice this of course includes some degree of retrospective idealization. The particular passage to which Dr. Winnicott refers is:

> But trailing clouds of glory do we come
>> From God, who is our home :
> Heaven lies about us in our infancy
> Shades of the prison-house begin to close
>> Upon the growing Boy . . .

The "prison-house" can be interpreted as the ego boundary of which the growing child becomes aware, in contrast to earlier primary narcissism. The passage thus refers to the development from the pleasure principle to the reality principle. Later in the poem Wordsworth stresses the value of retention of childhood memories:

> Though nothing can bring back the hour
> Of splendour in the grass, or glory in the flower;
> We will grieve not, but rather find
> Strength in what remains behind;
> In the primal sympathy
> Which having been must ever be . . .

Patient "Today I was playing with my daughter. A child has easy spontaneity. At the start I envied her ability to rely on herself. So my mother-in-law has retained something of childhood."

Analyst "It can be annoying when adults retain something of childhood."

Patient "When father did all the talking it left no one any scope. I felt hemmed in. No one had any time for me when I talked and so it was best not to say anything."

Analyst   "I am reminding you of the changeover from prattling to your need to think first so that the content would be appreciated and people would not laugh and you would not feel ashamed. It is rather like a stammer, this deliberate talk of yours, which holds people."

Patient   "Even now there seems to be hidden excitement. It is touch and go. Will the barrier break through? When I am safely out of sight? (Here the patient put his foot on the floor.)

Analyst   "You put your foot on the floor and I think that you feel at this moment that you could act, as for instance walk away. That is an expression of your true self."

Patient   "Yes. It is part of the restlessness. This is the crucial moment, the chance of a lifetime, and it is missed."

Analyst   "Lying on the couch has to do with your attitude."

Patient   "Yes, lying is symbolical of being controlled. It is peaceful and that is not what I want. I picture your suggestion that I should get up and play a game."

Wednesday, 1 June

Patient   "For the first time I feel that I am here myself. That means that I was unaware of time at the end of last session. I got carried away."

Analyst   "Your true self has its own time, in contrast to your false self which keeps in touch with clocks."

Allowing himself to become unaware of time illustrates "becoming the infant and allowing the analyst to keep track of time for him, thus providing secondary process function, representing infant care. (See pp. 559-560, 577, 597.) The maturational significance of such controlled regression is discussed in this book by Bruno Bettelheim (Chapter 9).

Patient   "When my daughter wakes I notice that she has no idea of the time. She imagines it is day in the middle of the night. Also I have been waking less regularly lately. Usually I know exactly what time it is. I had no idea of the time today and was awakened by chance by a noise. After I left here yesterday I felt excited. The barrier was almost broken through. The question still arises about occupying time by talking but there is no longer the same pressure. In the train I had nothing to read and it was difficult to know what to do unless I slept, but I noticed that most people are not worried by this and they are willing to sit an hour or more with no problem in regard to the occupation of the time. There is some progress here in that I am less worried. At the hospital where I was a patient I was preoccupied with the difficulty of filling in time. However could anyone live on his own, I felt. How could one cope with this problem of time? There is no question of idle chat which is sufficient for most people."

Analyst   "You are telling me that for the first time you might be able to be alone which is the only satisfactory basis for making relationships."

The origin of relatedness from narcissism is described in Dr. Winnicott's paper, "The capacity to be alone," (1958) in The maturational processes and the facilitating environment, *1965. In this paper Dr. Winnicott refers to the stage of narcissism as one in which the infant is "alone" in the sense of being undifferentiated from the mothering person. The capacity for a separate identity develops out of this kind of "aloneness" by introjection of the maternal object.*

Patient   "It seems a bit of a pity to have stopped yesterday when everything was in full flow. The problem is how to get back." (Here the patient had his pipe in his hands, playing with it.) "I wonder how long it will take to break through the protective barrier. Is it your fault or mine that it takes so long? Also is the treatment just beginning or just ending? How does one know?"

Analyst   "This matter of the barrier and its removal is not something suddenly happening now. There has been a gradual development in the course of your analysis which has brought you to your present position."

Pause.

Patient   "In that pause I had confused thoughts. It was abstract and could not possibly be reproduced."

Analyst   "This unintegrated state that you describe at any rate is your true self."

Patient   "In this confused thought is extreme annoyance, aggression, someone lying down in or on a bed, I don't know who it is. The idea came from a patient admitted today into hospital without my being told. I was dramatizing the scene. I fantasied that I went into the ward in a temper, removed the clothes off the bed, and pushed the patient out. I could see that it might also have to do with this couch here. I might turn up at the wrong time and you would be annoyed and turn me out. In a way that's what you did at the end of last hour. I was thrown out. Something that fits in here is the annoyance that I feel when I get home late at night and find my wife already gone to bed. I never complain of course but somehow I feel she ought to wait up."

Analyst   "The center of all this is the reaction you had to being thrown out at the end of last hour just when you yourself had turned up. You were in a vulnerable state."

Patient   "Something fits in here. I had to turn my daughter out of bed this morning. My wife never gets up till I call her twice. This annoys me although I am awake anyway. I always hope that she will get up and get the breakfast sometimes but it's no good making a fuss; that doesn't get one anywhere. Also at hospital this morning I was in a mood to discharge patients. I felt annoyed that they were there occupying beds. At the time it seemed quite reasonable but now it is obvious that this was related to the feeling that I was turned out from here."

Analyst   "There is also the question of the end of the treatment and your feelings about this."

Patient   "Also there is the whole question of discharging patients. What is the basis for turning them out? Is it for my sake or for theirs? Do we want them to be well or become independent as soon as possible or to be rid of them?" *Pause.* "There is also the feeling of wondering whether I shall change dramatically so that others notice it. Will there be results? Others must be affected by differences in myself. How different am I for others?

At the hospital where I was a patient people asked:
'What is wrong with you? Why do you need analysis?'
I could never explain. Would people possibly notice
an easing of tension if I were easier to talk to? The
crucial test is, will my wife notice? Probably she won't.
She has made up her mind that I am no use. I can't
expect her to change. It's too late."

Analyst   "Your daughter would be the one who would notice."

Patient   "About her I feel I had to wait for her to start playing
and I found it difficult to follow her. I kept on feeling,
'I don't want to play or read,' and was irritable, but
now I feel less pressed and I can even enjoy playing.
I don't know if she has noticed."

Analyst   "I think she must notice it if you enjoy it a little."

Patient   "I find I can now begin at last to enjoy my younger
daughter. She has not come into the picture before. Her
existence was only of academic importance. I never
felt that she belonged to me. In a way I would have
been really pleased to have found that she was not my
child. Nevertheless I can just feel able to anticipate a
change here. I am not sure I can attribute this to
psychoanalysis. It may be just an intellectual process.
I don't want to decide to take her on. A change in my
relation to her must happen to me emotionally."

Analyst   "To decide to take her on would be operating from
the intellectual which for you is the false self."

Patient   "This applies to all relationships. It is a matter of
deciding and then it's no good. This reminds me of
another person, which is mother. I feel guilty at having
neglected her recently. In fact I have not thought of her.
Why should I? But of course she pays. She is a sup-
porter and to that extent I can't cut her out. For a
long time she did not seem to be a mother-figure to
me. I blotted out the idea and did not even want to
call her mother. I don't know what to call her and this
fits in with the idea that she is not a mother-figure for
me."

Analyst   "The mother-figure for you has been your analyst since
a certain point in the analysis."

Patient   "I would like to know when mother ceased to be a
mother-figure. Can you help me?"

Analyst   I picked out various samples, such as when he went to his mother and found a baby sister on her lap and strained to stand on his own and also when at some point his prattle was not accepted, etcetera.

Patient   "This suggests to me that father was not able to play and he took everything too seriously so I had to try to be grown up. I have occasionally speculated about orphans. Have they the same difficulty when they have no parents of their own? This is an academic point.

Analyst   "When you have parents that you can take into yourself a lot depends on whether these parents were rigid in some way or other or whether they were adaptable. If you have only rigid parents to take in, you are rather in the position of orphans who have lacked some human aspect in their early care. You have been using me in the analysis to displace your mother and your father at various times."

Thursday, 2 June

Analyst   (Patient quarter of an hour late.)

Patient   "I find myself in a quandary. I ought to be able to start in a different way, since two days ago I seemed to find a new way of working. I don't like to go back to the old way of having nothing to say, and the formal opening, etcetera, etcetera. I ought to start out directly. I know this is not a realistic feeling, etcetera, etcetera. I had the idea that it is important to break through the barrier problem, to find the quickest way. You said the more formal approach has achieved something of itself, but nevertheless it must be slower. One thing I noticed this morning was that I was more aware of having dreamed. I forgot the dreams soon after waking but not immediately, and I was conscious of a lot having gone on. I had the feeling 'this is more like normal.' "

Analyst   "You felt there was life going on in you while you slept, so that the dissociation we spoke of the other day was less complete. So part of the function of the dreaming was achieved, the formation of a bridge between the inner world and waking life."

Patient   "I suppose I could have tried, I could have written down the dreams, but it seems to be a part of the psychoanalytic technique to dismiss any form of aid except just talking — it's easier to believe in work done by other methods — especially as I distrust talk as something that father was good at, you might say to the exclusion of other things. I remember the recent discussion when I turned down the idea of my being an analyst; this was more a feeling of hostility to the idea of talking."

Analyst   "It does seem that if a conscious effort is made to help the analyst there can come about new defenses, but I would not say that there is no place at all for conscious effort."

Patient   "I would like to find another way, for instance to find that you know what's happening, something less laborious than my writing things down and then reproducing them."

Analyst   "The bridge provided has to allow of two way traffic. I am not sure at present whether I am talking to your true or your false self, using the language of recent sessions."

Patient   "It's the false self. People hear in two different ways — one might say two aspects of the personality like intellectual and emotional. It's feasible to be distracted and yet be talked to at the same time — one part takes the emotional and the other takes this intellectual aspect of the same sentence. When things go well both recognize the situation, both work together. In a way I feel concern about lack of emotion — I can only be intellectual."

Analyst   "At the start when you talked, this talking had its own importance, as I have said, apart altogether from content. It meant you were alive, awake, eager."

Pause.

Patient   "I felt anxious just then. One difficulty is that a breakthrough might release so much and then I would become changeable with each emotional facet as it presents so I keep busy talking and this gives no time for me to take in what you say. I have a vision of being careful not to do all the talking so that you might not bother to listen."

Analyst   "What would happen then? This would be one-sided like the alternative of waiting for you to provide all the talking."

Patient   "If I were to talk without inhibition there would be no point in my coming here. I could talk to myself. I had a thought about last night when it was difficult to talk with my wife. The thought was that there was no reason why I should stop if I were talking without inhibition, going over the same things and not progressing with an idea. There would be no point in stopping. I would get no pleasure. There is no emotion in it."

Analyst   "I would remind you here that you were late and I am not sure whether this had any meaning to it today. It could be something that is more nearly related to yourself than your talking is."

Patient   "No, I think it was not significant or perhaps it was just rude. I can see that I could have saved a few minutes but the important thing is that I could have been more worried about being late. In that way it does come in. I felt coming here, 'I wonder if Winnicott is offended?' This is a new departure. Previously I have been only concerned with the idea of being punished. This time it was less the effect on myself and more the effect on you. Would you be upset? Today therefore there is some point in apologizing. Previously if I apologized it was only to cover up what had happened."

Analyst   "You seem to be less under a compulsion."

Patient   "My feelings are less remote than they were two years ago when it was simply intellect. I felt I ought to be concerned. Now I do not think about it but if I am late I am concerned about upsetting you." *Pause.* "I was thinking then, I wonder if others will notice the change that came over me in the last few days."

Analyst   "You would like this. It would feel more real."

Patient   "Especially if my wife noticed the change, that is what would really be the acid test of progress, she being so unwilling to recognize psychoanalysis as useful." *Pause.* (Right finger to mouth.) "I was feeling then that I recognized there is a danger in being concerned about others' feelings. Previously when I had a more intellectual concern I could afford to ignore what others thought. I could say 'be damned' to everyone else. But if I share with others then I become more concerned and must expect to have my imperfections noticed. I used to dismiss all this by saying I am ill, but now that I am not ill any longer I have to face up to being imperfect if it is me."

Analyst   "There is something perfect because unused or unexperienced that you wish to preserve as perfect in yourself, and if you are not ill then what you fear is that you will be found to have failed in the preservation of this perfection." (This interpretation was almost certainly wrong at this point.)

Patient   "I do not seem to be concerned at the moment with the idea of breaking something perfect. I mean that I cannot use that just now. I was thinking of something else and I only clocked in halfway when you were speaking. I was remembering that this afternoon I started to read a book about the eighteenth century in U.S.A. The characters were dressed in the style. I remembered that I had forgotten to bring this book back with me from the hospital and so I shall not have it tonight, therefore, and this is the thing, I shall have to plan what to read. This is a minor catastrophe. It is a story of a tall and thin man who studied at Harvard. He gets drafted into army life which changes his whole career. My own job is due to end. A change in my life is therefore coming through the agency of forces outside my control. I have the same difficulty here sometimes about abrupt changes." (Right index finger to mouth.) "Also I was forgetting the important point is escape. Reading provides an escape for me especially at the present time because there is something to escape from, the environment."

Analyst   "What do you feel would happen if you were well this evening and if your wife were to respond?"

Patient   "Firstly, I would talk more easily. Secondly, she would be more interested in my hospital affairs. Thirdly, I would be more interested in her doings. Conversation would flow. We would be happy. We would sit and chat for one or two hours. But what will happen is that we will talk with strain and tension or there will be silent tension. For me I feel silence like an active denial of talking. It is a deliberate act. If I reprimand her she will have nothing to say. It means I do not want to talk. I have gone away."

Pause.

Analyst   "You think that we are near the time for stopping and you do not wish to embark on something new."

Patient   "Yes, I was thinking if my wife saw a change in me how important it would be."

Analyst   "But here as you are implying is the one place where you cannot act. I would say this, that the one thing you cannot do is to act not-acting."

Monday, 6 June

Analyst   I announced at the start that I would need to go out for ten minutes towards the end of the session.

Patient   "Ten minutes ago I can say that I did not want to come. Coming is a nuisance. Now that it has become less urgent I only come because of the job being incomplete. There is less drive and then I have the thought of the time that my job ends in ten days so that alterations will have to be made in the times, and it suddenly came over me how soon this is. It will be convenient if I can stop instead of making alterations. I do not feel prepared to discuss them just at the moment. Last time it seemed that the stream of excitement dried up so that I am now not sure whether or not I am on the brink of a change. This gives me a reason for wanting to go on. I think I unconsciously am alarmed at what was happening and so unconsciously I dried up. It was a good example a couple of nights ago showing me that I have still a long way to go. A garden fête at the hospital, and I felt out of place, but I could see everyone else being gay. When I returned to the small room with two or three others in it I felt safe again. Again I seem to be drying up. There seems to be a picture of myself lying down and finding words coming out but in fact nothing was happening. Today all the time I am feeling

I would like to be liberated from here but the question is, would I be able to enjoy the liberty?"

Analyst   "The question of liberty here does not arise at the present moment."

Patient   "I seem to be aware of an ending."

Analyst   "An important thing comes into that, which is that the operation of time is traumatic to you. When your true self appears then the only meaning for time that you can endure is if you begin and end something yourself. This would be one of the blocks in the way at the moment that you realize that your true self is in danger of being affected by my time which goes by the clock and this danger is very real."

Patient   "This gives some relief. Even as a patient at the hospital I see now that I was very much affected by my dismissal at the end of the hour although at the time I was not aware of this. Now I realize that I experienced fury at being stopped; extreme annoyance, and I was even aware of this when my sessions were cut from three to two."

Analyst   "You are telling me then that fury has been going on inside you all this time but that it never shows."

Patient   "It makes me think of a situation in which my father would set a timetable for playing. This was uselesss. I could not play when he said it was time to play and stop when he said it was time to stop. My father would sometimes say 'You can't play now.' "

Pause.

Analyst   "There is one thing left over from last time and I am wondering whether it was important. At a certain point you took your right finger to your mouth. I am not quite sure when it came but it might have been significant. I think that it was your left finger that you sucked."

Patient   "No, I think it was my right finger I sucked. I know about this because there is a scar on that finger and I remember that I cut it and used the fact that it was difficult to suck it while it was bandaged as an artificial break to the finger-sucking.

Analyst   "I do not know of course how you came to hurt your finger but in a way you describe what seems to stand instead of a threat that it would be damaged if you did not give up finger-sucking."

Patient "I do not remember the accident but it fits in here that I have been smoking less for a week. I have often intended to reduce smoking but never with success. Whenever I set myself to stop, something else said to me: 'Why stop?' but for the last few days it has been different. Much easier to stop. I allowed myself to run out of cigarettes and I did not find it distressing and afterwards was able to control smoking. There seems to be a logical association between smoking and finger-sucking; both come in response to stress. Also when you said that you would be breaking the hour for ten minutes, first of all I felt, 'Good, that's something novel. Now I will be able to have a smoke.' Now it occurs to me that the first reaction was to deny that I was alarmed at what you said. Your going out of the room would leave me with the problem, what shall I do?"

Analyst "One can say that the cigarette is half symbolical of me; something that can be used instead of me, but half of it is an indication of stress. Something used compulsively. So it seems possible that what you did with your finger was significant. And also that my breaking into the hour cannot possibly be good from your point of view although you seemed to accept it very easily. It makes you look round for ways of dealing with strain." (At this point he was playing a game, banging his little fingers together.)

Pause.

Patient "I cannot remember when your holidays start. The question is, will it be worthwhile fitting in something, making new arrangements, when I start to do the new job, as this will only give a little while and it might not be worth the bother. I shall know whether I have the job on a permanent basis by September when you return. I have a feeling that it would be good not to try these four weeks so as to make a longer break in which I might be able to find out if I want to come or not. The question is, is this honest? Is a long time away really a help in making a decision of this kind? I remember that you once said that all the years between the two treatments I had kept my development in abeyance so that from the point of view of a treatment they were wasted years. There is also the thing that coming along means a constant probing into the private life."

Analyst "Included in all this is the idea that you might really be able to come to your own conclusion about this matter."

Patient "Yes, but I am not clear about whether I just do not want to come or whether I am trying to avoid something."

Analyst "There is one thing that we have been talking about which you may be trying to avoid which has to do with fury which is going on inside you and which is not felt at the appropriate moments."

Pause.

Patient "The idea occurred to me then that I might have thoughts that belonged to me. It would take time to explain it. Something *could* be kept to *myself*. It is not absolutely necessary to bring Winnicott into it. This is all part of a gesture to not come."

Analyst "Not coming would seem to indicate that you cannot be sure of the right to keep something secret."

Patient "Earlier on I used to talk all the time and try to say everything. It never occurred to me not to want to say something. So this is a novel idea of having secret thoughts. In the relationship with the girl every detail came into the analysis. It always felt to me that it all belonged to Winnicott. Now I seem to want to do something for myself. Talking here about things is a deterrent to freedom outside."

Analyst "So this is really what you mean about not coming. It is part of your wish to find out what you are like."

Patient "Previously everything was talked out and I had no desire for privacy."

Analyst "I think the point was that you had nowhere to put it."

In a review of "Memories, dreams, reflections," by C. G. Jung (Int. Journal of Psycho-Analysis, *Vol. 45, 1964, pp. 450–455*), Dr. Winnicott points out that in so far as there is splitting of the ego we find dissociation rather than *repression, and that under those circumstances the patient feels as though he has no place to hide secrets. The capacity to repress and to hide secrets depends on a certain degree of integration and synthesis, "unity," of the personality.*

Patient	"The intellectual was simply an area for discussion; not a place where anything could be hidden."
Analyst	"So it seems that you have turned up and you have an inside and an outside."
Patient	"If I were to change my analyst I have always felt that all would be wasted but that has to do with my intellectual self. The only place in which I had to hide was in someone else that I would confide in. I am reminded that as you went out of the room, though I was prepared for it, it came as a surprise. I was at a loss. I rationalized it by noticing that I had forced you into offering me a cigarette. I was amused because of the way in which this indicated loss and deprivation."
Analyst	"The cigarette that I offered really got in the way of your fury."
Patient	"Yes, I nearly refused as an angry gesture." *Pause.* "It's difficult to decide what to say next. Now I have dealt with the mechanism of interruption, I now have to deal with the interruption itself, which is more difficult. I have to start all over again. I can resent the idea of being compelled to talk."
Analyst	"The idea of being compelled to talk seems to rule out the idea of your talking because you want to."
Patient	"Also whether I want to stop or not. The thing is, will I find myself in a situation in which I need to come; something to do with time? I never really enjoy myself because it is dependent on my coming here."
Analyst	"It becomes more and more clear that not coming has to do with your discovery of yourself and of your capacity to keep a secret, and it is only from not coming that you can discover a spontaneous wish to come."
Patient	"That seems true but it is not real for just now. I cannot recognize that I might just want to come; something I am not used to yet."

Tuesday, 7 June

Patient "Nothing seems to come. Having found a possibility of talking differently there ought to be another opening and I feel disappointed." (Here the patient put his right fingers to his mouth.)

Analyst "I feel that you do not give yourself time. If you are communicating from your intellectual self, then of course there is no point in waiting and it is natural for you to engage immediately on arrival. If, however, it is your emotional self that is here, then it is unlikely that you would have the impulse to speak exactly at the same moment as I become available."

Patient "Yes, it is a kind of protest about there being only the three sessions in the whole week. If I am operating emotionally then I must have the right to come when I want, so that to be expected to start straight off is an adjustment to try to meet an unsatisfactory timetable. What I fear is that I will protest by not talking at all for the whole hour."

Analyst "It is like letting me know that you want to be away but coming in order to let me know."

Patient "If I do not start I have a definite fear that I won't be able to begin. Each second provides a mounting difficulty and I also talk because I can't bear the time wasted though of course trivialities may be a waste too. This applies in my relationship with other people. I have a need to find something to say though I probably feel like saying nothing for hours. I would like a relationship in which it was not necessary to talk or there could be a jumble of words and phrases and that would be no use. This happens with my wife. I try to say what comes, try to be natural, but there is nothing but a jumble of ideas. This seems artificial, glib. I am talkative, trying to be lighthearted, but the result is confusion. This is why people lose interest in me. At times that could happen here and you would not be able to take in what I was saying because it would be too confused. That is why I edit everything."

Analyst "But editing produces annoyance in you."

Patient "I really want to talk like a child; like my daughter, for instance. It is sometimes difficult to follow her but that of course is common with children of her age."

Analyst "With you as a child I am not sure that there was anyone who recognized that it was natural for your conversation to be difficult to follow."

Patient "Possibly I was rebuked for nonsense. Probably by father, who would call me long-winded. There was some special time at nine or ten, but it may have happened earlier as well."

Analyst "You see how concerned you are about my attitude if you should talk like a child. And child talking is really more like acting or doing, whereas in the conversation of an adult the content is more important."

Pause.

Patient "Now as before I am trying to get away from the intellectual approach which is a barrier but in doing so I am in danger of falling asleep. I am not sure if I can afford to neglect this intellectual compulsion if I am to keep awake."

Analyst "Going to sleep, however, is really you."

Patient "But it blots out everything else. If I were to sleep the whole hour — "

Analyst "Even that would be something. You would not sleep anywhere. It is because you are here."

Patient "Perhaps I would sleep anywhere and I have noticed a tendency both with my mother and with my mother-in-law. However, here there comes the social need for me to be awake. I feel I do not want to bother to be sociable. I have gone to sleep in that way and it has annoyed my wife who says it is bad manners." *Pause.* "One difficulty about sleep, I risk wasting the hour and feeling guilty about letting you down, so I can keep awake to some extent for your sake."

Analyst "But you cannot take it for granted that I am here unless your intellect is active — (Here the patient slept and snored, and then was suddenly awake.)

Patient "It does seem not only guilt; also a challenge to you expressing contempt."

Analyst "That is you and is real." (Renewed sleep.)

Patient "It seems as if you are challenging me to go to sleep if I want to as if you are giving permission but it won't get us anywhere. Talking is the medium of progress."

Analyst   "This reminds me of your father."

Patient   "Yes —— um —— um — " *Pause.* (Probably asleep.)
"Especially disconcerting that I keep thinking of things
about hospital and wasting the short time I have here
asleep." *Pause.* "Sometimes I think about hospital problems to avoid something else because I can say about
them that I need not discuss them, but if it is not about
work I feel I must tell you."

Analyst   "You as editor have strong views on what is suitable for
publication here."

Patient   "Like yesterday when I said I don't want to come and
I feel guilt about it. It's rather subtle but it's not the
same thing showing that it is not worthwhile coming."

Analyst   "In regard to your intellectual self there is the editor
and I am interested in what kind of editor he is, and
what does he think important?"

   Pause. (Momentary sleep.)

Patient   "I had a dream then that as an alternative to saying
nothing I was talking too much and people were
annoyed at the liberty I was taking, expecting them to
listen to me going on talking."

Analyst   "You are therefore talking about curbing a compulsion
just like stealing." (Probably asleep.) "You have a claim
on me to listen to you and a claim on my time." *Pause.*
"I would add, a claim to be able to waste my time; as a
symptom this makes sense and indicates that you feel
you have been deprived in all these ways."

*The claims on the analyst's time and attention, against
which the patient defends himself, are derived from
deprivation. The capacity to make such claims on the
environment, in this instance on the analyst, indicates
that at the time of the original deprivation the patient
was able to perceive that the failure came from outside
himself. Thus when he reaches a repetition of the experience of deprivation he is able to seek a remedy for it from
outside of himself. Dr. Winnicott has described this process in "The Psychotherapy of Character Disorders,"
(1963), in* The maturational processes and the facilitating environment *(1965). In that paper he points out*

*that it is an essential part of the therapy of character dis-
orders for the patient to become angry at the repetition
in the transference of original experiences of deprivation.
This correlates with the next interpretation, about the
"fury" which is thought to be one determinant of the
symptom of sleeping during the analytic hour. (See note
p. 595.)*

Patient "In spite of all this there is a deadlock. It is either hospital problems or sleep. What I am concerned with is the
present and the question that I am asking is, how does
this sleeping join up with now?" (By this time he was
fully awake.)

Analyst "At this point I can remind you of the fury which you
found exists in you and which does not find expression
and which is likely to be underlying the symptom of
sleep."

Patient "It's funny, I was just thinking that I was protecting
you from an outburst of temper. I was thinking, I have
shown very little temperament here. There has been a
half-hidden feeling which I now see as extreme fury. I
fear a violent outburst. Perhaps I may find myself expressing tremendous anger which ought to have been
expressed perhaps with father at an earlier date. Somehow I missed the boat."

Analyst "I can now speak to you again about father standing
between you and mother. I would remind you of the cut
finger which you produced as an accident and used for
breaking yourself of finger-sucking, being as it were
unable to fight father coming in between and threatening you, although in fact you felt the threat. Father
missed the boat as a strong person coming between you
and mother and between you and what was symbolical
of mother."

Patient "If he got in between it was in a way that was not
recognizable at the time. I feel restless now. I really do
not want to lie down. That means falling asleep. I would
really like to turn over on my face."

Analyst "Evidently you have taken it as assumed that I have
prohibited your turning over on your face." **(This is
what we have been leading up to for years.)**

Turning over on his face represented identification with his father, in intercourse with his mother.

Patient "I remember that at about twelve to fourteen years old lying on my back meant death. It was when I was at school. It seemed that it meant being helpless, lying in a coffin. It was all right if I was awake, outdoors under a tree, but in bed dangerous."

Analyst "Did it perhaps get connected up with the woman's position in intercourse?"

Patient "No, I don't think it's that at all."

Analyst "Then we look at other things. I would like to remind you as I have done before that in the first analysis you had a very important symptom which was the inability to lie down, and that the end of that analytic phase came when you were able to lie down and to tolerate the anxiety associated with it, which at that time had to do with having been satisfied as an infant by a perfect mother, the satisfaction producing annihilation of the object. In other words, you had no knowledge until the analysis that if you waited there would be a return of desire and therefore a return of the object of your desires." (On previous occasions when I have reminded the patient of this he had been vaguely able to remember but the reminder did not produce any new material.)

Patient "It had a special significance then because it was so near to my actual fear of lying down which persisted up to that date from the twelve-year-old period."

Analyst "I wonder if you are able to tell me anything about the twelve to fourteen years."

Patient "At that time my father began to be ill but he did not know. The first time was at a fête when someone was making a lightning sketch of him and I suddenly saw that he looked old and tattered. I remember that I was completely shaken. He did not look well and I realized that I could no longer take his being alive for granted. Soon after he became ill (the beginning of the long illness — cancer of the lung). So I see now that I did not see then that subconsciously I had reason to doubt his immortality for the first time at that fête. I had no way at that time to explain the whys and wherefores. This

	might be all wrong, but it is how I remember it today."
Analyst	"From that time onwards therefore you had to protect father from your fury and at an age when defying your father would be quite natural and part of the process of growing up. About adolescence I would say that although father has won over you in regard to your early childhood relation to mother, he now comes along as someone you can defy when investigating relationships with mother substitutes. I would say that at the time it threw you over into an exaggeration on the homosexual side although this did not develop into anything."
Patient	"I don't think I remember about that."
Analyst	"Well, at the time when you first came to me you were dressing in a way which was quite different from the style which you adopted when you left me. For instance, you wore a pink tie."
Patient	"Yes, I remember the flamboyant ties, but it was also an act of defiance. I was not really at ease with them but I mistrusted myself. I would say that all the time I was afraid of what father would say."
Analyst	"You have probably heard the term, the return of the repressed. The main fury and your defiance of your father was not available but it turned up in this way."
Patient	"You remember, don't you, that at the time I came to you first he had already died?"
Analyst	"Yes, I know, but you had not accepted his death and indeed it was in this phase of the analysis about a year ago that you accepted this fact."
Patient	"As a matter of fact I am only just beginning to accept it now."
Analyst	"It is impossible to accept the death of your father unless you are able to encompass your anger with him and the death of him in the dream in which you kill him. He, being ill, had to be protected, and your protection of him has kept him alive all this time."

Friday, 10 June

Patient	"I have been to my daughter's school open day, and found it very bewildering. I had to make the effort to be interested but after an hour I became agitated. It is im-

possible to be normal there, and this is in marked contrast to what I feel at hospital. In the classroom I did not know what to look at and meekly followed the others. I felt I ought to be fascinated. I was upset at not being affected. The building I found more interesting. It reminds me that at one time I nearly was a teacher and I am horrified at the thought —

"In contrast I have been excited and even fascinated to realize how much children of five and six are capable of thinking, the way they manage abstract ideas like learning to read and write and various skills. I seem to be finding out for the first time what adults take for granted and I was able to picture myself in the school as a child although unable to take part as an adult."

Analyst   "I would like to remind you that yesterday you were speaking of difficulties starting at the time of your father's death when you were adolescent."

Patient   "I am reminded that you said that it was only recently that I had allowed my father to die, and I said, 'Has it happened yet or perhaps it is happening now?' Now it is as if I have accepted this and that has taken me back to the period earlier than the age at which father died when things first seemed to be unreal. Probably at the time of learning to read. The sort of age that my daughter is at now."

Analyst   "So that as a child you felt unreal at school learning to read, etcetera."

Patient   "It was difficult to work with children. It is the same difficulty now fitting in with what others are doing, though I missed joining in. I want to be social but something gets in the way and I cannot be. This has to do with the age five or six, the time when I started to be on my own and I never got back into line again. Today I ought to have wanted to go but I didn't."

Analyst   "What about your memories of five and six? For instance, about the first day at school?"

Patient   "Only vaguely but I was seven then. You remember that mother ran a school and it was not until seven or eight that I went to a prep school. When I was five I went to mother's school with the two sisters and the children of neighbors."

Analyst	"So that the other children at this school run by your mother were intruders in your home."
Patient	"For a long time, in fact, I refused to take part. One motive was resentment and this is a new idea to me. Resentment that the other children moved into my family. Quite simply I moved out."
Analyst	"You remember having withdrawn at some sort of date as when you found your baby sister on your mother's lap."

Pause.

Patient	"Now I feel a tendency to face the situation, to look forward but not accept. This has to do with my going to sleep. It is the same as not going to school, and the same as withdrawal at the age of four or five." *Pause.* (Probably asleep.) "I have difficulty in keeping awake here. That is the same as running away from school. I never reach a dilemma but run away."
Analyst	"You are protecting everyone from your fury, saving the world. If you do not go away everyone will die."
Patient	"Why?"
Analyst	"Because of the fury we were talking about."
Patient	"Occasionally I wonder if I had feelings at that time of destroying the other children that came to mother's school."
Analyst	"By withdrawing you do two things. You keep omnipotence and also you save the lives of the children."

Pause.

Patient	"Just now I feel the obstacle is so great that I will not be able to get over it."
Analyst	"We have found that in adolescence you had to protect father from your fury but at the age of four and five in a sense there was no father to save the situation because he avoided the role of the strong father." (During this interpretation the patient quickly went to sleep.)
Patient	"I seem to have been going to sleep several times today. This must be important."
Analyst	"I think you did not hear what I said. I spoke about father being ill so that you had to protect him." (I repeated the interpretation.)
Patient	"It occurs to me that it may be a pointless observation, rather abstract, that the difficulty here is that there can-

not be an ordinary withdrawal as in a social gathering in which I do not have to talk if I don't want to. Here I have to go further to escape from a situation. Not talking is too well understood."

Analyst   "Not talking is equivalent to killing."

Patient   "Part of silence is a need to keep some feelings away from here. I have the right to not say things but I am not aware of the deep feelings. I can only take for granted the word fury."

Analyst   "Yes, we do not know yet for certain."

Pause.

Patient   "It seems also as if from an early age, say four or five or six, I substituted an intellectual for a real emotional self, because the latter was not able to make itself felt."

Analyst   "And the latter is consequently inexperienced."

Patient   "It is more difficult to concentrate and to keep awake today. Does that mean that there is something especially dangerous? This is partly related to the fact that by changing the job I am uncertain how long I will be able to come at the usual times though of course if I need to come I will be able to." *Pause.* "There is another idea about silence. That it is unproductive. You said that it can be useful. Today I seem to be challenging you. All right, you say it is useful. Let's see what happens if I do not speak. Prove yourself! Probably there is some anxiety about the idea of your having been able to make use of the silence. When challenged then there is no escape from not coming. There is no way of bringing not-coming."

Analyst   "I think here I am mother and you are four or five years old."

Patient   "It is very important that mother did not know my feelings because there was something I dare not tell her as it would involve her destruction." *Pause.* "My only hope in those days was to grow up suddenly and so avoid a great deal of unpleasantness. I tried to become an adult from the age of five. I wanted to be sociable but to do without the intermediate stages between early childhood and being grownup. That was the only safe way that was possible."

Analyst   "The whole period which people call latency period seems to have been wiped out. Father's death at a later age seems to have been a version of its own during that period." (I felt from the failure of response here that my interpretation was probably not right. The patient was nearly asleep.)

Patient "It occurs to me now that two weeks ago when I was suddenly able to talk freely and was unaware of time this was to some extent artificial, a trick. The point is that it hid the idea of not talking at all. I am starting to discover what is behind the not-talking in the past. I have always thought of this symptom as just a nuisance though you have spoken about it as potentially valuable. I believe that it was concealing something only now I mean what I am saying, that the silence itself is the significant thing."

Tuesday, 14 June

Patient "Last time I slept a lot. If I let myself go then I would sleep all the time. I feel this may have been very important, an avoidance of something, unconsciously, perhaps something was getting near that was dangerous. There are two things: first, today I am more tired, but second, I feel that there is less risk of going to sleep, because being really tired I'm not likely to get to dangerous things. It's a curious position. I don't feel externally that I have made progress lately, that is to say I don't feel better, but nevertheless I wonder when and if I should expect to reap the fruit of the work done here. If I have to stop, will all the recent work be wasted, or can it be consolidated? Psychoanalysis while it goes on produces an area of disturbance, I know, so that I cannot expect to feel well while I'm coming."

Analyst "Do you remember about last time, and the work we did on the subject of silence and its positive meanings?"

Patient "I only vaguely remember. I don't talk with my wife because she will not argue and so offers no struggle. We talk only about minor things. I have given up trying. It's not urgent now and experience shows its fruitlessness. It isn't worth trying. She's deliberately not talking

	and I am forced to play the same way. Not talking is an active thing."
Analyst	Here I collected together all the recent work we had done on silence.
Patient	"It's curious, all we had talked about had disappeared. It still seems remote."
Analyst	"So you are referring to the need you have for me to remember, even when we agree."
Patient	"About agreeing, I feel I'm only too likely to agree. I tend to accept unless I definitely reject. I willingly accept and seldom flatly disagree. I hardly ever argue."
Analyst	"I would remind you that you said I would be like cotton wool, if you hit me your arm would go right in and it would get lost."
Patient	"I had a mental picture then — a fight with you. (I kept you at a distance.) This would be the ideal if you would not be aggressive all the time but would be in an aggressive state — a kind of boxing match, but the blows would bounce back off you. There is some dislike of you here. You adapt completely and produce a negative atmosphere — this is too much like my father. I have an abstract picture of a mother who adapts too easily, trying too hard to be perfect." (This is the mother's exact description of herself at the time of the patient's infancy, given to me before I started the first analysis.) "The result is soft and distasteful."

In the paper "On communication" (1963) in The maturational processes and the facilitating environment, *Dr. Winnicott says that after development of the ego has progressed to the point that the infant is able to retain the memory of the object as potentially satisfying while recognizing its failure to behave satisfactorily, the frustrations that are inevitable because of the operation of the reality principle can have value, "in educating the infant in respect of the existence of a not-me world." In the case of the neonate, maternal adaptation must be near-perfect, as Freud pointed out. ("Formulations on the two principles of mental functioning," Standard ed. vol. 12 (1911), pp. 219–220.)*

As the maturation of the infantile ego progresses,

*the mother's persistence in providing near-perfect grati-
fication changes over from an adaption to the infant's
needs to a trauma. Such infantilization of the developing
child represents an intrusion and a hindrance to the
child's differentiation and individuation. In "The antisocial tendency" in his* Collected papers *(p. 312), Dr.
Winnicott points out that "It is sometimes said that a
mother must fail in her adaptation to her infant's needs.
Is this not a mistaken idea based on a consideration of id
needs and a neglect of the needs of the ego? A mother
must fail in satisfying instinctual demands but she may
completely succeed in 'not letting the infant down,' in
catering for ego needs, until such a time as the infant
may have an introjected ego-supportive mother, and may
be old enough to maintain this introjection in spite of
failures of ego support in the actual environment." This
very important distinction between satisfying id needs
and adapting to the needs of the developing ego underlies Dr. Winnicott's concept of active adaptation to the
needs of the regressed patient, and distinguishes this concept from supportive psychotherapy.*

*Herbert Rosenfeld, in "On the treatment of psy-
chotic states by psychoanalysis: an historical approach,"*
Int. J. Psycho-Analysis *(1969), Vol. 50, pp. 615–631,
says that "Winnicott's views" on the treatment of schizophrenia "are identical both in theory and practice" with
the early recommendations of Pearce Clark and Fromm-
Reichmann. Rosenfeld summarizes these recommendations as follows: the analyst should imitate an early
omnipotent magical infant-mother relationship, fostering a positive relationship and promoting a nonambiva-
lent positive transference. In "Clinical varieties of transference" (1955),* Collected papers *(1958), Dr. Winnicott states that active adaptation to the needs of the
regressed patient necessarily is incomplete, since the
patient is not in fact an infant and the analyst is not in
fact the patient's mother. The form of the failures of the
analyst's attempted adaptation are determined by the
specific needs of the patient, and therefore are to some
degree repetitious of earlier failures. Instead of the classical negative transference of the neurotic patient, in a*

*successful analysis, the regressed schizoid patient experi-
ences objective anger about the inevitable failures in the
analyst's adaptation. This anger has value. At the time
of the original infantile trauma the ego of the patient
was not sufficiently differentiated to experience anger,
and instead suffered disruption of continuity of development, with resulting ego defect.*

*Considerable ego development is required in order
for anger at the analyst's failures in the present to be
experienced rather than a repetition of traumatic disruption. Once it can be experienced, however, it enables
further maturational progress and frees the patient from
dependence on the analyst. This is really a long way
from the view that Dr. Rosenfeld attributed to Dr.
Winnicott, simply fostering an unambivalent positive
transference while giving "complete acceptance" to
compensate for narcissistic injury.*

Patient	"I remember a striking difference between the desire to be silent last time and the desire to get away from chattering. Chatter has limitations. It has an edge to it even if it has no meaning. I like the idea of chatter, but pure chatter has no edge, no purpose. Chatter is talking without object. The effect is only a temporary amusement." *Pause.* "I was silent then because I recognized it as a good thing in itself sometimes not to talk. Not to talk for talking's sake. In the past I made too big an effort to try and say everything." *Pause.* "I feel that if I don't talk there is a danger of never talking at all, and then going to sleep. I can't trust silence."
Analyst	"Did you sleep just then in the pause?"
Patient	"No, not really."
Analyst	"There is something real here, in your silence, that it is you yourself, where as talking for talking's sake means you are not sure you exist."
Patient	"The difficulty is that if I don't talk or don't want to talk this needs an interpretation. In general I don't like talking." *Pause.* "Tiredness has something to do with not talking. It provides an excuse, so that at the moment I don't have to talk, nor do I have to explain why." (Patient yawns.)

Analyst   "You are needing an interpretation from me, and I will say that you are making a claim on me." (Patient asleep.) "I think you wanted to hear my interpretation but you went to sleep because you were afraid of it. You perhaps fear the right interpretation."

Patient   "I assume that the interpretation is right, if it is made. The fear is of what I might find to be true. I had not thought of the possibility of your making a wrong interpretation (it would then be only an opinion, which I would accept as an opinion by not accepting it as an interpretation). So it's not so much the interpretation that I fear as discovery of something, as if I were to be hit over the head."

Analyst   "You recently said that silence could be hitting."

Patient   "I had a curious idea then, that somebody was eating something, you eating ideas, so if you produce something (an interpretation), you are vomiting. Therefore accepting an idea from you is distasteful. There is the danger that I don't recognize these ideas till they are half consumed, and then I find out and vomit. For a moment I had a very clear picture of all this, of you sitting at a meal, with a plate of food which you eat, and while you eat the food increases, which means that you are bringing it all up, slowly." *Pause.* "It seems very difficult, this not talking, it's dangerous, nothing happens. Can you make use of it? It's only too easy never to talk. I remember now, as I left yesterday I wondered, is it worthwhile to carry on if not talking is life?"

Analyst   "This connects with the idea of being loved with sanctions, or being loved meaning having your existence valued."

Patient   "I feel about that that I can try to believe and assume that I am loved, but what if it isn't true? I almost find myself in water without being able to swim, and no one to support me."

Analyst   "Exactly, you've said it — that's what happened to you."

Patient   "There is a big difference. I ought to try (although it's impossible) not to do things myself but to make others do things in abstract, *without* their actually doing them. This is a contradiction, it can only happen by magic."

Analyst   "What you miss is the fact of mother's identification with you, her baby."

Pause.

Patient   "Sleep is not purely negative or avoidance. It provides an element which gives you a chance to come forward."

Analyst   "Yes, my only chance."

The mother's adaptation to the infant's needs provides what Dr. Winnicott has called "the facilitating environment," in which optimal personality development can occur ("From dependence towards independence in the development of the individual," in The maturational processes and the facilitating environment, *London: Hogarth, 1965, 83-92). Continued failure of the facilitating environment — continued maladaptation to the needs of the infant — has been termed "cumulative trauma" by Khan (Khan, M. M. R. (1963), "The concept of cumulative trauma,"* Psychoanalytic study of the child, *New York: Inter. Univ. Press, 286-306.)*

Wednesday, 15 June

Patient   "After I left yesterday I was thinking about our conclusion. I've been a long time facing the problem, to find a hopeless prospect of being loved or wanted for myself rather than on account of what I do or achieve. I had discussed this before, when we were on the subject of perfection. I did not recognize the possibility of being wanted or respected for myself, so perfection was the only alternative, and anything less meant complete failure. So when I first complained that I was ill I was appalled at the dilemma, as I felt so far from perfection, which meant absolute failure. Before that I avoided the direct onslaught by retiring into myself, and so avoided problems of being wanted or loved, or of being perfect. I did not believe in being loved and so the talking difficulty arose because there was no point in demanding what I wanted to get without demanding it.

"Then I wondered, having discovered this situation, what was the next step to take, what would solve the problem? No practical step would help because by the nature of things I could not take action. In this dilemma is it possible to get over the fact that for so many years I have missed something, missed or failed to recognize being loved if it was there? Also it struck me that mother might have suffered from the same disability, if she had no hope of being loved for herself — hence perhaps her desire for perfection.

"Also, what role did father play? I cannot picture him in the same category. He seemed to have no problem." *Pause.* "At the start I wondered whether to talk about yesterday or not; it is difficult to talk about without making it too intellectual."

Analyst   "This is where silence comes in, if it is understood."

Patient   "But how in silence can I demonstrate how important it is? Also at the end of yesterday I was impressed by the discovery, perhaps by its drama more than by the truth of it, that is to say its definiteness, rather than by its subject matter. It seemed very important but too simple to explain everything."

The silent communication between infant and mother depends upon the original symbiotic unity. From the infant's point of view this begins with a totally undifferentiated state in which the mother is perceived in terms of part objects, and gradually progresses toward incorporation, introjection, and identification. From the mother's point of view, under optimum conditions, complex mechanisms of empathy and identification, with perception of the infant as a whole person in time and space, are present from the start.

Patient   "It seemed to follow (I have recognized it for a long time) that I have been obsessed with a need to try to please everybody, this being all part of perfection and of the drive to find love and respect. I have been concerned not to upset people, more than with the positive aspects of relationships. If I said something definite I was disturbed if this was not accepted. There was an example today, discussing a case over the phone with a G.P. He wanted advice about a child, and he argued with me instead of taking what I said for granted and

I was very upset. It was simply a case of a three-months-old baby that possibly has rubella, and the G.P. was critical of the diagnosis. I felt I was being shouted down. He was more definite than I was and I felt wrong, uncertain, and then annoyed. I could have been firm."

Analyst   "Yesterday when I made my simple interpretation there was the content of what I said but also the firmness of my attitude and statement. You were affected by my feelings displayed by the way I did it."

Patient   "I enjoyed the categorical nature of your statement, because I can't be like that. Often you seem cautious, you don't commit yourself, you are reasonable and admit when you are wrong, but I find that less satisfying. It would be better for you to be gloriously wrong than vaguely right."

Analyst   "Well, I was definite and that was satisfying. We now have to consider, was I gloriously wrong?"

Patient   "It's difficult to remember things, but what you said fits in in the back of my mind. The meaning is vague but the memory is of something definite and decisive. My own not being decisive is not only a fear of being wrong. It turns up in the taking of case-histories, and in my not remembering people's names. There is a definite reason — as an excuse I am vague. There is an obvious thought here — being decisive is father. Part of my distrust of it in myself is that I do not want to be identified with him. If I am too much like father then, if I am loved, it is on account of my being like father, not because of myself."

Analyst   "Do you know of mother's early history? Had she childhood difficulties?"

Patient   "My own memory of mother's mother is colored by the fact that she was elderly when I knew her, but she was a difficult person. This is not the representation of what she might have been in mother's childhood. There is also what mother said, and this is her subjective account — I might have the idea now of making my difficulties go back to my grandmother — but she had an anxiety drive. As I see my own difficulties now, they arise out of the fact that mother was a more powerful personality than father was. I am aware that father was too perfect — this doesn't ring true. If father was decisive I was happy though I disliked it. I respected it. Now if mother starts to be definite I am irritated. It's not right coming from her. About mother I can speak of contemporary feelings, but in regard to father it all dates back to the time before I was conscious of the problems we have found here." *Pause.* "I had an idea here, about father. His being decisive had one disadvantage for me. It left no room for play."

Analyst "So that — ."

Patient "I am trying to pick holes in father, trying to find a chink in his armor."

Analyst "What was later good in father may have been bad from your point of view when you were an infant, especially as father took a motherly interest in you from early days, as you have told me. But I would say that eventually father's human decisions would be preferable to mother's rules based on the idea of perfection. You could be defiant with father, but you can't do anything about rules."

Patient "I feel there is one thing to be avoided, not to accept anything too readily, since so little can be done."

Analyst "Also to avoid a positive relationship, both ways, between you and me." *Pause.* "I think you slept?"

Patient "Yes, the first time today. I was aware of getting sleepy. It's difficult to face up to the situation, I mean the content of your interpretation." (That is to say, as opposed to the decisive manner in which he felt it was given.)

"I still feel, 'also I'm trying to avoid.' I cannot get to the not-wanting-to-talk as a positive thing."

Analyst "When you sleep you drop me. You never had mother and so could not drop her." (Patient sleeping?)

Patient "I feel at the moment that what goes on in my mind is far away from what we are talking about — a vague daydreaming — difficult to get hold of — it's about children playing."

Analyst "Father didn't give room for play."

Patient "And mother didn't know how to play so she was unable to."

Analyst "So it is very important I don't drive you to the point by being decisive."

Patient   "Also I am speculating about my perhaps not being able to come after next week because of the change of job. I might not want to come because you have become the nasty man who discovers what I don't want to have discovered. So I get sleepy and express my disapproval. It's childishness, that way of putting it, but it's important that you have become the ogre of childhood play."

Analyst   "So you have been able to reach play with me, and in the playing I am an ogre."

This interpretation joins the metapsychology of play with that of transference. "Illusion" is central to both play and transference. External objects are imbued with qualities derived from inner psychic reality. "Illusion" differs from delusion in that the actual qualities of the external object continue to be acknowledged while it is perceived subjectively. In this instance the patient retains his awareness of the actual identity of himself and of the analyst while becoming aware of the feeling that he is a helpless victim of an ogre. The self-observing function is intact. If this had not been true, and the patient had been overwhelmed by the reality of the ogre-victim images, he would have had a so-called delusional transference. Such a transference is workable when it can be contained in the analytic hours, and the patient regains his awareness of the reality of the analytic relationship as he leaves the session. The term transference psychosis is often used to refer to the situation in which this does not occur, and in such instances the patient may need temporary hospitalization during analysis. Dr. Winnicott's statement that it is important that he not drive the patient by being decisive, aims toward delineating the actual identity of the analyst from the patient's transference projection. It is therefore an interpretation which helps to define the psychoanalytic setting.

Friday, 17 June

Patient   "I used to think it important to discuss how I was feeling; now it seems relatively unimportant. Feelings and moods are variable, transient. They depend on variable factors. More important is to get at the things behind the moods."

Analyst   "Yes, you are saying something I hadn't thought of before. Your mood was the nearest you could get to your self."

Patient   "One thing that emphasized the unimportance of my mood has been the fact that I find other people are not impressed by how one feels."

Analyst   "When people say, 'How are you?' they definitely don't want you to say you have a pain in your elbow. It is not appropriate to follow up the idea in the question."

Patient   "This has to do with things my wife and I have had rows about, and I have rebuked her for not asking me how I feel. She says, 'What's the point? You are always miserable.' There is something else. Before I came I felt some confusion as to the reason for my difficulty or reluctance in talking. There are two factors: the fear of the fury, and hopelessness about being loved. I suppose if one is right the other must be wrong. In the last two times anger has disappeared."

Analyst   "There can be a connection between the two. You must have some hope in order to be angry. To be angry you have to be able to keep in mind that which you hoped for while reacting to its absence."

Patient   "In that case the idea of my being completely hopeless is an exaggeration. One exaggerates to get to a simplification, to find one cause for all one's troubles."

Analyst   "We have often found that when we clear up a point that leads on to the next."

Patient   "I am really aware that one thing cannot solve everything."

Analyst   "There is a difference between the fury and the deprivation. You reached theoretical fury but real deprivation in the past weeks."

Patient   "Yes, the fury was somewhat theoretical, except that I felt vague annoyance. I felt there might be anger somewhere. Another thing about anger; it's always a temporary mood, never lasting long. Is that what it is like or must there be buried anger that I cannot sustain?"

Analyst   "We see you going to and fro from anger, which produces its own dangers, and hopelessness which is not so much dangerous as that it makes you feel life is futile." *Pause.* "In the analysis you came to certain dangers, associated with anger, and so you went back to hopelessness."

Patient   "Anger is more productive that hopelessness which is negative."

Analyst   "You feel more real when you are angry even if the ideas that belong to anger involve a sense of danger."

Patient   "Anger involves an object, but hopelessness — well there's nothing to pursue. So anger entering into discussion today might possibly be more useful. I feel excited at the idea of reaching to hopelessness, but I seem to have come to a dead end, so for two days the anger has got lost. I feel I'm getting a bit repetitive. The idea occurs to me that I might be boring by constantly going over the same thing. Socially I know I'm boring by being monotonous but I can't help going on doing it. The alternative is hopelessness, silence, absolute."

Analyst   "There can be anger at realization of deprivation, when you feel hope and hopelessness almost at the same time."

Patient   "Hopelessness is only relative because if complete it isn't recognized."

Analyst   "Yes."

Pause.

Patient   "I find now that I ought to be starting thinking about the next stage, making use of these discoveries. I notice that in contrast with the past few weeks I am no longer sleepy. This is disappointing if sleepiness is evidence of something emerging. If I'm awake I start thinking clearly about the future and this can be unproductive."

Analyst   "The new situation comes from the idea which is the opposite of deprivation, that to some extent, here and now, I have love for you — a new version of the series of events in your analysis that started with the fluid medium. Here I mean love with no ifs and no sanctions, nothing more nor less than my capacity to be identified with you."

Patient   "It occurs to me that I've just arrived at the situation that I was in when I first started to come to you, that is for the first analysis. I could not think what the devil to talk about."

Analyst   "That is to say, that had I known about you (and I would have had to have been a magician) I could then have made the comment I am making now. I could have said, 'The only way you can start is by my coming to you with love, and you cannot say this because you don't know it.' This was dramatized at the start of the second analysis when you had no idea of wanting me, and you would not have come to me had I not come and fetched you. Of course I do not alter the fact of the first deprivation, that of your early infancy, I only offer a token of loving."

Patient   "I feel that I could not start because I had nothing to work on. I never had the idea that things ought to start from you."

Analyst   "So we come to a positive meaning for silence — the expression of the idea that the start must come from me."

Patient   "This is not new. I remember before feeling hopeless about producing anything, but I thought it was that I would *like* you to produce something first. Now I see it is more than just convenience."

Analyst   "If you like me to start it is already no good for me to start, because in doing so I only follow your wish. To make adaptation to your *need* I must come to you with love before you know about the need."

On the basis of identification with the infant, the mother makes active adaptation to the infant's needs.

Maternal adaptation provides the object that can be linked with the need. This is the prototype of interpretation. From then on the infant can use the memory of the object or other adaptive measure that was provided by the mother as something for which to wish. This link of "need" with object leading to a "wish" may never have been firmly established in the schizoid case, or can be lost in regressive disintegration. Through identification with the patient (here called "love") the analyst is enabled to adapt to the patient's needs, for example by interpretation. This establishes, or re-establishes, connection between id needs and external reality.

In this case when the patient was hospitalized, Dr. Winnicott offered to resume the analysis. In doing this he "interpreted" the patient's breakdown as an appeal to the analyst. Before this "interpretation" the breakdown was a meaningless event. By the "interpretation" the breakdown was given both meaning and value. From then on the patient could begin to "wish" for treatment rather than only having a "need" for treatment manifested by symptoms. (See pp. 661-662.)

Patient   "This reminds me of my relationship to women, which only starts when the woman takes the initial steps. I feel hopeless about making a conquest. If I try I start with the assumption that it will be hopeless. I don't see why it is important that the drive should come from outside except that at an early stage it didn't."

Analyst   "From your point of view, whether true or not, your mother was unable to surrender herself to an identification with you, her baby. You will see what I mean if you think of the word confined, which implies that the mother, like the infant, is caught up in a process, and which shows the mother's temporary identification with her infant, which is almost complete. In the same way I am caught up with you in the process of your analysis and of your going back to infantile dependence and your emotional growth forward again. Only if I am caught up as you are in these processes can you start to exist." *Pause.* "This leads to a consideration of the analyst's motives."

Patient   "Yes, I was actually thinking, 'I wonder in broad terms what you are out to do, what faith you have in your ability to do something.' A friend, a doctor, was recently talking about his future, and he said he thought of trying psychiatry; he said it might be profitable. He had no belief in its being any good and he said, 'It's a waste of time really.' I was annoyed about the waste of time idea, but I too had doubts as to whether or no there was any truth in it. I wondered, 'Do you regard psychoanalysis as an experiment, not knowing the outcome?' "

Analyst   "I might be doing it for money and I might be doing it without belief in my ability to get anywhere, but what concerns you is: Do I suffer with you if the analysis is a failure?"

Patient   "Yes, because it's so easy if you decide psychoanalysis is a good line to take up. You might not believe in it but you might carry it on as a technical exercise, and be prepared to jettison the work if you find something else more promising."

Pause.

Analyst   "In comparing the analyst's job with that of the doctor you are noting a difference. The doctor deals with illness, and if he cures the patient of the illness he has finished. The analyst, on the contrary, needs to have a positive feeling, something in his relationship with the patient that does not end with the cure of the illness. This concern for the existence of this human being underlies any wish the analyst may have to cure the patient of illness."

Patient   "We came to this once before, I remember some months ago, soon after I restarted with you, after we had talked over the immediate causes for tension, this was all tied up with the question, 'Why have psychoanalysis at all?' Since if relief from symptoms is all that is required, I needn't have come. This answers a problem I have never answered before: how to decide whether anyone does or does not need analysis. It hinges round whether it will be discovered that the symptoms are the important thing or whether they are a minor problem as compared with something else. I had one thought this morning, before I came, how much ought I to be ambitious, to struggle, or have I reached a stage at which the best policy would be to live within one's limitations? I wondered whether once having given up one's ambition, would one then be satisfied, or at least find a workable existence?"

Analyst   "You are getting to a position from which you can consider these matters."

Patient   "Is there a state of trying too hard so that one does not exist at all? There is an analogy, if I look at a picture and do not enjoy it, should I go on trying or just pass on to one that I enjoy and get pleasure from and ignore the idea that I was supposed to get something out of the other?"

Analyst   "The idea of yourself existing just comes in here, in contrast to the idea of your living up to someone else's expectations."

Patient   "Expectations can come from inside."

Analyst   "Yes, surely, from people inside who are to some extent built on outside people, such as father, that you have wanted to please. But you have had to maintain these introjected people because of your own lack of sense of existing in your own right."

Patient   "That summarizes it, in trying to achieve being myself I have had to use artificial props, and these are no longer necessary. I feel just now aware of a much more positive hope. I can visualize a situation arising, a foreseeable future, not so remote, it could be that it will be possible to say this has occurred. I used to feel there was no prospect that I would *actually* start to exist. It was like a challenge to you — do your worst, but I had no belief that something would actually happen."

Tuesday, 21 June

Patient   "You might start by asking about my new job. I have a feeling of dislike of the idea of that, I don't know why. It's the idea of being congratulated by you. It would be the same with my mother and my sister. It seems that it would be an intrusion. You would have no right to make a comment. It would not matter if it came from people who work with me or some casual acquaintance, that would not be actively intruding."

Analyst   "There is a link here with the theme of being loved without any ifs. The idea would be conveyed that you would be loved because of your success, which for you is the negative of being loved."

Patient   "Yes, in general any remark you make about outside things here is out of place, undesirable. Mother fits in here because she is partly responsible for my coming to analysis, but I don't see how my sister comes in. I mean the sister who is having analysis."

Analyst   "How does she seem to be just now?"

Patient   "She is fairly well, working. I find talking to her a strain. Her treatment is incomplete; her behavior is unreal."

Pause.

Analyst   "You are inevitably comparing your sister's condition with your own. If you were to make a deep change you would be concerned as to whether your sister had made the same change."

Patient   "I'm not sure; it might be. I'm just thinking about it. I was thinking before I came today, there was a demonstration of cases at hospital for postgraduates; it happened to be a demonstration of mental cases. There was a discussion and one thing that came up reminded me of my anxieties when I first went into hospital myself as a patient, that is to say, before the second analysis. Was I a schizophrenic? Whether the unreality feeling was part of a true schizophrenic? These unreality feelings were discussed in the case demonstration. I thought I had dealt with this, but now again I have to consider this part of my problem. The doctor doing the teaching said that psychotherapy was of very little use in the treatment of schizophrenia. You once said that I had a psychosis rather than a neurosis, and I find the idea disquieting."

Analyst   "Yes, I did say that."

Patient   "I am anxious about the natural history of the illness. It might imply that there is worse to come; there are natural remissions in schizophrenia and I must perhaps anticipate relapses. The relapse rate is high, even when patients have improved through physical treatments. So perhaps we are only delaying the final breakdown; because, though I feel well at times, I have moments of unreality. I have avoided putting a name to it because I regarded schizophrenia as a pretty hopeless proposition. On the other hand I find myself arguing against the assumption that schizophrenia should be treated by physical methods. It seems wrong to treat a thought disorder by an empirical method. A few of the doctors argued even that schizophrenia was an organic illness with a physical pathology. The basis of the argument was that certain drugs produce schizophrenia attacks. So I feel anxious that I might prove untreatable."

Analyst   "You are faced with two alternatives, and these involve pretty big issues. On the one hand you can be treated, in which case all these doctors are wrong, and the official view of schizophrenia is wrong, or the psychiatrists are right and you are untreatable."

Patient   "Again, in a discussion with my wife, she would have helped if I had not had psychoanalysis. One argument originally used was that I might get much worse, but she would not accept blame if I got worse through not having psychoanalysis. Again I remember at the time I was in hospital I had a fear that I would get so out of touch that no treatment could possibly be effective."

Analyst   "When you were so very ill you were dependent on the fact that I and your mother and your sister held views about the psychological nature of your illness, and it is this that joins us three together."

Patient   "Another alarming feature is the feeling that a breakdown might occur if I were to meet any new stress, so I wonder if I must be careful in choosing a job, avoiding the danger of emotional stress. The disadvantage here is that this produces a state of boredom."

Analyst   "Boredom itself is a form of stress, too."

Patient   "Yes, but the anxiety is about the shelving of the problem. I'm worried at the idea of going on shelving the main problem. I offer as an excuse that I've got to justify being irresponsible which comforts at the moment and gives relief from the alternative of recognizing that I have a schizophrenia symptomatology. So frank schizophrenia is a variation of normal behavior. Therefore schizophrenia episodes are in fact nothing to worry about."

Analyst   "If schizophrenia is related to the normal in this way, that would rule out the theory of an organic illness."

Patient   "That would be comforting."

Analyst   "So in the psychoanalysis of yourself you are finding out the answers to this vast general problem of schizophrenia illness."

Patient   "Also I wonder if I'm not too much of a burden on

other people. My wife talking about my breakdown implied that if I were schizophrenic then she could not tolerate still living with me, if I was so ill as that. So I have a conscience about my burden on her being so very great. Also some of this anxiety about others comes into it, especially if there is a possibility of my doing psychotherapy in the future. If I have to accept the idea that the majority views on schizophrenia are mistaken, then it would be immoral for me not to do anything about it. Here is an immense task, needing missionary enthusiasm, which I've just not got. If I find a lot of people doing something wrong it's not comfortable to be doing nothing."

Analyst   "You are dealing with an abstract problem of the general theory of schizophrenia, when the true problem is your own self and can you get well?"

Patient   "It's not easy to accept that that's fair."

Analyst   "The first two others, after yourself, would be your mother and your sister."

Patient   "Yes, if one assumes that my illness is schizophrenia then their's is also, and after all there is the family element too, (I mean familial not necessarily inherited). There is implied here an anxiety about the state of my own children, though I have assumed that it is not likely they are affected in the same way, though I have no rational grounds for such an assumption. It just seems unlikely."

Analyst   "There is the question of your wife. For instance, would you say she is accessible or inaccessible, on the whole, to her children?"

Patient   "She's inaccessible to me, when she suddenly disliked my illness, but she is not so with the children. I wish she was therapeutically more stout."

Analyst   "Perhaps you chose your wife because she was different from your mother in an important way."

Patient   "Yes, she has a large amount of common sense, which is absent in my family. Although she is prepared to plunge into the unknown, nevertheless she keeps her feet on the ground. She knows what she wants, and she goes out to get it. So I recognize that I chose her because of the contrast relative to my own family."

Analyst   "So the children are not likely to be affected, although it is difficult for you that you cannot get from her what the children naturally derive from her sense of reality.

Patient   "Suddenly then I remembered a quotation from a paper I read three days ago: 'People wrapped up in themselves make a very small package.' That is myself, or what I am trying to avoid. I am able to despise myself for my limitations. It occurs to me that a reason for my distrust of psychiatry is part of my whole attitude to psychological medicine and to schizophrenia. It is based on a wrong attitude. This is something I was subconsciously aware of before the breakdown. If I accept the idea of working with the majority then I have to accept what is wrong along with all the rest — ."

Wednesday, 22 June

Patient   "Feelings continued after last session. I had anxiety about what is likely to happen, having arrived at a label; what will happen in the future? The implication might be that the treatment must go on for a long while. Anxiety was mixed up with some relief and even amusement. Relief because a name to the illness makes it less obscure, easier to deal with, so I felt more confident; but amusement at the idea of the fools who argued that schizophrenia can't be treated by psychotherapy, and at the idea of how many are not aware of the nature of schizophrenic illness. It's amusing to see what expression they would have if told that I myself am schizophrenic. I managed to get so far in medicine as to fill a resident post. They might even be horrified, people I have worked with recently and medical colleagues, especially those who interviewed me at the beginning and who wanted a report from yourself. They would have forgotten by now."

Analyst   "If all goes well people forget. If things go badly they remember?"

Patient   "I feel anxious now, insecure about my new job, and so on. I've no means of knowing."

Analyst   "You are also wondering about my capacity in my job here."

Patient   "Of the six or seven consultants I work for only one is on the selection panel. I still feel I need to be helped on a bit. In my work I've still to be dependent on being pushed forward. To compete on equal terms makes me feel insecure. I've not had to except in the first job (when I broke down). Also in the present stage there is the disadvantage that one does not apply for a new job till one is out of a job, so I might be unemployed, in which case it would be very difficult being at home all day. Finally, I'm still worried about the question of the future. I'm up against practical problems. I'm not in favor of being a G.P., but there seems to be very little alternative prospect. A reason why general practice does not appeal is that the G.P. is self-dependent."

Analyst   "People tend to ignore this aspect of general practice, the G.P.'s isolation."

Patient   "Yes, for instance it is all right to refer a hospital patient back to the G.P. but not thought good for the G.P. to refer a case back to hospital. This makes a paradox. One thing that alarms me about being a G.P. is this measure of security, that is as a permanent job. It is in any case distressing to be committed. It is the insecurity of hospital appointments that is the attractive feature. One need not make any decision about the future yet, but one can go on temporizing. But once a G.P., it's G.P. for keeps.

     "To revert to the topic of yesterday, there's something I forgot. It escaped me at the time. It has to do with what would happen if I had an easy steady monotonous job; then I should suffer from lack of interest. I'm worried about choosing being a doctor because there are difficult problems to be tackled the whole time, and no regular hours. I wonder if I'm right to choose medicine at all because I have to face perfect security, long hours, inadequate pay for the responsibility taken; but there was no alternative at the time of choice. You've got to have missionary enthusiasm to be exploited. There is also the problem of how much administration is to be done by medical personnel. A doctor hates to be told what to do by lay persons, but doctors would hate to do the organizing themselves. I seem to like to have a perfect administration as a background. I feel I despise myself over this weakness of dependence, while resenting interference."

Analyst "Your dependence on the administration is a dependence on people."

Patient "This is part of my dispute with my wife. I like to regard her as the administrator, who sees I do the right thing at the right time. She expects me to do all that. My organization would break down if she were not there to look after it. She resents this."

Analyst "In regard to your present job, is that more administrative?"

Patient "I'm not sure yet. At first I found it somewhat easier being in an advisory capacity, with less day-to-day anxiety about direct responsibility. I worry if a consultant says, 'See this patient is admitted to the ward,' because the task falls to me to arrange it. This is worse than a medical problem."

Analyst "This is like the problem of environment and of yourself in an environment."

Patient "I don't think I'm clear about what you said. I feel anxiety about administrative work — like looking after children — you can't just let things go. If you've got children they've got to be dealt with. You can't say one afternoon, 'Well, I've had enough.' This is the awful thing about administration. I wonder if this is an expression of my mother's feeling of inadequacy as a mother, that she herself is insecure, so that I am more insecure as a father. In the same way that administrative problems are like children, so is chess. It is difficult to tackle chess problems, it occurred to me a long time ago, because you decide on a move, which is difficult enough, but the next move depends on what someone else does. It is therefore a living problem. In tennis it feels different to me. Before I can confidently tackle a problem I like to have the situation tied down so that there is no urgency — no dynamic insecurity."

Analyst "This could be carried over to the analytic situation, with analyst and patient."

Patient   "Yes, and someone with whom what you do affects his whole future. This is the most worrying but the most interesting thing about psychotherapy."

Analyst   "You are hoping to integrate the two aspects which are at present not integrated in you."

The "two aspects" refer to the same ideas as those which underlie the concept of "true self" and "false self." The "true self" exists in an environment, the important features of which are accurately represented by the corresponding internal mental representation. The personality can therefore operate as a whole unit. The "false self" is close to the "as-if personality," and refers to a split in the ego whereby the schizoid individual relates to the outer world as though acting a part in a play. Such relating feels unreal, no matter how satisfying. Instinctual impulses remain attached to internal object representations that are relatively remote from perceived external reality. When such a situation exceeds a certain quantitative level, the patient gives up relating to external reality altogether, losing the defensive false self. At that point the diagnosis changes from schizoid personality disorder to frank schizophrenia. External factors play a part in strengthening or weakening the link between internal and external reality and therefore between the parts of the patient's ego that are oriented toward internal and external reality, both in infant care and in analysis.

The deepest anxiety concerns disruption of homeostasis: in the extreme this involves annihilation. The false self defending the true self corresponds to the "protective shield against stimuli" (Freud, S., "Beyond the pleasure principle" (1920), Standard edition, Vol. 18 (pp. 3-64), and to schizoid psychic structure. But Dr. Winnicott points out that the isolation of the central self is part of healthy psychic structuring as well as a manifestation of schizoid ego splitting. In this Dr. Winnicott's formulation is consistent with Freud's description of the "protective shield against stimuli" that is part of normal development.

The true self includes the mental representation of the physiological homeostatic processes, which must be isolated from environmental intrusion as a condition of survival. The concept of homeostasis implies constancy that is maintained despite environmental changes. Guntrip (Schizoid phenomena, object relations, and the self. New York: Inter. Univ. Press, 1969, p. 237) *regards the isolation of the central self as a manifestation of a defensive split in the ego. Although such a split is universal, Guntrip believes that this is because no one has perfect mental health. He believes that there would be no such isolation in the theoretical perfectly integrated personality. Guntrip says that if the core of the healthy personality is isolated, any meaningful difference between health and illness is lost.*

The difference between Winnicott's and Guntrip's position depends on the definition of the term "ego." If the ego is regarded as a hierarchal system that includes the totality of homeostatic mechanisms, it then includes the physiological systems that maintain homeostatic balance which must be unaffected by the outside world as a condition for survival.

Patient	"At the time that I felt most acutely ill I was like someone in a bog, or trying to climb up a cliff of sand or gravel, and each step losing ground, surroundings being far from static, a dramatization of dynamic insecurity. But I knew even then that I yearned for a basic security, I was aware of never being happy, so I wanted the ability to deal with the dynamic situation."
Analyst	"You wanted a basic security, and longed not to need this same thing, basic security."
Patient	"It was an intellectual awareness. Now it is more that I *feel;* it's not just knowing, or of being in the direction of knowing. Still it seems too much like a gamble in which the risk if I fail is too high. This is not my idea of desirable excitement. It was often said that father used to tease me because if I had to make an answer giving choice I always said 'Both.' I was always horrified at the idea of missing something. That fits in with my inability

to cope with dynamic insecurity. Gambling is an unsatisfactory solution to that problem, not a sensible decision, a wrong method."

Analyst   "Your alternatives are to be an individual taking the environment for granted, or to be environment-minded, and to lose individual identity. You are telling me that you cannot solve the dilemma of these alternatives." (Patient asleep.)

Patient   "I feel bewildered, out of my depth. Yes, I slept. Sleep is one way of getting round a dilemma." *Pause.* "One thing occurs to me, associated with sleepiness. It has to do now with bewilderment, when I'm faced with being unable to cope, desperate, hopelessness that I can ever get better — then I go sleepy."

Analyst   "You have an intellectual understanding that for a solution of the problem something depends on me, but in fact your problem has not been solved, and you are left in a state of bewilderment."

Friday, 24 June

Patient   "I find it difficult to start today. I seem to be in a stationary condition. There is no prospect of something happening. It strikes me that, broadly speaking, in spite of the ground covered, I feel the same as when I came two years ago, though more confident and less depressed. I feel just as unreal as at the start. A factor may be that the stage in my work is unsatisfactory. I have less contact with patients now, more time to spare, with no definite place to be. Living at home now may make it less easy to keep up contact with the other doctors, whereas as a resident this was easy. At home it is a little easier. We don't fight or struggle now, but it's no more satisfactory, and it means I have not progressed if I can't deal with my present situation better." *Pause.* "Also I felt after I got here, it would be nice to lie and say nothing, and see what happens, but probably nothing would happen. You would sit there and accept my silence, and this would leave me unsatisfied."

Analyst   "There is something you want, but you feel hopeless about whatever it is happening."

Patient   "I find a link between this and the topic we have recently discussed about being hopeless about being loved. In a way I can bear this out in practice; in situations outside here if I were to take it easy and wait nothing would happen. So I can't just leave it. The outlook would then be hopeless." *Pause.* "Also I could add something about being hopeless about being loved. I feel hopeless about my being able to cope with the situation should love arrive."

Analyst   "You would not be sure you could accept it."

Patient   "I never have been able to accept it and have feelings, and so I have doubts."

Analyst   "If I loved you then the test comes as to your personal difficulty, but while none is available you are untested and you can then keep the idea that it might just possibly be all right. You are saying you have no experience in this field, that you just can't know." (Patient sleepy.) "You are telling me about this deep split in your nature, so that your impulses make no contact, but your acceptance of reality is with a false self that does not feel real."

Patient   "Yes, if that is the situation what can be done about it? Will recognizing it alter it? It is easy to understand but how is it possible to deal with absence of feeling?"

Analyst   "Let us say, then, that this is where you are, and you see no way out." (Patient sleepy.)

Patient   "But this sleepiness is not directly related to what is being said. It is more the general situation, a reaction to the hopelessness of the situation."

Analyst   "By the nature of it, you cannot see any possible outcome."

Patient   "For two years we have uncovered interesting ideas and all that, but we are no nearer tackling this all important problem." (Sleep.) "I had a curious impression then, almost a dream. Someone was trying to get into touch with me about hospital matters. What would you do if this happened? If the external world were to come into the analytic situation?"

Analyst   "The dream is about the topic that we were discussing exactly. You bring about a contact that initiates from the hospital, and this is all right because it is not about you. Here nothing is any good unless it is about you and you have no hope then. It shows that what you are fearing here is being awake while feeling no hope about contact with me here."

This correlates with the patient's impression that his mother was present but emotionally inaccessible, acting the part of a perfect mother. The revival of this situation in the transference is associated with sleep as a defense against the tantalizing environment.

      "It is difficult for you to remain here and to be cut off from contact, in fact isolated."

Patient   "Yes, when I hear you talk loving words the idea of you and I being here together becomes remote."

Analyst   "The precondition for the next stage is this difficult one in which you are here with me and yet isolated." (Patient sleeps for several minutes.)

Patient   "It seems almost as if part of the difficulty about talking here is that unconsciously I am so to speak deliberately isolating myself. I have a need *not* to establish contact."

Analyst   "Yes. You seem however, to be going at an abstraction, trying to make the abstraction real."

Patient   "Yes, that's what I'm trying to do, to convert the abstraction into a reality. It is tempting to evade issues by going to sleep, but it is not helpful to do so, and in a way I feel I've got you ranged against me here, for you have pointed out that sleeping can be valuable because of the dream that may go with it. I feel that sleeping produces a stalemate."

Analyst   "The alternative is very difficult for you; it is to be awake here, but not in contact."

Patient   "Yes, there seems to be only one solution, sleep, with the idea that I will wake and find everything changed and the problem solved." (Sleepy. . . . Here he put his hand on his face and forehead, a rare occurrence, perhaps the first time it has happened.) *Pause.* "It seems at times, but I've said it before, that every now and again I take stock and find I've been asleep and then I want to punish myself because I'm useless. It's wasting time."

Analyst   "A moment ago you put your hand to your face. If I were a sensitive mother and you an infant I would have known your face wanted contact and I would have brought your face against my breast, but you had to be the mother and the infant and your hand had to act the part of mother." (Sleep overcame him at the beginning of this interpretation.)

Patient "I'm still up against not being here. I don't feel it's any use."

Analyst Here I repeated the interpretation.

Patient "I grasped that but I ought to have been speculating about what you would do; I would be horrified if you actually did anything. You seemed to imply that you would have to make a physical contact."

Analyst "Do you remember the headache that was outside your head, and my interpretation about having your head held, the day you had held a child's head?"

In "Withdrawal and regression" (1954), Collected Papers, Dr. Winnicott reports that the patient complained of headache that felt as though it were situated just outside of the head. The pain being "outside" of the head represented a need to have his father hold his head because of grief over the father's death. The mother was unable to provide such care in a way that the patient could accept.

Patient "There is a paradox, which fits in here, which I have discussed with my colleagues, about patients attending outpatients' department. I don't want to go on seeing people for whom I can't do much. But many enjoy coming to hospital, and even the long wait. Now I'm doing outpatients more, and each time I have to make a decision about future attendances. It has struck me that what they want is to have their hands held, that is to say, they are not content with verbal contact; they need some physical contact."

Analyst "And they miss it, don't they, if they are not physically examined?"

Patient "They feel it's a waste of a visit if they are just spoken to. Even a minor examination makes all the difference."

Analyst "I suggest that the subject is the loneliness which is more or less universal, and that that is the same subject as that of your being here, but isolated, not in contact with me." (Sleepiness?)

Patient   "I'm trying to sum this up. This idea of physical contact. This sleepiness of mine today is new, that is to say, it is happening in a different setting. All this sleepiness today arises out of the conflict, wanting physical contact and being horrified if I got it."

Analyst   "Do you remember, in the incident of the headache outside your head, you said that if I had actually held your head you would have felt it as a mechanical application of a technique? What was important was that the need was understood and felt by me."

Patient   "At the level of feeling, I need physical contact, but feel horrified at the idea of getting it here. But I feel I ought to want it somewhere."

Analyst   "The girl gave you physical contact which was important to you, but it was contact that belonged here but it was obtained outside. Now you have a conflict between needing and being horrified. As an infant your need was quite definite and simple. The question is how much are you an infant here and now, and how much is it true to say that we are talking together about an infant?"

In this interpretation physical care, as gotten from nursing during somatic illness or in the course of love making, is psychologically linked with the care received from the analyst in the transference regression. The girl with whom there was actual contact unconsciously represents the analyst in the present and the mother in the past. (See Little, M., "Transference in borderline states," Int. J. Psycho-Anal. Vol. 47, 1966.)

Patient   "It is an important stage of progress to recognize the need for physical contact. At first it was only an intellectual abstraction, the question whether as an idea it was attractive or not."

Analyst   "Now, however, you are talking about real needs."

Patient   "This may be rather obvious, but in some cases the contact I need can be verbal, that is if it comes at the right time. There are times recently when I've gone home and found my wife not concerned, offering no greeting. I have felt upset, but have not made a fuss because I know it's no use. But I have thought that if something had come from her at the right moment it need only have been a word."

Analyst   "I would say that a correct interpretation that is well-timed is a physical contact of a kind."

Patient   "Something occurred to me. I have noticed in the last few weeks quite a big change. Originally, a year ago, I enjoyed the cinema because for a few hours I could ignore my problems, identifying with the film characters, and therefore resenting the intervals with lights up. Now if I go to the pictures, which is rare, I feel worse when I go home, more out of contact and so bad-tempered. I don't any longer want to be lost in the film characters. Now it's all right if I go *with* someone, so that when we come out we have had the experience in common. I'm aware now that I used to go to the cinema to dig myself further back into remoteness. It is annoying that my wife will not discuss films. Either she has not been to the film yet, so she doesn't want to know the story, or else she has been, and that was some time ago and she has now got bored with it." (Because of the children the two can but seldom go together to the cinema.)

Tuesday, 28 June

Patient   "I have nothing to say and this seems to have some positive quality."

Analyst   "A thing in itself."

Patient   "Yes. Ever since we talked about schizophrenia I have been more aware of altered feelings. I have been on the lookout. It has made me more critical about recognizing normality. Previously I was prepared to accept that the analysis might enable me to return to what I was like several years ago but this would be a return to unreality, and now I assume that I have always been abnormal. So there is nothing for me to compare the normal with. So carrying on all right is no longer adequate. Again this contributes to my feeling of hopelessness. If I have got to get somewhere I have no experience, so a prospect of arriving is less tangible. We can remove obstacles here but what about positive steps? The first time I came to you I was not aware of any problem. My sole aim was to get somewhere different, to make progress possible. Mother offered me treatment for no very good reason. She said it could benefit me without my being aware of need. Perhaps mother knew something was wrong. At the moment I appear rather a fraud asking to be made different. This is something unparalleled in ordinary medicine."

Analyst "There basic health is taken for granted and the attempt is to alter illness."

Patient "Before I started I had an idea of positive health on the credit side but since I have become a doctor I feel that has gone by the board for health has no meaning. It would be an intellectual idea having missed something and to feel convinced that it can be altered."

Analyst "The only thing that would be satisfactory would be if it happened." *(See p. 479 and Note pp. 665-666.)*

Patient "My baby daughter had a first birthday and I forgot, although I talked about it the night before. The older daughter mentioned it as soon as she woke and I was shaken by my own absence of excitement. How can I learn to get excited? A fundamental subjective process cannot be instilled, yet that is what I have come here for." *Pause.* (Sleep?) "At the moment I am up against a difficulty not knowing where to go or what is the next step. I could be silent for a long time not as a joke but simply because I have nothing to say."

Analyst "You seem to be leaving out of account that this is experiencing something, being here but not having any contact with me."

Patient "I am aware of the general nature of the problem but I am not aware of the special aspects at the moment. It occurred to me that there is no good reason in treatment to refer to specific problems. Just now there is no point in saying what comes into my mind. I had forgotten that it was the expected idea (free association). It is unhelpful to remember things. I am trying all the time to avoid pointless use of words."

Analyst "In this case free association is not talking and being out of contact."

Patient   "Ideas disappear as before, but now in order to think I have to be remote. It comes back to me that I cannot chatter, only by a very great effort, so what I say is not chatter but is forced words. There is no spontaneous lightness. I have the feeling of unreality because of the effort to be spontaneous. Effort is artificial in itself."

Analyst   "Being remote is real although it brings you out of touch."

Patient   "Outside there is the same loneliness because of lack of contact. Other people are put off so they don't make friends. My wife felt like that about me. She complains that I don't notice things. An example is that when someone talks my first reaction is to say nothing. There is nothing to say. But I want to be friends so I talk in an effort to be friendly but I am aware that it is hopeless all the time." *Long Pause.* "When I woke I felt I was smothered with hair."

Analyst   "Possibly something to do with mother and yourself."

Patient   "It feels like that but what then? I feel that there is a connection between mothering and smothering."

Analyst   "A mother may be able to be in touch with you when you are remote."

Patient   "If that is so, it is rather difficult. Outside here there is no one to know what I need. In here when I hint that I want you to say something you never will. You seem pledged not to. It is a hopeless position to know that you have decided not to do the one thing needed."

Analyst   "How am I to know what is needed? You are making a search for the experience of not being met because no one was there to be in touch with you."

Patient   "How does this get anywhere?"

Analyst   "I think you are near feeling anger, which is all the time implied if you are reaching moments at which there was failure." (Patient asleep.) "You had a need then to be held with someone else in charge while you slept."

Sleep at this moment can be seen to have two meanings:
1.) A defense against anger at not being "held" well. In the anger at the analyst's failure to provide maternal care the patient comes to deeper realization of the reality of the need for such care.

2.) *Satisfaction of the need to be held by the analyst, represented by the couch.*

Patient   "I am up against a difficulty that the mechanism here is essentially verbal. It is difficult to picture progress along a verbal level. It is too much like magic for me to expect to benefit from it. Yet in a way perhaps it is not so illogical."

Analyst   "The couch is me more than if I were to actually hold you. The clumsiness of the whole matter would remind you only too well that you are not the infant you feel you are."

This illustrates the general principle that infantile needs can be satisfied in an adult only in a token or symbolic way.

Patient   "In mother's house or in my mother-in-law's house I not only have nothing to say but I go sleepy. In terms of what we said perhaps I am appealing for support, and I have a desire to sit or lie down. It seems that I cannot bother to be awake." *Pause.* "It occurs to me again, I am wondering whether the sleep represented a recognition of a failed desire to be fondled as a baby. I am dead to something. The difficulty is the fear of the anger. We have talked in the past about hidden anger. This reminds me of a situation of feeling annoyed with myself for being so cautious, not allowing anger to escape. I could stand a release of much more anger and I am annoyed at holding up so big a barrier to progress which depends on letting it go."

Analyst   "There is a need for you to feel sufficiently integrated to stand the effect of being angry."

Anger becomes possible when the patient becomes aware simultaneously of the actual analytic situation which can meet primitive needs in a token way only, and of the primitive needs themselves, directed toward the analyst. The disparity between what the patient needs and what the analyst can offer is an important source of insight as to the nature of the primitive needs. This disparity can only be reduced by acceptance by the adult of token or symbolic gratification.

Patient	"Now I feel I could stand more disruption."
Analyst	"If I am right in all this you are angry with me for not holding you, which is the original failure coming into the present."
Patient	"I feel here too that when I have nothing to say there is some mechanism saying, 'You are all right; is it worthwhile risking a disturbance? You might be able to manage.' It is no good appealing to this voice. I am prepared for the risk but the other part of me is too cautious."

Wednesday, 29 June

Patient	"I had a dream last night. It has faded. It hinged round something near a true story of my wife and a man. It was nearly a nightmare. Perhaps I was fighting with him or struggling. The last two or three nights I feel I ought to have fought him more vigorously at the start, to have been less weak. The dream is a dramatization of what I wish had taken place."
Analyst	"There seems to be something strengthening in you, enabling you to reach the struggle which has always been implied."

This represents a period of developmental progress, from the need for infantile nurture, which had been revived in recent hours, and toward the problem of oedipal rivalry. The recent awareness of wishes for infantile nurture can be said to have released this period of psychosexual maturation.

Patient	"Yes, sometimes I have the feeling that my relationship to my wife might alter. I have felt that if I approached her now and became more affectionate she might possibly find me more acceptable. I have heard less about the man. Perhaps she is not seeing much of him. I have no more to go on than a subjective feeling."
Analyst	"Often we see you get towards the idea of a struggle

between two men and then a retreat from this position. Now you seem to have come up to it again."

Patient   "I remember that we discussed a time or two ago about my wanting to be mothered or fondled and so on, and as I went away yesterday I thought perhaps I have wanted this from girls, and my wife has not any interest in this but would like to be fathered. On the bus I thought, I have a fear of being mothered. You remember the music teacher in the first analysis with you. To be mothered would be all right if it were by the right person. My mother-in-law is the wrong person. In part I despise myself about childish or effeminate attitudes. Unfortunately I chose my wife who just does not like mothering. If someone appeared only too anxious to supply affection and motherliness then if I play with the idea of this I am filled with alarm."

Analyst   "With me you get certain limited examples of mothering but these lead you to see the absence of mothering from the right person at the right time."

Patient   "I am not sure I understand this process. Whether in analysis one goes through what one has missed in token form like embryo in evolution? I can understand that. It seems more reasonable."

Analyst   "There is a relationship between what you feel about women and what you feel about analysis. When I do well you feel strengthened to meet the failures which have distorted you and angered you about this. Anger simply was not there because you were not organized into a strong enough position to be angry."

Patient   "So I can only see two alternatives. One is to go through a mothering process and the other is to be angry because of the absence of good mothering at the right moment."

Analyst   "We shall see in the course of the treatment." (Patient asleep.) "It seems that when you came towards the idea of a clash with father you were thrown back on the question of whether it was worthwhile, and your relationship to your mother was not strong enough or well enough founded so that you were thrown back on the weaknesses in this relationship." (Patient sleepy.)

Patient   "I was not actually asleep. I had paused because you

	were going too fast. I was not keeping up so I stopped, which was a reaction to your going too fast."
Analyst	"If I went on ahead that would be teaching and not psychoanalysis."
Patient	"It is difficult for me to accept responsibility that I have to set the pace but I can see why that must be."

Pause.

| Analyst | "Just now when I went too fast I was exactly like your mother at her worst, or at any rate as you felt her to be at some critical early time. The present was the same as the past and implied in it all is anger with me." |

Dr. Winnicott had interpreted too rapidly for the patient to follow. This was interpreted as a repetition in the treatment of inadequate maternal adaptation, or failure of maternal care, or failure of the continuity of the "holding environment." The patient's reaction to this was to withdraw, stop participating in the analysis, and to experience episodes of sleepiness and sleep. The withdrawal and sleep are interpreted as methods of defending himself, his "true self," from impingement by the analyst. This "impingement" is interpreted as a repetition in the transference of the same kind of "impingement" which led originally, in infancy, to the establishment of the split or fragmentation whereby a "false self" defense was established for the protection of the inner "true self." The division into a true self protected by a false self can be compared with Freud's "rind" concept of ego development to be found in Beyond the pleasure principle *(1920).*

The original traumatic "impingement" is presumed to have occurred in early infancy, before the ego was sufficiently differentiated for full knowledge of the fact that the "impingement" came from the outside world, and therefore for the full experience of anger appropriate to being subject to intrusive assault from the external environment. The patient's experience of anger within the transference was inhibited, but to the degree that he was able to feel anger, it is assumed that he was experiencing it not as a repetition of an earlier experience, but as something newly achieved.

The anger is justified in the present, by actual behavior of the analyst which reproduces trauma that originally disrupted development because it occurred before the ego was sufficiently developed to experience anger.

The patient has become able to answer the question about which he had felt hopeless earlier. (See p. 479.)

Patient	"There is a practical problem here with the small daughter who is fed on the bottle. We have tried to wean her on to a cup but she is not enthusiastic. I am torn between pushing her on and avoiding allowing her to become backward, relying on the bottle until she is too old and people would criticize and say it was absurd, but on the other hand I want to avoid the trauma of taking it away from her. There are two schools of thought : push and not deprive. Also in hospitals when children come in with dummies the first thing the nurses do is to deprive them of the dummy. Now it seems to me that this must be a bad policy just when the children are deprived of their home environment. It must make the separation harder so with my own child I can see how my own background contributes to the dilemma."
Analyst	"The children at hospital are usually older than a year and at a year, which is the age of your little girl, it must be even more true that hurrying can do harm. But in regard to yourself the trouble was at a much earlier stage when you simply could not do with being pushed on, and with failures of adaptation."
Patient	"It is better to meet the scorn of other people than to risk hurting a child."
Analyst	"The scorn of other people just does not count when you are in charge of so small an infant."
Patient	"The conclusion is that the idea of a struggle with the child is bad. Later the child knows what is happening and the struggle is less harmful like when a child refuses to eat or to learn. I see now that there can be value in a struggle later when things have gone well at the beginning. *(See Note pp. 295-296.)* There is the question of my wife's attitude about my sister's children who are naughty. She fears that the familiar pattern is reappear-

ing. I do see now that she is actually alarmed at the struggle which is not abnormal at their age as it means that they have not given in. All this seems remote from my problem but I suppose it has some bearing on it. The question is how to get back. To sum up, my own problem is how to find a struggle that never was. In the dream it was the struggle that was missing."

Analyst   "You were not able to get the relief that the triangular situation brings when a child is in a clash with father; relief from the struggle with mother alone."

Patient   There was a renewal of the stopping here when he said, "This is like going out. An annihilation of you is implied." *Pause.* "I realize here from time to time that there is danger in too much excitement because the idea of excitement involves rushing away. Anger is the same. If I was suddenly excited I would get up and tell you things and do things. Excitement is no good here."

Analyst   "The risk is too great for you because of the clash."

Patient   "A feature of excitement is irritation that it is not private. This applies to sexual matters. I have always had a difficulty that in sexual relationship with a girl there is no privacy because there are two people. It is undesirable. On several occasions I have felt loneliness suddenly when in relationship with a girl as if I had stopped seeing her. Also I upset my wife the first holiday we went on after marriage. We went with people and I did not want to be with her alone. I did not want to be excluded from the others, or else I feared what would happen if there were only two of us."

Analyst   "A bit of each."

Patient   "I also realize the difficulty with my wife about treatment here. I want to talk to her about here; I want somebody else in on it. I don't want one to the exclusion of the other. The trouble with mother is that it excludes father."

Analyst   "On another occasion you said that what you needed was for the two parents to recognize you as an infant so that there would be the three of you."

Patient   "The idea of mother being perfect seems to exclude father. The word 'mother' and 'smother' seem to me to be related."

Analyst   "You are trying to deal with mother's hate mixed up with her love."

Patient   "Not that way. She eliminates the struggle with father because he joined in her plot being clever about it."

Friday, 1 July

Patient   "The first thing that comes to me is something I noticed last week. Some doubt as to how to begin because you said I try too hard at the beginning, and so it struck me that to talk at the beginning is almost wrong. I ought to be wary about this."

Analyst   "You feel it is unnatural to be the one starting."

Patient   "The last two times I started with a tremendous rush, but on the whole I was thinking about this on the way here; that would be a natural form of behavior."

Analyst   "Being as careful as you are certainly prevents both silence and surprises."

Patient   "Also I remembered that I had a clear dream last night although I have forgotten it. It's curious; I remembered it one hour after waking; I then lost it. There are two things in association with the dream. There is a semblance of truth and also a struggle in it but this may be artificial."

Analyst   "A bridge between your inner reality and external life, although you have forgotten this dream now. *(See Note p. 542.)* Do you think of it as having been pleasant or unpleasant?"

Patient   "Not as unpleasant as previous dreams."

Analyst   "There seems to be a struggle."

Patient   "Yes, I think it was with the wife's boy friend." *Pause.* "At the moment I am skirting round the various ideas to find somewhere to start. Ideas come and then get dismissed as incoherent, unimportant."

Analyst   "What you are preventing is taking up unformed ideas and seeing where they get to. Perhaps they might not even get as far as being words but might be just sounds."

Patient   "It is a jumble of words, not meaning anything. Odd bits and pieces — tokens."

Analyst   "I am thinking of the period that we have spoken about before you could express ideas, when prattling or even just babbling was what you could manage. There is a question of what kind of audience you have and what you feel I am expecting."

Patient "There is also a fear of letting you have things that I have not had time to go through first. I am anxious lest you should be misled and chase the wrong ideas. Also there is a possibility of a deeper fear that I might get to an uncomfortable situation." *Pause.* "A lot of these ideas are related to things to do with work. There really is no real cause for anxiety. In the past in this sort of situation the interpretation was that I did not want to bore you with hospital matters. Now there is more the element of deliberately keeping you out of them. I don't want you reaching to all parts of my world. I have a feeling of danger that you might become too omnipotent. There must be some way to keep you out."

Analyst "You are telling me about positive elements in keeping me outside, which means having the right to your own inside. I think there may be something to do with mother here." (Patient sleepy.)

Patient "Today I seem sleepy and there is some excuse. Friday's a busy day and so on, but that isn't all."

Analyst "I am not sure that you know what I was saying."

Patient "Yes, I think I do know, but I was thinking of something while you were talking."

Analyst "I think I ought not to have wakened you."

Patient "I feel accused. I don't want to be caught."

Analyst "You were having a secret sleep and you feel that I discovered this secret."

Patient "There are various reasons. For one thing I insult you by sleeping; for another, I don't like the idea of you apologizing for sending me to sleep. There is a pattern of not wanting to find you too ready to withdraw and to apologize and so on. It puts me in the position of having to look after you."

Analyst "And also spoils the idea of a struggle."

Patient "If I apologize to my wife she gets annoyed. Apologies can be overdone. An apology commands acknowledgement. It cannot be left; it expects some further action." *Pause.* "I suppose I distrust sleep. This is not the right place for it. It will be noticed and so I have to wake myself in order to forestall comment."

Analyst "If you sleep you leave me like a few days ago when you said that you stopped because I was going too fast."

Patient "Yes, I could not keep up, so it was not worth trying. At the moment I am thinking in terms of progress in the analysis. Sleep is irritating in that while I am asleep there can be no communication here. Somewhere or other finding it difficult to talk here is related to difficulties outside which are rather new. I had a busy day today. I got behindhand with notes and things. It is a cause for worry. And it is new that these external worries are reflected in disjointedness here in the analysis."

Analyst "This is another example of there being less distinction between two aspects of your life."

Patient "Usually external problems stimulate me here. Now they only lead to confusion and sleepiness. It is outside things that are getting too confused." *Pause.* "I had an idea then associated with all this running away. Firstly, silence and sleep are the same as running away. Secondly, which is new, I feel today I got into a mess and I would like to run away from this situation. Once I talked to you about brushing past you but I did not at the time recognize that I was fed up. Now I feel that there was confusion that cannot be coped with, and I wanted to go away and try again next time. It reminds me of a situation of a child dreaming. People say it's only a dream. The thing is to wake up. It's the same sort of quality. I would like to wake up, that is, get up, go away."

Analyst "The dream seems to take you towards the uncomfortable."

Patient "One idea is that you are critical of me for not playing my part. Also that I waste your time and I ought to justify coming here."

Analyst "How far has the hour been disrupted by my breaking into your sleep? It seems to me that what I did was rather like the original trauma that disrupted you."

Patient "The danger was that I was encouraged to be precocious. I could read very early indeed and it strikes me now that this has a doubtful advantage."

Analyst	"By early reading you lose being read to while going to sleep."
Patient	"It occurs to me, one thing that has annoyed me about my wife for two years is that she is unwilling to talk last thing at night."
Analyst	"Possibly she might talk and you go to sleep while she is talking."
Patient	"But it is irritating to me that she has made a blunt declaration, 'I am not going to talk.' Communication is at an end. There is something also in it of an idea of myself needing her to be available until sleep. It is a hazy idea but I find I am annoyed that she won't say goodnight. I would like conversation to be available until one of us goes off to sleep."
Analyst	"There is a positive element then in my talking and your going to sleep. The lack of this positive element might have contributed to your finger-sucking." *Pause.* (Here his hand was over his mouth and face.)
Patient	"Also if I make you too anxious about waking me I might produce a situation in which you are scared to do anything. It is an indefinite danger arising out of my sleeping that you might do nothing and I would never wake. This is all part of my anxiety about your being too apologetic and not being in command."
Analyst	"There are two things I do. One is when I am good enough I displace your mother and others who failed. When I am bad I reactivate the bad past and it comes into the present."
Patient	"Part of the anxiety is that if I put myself in your situation, and I thought of this while coming here in the train, I would not be able to manage these difficult matters. Recently you drew attention to the effects of your own actions. If I were doing the same thing what I did would be full of blunders. It seems you have got to be on top of everything."
Analyst	"Certainly I make mistakes but there are times when these can be valuable if acknowledged."

Tuesday, 5 July

Analyst	(I was late on this day, which was already a postponed

time. This had no perceptable effect on the material. There was an exceptional noise because of a cocktail party next door.)

Patient   "Oh! coming here today I was not thinking about how to start because there is no immediate or pressing problem except the vague problem of aim."

Analyst   "These words, 'vague problem of aim,' seem to me to be quite fundamental to your illness."

Patient   "I am not sure what I am aiming at."

Analyst   "There are many ways in which this has appeared, one of which was that in the second analysis you were not able to come directly to me but I had more or less to go and look for you. Also you have said that in your first analysis you had no aim. At the beginning, like other infants, you had no aim and this problem has remained with you."

Patient   "I am not sure what you are meaning about 'at the beginning.'"

Analyst   "Put very crudely, when a baby has tasted milk he knows that his aim is to get at milk, but if no milk is presented the aim remains undirected. This idea can be spread over the whole of the details of infant care. It seems to me that your words, 'vague problem of aim,' state the whole thing and there is no solution for you except that something comes from me."

Patient   "This seems to be a general expression of a lot of problems in my life where I have no aim or objective. What sort of a job I am to take, for instance, and about the whole of my future. So far everything has depended on accidentals."

Analyst   "Possibly that is the only thing that your mother failed you in, in meeting your original impulses and giving your aim a direction. In this way you have an exaggeration of a difficulty that is inherent in human development. It seems that mother was unable to be sensitive enough at the very beginning in the way that she could only be by an identification with her infant."

Patient   "I don't quite see how."

Analyst   "You will remember when you put your hand to your face and I said, 'If I were a sensitive mother of an infant

I would know that your face needed contact.' " *(See pp. 656-657.)*

Patient   "So the question now is, should I try to rectify the error or recognize that something is missing in my development?"

Analyst   "You have two alternatives: either finding me good enough or finding me failing you, in which case anger is implied although you have not reached this stage."

Patient   "I have to decide to find out whether it is possible to correct the omission."

Analyst   "A thing that comes from this is that psychoanalysis takes you back not to something good that has been forgotten but to a failure or an absence of something."

Patient   "It seems that I have to learn how to manage to find an aim. By contrast with my present aimlessness I feel I ought to have an aim now."

Analyst   "What you are saying is that you feel hopeless and you are saying what you feel hopeless about. It is about this matter of aim."

Patient   "Now is the time to alter. Perhaps I have to make a conscious decision."

Analyst   "I think not."

Patient   "So perhaps I have to go to you for something."

Analyst   "Just here you have a dependence on me and you are saying that at the moment you feel I am failing you. You are working away at the idea of the start of the hour, but it is the work done in the middle which elucidates this problem."

Patient   "I would like to say that the start is not always awkward. In the last few weeks the difficulty in starting has been less or even absent."

Analyst   "You remember you said that on two occasions you felt that you started with a torrent. The changes come through the work we do in the whole hour and the change to be expected is that this problem of aim may disappear. What we do in the hour depends on the matter of subtleties in our relationship."

The "subtleties" in the relationship between the analyst and the patient to which Dr. Winnicott refers in this interpretation consist of his responses to the patient's expression of needs which the patient is not yet able to experience as wishes or desires. The analyst can respond to such expression on the part of the patient by a reaction which in some way or other meets the patient's need, and in that way lets the patient know what aim, object or direction can be given to a previously inchoate need. At the same time the inevitable gap between the analyst's reaction and the primitive needs of the patient who is regressed in the analytic setting are acknowledged, and the patient's anger at such a gap is recognized as legitimate both in the present and in the past.

Patient	"I recognize the need for subtlety. This presents a new difficulty or emphasis. There is not much point in my asking specific questions or bringing up concrete matters. An example occurred to me while I was waiting. I might discuss a specific topic but what would be the point? The topic has not much to do with me and it might cover up the difficulty about talking and be a bad way to start talking."
Analyst	"A specific question limits itself."
Patient	"I wanted to ask your opinion on an interesting topic but it seems unlikely to get me anywhere."
Analyst	"The question may contain something valuable although I do see what you mean that if I simply answer it I am being of no use."
Patient	"But I think it is not so much that I want to know the answer as that the question might interest you yourself. So that might start you talking, just in the way that one deals with some chance meeting with a person, finding out their line, etcetera. It is an opening gambit to be abandoned later. The question was about a letter in the *British Medical Journal* this week. It had to do with the treatment of skin disorders by hypnosis. This seems a curious idea that a specific defect could be cleared up piecemeal. I have read something by Freud about hypnosis a long time ago which suggested that he started using it and abandoned it but it seemed to me he never gave much of a reason. The idea of hypnosis suggests that I am trying to get something out of you, a short

cut, or that you should take the initiative. So the question might have importance on its own."

Analyst   "If I become the dominating figure then that eliminates the problem of your having your personal aim met. This seems to represent again your extreme hopelessness that we might meet in a subtle way on equal terms."

Patient   "About hypnosis, I always felt that it just could not happen to me. I cannot imagine how anyone could set about it. I would be so sceptical from the start. It is out of the question that I should get into a hypnotic state."

Analyst   "It is interesting in view of the fact that sometimes you look as if you are asking for it when you go sleepy and want me to dominate, but this brings out what you have yourself expressed, which is that there is very great hostility wrapped up in this sleepiness. Nevertheless the whole of this is a continued expression of your hopelessness about our meeting in a way in which there is a subtle interchange."

Patient   "I must have been aware of the idea of a subtle interchange because I recognize that I have been looking for just something like that, without really knowing it. I could express my difficulty with women in this way, that I can only think of two ways of establishing a relationship. By one way it all comes from me; by the other way, which of course doesn't happen, it all comes from the girl, and I would not like it if it did. So I must have been aware that there could exist a satisfactory compromise which is described by these words, 'subtle interplay.' "

Analyst   "This which we now call subtle interplay has been happening all the time in the analysis. It is not something that might happen tomorrow but something that is happening now."

Patient   "In a way, yes, but it so frequently gets broken off or does not develop. We break off and start again."

Analyst   "At these points of breaking off I am doing exactly what was done badly originally and you are affected in the present as at the beginning."

Patient   "It occurs to me now that often I come here hopeless about starting and cannot see any way in which there could be a solution. Then half way through I notice suddenly that I have been doing what I thought to be impossible — talking and getting somewhere. It is as if I suddenly wake up and notice that I am doing something I thought out of the question."

Analyst "We are both engaged in this matter of subtle interplay. I think that the experience of subtle interplay is pleasurable to you because you are so vividly aware of hopelessness in this respect."

Patient "I would go so far as to say that it is exciting."

Analyst "The word 'love' means a lot of different things, but it has to include this experience of subtle interplay and we could say that you are experiencing love and loving in this situation."

Pause.

Patient "Again I notice something today that seems different. Could it be that there is more noise than usual?"

Analyst "There is a great deal of noise today because of a cocktail party next door, and also the children that we are used to are in a more excited state and are playing more noisily than usual. I noticed that you did not make any remark about this at the beginning."

Patient "I noticed it but it did not seem worth mentioning."

Analyst "The fact that you did not comment on this at the beginning now comes in as a positive contribution to the hour, because that would have been simply getting away from the vague problem of aim. You would have started by reacting to an external event."

Patient "This expresses part of my difficulty with my wife. When I try to talk to her I do just this thing. I talk about concrete things that I know she is not interested in, and it gets nowhere. She must be aware that I am casting about for some way of breaking the silence and she rejects it all. She refuses to contribute. At times I feel like scolding her for not recognizing my need for chat. In fact I have scolded her."

Analyst "I am not in a position to judge what your wife would be like if you were normal but here we have your wife on strike against being a therapist."

Patient "I have no means of judging what she would be like if I could take all these things for granted." *Pause.* "Here I am up against a difficulty in that she expects me to take a more decisive line. I feel there is no point. It has got to come naturally and she won't understand that attitude. I have been speculating, if I were to go home unexpectedly and were to find her boy friend there. In the past I have just walked out. Ought I to take a stronger line, I wonder, and insist on his going? But I don't know if there is any point in being more decisive. I don't really know what I want to happen. I imagine a situation in which there is a test, but what is the test and what is the answer that I want? Do I want her to be sorry? Do I want to be tough with the man? Do I want to challenge her actually to defy me? I don't like the idea that I am not able to face up to the situation if it should arise."

| Analyst | "The thing that is absent in your relationship to your wife is subtle interplay, which we know in part depends on your inability to take this for granted. In a sense we have now to come round to an answer to the question because it could quite reasonably be said that Freud abandoned hypnosis and developed psychoanalysis because he saw the value of subtle interplay between analyst and patient and realized that this very thing was eliminated in hypnosis." |

Wednesday, 6 July

| Patient | "I was just thinking. It occurs to me to say that I had a dream last night. There is only a bit that I remember at the moment. I was having an exam (I am not sure of its nature) at the hospital. It was conducted by Professor 'X' of my medical school. The practical was being done on patients that are in my care so the examination was rather of the nature of a chat — a discussion without the examination of patients. It would have been silly to have examined them because I knew a lot about them anyway. In a way I have a sort of exam next week, the interview about the job that I am already doing as a locum; and also about a hospital. There is a connection with the fact that these interviews about jobs have nothing to do with medicine. It is a curious tradition that one is never asked questions about clinical medicine." |

Analyst   "I would take out of the dream the word 'chat.' You remember how it came in recently. There seems to be some sort of idea of a contact with the professor in a play area."

Patient   "He is a genial man reputed for being friendly. I have just remembered that I saw him recently when I dropped in at my hospital. As a matter of fact, I was disappointed because he did not recognize me though I could hardly expect him to as I was only a student. But some of the other staff might have. Perhaps he is snobbish. He could represent a fatherly figure for me."

Analyst   "He is a man that you would like to be able to have an easy relation to."

Patient   "Yes, but he is inaccessible. At the moment I do not feel like challenging him."

Analyst   "The fact that he is a genial figure makes the position tantalizing."

Patient   "Yes, because others there do seem more willing to recognize students."

Analyst   "If an exam were to be on your own patients you would come off rather well, would you not?"

Patient   "Professor X would be critical. He sets a high standard; you can't bluff him. Also it comes in that although he has a genial personality he demands a very high standard of work from his house physicians so that they have no time off at all. At the time when I first worked I needed weekends, and the prospect of a job under Professor X would have been gruesome with no time off at all. I feel alarmed at the idea. It's curious that he should demand such a standard for his house physicians and not tolerate the same thing for his own patients. A curious tradition, asking too much and taking advantage of the fact that such jobs are very much sought after. So there is a good deal of resentment about his genial character. I almost blame him for my not trying to get a job there because of his needing work without relief."

Analyst   "So you would really have liked a job at your own hospital."

Patient   "Yes, there are great advantages to be got from that. It's a matter of prestige, but in regard to experience the job is not good — fewer patients and less responsibility —

but you can't overlook the prestige element. Also there builds into this a film that I saw last night, 'The Women's World.' The president of a large motor works invites three leading salesmen and their wives to stay with him. On the behavior of these couples during the holiday he is to decide who to give an important job to."

Analyst   "What a terrible situation!"

Patient   "It's like my own position — one interview and three other candidates."

Analyst   "So the word 'struggle' comes in as well."

Patient   "I hadn't thought of that aspect. All the time in my hospital jobs I have not struggled for anything. I have hoped to be fitted in. It is an uncomfortable feeling. I don't seem to have the ability to fight my own way."

Analyst   "The idea of struggle and of the rejection of the unsuccessful candidate certainly comes in at the present time through the film."

Patient   "Yes. One of the characters in the film said, 'What a pity we are forced to hate friends.' "

Analyst   "So you are forced to hate the other three who are applying."

Patient   "I was not aware of that but I see it in the background. I have never been able to recognize this hatred. There has always been a lack of jealousy and for some time I have known that it ought to be there. So I turn my hate against the system that compels one to compete. I remember in my first job I competed with three others and I was pleased to get it. I never thought of the others as people. They were just competitors. I got an intellectual satisfaction."

Analyst   "You were not in a position then to triumph over people."

Patient   "I was only dimly aware of primitive rivalry. It seemed too childish to allow myself to gloat over the unsuccessful. As a small boy I might have gloated when favored at home but it was undignified, and this is not proper adult behavior."

Analyst   "Did you get there in childhood even?"

Patient   "The first idea that comes to me is that on occasion I got father's ear in competition with my sisters and gloated at having beaten them."

Analyst	"Do you think that has had to do with your being a male when they were girls?"
Patient	"That may well have been. I feel that competition is robbed of significance because girls are different so it is not on fair grounds. If it had been with a brother that I competed that would have been a real victory."
Analyst	"But you are implying an inherent victory. Simply that by being a male you have a superiority."
Patient	"Yes, I suppose." (Doubtful.) *Pause.* (Thinking.) "I am stuck here. I think we are pressing too far."
Analyst	"It may possibly be my fault."
Patient	"I made too much of the absence of competition. Parts seem genuine enough. There is a general lack of concern."
Analyst	"It seems that there is something here which may be true but it is not the main thing at the moment."
Patient	"I am not sure at all how much being a male really fits in except to emphasize loneliness. Also an inability to face up to competition is one thing I came here to see about."

Pause.

Analyst	Here I started an interpretation —
Patient	"Sorry, I lost which subject we were talking about. You mean, does coming here exclude others from coming? I am not convinced as I think that is something that you have brought up. Or if it is there I am not willing to recognize it. Perhaps there is something more in it because my wife's criticism of my coming here and my own criticism of psychoanalysis is that it is a treatment only available to a very few. The treatment is not justified as it is only fortuitously available and I have never really answered this question. I just ignore it. I need the treatment and that's that. At times the idea is uncomfortable." *Pause.* "Something I was thinking is perhaps an extension of the idea of wanting to be helped and being ashamed of it. I remember the criticism felt by the patients at the hospital of the role of the P.S.W., who did not seem to fulfil two important functions which are hers. She did not keep in touch with relatives and she was not able to inform them when approached, and also she did very little to help patients into jobs, rehabilita-

tion, and so on, after they left. This did not apply to me. The idea was, go out and find one if you want a job. I felt irritated. The idea of someone not doing what they were supposed to do."

Analyst "This is again to do with struggle."

Patient "It is the same with the work done by almoners in hospital. They are part of the family supplying parental responsibility, but I wonder if it is not looking after the patients too much. This is part of a criticism of the welfare state. I am annoyed that I myself expect and want a hospital organization to take over and look after patients so that they get social as well as medical care. In the same way, on leaving medical school the newly qualified doctor wants a job fixed up. This means weakness, immaturity. I do not feel clear about it."

Analyst "Included in it all is your inability to stand triumph, to accept your own aggressiveness."

Patient "About medical patients I find myself oscillating between complete care and complete abandonment. On the one hand I am pushed by the feeling that it is nice, comforting, to give social care. On the other hand I feel critical. This is mollycoddling. The weakness in me is that I can't formulate my own opinion. A lot of my indecision is part of this not wanting to accept responsibility for myself and my own decisions because they are made by other people's decisions. I hide the difficulty about deciding things by saying it doesn't matter what I feel about it." *Pause.* "At the moment I feel I have wandered round. I have been too dilatory. I have not put pressure on one object. I feel confused. One thing is that I feel I have failed to impress you. Perhaps I was hiding that the criterion is whether I impress you or not."

Analyst "There seem to be two alternatives. Either there is something in the dream theme that I have missed and I have taken up the wrong points, or the other alternative is that I am right and that you are strongly resisting the idea that I put forward that the central theme is the hate of rivals. I have an idea that you feel I ought to be backing you up in the interview next week, as in fact I did do in your original interview. I am getting at this through the dream of Professor X."

Patient   "The idea occurs to me that he might be one of the assessors or someone like him although this is very unlikely. Also I recognize that it is farcical complaining, because I am relying on the fact that I am already working in the job so that they have some obligation towards me. I have wormed my way in. I feel guilty because I ought not to rely on prejudice in my favor."

Analyst   "Because this again eliminates the struggle and the overthrow of rivals which is what you are trying to get to."

Patient   "I can't afford to be honest and so I use unfair weapons, but it is not satisfying."

Analyst   "It is difficult to know which would be satisfactory to you :
1.) To fight.
2.) That your work should be better than that of the others.
3.) To worm your way in, and
4.) That you might be the better man.

"How would you feel if it were true that you were the best man in a general way of the candidates applying?"

Patient   "I don't know. Then there would be no competition."

Analyst   "It is quite clear that the satisfying alternative is the first, but you are unable to dream the dream in which you fight to kill your rivals."

Friday, 8 July

Patient   "The first thing that occurs to me is that I dreamed again the night before last of an exam. It was Professor X again, but the exam was more related to cases. Last night I dreamed of an exam again but it was not Professor X. It seems that the subject of a test or viva must be more important for me in the unconscious than I am prepared to admit. Three nights in succession I have dreamed in this way. It is curious that I notice that I remember the dream on waking and then again an hour later recapitulate. After that I forget the dream completely till I arrive here, then I remember, but by that time the subject matter has become elusive. It is curious how dreams like this come back. Just as I become fully awake the dream is there but I am still drowsy. Then it fades as I become alert."

Analyst   "All the time there is the external fact of the interview next week."

Patient   "Last time we spent a lot of time discussing this subject, but I am hazy about the form of the discussion."

Analyst   "Perhaps you remember that an important part of the discussion was the relationship between you and those turned down."

Patient   "Oh yes, I remember now. I notice today, it occasionally cropped up while I was doing outpatient work. In the rush I found myself tending to think of patients more as units than people — items of work to be got through. I found myself hoping or expecting to find nothing wrong, just to save myself from having to deal with them, and constantly had to pull myself up and to remember that these are people come for advice. I cannot expect them all to have nothing wrong. I repeatedly pulled myself up."

Analyst   "The matter of people compared with units is like the people who are rivals but who do not turn up in the last two dreams."

Patient   "The other side of the picture is of course that I only see people in the outpatients who have been twice or more before, so I am looking at the results of investigations, seeing whether there is a need for further treatment or whether to tell them they need not come again, or the people need regular checkups. So I do not feel so bad about it, but I have to keep my eye open for the genuine patient. It is a curious situation that the conscience comes into it. There seem to be two kinds of consultant that I work for : One aims at seeing patients and discharging as soon as possible to the G.P. The other tends never to discharge so the outpatient department is filled with old patients. In the first case I have to put on a restraining hand and in the second case it is the opposite. I find I tend to favor getting rid of patients, partly because I do not like long lists, and I justify myself by saying that I am saving the people unnecessary journeys. I find myself in the patient's position and reflect, 'what would I like?' and so on. So it's like coming here. I really only just now realized that I am coming to your outpatient department and the object is to not have to go. It is a reflection on my need to make sure that you are aiming at getting rid of me."

Analyst   "This business of your putting yourself in the patient's place and all that is one example of the subtle interchange."

Patient   "That is what I try to do. Both extremes may be justified but I try to strike a balance. I could have the entire population attending my outpatients. A guiding point is what is reasonable when one uses the patients' own feelings."

Analyst   "This is a description of myself with you."

Patient   "Yes, and with some patients one has to be on the lookout as they want to leave off, but one can see that they are not well. So here it is not just how I feel. I have to rely on you to know more than I do."

Analyst   "The principle is that you come here in order not to have to." *Pause.* "I cannot yet see the relationship between this and the dreams."

Patient   "One comment is whether one's attitude to people is suitable to the job. One's conscience comes into it."

Analyst   "You say that the interviews for jobs do not take into account medical acumen. I wonder whether you feel that they also omit an assessment of your conscience in regard to patients."

Patient   "They cannot assess this. There are only two ways of assessing this — the opinion of the consultant for whom one works and that of the patients. I feel in a way that I am still a fraud. I do not feel half as capable as others think I am. In medicine it is mostly bluff, and I have to ask myself, do I bluff more than the average?"

Analyst   "This is really an examination of myself. You are the one who has the chance to find out, as my patient, whether I bluff."

Patient   "The patient can say how good my bluffing is. He may notice I am mystified and seem lost. It is bound to happen because I am not a good actor. I cannot disguise myself. If I cannot make head or tail of a story I feel hot and bothered and show it. This is the same as wondering how you cope when you are lost here."

Analyst	"Do patients prefer the actor or the doctor who shows when he is confused?"
Patient	"Well, the actor is rather popular, but patients get put off by bad acting."
Analyst	"Joined up with this is your dislike of my being apologetic."
Patient	"I don't like apologizing when I am not certain. Also dealing with other people, doctors and almoners, etcetera, I personally feel that I look vacant. The thing is, do they notice it? I am sure they don't notice it nearly as much as I feel they do. I just hope they accept it as a mannerism or a pose."
Analyst	"I would like to remind you of the time when you stopped because I had gone on beyond you. (See p. 665.) I suppose this feeling that you look vacant is rather like this stopping or withdrawing or sleepiness that happens here."
Patient	"Or I pretend to understand when I am at work but here mannerisms and stunts would be noticed as such. I find that satisfying and even useful. And when I am not here I forget that others are not so observant as you are or that they do not know me and just would not notice. It is as if I imagine others act for you in your absence. Part of my sensitivity away from here is related to coming here where I am the topic."
Analyst	"Yes, here you are the topic but there they have their own thoughts as well, and their own topics."
Patient	"This brings me back to the job and the examinations. I think I fear this interview. It means much more to me than the job. It is a judgment on me. Am I generally any good or not? So I am concerned about the others because some will fail if I get the job, so it is a judgment on me for not considering whether the others are more qualified than me. This is a subjective approach. As I have been locum in the job I am known, and if they do not employ me it is rather like a rejection, so that I am likely to keep the job. I feel in general that I would prefer not to apply for a job in the same group so as to avoid this problem. It is unfair to the employers if they have an obligation to be good to an employee. I am trading on that. If I turn out to be no good I am taking a mean advantage

applying for this job. I have accepted some responsibility for the choice of myself."

Analyst   "There are three subjects : One is yourself, another is the job, and the third is the other candidates. What you are not mentioning is the fact that these people that you may be turning out could be friends. This came into the film." *(See also pp. 538-540.)*

Patient   "I do feel I do not want to go on, not today at any rate. I would like to come back tomorrow. I feel uncomfortable ; I have had enough ; I would like to run away."

Analyst   "The thing in front of you that is difficult for you is that you might be involved in triumph. This particular aspect of the interview is unacceptable to you, that there shall be a struggle and that you will fight and kill."

Patient   "Yes." (Sleeps.) "When you were talking about triumph it occurred to me that part of the anxiety when things are too difficult or when I have too much responsibility in a case is that things have suddenly gone too far ahead so I find myself alone on my own with no one to lean on out in mid air and so on. Running away means retreating. I want to go to mother's lap almost exactly as you described some time ago about a child walking to his mother and horrified to find himself on his own. Walking means separation. I can accept triumph if there is someone to share it with even if I have to imagine someone, but that is hazardous. The imagination may fail and I will be left holding the baby."

Analyst   "To some extent this has to do with your being an only son. Do you remember my speaking of this before?"

Patient   "No."

Analyst   "The fact that you had no brother may be an important factor. You said that in competition it took some of the gratification away if your rivals were sisters in relation to father."

Patient   "I feel that triumph is hollow if there is no one to show it to."

Analyst   "The difficulty here is between reality and fantasy. In a competitive game you can share your triumph with the other competitors if you win, but if it is a dream and your aim is to kill — (Patient deeply asleep.) — then you cannot share triumph with the rival."

(The question seriously presented itself as to whether I had made a technical error taking the subject over to rivalry, that is, going on ahead too fast.)

Patient "The last few minutes it has been very difficult to keep here at all. Perhaps I slept. I feel annoyed with myself for wasting time. There is absolutely no excuse." (Sleeps again.)

Analyst "There is the interview next week. The fact seems to be that this interview is in advance of you in your analysis. You are not really worried about the interview as such, but what it means to you, in terms of your relation to me, is something that you have not arrived at, and so you stopped. You cannot dream of killing the rival. Circumstances are behaving as I behaved the other day when I went on ahead."

Inhibition of dream and fantasy life leads the patient to experience the external event, the interview, as though it were the realization of a dream. He therefore finds himself anxious and inhibited in reality. (Compare Note p. 525.) This same factor, inhibition of fantasying, can lead in some cases to acting out in reality.

Patient "If I were applying for a job in the usual manner on equal terms it might be easier."

Analyst "It might, but I am not sure whether you could manage such a thing easily at the present moment in your analysis."

Patient "It is hypothetical. It might be. I am not worried about either the interview or the job as such. It is a combination of uncertainty with the feeling that there ought not to be uncertainty."

Analyst "I think that you are not ready for open competition."

Patient "If it were an outside job I could afford to be indifferent. The trouble is that this is 'in the family.' "

Analyst "Yes, just that."

Wednesday, 13 July

Analyst On Tuesday, 12th July, the patient rang up at the time of his hour to say that the combination of the hot weather and his being very tired made him wish to miss a session.

Patient   "I felt exhausted last night. By the way, I didn't get the job. That and the heat made me unwilling to come. A local hospital has very little to say in the choice of its resident staff. About the interview I felt unusually agitated, more than I have done on previous occasions. It is curious, because there was no reason. I felt that I was not the same person as in other interviews. For half an hour I was excessively bewildered and then felt relief. To get this job would not have been quite satisfactory for me. I had the feeling that it would be unfair taking an advantage. At least now with another job I shall be able to satisfy myself that I am on my own feet. Some of this may be myself reassuring myself. The advantage of this job was that I would be working in the same group and therefore must seem to be popular. It is not after all so impressive as one might think."

Analyst   "You were saying these things before the interview last week."

Patient   "This afternoon I feel more in favor of a break from treatment for a time. There are snags both ways. The advantage is that I would have more scope in selecting jobs. I feel that now coming to analysis depends on the job more than the other way round. The disadvantage would be that the process of analysis is incomplete so that I ought to get it completed before having a gap. I feel like trying it out. It's difficult for me to judge."

Analyst   "There are certain things that you have told me in previous sessions. You can see I am able to judge better than you. For instance, I can point out to you that in your description of the interview what has been left out is that you have been killed."

Patient   "I noticed a curious thing. One of the other candidates came in to see me in the morning before the interview. I wondered why he did it. He said did I think he might get the appointment and so on. It was silly to ask me. I wanted to say no, so as to limit the field. I felt hostility towards him. I think for the first time I felt hostility in such a situation and did not want to talk to him and he did not want to talk to me."

Analyst   "You seemed to be having the natural feelings belonging to this situation."

Patient   "I was warned by the staff that their favoring me would not carry much weight. After I came out I felt more friendly to the others. When one had been selected there was a change of atmosphere among the three who were left. We had nothing to quarrel about any more."

Analyst   "So you entered more than you usually have been able to do before into the rivalry situation."

Patient   "That applies in general too; I am more able to feel rivalry when it is present. I am able to summon up more hostility about my wife's boy friend. Not that I have seen him recently. My wife avoids our coming into direct conflict. If we were to meet now I would be more positive in my hostility. Certainly not begging for mercy. In general I am tending to lay down the law more firmly. In my work this is partly due to an increase in experience so that I am able to be more authoritative. Today doing a ward round with the junior I was able to make a definite diagnosis where he was not certain. And I did so without being apologetic. Some months ago the idea of being in authority was something I could only accept in theory. Now it feels more logical and it is less of an act; more natural. This was a clear-cut case; I could not help thinking why he did not notice what I noticed."

Analyst   "So experience does not make you clever all the time; it makes the truth seem more obvious."

Patient   "I wonder how I could not do it before." *Pause.* "At the moment I notice that you are not making any comment on whether I go on with analysis or not. Perhaps I do not want to feel I am coming here only because I want to even if I have a good reason. It would be easier if I did not have to accept responsibility for this sort of decision. A criticism against coming here is that I would be able to say no; nevertheless I would like your view. How important is it for me to go on coming?"

Analyst   "I will say definitely that I prefer it if you can continue. Nevertheless there is the point that I am also pleased about the progress which means that you might be able to put the job before the treatment."

Patient	"Am I justified in thinking it could be done?"
Analyst	"I do just think it possible."
Patient	"At the hospital where I was a patient, when I spoke about taking a job they said, 'You can but you need not.' This implied a gamble. Now that I have made progress here is it still a gamble?"
Analyst	"I think that it is all right for you to leave off but there is more for you to get out of analysis around the subject of rivalry, which you are only just beginning to be able to accept with its full implications. So I will say again that it is better if you can come in September and get on with it."
Patient	"I remembered this evening on the way here one of the chief jobs they offered me is in X, and I found myself not being very keen because it is further out. It is funny I never thought about whether I could get here from it or not, only that it was too far from home."
Analyst	"No doubt you have a good deal to discover in yourself as a result of the changes that have come about in the analysis recently."
Patient	"In the old days in the first treatment you said that it was quite a good result for war time. Would you be making the same sort of comment now? Good but incomplete? A breakdown is likely to occur later on?"
Analyst	"No, I would not say that now."
Patient	"Quite good enough is not good enough if I am due for a breakdown. How far is a breakdown inevitable? Probably it was when I left off the first treatment as I have never felt normal. I am concerned now that I do not really know what I want to do with my life."
Analyst	"I am saying clearly that I do want you to come in September. If you do not come I can see that there are advantages to be got out of the break."
Patient	"I can keep comparing my views on psychoanalysis with my views of it ten years ago. I used to express strong views that psychoanalysis was unscientific, feeling that analysts were too dogmatic, almost sectarian. If one disagreed with an analyst one became a heretic. So psychoanalysis seemed a bad thing. I held this view until I broke down. Now my experience is such that I do not know where I got those views from. It may have been

mother's fault. This is quite a recent idea that I have had. Her rigid adherence to Freud and analysis I find is not shared by most analysts. Analysts as a whole I find do not say that Freud is right and everything else wrong. They think as they go along. My wife quotes my words belonging to the time when I was hostile when I expressed fervent hostility to psychoanalysis, so my coming here now is regarded by her as a backsliding, doing something against my own principles. Also, ten years ago one thing that disturbed me was a book of Freud's in which he dabbled in anthropology. I can't remember — "

Analyst   *"Totem and Taboo?"*

Patient   "Yes. He was arguing from theory reconstructing the past through the present society. I have not read it for a long time, of course. I wonder if I would consider this a valid criticism now."

Analyst   "It interests me that you refer to *Totem and Taboo* as unacceptable. Is not the theme of that book that the brothers come together to kill the father? The hostility between the brothers is suppressed for the purpose of the overthrow of the father."

Patient   (Laughs.) "I never thought that I might have an emotional bias when I was critical then. At the time I was critical that Freud said that the oedipus complex was important in primitive society, which was, in fact, matriarchal. It seemed unlikely, considering the boys did not know their own fathers. Even daughters had no specific fathers. So it would be impossible to apply the same set of rules, but I must say I am very hazy about this and I have not thought of it for a long time. Perhaps I ought to get it out again."

Analyst   "It is possible for anthropologists to criticize *Totem and Taboo,* but not, I think, along the lines that you were critical. I would say that the general view is that there was an awareness of parentage, only there were certain customs relating to the use of uncles and so on."

Patient   "The idea of original sin plays an important part in it, I think, unless my memory is at fault. I had great hostility to the idea that since the dawn of time children have been concerned about the sexual relationships of their own parents. There is almost a religious bias running through the book coloring the whole attitude. As I was brought up an atheist (that was father's doing), the idea that I might have to accept religious ideas came to me as rather horrifying and made me antagonistic to psychoanalysis."

Analyst   "I suggest that there is something you are leaving out of the subject presented in that book. The sin is associated with the killing of the father, but you are not saying anything about the central theme, which is that all those who were antagonistic to each other loved their mother, and it was love of the mother that made them want to kill the father in the primal scene."

Patient   "I am hazy about sin and the way it came into this book."

Analyst   "Original sin in this book seems to me to come in as the love of mother."

Patient   "I have an inability to accept the idea of a universal hatred of the father. The idea is unpalatable, but I think there is more to be gained out of this to do with the present situation. In those days I was attracted by anything that was not dogmatic, but now I would say that I definitely favor flexibility. My criticism of medicine is the dogma in it. This must be so because we have been taught it."

Analyst   "All this time you are paying a tribute to myself. You have often asked me to be more dogmatic, but as you have partly said, you value my flexibility and my willingness to try things out as I go along. This especially comes in in regard to the question, shall you leave off treatment or not?"

Patient   "The thing about dogma is that it cannot be wrong. The great master, Freud, the Pope, Stalin; the acceptance of dogma is something that takes the place of father. You assume that he cannot be wrong. A father-figure. It is a bad thing to let intellect rest on illogical emotions." *Pause.* "In a way, I seem to be ending on a theoretical note. Am I unconsciously but deliberately avoiding digging up something?"

Analyst   "There is an avoidance along the lines of using me in a general way as an analyst, or perhaps a mother-figure, and ignoring the fact that I am also a father-figure for you in your analysis. When I say I want you to come back I am a mother-figure, and this is valuable to you insofar as you are infantile. There is another way of looking at it, however, in which I, as father, say you must come back. Now you are in a position in which you can defy me. In a third way of looking at the matter, the analysis is mother that you want and I am father. Either I kill you or you kill me, because we are in rivalry. Often we discuss these matters, but here in the matter of whether you come back or not in September, there is a practical situation, and an emotional rather than an intellectual problem is before you."

END OF TERM

(Almost nine months later, the patient sent the following letter.)

4 April

Dear Dr. Winnicott,

I feel that I owe you an apology for not writing before. When I last got in touch with you I decided to stop at least until Easter while I was working at ——— and then let you know.

On the whole it has proved very satisfactory and my plans, so far, are to continue as at present until my appointment expires next August.

I am not at all sure what I will be doing after that. It is not yet possible for me to plan that far ahead. I am tempted at times to abandon analysis as I now feel so well. On the other hand, I do realise that the process is incomplete and I may then decide either to resume with you, or should that no longer be possible, to start with someone else. It seems to me to be a great step forward that I can accept that idea fairly easily.

Should we not resume later on, I would like to use this opportunity to express my gratitude for all that you have done.

Yours sincerely,

————————

Epilogue

24

Summing Up

PETER L. GIOVACCHINI

This book presents various viewpoints on psychoanalytic theory and technique. Differences are expressed on a few topics, but there is a surprising consensus on the crucial areas and important questions. For example, it is at least implicit (and in most of the chapters explicit) that the subject of psychoanalytic technique requires serious reevaluation. Although the advent of ego psychology has brought about exciting theoretical extensions and modifications, there has not been an extensive application of new theory to clinical practice; on the contrary, there has been a definite *therapeutic lag*. To a large extent, adherence to "classical" technique can be explained by the weight of Freud's authority, the penetrating power of his discoveries, and the relative youth of psychoanalysis. His discoveries are so immense that it would almost seem pretentious to tamper with them. Technical approaches are even more esoteric since the psychoanalyst learns most about therapy from his training analysis; and the training analyst, in turn, has learned from his own training analysis. Thus, early postulates regarding treatment have been handed down through several generations (not many); because of transference identifications, there is little tendency to make critical evaluations. The training experience for a large group of analysts has been a highly emotional, intimate experience — one with both advantages and disadvantages.

With the passage of time and the increased number of persons seeking psychoanalytic training, the personal aspects of the psycho-analytic institute have been replaced by a more formal, didactic atmosphere. The classroom has become a more important supple-ment to the personal analysis in teaching psychoanalytic technique.

Apart from what might be considered the natural evolution of the psychoanalytic educational system, important practical factors have forced many analysts to reexamine Freud's original tenets on the practice of psychoanalysis and its theoretical rationale. *Many of Freud's dictums on the limitations of psychoanalysis are no longer self-evident when placed in the theoretical context of ego psychology,* and some analysts have taken a different view of a large number of patients who would have been categorically rejected for treatment in the early days of psychoanalysis. Parenthetically, we are faced with a paradox. Freud divided patients into treatable transference neuroses and nontreatable narcissistic neuroses. He devised many of the indications for analysis, however, from the successful treatment of certain patients; today certain analysts would consider many of these patients as fitting into the category of narcissistic neuroses, including the psychoses.

In any case, the number and types of patients seeking treat-ment and in some instances, directly asking for psychoanalysis have presented a distressing problem to the analyst who is trying to adhere to Freud's initial tenets. Parallel with this, the scarcity of patients who would be considered treatable is similarly distressing. These problems are reflected in this book; although they are not always spelled out precisely, they are alluded to many times in a strikingly homogeneous fashion. The chapters that deal with technique eventually raise the question of how to deal with patients who would have been excluded from psychoanalytic treatment in the so-called classical tradition.

In selecting clinical material, it is especially significant that *all* of the authors chose to discuss patients who would have been classified as narcissistic neuroses — patients who suffer from relatively severe characterological pathology. As an experiment, if a group of experienced analysts had been asked to write about psychoanalytic treatment, it might have been astonishing if all of them had described, even in the broadest terms, the same type of patient. Although the number of contributors to this book is comparatively small, this, in effect, is exactly what happened. This can be considered the unexpected outcome of a spontaneous, unintentional experiment. Consequently, patients who suffer from severe psychopathology were not excluded from discussion here about the psychoanalytic viewpoint. *Formulations and theoretical evaluations were, for the most part, made in a context that differs from Freud's original hydrodynamic psychoeconomic and id-oriented psychodynamic frame of reference. The type of psychopathology was often responsible for this metapsychological shift.*

In ego psychological terms, the patients described here showed remarkable similarities even in a microscopic fashion, so to speak, as well as in a grossly phenomenological fashion exemplified by a wide range of maladaptive behavior; these patients exhibited problems in their general adjustment to the external world rather than discrete symptoms. They tended to be vaguely dissatisfied, revealed a paucity of meaningful object relationships, and saw little purpose or direction to life. There seemed to be defects in both perceptual and executive ego systems that were reflected in a poorly structured self-representation. Most of the patients described here suffered from identity problems, which in extreme cases reached panic-like proportions, resulting in what has been called an existential crisis.

In contrast to the psychoneuroses, our patients suffered from pregenital fixations usually with developmental disturbances in the symbiotic phase. Attempts at adaptation included fragmentation and splitting mechanisms. They had a prominent need to fuse with external objects, especially during the transference regression.

GENERAL CONSIDERATIONS

From a broad viewpoint the therapeutic management of these patients centered on two principles : some authors wrote of technical maneuvers that were basically modifications of analytic technique, whereas others believed that an even stricter adherence, without parameters, to the psychoanalytic frame was required, especially for cases suffering from severe psychopathology.

The deviations described were minimal for the most part, and the therapist did his best to remain in an analytic context. These maneuvers were usually employed in extremely difficult situations with very disturbed patients, and they were designed to achieve sufficient stabilization so that analysis could proceed. In examining the therapist's behavior, the transference-countertransference interaction is highlighted; the analyst conducted himself in such a fashion that was in some way, antithetical to the patient's transference expectations. On other occasions, the analyst functioned as an ego adjunct, supplying integration by reinforcing reality-testing and helping the patient master difficult situations; at times, this meant helping the patient control disruptive inner impulses by strengthening repressive defenses or controlling the extent of regression.

Sometimes, the analyst's response *seemed* to be a purposeful deviation with a supportive intent. Some of the chapters described "interventions," apparently out of context, where the patient was told that his behavior demonstrated a need to impress, test, or frighten, or that it indicated feelings toward the analyst. These may be highly charged dramatic moments, but on closer examination are seen to direct the patient's attention to the transference implications of his behavior.

These confrontations gradually merge with the viewpoint that deviations from analysis are not necessary in the treatment of patients with severe psychopathology and, in some instances, may even be detrimental. The analyst with this orientation believes that all symptoms and behavior must be understood in terms of their adaptive value, especially in the transference context. Although the patient may feel disturbed, to perceive his feelings and attitudes as having even a modicum of meaningful purpose has a positive, integrating effect. Analysts with this viewpoint tend to be more optimistic about treatment in general and the range of treatable conditions. The influence of the environment is placed in a deterministic context and viewed in terms of the patient's motivations and adaptive manipulations.

Of course, no analyst would assert that all patients in any setting are treatable, and some of the most classically oriented analysts discuss the limitations of analysis in terms of environmental intrusion. However, even here it must be remembered that *the limitations of analysis are not attributed to intrapsychic factors, but rather to extraneous, outside influences. These analysts would rather abandon their approach entirely so long as such intrusive elements persist rather than modify their technique.* Later, these patients may seek analysis, having understood that the analyst was more interested in preserving the analytic setting than in instituting some other type of treatment.

Other analysts write about the content of their interactions which were specifically designed for patients suffering from severe psychopathology. In some instances, the therapist attempts to view all of the patient's productions in terms of their transference potential. This does not mean that he interprets everything the patient brings to him; rather, he attempts to evaluate what might be considered the amount of transference projection present in his associations. The transference focus thus becomes an observational viewpoint and the analyst attempts to help the patient look at his own productions in a similar manner. Patients who have special difficulties in distinguishing between themselves and the external world can gain considerable security by recognizing their responsibility in determining the events in their lives, as well as their reactions and attitudes.

Technical discussions often deal with the question of what should be interpreted. Some therapists do not believe that the genetic interpretation (for example, telling the patient that he is reacting toward the analyst as he reacted toward his father) is particularly useful for patients suffering from ego defects; to them, the past does not possess tangible reality. Feelings have to be expressed in the present so that distinctions can be made between what emanates from within oneself and what is outside. Consequently, some analysts try to limit their interpretations to the here-and-now aspects of transference-countertransference interactions; they try to scrutinize the patient's feelings toward themselves as examples of projections and *current* adaptations.

All of these topics are discussed in considerable detail in this book. Statements made by one analyst may contradict something said by another. Still, as mentioned at the beginning of this chapter, there was considerable agreement on the value of extending the psychoanalytic method, although there are many differences on the *specific* selection of patients.

DIAGNOSTIC FACTORS

Chapters 5 and 6 are primarily devoted to the criteria for psychoanalytic treatability; the approaches of these two analysts differ substantially, leading to further consideration of diagnostic procedures.

Besides the matter of indications for analysis (which, in one sense or another, is discussed throughout the book), there is the additional and broader matter of the diagnostic aspects of the psychoanalytic method in general. In addition to making distinctions among various emotional disorders (such as characterological problems, psychoses, and psychoneuroses — distinctions that are harder to make as we learn more and accumulate experience), the differential diagnostic potential of the psychoanalytic method should be examined. Early in his career, Freud discussed the distinctions between hysterical conversions and organic afflictions. Today psychoanalysts are often consulted to determine whether a patient's complaints are psychogenic or primarily organic. It is not unusual to find a psychoanalyst as chief of a liaison service in a department of psychiatry of a general hospital.

A colleague told me about a young woman who had been referred to him by a neurosurgeon for psychiatric consultation. The surgeon believed there were sufficient signs to warrant intracranial exploration. On the other hand, because the patient had indulged in considerable sexual acting out, he was suspicious about her general emotional stability. Her headaches and other symptoms may not have had an organic basis. My colleague did not believe the patient was psychoanalytically treatable. In the first place, she did not want to be analyzed; she indicated by her feelings and behavior that she was overwhelmingly frightened to look within herself. There were indications that she was terrified about dying and was using emotional difficulties to defend herself against what she felt might be fatal brain pathology. Still, she did not want to tamper with her psychopathology because she wanted to avoid acknowledging the possible underlying organic process. If a psychoanalyst understood her psychodynamics, then, he could reinforce a neurological diagnosis.

Two questions come to mind: First, if this formulation is correct, does it necessarily mean that there is organic pathology? Could the patient be reacting to the *fantasy* of having neurological pathology rather than an actual disorder? It does not seem likely that the psychoanalytic approach or point of view can offer anything specific to resolve this question, and, as we know, Freud had to face an analogous problem in determining whether infantile sexual traumas were fantasies or actual events in his hysterical patients. Can the psychoanalyst make judgments about reality factors that include organic diseases? Second, could the patient be developing symptoms of an organic disorder in order to avoid facing overwhelmingly disruptive emotional problems? In this case she may not want analysis because it is too threatening in uncovering her psychic pain; although an organic disorder is less threatening, it may have become dangerous with the suggestion of intracranial surgery.

There are, of course, many cases in which a psychoanalyst has made a correct organic diagnosis, even though the referral was made only for the treatment of psychopathology. *However, was such a diagnosis made because of the consultant's psychoanalytic frame of reference or was he, in fact, using his medical and neurological knowledge — in some instances, without being consciously aware of his medical diagnostic orientation?* If this is true, he is not functioning exclusively as a psychoanalyst. I believe these points should be emphasized because my discussions about psychoanalytic consultations with chiefs of liaison services indicate that they are not well known and accepted.

The psychoanalytic method is designed for a specific purpose, and questions about its diagnostic applicability to other areas are not settled. Recognizing its present limitations may, in the future, lead to discoveries that will be more tangibly useful in the organic realm than seems possible now. On the other hand, recognizing its current limitations does not, in any way, devalue the psychoanalytic approach; it merely delineates the boundaries. But within these boundaries, which include, from the viewpoint of most of our authors, the vast area of characterological disorders, the psychoanalytic approach is remarkably effective in augmenting our understanding of and influencing our ideas about treatability. The authors did not stray from the psychological frame of reference in discussing their ideas about the "selection" of patients.

THEORETICAL CONSIDERATIONS

The topographical hypothesis and the psychodynamic frame of reference have led to many useful deterministic concepts that clarify the seemingly bizarre and puzzling behavior of many psychoneurotic patients, especially hysterics. Attempts to use such a theoretical approach with other types of patients, however, have not been as fruitful.

The patients described here have suffered from characterological problems. They could not be conceptualized in terms of the return of a forbidden repressed impulse, the generation of signal anxiety, and the construction of a defense that is then reflected in symptomatic behavior. Instead, our clinical material encompassed problems that deal with the structure of the psychic apparatus. These patients did not have a disharmony between two areas of the mind, but they had something faulty in the anatomy, so to speak, of a particular segment of the psyche. Since the id, generally, is believed to have less organization and structure than the ego, the latter is thought to be responsible for synthesis and adaptation; and characterological defects are formulated in terms of ego pathology. Consequently, psychopathology is conceptualized from the viewpoint of ego psychology within the framework of the structural hypothesis.

The relationship of various ego subsystems to one another and the external world is examined rather than the conflicts between the ego and the id. All of the authors also seem to use ego-psychological concepts, saying very little about energetic factors based upon hydrodynamic discharge principles. The concept of psychic energy must be included even in formulations that do not emphasize intrapsychic conflict. Still, in the cases suffering from structural defects, one is more likely to encounter an inability to function rather than an undischarged tension. Failure to master one's problems results in discomfort and tension, but this is different from a quantum of energy seeking discharge.

Patients, today, focus upon their relationship with the outer world, and one can correlate their adaptations and their self-esteem with their sense of identity. The goal-directed, purposeful qualities of problem-solving behavior are discussed in terms of energy distribution which, in turn, is related to the integrity of the perceptual and executive ego systems. The complex demands of the adult world require fairly sophisticated responses. The ego has to have well-structured, adaptational techniques at its disposal, techniques that require energy in order to be activated. The more complicated the adaptive response, the more energy it may require. Briefly, secondary-process activities use ever increasing quantities of energy, depending upon the degree of complexity; they also demand more of the psyche than reactions based chiefly on primary-process elements.

Another important aspect of psychic equilibrium is the conservation of energy. A sophisticated response that leads to successful mastery uses energy efficiently, whereas maladaptive and poorly integrated defensive responses waste energy and lead to psychic exhaustion. Such exhaustion frequently happens to patients who suffer from severe psychopathology — patients who have poorly developed executive techniques and find it difficult to relate to what they feel are the inordinate demands of their environment. These patients often seem to be literally exhausted, and they manifest considerable confusion, even when confronted with a situation that would appear quite commonplace to another person. Without the memory traces of gratifying experiences that lead to efficient adaptational techniques, these patients have to resort to more primitive approaches to the problems of everyday life. During treatment, one is impressed with their lack of *functional introjects* and with the fact that their primary-process-oriented defenses are designed to preserve them from states of energy depletion.

I believe that the regressed state experienced during treatment can be compared with dreaming. Sleep is restorative; facing the problems of everyday life uses up energy that has to be replaced metabolically by nourishment and rest. During sleep intricate secondary-process activities are decathected; therefore, the energy required to sustain them is no longer used. The sleeping person is not confronted with the need to master the problems of the external world. Still, at some level the psyche is active, and internal tensions and demands have to be met. However, these inner demands do not require highly organized, well-structured responses. For example, dreaming can be thought of as an adaptational mechanism. From the theoretical perspective outlined here, the dream constitutes a method of resolving inner problems that demands less secondary-process-oriented solutions and thus requires less energy than more reality-oriented adaptative and defensive techniques. One can conceptualize dreams as states leading to energy conservation that enables metabolism to exceed catabolism, thus providing a restorative element.

Freud described dreaming, as above, in deterministic, functional terms. However, our formulation does not require a discharge hypothesis with a hydrodynamic analogy. Since this book emphasizes psychic structure, our formulation consists of a hierarchy of executive ego-system responses, responses that are determined by the introjects of either gratifying or frustrating experiences. Complicated needs call for responses with considerable organization, and these require more energy than responses to relatively simple needs. On the other hand, a more gratifying response is relatively efficient in conserving energy, whereas a primitive, maladaptive response — even though it has less secondary-process organization and requires comparatively less energy to evoke — is frustrating and wastes energy.

In the sleeping state dreams usually constitute a successful response to inner disturbances which, if unchecked, could awaken the sleeper. As Freud demonstrated, the relative lack of consciousness during the sleeping state does not permit the operation of intricate adaptations and defenses that require considerable energy; consequently, during sleep the psyche conserves energy but is vulnerable. The sleep regression exposes the psyche of patients who suffer from ego defects to trauma by cathecting threatening and disruptive introjects. Dreams resolve the inner disruption caused by the loss of sophisticated defenses and adaptations by the primary-process (less energy-consuming) elements Freud described. In ego-psychological terms the dream accomplishes a "detoxification" of disruptive introjects and permits the person to continue sleeping and to benefit from whatever restorative qualities are inherent in sleep.

Many of the patients discussed in this book said that an analytic session often had the same restorative effect that sleep ordinarily has. I have frequently had patients who felt both physically and emotionally exhausted at the beginning of a session, and their general appearance conveyed a lack of energy. At the end of the session they would feel cheerful, buoyed up, and energetic. This sometimes happened even though nothing of apparent significance occurred during the session. Since the analytic setting stimulates regression, in some ways it resembles sleep. Patients frequently lose their awareness of the passage of time, and a session may appear interminably long or inordinately short. Secondary-process-directed logical thinking is replaced by primary-process-oriented free association. Complex adaptive and defensive maneuvers are, to a large measure, relinquished, and sometimes there may even be a clouding of consciousness. As in the case of sleep, the analytic regression is characterized by relatively more primitive defenses and adaptation; since the regressed state can conserve energy, it can have a restorative effect. During sleep, the dream and the dream process represent a primitive adaptation; during the analytic regression, the transference projection serves almost the same function.

Since projection is a relatively primitive defensive adaptation, one can surmise that this operation requires less energy than those that utilize more reality elements. Patients with characterological problems eventually project early introjects onto the analyst; in so doing, they gain some freedom from their disruptive and constrictive effects. The transference projections thus achieve a detoxification similar to the dream and require less energy to keep such introjects under control than other, more intricate defenses.

Thus, pregenitally fixated patients derive considerable benefit from the analytic process in general, apart from insight-promoting goals. The analytic setting, insofar as it leads to regression, has a replenishing effect and makes available sufficient energy so that the work of analysis can proceed in the direction of acquiring further ego integration and freedom from the disruptive effects of archaic infantile introjects.

THERAPEUTIC CONSIDERATIONS

Since all of the contributors to this book devote the major part of their lives to treating patients, the theoretical considerations mentioned above are relevant to the extent that they lead to further understanding of the therapeutic interaction. In my summary here I will discuss certain theoretical aspects of the therapeutic process — a subject of universal analytic interest.

Psychoanalytic treatment traditionally deals with the analysis of defenses; however, we must further amplify the concept of defense. Ordinarily, defenses are believed to be psychic mechanisms that are reactions to unacceptable id impulses and whose function is to achieve repression of such impulses. Once again we are dealing with concepts of intrapsychic conflict, which have received very little attention in this volume. The contributors have said very little about the undoing of repression, the recovery of traumatic memories, and the lifting of infantile amnesia. Instead, they discuss the patient's interactions with the outer world and indicate that these conflicts seem to be derived from failures of adjustment. Behavior designed to compensate for such failures seems to dominate the clinical picture, giving it defensive characteristics. In this sense, the defense is conceptualized as an adaptive mechanism, not to achieve repression of disruptive inner forces, but to deal with the complexities of everyday life. These patients find themselves emotionally unable to handle ordinary tasks and form meaningful object relationships.

Perhaps this distinction is simply semantic and the term "defense" should be reserved for the classical concept of dealing with intrapsychic conflicts. One could use another expression to designate these patient's interactions with their environment that characterize the nature of their psychopathology. On the other hand, in terms of mental mechanisms, there are certain similarities between the responses of the classical psychoneurotic and those of the patients discussed here. It is at least possible to conceptualize a continuum if the defenses are hierarchically arranged. For example, our patients make frequent use of splitting mechanisms and projections in their interactions with their environment. Both of these mechanisms are, so to speak, directed outward, and a part of the self is denied much as an impulse may be repressed. These are global reactions, in contrast to the selective, discrete aspects of repression — reactions that emphasize the general lack of ego structure.

One can postulate a spectrum ranging from the denial of a part of the self to the repression of a specific class of id impulses. A relatively amorphous ego cannot support a highly structured function such as repression. Thus, the denial of parts of the self and the repression of an impulse — the progression from a large segment of the psyche to a well-circumscribed element — reflect the composition of the ego as it moves from a relatively unstructured to a structured position. In our clinical experience, the transference regression reveals specifically how early traumatic introjects affect development in general and some ego systems in particular. The role of defense becomes important in this context because the psyche has to protect itself from inner disruption as well as deal with the problems of the external world, as has been discussed.

The archaic introjects, usually derivatives from the maternal relationship, determine the course of ego development. For example, if the nurturing experience has been gratifying, the child will develop confidence that his needs will be met; as mentation develops, he will find himself valued. His self-representation will feel secure in the belief that he will be taken care of and loved. The archaic introjects, thus, determine the character of the self-representation; one may feel secure, loved, and valued or one may feel hateful, rejected, and manipulated for the mother's narcissistic needs and not related to as a distinct person. The latter orientation will inhibit emotional development and make the acquisition of potentially gratifying experiences and introjects difficult. This, in turn, will increase the number of conflicts because the psyche will not develop the resources or techniques that would enable it to turn to the outside world for help. This inability to gain help from the environment will operate in a negative feedback fashion and cause the self-representation to feel even more vulnerable, helpless, and unworthy.

Many of our patients' behavior can be understood as a defensive (in the broader sense) reaction to this vicious circle. The patient has to protect himself from his self-hatred and vulnerability as well as compensate for his isolation and inadequacy in coping with external situations. One often notes an angry denial of feelings of inadequacy and a withdrawal from current values, an orientation that frequently leads to destructive and self-destructive acting out. Other patients reveal their vulnerable sense of identity directly by feeling confused, depressed, and hopeless and more or less paralyzed in their pursuit of goals.

There is a certain homogeneity in the types of reactions that help overcome such states of helpless vulnerability and inadequacy. Many of these patients seek omnipotent rescuing; they tend to idealize a person or a cause and to recapitulate the symbiotic fusion, but with a savior instead of a destructive maternal imago. This reaching out for magical salvation to absorb infinite goodness within the self and to counteract the malignant badness they feel gnawing within is clearly reenacted in the transference. As a rule, however, this projection of omnipotence cannot be maintained, and if the analyst attempts to gratify the patient's needs for rescuing, the result can be catastrophic; the patient's disappointment and sense of failure could become vehement and assume suicidal proportions.

Because of characterological constrictions, many of our patients attempt to "construct" an external world that will be congruent with their psychic structure; to some extent, of course, everybody does this. The way in which the perceptual system perceives reflects the ego's total integration and is determined by a series of memory traces that encompass the meaningful experiences of the past. Thus, the world is viewed according to one's orientation and its level of complexity is consistent with the ego's integration of perceptual experiences and executive factors. Patients with a limited and distorted developmental experience have a constricted and defective perceptual system. The reality experience of these patients differs from that of persons who have not had similar developmental problems.

Segments of the external world sometimes cannot be perceived because the perceptual apparatus is not sufficiently structured. Some observations require a telescope and others a microscope, but many patients have only a narrow perceptual range. This optical analogy, as all analogies, is not strictly accurate, for there is more than just quantitative factors and the registering of perceptions. The ego perceives in its own distinct qualitative fashion, reflecting the patient's background. *Those reality elements that are not part of past experiences cannot be integrated within the ego and brought alongside a memory system so that the executive apparatus can draw from this memory store and institute an appropriate response.*

In these instances, the memory system lacks the necessary elements that would make a given perception plausible and meaningful. For example, experiments with monkeys have clearly shown that if the animal is deprived of visual experiences from the time of birth, but later allowed to see, he will never be able to perceive in more than a rudimentary fashion. Humans who are blind from birth but whose sight is anatomically restored later on have similar visual constrictions; they cannot see beyond crude forms or construct ordinary perceptions — such perceptions seem inordinately complex and beyond their capacities of discrimination. Thus, the range of the perceptual system depends upon the amount and quality of past experiences. In the sensory area, there also seems to be an appropriate time for such experiences; if they are missing during a certain formative, maturational span, later exposures do not seem to be particularly effective. These sensory constrictions, in turn, lead to the constriction of skills and adaptations in the executive area. In addition to limited sight and hearing, skills that depend upon such modalities, such as reading and talking, may also be impaired.

Reality-testing is an ego function that should be considered from a relative rather than an absolute viewpoint. However, in a broad, general sense, there is a norm from which rigid perceptual deviations and omissions and corresponding executive responses are considered psychopathological or, at least, unique and idiosyncratic. Our patients demonstrate that their perceptual system has only permitted them a particular inflexible view of the outer world toward which they have to respond in a specific fashion. Clinging to stereotyped reactions protects them from suffering an inner disruption that would result from the painful awareness of their ego defects. Again, their rigid and segmented fashion of relating to the outer world can be seen as a defense in the broader context we are using here. Insofar as the environment is perceived and reacted to according to inner organization, this defensive adaptation can be referred to as *"externalization,"* used here in a somewhat different sense than by other authors who have not, as a rule, attempted a precise definition in terms of ego concepts.

For example, some patients reveal that they have always been immersed in turmoil; they seem to live in a perpetually rough environment and to encounter one after another tumultuous and sometimes violent situation. To generalize from their experience, it would appear that they view the outer world as a seething cauldron. Such things as peace and quiet, sympathy, love and understanding are totally lacking. One patient described his situation rather graphically. He saw himself as a person who was raised in an environment where he had to lift heavy weights constantly in order to survive. As a consequence, he felt he should develop some very strong muscles, particularly the biceps. Then he would be able to adjust to a world that demanded a weight lifter's strength. However, he saw that if his environment required the well and delicately coordinated muscles of a tennis player, he would perish in spite of his strength. He was describing a "hypertrophy" of certain anatomical features that would be adaptive to only a given setting. Consequently, he felt he had to limit his actions to that setting alone since he did not have sufficient flexibility to adjust to any other.

Another patient told about the following recurrent fantasy, which she believed she might have once seen in a movie or heard on a radio soap opera. The heroine of her fantasy is a young child whose poverty-stricken, cruel parents have dressed her in rags. One day a beautiful and charming heiress, touring the slums, finds herself very much drawn to this urchin. She decides to adopt her and makes the necessary arrangements by purchasing her from her parents. Then she brings the child to her mansion where she provides all kinds of candy and food; she also gives her a roomful of toys, all of which the child stares at in wide-eyed amazement. The heiress then leaves her alone to contemplate her good fortune. Once the heiress has left the room, the child tiptoes to the window, opens it, climbs out, and then runs back to the slums as fast as her little legs can carry her.

Both of these patients exemplify a fixation to a particular environment. They have developed adaptive techniques to cope with a given environment, but these techniques are limited and cannot be transferred to another setting. Of course, this inadaptability leads to many restrictions; even pleasurable, gratifying experiences cannot be integrated within the egos of such patients.

Obviously, the world these patients relate to is that of their early traumatic childhood. To the extent that this world is constricted and distinct from the world of reality in general, the patient will have difficulty getting along in a larger context. In a more varied and richer environment the child will develop a wider assortment of flexible, adaptive mechanisms. His mobility will depend upon his range of adaptations; in some instances, there is an apparent paradox in some of our patients who seem to be able to cope with traumatic circumstances quite well but not with situations that others would find pleasurable and secure. This adaptive externalization is not the same as masochistic adjustment although, phenomenologically, it may appear similar. These concepts of defense are basically characterological and enable us to understand how the patient will behave in the therapeutic setting. He will attempt to structure the analytic relationship in a way that resembles how he structured his early environment. Keeping this point in mind will add to our understanding of the transference and bring into focus the characterological shifts that occur during analysis.

Many of the contributing authors investigate the question of what happens to the patient's mind during the course of psychoanalytic treatment. The modification of inefficient and constrictive adaptive techniques and the acquisition of new or more flexible ones is a propitious therapeutic outcome synonymous with a higher, more expanded state of ego integration. How this comes about is the theoretical essence of the analytic process. The authors all agree that the indispensable vehicle for characterological change is the transference, and many believe that interpretation within the transference context is the way in which patients achieve greater flexibility and autonomy.

As discussed above, the patient initially views the analytic relationship in terms that are familiar to him within the limitation of his perceptual system and his unrealistic, sometimes magical, expectations. The analytic setting, in actuality, neither corresponds to the patient's viewpoint nor is it designed to contradict it. Because of its so-called neutrality it provides an atmosphere that makes it easy for the patient to project infantile imagos. The analyst makes himself available for the patient's projections. How he does this is not easy to describe and, may, to a large extent, depend upon personal factors that determine therapeutic style.

Some of the therapeutic encounters reported in this book give the reader a definite impression of how a particular analyst works, that is, his specific style. Even though there is considerable variability in the accounts, I believe there is, at least, one common denominator: The analyst does not react to the patient's productions primarily in terms of their content. If the patient despairs, the analyst does not respond with despair or pity or by trying to reassure him. Although the analyst may have felt concerned and, at times, showed it, his spontaneous reactions unsually indicated that he was interested in the patient's material because he believed it was a phenomenon worthy of study and possible to understand. His reactions would demonstrate to the patient that all was not hopeless, inchoate confusion; thus the patient would gain security in learning that there was direction and purpose to his feelings. By introducing the observational frame of reference (the secondary process), the analyst brings organization to a situation that would otherwise be hopelessly muddled for the patient. The analyst's calm, non-anxious, interested attitude supplies the framework that enables the patient to relax his defenses. He finds himself able to rely upon the organization provided by the analytic setting so that he doesn't need to depend as much upon his own inefficient and primitive adaptations. The analyst thus becomes the representative of the patient's integrative ego system, and the patient, in turn, can permit himself to regress.

Regression causes the patient to revert to adaptational techniques characteristic of his infantile past. The perceptual system also perceives in terms of earlier developmental phases. The use of archaic defenses, such as projection and primitive modes of perceiving, establishes the transference relationship.

I was particularly impressed that much of the clinical material showed that the analyst was in charge of the situation, so to speak. I am referring to both the calm organization that he brings into the treatment and his inquiring attitude and attempt to understand the patient's productions in the deterministic terms of their intrapsychic origin in order to indicate to the patient that he is not responding personally to the patient's projections. Regardless of the patient's confusion and anger, the therapist maintains an even keel; he feels no injury or retaliatory anger. If he maintains his analytic equilibrium, the analyst is in a dominant position, but one that promotes understanding.

Since the patient feels free to regress because of support provided by the analyst's secondary process, the patient is inclined to trust and respect the analyst's opinions even when he is consumed with destructive feelings. At some level, the patient knows that many of his feelings toward the analyst are due to infantile projections. *The patient's trust in the analytic setting that permits regression and primary-process-oriented transference projections enables him to view his feelings as intrapsychic phenomena rather than as provoked by outside sources.* Thus, the patient experiences an interplay of feelings that are evoked by the transference regression and the integrative aspects of the analytic setting. This interplay leads to the establishment of an observational frame of reference, in which both the patient and analyst participate and learn how the patient's mind works.

The contributors to this volume repeatedly demonstrate their respect for the patient's psychic productions; they also indicate their faith in the resiliency of the mind. Even though many of the patients experienced severe childhood deprivation that led to primitive fixations, most of these analysts believe that the psychoanalytic process could undo the fixation and bring about true characterological development.

Characterological fixation is caused by disruptive and constrictive introjects. The ego has to use — and sometimes exhaust — its energy to construct defenses against them. Therapy is designed to undo the effects of these traumatic imagos and to replace them with benign introjects that contribute positively to the identity sense, leading to the acquisition of efficiently functioning adaptive techniques. These beneficial changes, most therapists agree, involve two processes: regression to a stage that corresponds to the developmental phase when the traumatic introjects were formed, and identification with certain aspects of the analytic interaction.

Regression within the transference context eventually brings the patient back to a period when his character was in a rudimentary, formative state. In spite of the disorganization experienced by the patient due to the relative lack of psychic structure, the destructive pressure of his introjects is attenuated since they are also less structured. In many instances, such deep states of regression are accompanied by little or no anxiety; even if the patient becomes panicky or acts out, such reactions are short-lived. The constancy and non-anxious quality of the analytic setting make even the most extreme regressions tolerable and, at times, comfortable. Trust in the analyst, which in the transference may become elaborated into omnipotence, and the diminishing influence of hostile introjects cause the patient to experience primitive stages of organization in a relatively non-disruptive fashion. Furthermore, the ego is more receptive to outside influences when it is less structured and when archaic imagos are somewhat decathected. The ego no longer needs to defend itself so vigorously against them, or else it uses more primitive defenses which require less energy. Thus, energy becomes available for other purposes.

Regression in analysis does not exactly recapitulate the corresponding developmental phase. There is always an uneven and selective factor in the regressive process; not all ego systems are affected to the same degree. No matter how regressed, most patients can still communicate verbally, control their excretory functions, feed themselves, and so forth.

This selectivity may be the essential feature that leads to characterological change. Whereas some parts of the ego are primitively oriented, others that are primarily oriented toward relationships with the outside world continue functioning at a mature level. In such ego states, one finds the *tabula rasa* of childhood with its heightened receptivity combined with the aggressive discrimination of the adult. With the additional energy released by the diminished need to defend against hostile introjects, the ego is in an excellent position to form new constructions that will lead to higher stages of integration. The patient's heightened receptivity during certain types of regression makes him especially sensitive to certain elements of the analytic interaction. Opponents of analysis, especially during its early days, said that its effects were due to the suggestive influence of the analyst and, thus, only transitory and impermanent.

A careful examination of much of the clinical material presented here does not impress one with the suggestive influence of the analyst. In spite of the patient's needfulness and the fact that he seeks guidance, he maintains his critical faculties and evaluates what is offered to him. Furthermore, the authors have been especially candid in indicating that what they offer the patient is more than mere suggestion, and, unlike suggestion, does not impinge upon the patient's autonomy. Most of the time, these analysts do not communicate much to their patients outside of the intrapsychic realm. The content of their verbalizations is not exhortative nor does it try to persuade the patient to behave a certain way. When an individual suggests something, he is trying to convince someone about moral standards, judgment, or behavior, but the clinical accounts presented here generally show that the analyst had no interest in imposing such standards.

The analyst, however, does want to convey an *attitude* to the patient. First, he communicates his non-anxious demeanor, and the patient gradually incorporates this orientation. Next, he demonstrates his exclusive interest in trying to understand how the patient's mind works. The patient thus finds that someone is unambivalently (at least more so than he has ever experienced before) interested in him — someone who does not react disapprovingly or punitively. The analyst wants to know why the patient reacts as he does; he does not simply accept the patient's behavior as if it were the natural consequence of his inadequacy or a reaction to insurmountable external circumstances. The analyst is introducing the observational frame of reference, and gradually the patient will begin to look at his productions in the same way.

Although some of the authors discuss certain qualities that they believe are required for analysis, their case material often indicates that these qualities are not present at the outset but that they develop gradually throughout the course of analysis. For example, some of the authors pointed to the ego's self-observing function as a prerequisite for analysis, but the analyst's attitude and approach will often determine whether the patient adopts an introspective attitude.

The patient's incorporation of a non-anxious observational frame of reference occurs in stages and may parallel general ego mechanisms of incorporation. Briefly, the following sequence takes place: The child or the patient first incorporates experiences with the outer world in a global fashion (symbiotic fusion), then progresses to the formation of discrete introjects, which later become amalgamated as modalities and become parts of the ego's perceptual and executive apparatus. When the patient repeats this sequence in various phases of regression, he eventually reaches a stage where his observational frame of reference is well entrenched. Since he gains this point of view from the analyst, I propose to call it the "analytic introject"; I believe this term is more in context with our ego-psychological focus than "working alliance" or "therapeutic alliance" and does not necessitate artificial distinctions between transference and nontransference elements.

Ego regression for a patient who is suffering from severe pathology has been conceptualized as a recapitulation in the transference of early developmental phases. The correction of the transference distortion by interpretation permits the patient to "emerge" from the symbiotic phase with an intact autonomous identity and to structure his personality without the earlier conflicts and constrictions. Since the patient has fused with the analyst, he retains a portion of the relationship within him as an introject after he has resolved the symbiotic fusion. To the extent that the analyst does not coerce, manipulate, or otherwise impinge upon the patient's autonomy during the regressed state of transference fusion and constantly conveys by interpretation his wish to understand the operations of the patient's mind (that is, his determination to remain in the observational frame of reference), the patient incorporates this aspect of the analyst, thereby enhancing his individuality rather than submerging it. Through amalgamation of the analytic introject, the patient adds to his perceptual system; it expands its capacity for self-observation and can see the outer world from a different perspective.

The expansion also includes external objects. The acquisition of the analytic introject and the decathexis of traumatic objects, which was the outcome of the transference regression, makes it possible for the ego to introject new, adaptive experiences to replace the old, constrictive, archaic imagos. Whereas the old introject had to be defended against and thus resulted in fixation, the newly acquired introjects are *functional introjects*. They represent persons and *experiences* that enhance the ego's functional range. In a sense, the patient is once again able to learn, that is, to incorporate experiences into the memory system that will be useful to him at a later time.

Introjects are revised with each experience that is in context with them. They can also be viewed in terms of a structural hierarchy. The early introjects represent the core; accretions are made as the individual experiences increasingly complex and sophisticated adaptational techniques. When the initial introject consists of only a modality (a method and function rather than a concrete person), such as the analytic introject, later accretions also contain mainly functional elements rather than concrete content. Obviously, the acquisition of functional introjects leads to a flexible ego with an increased range of adaptations. A functionally oriented ego adapts better to the inner and outer world. If there is little conflict, the ego can develop further with little impediment.

Some of the authors find it useful to conceptualize an emotional developmental drive that is analogous to the individual's innate maturational potential. The interaction of this drive with the environment — like maturation — is responsible for the structuring of the psyche. Environmental failure (constrictive traumatic introjects) can lead to fixations or distortions of emotional development. Regression within the structured analytic setting diminishes the effects of the frustrating environment. The analyst's understanding, to some extent, makes up for the lack of understanding the patient suffered during childhood. Thus, through formation of the analytic introject — a basically gratifying experience — the previously repressed developmental drive is, in a manner of speaking, released.

For the first time in his life, a deprived patient will find that he is understood and that the analyst is reacting to him in terms of himself rather than as a narcissistic extension of the analyst. At the same time, the patient's impetus for emotional development is no longer impeded and he develops the ability to turn to the outer world for potentially beneficial experiences. Most of the authors represented here believe that the effects of constrictive damage in the early environment can, to a large extent, be undone. They conceptualize the developmental drive as being hardy and not particularly phase specific. Some of the authors believe that there are limitations to what can be accomplished with seriously ill patients, but they also believe there is potential for further structuralization, which can be achieved by analytic means.

TECHNICAL FACTORS

The latter part of this book presents clinical material and discusses various technical issues. From the description of specific interactions, certain general principles about technique can be formulated. I believe that all of the authors would agree that the essence of psychoanalytic technique is insight-promoting interpretation of the transference relationship. The usefulness of interpretation alone, however, has been debated. From such discussion various technical concepts are more clearly defined.

Some psychoanalysts believe that the development of the transference neurosis can lead to the resolution of basic problems, thereby achieving a psychoanalytic cure. The transference neurosis is defined as a contemporary edition of the infantile neurosis and refers exclusively to the oedipal situation. In order for transference to take place, there must be a total transfer of infantile feelings toward the analyst with virtually nothing left over for external objects.

These formulations were not particularly emphasized in this book, and the transference neurosis in the above sense was not described. Instead, the therapists encountered either irrational reactions toward them that alternated with similar reactions toward external objects or reactions in which the patients idealized or denigrated the therapist and reacted in an opposite fashion to someone else. These patients also experienced feelings that differed from those postulated for the transference neurosis to the extent that their projections consisted of either primitive pregenital feelings that are usually destructive in nature or attempts to magically fuse with the analyst. Genital sexual elements seemed to be minimal and contributed very little to the transference projections.

The transference neurosis, as traditionally described, distinguishes the patient who suffers from severe psychopathology from the classical psychoneurotic patient. Still, are these differences as distinct as they appear on the surface? The basic feature of any transference phenomenon is that it consists of *infantile* feelings. In our theoretical formulations concepts regarding object relations are more important today and infantile feelings have to be understood in this context. If one also thinks of object relationships in terms of a hierarchy, one can view them as a developmental progression from pre-object to a part-object and finally to a relatively whole object relationship. Therefore, any projection of infantile feelings has to correspond to some phase of object relationships antedating whole objects since the latter signify the accomplishment of maturity. Consequently, all transference phenomena, by definition, refer to feelings toward part-objects.

Because of the part-object quality of transference, one can conclude that no transference can be directed *exclusively* toward the analyst; a part-object relationship implies that feelings are divided between one part-object and another. The analyst is assigned a specific role and others are assigned different roles. True, the degree of splitting objects during transference regression depends upon the depth of the regression which is, in turn, determined by the fixation point that characterizes specific psychopathology. However, even in better integrated personalities, there must be some part-object element in order for transference to occur, and when such patients regress they cannot direct their feelings exclusively toward one person, the analyst.

Similar considerations apply to the concept of the transference neurosis. Oedipal feelings represent the mature end of the psychosexual scale and indicate only a slight regression from structured genital feelings. In our experience, patients who limit their regression to the oedipal phase are extremely rare, if they exist at all. Even when the oedipal level is reached at the final stages of analysis, there are often transference projections of pregenital elements. Despite the possibility that these more primitive projections represent defenses against the Oedipus, they are still directed toward the analyst and must be considered within the framework of transference — at least, as a defense transference. Consequently, the transference neurosis is only one element in the unfolding of the transference. Although its resolution may be the essence of therapeutic success in some patients, many other transference projections must be analyzed before the patient can finally experience the transference neurosis and work it through.

Therefore, even more pregenitally rooted, part-object-directed feelings can be worked with during analysis, and objections to analysis of patients who do not develop a transference neurosis or who do not direct their infantile feelings exclusively toward the analyst must be perceived as implying that there are absolutes rather than differences of degree.

Borderline and psychotic patients, according to the experience of our authors, develop transference when it is defined as indicated above. The question is often raised as to whether such transferences, including psychotic transferences, are therapeutically operable (that is, can they be resolved through interpretation that leads to insight?). To some extent, this has been answered by discussing the acquisition of the analytic introject. However, with patients who suffer from severe regression — where the predominant aspects of the transference projection consist almost entirely of narcissistic elements and even part-object aspects are absent — it has been asked if the patient has sufficient ego structure to perceive the analyst as being even minimally separated from himself. A narcissistic object relationship is not thought to be a true object relationship in the sense that it can be worked with therapeutically.

Many of the cases described here reached deep regressive levels and responded to analysis. This is an empirical argument for analysis; it has brought into focus the importance of the symbiotic phase, fusion mechanisms, and interpretation within a psycho-pathological framework and fixations. Because the symbiotic phase of development seems to be etiologically instrumental and is recapitulated in the transference, it is discussed in considerable detail. It has many technical implications, but insofar as fusion occurs with a therapist who has maintained a calm, observational frame of reference, it is possible to learn from this fusion and progress to states of individuation.

The technical question of whether all or only some transference is analyzable has led many of us to regard therapeutic amenability in terms of the interaction between the therapist and patient rather than unilaterally in terms of the patient's psychopathology. Acting out has been viewed in this context and defined as behavior that the analyst cannot tolerate. Some analysts perceive therapeutically noneffective transference as a form of acting out. If a patient's transference goes beyond the limits that an analyst can tolerate, it is thought to be unanalyzable. Another therapist, however, may have different limits of tolerance and thus be able to work with that patient's transference projections. Transference resolution as well as the broader matter of treatability in general are relative and are not strictly determined by the depth and quality of regression. They are, to some extent, independent of the narcissistic or part-object quality of the transference projection and have to be considered in the context of the therapist-patient interaction.

The analytic setting creates an atmosphere that implicitly facilitates the development of transference. Reading the clinically focused chapters led me to feel that the analyst's *expectation* about the formation of a workable transference was significant in determining the course of the therapeutic process. Every association has a transference component. By relating himself primarily to that component, the analyst is covertly encouraging its further development. The analyst conveys his expectations by examining the given relationship between the patient and himself; this may be done either silently or by active interpretation.

The contributing authors did not question the efficacy of interpretation; they obviously thought it was an important therapeutic tool. They did not particularly explore the effectiveness of a non-transference interpretation; many of the chapters implied that even though such an interpretation may have some supportive value, it does not lead to analytic resolution.

The transference interpretation refers specifically to the

patient's distorted perceptions of the analyst; it includes that which is being distorted in the context of an object relationship. Thus, the patient learns how his archaic introjects bring about his current reactions. By incorporating the analyst's viewpoint, the patient is, in effect, establishing an analytic introject in his memory system that mitigates the effects of his infantile introjects. Thus, he expands the operation of his perceptual system and strengthens his reality-testing.

A particularly effective type of interpretation that does not *seem* to be a transference interpretation is one that refers to an event in the external world. The patient is unaware of the event's significance and its implications in producing the behavior that characterizes his psychopathology. I have called these interpretations "linking interpretations" because they link an experience in the external world (like a dream stimulus) to behavior in the office directed toward the analyst.

For example, a young housewife in her middle twenties, stumbled into my office. As she lay on the couch she dropped her purse, and its contents scattered all over the floor. Frantically she started to gather them up but then became quite anxious when she could not find her car keys. This seemed particularly strange because the keys were lying close to my feet and were clearly visible. Knowing something about her confusion, I asked her why she wanted to impress me with her helplessness. This question had a calming effect; she found her car keys and then relaxed on the couch. I asked if anything in particular had happened that made it necessary for her to reveal what she felt was her weakness and vulnerability. She said that she could not think of anything and then went on to tell about what seemed to be routine events of that particular day.

It was a cold and icy day, and the patient had arranged to pick up her neighbor's children from nursery school. It was the patient's turn to drive, a task she abhorred because she was often terrified in traffic and believed she was a very poor driver. She was upset about what she perceived as her incompetence in general and especially this manifestation of it. She was also distressed because, at times, she had to drive in order to keep her appointments with me. On this day she was especially afraid because the streets were icy and driving was hazardous. As she came down the stairs of her apartment house, she met her neighbor who spontaneously offered to pick up the children because the patient's automobile was further down the street than the neighbor's. At first, the patient hesitated but then accepted the offer with great relief.

It became apparent that her behavior in my office resulted from the tremendous shame and guilt she experienced when she accepted her neighbor's offer of rescue. Her feelings of vulnerability and helplessness increased, and because of the transference projection she believed that I would sternly disapprove of her weakness. Since she was afraid of my reaction, she attempted to placate me by further emphasizing her incompetence and clumsiness; her inability to find the car keys represented her fear of driving and, by extension, her general inability to function. Of course, there were other related meanings to this defensive modality (including the need to avoid frightening sexual feelings), but these were not obvious at the time.

Pointing out the stimulus to and the meaning of her behavior constituted a linking interpretation. This is still a transference interpretation, but the interaction between the patient and therapist was extended outside the consultation room to the origin of the particular behavior that characterized the given transference projection. Linking situations in the external world to currently experienced feelings in the analytic setting prevents interminable primary-process rumination and leads to cohesion by making the external world comprehensible in terms of the transference interaction. In these instances, the analytic setting provides an integrative experience, extending the patient's secondary-process perceptions of his behavior both inside and outside of analysis. By recognizing the irrational determinant of his reactions, the patient can maintain control and limit his feelings to manageable proportions.

Here, I have spoken of interpretation from an operational and transference viewpoint. Sometimes, the analyst makes a statement to the patient that does not seem to be a transference interpretation but nonetheless provides integration. This type of communication, which is illustrated several times in this book, consists essentially of some remark about the analytic setting. The analyst may tell the patient how he, himself, feels or that he finds some aspects of the patient's material particularly interesting. At other times, he may prohibit certain behavior; he may not allow the patient to sit up, smoke, or do anything else that the analyst feels will disrupt the treatment.

Although these interactions may appear to be manipulative, there are several essential differences. For instance, the analyst is not trying to tell the patient how to lead his life or what is best for him; he is merely defining, in a sense, the boundaries of the analytic setting. This may take the form of delineating the limits of the analyst's feelings, informing the patient that he will maintain a certain degree of constancy. At the same time, the analyst is indicating that he is available for the patient's projections; by showing his interest in the material the analyst is also emphasizing that he is not afraid of being destroyed, a fear that the patient may hold because of his inner destructiveness.

The prohibition of certain types of behavior is not a manipulation or an attempt to set up standards of conduct with moral implications. Usually the analyst tells the patient the conditions *he* requires in order to be able to conduct analysis effectively. For example, the analyst may not feel comfortable and consequently not be able to function in his analytic role if the patient sits up. Other types of behavior may also be objectionable to the therapist and therefore disruptive of the analytic setting. The therapist's requirements are not rationalized as being therapeutic maneuvers and "good" for the patient; they pertain only to the analyst's needs, and, in some instances, their origins may be idiosyncratic. Hopefully, the analyst's needs are minimal. If the patient finds it impossible to conform to the given conditions, he may have to be transferred to another therapist whose idiosyncrasies are more congruent with his own. In any case, there has to be sufficient comfort (sometimes referred to as rapport) between the therapist and patient so that the analytic setting maintains a degree of constancy.

I would like to illustrate the type of prohibition I have in mind. One of my patients, a young man in his middle twenties, complained that the couch was too soft and hurt his back. He believed he would be more comfortable if he lay on the floor. After he made this suggestion I wondered how I would feel about it if he left the couch. From a logical viewpoint, there seemed to be nothing wrong with his idea. Why should I interfere with his autonomy just because his idea seemed strange and unconventional? True, there were undoubtedly many transference elements in his behavior, some of which I already understood. I interpreted a few of these implications, such as his masochistic need to be submissive and demean himself. The patient understood this need but nevertheless believed that his back would feel better if he lay on the floor, and so he did this.

For a while I did not interfere, and the material proceeded smoothly without any discontinuity. My thoughts, at first, went as follows: Why shouldn't he lie on the floor if this is what he wants to do and feels more comfortable, despite the irrational factors underlying his wish? After all, a large portion of patients' material and behavior has irrational motives, and it is precisely such motives that lead patients to seek treatment. Furthermore, how am I going to learn about his primary-process elements if I forbid their manifestations?

In spite of these reflections, I found it difficult to follow the patient's associations because I began to experience a vague sense of discomfort. This discomfort increased and, without deliberation, I was about to instruct the patient to get back on the couch. However, it was not necessary to do so because, apparently, I must have communicated my uneasiness to him, for he began to feel uncomfortable on the floor and spontaneously returned to the couch. Later in the session, I understood the sources of my feelings. I found it difficult to tolerate a person lying at my feet. The patient may have wanted to demean himself masochistically, but letting him lie at my feet meant that *I was participating* in his debasement. This was therefore a kind of acting out on *both our parts;* it led me to feel uncomfortable and subsequently disrupted the flow of material. Perhaps, another analyst could have worked with this patient lying on the floor. In that case, he would not have felt uncomfortable because he would not have felt that he was participating in the patient's submission.

These issues raise subtle technical questions about the definition of the analytic setting and acting out. From this example, one can conclude that acting out is not a unilateral phenomenon referring simply to the patient's behavior. *Acting out or, at least, disruptive acting-out involves a reciprocal relationship between the therapist and patient and does not emanate either primarily or solely from the patient.* This viewpoint lessens the need for moral assessments or viewing certain clinical phenomena as bad and others as good for treatment. Concepts such as resistance and motivation as well as acting out are not used as weapons to blame the patient and thus classify him as untreatable. Therapeutic amenability is conceptualized in terms of the construction of the analytic setting, and judgment about treatment involves technical issues that bring the analyst's motivations, as well as the patient's, into focus. Acting out thus becomes a relative concept, and its prohibition ought to be considered in the larger transference-countertransference context.

Defining the analytic setting is a technical maneuver that, on the surface, differs from the transference interpretation. The analyst tells the patient something about himself or the analytic procedure; he does not make observations about the patient's behavior or feelings toward himself. Defining the analytic setting seems to be a particularly valuable technique in treating patients who suffer from severe psychopathology. It often leads to sharpening the patient's ego boundaries by delineating the limits of regression that are compatible with treatment. However, even in cases where there is relatively good ego structure, this technique, in addition to interpretation, is valuable.

Closer examination reveals that defining the analytic setting is a special type of interpretation. By pointing out the limits of his reactions the analyst indicates to the patient that, in some way, his own reactions differ. Either the patient had not been aware of this difference or else he had other expectations about the analytic procedure. Pointing out this difference or correcting the patient's misconceptions about the analytic process leads to a point where the patient's attitude can be contrasted with the analyst's, and this contrast constitutes a transference projection.

As repeatedly emphasized throughout this book, patients who suffer from severe pathology often fuse with the analyst. Regression in treatment reactivates the symbiotic stage, and the dominant transference state is characterized by fusion. Differentiating the setting emphasizes elements that have been blurred by fusion and once again points out the transference. These matters are discussed in considerable detail in Chapter 14.

Besides specific technical maneuvers, this book discusses broad areas of psychoanalytic technique. For example, the attitudes of some of the authors about regression seem to be distinct — somehow they seem to be more positive than usual. I believe they are advocating the extended use of regression. By not overtly encouraging but by respecting the patient's right to regress, therapists can create an atmosphere in which the investigation of psychopathology is less threatening. Acknowledging the patient's need to withhold and, in some instances, to keep secrets augments his autonomy, and therefore the patient sees analysis as less peremptory.

Some of the authors describe episodes of disruptive and non-disruptive regression and contrast the two states. During analytic regression the imago of the analyst is retained and, even in primitive fused states, continues to be operative. The patient still feels anchored in an object relationship; although the regressed state has painful and stormy elements, he derives some security from the regulatory constancy of the analytic setting. These aspects of the regressed state emphasize the *intrinsic support* analysis provides and its integrative potential.

In this book, the subject of psychoanalytic treatment has been viewed from many perspectives by authors of different backgrounds and orientations. All of them seem to be dedicated and to have faith in the analytic process. Some questions have been answered admirably and in the process of reaching conclusions, new questions have been raised. To all of us who have participated in writing this book, the subject of psychoanalytic treatment is fascinating and vital. As we explore further the concepts underlying our relationships with patients, our respect for the resiliency of the human psyche becomes deeper. The patient is not viewed as a tragic example of human misery. Instead, his psychic productions are seen as worthy of inquiry; gradually he begins to understand that something inside of him is puzzling and fascinating, and he learns to value what he discovers. Both the patient and analyst continue to achieve higher levels of ego integration, and the observational frame of reference becomes increasingly entrenched as a characterological modality; the analytic viewpoint becomes a way of life.

A separate index was prepared for Chapter 23. It begins on page 745.

730

733

blissful, 359
of libido and aggression, 140
with object and isolation, 332
painful and threatening, 358

Geleerd, E., 70, 79, 92
Genitality, premature stimulation of, 262
Gerard, R., 171, 187
Gill, M., 140, 168, 173, 258, 259, 288
Giovacchini, P., 3–13, 10, 12, 120, 130, 140, 142, 148, 168, 169, 173, 182, 187, 222, 225, 226, 222–235, 290–304, 337–350, 361, 363, 364–378, 383, 403, 435
    on ego integration, 119
    analysis of a marital partner, 431
Gitelson, M., 295, 304, 365, 378
    on Klein's view of origin of oedipus complex, 53
Glisan, M., vi
Glover, E., 9, 10, 12, 17–32, 36, 50, 51, 58, 63, 92, 103, 112, 261, 288
Glover, J., 24
Gratification of defensive demands of regressed patient, 273
Gratitude, 48
Greed
    and aggression, 47
    and anxiety, 47
Green, M. R., 202, 215
Greenacre, R., 341, 350
Greenson, R., 10, 12, 202, 204, 215, 293, 304, 365, 378, 383, 388, 403
Grinker, R. R., Sr., 54, 58
Groddeck, G., 35
Gross, A., 202, 203, 204, 215
Guilt
    and reparation, 41
    reparation and sublimation, 48
Guntrip, H., 52, 58, 72, 73, 92, 367

Haley, J., 130
Harley, M., 79, 92
Hartman, H., iv, 139, 169, 172, 174, 181, 183, 187, 263, 288
Hawthorne, N., 205, 206
Head banging, 148, 171
Heimann, P., 56, 58, 261, 263, 264, 265, 280, 288

Heisenberg, W., 182, 187
Help, inability to extract from environment, 709
Heredity, 30
Hinsie, L., 191, 199
History taking, as an intrusion, 225
Hitler, A., 37
Hoffer, W., 57
Holzman, P., 268, 272, 288
Homosexuality, and narcissism, 183
Hopelessness, 208
Horney, K., 54
Hospital
    to control acting out, 280
    maternity, 315
    mental, 316
Hospitalization, 118, 183
Hug-Helmuth, H., 35, 40
Humor, 181
Hydrodynamic model, 166
Hypertrophy, as related to adaptation, 711
Hypnosis, influence on Freud, ii
Hypochondriasis, 109
Hysteria and underlying schizophrenia, 247

Identification
    partial and transient, 374
    patient with analyst, 115
    projective, 46
Identification systems, defined 254
Identity
    and autonomy, 197
    based on reliable and predictable environment, 125
    in borderline states, 263
    concept of, 339
    defective self-representation, 356
    due to fusion with analyst, 356
    male, in girl, 176
    problems, 337–350
    professional threatened, 339
Identity problems, and existential crisis, 699
Illness
    denial of, 316
    need to experience as precondition to recovery, 316

734

therapeutic process, 172
trial period, 122
See also Treatment
Psychoanalyst, professional identity, ii
Psychoanalyst-patient unit, 314
Psychoanalytic approach, compared with general psychiatric approach, 24
Psychoanalytic consultation
initial duration, 102
and ego, 101
and patient's autonomy, 101
technique compared and technique of analysis, 100
Psychoanalytic research, future of, 30
Psychopathology
selective aspects, 159
blaming the outer world for, 228
Psychoses, 41
analysis of psychiatric core, 425
autistic, 160, 201
borderline, 310
defenses in, 47
isolated to office, 229
prevention of, 315
symbiotic, 160
treatment of, 414–435
Psychosocial moratorium, 193
Psychosomatic integration, 319
Psychotherapist, psychoanalytically oriented, defined, 26
Psychotherapy
distinguished from psychoanalysis in terms of interpretation of conscious or preconscious, 25
focus upon secondary process, 25
and suggestion, 17
Psychotic episodes and creative functioning, 185

Racken, H., 85, 264, 265, 289
Rank, O., 9, 12, 55
Rapaport, D., 140, 169, 171, 188, 263, 289
Rapport, 724
Reality principle, 326
Reality testing, 49, 170, 171
in borderline states, 263

and premature deep interpretation, 69
and projection and introjection, 45
in psychoses and borderline states, 267
Referral, for analysis, 103
by wife, 241
Regression, 141, 316, 355
and adaptation, 191–192
in analysis, 164, 259
and defensive ego splitting, 162
defined, 191–192
differentiated from ego synthesis, 184
and ego development, 193
and equation of love and hate, 319
fear of, 162
as freedom from rigid defenses, 198–199 ·
and fusion of patient with analyst, 314
goals of, 419
induced by L.S.D., 179
accompanied by obsessive-compulsive symptomatology, 423
and id satisfaction and ego development, 190–191
and survival, 192–193
transference recapitulation of early developmental stages, 159
unequal, 414–415, 715
Reich, A., 365, 378
Reich, W., 9, 12, 35
Reichard, S., 8, 13
Reider, N., 268, 289
Reik, T., 204, 209, 215
Reisen, A. H., 141, 152, 161, 169
Rejection of any interpretation activity, 240
Religious mysticism, narcissism in, 183
Reparation, 41, 48
Repetition
and ego stability, 321
and integration in transference, 314
Repetition compulsion, 423
Replication of analysis, in first interview with fragmented patients, 232–234, 242

740

Timing, of reliving infantile trauma, 190, 193, 195
Toilet training, 321
Tolerance and analyzability, 721
Topographical hypothesis, useful in hysteria and not in characterological disorders, 703
Training analysis, 697
Transference, 40, 314
  acting out in, 256–257, 280
  acting out in, defined, 268–269
  acting out in borderline states, 335
  ambivalent, ii, 24, 275
  analysis of, 18, 24, 25, 40
  delusional, 114, 166
  dependent, 99
  distinguished from a defense, 360
  question of exclusive projection to analyst, 719
  expectation, 299, 721
  fusion of patient with analyst, 125, 127, 135
  and genetic reconstruction in borderline states, 275–276
  idealization of, 278, 279
  interpretation and therapeutic progress, 67
  narcissistic occurrence in the narcissistic neuroses, 351
  negative, 257
  negative and projective identification, 264
  non-transference aspects, 721
  and omnipotence, 283
  outside of therapeutic relationship, 282
  paranoid, 113, 330
  positive, 283, 314
  projection upon whole or part objects, 301
  proxy, 241
  in psychosis, 70
  psychotic, 255, 330, 334, 335
  psychotic, defined, 268
  psychotic and pathogenic early object relationships, 272
  rapid changes of in borderline states, 267
  regression, 268

  regression and reality testing, 267
  resistance and instinctual gratification, 269–270
  short duration of transference cure, 425
  symbiotic, 74
Transference neurosis, 307, 308
  and archaic introjects, 139
  defined, 718–719
  and narcissistic personality disorder, iii
  and transference manifestations, 68
  and transference psychosis, 80
Transference psychosis, 74
Trauma
  definition of infantile, 157
  leads to dissociation, 401
  seduction in hysteria, 401
Travelogue narrative, instead of free association, 271
Treatment
  changing attitudes towards, iii–v
  forcible technical device, 113
  interruption of by patient, 129
  necessity for non-analytic, 423
  play therapy, 35, 40
  of psychoses, 414–435
  termination of, 128
  varieties, organic, manipulative, psychoanalytic, supportive, 4–7
Trichotillomania, 150
Trust, in analyst and freedom to regress, 715

Ulcerative colitis, 104
Umwelt, 172
Unconscious
  system, 18, 24
  timelessness of, 210, 325
Unity, 310
University of Illinois Department of Psychiatry, vi

van der Walls, H. G., 78, 93
Videotaped interview, defensive use of, 227
Von Uexküll, J., 172, 188

Waelder, R., 62, 63, 93

742

743

The main index for this book begins on page 729.

displacing introjected parents, 611–612

empathy contrasted with involvement, 474

fatigue of, patient's need to control, 586–589

hate for patient, 543

identification
— with dead father, 579
— with patient, 642–644
— with patient, and love, 641

initiative, 635, 642, 672, 675

integrative
— activity, 466, 511, 515, 528
— function, 465, 473, 483, 511, 535, 549, 568, 576
— and amnesia, 488, 631

limited adaptation, function of, 662, 664, 673

love for patient, 543, 606, 642, 644, 655, 676

mistakes, 462, 463, 509, 520, 535, 598, 615, 665, 671, 681, 687
— example of use of, 598, 665

motives of, 492, 643–644

note-taking, 511, 543

responsibility of, 460, 479, 592

role of, 539, 549, 557, 568, 671, 684

survival, 477

as symbol, 480, 661

Analytic introject
and ending of analyses, 564
identification, and expansion of ego capacity, 550

Analytic process, 459
and change in fantasy, 532
and medical practice, 644, 660
and passivity, 575, 672
and teaching, 665

Analytic session
and analytic introject, 564
beginning of, 514, 521, 613, 668, 675
as castration, 572, 578, 616
end of, 490, 498, 514, 548, 552, 572, 578, 597, 610
and intellectualization, 621

Anger
and ego integration, 631, 640, 641, 665, 673

at failure of holding, found in regression, 661

justified in present, 665

repression of, 619

and sense of reality, 641

Anxiety, 477, 527, 682
annihilation, 485, 527
castration, 467, 488–490, 505, 527
— and talion principle, 572
depressive, 477–478, 498, 517, 526
and object relations, 485
paranoid, 545, 549, 572
schizoid, 478
— See also Ego; False self; Object
and symbol formation, 571
See also Resistance

Art and transitional area, 559–560

As-if personality, 652
See also False self

Autonomy, 558, 581, 620, 676
and degree of psychopathology, 592
and spontaneity, 502

Bedtime, being comforted, 671

Bettelheim, Bruno, 608

Boredom, 465, 647
and instinctual inhibition, 603–606
See also Resistance

Bowel training, 510

Breakdown, positive value of, 642–643

Cannibalism, 465–476, 498
and castration, 521, 522
and end of analytic session, 498

Castration
as defense against more primitive anxiety, 527
and end of analytic session, 572, 578
and phallic woman, 491

Child
as defense against delusion of phallic woman, 564
as female penis, 505

Choice, and change from need to want, 558

Clark, P., 632

Communication, silent, 636

Competitiveness
with females, 489
with males, See Rivalry

three functions, 587
timing of, 466–467, 550
See also Transference
Interpreting, reasons for, 587
Intimacy, and names, 525–526
Introject, analytic, 539, 549, 669
displacement by analyst, 671
and ego defect, 645
maternal, 669
parental, 612
— assimilation, 602
primitive, 465
Introjection, 498
in depressive and schizoid character, 526
identification and identity, 645

Jealousy, 679
Jones, Ernest, 465, 522

Khan, M. M. R., 456, 635
Klein, Melanie, 473

Lateness
of analyst, 463, 582, 671–672
of patient, 460–461, 582, 614
and projection, 502
Little, Margaret, 658
Loneliness, 593, 657–659, 661, 667
Love
conditional, 645
versus demands, 634–635
and idealization, 566–567
inhibition of, 471
and mutuality in analysis, 676
and sadness, 469
and sex, 458
and spontaneity, 468

Magic, and mother's identification with baby, 635
Marriage
mutual adaptation, 530–531, 553, 560
— disrupted by analysis, 530
choice of partner, 648
repetitive patterns of, 538
Masochism, 464, 675
Masturbation, 468, 482

and elimination of competition, 485
and fantasy, 481–482
and need for independence, 590
Maternal care, 467
absence of, 638
continuity of, 470–473, 477, 595–596
and reality contact, 642, 672
tantalizing, 656
Milner, Marion, 594–595
Mood, and true self, 640
Morality, development of, 517
Mother
castrating, 506
See also Adaptation; Environment; Identification; Maternal Care; Transference
Mother's withdrawal, and infant's need to control, 596–597
Mourning
impeded when hostility is repressed, 626
and object loss, 526
and patricide fantasy, 540, 626
Mutuality, versus domination, 675

Need and wish, 558, 620, 642–643, 661, 674
Negation, and ego development, 558
Neurosis and psychoses, 646
Note-taking, 511, 543
Number, concept of, 523, 534

Object
annihilation by satisfaction and loss of object cathexis, 476, 477, 625
constancy, hope and anger, 470, 640
loss, depressive and schizoid, 526
relatedness, origin of, 467, 608, 672
relation, narcissistic, 569
survival, 502
Oedipal
development, failure of, 668
rivalry, 663
— avoided, 571
— and regression to dependence, 592
See also Rivalry

triangle, composed of patient, analyst and analysis, 548
— development in transference, 545
— developmental significance, 483, 485, 496–497, 520, 530, 546, 548, 600, 667
— and phallic woman, 525
Oedipus complex, 459
adaptive significance, 525
conflict, developmental significance, 520, 538, 546–548
Opposition
need for, 669
organizing function of, 557, 604, 631
Oral erotism, 523
Orality and sleep, 527
Original sin, and love of mother, 692

Parents
combined and differentiated, 497, 524–527, 534, 550, 668
rigidity, 612, 656
See also Phallic woman
Passivity, 497, 506, 643, 675
as a defense against impotence, 579
defensive, 497
and need for analyst's initiative, 642–643
Paternal authority, 524, 538–539, 638
sought in women, 540
Patricide, 540, 692
fantasy, developmental significance, 540
fantasy, and homosexuality, 626
Perfection, 567
as a defense, 493
— against failure, 635
and love, 566–567
Phallic woman, 490–491, 495, 503, 524, 532, 540, 546
defensive meaning, 509
need for, 540
Physical contact and understanding, 656, 659
Play, 467, 479, 495, 638–639, 678
internal and external reality, 559–560
and interpretation, 474

and speech, 467
symbolism, inhibition and acting out, 571
and transitional area, 495, 511, 537, 559
and transitional object, 480
Position on couch, 550, 624
Potency, 504
and love, 579
Prattling, 466–467, 594, 598, 613, 678
and ego integration, 472–473, 668
and regression in a holding environment, 594
and spontaneity, 613
Pregnancy, meaning of, 505
Preoccupation, of parents, 598
Privacy, 667
and mental structure, 619, 669
Projection, 539
on to a social taboo, 548
Psychosis, transference, 639
Punishment, 524

Rage, return of repressed, 626
Reaction formation, 460–461
to environmental impingement vs. awaiting personal impulse, 676
Reading, precocious, 671
Reality
sense of
— and anger, 641
— and diagnosis, 651
— and false self defense, 655
— and loneliness, 661
— and maternal adaptation, 642
testing, 639
Rebirth fantasy, 460
Regression, 472–473, 506, 523, 631, 662
in analysis, 472, 499, 526, 576, 591, 608
and ego defect, 526
to failure of maternal adaptation, 673
and maturation, 526, 608, 662–664
and needs and wishes, 674
and past time, 665
and physical contact, 661–663
from rivalry to dependence, 590–591

and somatic illness, 499
to success and failure, 673–674
and time sense, 608
two kinds, 673
and vulnerability, 610
compared to withdrawal, 576–577
Reparation, 461, 470–473, 502
and aggression, 473
failure of when infant has multiple
caretakers, 470
Repressed, return of, 626, 629
Repression
capacity for, 619
and dissociation, 619–620
Resistance, 463, 521–522, 682, 686
and ego boundary, 669
and overdetermination of behavior,
545
and sleepiness, 486, 686
and suppression, 522
Responsibility of analyst and patient
in relation to ego state of patient,
592
Rivalry, 496, 527–529, 556, 663
and aggressiveness, 681
degrees of, 572
and destructiveness, 682
developmental significance, 524–
525
and ego development, 679
and Freud's "Totem and Taboo,"
691
and friendship, 538, 540
inhibition of, 682
and instinctual inhibition, 628
and killing, 687
and siblings, 628, 680, 686
and triumph, 686
See also Oedipal
Rosenfeld, H. R., 632
Ruthlessness, 461, 502
and depressive anxiety, 532

Sadism, 470
oral, 473, 521
— and thumbsucking, 617–618
Safety, after satiation of self and
object, 502

Satisfaction
and object cathexis, 477
and loss of object cathexis, 625–626
See also Object; Need and wish
Schizoid illness
personality and schizophrenia, 458,
652
reaction, 478
See also Ego; False self; Object,
relatedness; Schizophrenia
Schizophrenia, 458, 528, 646, 652
and anxiety, 528
etiology, 647–649
treatability, 646–649
Secrecy
and ego boundaries, 523, 619–620,
669
and ego integration, 620
and mental structure, 619
patient's, 523–524
and recognition of wish, 620
Self-observing function, 639
Sexuality, female, 504–505
Silence
and adaptation, 635
analyst's, 636
and identity, 660
and need for analyst's initiative,
641–643
patient's, 523, 629, 661
positive value, 628–630, 633–634
Sleep, 524, 657
and ambivalent transference, 622
and analyst's speech, 671
in analytic session, 524, 527, 547,
665
— and negative transference, 466,
520, 624, 628, 638
— and positive transference, 606,
635, 638, 655, 658
and anger, 516, 520, 661
and castration anxiety, 578
compulsive, and orality, 525–527
and conflict, 501
as defense
— against anger, 624, 628
— against anxiety, 487, 488
— against environmental impingement, 670

and control, 617
and ego integration, 468
and start of session, 620
subjective, and true and false self, 608, 617
Toilet training, 510
Transference
aliveness and deadness, 579, 599
analyst as female in, 485, 504
anger in, 665, 673
anxiety and compliance in, 545
defiance, 563, 574
delusional, 634
dependence, 460–464, 473, 498, 528, 551, 590, 597
— and acting out, 461
— and sleep, 622
— and somatic illness, 499
displacement, 474, 493
equality, 567
idealization and denigration, 549
interpretation, 474–476, 535
— and dissociation, 549
— of link with physical contact, 658
maternal, 462, 510, 536, 590, 599, 600, 611
— and exhibitionism, 510
and mother's ambivalence, 669
— anxiety, 494
negative, 545, 631
— as an achievement, 661, 665
— and Oedipus conflict, 545
— and sleep, 622, 638
— and sleepiness, 486, 488
positive and ego state, 642, 656, 676
psychotic, 639
regression, 472, 499, 631, 658
rivalry, 535–537, 582
sequence of development toward oedipal rivalry, 535
and sleep, 656
and somatic illness, 459, 498–499, 658
split, in relation to two objects, 535
use of external situation in, 545
Transitional area, 495
and analyst as symbol, 480
and analytic setting, 549, 552
and mutuality, 675, 678

See also Dreaming; Ego; Play
Transitional object, 666–667
and analyst as symbol, 480
and transitional phenomena, 467–468
See also Dreaming; Ego; Play
Transvestitism, 507
Trauma
cumulative, 635
infantile, 665–666
reactivation by analysis, 665, 670–671, 675
Triangular relationship and hate, 483, 485
See also Oedipal rivalry; Rivalry
True self, 652, 665
and action, 506, 607–609, 620
and antisocial behavior, 506
and environmental impingement, 654
and false self, and identity, 577
isolated and inexperienced, 629, 655, 659, 661
and mood, 640
and parapraxis, 598
and silence, 661
and sleep, 622
and time, 608, 617
and twiddling, 467
and unintegration, 609–610
See also False self; Spontaneity

Unconscious
and conscious motivation, 545
cooperation and autonomy, 581
Unintegration, 577, 594
Unreality feelings, 646, 652–655
Urination, and crying, 606

Wastefulness, fear of, 656
Winnicott, Clare, 456
Withdrawal, 464, 466, 541, 577, 628, 656, 660, 665
as defense against dependence, 464
and omnipotence, 628
to protect loved objects, 628–629
and regression, 577
and sibling rivalry, 628